HUGH DALTON

BEN PIMLOTT

M

MACMILLAN

Copyright © Ben Pimlott 1985

First published in hardback 1985 by Jonathan Cape Limited

First published in paperback 1986 by
PAPERMAC
a division of Macmillan Publishers Limited
4 Little Essex Street London WC2R 3LF
and Basingstoke

Associated companies in Auckland, Delhi, Dublin,
Gaborone, Hamburg, Harare, Hong Kong, Johannesburg,
Kuala Lumpur, Lagos, Manzini, Melbourne, Mexico City,
Nairobi, New York, Singapore and Tokyo

British Library Cataloguing in Publication Data
Pimlott, Ben
  Hugh Dalton.
  1. Dalton, Hugh   2. Statesman—Great Britain
  —Biography
  I. Title
  941.083'092'4   DA585.D3

  ISBN 0-333-41251-6

Typeset by Ace Filmsetting Limited, Frome, Somerset
Printed in Hong Kong

HUGH
DALTON

Ben Pimlott is well known as a political historian and commentator. He is the editor of the *Dalton Diaries* (the first volume of which was published in 1986), author of *Labour and the Left in the 1930s*, and editor of *Fabian Essays in Socialist Thought*. His articles and reviews appear frequently in the *Guardian*, *New Society*, the *TLS* and elsewhere. He teaches politics at Birkbeck College, University of London.

To
JEAN

CONTENTS

Contents

ILLUSTRATIONS

PREFACE

This is the story of an unusual and contradictory man, and of his political adventure. It is not a work of piety. Nor is it 'official'.

What should the aim of such a story be? Biography may be distinguished from fiction by what Virginia Woolf called 'the creative fact; the fertile fact; the fact that suggests and engenders'. In biography, you strive to be accurate, and although you may speculate a little, you do not say what you know or suspect to be untrue.

On the other hand, it is wrong to see biography as a search for the 'whole truth' about a character. Some distinguished biographers have presented themselves as humble explorers, seeking only to discover and inform. This is misleading. Biography is not mere reportage. The form is literary, the method interpretative: it is significant that 'portrait' should be the common metaphor. The author attempts to build, not a distillation of important facts, but an impression, using a *pointillisme* of detail, quotation and comment. The impression should be recognisable, and revealing. But it is not achieved by deductive reasoning; nor is it testable.

A better aim than 'truth' is 'understanding'. The biographer tries to understand by making connections. Here, the facts that matter are not just events in the life under scrutiny; they include facts about friends, enemies and society in general. The facts do not speak for themselves; they acquire significance only in the context in which they are placed. 'Understanding', in this sense, is subjective. It entails no single or correct body of knowledge, waiting to be presented.

If biography is about understanding, everything becomes relevant. If it is merely about facts, there is room for a dangerous and improper distinction: between public facts and private facts, which can be put in separate boxes. Thus, some have argued that it is possible to exclude private facts altogether. This is a strange contention, especially when applied to political biography. For it is surely apparent that in politics every publicly-expressed passion – of patriotism, class sentiment, concern for the poor or whatever – has a private dimension; and that 'political character' is always a package in which 'public' and 'private' traits are intertwined.

For the biographer, the scope for linking public and private depends critically on the nature of the evidence. In this respect I have been exceptionally lucky. For most of his adult life, Hugh Dalton kept a diary – mainly a record of political events and experiences, but with private thoughts often peeping through. This remarkable document has become an Aladdin's cave for historians, and it has been my single most important source.

My first debt, therefore, is to my subject as a writer. My second is to the London School of Economics, which invited me to prepare an edition of the diary (the copyright of which it holds) for publication. My third is to the Leverhulme Trust Fund, whose generous financial support made such a project possible. Two annotated volumes of diary will appear shortly. The special opportunities provided by this undertaking helped immensely with the present work; for much of the time, indeed, authorship and editorship were different sides to the same enterprise.

For other funding, I am grateful to the Nuffield Foundation for the award of a one-year research fellowship, clearing vital space at the beginning, and to the British Academy and the Nuffield Foundation (again) for smaller grants towards expenses.

Many people helped my research, and I wish to express my gratitude to all of them. It is impossible to mention every name, but I would like, in particular, to thank Dr Angela Raspin for her expert guidance on a wide range of queries relating to private papers; and Dr Dorothy Tarry, my research assistant on the diary editing project, for her imagination and skill in the pursuit of elusive sources. I am also grateful to Mr H. E. Cox, Librarian of the Mirror Group Newspapers Ltd, and Mrs Irene Wagner, former Librarian of the Labour Party; and to Dominic Lawson, for some sharp-eyed detective work on Dalton's early election campaigns. The staff of the British Library of Political and Economic Science (B.L.P.E.S.), the Public Record Office (P.R.O.) at Kew, and the Bodleian Library, Oxford gave valuable help over a long period. I am especially grateful to the Reading Room staff of the British Library in Bloomsbury, where much of this book was researched and most of it written. I am very much aware of what I owe to the service provided: the best example of practical socialism I know.

I would like to thank Mr James Callaghan for letting me see Dalton's marked copy of Keynes's *General Theory*; Susan Crosland

and Marjorie Durbin for making available relevant items from the papers of, respectively, Anthony Crosland and Evan Durbin; Michael Dalton, Joyce Parker and Morag Simpson for advice and information about Dalton genealogy; Elizabeth Durbin for sending me draft chapters from her forthcoming book *New Jerusalems*; Lord Kahn for an energetic and enlightening tour of Cambridge economists known to Dalton; Michael Lee for sending a copy of his invaluable mimeographed study of the Anderson Committee; Marion Miliband for lending me the Visitors' Book from West Leaze; Donald Moggridge for sending me material from Keynes's *Collected Writings* in proof; David Roberts and Andrew Sargent for lending me copies of their doctoral theses; Dr Urwick, Dalton's medical adviser, for a note about his patient's illnesses and their treatment; John Vaizey for helpful advice; and Philip Williams for showing me chapters from his biography of Hugh Gaitskell before it was published, and letting me see relevant papers in his possession. I am extremely grateful to Mr J. S. Peart-Binns, who made available draft chapters from his own unfinished biography of Dalton, and lent source material acquired during his researches. I would also like to express my gratitude to an American friend, Peter Reichard, who, not long before his tragic death, stimulated a new line of thought by sending me as a gift *The Great War and Modern Memory* by Paul Fussell, a book I came greatly to admire.

For access to items of correspondence (mainly letters by Dalton) thanks are due to: Hilde Auerbach, Michael Barnes, Florence Davis, J. Feeling, Michael Foot, William Gregory, Frank Hardie, A. C. King, Lord Mayhew, Joyce Parker, Jasper Ridley, Lord Robens and Lord Walston. (These small collections are referred to in the Notes by the name of their present owner: e.g. 'Auerbach Letters', etc.).

A vital source has been the informal, untaped interview. I am grateful to the following, who agreed to see me and then gave generously of their time: Brian Abel-Smith, Austen Albu, Tom Anderson, Hilde Auerbach, Anne Barnes, Michael Barnes, Amber Blanco-White, Lord Boothby, Jim Boyden, Lord Brockway, Lady Brook, Sir Robin Brook, James Callaghan, Douglas Carter, Robert Carvel, Arthur Cheesemond, Sir George Chetwynd, Harry Clements, Dame Margaret Cole, Susan Crosland, Nicholas Davenport, Olga Davenport, Florence Davis, Margaret Dean, Sir Geoffrey de Freitas, Pauline Dower, Marjorie Durbin, Matilda Edelman, Sir Trevor Evans, Lady Foot, Sir Dingle Foot, Michael Foot, Heather Forbes Watson, Ian Forbes Watson, Lady Fraser, Sir Robert Fraser, John Freeman, Baroness Gaitskell, Lord George-Brown, Margaret Gibb, Rosalind Gilmore, Lord Gladwyn, Jo Gordon, Alexander Grant, Mary Grant, Harold

Guthrie, Sir Noel Hall, Sir Patrick Hancock, David Hardman, Pat Herbert, David Hopkinson, Denis Howell, William Hughes, Douglas Jay, Peggy Jay, Roy Jenkins, Lord Kahn, Lord Kaldor, Bernard Keeling, Ann Kendall, Fred Kendall, Sir Geoffrey Keynes, A. C. King, Lord Lambton, S. Levenburg, Sir Harry Lintott, Lord Longford, Grant McKenzie, Enid MacLeod, G. J. Macmahon, F. Macmanus, John Maddison, Mary Maddison, Lord Mayhew, James Meade, Dame Alix Meynell, J. R. S. Middlewood, Ian Mikardo, Marion Miliband, James Mudd, Robert Nield, Lord Noel-Baker, Sir Thomas Padmore, John Parker, Joyce Parker, the Hon. Helen Pease, Sir Dennis Proctor, E. A. Radice, Joan Radice, Sir Victor Raikes, Jack Rathbone, Lord Robbins, Lord Robens, Sir Austin Robinson, Kenneth Robinson, A. L. Rowse, Harry Russell, Lord Sandys, Baroness Sharp, Lord Shawcross, Morag Simpson, Josephine Smith, Sir Robert Somerville, W. H. Spedding, Lord (Michael) Stewart, Lord Stockton, Lord Strauss, Bickham Sweet-Escott, George Taylor, Lady Trend, Lord Trend, Lady Vaizey, Lord Vaizey, George Wagner, Irene Wagner, Lord Walston, Gwilym Williams, Len Williams, Lord Willis, Lord (Harold) Wilson, Olive Wilson, Baroness Wootton and Sir Woodrow Wyatt.

I would like to thank those who provided information or answered particular points by correspondence: G. C. Allen, Hugh Berrington, H. A. R. Binney, P. Bolton, Nick Bosanquet, Mrs J. M. Brown, Eveline Burns, David Butler, Colin Clark, Lord Cockfield, Cyril Coffin, Denis Craig, Peter Croft, Ken Dallas, Mrs E. Davison, A. Essex-Crosby, Justin Evans, Dr U. R. Evans, W. L. B. Fairweather, Hugh Farmar, Ruth Gilmour, Sir Arthur Gosling, F. Gutteridge, E. L. Hargreaves, Pat Haynes, J. H. Hopkins, Sir Alan Horne, Pearl Jephcock, E. Joiner, Major W. G. McMinnies, Philip Mantle, Freda Mantner, Sir Harold Mitchell, Sir Edmund Parker, E. F. Penrose, Sir Anthony Percival, Ishbel Peterkin, Alice Prochaska, Peter Pulzer, C. A. Reeves, M. J. B. Riches, Jasper Ridley, Lord Roberthall, Rachel Sharp, W. A. Sibbs, Clifford Smith, Patrick Strong, L. B. Sutherland, Lord Taylor, Herbert Tout, George Wansbrough, A. E. Welch, L. P. Wilkinson, Sir Hugh Willatt and Klaus Ziegel.

I am grateful to the following for permission to quote copyright material: H.M. the Queen (Royal Archives); Mr Julian Amery and Hutchinson Group Ltd (*Approach March*); Lord Attlee (Attlee papers); the British Library of Political and Economic Science (Dalton and Passfield papers); the Brooke Trustees (Brooke papers); the Controller of H.M. Stationery Office (Crown copyright records in the Public Record Office); Susan Crosland (Crosland papers); Gerald Duckworth & Co, Ltd (*The Autobiography of Goldsworthy Lowes*

Dickinson); Macmillan, London and Basingstoke (*The Life of John Maynard Keynes* by Sir Roy Harrod); Professor James Meade (Meade papers); Frederick Muller Ltd (Dalton's published memoirs); the Public Trustee (Dalton letters not in the B.L.P.E.S.); Virago Press Ltd and The London School of Economics and Political Science (*The Diary of Beatrice Webb*, Vols 3 and 4); and the Dean and Canons of Windsor (Vidler papers). I am also grateful to the owners or holders of papers quoted: Balliol College, Oxford; the Bodleian Library, Oxford; the British Library; Churchill College, Cambridge; the House of Lords Record Office; King's College, Cambridge; the Labour Party Library; McGill University; New York Public Library; Nuffield College, Oxford; Lord Ponsonby of Shulbrede; Rhodes House Library, Oxford; the Royal Economic Society; Sheffield City Libraries; the University of Strathclyde; the Trevelyan Family; and Trinity College, Cambridge.

For permission to reproduce illustrations I wish to thank: the B.B.C. Hulton Picture Library (nos 20, 26, 41 and 52); Central Press Photos Ltd, the Photo Source Ltd (no. 21); the *Daily Mail* (no. 33); the *Express & Star*, Wolverhampton (no. 54); Heather Forbes Watson (nos 1–7, 12–14 and 18); Fox Photos Ltd, the Photo Source Ltd (no. 32); Philip Greenall (no. 49); F. Gutteridge (no. 16); Keystone Press Agency Ltd, the Photo Source Ltd (nos 31, 40 and 44); Popperfotos Ltd (no. 37); W. H. Spedding (no. 17); the *Standard* (for the Vicky and Low cartoons); the *Western Mail & Echo*, Cardiff (no. 47). Other photographs are from family sources, the British Library of Political & Economic Science (B.L.P.E.S.), and the Labour Party Library.

Several people kindly agreed to look at chapters in draft. Rodney Barker bravely read the whole of an early version; Sir Robin and Lady Brook, Robert Carvel, Hugh Davies, John Freeman, Nick Hartley and George Jones read and commented on segments. They cannot, of course, be held responsible for anything I have written, but I should like to say how much I have appreciated their interest, and how greatly I have valued their suggestions.

I would like to thank my colleagues, present and former, in the Politics and Sociology Department at Birkbeck for all their encouragement and help, and for providing as pleasant and fertile an environment for writing as one could possibly wish for; and I should mention, in the same breath, my evening class graduate students, with working experience mainly in administration, journalism and politics, who have provided an invaluable testing ground for many of the ideas in this book.

For secretarial and other much needed assistance I am grateful to

Greta Edwards, secretary and chief code-breaker on the diary project; and to Audrey Coppard, JoAnne Robertson and Susan Proctor.

At Cape, I have received the kind of attention and guidance for which an author cannot normally hope. I would like to thank, in particular, Graham C. Greene and Tony Colwell, whose interest and enthusiasm helped to keep me going; and Jill Sutcliffe, whose sense for language and care over detail have been a priceless asset.

I owe a very special debt to Anne-Marie Rule, who has done much more than type successive drafts of the manuscript with her usual intuitive accuracy. Her words of encouragement, her kindness and friendship, have been, as always, a unique source of sustenance and strength.

I salute my sons, Dan and Nat, and thank them for the pleasures they bestow. Most of all, I thank my wife, Jean Seaton – dear comrade, critic and support – whose instinct and understanding have helped to shape my thoughts at every stage, and to whom I owe more than I can express. This book is dedicated to her with love.

Gower Street,
London WC1

November 1984   B.J.P.

PREFACE TO THE PAPERMAC EDITION

The publication of the Papermac edition has provided a welcome opportunity to correct a number of misprints and factual errors. I am most grateful to readers who wrote to me pointing out mistakes and I have, in almost every case, heeded their advice.

September 1985   B.J.P.

I

Behind the Night

I

The Royal Connection

When, in his forty-eighth year, Canon John Neale Dalton became a father for the first time, he was anxious that his son should have as good a start in life as it was possible to arrange. The child was born on 16th August 1887 in the comfortable surroundings of the Gnoll, Catherine Dalton's father's country mansion, set in fine gardens near Neath in Glamorgan. The Canon lacked the ample resources of his father-in-law, so he wrote to his sister Eliza in Oxford, combining paternal pride, fraternal solicitude and a request for family possessions:

> Although I daresay you have already heard I write these lines to tell you that Kitty has a little boy, such a jewel. He crows away when he is pleased, and has a temper and will of his own. We hope to name him John Edward Hugh. Two old family names and one of Kitty's brothers. I do hope your own health has been better. I often think of you. Are you going to leave Oxford? If you feel inclined to part with the old nursery wardrobe from Greatham, or any other pieces of the old furniture, I should so like to take them of you. If you will get them valued by a furniture man at Oxford or tell me what you think them worth I shall be so happy to send you the value. The wardrobe would come in especially useful just now, when we must begin to think of furnishing our nursery.[1]

But if (for the purpose of writing to a sister), Edward could be presented as a family name, there was also another, far grander association. Edward was the name both of the Prince of Wales and of his eldest son, Prince Albert Victor Edward, known as Eddy. After some further thought, therefore, the Canon re-arranged the names, placing the royal one first. Writing to Prince Eddy's younger brother George, later King George V, on 11th September, he explained the new ordering and its significance:

> I am sure that you will be glad to hear that I have a little son. He was born August 16th and we hope to have him christened here on my birthday the 24th September. Eddy is going to be Godfather, and 'old voice' [Hugh Evan-Thomas, Catherine's brother]: and his names are to be Edward Hugh John Neale, after his godfathers and myself. If ever there is another boy I hope you will consent to be Godfather, and we will have him called after you. But this is counting one's chickens before they are hatched: and going altogether too fast![2]

Prince George, on board H.M.S. *Dreadnought* at Trieste, replied promptly and politely:

> I am delighted to hear that you have become a father, receive my most hearty congratulations and I am very pleased Eddy is Godfather. I shall be proud to be the same to the next one. I hope Mrs. Dalton and the baby are very well. I hope you are spending a pleasant time in Wales now, it must be delightful in the country. Well now to tell you what I have been doing. I left England with Louis Battenberg as you know on the 11th August and arrived at Gibraltar on the 16th . . .[3]

The baby was duly christened Edward Hugh John Neale Dalton at St George's Chapel, Windsor. To the Canon's great regret Prince Eddy was not present, being away in Denmark, and so had to become a godparent *in absentia*.[4] The young prince seems to have been pleased about his new status, though characteristically tardy in the exercise of the duties which it entailed. On 8th October, a fortnight after the christening, he wrote apologetically to Canon Dalton:

> You will I hope receive in a few days my gift for my Godson which was not ready before, or I would have sent it for the Christening on the 24th of last month. I hope you will think the cups suitable, as I got them in Copenhagen, and they took my fancy at once; and I think they ought to come in useful when my Godson grows older as I used to have the same kind of cups for drinking out of as a child. I suppose you are back at Windsor again by this time, and I daresay were rather sorry to leave the pretty Welsh hills where you have been for the last few months.[5]

What became of the royal christening cups, or of any later gifts from Prince Eddy, is unknown – though Hugh (as the Canon's son was always called) is believed to have sold off royal possessions during the Second World War, much to the displeasure of King George VI, Prince Eddy's nephew.[6] Hugh may not have remembered his royal godfather, but if he did, he did not cherish the connection, and nobody outside his immediate family was ever aware of it. In adult life Hugh's attitude to monarchs and princes as a type, and to the Windsor family in particular, combined suspicion with contempt in roughly equal doses; while the British Royal Family came to regard Canon Dalton's son with a loathing far greater than its dislike of any other Labour politician – a development which, as we shall see, was not without historically important consequences.

In 1929 Beatrice Webb (who usually had a fine sense of such things) placed Hugh Dalton in the 'upper or upper middle class: old governing class of the 19th century'.[7] This was close, but not quite right. There had been respectability and public service on both sides of Hugh's family for many generations, and considerable wealth on his mother's side – but little involvement in governing.

The writer A. C. Benson, best man at the Canon's wedding, wrote of his own family that it was ancient but obscure. 'My ancestors had been mostly clergymen, doctors, lawyers', he recalled, '. . . we had portraits, miniatures, plate – in no profusion, but enough to be able to feel that for a century or two we had enjoyed a liberal education, and had opportunities for refinement if not leisure, and aptitude for cultivating the arts of life.'[8] Benson might also have been writing of the Dalton family, which had been composed of minor gentry, merchants and clergy for several hundred years – maintaining a social position which was increasingly based on education and business skills rather than on land.

The earliest known Dalton followed Henry II from Normandy in 1153, receiving a grant for the manors of Dalton and Byspham in Lancashire. Hugh Dalton was descended in the direct male line from a sixteenth-century Dalton younger son, Roger, who became Member of Parliament for Lancaster, and moved south, settling in Oxfordshire. During the Civil War the loyalty of this branch of Daltons nearly resulted in the family's obliteration. Ten Dalton brothers, cousins, nephews and uncles were killed fighting for the King at the Battle of Worcester in 1651. The surviving heir, Walter Dalton, fled to Carmarthenshire – and it is recorded that he lost three sons through hardship sustained in the flight.

Reduced in property, Hugh's Dalton ancestors entered the learned professions or took part in the expanding East India trade. It was in the eighteenth century that there emerged characteristic features and traditions, still apparent when Hugh was growing up. James Dalton, great-grandson of the fleeing Walter, moved from Wales to become Rector of Great Stanmore in Middlesex – establishing an enduring family connection with the Church of England. James's sister married a Thackeray, forebear of the novelist, while James's son, born in 1755 and apprenticed as a draper, set up a shop in London for the sale of silks and satins from the East. Thereafter Daltons always cherished their involvement with the Drapers' Company in the City. Both the Canon and Hugh served as Masters, regularly attending dinners and associating themselves with the Company's charitable works.

A marriage in the next generation introduced a new, more powerful sense of moral purpose. In 1806 James Dalton's grandson John, also a cloth merchant in the family business, married Hannah Neale, a member of a wealthy pottery family which had become closely associated with the evangelical Clapham Sect. The interests of the Neales – religion and mathematics – now entered the Dalton family as a dominant gene. The piety and earnestness of the Neales were summed up in a story about Hannah's theologian brother Cornelius (Hugh's great-great uncle) who was alleged to have had one almost uncontrollable vice: an interest in the reading of fiction. After leaving Cambridge as senior wrangler in 1812, the young Cornelius Neale succeeded in breaking this obnoxious habit; his wife found to her inexpressible joy that he had thrown the Waverley novel he had been reading to the other end of the room, 'in a vehement recoil from anything which might interpose an earthly interest between him and matters of more serious moment'.[9] James Neale, father of Hannah and Cornelius, had been one of the first and most active members of the London Missionary Society. Hannah's children were brought up in the same mould: of seven sons who survived infancy, four entered the Church, three having left Cambridge as wranglers.

The eldest of the seven, John Neale Dalton, grandfather of Hugh, graduated from Caius College, Cambridge in 1834, and married his Dalton first cousin, who bore him five boys and four girls. One son, called Cornelius after his great uncle, achieved distinction as a barrister and civil servant, a member of Royal Commissions, Comptroller-General of the Patent Office, and spare-time author – eventually receiving a knighthood.[10] Two sons entered the Church, following in their father's footsteps. One of these remained a country parson all his life. The other, John Neale Dalton, was Hugh's father.

Thus by the mid-nineteenth century the Dalton family had become well-established, with many scions. It was neither rich nor (to use

Beatrice Webb's term) upper class. There were no big estates, no country mansion or town house. The schools and colleges attended by Daltons were not those patronised by the wealthy. Yet there was enough money – from the family drapery business, and through the Neale inheritance – to educate large families of sons to take their place in the professions or the Church. In this respect, Daltons were little different from many other similar clerical families inhabiting the rectories and vicarages of rural England.

But there was something else. Mainly through the Neale connection, Daltons had joined the fringes of the network since labelled by Noel Annan 'the intellectual aristocracy', which had begun to establish a nationwide dominance of English cultural and scientific life. Daltons were not Darwins, Huxleys or Raverats. Yet they had been going to Cambridge and graduating well for several generations, developing traditions of intellectual inquiry, public service and personal self-advancement that typified Annan's families whose children 'were encouraged to take part in, and succeed at, the competitive examinations at school and university which others of their class had devised'. Like Annan's intellectual aristocrats, Daltons were keen walkers – worshipping beauty in Nature, while retaining what Annan called 'an evangelical distrust' of beauty in art.[11] Daltons were related to Thackerays; Neales were cousins of Wedgwoods and Stephens. Hugh Dalton cared little for his own personal heritage, but his similarity in family background to others who made up the intellectual and political *avant garde* at Edwardian Cambridge helps to explain why he so quickly found his place among them.

If ambition allied to public service was a tradition brought into the family by Hugh's great-grandmother Hannah, the most perfect expression of that tradition among Hugh's close relatives was to be found in his civil servant uncle, Cornelius Neale Dalton. By contrast, Hugh's father followed a path that at first seemed destined no further than a rural rectory. Born in 1839, the younger John Neale Dalton was educated at Blackheath Proprietary School and as a scholar at Clare College, Cambridge. Having obtained a Third in Classics and a First in the Theological Tripos, he was ordained in 1865, taking a curacy in his father's parish of Milton Keynes. Four years later, at the age of 30, he became curate to Canon Prothero, at Whippingham in the Isle of Wight.

This was scarcely a remarkable trajectory, nor one apparently aimed at high achievements. Yet appearances may be deceptive. Whippingham was not an ordinary parish, nor Prothero an ordinary parish priest. Can it have been an accident of geography that, in taking his first appointment away from home, John Dalton should have chosen the parish which contained the royal residence of Osborne, frequented by the Monarch herself? Or was the young clergyman already aware of the opportunities offered by Canon Prothero's close links with the Chapter of St George's Chapel at Windsor? In later life, John Dalton was known for his intrigues and calculations. It would be wrong to assume that his arrival at Whippingham did not have about it an element of far-sightedness. Dalton can hardly have anticipated the particular opportunity that this curacy was to provide; but he would have been aware that it would quickly bring him to the attention of Queen Victoria.

'A showery morning', the Queen wrote in her diary on 5th February 1871. 'Did not go out, before going to Church at Whippingham. Mr. Dalton, the Curate, preached.'[12] Evidently she was pleased by what she heard, for the same year the Queen engaged Dalton as tutor to her two grandsons, Eddy and George, then aged 7 and nearly 6 respectively.[13] The appointment was not regretted, and three generations of royalty came to regard John Dalton as a source of advice, understanding and, in the case of King George V, lifelong friendship. John Dalton lived for another sixty years, the younger prince for sixty-four. In 1949 the Duke of Windsor recalled that Dalton retained his hold over his father right to the end, 'and would burst in on him at any time'.[14]

One can only guess at the impact of this preferment on the young clergyman whose previous experience had been restricted to country parsonages. As tutor to the sons of the heir to the throne, John Dalton acquired in the royal household a role that fell between surrogate father and elder brother – yet provided a relationship that in some ways was more intimate than either, for as he was an unmarried man without any other occupation, the princes absorbed all his time and attention. According to the future King's first biographer, four people chiefly influenced Prince George up to manhood: his parents, a certain Captain Stephen, and Dalton. Of these Dalton bulked largest between 1871 and 1885: 'He had during these years the lion's share of opportunity'.[15] For the greater part of fourteen years, the two young princes – shy and intellectually backward, isolated from their peers – were nurtured, trained and, to a limited extent, educated by the former curate, who made their upbringing his life's work.

Dalton's regime, based on a meticulously strict routine and an obsessive concern with every error or transgression, would not commend itself to a modern educationalist. Queen Victoria, however, strongly approved. 'Saw Mr. Dalton who is a very good, sensible man and manages the little Boys very well', she wrote in her journal in 1874.[16] Two large albums were kept, in which details of progress and weekly reports were recorded. 'Prince George this week has been much troubled by silly fretfulness of temper and general spirit of contradiction', Dalton wrote in a typical entry, when the boy was eleven.

How did the princes react? According to Harold Nicolson, official biographer of George V, '[Dalton] possessed a resonant voice and much enjoyed listening to it; his handwriting was neat and scholarly; his passion for tidiness and order left an indelible impression upon Prince George's habits of thought and life'. Yet this damning assessment was not entirely fair. Even Nicolson noted the tutor's refusal to be cowed by his employers, and his readiness to point out the harm that was being done by the restless journeyings of the Prince and Princess of Wales.[17] Correspondence from George in early adolescence clearly suggests a strong mutual affection between tutor and pupil. 'On Tuesday I went cruising with Papa in the "Hildegarde" and we won the cup, and all the sailors cheered and Papa gave them each a glass of champagn [sic], which they liked very much indeed', the twelve-year-old prince wrote to Dalton in a typical letter, full of cheerful exuberance. 'The "Thunderer" came in to Cowes last night with Lord Charles Beresford she looked a beautiful great monster as she came in.'[18]

The difficult one was Eddy. Both boys were slow learners, but George was keen and willing, a respecter of authority and passionate in his personal loyalties. Eddy, by contrast, was regarded by tutor and parents alike as wilful and obstinate, passively resisting the endeavours of those who sought to fit him for future responsibilities. Plans to send Eddy to public school – an unprecedented step for royalty – were dropped when Dalton persuaded the Queen that this would separate the prince from the supposedly benign influence of his younger brother, and that the 'evil associations' of school life presented risks too serious to take. In the end it was agreed that, rather than school, the two princes should be placed together on a training ship, the corvette *Bacchante*, for an extended cruise around the world. This decision was taken after Dalton had first tendered, and then withdrawn, his own resignation in a row which caused a minor constitutional crisis over the question of whether it was desirable for both princes to travel on the same ship.[19]

The *Bacchante* voyage was a turning-point in the lives of the princes and their tutor. It removed the two boys, now aged 14 and 15, from all family influences for a period of three years (with one short interlude), during which Dalton was able to ensure that his own dominating companionship should have no rival. Away from the interference of his employers, the young clergyman dealt as he wished with anybody who had the temerity to befriend his charges. When the Senior Midshipman showed signs of familiarity, Dalton engineered the removal of the unfortunate young man from the ship.[20] Others, taking note, kept their distance. Not surprisingly, cadets regarded Dalton as a martinet and a kill-joy, and he was seen by officers as 'an incubus' of rows in the ward-room.[21] Perhaps it was loneliness caused by Dalton's policy of segregation that drove Eddy into a state of depression and apathy. So far from providing the desired stimulus, the cruise proved enervating, and Dalton was soon reporting home that the eldest son of the Prince of Wales sat 'listless and vacant', wasting as much time as ever, showing a weakness and lack of will-power, not only in work, but 'also in his hours of recreation and social intercourse'.[22]

The Dalton regime cannot have been wholly oppressive. George seems to have enjoyed the trip, which provided the background to his future career as a 'sailor-king', with a lifelong devotion to the navy. The member of the royal party most affected by the years at sea, however, was not George or Eddy but Dalton himself. For the tutor, the voyage was a welcome relief from a world of regal opulence and aristo-cratic selfishness in which he had been forced to play a very humble role. At sea, Dalton was his own master, as well as master of the most important members of the ship's complement. He enjoyed the royal welcome given to his party at every imperial stopping place across the world. Most of all, he enjoyed the idea – more perhaps than the reality – of the rugged, male comradeship of H.M.S. *Bacchante*. 'Oh dear, how often my thoughts go off to you, and I wish I could be, if even for a few minutes, with my little Georgy', Dalton wrote shortly after the trip had ended.' ... I often fancy I can see you going along on the sea; and I turn up on deck at Evening Quarters, or in the changing of the watches during the night.'[23] Seventy years later, a clerical colleague attributed Dalton's irritating habits as a Canon of Windsor to the fact that he had been 'taken from his country curacy to live among sailors, at sea, where he was out of association with the clergy'.[24] Canon Dalton's house was soon cluttered with naval mementoes: model ships and sailing prints and pictures of ruddy-faced matelots. A sailor-servant on the *Bacchante* became his personal retainer in St George's Chapel for the next half century.

There were many stories about Dalton's nautical affectations. A former pupil at St George's Choir School, Windsor, recalled telling a master who had put a lit pipe in his coat, 'You're on fire, Sir'. 'Now Canon Dalton would have put it differently', came the reply. 'Canon Dalton would have roared out: "I say, Fox-Strangeways, there appears to be a slight conflagration manifesting itself from your port-side pocket".'[25] Time and again, in later life, Dalton would hark back to the *Bacchante* and its supposed pleasures. 'You will think me an old grumbler', he wrote to George early in 1888, 'but I often wish myself at sea again. A happier three years I never had than when I was afloat: and happier I never expect to have.'[26]

But the most dramatic effect of the trip was indirect. It was the *Bacchante* voyage that caused Dalton – apparently a confirmed bachelor – to decide upon matrimony. Dalton's embargo on close social contacts did not extend to one midshipman, Hugh Evan-Thomas, under seventeen at the beginning of the first cruise. Dalton developed a liking for this young cadet, who became an accepted member of the royal group. Evan-Thomas showed Dalton letters which he had received from his sister Kitty. These so intrigued the older man that on his return in 1882 he asked to meet the writer. Within three days, the middle-aged clergyman had proposed marriage to a young girl half his age.[27]

There was no immediate wedding, perhaps because the Canon's royal responsibilities were not yet at an end. Over the next three years, Dalton accompanied Eddy first to Lausanne, and then to Cambridge where the prince spent two undergraduate years. By this time the burden of the ever-vigilant tutor must have become exceedingly irksome. Early in 1885, Queen Victoria wrote in her diary: 'After tea saw, and talked to Mr Dalton, whom I found very sensible about Eddy. He is now going to read with him his dear Grandfather's Life'.[28] If that was not bad enough, Dalton's stream of adverse reports continued unabated. ' ... I cannot, I confess, help being much grieved by the unsatisfactory account you are unfortunately obliged to give me of Eddy', Princess Alexandra, the Princess of Wales, wrote during the Lausanne trip. 'It is indeed a bitter disappointment that instead of steadily improving as we hoped ... he should have relapsed into his old habits of indolence and inattention'.[29] But Dalton's tutelage did not go on for ever. In June 1885 the Queen wrote that the tutor, who had watched and guided the boys so well, had just left Eddy,[30] and on 6th July, the Prince, now aged 21, joined his regiment at Aldershot.

In October, Dalton's services were rewarded with a canonry at Windsor, carrying with it the life tenancy of an elegant house in the Chapel Cloisters.[31] On 16th January 1886 he married Catherine Alicia Evan-Thomas. It must have seemed a strange match. Apart from the distance in ages, Evan-Thomases and Daltons belonged to different worlds. The Canon was a parson's son. Kitty's father, Charles Evan-Thomas, was a landowner (and, for a time, a coal-owner)[32] who had just become High Sheriff of County Brecknock. Charles's elder brother Henry Thomas traced his descent from Elystan Glodrydd, Prince of Fferllys, and Thomases had been seated at Llwyn Madoc, County Brecknock, for several centuries. The Gnoll, Hugh's birthplace, was a recent acquisition – inherited from an uncle, Henry Grant, whose father bought it and its estate in 1810 for the huge sum of £100,000.[33] Charles had come into sole occupation of the property in 1880, by which time he and his wife Cara had eight children, including Kitty and Hugh. Charles's son Hugh Evan-Thomas, midshipman on the *Bacchante*, later became Commandant of the Royal Naval College, Dartmouth, and an Admiral, commanding the Fifth Battle Squadron at the Battle of Jutland in 1916.

Dalton's royal association may have overcome any doubts about his age and origins, and the marriage seems to have aroused no objections from the bride's family. Yet it was scarcely a propitious alliance. Kitty was a young woman going out into the world for the first time. John was withdrawing into effective retirement, his life's adventure over. For the next forty-five years his massive personality dominated the Chapel Chapter as it had once dominated the princes. Yet his real importance having already ceased, much of what remained seemed petty and frustrating.

The princes did not depart entirely from the Canon's life. They often visited him at Windsor. 'Papa wishes me to tell you, that both Eddy and I are coming to sleep at your house on Saturday night when we come to tea at Windsor, as there is no room at the Castle', George wrote a few weeks before the birth of Hugh.[34] Nevertheless there was a gap in the Canon's life, and it was natural that he should look to his own children to fill it. What more understandable, therefore, than to name the first child Edward, and to hope for a second boy, in order that he might be called George? Alas, fate did not oblige a second time. Another baby died in childbirth.[35] A second surviving child, born in 1891, turned out to be a daughter. When the Canon heard the news, so it was said, he turned on his heels in disgust and left the room.[36] The child was named Alexandra Mary, after the Princess of Wales and Mary of Teck, at that time betrothed to Eddy, and later married to Prince George. George agreed to be godfather as he had promised, and the little girl was always known as Georgie. There were no further children. Six years after the departure of Eddy and George from John Dalton's care, their places had been taken by Edward Hugh and Georgie. Yet, as the royal princes grew away from him, the Canon seems to have regarded his own son and daughter as meagre compensation.

Perhaps it is fanciful to see Hugh cast, from birth, into the uncomfortable role of substitute royal prince. What is beyond doubt is that the atmosphere of royalty and the Court enveloped his family, dominated his childhood and played a large part in shaping his attitudes. In his memoirs, he noted cryptically that he had been brought up 'under the shadow of the Castle'.[37] This was true in a very literal sense. The Cloisters are squeezed between St George's Chapel and the battlements of the great royal fortress. No. 4, where the Canon lived, is part of a high terrace which merges into the Castle's Winchester Tower. The house itself, Georgian in interior style, contains large rooms on three floors, with a study at the top, cellars beneath, and extensive servants' quarters. Wide windows face north towards the river with a fine view of Eton College Chapel. At the back, the land slopes sharply down towards the Choir School, leaving room only for a small garden, physically over-shadowed by the massive perimeter wall of the Castle. Hugh spent the first eleven years of his life in this house, apart from visits to his grandmother in Glamorgan. It remained his home, in school holidays and university vacations, for another twelve. Every childhood and adolescent recollection must have been coloured by the memory of Windsor – and by the power, mystique and historic inheritance of the Royal Family around which the Windsor community revolved.

Was he happy there? Hugh wrote kindly of both his parents in his memoirs. On the other hand, Georgie's children recall that their mother found Kitty Dalton cold and remote,[38] and Hugh appears to have been little moved by her final illness and death in 1944. As she lay dying he wrote, clinically rather than bitterly, 'she has combined great physical toughness with low mentality and very little imagination'.[39] There is little evidence that, either before or after the Canon's death, she took much interest in her son's unusual career. Hugh recalled 'happy memories of days spent at the Gnoll', his grandmother's house, where he could enjoy the large garden and grounds – but not happy days at Windsor. Instead he wrote: 'I suppose that these surroundings stimulated in me a certain irreverence towards authority'.[40]

Dalton's memoirs are generally most significant for what they leave out, and the absence of any positive reference to Windsor, combined with Georgie's recollections as related by her children, adds to an impression of a childhood that was lacking in warmth, intimacy or fun. Canon Dalton was well acquainted with the ways of growing boys, but he knew little of babies and small children. Stories about him and his new son suggest an absent-minded approach to the whole business, as though the child was only partly in his thoughts. The Canon was to be seen walking at great speed alongside a pram pushed by his wife, trying to hold back his own pace. 'He could not help shooting ahead, and then, finding he had left the pram far behind, would shoot back again, say a few words, and shoot off once more.'

It was also alleged that when the Matron of the Choir School asked what the baby looked like, Dalton replied, 'Been to the Zoo?' The Matron said she had. 'Been to the Monkey House?' asked the Canon. 'Yes'. 'Then you've seen my son.'[41]

One of the Canon's main concerns was that his infant son should be as much like Prince George as possible. 'My wife and the boy are very well, thank you', he wrote to George in December 1887. 'He grows vigorously. He has bright blue eyes, and light hair, your colour. I want you to see him ... ' The following May, the Canon again referred to the child's light hair and blue eyes, writing wistfully, 'I hope he will make a good sailor boy some day'.[42] Eagerly, he begged the princes to take a look. Eddy responded in November 1888. 'I ... think my God son a fine looking boy by the photo', he wrote, 'and hope I may have an opportunity of seeing him myself when next I go to Windsor which I daresay will be before very long.'[43] When George returned from his own long voyage, a large royal party descended for an inspection. Prince George noted in his private journal:

> At 5.0 we all went to evening service in St. George's Chapel, and then Papa, Mama and we five went to [tea] with Mr and Mrs Dalton, she is very nice and they have such a nice little boy 15 months old, his mother is also living with him and she is 82. They have made their house most comfortable.[44]

This may well have been the last positive comment about Hugh Dalton ever to be written by a member of the Royal Family.

When did Royalty first come to dislike him? A favourite story – often repeated by Tory enemies and in the press – was that Queen Victoria had him to tea, and observing him stuffing himself with food, remarked 'what a horrid little boy!' Hugh denied this version, and gave his own. When he was four, Hugh later claimed, he attended a Christmas party for hundreds of children at the Castle. The Queen passed slowly along each table, saying a few words to each child:

> I had just greedily grabbed a lot of grapes and piled them on my plate. When the Queen reached me, she said: 'What a lot of grapes you've got.' And I replied, shrilly but audibly, 'Yes, Queen.' Then she said: 'I expect you'd like me to go away, so that you can eat all those grapes.' And I replied again, 'Yes, Queen.' Whereat she turned to her Lady-in-Waiting and said: 'What a loud voice that child has, just like his father!'[45]

The important thing, however, is not whether the 'horrid little boy' version was true or apocryphal, but that it should have been widely believed and repeated. It is possible that the story was resurrected, or invented, when Dalton was already a socialist politician, as a weapon to be used against him. It seems more likely that versions continued to be current in the tiny Windsor society throughout this period – reflecting the attitudes of colleagues, neighbours and the Royal Family as well.[46]

Within Hugh's own family, opinions varied as to whether he was horrid or not. 'My bright little grandson is much grown and a very amusing companion to his poor old grandmother', wrote the Canon's mother, widow of the Rector of Milton Keynes, when the boy was three. 'He has just been in this room with us for an hour, full of chatter and now gone for his walk, which I shall hear all about when he pays me his afternoon visit.'[47] On the other hand, some relatives felt that the child was allowed to behave too much as he pleased.[48]

The notion that Hugh was over-indulged (not necessarily the same as being unequivocally loved) was certainly shared by his younger sister, Georgie. Georgie has also provided the strongest testimony of Hugh's juvenile horridness, at least in the domestic context – none the less powerful for having reached us second-hand, through her own children.[49] Hugh may or may not have had a happy childhood. Georgie's childhood was undoubtedly the most miserable part of her life; and in her mind, at least, Hugh was the major cause. We do not have Hugh's side of the story, though occasional references in his diary show that he regarded his sister as childish, emotional and self-centred. Georgie's side presents Hugh as a tormentor, operating against a background of difficult family relationships, in which he knew himself to be the favoured child.

Georgie remembered an affectionless childhood, in which she saw little of her parents and was conscious of having only a small importance in their lives. She recalled her father, fifty-two when she was born, as a remote and detached figure, living among books and memories in his attic study and barely acknowledging her existence. Her mother, wishing to have as little to do with the children as possible, delegated responsibility for child-raising to a cold and unsympathetic nurse, called Nanny Larcomb. One speciality of this grim keeper was to tie the little girl's hands to improve her posture. Another was to fix her hair to a button on her dress, to make her sit up at table. As Georgie was taught by governesses at home and never went to school, she saw little of other children apart from her brother. Nanny Larcomb filled every waking hour, and the nights as well, for they shared a bedroom until Georgie was grown up. The tyranny was only relieved when the First World War enabled Georgie to get an office job in

London, and find a husband.

There are two possible strategies for the oppressed: to unite against the oppressor, or, by forging an alliance with the ruling power, to participate in the oppression. Hugh seems to have chosen the second. Nanny Larcomb is not mentioned in his memoirs – though presumably she featured nearly as much in his life as in Georgie's. According to Georgie's account, however, the nurse's treatment of the two children was unequal. Decades later, Georgie would mimic, with a special venom, the tones of the fierce old retainer saying, 'Oh, the dear boy', at Hugh's every whim and gesture. Georgie also recalled with bitterness how Hugh's fraternal persecutions went unchecked. 'As soon as I got anything nice', she would relate to her children, 'Hugh came along and smashed it to bits.' Dolls were broken; toys were appropriated and vanished forever. In between these bandit raids, Hugh reflected the general scorn of the Dalton household by ignoring her completely.

Georgie never forgave him. Regarding her brother as selfish and vindictive in the nursery, she refused to take his later politics seriously or to regard his socialism as anything other than a ploy. She maintained that he joined the Labour Party because it offered a world where the competition was slight and where he could the more easily advance his own fortunes. 'He was always very ready to grab a chance', she would say. Georgie's children were brought up to regard their uncle as arrogant, sharp and nasty, a reprobate whom it was better not to know. Georgie is remembered by those who knew her as a lively, generous, warm-hearted woman, devoted and loyal to family and friends. The antipathy that existed between brother and sister is therefore all the more intriguing.

How much effect did it have on Hugh's later attitudes? Logically, Georgie should have been the rebel. Instead she dealt with the loneliness of her childhood in other ways. As a mother, she sought to give her own children the love and warmth she never had; holidays, outings, celebrations, social events, gained a special meaning. In her political attitudes she reacted, not against the Anglican Toryism of her father, but against what she regarded as the affectations of her brother. 'It's a pity he got in with the wrong set at university', she would say, recalling that Hugh's undergraduate socialism did not extend to charity at home; while she was recovering from a serious riding accident he was too preoccupied with exciting Cambridge friendships to show sympathy or take notice of her at all. Georgie married a future President of the Confederation of British Employers, who shared her dislike of Hugh and his politics. When the old Canon in his dotage began to vote Labour out of paternal loyalty, his daughter remained staunchly Conservative. Unlike her brother, she was firmly attached to the Royal Family and to all it represented. Her daughter, Heather, saw Hugh on only one occasion: at a royal garden party in the late 1940s. She remembers that her mother said, 'Don't look round'. Both averted their eyes as the Cabinet minister uncle passed by.

Hugh may have been strengthened in his ideals by the knowledge that his sister rejected them. Yet it is likely that his life-long attack on wealth and privilege was also a product of the Royal backcloth to his family life. If Georgie found Hugh an intolerable competitor within the Dalton household, Hugh must have been well aware that his was not the first claim on his father's affections. Indeed we may guess that Dalton family life was, to a considerable degree, burdened by the Canon's thoughts and anxieties about the princes.

Missing from Hugh's own account is any mention of Eddy. Yet Eddy must have been a cause of mounting concern to the Canon during the first four and a half years of Hugh's life. We have seen that Eddy, in direct line to the throne, had progressed slowly. Some believed that the young prince's resistance to work was 'a fault of nature', or that he was 'almost wanting'.[50] Others blamed Dalton. When Eddy joined his regiment in 1885, his royal cousin the Duke of Cambridge wrote angrily that the instructor at Aldershot had been astounded at the young prince's ignorance. 'It is clearly Dalton's fault, for it is not that he is unteachable, as Major Miles, having found him thus ignorant, is equally astonished how much he has got on with him and thinks, under the circumstances, his papers are infinitely better than he dare to expect.'[51] More than sixty years later, Queen Mary, who had been betrothed to Eddy before eventually marrying George, made a similar complaint. What she had against Dalton, she declared, 'was that he never tried really to educate the Princes. It was disgraceful that "the King" had not been taught more.'[52] Whether or not this was just, the tutor must have been sensitive to the charge – especially as Eddy began, in his early twenties, to go very wrong indeed.

In the five and a half years that followed his release from Dalton's custody, the backward and hitherto lethargic young man (now Duke of Clarence and Avondale) gained a reputation for a dissipated and unstable life-style which had some particularly disturbing features. In recent years Eddy's name has been linked to the Jack the Ripper murders in Whitechapel in 1888. The evidence is so flimsy that it may be discounted. On the other hand, there is fairly strong circumstantial evidence to connect Eddy with a series of trials, and a libel action, in

1889 and 1890, involving members of the aristocracy and a male brothel specialising in telegraph boys.

One of the leading figures in this affair, which became known as the Cleveland Street Scandal, was Lord Arthur Somerset. Somerset was Extra Equerry to the Prince of Wales, who at first refused to believe in his friend's implication, 'any more than I should if they accused the Archbishop of Canterbury'.[53] Somerset fled the country to avoid prosecution. Thereafter, Somerset always claimed privately that he was shielding another – widely presumed to be Eddy. Somerset's solicitor, convicted and imprisoned for aiding Somerset's escape, was not struck off the rolls by the Law Society, supposedly because of the royal involvement. Though there were veiled references in the press – Eddy's moral laxity, generally of a heterosexual nature, was in any case the subject of Society gossip – the extent of the prince's direct implication was never proved. But the view that there had been a skilful cover-up to save the name of the Royal Family was held by many people at the time.[54]

All this must have been deeply distressing to the Canon, who can only have regarded the waywardness of the prince as a personal failure. However, the Eddy problem was soon to be solved once and for all. In January 1892, the Duke of Clarence died of a fever – apparently influenza, though other theories have been advanced.[55] Queen Victoria recorded two months later that Dalton 'has felt dear Eddy's death dreadfully'.[56] Yet the real burden fell on the young Prince George, now 26, who had to face not only the loss of a brother and close companion, but also the realisation that he now stood in direct line of succession to the throne, after the Prince of Wales.

In his grief and anxiety, the future King turned to the man who knew and loved him best. The Royal Archives contain twenty-three letters from Prince George to Canon Dalton written in the year that Eddy died. What was the impact on the Canon's children? Hugh's memoirs are again interesting for what they leave out. Though there are accounts of meetings with Queen Victoria and the Prince of Wales, there is no reference to George's frequent visits to the Cloisters. Perhaps this was because the Prince took little interest in the Canon's son. George would write announcing his intention of coming to tea, and even express a wish to see the family. But his letters never mention Hugh by name, and there is no indication of anything more than a well-trained politeness.

Did George dislike the 'horrid little boy' of the Queen Victoria anecdote? Was Hugh ushered out of sight when the Prince arrived? Did the young Hugh resent these royal visitations, and the flurry of excitement which they must have caused? In the end, Hugh's attitude to his father's royal connection remains mysterious. Yet if the Windsor surroundings stimulated in him 'a certain irreverence towards authority', Prince George, honest, reliable, humourless, utterly conventional, and leaning heavily on the fatherly affections of the Canon, was the member of the Royal Family most frequently in view, and the one most likely to have been responsible.

If Hugh's politics, and perhaps also the quality of his relationships, owed much to his father's career and special loyalties, other attributes seem to have been acquired by direct inheritance. Canon Dalton was more than a clergyman and a pedagogue. He was also a Chapter House politician of formidable presence. Indeed, the roots of Hugh Dalton's adult taste for machination may be found in the wars of party and faction that dominated the Trollopean world of St George's Chapel.

Because of the royal connection the Canon's position was uneasy, and he seemed to be set apart from other Chapel clergy. The spheres of Chapter and Court were not the same. Chapel appointments were in the monarch's personal gift. Yet social and hierarchical barriers separated the Chapel clergy from the Household. Hence Canon Dalton's access to the Royal Family was a source both of political strength and of jealousy in the enclosed clerical society to which he now belonged.

Some colleagues felt that Dalton displayed qualities ill-suited to a man of the cloth. Others liked to believe that his outward manners concealed an inner state of grace. About one thing there was agreement: Dalton aroused love and hatred but never indifference.

Opponents pointed to his ferocious temper. 'Sometimes he would abandon the more gentle manner of priestliness', a young friend recalled, 'to stamp and roar as a merciless pagan, angry with the rest of the world'.[57] What clerical colleagues found particularly perturbing was his disregard for scruple, once he had fixed upon an objective. 'He would scheme by questionable means', admitted one beneficiary, 'to see what he had in mind was carried out'.[58] Worse – in the eyes of many – he viewed this trait as a subject for pride rather than for shame or repentance. 'Thank heaven there are two things I have never had', he would gleefully declare, 'nerves or a conscience'.[59] Successive Deans of Windsor had reason not to regard this as a joke. The Chapter House operated a system that was supposedly a form of democratic self-government. Dalton ensured that in practice it was a dictatorship. For two generations he was effective ruler of the Windsor clerical community. One colleague recalled that the Statutes allowed very limited powers to the Dean. 'In Dalton's time he had practically none ... any member of the Chapter who timidly ventured to oppose a Daltonian project was, literally, shouted down'.[60]

Dalton first established his dominance in 1891, when a strong Dean was succeeded by a weak one, Philip Eliot. For the next twenty-six years the Canon's influence was all-embracing. In 1917 – to Dalton's intense rage – Eliot was followed by Dean Albert Victor Baillie, who sought with little success to assert his authority in the Chapter. Baillie wrote of his experience of Dalton with notable bitterness, posing a question that puzzled many others: 'Why was Dalton so provoking?' His interesting – and significant – conclusion was that the old Canon had become a rebel against what he regarded as the humbug of Victorian respectability in the Church of England. According to Baillie, Dalton had decided 'that all clergy were unreal, conventional and weak'.[61]

Yet for all his bad temper, intolerance, delight in the shocking and outrageous, and capacity for deliberate rudeness, Canon Dalton had a reputation for great kindness towards those whom he took it upon himself to help. Among papers in the archives of St George's Chapel there is a remarkable letter from a former Assistant Organist, M. C. Boyle, befriended by Dalton when the Canon was in his eighties. Boyle recalled that despite a great difference in years (82 and 22) there developed between them 'a beautiful platonic relationship more like that of a father and his son'. Dalton urged Boyle to read for a Music degree, paid all his fees for a crammer in London, paid his salary at the Choir School to enable him to take time off for three months, and finally paid all his fees at Oxford. Yet the Canon was by no means a rich man.[62] What was the explanation? One aspect was a particular, and perhaps romantic, interest in young men. Another was what one friend described as a special compassion towards those of lower rank. 'A recalcitrant servant, a working-man tempted to petty crime, a poor or a knavish boy were all certain of his help and sympathy, but let an equal thwart him or ask for his pity and he would rise to destroy.'[63]

The Canon's lifelong interest in knavish boys was put to creative use in 1892, when he devised a scheme for moving, expanding and re-organising the tiny Chapel Choir School. Sixty years later, a former headmaster described Dalton as 'the real founder of the Choir School as it now exists'.[64] There are many stories that reflect Canon Dalton's benevolent interest in this establishment – generally presenting him as a terrifying, but fundamentally benign, figure whose sense of fun was not one which small boys always found reassuring:

During the Easter holidays, when the Court came into residence, six boys had to come back in order to sing in the Private Chapel in

the King's private apartments on Sundays. On these occasions ...
it was customary for members of the Chapter to give hospitality to
us for the week-end. I shall never forget the first time I had to go
and stay with Canon Dalton. In fear and trembling I was taken to
his house one Saturday afternoon, to be greeted by the Canon with
the words, 'Ah, he's come, and he will be whipped, and whipped,
and whipped.' Another boy was to stay there and our terror was by
no means lessened by our bedroom. No electric light, an enormous
four-poster bed with curtains, and terrifying oil portraits on the
walls. The two little boys said very short prayers, cleaned their teeth
and popped into bed, and then hugged each other all night for fear
that the terrifying lady in the picture over the mantel-piece would
come down from her frame and get us.[65]

How much was boyish imagination, and how much reflected the
real peculiarities of the household in which Hugh Dalton grew up?
Stories about the Canon all had one thing in common: eccentric
behaviour, either reflecting indifference to conventions, or else
deliberately designed to shock.

Former choristers liked to recall the time when, in the middle of
reading the lesson at morning service, Canon Dalton paused to cough
'and in doing so ejected his dentures with extreme velocity, made a
brilliant slip-catch with his left hand and replaced them with complete
equanimity'.[66] Most anecdotes showed the Canon savagely debunking pompous colleagues. When one canon appeared in the Chapel
vestry before a service adorned with decorations, Dalton eyed him up
and down with mock seriousness, and then declared at the top of his
voice, 'My word you do look a swell!'[67] Deans were his most frequent
victims. On the day that the much-persecuted Dean Eliot returned to
St George's Chapel after an absence caused by an attack of phlebitis,
Dalton interrupted his intonation of the Vestry Prayer to ask loudly,
'How are the flea bites?'[68] There was also a famous incident during
the instalment ceremony of Dean Baillie, when the Canon officiating
referred by mistake to 'Queen Victoria' instead of 'King George'.
Dalton declaimed from his stall, in a voice loud enough to be heard all
over the Choir, 'silly old fool'.[69]

Dalton's voice was the subject of widespread comment and admiration – and of pride to its owner. Before setting out for services in the
Chapel, King George V would enjoin the Royal Family, 'Let us go to
hear the old Canon roar'.[70] 'We used to say that he possessed the
tones of a lion and a mosquito as well', recalled Russell Thorndike, a
former chorister. 'To hear him read the lessons was a thrilling experience, especially the one about King Rehoboam – "My father hath

chastised you with whips, but I will chastise you with scorpions". He made the "whips" crack, and the scorpions really crawl and sting.'[71] Two other readings were especially prized. One was the Judgment of Solomon. A former choirboy who became a bishop describes how, when this lesson came to be read, the Canon would throw himself into the dramatic situation, imitating the two mothers arguing before the King, and building up to the great climax: 'It shall be neither mine nor thine, divide it', which he barked out with all the venom and hatred of the disappointed woman.[72] Nothing, however, compared with Dalton's reading of the throwing of Jezebel out of the palace, to be trodden under foot by Jehu's chariot. His blood-curdling reading of the words 'Throw her down' was a particular joy to the choristers.[13]

Hugh's career was based on an ability to declaim in a manner very similar to that of the Canon. Indeed there were so many transmitted characteristics that it is useful to consider them collectively. Hugh gave his own inventory:

> I inherited and learned much from my father that has helped me to make my own way through life – good physical health, after an uncertain start, and great stamina, a strong voice, a strong temper, strong views, some obstinacy and, I hope, a capacity for friendship on equal terms with a wide range, in age and class and type, of men and women and, I trust, beyond all else, an abiding loyalty to firm friends.[74]

We have noted the generous interest in younger men; the delight in intrigue, combined with an appearance of cynicism which actually hid some powerfully held beliefs; above all, the irreverence towards petty authority, and the instinct for attacking pomposity and humbug, which in the Canon took purely social, and in Hugh political, forms. To these might be added, less attractively, a streak of malice; and a retreat in old age into sentimentality, nostalgia, and a comic role. Hugh was often described as a 'traitor to his class'; yet the closer one looks the more he appears, not as a rebel against his father's attitudes and persona, but as a version of them.

In only two important respects – his father's religion, and his father's devotion to the Royal Family – was there a reaction. Only the last really divided them. In later life, Hugh was always reticent on the subject of the Monarchy. Yet in seeking an explanation of his attack on the very foundations of the Monarchy's position – its inherited privileges and vast wealth – and in seeking to account for the young Hugh's single-minded and successful pursuit of power and fame, the existence of a royal 'brother' whose presence pervaded the Windsor community and who had so prominent a place in his father's private emotions, should be borne in mind.

II

Boyhood

When Hugh was eight, he started at the Choir School which his father had helped to reorganise. He was the only day boy, and unlike the majority, he was not a chorister.[1] St George's was a pleasant and intimate establishment – recently increased in size from twelve to twenty boys, under a new head. Russell Thorndike, Hugh's direct contemporary, wrote a book about his happy memories of St George's.[2] Another boy, who entered the school in 1898, described being taught by a kind mistress, and going through a ceremony to join the Stamp Club involving singing a song with a piece of stamp paper hanging on his nose.[3]

According to Thorndike, Hugh excelled at work, and came top of his class.[4] But St George's was too small to offer more than a basic education, and its syllabus was not geared to the requirements of the most famous public schools. Hence, Hugh was taken away after three years and sent as a boarder to Summer Fields near Oxford – a preparatory school of a very different order.

Summer Fields was one of a number of forcing houses for little boys that had sprung up in the late nineteenth century to cater for the social and educational aspirations of the upper middle class. Such establishments were private businesses, often family concerns. Market pressures were fierce, and there was a constant need to demonstrate to parents that they were getting value for money. The touchstone of success was the annual competition for scholarships to public schools. The most prized awards were those to Eton.

There were about 125 boys at Summer Fields when Hugh entered it, watched over by the Rev. Dr Eccles Williams, the headmaster, whose voice 'would break with emotion at end of term sermons and harden at times of corporal punishment'. Flanked by the Rev. Hugh Alington, 'the Bear', who taught Xenophon and the plays of Euripides furiously with a cane,[5] Eccles Williams focussed the attention of the whole school on a single objective, regarded as the ultimate attainment: the Eton List. Sham Eton papers were taken and a list of awards given, with real prizes, including boxes of chocolates and a gold sovereign.[6] There were rival establishments, similarly directed: St Cyprians, Horris Hill, Waynflete, the Dragon. But none had quite the single-mindedness, the delight in victory and contempt for defeat, of Summer Fields. One effect was to put the school at the head of its own chosen league, and year after year it took the top Eton award. Another effect was to instil feelings of competitiveness that lasted a lifetime. A century after its foundation in 1864, Summer Fields was able to claim 33 Members of Parliament, including two Prime Ministers, two Chancellors of the Exchequer and a Foreign Secretary, among its former pupils.[7]

Clever boys flourished under the Eccles Williams regime. For juvenile prodigies like Ronald Knox, Dalton's contemporary and first in his election to College at Eton, the system could be enjoyable and productive.[8] For others, it could be the cause of the deepest feelings of failure and inadequacy. One man who had been at the school shortly before Dalton, recalled: 'I was simply a very stupid little boy, whom the Summer Field authorities rightly guessed could not be educated up to scholarship standard in four terms. They therefore took little interest in me, except that they beat me, as they did everybody else.'[9]

To move from the relaxed atmosphere of St George's into this scholastic factory, as a boarder for the first time, must have been an uncomfortable transition – made worse by Hugh's physical delicacy. Letters from Prince George to the Canon twice refer to Hugh's illness and recovery in 1897.[10] This may explain why, at a school that did not normally take new boys above the age of ten, Hugh should have waited until eleven before entering. Now his health broke down badly, and over the next two years he spent much of his time in bed with asthma and bronchitis, missing work and games. In his memoirs, Dalton described Summer Fields as 'quite a good school, then as now, with a tendency to cram'.[11] But he cannot have liked it much. A near contemporary has described the experience of being ill at Summer Fields:

The medical supervision of the school was in the hands of a terrifying matron who, if one's draught was unpalatable, was wont to hold one's nose while she administered it ... I was only in the sick-bay once myself, when I had developed roseola twice, having the second rash in me while I was still recovering from the first. This the authorities told me was impossible, and my maladies were regarded as suspiciously as most of my other behaviour; as Talleyrand asked when the Turkish ambassador died during the negotiations: 'What does he mean by that?'[12]

Hugh recalled that at Summer Fields he was clumsy and ungainly, 'a mild and well-behaved person, somewhat lacking in energy and vitality'.[13] How did others find him? Ronald Knox's attitude reinforces the 'horrid little boy' image. According to Knox's biographer, Evelyn Waugh, there were only two features of Summer Fields about which Knox ever complained: 'one, the daily distribution by the matron of three sheets of lavatory paper to each boy, a practice which he found niggardly and indelicate; the other, the presence of a loutish little boy called Hugh Dalton.'[14]

Hugh performed poorly at outdoor games, perhaps because of his delicate constitution, and was never included in any school team. At work he was above average, but was not considered a high-flyer. Little boys were closely observed on arrival for signs of talent: Hugh was placed in the second stream. Because of his Church background he did well at divinity and from the beginning he showed his family's traditional aptitude for mathematics – gaining prizes in both subjects in the summer of 1900.[15] But he was no match for boys like Knox. School lists reveal Hugh's erratic progress, generally in the top half of his classes, which were not the best ones. He came bottom (out of eight) in the Lower Fourth at the end of 1899 – perhaps because of illness. Thereafter he began to improve. Yet his weakness at classics, the key subject for public school scholarships, kept him out of the Fifth Form where boys were groomed for the Eton List. By the end of his last year he was fourth in the Upper Remove (the second form). He was in short an unremarkable boy, of whom no particular distinction was expected.

Nevertheless he was put in for a scholarship to Eton in 1901. Twelve out of seventy competitors were successful.[16] Hugh came seventeenth. Given that the Eton exam attracted the most talented pupils – or the most efficiently crammed – from the most competitive preparatory schools in the country, this position was scarcely an indication of ignorance or stupidity. But in the context of the Summer Fields scale of values, and perhaps also of his father's hopes, it was a bitter defeat. That he should have taken the exam at a later age than most suggests that, whatever the school's opinion of his son, the Canon (who had sent Hugh to Summer Fields in a record year for Eton awards) had the Eton List in mind. The knowledge that five Summer Fieldians, several of whom were younger, had been placed higher on the List, must have been galling. So must the School authorities' conclusion that they had been right all along. The School magazine makes it clear that Dalton's performance was regarded as a vindication of previous assessments. His work, this publication revealed, had improved immensely during the year, and he should regard his placing as 'most satisfactory' considering the quality of those opposed to him. It should be borne in mind that he was a mere Upper Remove boy, 'whose achievement gives us great encouragement as to the standard of work in the body of the School'.[17]*

Hugh's failure to win a scholarship did not prevent him from going to Eton, but it made an important difference to his life once he got there. An Eton scholarship separated its owner from other boys of the same age, placing him in the intellectual and exclusive community of College. Each batch of scholars formed an 'election', entering together, working together and living together throughout their early days at the school. More was expected of Collegers; and correspondingly less of non-scholars, or 'Oppidans'. One observer described the contrast a few years earlier:

> The smaller section has proved itself every year more moral, more industrious, more distinguished in academical honours; the larger has become by degrees more idle, more extravagant, more self-indulgent, more entirely devoted to athletics and less to literary pursuits. It is scarcely a parody to say that an Eton collegian receives the best education in England, an Eton oppidan the worst.[18]

Half a century later, Hugh still regretted that he had not been in College where, he wrote, 'I would have found more mental stimulus and been a member of a more closely knit society'.

Hugh entered Luxmoore's house at Eton in the Michaelmas Term of 1901, when he was already fourteen (considerably older than most new boys), and merged unobtrusively into the anonymous mass of Oppidans. What he made of his environment at first is not clear, but he was not a typical Etonian. Though one of his mother's brothers had been at Eton, there was no tradition on his father's side of attending a school which generally drew its pupils from the sons of old boys. Bad at games, comparatively poor, unprepossessing – 'lethargic

---

* Fifth Form boys, who were expected to do well in the Eton exam, and Upper Remove boys whose parents insisted on entering them, were conducted to Eton in separate parties. 'The sheep were led by Dr. Williams', recalled one of Hugh's contemporaries; 'they stayed at the White Hart and wore straw hats with the school ribbon. The goats under an inferior master, stayed at an inferior hotel and wore caps' (Usborne, *Summer Fields*, p. 54). Hugh was presumably a goat.

and physically lazy' by his own description – a middle-class boy thrust into an upper-class, philistine, athlete-worshipping world, it would be easy to believe that he suffered physical or psychological persecutions.

'I was not unhappy, nor bullied, nor much beaten in my House, nor ever birched by the Headmaster', he wrote, ' – rather an easy lazy life, in short. Until my last year I was rather bored and indifferent.'[19] This was to refute a story, later well established in Tory circles, that Dalton's socialism was a reaction against misery at school. ('Whenever we got bored', one peer would recount, 'we went and kicked Dalton.')[20] Nevertheless, the double negative is interesting, occurring twice in the same passage. Perhaps he was 'not unhappy' during his first four years; but he does not seem to have enjoyed the greater part of his Etonian career, which was certainly a time of minimal achievement. So obscure were his adolescent schooldays that until his last year he is scarcely mentioned in the school records. He did not excel, and he did not at first rebel. One undergraduate contemporary observed that when Hugh entered Eton, he was 'like most "new boys" without any ideas in particular, save the one great principle of not falling foul of the public canons of taste'.[21] An Eton contemporary, still living in the 1980s, remembers him as 'a dull uninteresting boy ... lonesome and unattractive'.[22]

Unlike three other Summer Fieldians who arrived at Eton in the same year – Ronald Knox, Julian Grenfell and Edward Horner – Hugh was never a member of the brilliant College-based group that wrote plays and edited a magazine called the *Outsider*, one of whose contributors, Charles Lister, joined the Independent Labour Party while still at school. Hugh's closest friends were all Oppidans – R. C. Bourne and Algy Bligh, sportsmen rather than aesthetes, and Geoffrey Morris, later a classics don at Cambridge.[23]

Dalton moved from Luxmoore's house to Kindersley's early in his career. It was here that there occurred the major sensation of his schooldays. In June 1903, Kindersley's house was destroyed by a fire believed to have been started by an Etonian arsonist. Two boys died in the blaze, and others were injured. 'One great fellow is supposed to have gone off his head ... ' Julian Grenfell reported to his mother. 'Kindersley is absolutely dazed, and Caledon's hand is dreadfully burned.'[24] Flames and heat beat back the housemaster in his vain attempts to save a boy who had been trapped by bars across the windows on the lower floors. Forty boys escaped in pyjamas by scrambling down the wistaria and letting themselves drop into the churchyard.[25] Hugh was among them. 'My hair was singed', he recalled, 'and I smelt fire very easily for some time after that affair.'[26] News of the event quickly reached Windsor Castle, where the flames and smoke must have been visible. 'There was a fire at Eton early this morning in Mr. Kindersley's house and two boys were burnt, most sad', noted Prince George in his diary. 'Dalton's boy was in the next room to one of the boys but just got out in time.' As a sympathetic gesture – or out of curiosity – the heir to the throne invited Hugh and three Etonians with courtier fathers to lunch at Frogmore House, and to view the royal farm.[27]

Kindersley never recovered from this disaster, feeling a personal responsibility, and ever afterwards appeared a pale and broken man. In other ways he had already showed himself an unsatisfactory housemaster – the subject of opposition rather than respect. Unlike the cultivated Luxmoore, Kindersley was strong in muscular Christian virtue and weak in sympathy or intellect – good at games, sailing and carpentry, yet lacking in imagination and uninterested in those placed in his care. The food in his house was bad, the temperature in winter uncomfortably cold. On one occasion he tried to deprive the house of a library, calling it 'a room for idling'. He distrusted and quarrelled with senior boys. Dalton recalled that his own 'habitual irreverence towards authority' developed during his schooldays. Kindersley was undoubtedly a factor.

It was at Eton that Dalton first began consciously to form political attitudes. Kindersley was a Liberal and Free Trader. Dalton became 'a Joe Chamberlainite, a Tory Democrat, a self-confessed Imperialist'.[28] On one occasion, as chairman of the House Debating Society in his final year, he allegedly 'held the house spell-bound' with a defence and eulogy of Protectionism. On another, he delivered a long and impressive paper to the Eton Essay Society on 'The Need for Imperial Union'. Friends recalled that upon his mantelpiece 'Joseph Chamberlain occupied the place of honour that we might have expected would fall to Miss Gabrielle Ray or Miss Phyllis Dare, those goddesses of adolescent England'.[29] When he left Eton, he impudently presented his housemaster with a book about the Empire, supposedly to educate him.

Dalton's political stance was partly a way of attacking the dull and humourless Kindersley. Yet there were other elements as well, relating to aspects of Dalton's background that separated him from his contemporaries. He had grown up in a home steeped in idealised memories of Empire that had less to do with military glory than with the comradeship of midshipmen on the High Seas, an Empire of young pioneers boldly struggling in a common endeavour. Joseph Chamberlain's view of Empire accorded well with this heritage. There were other aspects that also had a strong appeal to a young man brought up against a background of great contrasts. Chamberlain combined a romantic attachment to far flung dominions with a radical rejection of wealth and privilege. He had asked, 'What ransom will property pay?' He had also declared – shockingly – that 'the Monarchy can't long endure'.[30] For Hugh, it was an enticing mixture.

Yet the rebellion involved in becoming a Tory Democrat at Eton was not great. Dalton's political awakening did not occur until he went to Cambridge. Meanwhile he rebelled in an area of far greater sensitivity than that of national or international politics, about which his fellows knew and cared little. He focussed instead on a subject of intimate concern to all Etonians: social convention. The reason was simple. He felt angry and frustrated at his own exclusion from the school's most exalted circles. Many years later, the writer and politician John Strachey had a stock answer when asked by dear old ladies why he became a communist. 'From chagrin, madam,' he would reply, 'from chagrin at not getting into the Eton Cricket Eleven'.[31] Dalton might perhaps have answered the same enquiry about his socialism: from chagrin at not getting into Pop.

Pop was a self-elected society of two dozen senior boys who governed the social life of the school. Because membership of Pop not only conferred exceptional powers, but was also a visible sign of a special kind of popularity, its importance to those who were in it and to those who were kept out is hard to overstate. 'Such was their prestige that some boys who failed to get in never recovered', wrote Cyril Connolly, at Eton just after the First World War; 'one was rumoured to have procured his sister for the influential members'.[32]

To be a member it was almost always necessary to be good at games. But this alone was not enough. Potential Pops had to combine athletic prowess with elegance, vitality, wit and charm. According to L. E. Jones, Dalton's contemporary, Pop included the most attractive boys – because membership elevated those lucky enough to achieve it to a state of grace. Pops were 'liberated from self-consciousness, social fears and suspicions, heart-burnings and anxieties', and were able thereby 'to step into the sunshine of easy self-confidence, frankness and gaiety ... ' Non-Pops, on the other hand, remained to a greater or lesser degree enslaved – victims of what Jones regarded as the besetting vice of the school, 'social unkindness'.[33]

Dalton reacted fiercely against Pop as an institution and in his final year deliberately flouted its rules of dress and behaviour. His revolt was symbolic: a *frisson* of social horror spread through the school when he appeared as Headmaster's Praeposter (whose duty it was to summon boys to the Headmaster's presence) wearing pumps.

Pumps were a privilege reserved to members of Pop. 'My pumps were an anti-Pop gesture', he recalled, 'a symbol of rebellion and irreverence'. He also tried to manipulate the incestuous politics of Pop from outside, managing to keep out one aspirant 'whose election, since he was in my House, would have caused me local inconvenience and rivalry'.

Dalton cheerfully admitted in his memoirs that he had been anti-Pop largely out of envy. He resented the existence of this self-regarding club which refused to have him as a member. He was aware, too, that there were reasons for his exclusion. In looks, personality, attainment, he was the opposite of a Pop. By his own account he was soft and self-centred, sluggish, sententious and sentimental. Yet it is striking that for the rest of his life the qualities he most admired in others were close to the Pop ideal: wit, urbanity, social grace, physical attractiveness. Some of those he loved best in later years had been Pops, Gladwyn Jebb most notable among them. Others, like Rupert Brooke and Anthony Crosland, would certainly have been in Pop if they had gone to Eton.

All the same, Dalton did taste some of the power Eton had to offer. In his last year he became Captain of Kindersley's. 'I have greater power in my House than Sir Edward Grey has in the Foreign Office', he boasted at his father's dinner-table. There was certainly nothing liberal or progressive about his regime. On one occasion, he proudly recalled, he beat the whole House because nobody would own up to having scribbled graffiti in the lavatory.[34]

His academic progress followed the same pattern as at Summer Fields. He made a slow start, then improved steadily, ending moderately well but still some distance from the top. When he left Eton he was Fifth Oppidan in Sixth Form – fifth among those who were not scholars. This had been his precise position in the Eton scholarship exam, when he had been five places away from admission to College. His strengths and weaknesses also remained unchanged. He continued to be bad at Latin and Greek, which dominated the Eton curriculum, and good at mathematics; he won the Assistant Master's prize in 1904, and was one of four Tomline Prizemen in 1906, on both occasions in the same subject.[35] In his last year he concentrated exclusively on mathematics. The *Eton College Chronicle* for 1906 mentions a paper on 'Dimensions' presented by him to the Scientific Society.

Although he seemed to be destined to follow his Dalton grandfather's path to Cambridge to read for the Mathematical Tripos, his private passion was for poetry. A contemporary recalled that 'at night his neighbours in the adjoining rooms used to wonder at the strange

chants that came from Hugh's room, where he was declaiming, perhaps, some sonorous passage from Erechtheus, some lyric from
Poems and Ballads'.[36] The combination of this enthusiasm with one
of his most notable inherited assets – the Dalton voice – inspired his
contribution to an Eton ritual called 'Speeches', at which members of
Sixth Form recited passages from great works of literature before an
audience of masters, parents and boys. Dalton first took part in this
event in October 1905, choosing Tennyson's 'Ode on the Death of the
Duke of Wellington'. The schoolboy reviewer for the *Eton College
Chronicle* was impressed:

> The opening at all events was most successful, for a first perform-
> ance has rarely been so attractive as Dalton's treatment of Tenny-
> son's fine ode, the length of which made it a task of real difficulty
> and a severe test of good speaking. This no doubt accounted for
> some hurrying of the pace about the middle, but both beginning and
> end were spoken with much feeling and with excellent articulation.
> The length also might excuse an appeal to the prompter, and it
> would be too much to say that there were no signs of shyness in this
> and in the sway of the body as weight was shifted from one foot to
> the other, but the voice was so pleasant and the words were so well
> felt that only experience is now wanted; and it was a feat to hold the
> audience to the close.

Dalton's second attempt in February 1906 was more ambitious.
He chose Swinburne's 'Triumph of Time' – a poem about unrequited
passion, betrayal, and death at the hands of the elements as a substitute for human love. What made him select this particular poem?
Swinburne's poetry was fashionable and slightly daring. These were
reasons enough. Yet for an adolescent who preferred Joseph Chamberlain to gaiety girls, and whose own mother was reputedly cold and
distant, there may have been some deeper reasons for picking lines
like these:

> I will go back to the great sweet mother,
> Mother and lover of men, the sea,
> I will go down to her, I and none other,
> Close with her, kiss her and mix her with me;
> Cling to her, strive with her, hold her fast;
>
> Thy sweet hard kisses are strong like wine,
> Thy large embraces are keen like pain.

The *Eton College Chronicle* critic was more concerned with Dalton's delivery, noting some features that later became distinctive, above all a clerical aspect to the performance:

> He has a pleasant voice and spoke clearly and with dignity, although the dignity a little suggested the pulpit. He avoided the hurry which marred two speeches in the programme, though he lost something of the fire of his author, and might perhaps have made more of the rhythm, for it is no good being afraid of metre with Swinburne. His gesture, save for an ungraceful stoop at one point, was pleasing, and the speech as a whole in spite of faults was decidedly good.[37]

'Fancy your boy going to Cambridge this year, how time flies', Prince George wrote to the Canon the following April.[38] Dalton left school at the end of the 1906 summer half with a closed exhibition to King's, Cambridge – his uncle Charles Evan-Thomas's College. 'I hated leaving Eton – I was near the top of the tree and I didn't want to come down', he recalled. But he had scarcely left his mark – as scholar, athlete or personality.

How had Eton affected him? He liked to claim that the impact had been slight. Yet he emerged unmistakably an Etonian in speech and manner, as in many of his tastes and attitudes. He was not ashamed or bitter about his education. Other middle or upper class Labour politicians affected a plebian style or sought to tone down the marks of their origins. Dalton made no such attempt, flaunting or even caricaturing his background as part of his defiance.

Eton did not make him upper class. A chasm of wealth and breeding separated him from the sons of landed and industrial families who set the standards of Oppidan life. It did not make him an intellectual, though his intellectual curiosity had begun to be aroused by the time he left. What it did do was to hoist him from the narrow assumptions of the clergy houses of his forebears. At the same time, Summer Fields and Eton together – scholastic package for the competitive middle classes – added to a sense of being second best and instilled a compensatory urge to succeed. Eton also gave him a measure of the future enemy. Later skills in Parliament as a pricker of Tory pomposity owed much to the experience of having slept in the same dormitories and shared the same desks as his adversaries.

Dalton always refused to attack Eton as an institution. Public schools, he maintained, should be democratised rather than abolished, so that their 'classless mingling' could provide one of the foundations of the Classless Society. The greatest virtue of such schools was that they took children away from their parents:

In my Utopia most boys – and, I think, girls too – would, for several years, go to Boarding Schools well away from their homes, so that their parents could not always be looking over the gate. They would live with one another, and with their teachers, well out of day-to-day parental interference.[39]

Was he writing about himself? Dalton was a boarder at Eton (a Tory rumour that he had been a despised day boy was untrue) but he was scarcely out of range of his parents, whose house was within sight of the school buildings. Did he wish to be more 'out of range' – like other Etonians? A mystery remains about Dalton's adolescent pre-occupations: how far he felt himself a failure or an outsider until his final year 'at the top of the tree'.

At the end of his school career he showed no sign of exceptional promise. It was the next stage, taking him far from the 'shadow of the Castle', that brought the change. In the summer of 1906 he went to France for a brief interlude, learning French in six weeks from a teacher who was unable to eradicate an uncompromisingly English accent.[40] When he returned he went up to Cambridge – and began a four year liberation which altered his view of the world and fixed his personality.

III

Golden Time

Dalton entered King's College, Cambridge in October 1906. It was a conventional path to follow: the connection between King's and Eton remained familial. A quarter of all Eton masters were Kingsmen, and many former Eton scholars treated King's as an extension of College. King's, however, had become more than just a finishing school for Etonians. In the late nineteenth century, the college had acquired a strong sense of its own moral uniqueness. J. T. Sheppard, later a King's Provost, drew a distinction between Trinity's preoccupation with intellect (a separation of the world into two clearly divided classes, the clever and the not clever) and King's 'unconquerable faith in the value and interest of each human being'.[1] Such niceties were the subject of earnest debate among those who regarded themselves as the élite in each establishment.

The concern of King's with human values was epitomised in G. E. Moore's *Principia Ethica*, published in 1903. Though Dalton did not read this until 1908, he soon became familiar with its ideas from conversations with friends. He wrote later of Moore: 'he made an enormous difference to my way of thinking and feeling about the most important things in life.' Dalton had abandoned Christianity on the playing fields of Eton. Moore filled the vacuum with a secular faith. Dalton quoted Maynard Keynes on Moore with approval:

The appropriate subjects of passionate contemplation and communion were a beloved person, beauty and truth, and one's prime objects in life were love, the creation and enjoyment of aesthetic experience and the pursuit of knowledge. Of these love came a long way first ... Our religion closely followed the English puritan tradition of being chiefly concerned with the salvation of our own souls.

This became the doctrine of King's, of Bloomsbury and of a generation of writers and artists.

Dalton was inclined to widen Moore's category of things good in themselves. The 'best states of mind', he felt, should be a category broader than simply those filled with love and with the appreciation of beauty. His memoirs contain a revealing passage:

> I myself would add, at a pretty high level, a wide range of *tense experiences*, e.g. winning a keenly contested race (or election), making a very successful speech (or musical or dramatic performance), climbing a high mountain, piloting a plane in new or very difficult conditions, writing a good short poem, solving with a sudden flash of insight an intellectual problem which had got one stuck. Into many such examples being and doing good both enter.

It was as an ethical guide, however, that he found Moore most appealing. He wrote that general rules of conduct, which he liked to feel were his own, were consistent with Moore's ideas:

> Thus, in broad terms, no one should prefer his own good to the greater good of others. Nor, within inner circles of loyalty, to the equal good of others. Nor, within the inmost circles of affection, even to the lesser good of another. We should so live as to realise the greatest good we can, in our lives, the lives of those we love, of our friends and of other members of any society or group of which we feel ourselves a loyal part.
> All this in an ever-widening circle of diminishing emphasis, since love, and all the lesser loyalties, mean preferences.[2]

The key word here is 'loyalty'. But the question remained: to whom should one feel loyal? Before King's, Dalton felt little attachment to any group – a 'lonesome' boy, holding aloof. From Cambridge on, his life was constructed around an organic conception of teams: friends, party and nation. Marxist or liberal appeals to the higher claims of the welfare of mankind always failed to move him.

Yet Moore was as much symptom as cause. King's was already preoccupied with values, as distinct from intellect; fashionably sceptical in religion; narcissistic and inward-looking in its human relations; and unashamedly snobbish in its view of the rest of Cambridge, let alone the rest of the world. In stressing values, King's was taking intellectual superiority for granted, and regarded an emphasis on mere cleverness as rather vulgar.

Such was the mood Dalton found when he came up – created by an earlier generation of bachelor dons who took a deep interest in those they taught, as nowhere else in Cambridge. All this contrasted sharply with Oppidan life at Eton, and for Hugh it opened new worlds of opportunity, understanding and affection.

On his very first day, Dalton met Rupert Brooke, and immediately fell under his spell. 'No Cambridge friendship of mine meant more to me than this, and the radiance of his memory still lights my path'.[3] So Dalton wrote nearly four decades after Brooke's death. Everybody who knew him well became aware of his deep nostalgia for this relationship. Young friends would be presented with volumes of Brooke's verse, or be asked to listen while favourite lines were read aloud ('He thinks it's *poetry*,' Hugh's wife Ruth would say with scorn). When Dalton went down from Cambridge in 1910, he destroyed all his own papers – but kept every message from Brooke, even the slightest postcard.

Dalton's friendship with Brooke was based on a similarity of background, and on common interests. In age, they were exact contemporaries to the month. Both had been brought up in cloistered communities (Brooke's father was a housemaster at Rugby). Both had a passion for poetry: Dalton went up to Cambridge 'rather drunk with Swinburne', an admirer of 'Atalanta' and of Housman's 'The Shropshire Lad', and he found that Brooke shared these tastes. Both, too, were filled with a powerful ambition to stand out from their contemporaries. From early in their first term, Hugh and Rupert were close companions, in and out of each other's rooms and parties, reading, reciting, talking together until late into the night.

It was not long before Brooke and Dalton found themselves at the centre of a small group of like-minded King's undergraduates, who together set up an informal society called the 'Carbonari' – the charcoal burners, after a band of nineteenth-century Italian revolutionaries. The Carbonari were an alternative Pop: self-consciously exclusive, yet standing for different values. They were intellectual and cultural rather than athletic, progressive rather than establishment-minded, generally middle-class and non-Etonian. Members included Arthur Schloss who, as Arthur Waley, became a legendary Chinese scholar and translator; Francis Birrell, who had been a Summer Fields contemporary of Dalton; Gerald Shove, who became a King's economics don closely associated with Maynard Keynes and the Bloomsbury circle; and Philip Baker (later Noel-Baker)* who followed Dalton into Parliament on the Labour side. The society met

* He is referred to as 'Noel-Baker' throughout this book, to avoid confusion.

weekly to read papers and poetry and to talk. Many of Rupert
Brooke's early poems were first read at these meetings.[4] Shortly after
Brooke's death in the First World War Dalton described to Edward
Marsh, who was preparing a memorial essay, the aftermath of
Carbonari evenings:

> Rupert and I and one or two others were generally the last to
> separate, and sometimes the dawn was in the sky before we got to
> bed. We walked round the Courts and beside the river for hours,
> trying to get things clear. For we wanted, half passionately and
> half humorously, to get everything clear quickly. Hitherto, we
> thought, we had been too young to think, and soon we might be too
> busy, and ultimately we should be too old. The golden time was
> now.[5]

Brooke and Dalton soon discovered another interest in common,
apart from poetry: politics, especially politics of an advanced or
slightly shocking kind. Here Dalton led the way – picking up in his
first few months at Cambridge the rudiments of a doctrine that was to
seize hold of him and shape the rest of his life.

Dalton was still a Tory when he went up to Cambridge. Later he
claimed to have had his first socialist thought as a child, in reaction to
an old nurse (Nanny Larcomb?) who reproved him for calling a
ragged pauper in the grounds at the Gnoll a lady. 'That's not a lady',
corrected the nurse, 'that's only an old woman'. From this, he maintained, 'I date my sense of social equality'. He also claimed to have
been greatly moved at Eton by a socialist sermon on conditions in the
slums.[6] These early lessons, however, were evidently of limited effect.

Material for his debut at the Cambridge Union Debating Society
was provided by his much greater interest in Tory Democracy. He
first spoke at the Union in the fourth debate of term, making out a
careful case in support of the British Empire. It was a modest success.
The *Cambridge Review* complimented him on 'a very good maiden
speech', and the undergraduate magazine *Granta* commented that
'Mr. Dalton (King's) should speak again – soon'.[7]

The change in Dalton's allegiances came quickly. After the Christmas vacation he made a fateful decision. He declared himself a
Socialist, and joined the Cambridge University Fabian Society. 'I
exchanged Joseph Chamberlain', he recalled, 'for James Keir Hardie
and Sidney Webb.'

Later he maintained that this decision involved only a small shift in
his actual opinions. 'Democracy was already one of the most emotive
words in my vocabulary. Nor was the Fabian leadership against the

Empire, and that reassured me'.[8] Why did he take the step? Part of the answer was that he had been captured by the most recent fashion, reflecting an exhilaration felt throughout progressive Cambridge after the landslide Liberal victory in the election early in the same year.

At the general election in January 1906, in the words of one historian, 'the full force of the country's reaction against the conservatives disclosed itself'.[9] Liberals obtained a large majority over all other parties, and the Tories and Liberal Unionists were reduced to a rump. More sensational still, 53 members were elected in the labour interest – 24 miners or Lib-Labs, and 29 under the auspices of the recently formed Labour Representation Committee. This was a new kind of House of Commons, with a new kind of Government. Under the premiership of Sir Henry Campbell-Bannerman, the Liberal Cabinet embarked on a programme of social reforms. Asquith and Lloyd George were the men of the hour, and behind them on the backbenches were young and radical members, such as Charles Masterman, whose *In Period of Change*, published shortly before the election, encouraged Dalton, Brooke and their friends to hope for a smashing of precedent and a break with tradition.

It was hard to be young and idealistic and not to be on the side of these advancing forces. Yet it was not the orthodox Liberal Party, or even its Radical wing, that won over 'advanced' Cambridge in 1906–7. The most rapidly expanding political group in the University was the Fabian Society. The national Society had been founded in 1884 for the purpose of 'reconstructing society … in such manner as to secure the general welfare and happiness'. It took its name from the Roman general Quintus Fabius Maximus, who preferred harassing operations against the Carthaginians to pitched battles.[10] The Fabians were socialist, humanist, intellectual and almost exclusively middle class. In 1900 they had helped to set up the trade union based Labour Representation Committee as a third socialist partner, in conjunction with the evangelical Independent Labour Party and the marxist Social Democratic Federation. The best known members of the Society were the novelist H. G. Wells, the critic and playwright Bernard Shaw and the social investigators Beatrice and Sidney Webb. Of these the Webbs were most influential.

Despite the socialism of its philosophy and the early link with the L.R.C., the Fabian Society did not consider itself tied to any particular party. Though the Webbs 'looked on the collectivising state and saw that it was good',[11] this did not make them automatic friends of the Liberals, and for a time Beatrice had hoped to achieve more by influencing the Conservative leadership. One of the last acts of

Campbell-Bannerman's Tory predecessor, Arthur Balfour, had been to set up a Royal Commission on the Poor Law. Beatrice counted it a considerable advance that she was herself appointed to serve on this body as a Commissioner. Applying themselves with characteristic thoroughness to the question of how best to deal with destitution, the Webbs began to develop a comprehensive social programme – and then to look for a political vehicle to push it through.[12]

The Webbs' Poor Law initiative provided the intellectual background to a growth of public interest in the Fabian Society during 1906. Yet the most direct cause of an increase in membership was a wider interest in Socialism that had been aroused by the outcome of the general election. In addition, the activities of H. G. Wells, currently at the height of his literary fame and popularity, sharpened the Society's proselytising edge. At the beginning of 1906, Wells had made proposals for raising the income of the Society to £1,000 a year, increasing the staff, improving the literature and extending the range of voluntary support.[13] Over the next two years, Fabian Society membership more than doubled, reaching two thousand, and new recruits committed themselves with the fervour of religious converts.[14] Members were required to sign the Fabian 'Basis', representing a minimum basis of agreement with the Society's principles. This document combined a revolutionary aim with a propagandist method. Objectives were, by any standard, extreme, including 'the extinction of private property in Land', the nationalisation of industrial capital, and (from January 1907) the establishment of 'equal citizenship' for men and women.

As the Society grew, members began to form themselves into groups: the Women's Group, the Arts Group, and Groups for Education, Biology and Local Government. One of the most successful was the Fabian 'Nursery' composed of liberated and somewhat bohemian young people for whom H. G. Wells was a particular hero. The Nursery had a social side. 'Naturally the Nursery is not exclusively devoted to economics and politics', wrote the Society's Secretary, Edward Pease; 'picnics and dances also have their place. Some of the members eventually marry each other, and there is no better security for prolonged happiness in marriage than sympathy in regard to the larger issues of life'.[15] It was against this background that the Cambridge University Society was established in the Lent Term of 1906 by a wild, brilliant, energetic young undergraduate called Frederic ('Ben') Keeling, accompanied by a small group of enthusiasts including Amber Reeves (later Blanco-White), whose parents were prominent Fabians in London.

Dalton wrote that Keeling 'netted him' for the Fabian Society, and it is easy to understand how and why. It was not long after his arrival that Dalton first met this strangely magnetic man, already in his third year at Trinity, whose 'round, red, warmly flushed, rather astonished face' betrayed an outgoing and friendly personality.[16] Keeling ran a club similar to the Carbonari called the Fish and Chimney, and Dalton and Brooke were soon invited to join. Keeling spoke often and impressively at the Union, always defiantly arguing the socialist case before a largely hostile audience, and in December he stood unsuccessfully for office. Earlier in the term, Dalton had listened in admiration as Keeling boldly declared that 'the first evil to be remedied is the tax on land, and the remedy proposed by Socialism is the nationalisation of land'.[17]

Students of political psychology will find much to interest them in Ben Keeling. A collection of his letters published posthumously in 1918 reveals a passionate idealist whose interests related directly to a tumultuous inner world. In an introduction to this work H. G. Wells described him as 'a copious, egotistical, rebellious, disorderly, generous and sympathetic young man'. He might have added that Ben Keeling was, in addition, a man whose fiery, creative temperament infused with his own excitement and crusading passion all who came his way.

For Hugh, joining the Cambridge Fabians at the beginning of 1907 was thus scarcely a sombre conversion. It was a decision to be right at the centre of the Edwardian undergraduate game at its gaiest and most carefree. Keeling had an instinct for the eye-catching gesture, the daring or unusual adventure. In the autumn of 1906 a big public meeting organised by the Fabians, with Keeling in the chair, sent a resolution to democratic politicians in Petersburg in support of the failed Russian Revolution. There was also a trip for Cambridge Socialists, 'including two girls' to London to take part in a meeting at which H. G. Wells urged middle and upper class Socialists to throw in their lot with the Labour Party.[18] One of the girls was probably Amber Reeves – clever, beautiful, wilful and advanced, and a part of what made the Fabians fashionable. Amber had discovered H. G. Wells through the Fabian Nursery, and promptly developed what Beatrice Webb called 'a somewhat dangerous friendship' with him – which led to the birth of a child.[19]

Signing the Fabian Basis may not have meant adopting puritanical habits. It did involve taking sides in an age-old undergraduate war. In the heartier colleges, Fabians often had a rough ride. Tradition-minded 'bloods' regarded Socialist intellectuals as fair sport: the famous debagging incident in Evelyn Waugh's *Decline and Fall* had many parallels at Edwardian Cambridge. On Saturday nights, bibulous rowing men were a species to be avoided; confined within their college walls, lynch mobs of oarsmen would restlessly roam in search of Fabian prey. Some potential victims got off lightly. When Ben Keeling's rooms were attacked, the enemy withdrew apologising: 'We don't want to fight with you, you're a damned fine fellow even though you *are* a Socialist; we know quite well you've got a lot of pluck.'[20] Others were less fortunate. According to a protest leaflet distributed in Cambridge in 1908, one man who was both a Fabian and a prominent member of the University Women's Suffrage Association, was seized by a group of sportsmen and immersed in a cold bath placed in the middle of Trinity Hall court. Another young Socialist, chased to his rooms, had his bed drenched with buckets of water while his tormentors bullied out of him a political recantation.[21]

Being a Fabian at King's was less dangerous than elsewhere, because King's valued its reputation for intellectual tolerance, and a number of King's dons had Fabian views. Yet even at King's there was an element of cocking a snook at those who found security in convention. This was an aspect that gave Dalton special pleasure. 'He had a gift for making people hostile to him', recalled Lord Noel-Baker. 'He half-deliberately said very socialist things in order to shock.' He did it once too often, and the enraged bloods got their revenge. After rumours that a 'disloyal toast' had been drunk at a meeting of the Carbonari, baying members of the snobbish Chetwynd Club dragged Dalton off for a ritual ducking in the college fountain.[22]

Though Dalton later claimed to have had 'athletes and aesthetes, intellectuals and innocents, politicians and playboys' among his Cambridge friends,[23] most of the athletes and playboys seem to have loathed him. J. C. C. Davidson, later a Conservative M.P., who went up to Pembroke in 1907, spoke for the whole of anti-aesthete Cambridge when he recalled Dalton as 'very arrogant, and detested by everybody and by no one more than myself'.[24] Dalton's unpopularity in this constituency arose less from his political attitudes than from the use he made of them to taunt his stuffier peers. Several decades later Dalton told a young writer 'how he and Brooke and their contemporaries thought of their generation as far superior to any that had preceded it'.[25] It was one of his most maddening features that he also regarded his Fabian group as far superior to run-of-the-mill Etonians at King's – and made his opinion evident.

Dalton in January 1907 was a Fabian by conscious act, but still at heart a Tory Democrat. It was by no means true, as one contemporary put it, that 'he suffered a complete rebirth: the last vestiges of the old man of Toryism were left behind him'.[26] Many Tory traces remained –

in his attitude to Empire, in his suspicion of Liberal moral stances, and in a paternalist view of political authority which, in some ways, tied in well with Fabian *dirigisme*. Nor did these ever entirely disappear. Nevertheless, it took only weeks of association with the enthusiastic Keeling-led Fabians for Dalton's new allegiance to develop into a serious commitment.

In February, there were two socialist visitors to Cambridge of special significance. The first was Wells, who delivered a resounding attack on the Marxists' 'mystical faith in the power of the masses'.[27] Dalton was to make use of Wells's arguments against far-left romanticism for the next half century. The second visitor was Keir Hardie, founder of the I.L.P. and symbolic leader of British working-class socialism. Wells had impressed Dalton intellectually. Hardie fired his emotions. 'In a crowded room I sat at his feet literally and spiritually', Dalton recalled. 'That night I became a quite convinced Socialist.'[28]

Perhaps it was not so simple. Yet Hardie's ability to inspire impressionable young men should not be underrated. Fenner Brockway, who met Hardie for the first time a couple of years earlier, gave a description of the encounter which also suggests a 'spiritual' conversion.[29] The gap between the lives and experience of Dalton and Hardie in 1907 could not have been greater. Partly for that reason, it is possible to believe that Dalton was deeply moved. Whatever the reality, Dalton always regarded 'Keir Hardie Night' in February 1907 as his own, personal, Damascus Road.

For most undergraduates it was not so much the nature of Keir Hardie's message that aroused excitement as the unusual conditions of its delivery. The Hardie visit to Cambridge became legendary as the occasion of a great symbolic battle between socialist aesthetes and college bloods. Greatly outnumbered in the undergraduate community, the Socialists generally avoided open confrontation. This time, however, they accepted a direct challenge and, through stealth and cunning, won the day.

Ben Keeling later gave this account:

My bed-maker ... told me a few days before the meeting that a gang of miserable rowing men had concocted a plot in the rooms at the bottom of my staircase to screw up Keir Hardie in my rooms while we had dinner. We therefore ordered a dinner ostentatiously for Keir Hardie at the college kitchens, and talked everywhere of his coming (by the wrong train), meanwhile secretly arranging that he should be met and taken to King's. On the afternoon of the meeting Mottram went to a theatrical costumier's and was made up as Keir Hardie – hat, grey beard and hair ... red tie, etc. I drove up with him in a hansom to the Great Gate, and was met by a number of Fabians, who shook hands with the great man. We made our way across the court amidst howls of a few hundred rowing men from various colleges and our other normal enemies. I then bolted to the Guildhall, where we had got a hundred trade unionists to help us hold the platform against the mob of undergraduates. Meanwhile, Mottram, Hubback, and Gomme kept up the fiction of a great feast in my rooms. The doors were screwed up, and a few hundred undergraduates howled with joy in the court.[30]

At eight o'clock the whole 'mock' Hardie group descended from Keeling's rooms by a mountaineering rope, and went to the Guildhall – only to be followed a few minutes later by the angry foe, who broke furniture and hurled eggs. This was all according to plan. In the meantime another group, which included Dalton, had picked up the 'real' Keir Hardie at the station, quietly given him a meal, and taken him to the Guildhall by another route.

So far the Socialists through greater ingenuity had kept ahead. Now the bloods launched a second offensive, bringing into action some sophisticated weaponry in the form of pipettes of stink-gas. By means of a construction of bellows and rubber tubing, foul-smelling fumes were pumped into the hall while a cornet blared out in an attempt to drown the real Keir Hardie's words.[31] Undaunted, Hardie finished his speech. Then Dalton, Keeling and their friends formed a bodyguard and marched the socialist pioneer to King's, where he talked about the working-class to a circle of triumphant Fabians. 'I admired his total lack of fear or anger, his dignified bearing, his simplicity of speech and thought and faith', wrote Dalton.[32]

Dalton's first year at Cambridge was spent making friends and acquiring new attitudes. In his second year, he emerged as a leading figure not just in King's, but in the University. The basis for this rise was the Cambridge Union, where he began to have an impact as a debater. His progress may be traced in the columns of University magazines. Earliest reports from Dalton's first year, when he was only permitted to speak late and briefly in debates, are short and to the point. They suggest an earnest but determined young man whose somewhat hesitant performances were built on careful preparation.

There was an initial problem about delivery: how to pace himself, and put the stress in the right place. 'Mr. Dalton (King's) seems to believe in pauses for effect', commented the undergraduate magazine *Granta* after his second contribution. 'The pauses, however, come with an unfailing regularity which defeats their end, and we wait in vain for the effect.' The *Cambridge Review* even made a criticism – apparently without irony – that was never to be heard in later years. 'Mr. Dalton', it declared, 'should speak louder and be more independent of written matter, and he needs greater emphasis and fire.'[33]

Some of Dalton's mannerisms suggested fear of his audience. There was the problem of his eyes, which had a habit of rolling involuntarily upwards, exposing the whites. He therefore took to staring at the floor. 'Mr. Dalton should look his enemies in the face', admonished *Granta*, 'and not scan the carpet'. He also had a habit of bowing his head when opposition was fierce, as if to protect his face from physical attack. In May 1907 he spoke in favour of the Government's land policy, arguing that 'Those wildernesses that are called sporting preserves are not wanted'. There were derisive jeers from the college bloods, as Dalton addressed the ground. Was he bent, asked *Granta*, or was he stooping to conquer? 'For some doubtless excellent reason Mr. Dalton insisted on arranging his body at right angles to his legs.'[34]

Yet there was also appreciation of his ability to marshal facts. 'If Mr. Dalton's manner was half as good as his matter he would be one of the best speakers in the Union', commented the *Review* after he had argued that there should be 'not a Conscript Army, but a Citizen Army'.[35] Even the content of his speech in opposition to 'sporting preserves' earned praise – though what Prince George, who entertained the Canon and his radical son to dinner at Frogmore House a few weeks later,[36] would have said about so impudent an attack on his own favourite pastime is a matter for conjecture.

In the autumn of 1907, Dalton's speaking markedly improved. Moving a resolution in favour of nationalising railways, he described 'in a breaking voice' a case of victimisation involving the removal of a railway porter from a congested district. The critics were impressed, especially by the simulated emotion. 'At times he is a little too sarcastic', commented *Granta*, 'but he has a manner of his own, and that is, in itself, a mercy.' *Granta* acknowledged his rising significance by referring to him in Union reports as 'Comrade Dalton', then 'Comrade Hugh', to be linked with 'Comrade Ben Keeling' or 'little Benjamin our ruler' as a leader of the socialist opposition. 'Comrade Hugh' still had a tendency 'to speak like a half-roused somnambulist', noted *Granta* in February 1908 but, it added, he had made wonderful strides.

Speech by speech, he was developing the style for which he would be known a generation later. He no longer bothered to conceal his pleasure, which at times seemed close to exquisite joy, when he succeeded in moving his adversaries to anger. Employing with precision a special weapon – a kind of silken, patronising sneer, patented

in his Windsor nursery – he would delight in making them roar.
'Young recruits in great political organisations are always touchy
about things they don't quite understand', he remarked in one debate, after catching out another speaker on a point of economics.
'"Comrade Hugh" should try not to get on his opponents' nerves,'
reproved *Granta*.[37]

IV

Comrade Hugh

Rupert Brooke at first held back from 'signing the Basis' and accepting full membership of the Fabian Society – although he had been a Fabian Associate since the spring of 1907. Then, in April 1908, influenced by 'Comrade Hugh', he decided to take the plunge. 'By next term', he wrote to Dalton, after a holiday illness, 'I shall be able to sit up and take a little Webb and milk'.[1] Soon, Brooke had become one of the most active and enthusiastic Fabians in the University.

The recruitment of Brooke greatly increased the social significance of the Fabians at Cambridge. The sense of living life for the moment which Brooke created in those around him – the feeling of Cambridge as a continuous, pastoral summer party – gave added glamour to the rapidly expanding Society. Meanwhile Cambridge Fabians were widening their contacts, making themselves better known to national leaders. Early in May a dinner was held in Keeling's rooms in Trinity beneath a huge poster of workers surging forward with clenched fists.[2] The occasion was in honour of Sir Sydney Olivier, Governor of Jamaica and Fabian elder, whose daughters were members of the Society in Cambridge. Brooke described the event as 'a very Socialist dinner of one course and fruit and twenty-five persons'. A notable guest at Keeling's table was H. G. Wells, whose close observations of the Cambridge Fabian circle – occasioned by his 'dangerous friendship' with Amber Reeves – were providing material for his lampoon of Fabianism, *The New Machiavelli*.[3]

In the summer of 1908 – the end of Dalton's second year – Ben Keeling, dominant personality in the group and the one around whom it revolved, went down from Cambridge. Before he left, he began to look ahead to a Fabian generation that would succeed his own – and both Dalton and Brooke featured in his calculations. 'The most important thing in the Society is the excellent nucleus we have got of first- and second-year King's men', he wrote to a friend. 'Dalton (second year) and Brooke (second year) are splendid men. Dalton will probably – certainly – be president next year.' The only danger he foresaw was that 'King's will rather monopolise the show.'

Keeling's valedictory message to comrades was about sex and the family. After reading a book by the socialist writer Edward Carpenter called *Love's Coming of Age*, he had become convinced that the family was 'at the crux of the social question'. Sex was much on his mind as his Tripos exams approached. 'My friends say I am obsessed with sex nowadays, perhaps that is true', he confessed to his future mother-in-law, a leading Fabian suffragist called Emily Townshend, with whom he had formed an unusually frank relationship. But it was the problem of family ties that really preoccupied him – no doubt because those in his own childhood had been particularly distant and disturbed. The family, he now decided, must be replaced by other forms of social organisation:

> It is one of my dreams that through my numerous and growing friendships with Cambridge and Oxford and other Socialists of my own generation, I may be able to do something towards creating a large enough body of opinion to make a development, in those other forms which are to supersede family organisation, possible. It does not take a vast number of individuals to clear a space in the jungle of convention sufficiently large for experiment – provided only we keep together closely. A hundred really determined individuals in more or less important positions, some of them with a measure of economic independence, can do a good lot to influence public opinion.[4]

Some aspects of Keeling's vision came directly from Carpenter's writings. Another influence was the early Fabians and their 'Fellowship of the New Life' forebears. Yet Keeling – facing the challenge of the outside world – was also responding to his years of university socialism, and the passionate intensity of the tight group of Cambridge men and a few women, in which he himself, Dalton and Brooke had all played central roles. 'Clearing a space in the jungle of convention' had been their task at Cambridge. How attractive was the idea of maintaining the comradeship forged as undergraduates, and continuing the task amongst the public at large!

What did Dalton think of Keeling's idea, with its suggestion of a select band of university socialists, rising to 'more or less important positions' in the community, and seeking by example to develop 'forms which are to supersede family organisation'? Dalton's own childhood made him sympathetic towards schemes designed to break the tyranny of family ties. As we have seen, he was attracted – at least in later life – by the idea of communal living for all children 'well away from their homes, so that their parents could not always be looking over the garden gate'. Like Keeling, he experienced Cambridge friendships as a liberating force. Dalton's adult life and political career – his indifference to domestic comfort, his practical faith in the power of intimate and equal friendships in politics – contained more than an echo of Keeling's notion of a tiny circle of Fabian comrades setting out to change the world.

That summer, Ben persuaded Hugh, Rupert and other friends to join him at a Fabian summer school at Llanbedr, between Harlech and Barmouth. First, however, Rupert arranged a house party around the pretty Olivier sisters.[5] But there was a personality problem, as he explained to Dudley Ward:

A. Y. Campbell has written infinitely vaguely ... but ends by being (for a poet) fairly certain he *will* come ... some time! But he ends 'If I should coincide with Dalton I hope you will defend me from him'. Now consider! A.Y.C. *doesn't* (seriously) dislike poor Hugh, does he? They'd get on all right, *half* coinciding, wouldn't they?

I asked Hugh if he knew and liked A.Y.C. 'Aeou yéés!' he yawned. 'Iye expect hé admires me! Letimcoem! Letimcoem!' So the emotions from that side are all right.[6]

Ben and Hugh stayed briefly with the Brookes at School Field, Rugby before setting out with Dudley Ward (another Kingsman) for Wales. Rupert followed a few days later. Apart from Keeling, Dalton, Ward and Brooke, male Cambridge was represented by Arthur Schloss, Gerald Shove and James Strachey, younger brother of Lytton and later a pioneer of British psychoanalysis.

Fabian schools then were much like Fabian schools today. There were, according to Mrs Webb, 'a dozen or so young university graduates and undergraduates, another strain of lower middle-class professionals, a stray member of Parliament or professor, a bevy of fair girls', plus a large remainder of nondescript old ladies who found the seven week stay on the mountainous coast of North Wales lively and quite cheap. For the undergraduates and fair girls, it was sheer delight. 'The young folk live the most unconventional life', Beatrice Webb tolerantly observed, 'giving the quaker-like Lawson Dodd, who rules the roost, many an unpleasant quarter of an hour – stealing out on moor or sand, in stable or under hayricks, without always the requisite chaperone to make it look as wholly innocent as it really is'. But if sex wasn't actually on the agenda, it was at least a matter for debate. ' "Is dancing sexual?", I found 3 pretty Cambridge girls discussing with half a dozen men', Beatrice wrote in her diary. 'But mostly they talk economics and political science.'[7]

The main value of the trip for Dalton was that it increased his contact with Beatrice and Sidney Webb. The Webbs had already met and entertained some of the Cambridge men the previous summer. Beatrice had been gratified by their keenness, and by the respect they showed for their hosts. 'They are a remarkable good set of hard-working clean living youths', she had written. ' – mostly clever and enthusiastic and who look upon us as the Patriarchs of the Movement'. Just before the Llanbedr school, Beatrice and Sidney had seven of the Cambridge men and Amber Reeves to stay for three days at a holiday farmhouse which the Webbs had taken near Leominster. Beatrice found Amber 'an extraordinarily vital little person – but egotistical and vain and a dreadful little pagan', and the men 'all nice fellows and two remarkably brilliant persons'.[8] She wrote in her diary that the Cambridge Fabians were the most outstanding set that the Society had yet attracted. 'Two are remarkable men', she noted, ' – Keeling and Dalton – the one a fervent rebel ... and the other an accomplished ecclesiastical sort of person – a subtle wily man with a certain peculiar charm for those who are not put off by his mannerism.'[9]

It was the 'subtle wily man' who impressed her most. She amplified her description of the twenty-one-year-old undergraduate, only two years out of Eton, in a letter to her sister:

> One of the Cambridge Fabians, Dalton (the son of the Dean of Windsor [sic]) is one of the most astute and thoughtful of our younger members – by nature an ecclesiastic – a sort of lay Jesuit – preparing for political life.[10]

So Cambridge politics was not just a game. This sentence is the only concrete evidence that Dalton was already contemplating a political career, yet it is unmistakable. What did she, or he, mean by 'political life'? Was he hoping to become a Liberal M.P., the only realistic parliamentary option for a middle class young man of radical opinions in Edwardian England? Or did he imagine a non-parliamentary 'political life' in keeping with Keeling's vision? That might, perhaps, account for Beatrice's description of him as 'a lay Jesuit', carrying the suggestion of a secular priesthood.

At this stage such thoughts can have been little more than fantasy: Hugh had two full years ahead of him at Cambridge. For Ben Keeling, however, the future was already upon him. Despite his brilliance and vitality, Keeling remained deeply unsure of himself and desperately uncertain about which path to follow. He turned to Beatrice for advice, eager as always to listen to a strong, clever woman much older than himself. Beatrice considered his dilemma. Then she took him firmly in hand, and he responded, allowing her to shape his life.

Keeling left Cambridge and moved to a house in the Walworth Road in the heart of one of London's poorest areas. The great energy which he had once devoted to building up the Cambridge Fabians was now directed into the organisation of Care Committees, of a kind that were being formed all over the capital under the aegis of the Labour Exchange Department of the Board of Trade. Beatrice's advice was constructive and sound, yet it is interesting to note how far Keeling's actual decision was influenced by feelings of guilt about sex: there seems to have been an element of a cold *douche* about the whole enterprise. Keeling's private torment – what he called 'this instability on the sexual side of myself' – remained a central theme in his correspondence with the understanding Mrs Townshend. One of his letters described how in Wales he had tried to walk off a 'curious, absolutely involuntary, driving, haunting desire' for a girl member of the Fabian party, and had then returned home 'conscious of an almost restless energy in me'. Political or social activities of a humble nature had become a way of compensating for the shamefulness of his emotions.

Keeling's relations with women, towards whom he usually behaved badly, always filled him with the deepest remorse. That autumn, there was a new and interesting lament. 'I caused years of suffering to the mother who bore me and now I have caused indefinite suffering to F. [a girlfriend], yet I would willingly atone for either of these courses of action by any work of expiation', he wrote in September. 'I would consciously select a life of narrower interests, less effective work, less dear friendships and loves if by so doing I could increase the well-being of my fellow-men.'[11]

There was a lot of 'little Benjamin our ruler' in Comrade Hugh and vice versa. In personality, Keeling and Dalton were very different – as Beatrice Webb's description indicated. Keeling was the more evidently passionate and (to use his word) unstable of the two. Yet they had in common a love of the limelight, and 'an almost restless energy' as the driving force behind political activity. More important, the theme of expiation, so powerful a force in Keeling, influenced Dalton in significant ways as well.

Keeling, brooding darkly on his own future, alternated quixotically between a career as a tribune of the people, and a proletarian metamorphosis. The second idea was much affected by conversations with

Dalton. 'I have been thinking', Keeling wrote in his journal at the end of 1908,

> ... about the possibility of starting out to earn my living in the 'wild places of the earth' (as dear Hugh says) with £20 in my pocket, trying to work my way round the world in two years or so, starting in the spring.[12]

The phrase 'wild places of the earth' was taken from a poet whose work Dalton had recently been reading with admiration: the Canadian writer of popular ballads, Robert Service. A few months earlier, Dalton had urged Brooke to read a collection of Service's verse called *Songs of a Sourdough*.[13] One of these 'songs', entitled 'The Call of the Wild', expressed in vivid language an escapist dream that fitted in well with middle-class Fabian fantasies of expiation. The idea of living rough and working in remote parts of the world may have come directly from this poem. Service does not mention 'wild places', but 'the wild' and 'silent places' occur in consecutive lines:

> They have cradled you in custom, they have primed you with their
>   preaching,
> They have soaked you in convention through and through;
> They have put you in a showcase; you're a credit to their teaching –
> But can't you hear the wild? – it's calling you.
> Let us probe the silent places, let us seek what luck betide us;
> Let us journey to a lonely land I know.
> There's a whisper on the night-wind, there's a star agleam to
>   guide us,
> And the wild is calling ... let us go.

There is another couplet, earlier in the poem, that makes the point even more clearly:

> Have you suffered, starved and triumphed, grovelled down, yet
>   grasped at glory,
> Grown bigger in the bigness of the whole?[14]

Fabians in general (like Annan's intellectual aristocrats) enjoyed walking, hiking and mountains, and for Dalton, as we shall see, the 'call of the wild' had a particularly powerful appeal. Was there a connection between his love of long walks in rough countryside and the adventure of entering working-class politics and making contact with idealised workers in their natural state? In Keeling, the links between

seeking out wild places, 'grovelling down', and 'grasping at glory' were
direct. ' ... I rather fancy that in a few months I shall be thousands of
miles away, finding out what it really is to be a proletarian', he wrote to
Mrs Townshend in February 1909.

That Dalton responded to Keeling's latest enthusiasm is suggested
by a letter to Mrs Townshend, shortly before his move to the Walworth Road, in which Keeling announced his decision to select a
working-class borough and 'settle down there next October or
September'. Keeling went on to make clear that he had not abandoned
the idea of a secular order:

> The Fabians here are very keen on my taking this line [i.e. moving
> to a working-class borough]. As it happens, the two leading men
> now both have a chance of securing a measure of financial inde-
> pendence as soon as they finish up here, and if I succeed in showing
> that there is a useful career on the lines I suggest they will probably
> come and join me. I hope my friend Dudley Ward will come and
> live with me at once and give me some help. I have hopes that I
> might secure a regular stream of Cambridge Socialists for South
> London. It would really be a new movement – no damned ideas of
> religion, philanthropy or 'social service', but a plain carrying out of
> what will in future become normal activities of citizenship. By God!
> If we could capture a Borough Council or a Board of Guardians we
> could shift something.[15]

This tells us more about Keeling's fevered imaginings than about
Dalton. There was no 'regular stream of Cambridge Socialists', nor
was there likely to be. Yet it indicates that Keeling did not dream
alone. Who were the two leading men? Dalton, secretary of the
Cambridge Fabians, and currently president-elect, must have been
one of them. Had Dalton, the 'lay Jesuit – preparing for political
life', been indulging in a reverie about working alongside Keeling as
part of a socialist brotherhood?

At the start of the 1908 Michaelmas Term, Dalton succeeded Keeling
as president of the now well-established Cambridge Fabians, and the
series of socialist speakers continued. One guest was Ramsay Mac-
Donald; Dalton was not impressed. He was much more interested by
Goldsworthy Lowes Dickinson, who gave a series of four lectures on
the Ideals of Democracy.

Dalton always claimed to owe a great debt to Dickinson. Many
years later, he gave this description of 'Goldie', one of the most celebrated of King's dons: 'He lectured on political ideas, was easily

interested in young men and, from my first year, he took an interest in me which continued till his death in 1932.'[16] Dickinson ran another select group for the reading of papers and discussion of ideas, known as 'Dickinson's Society', whose dozen or so members, half under-graduates and half dons, included both Brooke and Dalton. At meet-ings of his Society, Goldie would stand by the fireplace, according to one member, 'rubbing himself and saying clearly for each of us what in our muddled way we could not say clearly for ourselves.'[17] One of the first non-Etonian fellows of the college, he was a prototype of the new kind of King's don who treated undergraduates as equals.

Dickinson was well read in political science, set in a classical mould, with a liberal commitment to rationality in the ordering of public affairs. From within the comfortable and secluded world of King's, he concerned himself with the idea of poverty, and the problem of how to deal with it was central to several of his books. In the 1890s he had become (by his own account), 'a kind of academic Socialist, partly from my reading in French socialism, partly from the writings of the Fabian Society', and he arranged that leading Fabian scholars should lecture at the college.[18] Mary Agnes Hamilton (a Newnhamite who was up a few years after Dalton, and became a Labour M.P.) wrote of Dickinson that 'Listening to him, talking with him, remains the best that Cambridge gave me.'[19] Dickinson's close friends included the novelist E. M. Forster, who wrote his life.

As with Keeling, so with Dickinson, political passion was closely bound up with a private world of sexual unhappiness. In Dickinson's case sexual difficulties took a more extreme form. A moving and sensi-tively written autobiography, published posthumously, reveals Dickinson as a homosexual afflicted by a lifelong obsession with the idea of being trodden under foot by young men wearing leather boots. The link between Dickinson's sexuality and his politics will be con-sidered in the next chapter: though it is relevant to mention here a rejection of convention, and a desire for self-abasement through the service of his fellow men.

It is also relevant that Dalton came to know Dickinson at a time when the King's philosopher was experiencing an unusual sense of personal fulfilment. Dickinson's main relationships had been with near contemporaries (in particular with Roger Fry and Ferdinand Schiller). During the second half of Dalton's Cambridge career, how-ever, Dickinson fell in love with a young undergraduate called Oscar Eckhard, who had been a contemporary of Rupert Brooke at Rugby. Later Dickinson recalled the years of the Eckhard relationship as the happiest he had known. 'It was like a new youth', he wrote. 'I hardly knew why I was so happy'.[20] It was in this period, when Dickinson had most to give, that Dalton came under his intellectual and political influence.

Dickinson, like several other King's dons, was closely associated with the circle of friends from which the Bloomsbury group later emerged. Dalton never became a member of this group. One reason was that he lacked the finer sensibilities required for election to the Apostles, the semi-secret Cambridge society from which the essential Bloomsbury spirit was derived, much as he had lacked the necessary graces for election to Pop at Eton. This failure may help account for his hostility, in later years, towards a number of Bloomsbury figures. What made the exclusion especially painful was that the Apostles, and Bloomsbury, took up Rupert Brooke, whose looks, charm and style were so close to their ideal. It was Brooke's increasing association with a literary world in which Dalton played no part that gradually separated the two friends.

Although Brooke had long been marked out as a future member of the Apostles, having known the brothers of both Lytton Strachey and Maynard Keynes from schooldays, he did not actually join until the spring of 1908 – at about the same time that he joined the Fabians. Of the two societies, the Apostles mattered much more to him; he felt keenly the social importance, and derived deep pleasure from the friends and contacts acquired thereby.[21] The pleasure was reciprocated. Lytton Strachey, in particular, was delighted by the new recruit. He had described to Virginia Stephen 'a young undergraduate called Rupert Brooke – isn't it a romantic name? with pink cheeks and bright yellow hair – it sounds horrible, but it wasn't.'[22] For Dalton, on the other hand – tall, noisy, and physically clumsy – there was no similar feeling. Strachey met Dalton in Cambridge in the summer, but had no wish to become better acquainted.

The attitude of the Apostles to Dalton was important, because of Maynard Keynes. In 1908 links between King's and the future core of the Bloomsbury group were being strengthened – mainly because of Keynes's return to Cambridge. In a state of deep emotional upheaval, and with his main affections shifting from Lytton Strachey to Duncan Grant, Maynard Keynes had resigned from the India Office and taken up a Fellowship at King's. When Keynes arrived, the Long Vacation period of residence was in progress, and he was brought into contact with the best known King's undergraduates. 'We hear at once of new figures', records Keynes's official biographer – 'Gerald Shove and Hugh ("Daddy") Dalton'. But it soon became clear that Dalton was not at the head of the list. Keynes hugely enjoyed the social delights of King's, and Dalton was one of those with whom he associated. When Brooke gave a supper party attended by Hilaire Belloc and Desmond

MacCarthy, Keynes noted the other guests: 'The usual collection of people, Gerald [Shove], Master B[irrell, Francis], James [Strachey?], Daddy [Dalton] and me.' Brooke, Birrell and Shove joined the select band of Keynes's special friends. Dalton, however, did not.[23]

In his fourth undergraduate year, Dalton was taught economics by Keynes, and became a member of a small society formed by Keynes at which papers were read. Later, Dalton was fond of quoting a remark of Brooke's which expressed the collective narcissism of this group: 'A world containing you and me and Maynard Keynes is obviously better than a world containing three people just like any one of us.' Dalton claimed to have got to know Keynes better than any other don apart from Dickinson.[24] Yet Keynes regarded Dalton, not exactly with contempt, but with a kind of amused scorn, as a young man full of pretension who had little to offer that was original or interesting. Dalton felt this deeply; and, though he seldom admitted it, there was always a coolness in personal relations between the two.

If Dalton did not enjoy the close friendship of the greatest economist of his age, he did at least enjoy the patronage of Beatrice Webb. Beatrice was in an evangelical mood. 'When will all this wicked misery cease – misery that leads to wickedness and wickedness that leads to misery?' she declared early in 1908, after visiting workhouses and labour yards for the unemployed.[25] Her solution was a grand design to replace the Poor Law.

The Poor Law Commission had ended in conflict, with four out of eighteen members putting forward ideas which, on key issues, differed sharply from those of the majority. Led by Mrs Webb, the dissentients presented their 'Minority Report' which among other proposals sought the removal (or at least the reduction) of the moral stigma attached to pauperism, a recognition of poverty as deriving from distinct sources (sickness, widowhood, old age and so on) each requiring appropriate treatment, and hence the 'break-up' of the old poor law system – with each category of need (except need resulting from unemployment) to be dealt with separately by the committees of elected local authorities.[26]

These ideas Beatrice pressed on any leading member of the Liberal Government who would lend an ear. In March 1908 – while the Report was still in preparation – Winston Churchill, shortly to become President of the Board of Trade, dined with the Webbs and seemed favourably disposed towards their schemes. On their recommendation Churchill took on a young academic called William Beveridge, from the East End settlement of Toynbee Hall, to advise him about labour exchanges. Dalton was a witness of this particular Fabian initiative. 'That night Winston talked much, diffusively and overpoweringly, and listened little', he recalled. 'But he engaged Beveridge, as the Webbs had planned.'[27]

The Webbs' attempt to win over key ministers to their plan was, however, doomed to failure. Angry and frustrated, they embarked on a public crusade, establishing a 'National Committee for the Break-Up of the Poor Law'. A campaign of meetings, conferences and summer schools followed, and within a few months the new movement had sixteen thousand members.[28] The Fabian Nursery provided a vanguard.

Among early recruits to the 'Break-Up' campaign were Dalton and Brooke. It was their first experience of politics in the real world. In April, they planned a series of Thursday meetings, with discussions and papers on the Report. 'One on each part, perhaps', Brooke wrote to Dalton during the Easter vacation, 'and one on the Majority report (which, at least, James Strachey has read: and, I suppose, you?)'[29] In the summer, Rupert, Hugh and Dudley Ward hired a cart and made a tour of Cambridgeshire villages, spreading 'Break-Up' propaganda.[30]

The Minority Report campaign came as a culmination to Dalton's highly successful year as president of the Cambridge Fabians. The Society had ceased to be a small group of enthusiasts, and had become an established part of Cambridge political life.[31] This owed much to the Break-Up movement; it was also a result of painstaking efforts by existing Fabians to encourage others to join. Dalton was an especially determined recruiting sergeant. Another new member, Leah Tappin, a student at Homerton College for teacher training in Cambridge (and later, as Leah Manning, a member of the Labour National Executive and an M.P.), recalled his technique. Hugh had been informed that before coming to Homerton, Miss Tappin had already joined the Fabian Nursery. After negotiations with the highly suspicious Homerton authorities, he was permitted a chaperoned meeting:

> My first impression of Hugh Dalton was of a very tall young man, loose-jointed with cold grey eyes contradicted by a humorous mouth and the loudest voice one could possibly imagine. We sat in a kind of triangle, as far apart as possible, and Hugh spoke to me as if he were addressing a public meeting.

It was the start of a lifelong association – Leah regarding Hugh with adoration, and he repaying her with occasional acts of patronage and one major betrayal. 'I had much to thank Hugh Dalton for', she wrote. 'Without his friendship, I could not have penetrated very far into the life of the University or met some of the men I knew.' The University Fabian Society opened her eyes to many things, especially on sexual matters. 'I had never heard of homosexuality, but a frank, open debate on the subject which ... followed exactly the same lines as Wolfenden, made me understand suddenly my grandfather's out-raged feelings at the sentence on Oscar Wilde.'[32]

Dalton had now become a dominating figure at the Cambridge Union – unable to secure election to major office because of his views, but one of the best debaters all the same. His opinions were also beginning to crystallise – along the lines of Fabian 'gradualism': gradual in the sense of determined, rather than half-hearted. With knowledge, too, came confidence. In February 1909, at a debate with guest speakers from Oxford, he outlined his socialist programme. 'Step by step the process of nationalisation must proceed, gradually, tentatively, but steadily. Either a time limit would be set ... or perpetual annuities would be granted to present holders'. According to *Granta*, 'he did not attempt to scintillate, but gave the House a thoughtful and exhaustive summary of the ideals which he so sincerely and consistently advo-cated.' His *tour de force*, however, came at the end of May, when he opposed in a more light-hearted debate the motion 'that this House would welcome a revival of the Puritan spirit in English life' – quoting from Arnold, Shaw and Wells. At last praise for his performance was unstinting. ' "Comrade Hugh" is the ablest speaker with us who has not yet been President', considered the *Granta* critic. 'Tonight he gave us an intellectual feast.'[33]

After three defeats for the Union Secretaryship,[34] Dalton decided not to stand again. He explained his reasons in a letter to a contempor-ary, J. R. M. Butler, revealing characteristic features of the mature politician: firm expression, clarity, shrewd calculation, concern for friends especially young ones, bold principles. There was also an element of undergraduate priggishness:

> King's College
> Cambridge
> June 10th 1909

Dear Butler,
    As I told you yesterday, I prefer not to leave your letter un-answered.
    No, I shall not stand for Secretary at Christmas, or thereafter.
    Firstly, I think it very improbable that the Union will, on the fourth or any subsequent occasion, do what it has three times already decided not to do. Secondly, my continued candidature would impede those of younger persons, whom I desire should enjoy their opportunities to the utmost.

Thirdly, a certain sense of self-respect makes me unwilling persistently to offer myself to those who hold that candidates of other types are more fitted to be office-bearers.

May I say that I think it quite legitimate for anyone in Union contests primarily to consult his own interests.

Speaking generally, I should only be prepared to stand aside on any occasion, if I thought that my candidature endangered that of any of my very intimate personal friends.

But this is true only within that period of my career, when it is worth while, on other grounds, to be a candidate.

As I have said, I believe that that period is now at an end. You will realise, however, that I in no degree resent your having taken your opportunity of last term.

In questions of personal ambition working itself out through popular election the main guiding principle must, I think, always be that of 'Sauve qui peut'. But I appreciate fully your kindly intentions in writing to me on this matter.

Yours sincerely,
Hugh Dalton[35]

Fabian and Union politics were not, however, Dalton's only preoccupation in the summer of 1909. Since the Easter vacation, he had been much concerned by an ambition of a more personal nature. For their fourth year at Cambridge, he and Brooke faced the prospect of leaving the college and seeking accommodation outside. Dalton decided that nothing would please him better than for the two of them to share rooms.

Dalton and Brooke still saw much of one another. The same small group of friends seemed as close as ever. In the first half of 1909, 'Break-Up' campaigning and the prospect of Brooke's succession to the Fabian presidency had brought Hugh and Rupert together as much as in their first few terms. Yet their circles were no longer identical, and Rupert's 'Apostolic' and literary friendships were beginning to draw them apart.

As summer approached, Hugh began a series of anxious attempts to prevent their separation. He suggested a joint holiday. Rupert was evasive. Hugh raised the possibility of joint digs in the autumn. Rupert was more evasive still:

... [N]ext year is too immensely distant. I may indeed, not come up: or, for a term, or two terms only. Or I may even stay in College, under pressure, and amid a generation that knows me not. But, if I followed that alluring plan of solitarily reading Ben Jonson in a far hovel, you in another part of the hovel, would, I think, find me hideously unsociable. You have no conception of the disagreeableness of me towards those who dwell under the same roof. I am a hermit by disposition. And when the poetic fury takes me, I knock my head, like poor Mr. Horace, for hours against the wall; a disturbing noise. Yet Time will decide.

To another suitor, A. F. Scholfield, Brooke wrote: 'I promised Dalton, last holidays, that if I *did* share rooms, with anyone, I would with him (But I shant.)'[36]

So that particular dream was never realised. Rupert took a bedroom and sitting-room at a riverside cottage called the Orchard in the village of Grantchester three miles from the town. Hugh moved to digs at Newnham Croft.

Before these decisions were taken, Dalton had the satisfaction of beating Brooke for a Winchester Reading Prize in the annual competition in the Senate House. Brooke's rendering of Keats's 'Ode to a Nightingale' failed to match up to Dalton's declamation from Milton. Triumph, however, was swiftly followed by defeat. Dalton wrote in his memoirs that his interests at Cambridge were 'Personal Relationships, Politics and Poetry'.[37] There had been little time for Mathematics. Hugh was disappointed, but not surprised, when he was awarded a Third in Part I of the Mathematical Tripos. Rupert was taken aback and mortified to miss a First. 'The colour was drained out of him', observed Frances Cornford.[38] Both men resolved to make amends in the autumn.

For the time being the parties went on. It was a hot, humid July and there was a feeling of anti-climax after the term's adventures and its dismal end. With one year left, there was also a sense of foreboding. Carbonari, Fabians, Apostles moved round restlessly in groups – reading, playing, constantly discussing.

Rupert settled in at the Orchard. 'You may come & have a meal with me. I work a great deal', he wrote appeasingly to Hugh. 'I'm writing a very good poem about fish copulating.'[39] Ben Keeling paid a visit to Grantchester;[40] so did Will Crooks, working-class Labour M.P. for Woolwich.[41] Another notable feature of Grantchester that summer was the presence of a caravan containing the painter Augustus John and his family of 'ten naked children' – according to Maynard Keynes's report to Duncan Grant.[42] 'I fell deeply in love with all the children,' Rupert wrote to Edward Marsh, 'some of them with me.'[43]

At the end of July, Hugh, Rupert and one of the Olivier sisters went to the Fabian summer school at Llanfair, where they attended a series of lectures by Beatrice Webb. They lived in a nearby farmhouse rented by Hugh. Ben Keeling, hungry for companionship after a year in London, stayed for a week.[44] Meanwhile, Rupert planned a literary house party. His parents had rented the vicarage at Clevedon in Somerset – a large house with extensive grounds and a tennis court. Rupert gathered congenial friends. At the end of August Hugh, Gerald Shove, Francis Birrell, Gwen Darwin, A. Y. Campbell, two Oliviers and Eva Spielman all arrived. Rupert wrote to Marsh, urging him to join them ('You will find Francis Birrell, and Dalton, a leader of the *Demi-Monde*, whom you may have met & you may find the silent Gerald Shove.') Marsh accepted the invitation and was driven over by Edward Horner, Hugh's contemporary at Summer Fields and Eton. Maynard Keynes also visited briefly. 'Bring any volumes of Synge you can lay your hands on, also Yeats, and *Atalanta in Calydon*', Brooke wrote to Dudley Ward. 'You can ransack my rooms, and Dalton's.'[45]

Mrs Brooke viewed this gathering of her son's friends with a myopic eye. She found Gerald Shove gloomy and unreliable. For some reason, however, she took to Hugh. 'Now with Mr. Dalton I always feel safe; he's so very prudent in all respects. Though I wish he were not consumptive, poor boy.' This was an *idée fixe* for which there was no justification, but from which she could not be shaken.[46]

With the start of the Michaelmas Term, Dalton threw himself into academic work with a vigour which he had not shown since his arrival at Cambridge. With only three terms before Part II of his Tripos, he pushed University politics aside. He had now retired as Fabian president, handing over to Brooke. Having decided not to stand again for Union office, there were no peaks left to climb. Yet without holding any position of importance, he was acknowledged as a leading Cambridge personality. *Granta* ran a regular series of pen portraits entitled 'In Authority', generally restricted to athletes and holders of established offices. In 1909–10, the editor broke the rule to include Dalton, Brooke and Dudley Ward. The author of the sketch of Dalton wrote that Hugh had filled a large place in his own college, and in the University:

A fluent and graceful speaker, never at a loss for a fact or a retort, a fine judge of the modern school of English literature, and withal no mere intellectual, for he plays tennis and fives with keenness and some skill; above all, a genial companion and a true friend, 'Comrade Hugh' will always take a high rank among the younger generation of Cambridge men.[47]

Hugh was himself the author of the sketch of Rupert Brooke.

Before submitting it, he passed it to Brooke for scrutiny. 'You might *put in* that my real life only began since I went to live at Grantchester,' came the reply, 'that I have a Pet Cow called Betsy, that I can play country tunes on a pipe; that I used to have a very neat stroke for four past third man.'[48] Dalton amended his essay appropriately, adding embellishments of his own. In the version that was printed, he portrayed Brooke as a figure out of classical mythology, arcadian, sprite-like and ethereal, a symbol of undying youth. Rupert had written of country tunes on a pipe. Hugh turned this into 'simple tunes on a pan pipe':

> He brought with him to Cambridge a reputation both as an athlete and as a poet, a combination supposed by vulgar people to be impossible ...
>
> There is a vacant place reserved for him between Matthew Arnold and Arthur Hugh Clough, in the Poets' Corner in Rugby School Chapel ...
>
> He will tell you that he did not really begin to live till he went out of College at the end of his third year and took up his residence at 'The Orchard', Grantchester.
>
> It is said that there he lives the rustic life, broken by occasional visits to Cambridge; that he keeps poultry and a cow, plays simple tunes on a pan pipe, bathes every evening at sunset, and takes all his meals in a rose garden.[49]

For his final year, Dalton switched subjects from mathematics to economics. It was his first real break with family tradition: forebears had been wranglers or theologians; none had attempted a modern subject like economics. There were several reasons for the change. He had neglected mathematics for so long that it would be hard to get back into it or catch up. A new subject, in which a basis in mathematics would be helpful, offered a better opportunity and also a fresh challenge. But the most important reason was his Fabian passion. For a man who was interested in the reconstruction of society there could be no better foundation, nor one more in keeping with the Webbs' teaching.

Economics also happened to be a subject in which King's was particularly strong. Apart from Keynes, recently returned, there was A. C. Pigou, who had just succeeded Alfred Marshall as Professor of Political Economy at the young age of 31. Pigou was not a Fabian, but he was known to be sympathetic to many Fabian positions and he provided a solid intellectual base for Fabian arguments. He lectured on Money, and his pioneering *Wealth and Welfare*, published in 1912, was for Dalton 'a book that helped me, more than any other, to formulate my own approach from ethics, through politics, to economics.'[50] Pigou argued that inequality was wasteful as well as unjust, and provided a bridge from Moore's ethics to practical action which greatly appealed to Dalton and other contemporaries. 'The misery and squalor that surround us,' wrote Pigou, 'the injurious luxury of some wealthy families, the terrible uncertainty overshadowing many families of the poor – these are evils too plain to be ignored.'[51]

Pigou, 'tall and handsome like a Viking',[52] was an eccentric figure, much in the King's mould. Like Dickinson, he was easily interested in young men. 'Young friends were what he lived for ... ', wrote the authors of a memoir. 'He liked them to be intelligent or gay or athletic or handsome ... '[53] In addition to admiring Pigou's writings, Dalton approved of his criteria for picking undergraduate friends: 'good-looking, good on mountains, good moral tone.'[54]

In the general election at the beginning of 1910, Dalton offered his services first to Chiozza Money, a progressive Liberal who later joined the Labour Party. Then, in the last ten days, he helped William Johnson, a Lib-Lab miners' leader, who was standing for Nuneaton. During the campaign he spoke at meetings, canvassed and worked in committee rooms, helped by Rupert and Rupert's younger brother Alfred.[55] In scattered mining villages round Nuneaton, Hugh would quote from one of Rupert's as yet unpublished poems, which had been inspired by the poster on Ben Keeling's wall in Trinity: 'Yet behind the night, Waits for the great unborn, somewhere afar, Some white tremendous daybreak.'[56] The election brought a big drop in support for the Liberals, making them dependent on Labour and Irish Nationalist votes in the Commons to maintain their majority.

Late in January, the Brooke household was overtaken by a domestic tragedy. Rupert's father had been ill for some time. On 12th January Rupert wrote to Hugh saying that he was much worse;[57] later the same day he died. Rupert had immediately to take over his father's work as a housemaster, and therefore stayed in Rugby until April, not returning to Cambridge or Grantchester until May. During the spring vacation Hugh tried to persuade Rupert to join him on holiday in Devon.[58] Instead Rupert went to Lulworth Cove, in Dorset, where Lytton and James Strachey joined him in lodgings.[59] The literary, non-political, world was gradually strengthening its hold.

Before going back to Grantchester, Brooke visited Henry Nevinson, deputising as editor of *The Nation*, which had just accepted one of Brooke's poems for publication. Nevinson's description of his first sighting of the young poet reveals less about Brooke than about the symbolic role Brooke had begun to acquire outside Cambridge:

> Suddenly he came – an astounding apparition in any newspaper office. Loose hair of deep browny-gold; smooth, ruddy face; eyes not grey or bluish-white, but of living blue, really like the sky, and as frankly open; figure not very tall, but firm and strongly made, giving the sense of weight rather than speed, and yet so finely fashioned and healthy that it was impossible not to think of the line about 'a pard-like spirit' ... the whole effect was almost ludicrously beautiful.[60]

It was the beginning of a lionisation by smart literary society which lasted until Brooke's death. Fabian Socialism had always been more of a game to Rupert than to Hugh. Soon it was to recede into the background for good.

Hugh was about to be drawn apart from Brooke by something other than politics – his own departure from Cambridge. In Part II of the Economics Tripos, he only achieved an Upper Second. Keynes told him that he had wobbled on the borderline of a First, and that the examiners had been split over whether or not to give him one. It was a cruel blow. He made plans to move to London, to read for the Bar. Rupert stayed on at Grantchester, working for a Fellowship at King's.

First, however, there was another summer school in Wales – with Cambridge Fabians no longer in favour. 'The Fabian Nursery has not distinguished itself this year!' Beatrice Webb wrote at the end of 1909, after Amber Reeves had given birth to H. G. Wells's child, and Ben Keeling had been forced to marry in a hurry.[61] Now she felt depressed about the attempt to attract undergraduates to the Society. Dalton, Brooke, James Strachey and Clifford Allen were among the Cambridge contingent at the 1910 Llanbedr school. Beatrice felt that they were 'inclined to go away rather more critical and supercilious than they came'. She noted, with distaste, a comment by Brooke that undergraduates would only come on such a course if there were important people to attract them. 'They don't want to learn, they don't think they have anything to learn', she reflected. 'They certainly don't want to help others; unless they think that there is something to be got in the way of an opening or a career, they won't come. The egotism of the young university men is colossal. Are they worth bothering about?'[62]

Dalton recalled later that the Cambridge group had been cliquish, rude and ribald. There had been 'unedifying horseplay, too visible ... and jokes late at night, too audible, about the Webbs themselves'.[63]

Beatrice noted in her diary a 'bad element' of 'three or four critical *Cambridge* Fabians', of whom Rupert Brooke was one. 'Some persons delight in noise', she observed. 'Would it be possible to exclude the more boisterous "larky" entertainments and substitute, or at any rate include, something of the nature of religious music – or time for meditation?'[64] Some of the Cambridge party brought their own blankets and slept on the floor of a stable.[65] Rupert wrote to Dudley Ward describing the sight of Hugh standing over James Strachey, 'his huge penis steaming' in the early morning chill.[66]

So ended, as Dalton put it later, 'the best four years of my life thus far. Nor could I pick now on any later run of four that would outshine them.'[67] Nevertheless it was a hopeful departure. There had been no great academic achievement, no major office at the Union – in short no conventional laurels. Yet, having entered Cambridge as one of an annual batch of unremarkable Etonians, he left it well-known throughout the University. 'Hugh Dalton was the great man in my day at Cambridge', recalled a Tory opponent, who disliked him.[68] He had gone up a lone wolf, with no close circle to refer to, in a state of transition, not so much rebelling against, as beginning to detach himself from, his roots. By 1910 he was fully formed, identifying closely with the friends he had made and the values they shared in the little élites of Carbonari, Fish and Chimney, Dickinson's Society. 'I had acquired, I believed, after much furious striving "to get things clear", a coherent philosophy and a true scale of values', he wrote later. 'I was immensely proud of my chosen contemporaries, ready to defend them against all attack.'[69] He remained loyal to the memory of this group and what it stood for – as distinct from the overlapping Bloomsbury circle – for the rest of his life.

V

Ever Young

Few people are untouched by their student days. Dalton's four years at Cambridge remained so central to him that later events sometimes seemed like a re-enactment, an attempt to capture what had been lost. Of Rupert Brooke, Dalton was to write forty years later: 'He was to all of us who loved him, a child of Tir Nan' Og, the Land of the Ever Young.'[1] Brooke died in 1915. Dalton lived on, part of him always inhabiting a world of joust and innocence.

Was Dalton homosexual? There were people who, belonging to a post-Freudian generation, concluded that he must be, and two books published since his death seem to lend weight to this supposition.[2] In fact, no evidence exists that Dalton ever had a sexual relationship with another man, and his private life seems to have been one of blameless monogamy. On the other hand both before and after his marriage, his emotions were more stirred by men – increasingly by younger men – than by women. This preference affected his friendships. It also profoundly influenced his politics. In his view of the ideal, a concept of brotherly love and fellowship had a special importance, deeply rooted in his personality and in the environment of his youth.

Since the Canon, lover of knavish boys and princes, had similar affections, we should not attribute too much to Cambridge. Yet if Cambridge was not the cause, it was certainly a place where Hugh's feelings and ideas could gain nurture.

Dalton's generation was notable as the one in which women first appeared as a part of the term-time social landscape. Both the gaiety, and the emotional upsets, of Rupert Brooke and Ben Keeling revolved around girls rather than around men. The Fabians were in the forefront of the campaign for women's rights; partly for this reason, the Fabian Society was popular among female undergraduates. Hence Dalton and his friends had more frequent and more informal contact with young women, particularly intelligent young women, than the majority of undergraduates at the time. Where Apostolic 'Souls' of Lytton Strachey's generation had discussed the nature of erotic passion within a closed male group, the Fabian Nursery openly debated sexual questions in mixed company.

Yet there is no doubt about what may be termed the 'homosocial' nature of intellectual Cambridge before the First World War, and especially of King's, nor of the dominant role of values and attitudes which this entailed. Of the dons mentioned by Dalton in his memoirs as important influences upon him, three – Dickinson, Keynes and Oscar Browning – were at some time in their lives actively homosexual, and a fourth, Pigou, was well known for his interest in young men, 'intelligent or gay or athletic or handsome'. The homosexuality of particular individuals was less important, however, than a shared outlook that fed on and into a broader intellectual culture in which male affections played a central part.

In his brilliant study *The Great War and Modern Memory*, Paul Fussell points to 'a main pre-war tradition' of 'homoerotic' poetry running from Whitman to Hopkins and Housman.[3] In such poetry the eroticism was idealised, presented in a language of allegories and symbols. Within this tradition there was a *genre* – scarcely a school – of more evidently homosexual or 'Uranian' writing which contained as a central idea the worship of adolescent boys. The essence of both 'homoerotic' and 'Uranian' literature was sublimation: physical passion was rarely seen. There was a merging of the erotic and the spiritual or aesthetic, of the romantic and the comradely. Such writing provided the imagery of Edwardian Cambridge.

'The appropriate subjects of passionate contemplation and communion were a beloved person, beauty and truth', wrote Keynes in a passage already quoted. The contemplation of a beloved person, presented as an ideal, was a strong theme in the literature admired by Apostles and Carbonari. As Fussell points out, blondness was a feature of this ideal. A favourite poet among Carbonari was Housman, whose *A Shropshire Lad* Dalton and Brooke enjoyed reading aloud to one another. Timothy d'Arch Smith suggests in his book *Love in Earnest* that Housman's ideal of a beautiful blond adolescent was echoed in many 'Uranian' poems, with the 'love of fair English boys' presented as a form of patriotism.[4]

It was natural that Rupert Brooke, 'young Apollo, golden-haired', should be appreciated in a community strongly imbued with the homoerotic tradition. There were two Rupert Brooke myths. One, heroic, began with the news of Brooke's death. This popular myth, however, depended on an earlier cult that started the moment Brooke, already

well known to the families of both Lytton Strachey and Maynard
Keynes, arrived in Cambridge.

Strachey, who thought nothing of Brooke's poetry, was delighted
by his beauty. 'Whenever I began to feel dull,' Strachey wrote to
Virginia Woolf, 'I would look at the yellow hair and pink cheeks of
Rupert.'[5] Almost as important as Brooke's physical appearance was
the impression he managed to convey of wholesomeness. 'No one
ever looked so much like a poet as he did', writes Samuel Hynes, 'not
a *poète maudit*, but an ideal English poet, a Rugby-and-Cambridge
poet, a healthy, pink-cheeked, blond, games-playing poet.'[6] As Cyril
Connolly remarked about the not-so-distant world of a preparatory
school during the First World War, prettiness alone was suspect but
prettiness that was good at games meant Character and was safe.[7]
Brooke was an athlete, and as such was admired by sportsmen as well
as intellectuals, who therefore admired him all the more. But it was
the hair and cheeks that mattered most, making him god-like and
hermaphroditic in the eyes of some beholders. This was partly
deliberate. Rupert Brooke was 'a man who took poeticalness as his
destiny', suggests Hynes. As Hugh wistfully recalled, Rupert wore
his hair so long that a King's porter once mistook his sleeping form
in the college grounds for that of a woman.[8]

The cult was not restricted to contemporaries or near contemporaries. Brooke was attended by an older generation as well. One admirer
was the homosexual writer Arthur Benson, Master of Magdalene.
Benson was the son of an Archbishop. He was also – and here we begin
to encounter another matrix of influences and relationships – the same
A. C. Benson who had been best man at the wedding of Hugh Dalton's
father in 1886, when barely half the Canon's age. At Cambridge in the
early 1880s, Benson had been a welcome visitor to the rooms of the
undergraduate Prince Eddy and his tutor, and John Dalton had come
to treat Benson as 'an object of adoration'. It was John Dalton who,
perhaps wisely in the circumstances, dissuaded Benson from marrying
Erna Evan-Thomas, Hugh's mother's sister, impressing upon the
young man the mistake of early marriage.[9] As a result, Benson remained a bachelor all his life, a victim of bouts of nervous depression,
taking a friendly and occasionally romantic interest in the undergraduates placed in his care.

Arthur Benson was already in his late forties, and Brooke twenty-
one, when Hugh Dalton called on his father's old friend 'to sing the
praises of Rupert Brooke'. Intrigued, Benson engineered an introduction. Benson's account of this event is interesting because it contains
so many of the images characteristic of the homoerotic tradition – a
sprite-like arrival, 'healthily rounded' and 'frank' features, hair that

was not just long and fair but 'over-long' and 'golden', and (in somewhat bizarre combination) suntan and rosy cheeks:

And then I met him, in the rooms of another under-graduate, a pupil of my own. He strolled in very late, when we had almost ceased to expect him. He was far more striking in appearance than exactly handsome in outline. His eyes were small or deeply set, his features healthily rounded, his lips frank and expressive. It was the colouring of face and hair which gave a special character to his looks. The hair rose very thickly from his forehead, and fell in rather stiff arched locks on either side – he grew it full and over-long; it was of a beautiful dark auburn tint inclining to red, but with an underlying golden gleam in it. His complexion was richly coloured, as though the blood was plentiful and near the surface; his face much-tanned, with the tinge of a sun-ripened fruit. [10]

Brooke seems to have appreciated Benson's attentions. 'We had an infinitely affecting *tête-à-tête* last night', Brooke wrote after another meeting, several years later. 'He implored me to write to him. I nearly kissed him.' [11]

What was the effect of the Rupert Brooke cult on Dalton? Hugh knew Rupert as a close friend, not as a symbol or an apparition. Yet the values and images which created the cult within 'homosocial' Cambridge, and which before the outbreak of war took it beyond Bloomsbury to the highest reaches of Society and even to members of the Cabinet, were Dalton's values and images as well. When Dalton showed his friend the draft of his biographical sketch for *Granta*, Brooke was precise in giving instructions: rural seclusion, rustic simplicity, past athletic prowess should all be mentioned. It was Hugh who raised the image from a mortal plane by referring to a 'pan pipe', adding that Brooke 'bathes every evening at sunset'. ('Men bathing', as Fussell shows, was another favourite theme of 'homoerotic' literature.) [12] 'The radiance of his memory still lights my path', wrote Dalton in 1953, and we need not doubt it. Associated with that memory was a view of comradeship and personal relations in general which affected not only Dalton's adult friendships but also his concept of the political life and his socialism.

There was another important aspect to the late Victorian and Edwardian idolisation of handsome men: what d'Arch Smith calls 'a theme which haunts the whole of Uranian verse to the extent of its becoming a well-nigh universally used idea – the extraordinary longing for an attachment to a boy either of far higher or, more often, of a far lower social rank.' This longing was often combined with a desire to move such a boy, if he were of lower rank, away from his menial environment and into a better life 'wherein he could share the heritage of art, literature, the sciences, and eventually take his place as an equal, despite the fact that he had risen from the ranks.' Each writer had his own preferred category of humble boy. A recurrent type (incidentally one that, during the Cleveland Street Scandal, caused embarrassment to Hugh's royal godfather) was telegraph boys. Others, however, were almost as popular. For Edward Carpenter, prolific writer of Uranian verse, ideal types included 'the thick-thighed hot coarse-fleshed young brick-layer' and 'the grimy and oil-besmirched figure of a stoker'.[13]

We have already encountered Edward Carpenter, author of *Love's Coming of Age*, the book that convinced Ben Keeling of the need for 'forms which are to supersede family organisation'. It is to Carpenter that we now return.

Edward Carpenter was a former clergyman who had lectured at Trinity Hall, Cambridge and spent several years in the ministry before going north to learn about and teach the working-class through the University Extension Movement. He is of interest here for three reasons. First, because his extraordinary life and writings demonstrate so clearly the direct link between late Victorian middle-class interest in socialism or social revolution, and homoerotic (in Carpenter's term 'homogenic') love. Second, because of his powerful political influence on Dalton's Fabian circle at Cambridge. Third, because Carpenter happened to be one of Canon Dalton's oldest and closest friends.

In his memoirs, Hugh Dalton mentions this last fact almost in passing.[14] Its truth is more than confirmed by surviving correspondence between Carpenter and the Canon spanning more than half a century. The relationship, based on student days together at Cambridge, was evidently an intense one. When Carpenter, in a state of emotional ferment, decided to throw up a career in the Church in order to search for a different kind of fulfilment by living and working among ordinary people, John Dalton urged him to change his mind in terms that suggest the greatest intimacy, affection and concern. 'Let me conjure by all the influence I have with you, be that little or slightly more', wrote Hugh's father, 'and by all the hopes I have nurtured in my own soul of the work to be done by you and of the success that is to follow, let me solemnly conjure you not to pass this living when it comes to your turn as fellow of Trinity Hall.'[15]

Carpenter ignored this advice, and his life as a churchman ended. Soon most of those he knew in Sheffield, where he took up residence, were 'of the non-respectable class'. E. M. Forster wrote of Carpenter's move north, 'With him it was really a case of social misadjustment. He wasn't happy in the class in which he was born ... '[16] In his new environment, Carpenter began to develop a Whitmanite vision of male comradeship linked to a socialist religion. Later he adopted an explicitly homosexual life with George Merrill, a former barman who had been brought up in the poverty of Sheffield slums. (Merrill would manifest his humble and unmannerly origins by pinching the bottoms of visiting pilgrims, on one occasion Forster, who immediately wrote a homosexual novel, *Maurice*, inspired by the experience.) Carpenter's first and most famous work was a long poem, *Towards Democracy*; this was followed by other poems and expository tracts. His own sexuality was a major theme of all his writings, which attacked legal conventions and the very institution of the family, envisaging its eventual expansion into the fraternity and community of all society. Partly because he practised his own gospel of simplicity (growing vegetables, sandal-making and writing) Carpenter acquired a following, and became 'the leading exponent of the "New Thought" – of Whitmanism, Tolstoyism, William Morris Socialism, Hindu mysticism, neo-paganism and sexual reform.'[17] He was also an occasional visitor at London meetings of the Fellowship of the New Life, and its less utopian successor, the Fabian Society.[18]

Throughout Carpenter's unusual career, John Dalton continued to take a keen and fond interest in his friend's ideas, for which he had some sympathy and admiration. Hugh Dalton wrote of his father's strong sense of social equality. Perhaps this owed something to Edward Carpenter. At any rate, fifty years after Carpenter's original journey north, the Canon was at pains to stress the kinship between them. 'You have never during all the years that have passed been far from my thoughts, your many published works alone would have forbidden that', John Dalton wrote to his friend in 1920. 'Though our paths in life have been divergent ... yet still I can't help thinking that our outlook on life and its problems is not so wholly dissimilar as one might imagine it would be.' That he regarded himself as in some sense a disciple, is suggested in a letter of birthday greeting written a year later. 'I can never sufficiently thank you for all I am indebted to you', declared the Canon; 'for the intercourse I was allowed to have with you at Cambridge and afterwards has I hope left enduring influence on my mental and moral outlook'.[19]

Hugh was much affected by his father, and we may speculate that some of Carpenter's 'enduring influence' filtered through during Hugh's adolescent years. Was the Canon the owner of those 'many published works'? Was Hugh puzzled by the gulf that separated two of his father's most valued friends – one a preacher of social and sexual revolution, and the other the heir to the throne of England? Is it reasonable to imagine that by the time Hugh began to take politics seriously, he had absorbed (perhaps before any other socialist teachings) an impression of Carpenter's vision of the new socialist order?

Any knowledge of Carpenter which Hugh may have acquired at home would have been strongly reinforced at Cambridge. There, the most enthusiastic proponent of Carpenter's work was Ben Keeling. 'I have ... been reading Edward Carpenter's books a good lot lately', Keeling wrote at the end of 1907. ' "Love's Coming of Age" is the best book on the sex question that I know of.'[20] Sex and the family led Keeling to Carpenter's discussion of the re-ordering of society, and soon Keeling was treating the whole Carpenter *oeuvre* as a secular Bible. When Keeling journeyed to Leeds in 1910 to study the workers in their natural habitat, he mentioned Carpenter in declaring that, while he now discarded all dogmas, he retained 'a passionate faith in the development of a collectivist spirit in relation to property and breeding.'[21] Six years later, after a long and weary march back from the trenches of the Western Front, Keeling wrote home asking for a book by Carpenter. 'I enjoyed it immensely', he wrote to Mrs Townshend, a few days before his death in the battle of the Somme. ' ... I have always felt I understood Carpenter pretty thoroughly and he has influenced me much.'[22]

Carpenter had another key advocate at Cambridge: the favourite don of the Carbonari, and Hugh's patron, Goldie Lowes Dickinson. Like Hugh's father, Dickinson was a personal friend of Carpenter, as well as an admirer of his work. Dickinson had, indeed, followed Carpenter into University Extension teaching in the 1880s, and for similar reasons. Keeling was restlessly heterosexual, his interest in Carpenter stemming partly from Carpenter's liberated views on sex in general. Dickinson shared Carpenter's homosexuality, and Carpenter's refusal to accept conventional mores was one of the main reasons for Dickinson's admiration of him. 'He is himself the complete contradiction of the popular view that homosexuals are decadents, sensualists, etc., etc.,' wrote Dickinson. 'And that, in spite of the fact that he believes in and practises the physical relation very frankly.'[23]

Like the impulsive Keeling, Dickinson suffered from deep feelings of guilt. Unlike Keeling, he was for much of his life sexually ascetic. Keeling hoped to escape from a sense of guilt through acts of expiation. Dickinson tried to divert his passions into a creative outlet. The posthumously published volume that contains Dickinson's autobiography also includes a remarkable and impressively honest poem by Dickinson in the form of a Socratic dialogue between his Body (passion) and his Soul (idealism) which seeks to express the contest within him. The interest of this poem (in which the Body declares 'I want a youth', and the Soul replies 'Well, so do I!') lies in the writer's solution to the oppression of his sexuality – namely, in the enlightenment of undergraduates.

The poem begins with a self-mocking account of Dickinson's fetish, in which the poet describes his enjoyment at being, in a literal sense, trampled upon:

> He sits and at his feet I take my place,
> He plants them firmly on my neck and face,
> Both pleasing me and pleased himself at heart,
> Because he loves the dominating part.
> I sniff the scent of leather at my nose
> And squirm and wriggle as the pressure grows,
> While he, more masterful the more I gulp,
> Cries 'Quiet! Or I'll tread you into pulp'.

Meanwhile a more cerebral Dickinson fights for control, and conquers passion by sublimating it:

> Disinterested from my own desire,
> Secreting joy from grief and light from fire,
> With a detached and independent mind,
> I view the changing fortunes of mankind,
> From the first totterings of their infancy,
> Their boyish fights, their idle reverie,
> The lunacies of their romantic youth,
> Their blind and bloody quest of truthless truth,
> Till at their manhood's verge I see them stand,
> With the bright torch of science in their hand.

Finally the victorious Soul indicates the constructive role of suppressed passion in Dickinson's life:

> For you, my enemy, have been my friend,
> Driving me desperate to my proper end.[24]

Dickinson differed from Carpenter, who had ceased to regard physical passion as an enemy – even an enemy to be tamed – at all. But Carpenter, the apostate clergyman turned sexual revolutionary, might equally have written of sex as a power 'driving me desperate to my proper end'. Many people who were not homosexual admired Carpenter, ignoring his sexual philosophy or regarding it as simply one aspect of his thought. Dickinson was able to see that sex was fundamental. Dickinson's own account of Carpenter's ideas is a valuable reminder that one important middle and upper class road to socialism in late Victorian England was not through the intellect:

> His approach had not been that of economy theory. I doubt whether he had ever read Karl Marx through (how many Englishmen have, I wonder?). He arrived by a different route. He started with the love of men and of nature and in his desire to liberate became a critic of social institutions. When I say the love of men, the word *men* must be stressed, as all who knew him know; and the point must be emphasised because he cannot be understood unless his attitude to sex is understood.[25]

Was Dickinson also writing about himself? 'He started with the love of men and of nature and in his desire to liberate became a critic of social institutions.' Dickinson, it will be recalled, was a student of poverty. He was also an 'academic Socialist', interested in Fabian Socialism.

What should we make of this network of influences – Edward Carpenter and his friends or disciples, John Dalton, Ben Keeling, Goldie Lowes Dickinson – with their strange intertwining of sex, romantic friendship and utopian socialism? During his most formative years, Hugh must have received versions of the Carpenter doctrine from three men who greatly influenced his development: his father, a close contemporary, a valued teacher. But his own perspective was different, and we should not imagine that he was drawn to Carpenter, or socialism, for identical reasons, or indeed that he accepted the corpus of Carpenter's ideas. Hugh was never a utopian. He was much more interested in the practical schemes of the Webbs. Windsor and Eton contributed more to his socialism than feelings of sexual guilt, if indeed he suffered any.

We do not, however, need to regard Dalton as a follower of Carpenter to see the importance to him of Carpenter's diffuse influence. For Carpenter wrote not just of sex, law and social organisation. He also offered, no less than G. E. Moore, a religion based on love – the love of men for men. Keeling's socialism was, in part, atonement. Carpenter's socialism had passed through atonement to exaltation. Carpenter *celebrated* his communion with the working class, just as he had once celebrated a communion with beloved persons – such as Hugh's father – at Cambridge.

When Ben Keeling, on a final dance with death, turned to Edward Carpenter, the book he read was probably Carpenter's autobiography *My Day and Dreams* published in June 1916. If so, Keeling may have found comfort in a revealing passage about Carpenter's own undergraduate days in the 1850s. Two aspects of this passage are particularly striking. First, the bewitching perfection of university life. Second, the painful unreality of that perfection, and the sense of something missing in the relationships it offered – namely, contact with un-gilded humanity. Keeling might, indeed, have written in similar terms about himself, in relation to his own Cambridge generation:

What a curious romance ran through all that life – and yet on the whole, with few exceptions, how strangely unspoken it was and unexpressed! This succession of athletic and even beautiful faces and figures, what a strange magnetism they had for me, and yet all the while how insurmountable for the most part was the barrier between! It was as if a magic flame dwelt within me, burning, burning, which one could not put out, and yet whose existence one might on no account reveal ... Yet as time went on I think it must have become clearer to me that Cambridge never would afford in this direction the actual that I wanted. Expectation grew dry at the fount, and torpor and distress in the last year or two took the place of the romance of the years before. Somehow I think I must have dimly understood that the trouble arose partly from a deep want of sympathy between myself and the whole mental attitude, mode of life, and ideals of the university, and of the gilded or silvered youth who lived and moved within it.

It was against this background that, after Carpenter had thrown up his Church career and was wondering what to do next, 'it suddenly flashed upon me, with a vibration through my whole body, that I would and must somehow go and make my life with the mass of the people and the manual workers.'[26]

As Hugh grew older, he had nothing but nostalgia – at times, a very deep nostalgia – for his life at King's. If, for a moment, he was attracted to the idea, adapted by Keeling from the writings of Carpenter, of joining a family-less socialist brotherhood in a working-class borough, this owed something at least to a desire to stay with the athletic and beautiful faces and figures who had become his friends. For him, the aim was not to seek out an alternative world, but to extend the happiness of his existing one. Dalton's own autobiographical account of Cambridge life suggests a Carpenter-like socialist community in action: a world of comradeship and fraternal love without family distractions, held together by bonds of mutual loyalty and a quest to get things clear. If Dalton's view, later in life, of the perfect educational system was an extension of boarding school to all classes, his concept of an ideal adult society followed very closely the values and relationships of Edwardian King's.

How far did Dalton consciously connect the idealisation of male comradeship in Carpenter's work with homosexuality? Was he aware of the direct link which Carpenter himself drew between the supposed interest of homosexuals in young men 'of a far lower social rank', and socialism? In one of his most popular books, *The Intermediate Sex*, Carpenter wrote:

Eros is a great leveller. Perhaps the true Democracy rests, more firmly than anywhere else, on a sentiment which easily passes the bounds of class and caste, and unites in the closest affection the most estranged ranks of society. It is noticeable how often Uranians of good position are drawn to rougher types, as of manual workers, and frequently very permanent alliances grow up in this way, which although not publicly acknowledged have a decided influence on social institutions, customs and political tendencies – and which would have a good deal more influence could they be given a little more scope and recognition.[27]

Did Hugh read, and make sense of, Carpenter's curiously prosy poems, strongly in the Uranian tradition, like this one, called 'A Sprig of Aristocracy'?

Browned by the sun, with face elate and joyous,
Pitching hay all day in the wide and fragrant hayfields,
Frank and free, careless of wealth (preferring to do something
useful, and to champion the poor and aged) –
O splendid boy, with many more like thee,
England might from her unclean wallowing rise again and live.[28]

Dalton quotes less compromising lines from Carpenter in his memoirs, but does not comment on his work. The novelist D. H. Lawrence was allegedly much influenced by Carpenter's writings on homosexuality, but was always careful not to acknowledge this debt in order to safeguard his own reputation.[29] For a politician such an imperative was obviously much stronger. However, Dalton does refer in his memoirs to Carpenter as a man 'known to British Socialists as the author of *England Arise!* and *Towards Democracy.*'[30] *England Arise!* is a socialist anthem. *Towards Democracy*, on the other hand, is 'a long

Whitmanesque poem ... full of an ardent spiritualised humanism',[31] combining the themes of comradely love, 'Uranian' love, eroticism, spirituality and socialism. In this, most celebrated of all Carpenter's books, manual labour and the working-class are romanticised on the basis of an ethic of fellowship and equality derived from 'homogenic' love.

In June 1923, thirteen years after Hugh went down from Cambridge, Canon Dalton wrote to Edward Carpenter, now in his eighties, informing him of a wish 'to make my way over to you and bring my son Hugh with me, who for years has wished to make your acquaintance'. A few days later Hugh, whose main preoccupation at the time was the feverish pursuit of Labour parliamentary candidatures, wrote to his father that he had arranged to free the following Wednesday from all engagements so as to make the trip. As a result Dalton father and son motored over to Guildford, where Carpenter was staying, and spent an hour with the elderly sage.[32]

There were several possible reasons for Hugh's trip. One may have been a desire to please the Canon who wished to show off his socialist son. Almost certainly the main reason was that Carpenter's legendary socialist haven at Millthorpe lay within the boundaries of the Chesterfield constituency in Derbyshire. Hugh, who spent much of the same week at Labour Party Conference discussing with leading Derbyshire miners how best to ease out the sitting Labour M.P. for Chesterfield in order to gain the candidature for himself,[33] must have been hoping that Carpenter might provide contacts, or exercise influence.

A third reason may have been curiosity about a man who might have followed precisely the same career as his father, but chose self-abasement instead. We have considered various links connecting Hugh Dalton's life and thought with Edward Carpenter, but one – in some ways the most startling – has not yet been mentioned. In a memorial essay published in 1931, a few months before Canon Dalton's death, Edward Carpenter's friend Charles Sixsmith recalled the following incident at Millthorpe, some years before:

> Edward, tidying up some of his drawers, fished out a photograph of two little boys in Highland costume and with their names written by the boys underneath. They were our present King and his brother, the Duke of Clarence. He told me that he was invited to be tutor to the Princes and stayed a day or two at Windsor, speaking gratefully of the gracious way he was treated by Queen Alexandra.[34]

There is no reference to this encounter with the Royal Family in

Carpenter's autobiography, *My Days and Dreams*. Since, however, the latter book was published in 1916, by which time the younger of the little boys was on the throne, it need not surprise us that Carpenter, or his respectable publishers, should not mention such an event for fear of causing the Royal Family embarrassment. Sixsmith's intriguing recollection is, however, supported by the contents of an envelope in the Carpenter Collection at Sheffield Central Library. This envelope was added to the Collection in 1959 by one of Carpenter's executors, Gilbert Beith, a close friend of Carpenter and editor of the 1931 memorial volume. The outside of the envelope is inscribed and initialled by Beith, with a brief description of what was to be found inside, and a reference to 'when the job of being [the royal princes'] tutor was offered him and refused'. In the envelope are three photographs and an unsigned typescript note which reads:

These Photographs of Prince Edward and Prince George of Wales (later Duke of Clarence and King George V) were presented to Edward Carpenter by their mother the Princess of Wales (later Queen Alexandra) on the occasion of his visit to Windsor Castle in 1875, when she offered him the post of tutor to the two young princes, but which he declined for reasons of his own – which decision she much regretted at the time. Later, however, the post was accepted by the late Canon Dalton.

The first photograph is of Prince George. It bears the date 12th July 1875 and is inscribed 'Given to me by the present King in 1875. E.C. (1916)'. The second, of Prince Eddy, is dated a week later, 19th July 1875, and is inscribed 'Given to me by the then Duke of Clarence in 1875. E.C. (1916).' The third photograph, a family group, is inscribed simply 'Edward and George Christmas 1876 with Alexandra. E.C.'[35]
The date of Carpenter's inscriptions (1916) is easily explicable: preparing his autobiography in that year, Carpenter may have had occasion to sort through old papers, labelling and filing items for possible use. The other dates are more puzzling. By 1875, John Dalton had already been working as tutor to the princes for four years. So the typed note in the envelope is wrong in at least one respect: Dalton's appointment preceded, and did not follow, the gifts of the photographs – assuming that the dating of the photographs is correct, which, given the precision of the dates on two of them, seems likely.
Here we must speculate. Perhaps Sixsmith's recollection, and the notes on and in the envelope, were based on a misinterpretation of Carpenter's remark – though the statement seems too simple and dramatic to have been easily misinterpreted, and the photographs and

their inscriptions provide evidence of some direct contact with the princes. Perhaps Dalton asked Carpenter to join the Royal Household as an assistant tutor once he was himself already established there; though, in view of Carpenter's release from ordination vows in 1874, this again seems improbable.

Another possibility is that Sixsmith's recollection and the two notes in the Carpenter papers mixed up two separate things: a job offer, and subsequent gifts of photographs. If Dalton was offered the job which Carpenter had turned down, then we may presume that Carpenter had discussed his own possible appointment with his prospective employer in 1871, the year in which Dalton became the princes' tutor. In which case, we may imagine that a few years later Carpenter visited his old friend and met his royal charges and their mother, receiving the photographs during his visit, or visits.

If this is plausible, we should consider a coincidence of dates. The year 1871 was not only that of Dalton's appointment. It was also the year of Carpenter's crisis. In May 1871, Carpenter suffered a nervous breakdown and vacated his curacy in order to recuperate. In October, he resumed his lecturing and college work but not his church duties.[36] We may wonder whether a royal interview, and the kind of life it offered, coming at a time of doubt and conflict, contributed to his decision to make his life 'with the mass of the people and the manual workers'.[37]

Whatever the full explanation of the photographs and their inscriptions, Hugh must have reflected on the difference, almost a symmetry, in the lives of his father and his father's student friend: the turning-point in the lives of both John Dalton and Edward Carpenter occurring almost simultaneously, one rising to spend his life with the highest in the land, the other choosing to live among the lowest.

VI

L.S.E. and A.S.C.

Until he began an active political career after the Armistice, Dalton's life had none of the public display, the sense of being a star, which he had enjoyed at King's. After Cambridge he at last got down to the business of serious, sustained study, acquiring the skills upon which his later academic and political achievements were to be built. It was a productive time, laying seed-corn. But it was unglamorous. While friends published books and made their mark, Dalton had no spectacular successes.

Was he planning to be a politician? The possibility of such a career was still clearly in his mind, but he did little directly to pursue it. He even briefly considered emigration to Australia. Through a Liberal M.P. for whom he campaigned in the December 1910 election, he obtained a recommendation to become A.D.C. to the Governor of Victoria. He viewed the prospect with enthusiasm: but the Governor chose another A.D.C.

Dalton's first act on leaving Cambridge was political: an educational trip, in the Carpenter–Keeling tradition, to the north of England. Armed with letters of introduction he visited shipyards in Newcastle, steelworks in Middlesbrough, and a coalmine at Auckland Park in County Durham, later to be part of his own Bishop Auckland constituency.[1] For the time being, however, he took his undergraduate Fabianism no further, and instead set about acquiring a professional qualification. In the autumn of 1910 he moved to residential chambers in the Middle Temple and began to read for the Bar.

It seems to have been an unhappy episode. He could not, or would not, apply himself. Why did he try? Perhaps he was influenced by his uncle Cornelius, who had used the Bar as a stepping stone to a distinguished career in the public service. Unlike his uncle, however, Hugh felt no commitment to the Law. Very soon his interest moved elsewhere. The Middle Temple became a convenient base for pursuing the subject which had seized his imagination in his final undergraduate year – economics. He began to visit the London School, a few hundred yards from where he lived, attending lectures by Edwin Cannan, Graham Wallas and L. T. Hobhouse.

Dalton was attracted to the School by its pragmatic approach and progressive reputation. The Webbs had recommended it to him, much as they had pointed Keeling towards labour exchanges. There were also direct Cambridge links: Lowes Dickinson taught at the L.S.E. on a part-time basis, and the Director, a prominent Fabian called William Pember Reeves, was father of the talented and wayward Amber.

But above all the School recommended itself. The L.S.E. in 1910 was an institution well suited to his needs, intellectually and politically. Founded in 1895 with Webb inspiration and Fabian money, 'Sidney's child' (as Beatrice called it) had already become the most important centre for economic studies outside Cambridge. There was a bustling, ambitious feeling about the School at this time, after a period of rapid growth. The number of students attending lectures had trebled to 1,637 in the first six years of the century, and there had been notable additions to the staff – including H. B. Lees-Smith, later a Liberal and then Labour M.P., and R. H. Tawney. Edwin Cannan had been appointed to a new Chair of Political Economy in 1907. It was a sign of the increasing popularity of lectures that in the year that Dalton enrolled, temporary buildings had to be erected to accommodate new students.[2]

Cambridge friendships remained important, though gradually more distant as members of the Carbonari and Fabian sets went their different ways. Dalton occasionally returned to Cambridge to visit Rupert Brooke or to address the Union as an elder statesman. In November 1910 he opposed a pro- Tariff Reform resolution at the Union, speaking alongside Maynard Keynes. 'The hon. member has become an orator', commented the *Gownsman*.[3] He also kept in touch with Ben Keeling, whose shot-gun marriage was showing signs of strain. 'I gather Ben is going to be up for the week-end', Rupert wrote to Hugh from Grantchester, the same autumn. 'He came on Friday. I had not heard about "the typist"; but as I suppose they'll share a room, it will be all right.'[4] Keeling moved from London to Leeds, where he continued to work until he took a job on the recently established *New Statesman* at the end of 1912. Both Keeling and Brooke suffered bouts of emotional upheaval, and sought escape through foreign travel. As a result Dalton saw less and less of them..

Dalton's relationship with Rupert Brooke was still the one that

mattered most. Rupert departed on a world cruise in May 1913, not
returning until June the following year. Rupert's inconstancy became
the theme of their correspondence, with Hugh the pursuer and Rupert,
fawn-like and teasing, the pursued. Rupert wrote from Berlin in
August 1912:

> I gather from postmarks that Frau Neeve kept your card for four
> days, and my mother's for two. It has got here at length. You will
> have sought some other older man by now. To whom you will talk
> of law. Alas. But perhaps it is as well. For, yes, I am, as you say,
> dead ... I am under pretext of doing my dissertation here. Actually
> I have not done a word. I spend my time in making love to female
> dancers. They pirouette scornfully away ... [5]

Sometimes he adopted a playfully commanding tone:

> Next Saturday, 11th, I shall pass through London and stop for
> dinner with the C.U.F.S. [Cambridge Fabians] at the Inns of Court
> Hotel. I intend to sleep that night in your rooms. Tell me what you
> think about it. Answer immediately or I shall take other steps. [6]

Before Brooke set sail, Canon Dalton had supplied him with a letter
of introduction to the Canadian Prime Minister. In July 1913, having
crossed the Atlantic, Rupert sent Hugh a postcard:

> You'll be pleased to know I'm looking round the Empire, won't
> you? Rather in your line ... But they're a rough lot, Hugh. Their
> manners. [7]

In July 1911 Dalton won the Hutchinson Research Studentship
at the L.S.E. – the first academic distinction of his career. This
carried an annual grant of £100 and was regarded as the principal
research studentship awarded by the School. [8] The Shaw Research
Studentship, the other major award, was won by Eileen Power, who
was to become the greatest medieval historian of her generation.
Dalton continued to live at the Temple. But most of his attention was
now focussed on a study of the inequality of incomes, with Edwin
Cannan as his supervisor. The topic flowed naturally both from the
welfare economics of Pigou and from Fabianism. While others came
to believe that inequality was unjust for moral reasons or because of
their emotional revulsion against poverty, Dalton armed himself
against self-doubt or the accusation of soft-headedness by finding
ways of showing that inequality was inefficient.

Dalton always claimed that Pigou and Cannan influenced him more as academic economists than Keynes.[9] In some ways Cannan was a strange choice for mentor: cautious and increasingly unfashionable. Yet Cannan was, like Socrates, 'skilled in promoting a clearance of traditional rubbish from the mind'. He was not a systematiser and he was suspicious of orthodoxies. Politically, Dalton found him a friendly sceptic, a man who was not hostile to socialism but who felt that the onus was on the socialist to prove the practicality of his plans. Cannan told Dalton that one of the most important tasks for the coming generation was 'to work out schemes of Socialist organisation that should hold water from the point of view of productive efficiency'.[10] It was an instruction which the younger man tried not to ignore.

In 1913 Dalton began to publish the first fruits of his research in the L.S.E. student magazine *Clare Market Review* under the heading 'Some Problems of Distribution'. In a series of articles he attacked the principle and practice of inheritance. He also criticised the £5,000 pension still paid to the descendants of Lord Nelson,[11] an anomaly which as Chancellor of the Exchequer three decades later he took pleasure in ending. These articles are notable for the early development of ideas about inequality, for a firm, clear and witty style, and for their sycophantic praise of Edwin Cannan.

Dalton occasionally took part in student debates; but apart from a brief spurt of activity at the time of the December 1910 election, politics were not in the forefront of his mind. After the defeat of the Webbs over the Minority Report, the national Fabian Society had entered a period of recession. Upheavals in the Liberal Government, and the success of 'Lloyd Georgism', left Fabians struggling for a purpose. Meanwhile young Oxford recruits to the Fabian Nursery such as G. D. H. Cole and William Mellor were trying to promote revolutionary ideas that had little in common with the traditional approach of the Society.[12] Dalton and his Cambridge friends, who had looked to the Fabian elders for inspiration, had little sympathy for the new mood.

Some of the Cambridge Fabians were moving away from socialism altogether. Gerald Shove, Rupert Brooke and Dudley Ward, infected by Bloomsbury, had lost most of their earlier interest in politics. Ben Keeling, still as passionate as ever, was driven by a mixture of romantic idealism and re-awakened personal ambition to find merits in the Liberal Party. 'I am decidedly anti-revolutionist', Keeling wrote in June 1914, 'and I don't believe in most of the doctrines which distinguish the I.L.P. from the Liberals – the right to work, extreme antimilitarism, Little Navy and Little Englandism'. The Liberals had

improved social conditions. More important, the Liberals held out
the prospect of a political career. Keeling did not like the money,
social snobbery or 'undemocratic spirit' of the Liberal machine. But
he saw no practical alternative. 'I don't see that the Labour Caucus is
much better than the Liberal – while I simply can't swallow the doctrinaire generalisations of the Socialists', he concluded. 'I feel there is
in some ways more room for idealism with the Liberals.'[13]

Was Dalton thinking along similar lines? In his memoirs Dalton
acknowledged that he had been impressed by Lloyd George, but
claimed that the Liberals had never tempted him. There were too
many plutocrats, snobs and crashing bores in the Liberal Party, he
wrote (echoing Keeling). 'We did not want to get mixed up with all
that lot.'[14] Was this really the whole of his attitude? As Keeling recognised, the Liberals, for all their faults, offered the only opportunity
for entering parliamentary politics. Labour in Parliament was almost
exclusively working-class; it would have required second sight to
foresee post-war developments. If Dalton had not lost his desire for a
'political life' – and there is every indication that he had not – he must
have had his eye on the Liberals. Perhaps, indeed, he was closer to
them than he was subsequently prepared to admit.

It was at this time that Dalton first got to know C. P. Trevelyan, a
radical member of the Liberal Government. Three times – in 1911,
1912 and 1913 – Dalton made the journey to the Trevelyan estate at
Wallington, in Northumberland, to take part in the celebrated Trevelyan Man Hunts – annual hare-and-hounds chases through rough
countryside, much in the intellectual aristocrat tradition. 'The
Politician on the make is hunting for a place', Kenneth Swan, a
veteran huntsman, wrote in a doggerel verse after the 1913 event;
perhaps he had Dalton, one of his companions, in mind.[15]

Participation in a Trevelyan Man Hunt was of course no proof of
Liberal leanings: many huntsmen were just family friends, with no
political ambitions. Yet there are other indications that Dalton's
socialism was not uncompromising after he left Cambridge. In 1913,
he was reviewing books for a journal called the *Young Liberal*;[16] and
he himself claimed later that he had been offered a Liberal candidacy.[17]
Mary Stocks, who entered the L.S.E. a year before Dalton, recalled
an occasion at the School debating society when she spoke in favour
of a resolution on unemployment 'based on principles enunciated by
Mrs Sidney Webb, against cold opposition from Hugh Dalton, Leader
of the Liberal Party, who denounced the provisions as "academic"'.[18]
'Dalton changed from Fabianism to Liberalism, before the war',
Beatrice wrote in 1936, 'and came back to the labour party when it
was clear liberals had no future as an alternative government.'[19]

Perhaps this view of Dalton as a Vicar of Bray, adjusting his allegiances to suit the moment, was not entirely without foundation.

Yet Dalton was never a Liberal in any theoretical sense. If he flirted with the Liberal Party, the relationship was pragmatic. It was his socialism that had led him to the L.S.E., and the topic of his doctoral thesis gave weight to his socialist beliefs. Like Ben Keeling, he rejected 'doctrinaire generalisations'. Unlike Keeling (and unlike the majority of his Cambridge Fabian contemporaries) he was not content to leave socialism as a vague undergraduate enthusiasm. Dalton's study of the inequality of incomes was interrupted by the war; but his attack on the principle of inheritance, far more radical than anything the Labour Party was prepared to contemplate except briefly in the early 1920s, was well developed long before such ideas seemed likely to reap rewards in career terms.

During Dalton's student days at the L.S.E., he acquired the grounding in economic theory that was the basis of his approach to economic questions for the rest of his life. Meanwhile the School was important to him in another way as well: it provided him with a wife. Through the Students' Union he got to know an energetic young undergraduate called Ruth Fox. Like the young women Dalton had known at Cambridge, Ruth was a Fabian. But in other respects she was different from the pretty Olivier sisters or the carefree Amber Reeves who had helped to enliven the proceedings of the Cambridge Society. For Ruth, politics was a serious business.

The daughter of a retired Tory businessman, Thomas Hamilton Fox, and his half Scottish, half Greek wife Valentine, Ruth had been educated at Chantry Mount School, Bishop's Stortford, and by private tutors. She had entered the L.S.E. as a day student in 1909 – perhaps influenced by her father who, despite his Conservative beliefs, had become Treasurer of Beatrice Webb's Society for Promoting the Break Up of the Poor Law. At the School Ruth rapidly established herself as an efficient organiser and an effective speaker. After two years of fixing concerts, acting in plays, taking the floor in debates, she was elected Joint Secretary of the L.S.E. Students' Union. Soon Ruth and Hugh were closely involved in the foundation of an L.S.E. discussion group called the Query Club. Other members included Eileen Power and Bill (later Lord) Piercy. Eileen, Bill, Ruth and Hugh remained friends for the rest of their lives.

In 1913 Hugh nearly joined the staff of the School. A job became available in the social science department. Two candidates were interviewed, Dalton and a young social worker from the East End called Clement Attlee. Sidney Webb was Chairman of the Selection Committee. Although four years younger than Attlee, Dalton must have rated his chances highly: he was well known at the School and held its most prestigious award. But Attlee got the job. 'I was not appointed on the score of academic qualification', Attlee modestly recalled, 'but because I was considered to have a good practical knowledge of social conditions.'[20] It was not the last time that Attlee's closeness to the working people of London was to stand him in good stead.

Dalton felt that one reason for his failure was that Attlee was a qualified barrister, while he himself was not. The following spring he put this right. On 6th May 1914 he was called to the Bar, having obtained an undistinguished Third Class in the Easter exam. Three weeks later he married Ruth at St Michael's, Cornhill, in the City of London. It was a church wedding, perhaps as a concession to Canon Dalton, who performed the ceremony. Douglas Rouquette – a new friend, recently President of the Cambridge Union – was best man. Hugh was 26, his bride 23. They spent their honeymoon at Lockeridge in Wiltshire, acquiring an affection for Savernake Forest and the Marlborough Downs which they were to retain for the rest of their lives.

When they got back to London Hugh found a note from Rupert Brooke, home from the South Seas. 'I am as free as the wind on Thursday night. Are you? You can shelve your wife. Nothing shall occupy me on Thursday night till I hear from you. Write immediately to Rugby. All other times I am dining with E. Gosse, or H. James, or S. Olivier, and others of my contemporaries. How horrible it is to be a bachelor.'[21] The two friends dined together alone. It was their final meeting. A few weeks later Brooke was entertained by the Prime Minister at 10 Downing Street, and introduced to Winston Churchill who offered to help him get a commission should war be declared.[22] Dalton and Brooke now moved in different spheres. Early in 1915 Brooke wrote to Dudley Ward arranging to have letters circulated to a number of friends in the event of his death. Dalton's name was not on the list.[23]

Ruth and Hugh were on holiday in Ireland when war broke out. After their return Hugh did not immediately join up, though as more and more friends did so, he followed their example, becoming a member of the Inns of Court O.T.C. Unlike Ben Keeling and several L.S.E. lecturers (including R. H. Tawney and H. B. Lees-Smith, though not Attlee) who chose on principle to serve in the ranks, Dalton accepted a commission. He did not share Keeling's desire to be a private soldier so as 'to experience the life of the manual worker and to earn his living for a time by the sweat of his brow'.[24] He differed from Keeling in his attitude to the war in another way as well. Keeling joined the

British army as a pro-German, regarding Russia both as the real cause of the war and as a long-term threat. Dalton believed from the start in German guilt. Unlike many socialists and liberals, he never doubted the necessity of fighting or of winning once the war had begun.

Dalton's first experiences of war were humdrum rather than exciting or alarming. He was placed in the Army Service Corps, where he never rose up above the modest rank of Brigade Supply Officer, and remained well behind the fighting lines. It was an irksome and un-comfortable life but not a very dangerous one. He approached it with initial interest, then with mounting frustration. Although he had been commissioned early in 1915, he did not get beyond the training grounds of Salisbury Plain until early the following year. By this time some of the fiercest battles had been fought and many of his closest Cambridge friends (including Rupert Brooke) were already dead.

Dalton was posted to the 35th or 'Bantam' Division, one of the six divisions of the Fourth New Army, formed out of the original Fifth Army in April 1915. The 35th had been created from a nucleus of three 'Bantam' battalions – originally made up of well-developed men, including many miners, whose height fell below the standard accept-able for military service. The scale of casualties and demand for re-placements, however, were such that many later 'Bantam' recruits were unfit as well as small, the under-nourished products of urban slums.[25] Dalton thus found himself, already older than most sub-alterns, in a low status outfit attached to one of the least popular sections of the British Army.

At the beginning of 1916, the Division was directed to proceed to the Western Front. On the morning of his departure, Hugh left Ruth at their lodgings at Ludgershall, and set out on a three mile walk to Tidworth to join his comrades-at-arms. Before leaving, he acquired a small lined notebook. On the top of the first page he wrote:

22/1/16 Informed at 8.15 a.m. that B.S.O.s [Brigade Supply Officers] are going tomorrow, via Southampton.

It was the start of a habit he kept up with a few brief intervals for more than four decades. His diary began as a meticulous account of routine events. Gradually it became more relaxed, including thoughts and plans. His original intention was to provide raw material for corres-pondence. On 31st January he wrote that a diary was 'easier and more systematic than writing a letter'. Sending extracts to Ruth became a regular practice when he was away from home. Yet his diary soon acquired its own momentum, independent of any specific purpose, playing an important part in his life: a companion, a sounding board for ideas, perhaps most of all an emotional release.

Dalton left England in good spirits, eager for a new challenge. His mood was soon dampened as he discovered the disadvantages of being in a poorly regarded and badly staffed unit, and his early diary is filled with a steady growl of complaint, tinged with snobbery, at the stupidity, vanity and incompetence of fellow officers.

The Army Service Corps was responsible for the unknown, unsung, logistical side of modern warfare. A huge, bureaucratic network, 200,000 strong by the beginning of 1916, its matrix of communications and supply lines was spread through Northern France, feeding and equipping the troops of the front-line. There were a series of links in a chain of depots; provisions passed from one to the next, until they reached the fighting men. Goods were sent by train from base supply depots at the channel ports to railheads. Here a complete 'section pack grocery train', made up of trucks packed with one day's groceries for one division, were handed over to the supply officer of the divisional supply column, and the lorries of this column conveyed the rations to the refilling point. The rations were transferred to the horse-drawn vehicles of the divisional 'train', for conveyance to each brigade. Then they were carried on regimental transport wagons to selected spots convenient for the communication trenches, and from there they were taken by ration parties to the troops.[26] The life of a supply officer revolved around this daily exercise.

Dalton, however, was less bothered by the tedium of his job than by the people with whom he had to associate while doing it. A particular bugbear was his immediate superior officer, called Ewart, 'a selfish and conceited plebeian Scot', whose drunkenness, inefficiency and disagreeable habits were irritating from the outset. 'He is unreasonable, he is petulant, he is a confirmed grouser, he is ill-at-ease with gentlemen', Dalton grumbled when they got to France, though this did not prevent him from accompanying Ewart to the *Folies Bergère*, which Dalton found 'infinitely superior in every way to those one sees in London'.

Dalton soon discovered that the *Folies Bergère* was not the only thing he liked about France. Indeed he found almost all the inhabitants preferable to his own boorish companions. 'I am irresistibly attracted to France', he wrote, 'so brave, so rational, so calm, so competent'. Even a young woman tram conductor typified 'the calm competence of France', in contrast to the gracelessness of his compatriots. The British officer corps in Le Havre did however provide one point of interest. 'I learn that the venereal hospital here is full', he noted, wryly. 'The English section contains 26 A.S.C. officers and 2 Army Chaplains!'

On 26th January Dalton's company left Le Havre for Abbéville and then St Omer, beginning a long trek from one depot and refilling point to another. It was a routine that lacked even the virtue of regularity – a life of unpredictable moves, as rations arrived to be collected and delivered. Distant guns at the front were audible on 1st February and a few days later Dalton saw an enemy aeroplane in action: two bombs were dropped, killing three men close to St Omer railway station. On the 19th the sound of artillery became more ominous – a cannonade that lasted all day gave warning of the massive German assault on Verdun.

The nature of his job, arranging supplies and rations for a wide range of units, had one advantage: it enabled him to see far more of the organisation behind the lines than was possible for most junior officers – and to witness at first hand the muddle and confusion that frequently prevailed. The main psychological problem was the sense of being close to the action, yet with the full horror just out of sight: like a prisoner in his cell who hears the sounds of execution and wonders when his turn might come. The war was made the more nightmarish by the devastation of the countryside, and by the mental and physical scars of the wounded.

When the battle of the Somme started in June, he was sufficiently near to realise the colossal scale of the bombardment. He was fascinated by the guns. 'A fine roll of gunfire', he wrote on the first day. 'The chief feature of our artillery preparations this time is its thorough deliberation.' On the 13th he watched, awestruck, an Allied bombardment north-east of Albert. 'A great day', he commented. 'Some idea of "hell with the lid off"'. Noise deafening, especially at 10 feet from a big howitzer. Talk to 4 French officers of 75's, young and very charming. Show me their four kinds of shells – shrapnel, h[igh] e[xplosive], asphyxiating and lachrymatory, (the latter a dull green colour).' 'Firing tremendous again at night,' he wrote on 20th July, 'like the continual roll of the sea on high cliffs, with occasional sharper, louder and nearer blows.'

The noise and the splendour of the guns – from a fairly safe distance – helped to persuade Dalton to apply for a transfer to the artillery. For some time he had been meeting Royal Artillery officers and finding them greatly superior to Bantams. On 14th August he talked to an artillery officer called Colonel Fawcett, who said he would be glad to have Dalton in his Brigade. Dalton concluded that Fawcett would be 'a glorious fellow to work under'.

Meanwhile morale in the 35th Division was lower than ever. The

Bantams, thrown into battle, failed badly. In one attack more than half the men were allegedly crying like children '(which, indeed, is all that the latest Bantam drafts are!)' The company commanders reported that while they were prepared to go over themselves, their men would not and could not be made to follow them. Dalton attributed the demoralisation to excessive punishments for desertion and cowardice which, he felt, defeated their own purpose.[27]

Ben Keeling was killed in the trenches on 18th August, on another section of the front. Like many soldiers fighting in the most fearful battlegrounds, he had become coolly reconciled to the terrible odds against him. 'One seems uncommonly near the dead nowadays in the course of our tight rope dance, in which a certain proportion are always falling over into the abyss', he wrote home on 8th August, ten days before he died.[28] Dalton was not immediately aware of the loss of yet another friend. For the moment he was concerned with his proposed transfer, made the more desirable by the infuriating habits of fellow officers. 'Slight friction with Walker in Mess', he noted on 6th September. 'We all wish he wouldn't suck his teeth, or bring so many other vets to meals.' Dalton's spirits were not raised by the discovery that, if he achieved a transfer, this would involve no promotion.

Then there came a change: he was made 'Town Major' of a small township called Agnez, near Arras. 'This will be an amusing little job, and will be better than the monotony of the daily dump', he wrote. He welcomed the feeling of being in the public eye, and the opportunity to exercise political judgment. He had to deal with local crises – as, for example, when two inhabitants were in a dispute about the right to the manure of an artillery battery.

But such diversions did nothing to soften news of losses on the Somme, and of the road to Guillemont hidden by thousands of corpses. An officer fresh from the battle lines recounted:

– the ceaseless sweating diarrhoea in the shallow trenches, without change of underclothes, – the mad Germans eating their own dead after 8 days' exposure in a dug out, – the young subaltern, an only son, who never showed a sign of fear but had a true presentiment of his own death 24 hours beforehand, the nature of his wounds, the failure of the stretcher bearer to bring him right back, and his fortunate death, – the breakdown of another young officer — He thinks that after the War, when men have time to reflect, many will commit suicide, and many others will break down.[29]

On 13th October Dalton went on leave, having just heard that his application for a transfer had been rejected. He met Ruth at Victoria and went off for tea at the Temple. He had been away less than nine months, in the bloodiest phase of the War, within a few miles of the most terrible massacres in history – yet always just beyond the actual slaughter. In that time he had been almost constantly on the move, changing billet every few days, with no fewer than 39 stops. He had seen dead and wounded, prisoners and commanders, Indian troops and Africans, Canadians, Australians, and French. He had suffered rain, mud, cold, sickness and the tiresome habits of fellow, and especially senior, officers. But he had seen no fighting at first hand.

Dalton returned only briefly to France after his leave. When he got back to his Company, he wrote to Edwin Cannan at the L.S.E., angling for a job. The visit home had encouraged him to think about his post-war career. He decided not to go back to the Bar, but to stick with economics. 'Economics has always been my strongest intellectual interest, and to economics I shall mainly give myself, to think, to write and to teach', he wrote. He needed to make some money out of it, but he had 'a little besides'. If the worst came to the worst, he would lecture for the W.E.A. or University Extension, and write little books and do some journalism. 'But I would like something better', he told his supervisor. 'What I would like would be the job of your Assistant at the School ... What chance do you think there might be? Is there annoyance with me, because the war interrupted my thesis? I hope that two or three months may see it finished, when the war's over. I am keen to get it off my hands, even in a much abbreviated form, so as to be free for other writing.' He expected the war to run on 'till nearly the end of 1918', on the assumption that 'real internal troubles will come late to Them but later still to Us'. When he thought of the war in its broadest terms, he thought of dead friends:

> I was so proud of the intellectuals of my generation, and so full of dreams of what they might achieve. Most of the best and dearest of them are dead now, and it will be only a tiny, stunned fraction that will emerge at the end ... And we shall all take down with us to the grave wrecked hopes and agonising memories . [30]

In November, Dalton visited Arras, and saw Colonel Fawcett, the officer who had encouraged him to apply to join the gunners. Fawcett pulled some strings, and this time the transfer went through. On 25th January 1917, to his great excitement and relief, Dalton was ordered home to train for the Royal Artillery. The conversion of a supply officer into an artillery officer took place first at Horsham, then on Salisbury Plain, then at Lydd, in Kent, and finally in Shropshire, with

Ruth staying nearby. In June, he was instructed to proceed to France, in charge of 'reinforcements for Siege Artillery Batteries in Italy', and on 6th July he left England for a new, and very different, kind of warfare.[31]

VII

Blasting and Bombardiering

Though Italy had declared war on Austria as early as May 1915, it was not until August 1916 that hostilities were extended to Germany as well. At first this made little difference to the conflict that had been raging since the previous summer between Italians and Austrians in Trentino and on the Isonzo river. Then both the British and the Germans turned their attention to this little-noticed sector of the war. In the summer of 1917, ten newly raised 6-inch howitzer battalions were sent from Aldershot to the Carso sector, north of Trieste.[1] Dalton was part of this contingent, and among the first British troops sent to the Italian front.

Dalton's Italian war was in striking contrast to his experience in the Army Service Corps. Serving in France had meant drudgery and discomfort against a flat, dull landscape, with little to do that seemed either interesting or worthwhile. In Italy, he found light, warmth, vivid colours and rugged grandeur; and, as a fighting soldier, he discovered a new sense of purpose. He was immediately attracted by the open friendliness and handsome appearance of the Italian officers. He did not even seem particularly horrified by accounts of a quaint local custom:

> They take a captured Austrian and tie him to a stick in their front trenches. They then fasten this stick above the parapet in view of his comrades opposite and insert one of those small bombs, with a 1-minute fuse attached, into his fundament. (The bomb itself is not large enough for this to be a really painful operation.) They then light the fuse and retreat a short distance down the trench. It is an instantaneous death, but seems barbaric![2]

He was sent on arrival in Italy to an artillery emplacement on the

bank of the river Vippacco. Here his mood soared. The officers ate
their meals, shaded from the sun by a luxuriant growth of acacias,
above a broad, foaming waterfall. Watching the blue dragonflies that
flitted above the stream, he wondered whether 'anywhere, on any
Front, a British Battery occupied a position of greater natural beauty'.[3]
At Palmanova, an ancient Venetian town with sweeping views of the
Julian and Carnic Alps, he was put in charge of an Artillery fatigue
party which was helping the Ordnance to load and unload ammunition. What in France would have been a chore, became in Italy a
labour of love. He recorded a new plan:

> I shall write a book, if I survive, and call it 'With British Guns in
> Italy'. It will be a War Book, and sell well, and, with my later book
> on Italian economists, will establish me as an Italian 'authority'.
> It will contain some purple passages and some home truths about
> War, and some indelicate descriptions of sights, sounds and smells.
> I shall dedicate it to all who died for Italy in the War.[4]

Dalton's book on Italian economists never appeared, though he
made extensive use of the work of Italians, especially Eugenio
Rignano, in his academic writings. The rest of his plan, like most of
his precisely formed ambitions, was carried out to the letter. *With
British Guns in Italy* appeared less than two years later.

On 17th August 1917 Dalton was posted to the 302nd Battery, part
of the XCIV Heavy Artillery Group. He was made senior subaltern,
third in command, and responsible for one of the battery's howitzers.
He stayed with the 302 for the rest of the war, and never wished to
move again. 'The personnel of the Battery was splendid', he recalled,
'and I do not believe that in any other Battery the spirit of the men was
better, nor the personal relations between officers and men on a
sounder and healthier footing, than with us.'[5] Like other siege
batteries armed with 6-inch howitzers (short-muzzled guns), the job
of the 302 was to provide 'flying columns'. The guns were moved on
to the Front, a series of rounds were fired, and then they were quickly
withdrawn. Shells were of gas, or else they were explosive 'daisy-
cutters', whose purpose was to destroy barbed wire, making way for
advancing troops.

The widow of a corporal in the 302 remembers that Lieutenant
Dalton was very popular with the private soldiers and N.C.O.s. 'He
used pseudonym names and my husband was described as the baby
faced bombardier [when he was] waiting to go into hospital in Marseilles after being wounded in the left leg.'[6] William Spedding, an
artilleryman who served on the same gun, recalls that Dalton took

care to see his men every day and always had a word for each of them. He was cool in a crisis, friendly and well-liked, standing slightly aloof from the other (mainly regular) officers. Though Spedding never saw Dalton again after 1918, except in photographs, he retains a clear mental image of him – tall, sallow and already balding, and smiling sardonically. 'His manner was dry, and he looked at you in a funny way. He spoke very slowly, with a drawl.'[7]

Dalton's posting to the 302 took place on the eve of a major Italian offensive. The Italian Front, rightly seen as a vulnerable sector in the Allied lines, was also believed to offer a chance of breaking through the enemy defences. On 18th April there began a month of the most continuously fierce fighting in the whole Italian war. 'The guns massed along the Corada ridge searched the Austrian positions beyond Isonzo', wrote C. P. Trevelyan's historian brother G. M. Trevelyan, who was in command of the First British Red Cross Unit for Italy.[8] The Austrians replied intermittently. It was Dalton's first direct experience of a heavy bombardment. At night, when not on duty, he lay in his dug-out reading a recent book on the causes of war called *The Choice Before Us*, by Lowes Dickinson ('with nine-tenths of which I was in complete agreement'), as shells exploded among the wooden huts of the battery.[9]

The Italian offensive was an initial success. Earlier in the year, the Italian Third Army had failed in an attempt to take the Carso and Trieste from the Austrians, partly (so the British alleged) because of poor co-ordination between infantry and artillery and the lack of 'a proper creeping barrage'.[10] Now, at the eleventh battle of the Isonzo, the Italian Second Army broke through the enemy line near Anzza on a wide front.

The 302 was placed above San Marco with a beautiful view of the town. 'Exhilarated and absorbed by the progress of the fighting', Dalton wrote at the end of the nine-day battle, the first in which he had taken part. 'Great throbbing song of the Heroes in the air.'[11] Unlike soldiers on the Western Front, Dalton was able to experience warfare as a grand romantic adventure:

Here on the night of the 26th there occurred a scene wonderfully, almost incredibly, dramatic. The moon was rising. Shells passed whistling overhead, some coming from beyond the Isonzo toward the Ternova Plateau, others in the opposite direction from Ternova ... Suddenly there crashed out from the gloom the opening bars of the Marcia Reale, played with tremendous *élan* by a military band. The music came from Monte Santo. On the summit of the conquered mountain, the night after its conquest, an Italian band was

playing amid the broken ruins of the convent, standing around the
firmly planted Italian flag.[12]

By mid-September the Italian advance had been halted. One reason
was the February 1917 Russian Revolution and the collapse of the
Eastern Front, which enabled the Austrians to deploy larger forces in
the south than had been expected. 'The limit of human endurance had
been reached', wrote Trevelyan, 'and both sides settled down exhausted on the ground where they found themselves.'[13] A period of
watchful, uneasy silence followed. In the difficult terrain of the Italian
Front, lulls in the fighting were common, but they were always tense.
'You didn't like the quiet', Spedding recalls. 'You knew something
was up.'[14]

As the two sides viewed each other across the newly established line,
Dalton's thoughts moved away from the war. During his training in
England Ruth had become pregnant. The baby was due in November.
Hugh now concentrated on the possibility of getting home leave.
When he was promoted to acting second-in-command of the 302,
this advancement only interested him in that it might help or hinder
his chances of getting to England to see Ruth.

Meanwhile there were distractions: first, a brief tourist visit to
Venice, where he rode on a gondola, bought souvenirs and listened to
music in the Piazza S. Marco; then an unexpected visitor, as if from
another world – Philip Noel-Baker, formerly of King's and the Carbonari, and now serving with Trevelyan in the Red Cross. The two
young men greeted each other like lost brothers. Noel-Baker passed on
the gossip that had reached him from other parts of the Front: the
Italian High Command was believed to be preparing a new offensive.
Later, Noel-Baker, Dalton and some of the artillerymen of the 302
played water polo in the River Isonzo, and lay on the banks drying
in the autumn sun.[15]

There were other echoes of pre-war England. Dalton had a general-
ised dislike of British officers, apart from those he knew well. Senior
officers were the subject of his special contempt; so were officers with
'professional' skills. In France he had felt hostile towards vets. In
Italy his prejudice was transferred to doctors, who seemed to typify
middle-class boorishness and complacency. Having reluctantly
shared a table with some medical men, he recorded with disgust that
'their conversation at meal times is about sputum, faeces, sanitation,
gas gangrene and their own seniority'. Artillery officers were preferable, but they had their limitations as well. Dalton pronounced that
a lunch with a mixed British and Italian party had been a fair success,
'but English humour is very unvariable! (I note that my father is really

very typical of English jocular mentality!)'[16]

As a matter of fact, though his son did not know it, Canon Dalton's mood was far from jocular in the autumn of 1917. The reason was not, as one might have supposed, anxiety about Hugh, but fury at a recent political defeat of his own. The old man had just been passed over for the office of Dean of Windsor. Although he was now 78, the Canon regarded the decision to appoint Albert Victor Baillie, instead of himself, as a personal insult.[17] The issue had been a matter of deep concern to the whole Windsor community, and nowhere was embarrassment felt more keenly than within the Royal Family, where the King's former tutor had expected to find loyalty and support. Queen Alexandra, the King's mother, wrote the Canon a careful, soothing letter. At the end she wrote, as if turning to a matter of less importance, 'I hope ... that you have good news of y[r] Son!'[18]

Six hundred and fifty miles away, the Canon's son had come closer to death or capture than at any other time in the war. The expected Italian offensive never happened. Instead, late in October, there was a sudden increase in the Austrian bombardment. News came through that a thousand Austrian guns had been moved across from the Russian Front; and, even more alarming, that a German division had appeared in the Isonzo sector. Soon it became clear that a large number of fresh heavy howitzers were behind the Austrian lines. 'To listen to their shells whistling over one's head like express trains', wrote Dalton, 'and then, happily distant, deep crashes on percussion, is to realise most vividly the immediate military effects of the Russian disorganisation.'[19]

The attack which marked the beginning of the battle of Caporetto, what Trevelyan called 'that tremendous cataclysm which almost ruined Italy and bode fair to ruin the cause of the Allies',[20] began on 24th October. The whole might of the enemy was launched against the Italian Third Army, concentrating with a special intensity on the line between Faiti and the Vippacco. The 302 faced a steady bombardment of high explosives and gas, firing off round after round in return. The commanding officer, Major Graham, was wounded by a shell splinter. Dalton's own gun was half buried in a gigantic shower of earth as a shell landed nearby. Conditions were made worse by torrential rain and a sea of mud.

At first the line held. Then, as the pressure increased, the Front suddenly collapsed in the north, and the Germans began a rapid advance. On 27th October orders came through for the British forces to pull back to Villa Viola, behind Gradisca. Imagining that the 302 was about to be shifted northwards into the thick of the fighting,

Dalton composed his own strange epitaph – seeking to justify his life should it be abruptly ended:

> If I die in and for Italy, I would like to think that my death would do something for Anglo-Italian sympathy and understanding. Anything that I have written that is publishable, in my wife's judgement, I would like published, also in an Italian translation, in order that Italians may know how I loved their country and themselves.[21]

The extent of the Italian rout soon became clear. Eventually a shorter line was established and successfully defended along the River Piave. Before this was achieved, however, the entire Italian war effort nearly disintegrated. Close to the town of Caporetto, Italian regiments laid down their arms. Elsewhere there was a general retreat, with a massive movement of men and equipment across the Isonzo gorge and out of the hills. For the most part it was an orderly withdrawal. But in the final stages of the move westward to the River Tagliamento, discipline began to break.[22]

With the whole Italian Third Army pulling back, the three British batteries – the 302, 307 and 317 – were almost the last of medium and heavy calibre on the southern part of the Front, and Dalton's gun was the last of all to be withdrawn. After the order to leave had been given, Dalton marched his small group down to the Isonzo on the way to Villa Viola. Ammunition dumps exploded all around and villages blazed. The Italian army had preceded them, laying waste. 'I thought of Russia in 1812', Dalton recalled, 'and the Russian retreat before Napoleon, and Tchaikovsky's music.'[23] In Gradisca, burning petrol flowed in the streets. In Palmanova, flames roared in houses visited by British officers only a short while before, and sheets of black smoke, blown by a strong wind, spread across the fields. The peril facing the artillerymen was suddenly apparent. Roads were blocked. Rations had almost run out. Separated from his commanding officer, Dalton found himself responsible for the final contingent of British guns on the road, and in charge of about thirty men, already exhausted and in imminent danger of being cut off. Desperate for sleep, they had to lie down in a marshy field in driving rain. 'It was at this time', Dalton wrote, 'that I personally touched my bedrock of misery, both mental and physical.'

Next day brought little improvement. Delayed by mud, engine failure and a continuous traffic jam, progress was painfully slow. British morale was not helped by the evidence of defeat that greeted them along the road. In the town of Muzzano, weeping women crowded into the church while others gazed helplessly at the sky. Even more dispiriting was an encounter with Italian infantrymen, bitterly hostile to the war. 'Forward you militarists!', they jeered at the British. 'This is your punishment!' The congestion grew worse. Lines of vehicles, side by side and all pointing in the same direction, stood motionless, as if paralysed by the common fear of an Austrian assault.

Fear became panic on the morning of 30th October. Cavalry galloping along the road caused rumours of enemy patrols. A mob of terrified Italian troops poured past the immobilised guns and wagons. Italian officers were reported to be shooting fleeing soldiers in a vain attempt to stop the rush. Then the column began to move. Slowly they edged their way past wrecked military equipment and dead horses, towards the Tagliamento. As they approached, a new alarm was caused by a rumour that the bridge to safety had already been blown up. A crowd of women screaming in despair surged back up the road. At last the river came into view, with the bridge intact. The tractor pulling the British guns broke down three times during the actual crossing. Three times it was successfully re-started, and finally they reached the western bank. The Austrians arrived a few hours later, after the bridge had been mined by Italian engineers.

Dalton's party limped into Portogruaro in the small hours, exactly a week after the enemy attack began. The ordeal was not quite over. Dalton had been told to expect food, straw to sleep on, and the other British guns. He found nothing. 'There is only one thing more difficult than not weeping at such a time,' he wrote, 'and that is believing in an All-Powerful, "Loving Father"!' On 1st November the British gunners were transported to Carbonera, where the remains of the batteries had been turning up. Here at last it was possible to rest. Dalton went to bed and slept around the clock.[24]

The retreat had been the greatest danger and heaviest responsibility of Dalton's life so far. He had shown courage and initiative. But he had also suffered a deep psychological shock. Having closely identified with the Italian cause, he felt the unexpected Italian reverse as a personal humiliation. For several months he remained in a state of inner turmoil, turning over and over in his mind a variety of explanations for the defeat. Much of his bitterness was directed at the Germans, whose massive deployment had been the biggest single cause of the Italian collapse. Angrily, he rejected the British assessment: that the Italian Second Army was made up of cowards who fled in the face of a powerful enemy. He agreed with Trevelyan that if Allied reinforcements had come in the summer when the Italians had been attacking, there would have been a real chance of a conclusive break in the Austrian line. When the Italians finally succeeded in holding the enemy along the banks of the Piave some fifty miles south-west of the Tagliamento, he attributed this to the 'valour of the Italian soldier'. Later he wrote that after Caporetto, Italy had been wounded and bleeding, 'and the dramatic swiftness and horror of the disaster had bent her pride and almost broken it.' It was an apt description of his own feelings. For the moment his emotions were numbed, and he remained strangely detached from the devastations of war.

In mid-November he learnt that Douglas Rouquette, best man at his wedding, was dead. 'Poor boy', he wrote. 'What, at this stage of things, can one say? One can hardly go on feeling these incessant losses.' A few days later he met an Italian Professor of Nervous Diseases, who took him to his own 'hospital for nervosi' outside Ferrara. The wards were filled with mental casualties of the fighting. Dalton saw a young lieutenant with staring, terrified eyes; two soldiers whose heads wobbled ceaselessly from side to side in perfect rhythm, like the pendulum of a clock; men trembling under the bed clothes, gas cases struggling for breath, soldiers suffering from paralysis or speechlessness. 'Provided they are not minus limbs and bloody', Dalton wrote, 'I am not physically sickened, or even much horrified, but just tortured and conscious that all one's questions are impertinent, one's good wishes flat and empty, and that one is like a visitor to a zoo.'

It was some time before he recovered from the effects of Caporetto. As he did so his thoughts turned to the question of how he should occupy himself after the war's end. 'When it is over', he resolved, 'the survivors will need to show immense energy, cheerfulness and power of concentration.' Hitherto his ideals had been unrelated to actual experience of suffering or injustice. Now, having briefly encountered the horrors of war, he was able to imagine himself working with a new kind of commitment to prevent such a tragedy happening again. Staying in Ferrara, some of his confidence and belief in the future returned. Before he left he even harangued the bewildered page boy in his hotel 'on the immense power which he and his pals will one day wield in the world.'

Dalton's idealism was not unconnected, however, with a revived personal ambition. When he was told that he was likely to receive an Italian decoration for his part in the retreat, his mind turned at once to practical considerations. ' ... I shall value it', he noted, 'chiefly as adding to my reputation and hence to the insight the public attach to my words and deeds.' Delay in the delivery of the award made him impatient: while others were decorated personally by the Duke of Aosta, commander of the Third Army, no ceremony was arranged for members of the 302. 'The medal and brevet have gone God knows where!' he wrote in January 1918. 'Probably pigeon-holed in some damned G.H.Q. (British) office. I am furious at the whole thing.' If it was worth having, he should have been told through official channels. 'The fault as usual is wholly British', he concluded. 'I am sick of the damned race.'[25] The award turned out to be a bronze medal for military valour, in recognition of Dalton's 'contempt for danger' in carrying to safety the artillery pieces of his battery during the retreat.[26]

Before he received the medal, Dalton's war had entered a new phase. At the end of 1917 the 302, reassembled and re-equipped, was added to a special Group of Heavy Artillery which was being sent to back up the Italian Fourth Army in the mountains. In January the battery moved into position near Casa Girardi, high up in the Italian Alps, surrounded by 'a waste of flashing snow', with temperatures far below zero. Troops were issued with spiked shoes, fur-lined sleeping-bags and Italian great-coats. As camouflage, guns were white-washed and men wore white hoods and white overalls. There was a constant danger of snow-blindness. Another hazard was the din of the guns echoing in the mountains; one man went stone deaf as a result. The worst winter enemy was the cold. Everything froze overnight – boots, clothes, the ink in fountain pens, 'the lather on one's face before one had time to shave.'[27] Sometimes snow had to be melted to provide water for drinking and washing. Lack of water and primitive living conditions brought other problems. 'Lice were a regular feature', Spedding recalls. 'We used to hang our shirts up so that they would freeze solid to kill the lice. But it didn't work. When you put the shirts back on, the lice reappeared with the warmth of your body.'[28]

At the end of January, Dalton's long awaited leave warrant arrived. With bewildering suddenness, the privations of war were banished and he was in a train to Padua, and thence to England. It was an important trip, his first and only home visit during the Italian campaign, and one which united him with his new family. In November, while Hugh was recuperating in Ferrara after the retreat, Ruth had given birth to a baby girl, Helen. Now he was able to meet his daughter for the first time. 'Inspect my child and kiss the wife', he wrote after their reunion on Victoria Station.[29] It was a welcome respite, but too brief to counteract the effects of a bitter Alpine winter. Shortly after his return he suffered a physical collapse. 'Hugh has been in hospital with mountain fever, but is much better now, though still very weak', his sister Georgie wrote to an aunt in the summer.[30] The nature of his 'fever' and its duration are not clear, but he was able to spend a few days in Rome in May, perhaps convalescing.

Meanwhile the 302 had moved westward, this time to support

British infantry. Here it stayed, with the British Divisions of the so-called 'Asiago sector', for most of the remaining months of the war. With the winter over the weather became more clement, but the fighting soon became much fiercer. Dalton was scarcely back from Rome when a huge enemy bombardment began, followed by five successive waves of Austrian infantrymen – the biggest attack experienced by the 302 since Caporetto. The hut in which he slept was hit several times.

The offensive was eventually broken in June, and the battery was moved even further westward up into the Trentino. Once again Dalton was dazzled by the scenery, 'a series of great mountain ranges, uneven lines of jagged peaks, enclosing deep cut valleys, the lower slopes of the mountains densely wooded, the higher levels base precipitous rock.' The Austrian front line ran along one ridge of peaks and the Allied line along another. Between them lay No Man's Land – a deep valley into which patrols would climb at night, often with the aid of ropes. The 302 fired its shells across the valley, hoping – rather optimistically in Dalton's view – that they would find their target. As a mathematician he was angered by the failure of the regular officers to work out accurate formulae for the angle and elevation of the guns.

The Trentino excursion was brief, and the 302 was soon back on the Asiago Plateau. In early autumn there were two further moves: down to Mestre, within sight of Venice, then to a position near Udine, close to the bank of the Piave, in flat country. Here an enemy pilot spotted the position of Dalton's gun, but before the information could be reported home an Italian plane appeared and shot the Austrian down.

The final Allied offensive began on 26th October. The British guns fired gas shells continuously for many hours, then switched to high explosives. Next day British infantry attacked from a long island of sand in the middle of the Piave. On the 28th Dalton was sent across the river as a forward observation officer, to maintain contact with the advancing troops. His atheism was strengthened by the sight of the corpses left beside the road in the confusion of the Austrian departure. 'The more I look at dead bodies', he wrote, 'the more childish and improbable does the old idea of personal immortality appear to me!' He noted that dead men and dead horses rapidly gave off a foul odour, 'the latter smelling earlier and stronger than the former.'

That night he made his headquarters in a wrecked church, and sent back signals in morse code from the tower by means of a lamp. Next morning, British cavalry and infantry moved forward as part of the final advance. 'When I was relieved', Dalton wrote, 'I tramped back to the Piave, many miles now, and wading those of the channels that were still unbridged returned, tired and footsore but with a song in my heart, to my Battery.'

Allied troops continued to attack on a wide front, sweeping rapidly eastward. On 1st November Dalton was ordered forward once again, supposedly for a reconnaissance by car. Instead, it became a triumphal procession. The British party was greeted with delirious cheers as it entered villages from which the enemy had only just departed:

> And so it was that, first of all the Allied troops, we entered the little village of Nogaredo. And, as we came in, we sang, very loudly and perhaps somewhat out of tune, the chorus of *La Campana di San Gusto* ...
>
> > 'Le ragazze di Trieste
> > Cantan tutte con ardore
> > "O Italia, O Italia del mio cuore,
> > Tu ci vieni a liberar!"'
> >
> > (*All the maidens of Trieste sing with passion,*
> > '*O Italy, O Italy of my heart, thou comest to set us free!*')

> So to that village *we* were the visible liberators. All the villagers came running towards us, crowding around our car, weeping and cheering, pouring out their stories, touching and holding and kissing us. It is seldom that things happen with such dramatic perfection.

> The end was close. At 3 p.m. on 4th November the guns fell silent and the fighting ceased along the Austro-Italian Front. A week later the war ended in the West.[31]

Dalton left for England at the beginning of December. He would always remember his Italian campaign proudly. 'I had got some good out of it, though I did not think so at the time', he wrote later. Before the war, there had been a period of easy, pleasant drift, directed by little except Fabian arguments and Cambridge values. Now he had a sense of what needed to be done and a faith in his capacity to do it. 'It was the belief that politics, rightly handled, can put an end to war, which, more than anything else, drew me into the life of active politics when the war was over', he wrote in the late 1920s.[32] In his memoirs he added that, while he had no very clear idea of his next step, one thought was firmly in his mind. 'I badly wanted to go into politics, to help put right what my elders had put wrong.'[33]

Dalton's mood was different from that of many who came home determined to prevent war happening again. This was partly because he was exceptionally lucky. Only for fairly short periods was he in immediate danger. A remarkably large part of his war, nearly two

years in all, was spent training or re-training in England. In the Army
Service Corps the risks he ran were scarcely greater than those of
civilians. In Italy, the dangers he faced were seldom as great as those
confronting soldiers in the trenches in France and Belgium. Italy was
a relatively low risk sector for British troops, and artillery were far
less at risk than infantry or cavalry. Like other similar batteries,
the 302 was generally placed about a quarter of a mile from the front
line – close enough for casualties to occur regularly, but far enough
to escape the strains of a continuous bombardment. Spedding recalls
one day when three men were hit within the space of five minutes:
one in the knee, another in the thigh, and a third in the neck. But this
was unusual. More often, weeks would go by without any injuries
at all.

As a result morale remained high among the gunners, who were
conscious of their good fortune: Spedding recalls his own time in
Italy as 'happy days'. His picture, like Dalton's, is of a cheerful, close-
knit team, pulling together and making the most of tough conditions.[34]
The scenery helped: mountains, rivers and waterfalls instead of the
mud-filled landscapes of Flanders. So did the pace. It was a life of
movement and variety. In Italy, as earlier in France, Dalton was
seldom in one place for more than a few weeks. In France, this had
been a source of irritation; in Italy, it was an added stimulus, helping
to provide a sense of progress.

Unlike many of his compatriots, Dalton felt sympathy and loyalty
towards the peoples whose territory he had been sent to defend. This
Latinophilia was linked, rather strangely, both to hatred for Germans,
and to dislike of British stuffiness and British class assumptions.

Why did he hate Germans? For the most part he was facing Austrians, not Germans. He witnessed no German atrocities. Lord Noel-
Baker, who spent several hours with Dalton just before Caporetto
and knew him well both before and after the war, suggested that
Dalton's fierce anti-Germanism was a product of the trauma of the
retreat. Another reason was put forward by Dalton himself: he hated
Germans because they killed all his friends. Yet there may have been
more to it than either of these explanations.

Anti-German feeling was common enough among civilians during
and after the war, and among jingoistic right-wing politicians. It was
more unusual among combatants, or among radicals and internationalists of whom Dalton certainly regarded himself as one. In
Dalton's case it seems to have reflected in a surprising way a very
English preoccupation. Dalton's war diaries seldom deal directly
with politics. Yet they provide interesting evidence of rawness in
social areas. They also suggest that much of Dalton's pleasure at

being in Italy (and to a lesser extent in France) derived from a sense of liberation from English distinctions and class values.

When Ruth was newly pregnant in the summer of 1917, Hugh wrote:

> Any child of mine, I hope, will have the choice to marry a Latin, preferably an Italian, and not be confined for choice to stodgy, damned quasi-Teutons, with their fair ugliness, and their gawky manners, and their unbeautiful speech, and their unsunny country, and their lack of joy for life (but only guffaws) and of art of life (but only bad cooking and Bridge).

He added, 'But this is becoming an anti-patriotic tirade!' as indeed it was.[35] Dalton's mother played bridge and he regarded the game as a symbol of British middle-class stodginess and lack of imagination. But the biggest insult to the British was the reference to 'damned quasi-Teutons'. 'Quasi-Teutons, with their fair ugliness' linked the British to Germans (and distinguished them from the fair beauty of the Cambridge ideal), drawing attention to racial connections at a time when racial explanations of national behaviour were common. It is even conceivable that in linking Britons to Teutons, Dalton had in mind the Germano-British family which he had learnt as a child to resent: the most notable 'quasi-Teutons' of his youth had been members of the Royal House which had recently re-named itself, to avoid embarrassment, the House of Windsor.

There was no fully rational basis for Dalton's strong emotions towards Germans. What is evident, however, is that 'quasi-Teutonic' complacency and what Dalton saw as the blinkered caste assumptions of the British were tied together in his mind; and that class distinctions and militaristic values also seemed to be linked. Dalton was particularly hostile to senior regular officers of the British Army. In *With British Guns in Italy* Dalton described how the general who 'at that time nominally commanded us' ensured his own escape after Caporetto, installed himself comfortably in a hotel at Treviso accompanied by his staff 'all bright and polished and sleek', and did not even trouble to call a parade to congratulate the weary British veterans of the retreat. Dalton's account of the whole Italian campaign ends, interestingly, with a tirade:

> Youth was rejoicing that night in Italy, when the war against Austria ended ... Yet here and there were gloom, and drab, wet blankets, trying to make smoulder those raging fires of joy. In a few officers' Messes, especially among the more exalted units, men of forty years and more croaked like ravens over the impending loss

of pay and rank, Brigadier Generals who would soon be Colonels again, and Colonels who would soon be Majors ... They jarred intolerably. They seemed a portent, though in truth they were something less. They found themselves left alone to their private griefs, ruminating regretfully over the golden age that had suddenly ended, gazing into the blackness of a future without hope.[36]

Dalton contrasted the snobbish and hierarchical attitude of British regulars with the easy, even democratic, relationship that seemed to exist between Italian officers and men. In Italy, patriotism and socialism seemed close together. Fighting alongside the 'Latins', he saw himself as a defender of national integrity, democratic values, and the brotherhood of man.

There is another important aspect of Dalton's Italian war to be considered: his choice of the artillery. Dalton's transfer from the Army Service Corps had been a deliberate and informed decision. The artillery suited his style and temperament. Infantry received the flashes and the bangs. Artillery created them. The guns were the most powerful, and the most destructive, force in the land war. It was hard not to be filled with awe by their sheer size and impact – as Wyndham Lewis, editor of the Vorticist journal, *Blast*, later pointed out.

Lewis, who also served in the artillery, drew attention in his war memoir *Blasting and Bombardiering* to the hypnotic effects of the destruction wrought by the explosive shell. It was wrong, he suggested, to believe that the sole effect on witnesses was to create a sense of revulsion. The guns had a nightmarish ability to stir the imagination:

> It is they who provide the orchestral accompaniment. It is they who plough up the ground till it looks literally 'like nothing on earth'. It is they who transform a smart little township, inside an hour, into a romantic ruin, worthy of the great Robert himself, or of Claude Lorraine. They are likewise the purveyors of 'shell-shock', that most dramatic of ailments. And lastly, they give the most romantic and spectacular wounds of all – a bullet-wound, even a dum-dum, is child's play to a wound inflicted by a shell-splinter.[37]

Such observations were not restricted to professional writers. 'These things almost *please* one by their perfection of eeriness and horror', a young medical orderly wrote from France in 1915. 'Do you understand? They are like some gigantic supernatural artist in the grotesque and horrible!'[38] Neither this observer, nor Lewis, was arguing in favour of the dreadful romance of war. They were merely pointing out the futility of denying its existence. In the theatre of the grotesque, it was the bombardments of the artillery, what Lewis called the 'fearful flashing of a monstrous cannonade', that pleased most of all.[39]

Lewis's theatre was the grey terrain of Flanders, with its backcloth of twisted trees and pock-marked mud. It was in similar ground, behind the Western Front, that Dalton had first become entranced by the noise and power of the great guns. In the setting of the Italian mountains the romance was far greater. Indeed 'romantic' is scarcely a strong enough adjective for the emotions revealed in Dalton's extraordinary description of the Italian victory at Monte Santo in August 1917, and of its orchestral accompaniment, literal and metaphorical.

Wyndham Lewis may not have been aware of Dalton's account when he wrote his own. A better illustration of Lewis's point, however, could scarcely be found than in the cacophony of human voices, musical instruments and gunfire that celebrated the Italian advance. Dalton described how, after an Italian band had played the *Marcia Reale* from the ruined convent at the top of the captured mountain, the Austrians replied with a defiant bombardment:

But the music still went on. The Marcia Reale was finished but now in turn the Hymn of Garibaldi and the Hymn of Mameli, historic battle songs of Italian liberty, pealed forth to the stars, loud above the bursting of the shells. And many Italian eyes, from which the atrocious sufferings of this war had never yet drawn tears, wept with a proud, triumphant joy. And as the last notes died away upon the night air, a great storm of cheers broke forth afresh from the Italian lines.

The conductor of the band was none other than Toscanini, who had by chance been among the advancing Italian forces on the fateful day:

His presence had upon the musicians the same effect which the presence of a great General has upon faithful troops. They crowded around him, fired with a wild enthusiasm. Then Toscanini took command of what surely was one of the strangest concerts in the world, played in the moonlight, in an hour of glory, on a mountain top, which to the Italians had become almost a legendary name, to an audience of two contending Armies, amid the rattle of machine guns, the rumble of cannon, and the crashes of exploding shells.[40]

Dalton's war book, *With British Guns in Italy*, the first and best eye-witness account of the Italian Front by a British author, was pub-

lished in 1919. Appearing only three months after the Armistice, long
before the vogue for literary anti-war books, it reveals the attitudes of
a young officer who, while in some ways standing apart from his
generation, was in other ways very typical of it.

A striking feature of the book is the influence of Rupert Brooke and
of the values of which Brooke's name had become a symbol. Before
Dalton left for his dumping and refilling job in France, a popular
legend (the second cult) had already been built around the image of
the young poet martyred for England. The basis for this legend was a
collection of five War Sonnets published by Brooke in 1914. Later
critics have pointed to the weakness of these poems, based not on
experience of war but on a currently fashionable attitude towards it.
Dalton regarded them differently. Brooke's Sonnets, he wrote in his
memoirs,

> issued from him at a unique moment, in his life and that of us all.
> But having fitted so perfectly the mood of that moment, they have
> seemed to jar on later moods. Yet a strong felicity shines through
> them, and a very strong emotion.[41]

There is more than a flavour of the 'very strong emotion' of the
Sonnets in Dalton's war book. Cyril Connolly argued that Brooke's
verses were self-regarding: ' "England has declared war" he says to
himself "what had Rupert Brooke better feel about it?" '[42] Unlike
the Sonnets, written before Brooke left England, *With British Guns*
describes real experiences of battle. Nevertheless it is not hard to
detect a sense of looking at war through a filter of appropriate
response. What should Dalton, patriotic, progressive and egalitarian,
feel about it? One clear answer was 'what Rupert would have felt if
he was here'. When Dalton began writing about war, Brooke's poems
provided his main literary inspiration – so much so that his interplay
of arcadian images and patriotic sentiment came close to unintended
parody.

There is an echo of Brooke's most famous lines ('If I should die ... ')
in Dalton's scribbled note when the danger of being cut off by the
Austrians after Caporetto seemed most real: 'If I die in and for Italy,
I would like to think that my death would do something for Anglo-
Italian sympathy and understanding.'[43] *With British Guns* contains
other passages with an unmistakably, even comically, Georgian ring.
As for example when the author was recuperating in Ferrara after the
retreat, and soliloquising like a classical hero:

Then said I to myself, standing all alone at Quarto, 'Italy will not be defeated, nor even mainly saved from defeat by foreign aid. The strongest and best of her children will pull her through, even though they be not all the nation. But the rest will do their share also, and will follow, where the bravest lead. How young, and how uncertain of herself as yet, is Italy! And yet, how lovable, how well worth saving!'

There are also mock-Brookian rhythms and sentiments in a passage that Dalton virtually lifted from an early poem of which he was particularly fond:

For Italy was wounded and bleeding, and the dramatic swiftness and horror of the disaster had bent her pride and almost broken it. But though the future seemed black as a night without stars, the hope of a coming daybreak remained strong in the hearts of a few.[44]

This is almost a re-ordering of lines by Brooke which Dalton often recited at public meetings, a product of William Morris, Cambridge Fabianism and Ben Keeling:

Strain through the dark, with undesirous eyes
To what may lie beyond it. Sets your star,
O heart, for ever! Yet behind the night,
Waits for the great unborn, somewhere afar,
Some white tremendous day break.[45]

Yet, despite his dependence on Brooke for an idiom, Dalton was his own man. In many respects his war diaries and war book were conventional – displaying an uncomplicated eagerness for victory and belief in its necessity, a delight in military pageant and display, and an absence of war-weary cynicism. But there was also a detachment and aloofness, an intellectual readiness to stand back and observe. Dalton was quite unlike the young men who came into the army with all the attitudes and expectations of their class and then moved towards bitterness and disillusion. He had rejected his class long before the war. He already distrusted generals.

Dalton described himself as a 'very civilian sort of person' and in a very civilian kind of army he had remained so. 'Men over thirty grew so that they could not wear pre-war clothes', wrote Dalton's Cambridge contemporary R. H. Mottram, who served in the trenches and then in the Army Service Corps: ' ... [M]ore frequent, more serious and more catastrophic were the cases of men whose minds would never again fit their pre-war habits. The education of the war was profound –

it attacked the middle-aged who changed as they had never dreamed
of changing. A few weeks counted as years and left individuals unrecognisable. And it was permanent – there was no undoing it.'[46]
Dalton was twenty-eight when he went to war, thirty-one when he
came back: no young subaltern straight out of public school. He
acquired the familiarity with death and mutilation which separates
those who have known war from those who have not. Yet he was not
shattered or undermined. The war toughened him. He came home
with a more solid reason for rebellion and an angrier edge to his
ambition.

Nor should we take at face value Dalton's claim that the war left
him without close friends. Dalton's age group was in some ways the
worst affected by the war: not so old as to escape altogether, yet old
enough to have been available for action from the start; not so young
that the survivors could easily establish new circles of intimates.
Losses among Dalton's Cambridge group were heavy – Rupert
Brooke, Ben Keeling, Rupert's younger brother Alfred, Douglas
Rouquette were among the victims he cared about most. Later, Dalton
attributed not only his hatred of Germans, but also his passion for
encouraging the young, to his feeling that a whole generation of young
men had been tragically wasted. 'People have sometimes asked, since
then, why I had so few men friends of my own age', he wrote in a
revealing passage in his memoirs. 'The answer is the war. Before that,
I was rich in friendship.'[47] Yet of 13 members of the Carbonari at a
dinner in Rupert Brooke's rooms in 1909, 8 survived,[48] and Dalton
had in any case grown apart from most of his Cambridge friends, including Brooke and Keeling. After the war, Dalton's attitudes were
much influenced by a sentimental yearning for real or imagined undergraduate days. But the war was only partly responsible for his sense
of personal isolation.

It is impossible to understand the man as he later became without
seeing that for all his sadness at personal losses, his own war had been
a period of fulfilment. We can go further. If we are looking for a turning-point in his life we may find it here, during his service in Italy.
There is an important change of tempo between the French and
Italian phases. In France, we see a vigorous, pleasure-loving, reflective
civilian with half his mind on the interruption of an academic career.
In Italy there is suddenly a new mood – a love affair with a country and
its people, a comradeship with its soldiers, and a sense of commitment
that was reinforced by the trauma of Caporetto and its dramatic
aftermath.

The Italian campaign remained one sector where advance and
retreat still had a traditional meaning. Dalton's war ends, not with

exhaustion and relief, but with heroism, devastation, glory – and popular adulation:

> The fighting was over! That night of the 4th of November all the sky was lit up with bonfires and the firing of coloured rockets and white Very lights. One could hear bells ringing in the distance, back toward Treviso, and singing and cheering everywhere. It was an hour of perfection, and of accomplishment; it was the ending of a story ... The task of completing Italian unity was finished, so far as a series of wars could finish it ... The soldier had done his duty, now let the statesman do no less. Let wisdom and imagination make sure the fruits of valour.[49]

How natural the progression from this to politics! How small the difference between touring liberated villages in an army car, and barnstorming in a general election! Dalton ended his war 'blasting and bombardiering' until the last gun stopped firing. Then, having acquired a taste for conflict and leadership, he turned to the civilian arena. Still filled with the elation of victory and with scarcely a pause for breath, he began to battle his way towards a political triumph at home.

On 11th December 1918 Queen Alexandra sent Canon Dalton another letter. 'These awful years have been terribly full of misery and cruel anxiety', she wrote. 'I do hope that your prescious [sic] Son is all right and Safe now and you and y^r dear wife may soon welcome him home.'[50]

In fact, they already had. On the very day that the King's mother wrote, the Canon's son was campaigning on behalf of the Labour Party in the election which had been called by Lloyd George immediately after the Armistice. By pulling strings Hugh had secured a 'temporary' release from the army in order to take a secondment in the Whitley Councils Department of the Ministry of Labour. Meanwhile he had two weeks leave. Between 11th and 14th December he toured the safe Conservative seat of Saffron Walden, speaking for the Labour candidate Jimmy Mallon, a member of the Whitley Reconstruction Committee and shortly afterwards Warden of Toynbee Hall. Reformed, revitalised, and with a new socialist constitution, the Labour Party was fighting its first contest as a national body, independent of all pacts and alliances. 'I enjoy myself and am a great success', Dalton recorded, 'especially at S.W. itself which is very Tory and loves a soldier.'

When the results were known he studied them eagerly. The Labour Party had gained few seats, but it had substantially increased its vote.

The omens were good. He made some shrewd calculations:

> Four years hence Labour ought to poll a tremendous vote, and
> meanwhile win a lot of bye-elections. What is chiefly needed is
> (1) improved organisation in the constituencies, (2) an influx of
> brains and middle-class, non-crank membership. It is very weak
> now in knowledge on foreign and imperial policy, and army and
> navy. Also it will want some good lawyers, (but not too many).[51]

VIII

In Pursuit of Politics

Here was a good chance for a bold young man well-read in economics and politics, with a solid training in public speaking, and with a knowledge of the world. The Labour Party had only 63 seats in the new House of Commons. Yet the creation of a greatly expanded working class electorate and the continued disarray of the Liberals gave solid grounds for Dalton's belief that next time it would poll 'a tremendous vote', providing scope for 'middle-class, non-crank' aspirants alongside working-class trade unionists. Dalton was not the only member of his class to perceive the expanding Labour Party as a newfoundland, virgin territory ripe for plunder by resourceful colonisers.[1] In his case, however, there was no need of a sudden or convenient socialist conversion.

Before he could become a politician, he had to earn a living and establish a professional base. The prospect of returning to the Bar did not appeal to him. Instead he turned once again to the London School of Economics, where he had already spent three years before the war. If he could secure a teaching post, he calculated, it would be possible to continue the Fabian-orientated research which he had begun in 1911, and still have time for active politics.

One other possibility briefly occurred to him: the Foreign Office. 'This would be better than M[inistry] of L[abour]', he wrote, 'and worth staying for a year to get (1) knowledge and (2) a paper qualification for advising, and I hope guiding, the Labour Party in foreign affairs.' Pursuing this idea, he secured an interview on the basis of his Italian experience. He was asked whether he was willing to go on a mission to Italy and Albania. He answered affirmatively. At the same time, he was unimpressed by his questioner. How, he wondered, did the 'spectacle of ineptitude and ignorance' revealed at his interview reflect on the competence of the Foreign Office in general?

Nothing came of the Italian or Albanian schemes, perhaps because the Foreign Office had doubts about him as well. Soon he was concentrating all his attention on getting back to the L.S.E. 'It seems clear I can get in there in the autumn, as Cannan's assistant', he noted in mid-January 1919. '[Cannan] says it oughtn't to be difficult to make a reputation there, once I get my foot in ... ' An important factor was the large number of young economists who had been killed in the war.

Dalton's foothold was achieved at the end of the month. He accepted an invitation to give Cannan's Public Finance lectures the following term and in the autumn – a course of nine, repeated in the evening, for a fee of 40 guineas. With this settled, he determined to leave his job in the civil service as quickly as possible. Having decided to publish a book 'on something economic' as a stepping stone to a permanent lectureship, he set off on a brief holiday with Ruth at Corfe Castle, where he read a range of Italians – Papini, Soffici, Palazzasini ('Florentines who have passed through Futurism') and Panzini. They walked 65 miles, paddled, drank beer (in Ruth's case, milk) and looked for a summer hideout where Hugh could complete his thesis. When they got back to London, Hugh felt greatly refreshed, and 'full of inarticulate joy and relief' at having ceased to be a civil servant.

Meanwhile, he had begun to renew old acquaintanceships. He visited G. D. H. Cole, now famous for his Labour Research Department and Guild Socialist activities. The two men eyed each other cautiously. Dalton was impressed by Cole's knowledge, but found his interests narrow and disliked his wife. In March, Hugh and Ruth were summoned to lunch with the Webbs. It was a kind of interview, with Beatrice and Sidney putting them through their paces. A warmer reception was provided during a visit to Cambridge – Hugh's first since 1913 – where he saw Pigou and Lowes Dickinson and spoke at the Union, quoting Rupert Brooke's Sonnets. Dickinson urged him to become secretary to the Educational Committee of the League of Nations Union, but he declined. He also turned down a chance of doing a couple of days teaching a week in economics. Cambridge still made him uneasy, 'a place too full of the dead to give me either happiness or peace.'[2]

To Hugh's colossal delight, *With British Guns in Italy* was published on 5th May. 'I find it very elevating to the morale to be the author of a published book, on which one stands to lose no money!' he wrote. *The Times* called it a surprisingly optimistic work, whose author had been saved from cynicism by being sent to Italy where 'the beauty of the scene and the exquisite clearness of the atmosphere made hope always reasonable and things always worth doing.' Other favourable reviews also helped to build up his confident desire for a public life. He began to explore local Labour Party possibilities. Although the range of winnable seats had become wider than ever before, in many areas there was scarcely any local party machinery and little system in the choice of prospective candidates. In these early years a number of former Liberal M.P.s and other members of the professional class rich enough to contribute towards expenses were adopted without any competitive selection conference at all. Dalton was aware of the possibilities, and anxious not to be left behind.

In April he and Ruth attended a meeting of their ward Labour Party in Battersea. 'Must keep up contact with these people', he noted. 'It *might* be feasible to stand for this constituency ... ' Then a less promising but more immediate chance cropped up. A postman known to Ruth asked Hugh whether he might be willing to stand for the Westminster Abbey Division, where a by-election seemed possible. Though this was a hopeless seat Hugh accepted at once.

It was agreed by the Propaganda Committee of the local party that if he was adopted he should be bound only for a by-election. The crucial issue turned on expenses. Would he at least guarantee the £150 deposit? He agreed. After that, there were no hitches. Sidney Webb was chairman of the constituency executive, and made it clear that he thought Dalton would make a good candidate. Only nine members of the General Committee of the Abbey Division were present for the selection meeting. Dalton stressed the importance of 'the so-called middle-class coming into the Labour Party and doing their share of the work'. One question was put to him. Somebody asked if he favoured the public ownership of all the public utilities. He replied that he did.

After the selection, Dalton made another speech, mainly about foreign policy and public finance – already his two areas of specialisation. 'Even then', he wrote later, 'my ambition lay, without much preference, either towards the Foreign Office or the Treasury, but never, with any intensity, towards No. 10, Downing St.' This was the first step on a long road, and he viewed it with satisfaction. 'The Labour Party contains its good share of fools', he considered, 'but I am satisfied more and more that it is the best available Party, and will get better still.'[3]

Meanwhile his thesis on inequality was dragging on. He spent two and a half months during the summer working on it in Cornwall. 'I hope by October it'll be finally criticised by you', he had written to Cannan before his departure. 'I seem to have been muddling about with it since I was a small child, like Keynes with Probability! I want to get on with something shorter and snappier.'[4] But politics caused further delays, and he did not finish it until Christmas. Having passed it to Cannan, he began to inquire about possible publishers. Perhaps the School might put up the cash for a subsidy? 'I must make myself very agreeable to the Director on the off chance,' he wrote.[5]

Despite his adoption for Westminster, he continued to keep his eyes open for a possible general election contest. He secured a place, with Tawney and others, on the Labour Party Educational Subcommittee. This provided a good vantage point. Somebody mentioned that North Islington were looking for a candidate prepared to put up £250 per annum towards organisation. Dalton baulked at that. 'I tell him they'll have difficulty in finding such a person.'[6]

In the autumn, he began to receive overtures from Susan Lawrence, an L.C.C. councillor, about the possibility of fighting Cambridge. He had other Cambridge Labour contacts: Clara Rackham, wife of a don, and Leah Manning (formerly Tappin) a friend from pre-war Fabian days. Shortly before Christmas he went to investigate. At the Executive, there was little doubt that he would be chosen. 'Let's get him here at once; call it the Selection Conference,' Mrs Manning recalled saying; 'we don't want to bother about short lists and all that paraphernalia.' Clara Rackham suggested that Dalton might address a meeting. He did so, and was formally adopted in February 1920, speaking for an hour and twenty minutes, and talking of the 'hard-faced businessmen who had done well out of the war and of whom your member is one.'

So the Westminster contest never took place. Cambridge was a much more hopeful prospect. At a time when Labour's strength in any particular constituency was an unknown quantity, the large Tory majority did not seem unassailable – at least to Dalton. Determined to take the fight seriously, he borrowed a house in Panton Street belonging to the Cambridge musicologist E. J. Dent, and for the next year commuted to London.

Hugh went down well with the Cambridge Labour Party. Ruth was less popular. Leah Manning, who helped her run Cambridge's first Family Planning Clinic, found in Ruth 'a hard, resolute, streak', in contrast to Hugh's 'soft centre'. Helen Pease, daughter of Josiah Wedgwood (an Independent and later Labour M.P.), was struck by Ruth's apparent coldness. 'There is a way an affectionate wife looks at her husband – and she didn't have it.' A mystery hung over the daughter, Helen, who was seldom seen. 'We were puzzled by the fact that the child had been sent away to school at such an early age.' For some reason, Ruth was not prepared to talk about the child at all.[7]

In March, Dalton's thesis, turned into a book, went to the printer. It had been a hard labour, full of anxiety and frustration. 'What a travail over!', he wrote. 'It flatters my sense of my own obstinacy and persistence.' Now he was able to dedicate himself wholeheartedly to politics. Cambridge provided a useful testing ground. Ruth was his mentor. 'R[uth] says my speech wasn't very good', he noted after addressing a women's meeting. 'I thought it was. I made myself, and a number of my audience, cry over my peroration about women and battlefields.'[8] Once a man lurched out of a pub, downed a tankard of beer in one gulp, and challenged Dalton to do the same. 'Leah, go and get me a pint', he told Mrs Manning, and swallowed the lot without drawing breath, to the admiration of the assembled company.[9]

Cambridge was also a useful place to pull academic strings. In May, Dalton visited Pigou ('very affable and less gawky as he gets older') to discuss the Cassell Readership at the L.S.E., for which he was applying. At the end of the month, he got the job. This meant a salary rise from £400 to £750, and an increased status. 'R[uth] remarks that I am climbing,' he wrote. It was a notable ascent: within the space of eighteen months he had moved from the tenuous position of assistant, to one of the most desirable appointments in academic economics outside Cambridge – while pursuing his political career at the same time.[10]

Meanwhile he sought every opportunity to place his expertise and new standing at the disposal of the Labour Movement. 'I have written a memorandum on "Currency Policy in Relation to the Cost of Living" for a Labour Party Committee,' he told Cannan in August 1920. 'I have squared the Secretary, I think, to put some sense into this Report, which will be read by a lot of Trade Union Officials, who know nothing about money.'[11] A few weeks later he was pleased to find himself pilloried alongside Pigou by the *Daily Chronicle*, for allegedly inspiring a trade union report on money and prices. The report, declared the *Chronicle* severely, adopted 'Mr. Dalton's view that the increase of money rather than the decrease of goods is the dominant cause of the rise of prices!'[12] This was the kind of publicity he needed: linking him with the trade unions as an expert on financial matters, and reminding the Labour Party establishment that his 'independent' academic judgments could be used as ammunition against the Government and employers.

At the end of December 1920, he was able to reflect on some solid progress. 'Not a bad year for me really in which I've become Prospective Parliamentary candidate in a possible constituency,' he wrote, 'made a lot of speeches, learned a good deal about practical politics and organisation, published a fat economic tome, written an Economic Journal article[13] that few can understand and none refute, become a University Reader, and Examiner, and Doctor of Science, with a perceptive rise in screw, and brought myself in a few miscellaneous ways into the public eye.' But he was still near the bottom of the ladder he had set himself. ' … [I]t seems a long way to go to anywhere real yet, and life is passing, and in some moods it all seems very empty and silly.'[14]

Socially the Daltons now moved in a world of progressive intellectuals on the political outer fringes of Bloomsbury. Hugh's Cambridge candidacy brought him back into contact with some pre-war friends – Lowes Dickinson, for instance, and Gerald Shove, still at King's and closely linked to the Bloomsbury circle. Among other Bloomsbury figures, Dalton came to know Leonard Woolf, because of Woolf's involvement in Labour Party policy-making (and because Virginia had been a friend of Rupert Brooke). He also became increasingly friendly with Bertrand and Dora Russell, who lived in Chelsea, across the river from the Daltons' London base in Battersea Bridge Road. Dora listed Hugh and Ruth among their closest political friends in the early 1920s, 'not far away and frequent visitors.'[15] But Dalton saw little of Maynard Keynes – despite their shared profession, and Dalton's residence in Cambridge.

A new acquaintance who became a favoured protegée was Barbara Wootton, aged 23 in 1920, who had become an economics don at Girton, and was involved in Cambridge Labour Party activities. In 1922 she applied for a job at the Labour Party Research Department. Asked at the interview why she wanted it, she said she had been influenced by 'a multitude of converging considerations'. Hugh was appalled by this answer, and told her she should have said 'because of the unbearable injustices of our social system'. But she got the job and over the next four years Hugh and Ruth had her to dinner regularly to pump her about Party headquarters gossip.[16]

In the spring of 1921 the Daltons moved back to London, believing that the election would not be held for some time. Hugh continued to visit the constituency regularly, staying with the families of left-inclined dons. At the end of July he and Ruth deposited Helen, now three-and-a-half, in a private boarding establishment in Surrey ('a very successful arrangement') and went to Italy for a two-month holiday. Politics receded.[17]

In February 1922 the sitting member at Cambridge unexpectedly resigned, precipitating a by-election. It was Hugh's first taste of the political limelight and he thoroughly enjoyed it. 'He and Mrs Dalton worked unsparingly themselves, and this always creates a high morale', recalls a local Labour Party veteran.[18] Council election results encouraged a feeling of optimism. Hugh toured the wards in a car with a man ringing a muffin bell, giving children joy rides by twenties at a time. Ruth was disdainful of this kind of activity, throwing herself instead into organising and canvassing.[19] Other helpers included Barbara Wootton, Maurice Dobb (later a leading marxist economist), Kingsley Martin (later editor of the *New Statesman*) and the indefatigable Leah Manning.[20]

The Labour Party was on the brink of becoming the official Opposition nationally, and every seat seemed vulnerable. Dalton was fighting to win, and on 12th March, at a meeting which Arthur Henderson also addressed in the Guildhall, he abandoned his pledge to avoid personalities, smearing the Conservative for all he was worth. 'Imported Tory riff-raff are the liars who have come down on this town', he shouted from the platform. He then referred to his own military service in Italy, announcing that the Conservative candidate Sir Douglas Newton 'served his country during the war in Whitehall and not in the Army ... although he was of military age.'[21] This was to counter Newton's suggestion that if Labour or the Liberals were returned, the pensions of widows of men who died in the war would be stopped. In the streets, the Labour candidate was surrounded by children singing 'Vote, Vote, Vote for Mr. Dalton!', 'He's the man!' and 'Put the other down the well!' Dalton incited them to chant these slogans at very respectable-looking voters wearing Tory or Liberal colours, who pretended not to hear. 'The Campaign!' he wrote when it was over. 'I have never had 3 happier weeks.'[22]

It was to no avail. Newton won decisively, with 10,867 votes to Dalton's 6,954. Having not felt at all tired before the poll, Dalton was suddenly in a state of physical collapse, and despite the cheering and singing of supporters he wept openly after the result was announced.[23] The only consolation was that the size of the majority allowed him to abandon Cambridge without regret, and look for something better.

Yet in one sense Cambridge marked a high point in Dalton's early political career. Before the by-election came up, he had been at pains to cultivate the friendship and good favour of Arthur Henderson, Party General Secretary and arguably the most powerful political figure in the Labour Movement. In this, he had been more successful than he realised. He was aware of some progress; the previous autumn Henderson's son Arthur ('Little Arthur') had told him that his name had been submitted by the Party to the Cabinet as one of four nominees for the Advisory Committee on the Trades Facilities Bill. 'Little Arthur tells me that Big Arthur has a high opinion of me as an economist ...', Dalton noted. 'And indeed, it would appear that I am getting into the position of being one of the recognised authorities in the Party on financial questions.'[24] What he did not know was that Henderson had an equally great – if not greater – respect for his capacity in the field of foreign affairs. Evidence of this is provided by the diary of C. P. Scott, editor of the *Manchester Guardian*, who spoke at length to Henderson on 28th February, at the start of the Cambridge by-election. Henderson told Scott that Labour expected to get 200 to 220 seats at the next general election, and that this, together with 150 Liberals, would give a clear Liberal–Labour majority. They then discussed what form the resulting Government might take. Scott recorded the conversation:

> I raised the question of the competence of the Labour Party to man an administration, especially the Foreign Office and the Exchequer. Their resources he thought were much greater than was commonly supposed but it was noticeable that he relied mainly on men who have yet to be elected. For Foreign Affairs he suggested Ramsay MacDonald or H. Dalton, Labour candidate for Cambridge, or Tom Shaw, member for Preston, or W. Graham, member for Central Edinburgh; for Chancellor of the Exchequer Snowden or Sidney Webb.[25]

Dalton was 34. He had never before stood as a candidate, had held no public office, had no experience of foreign affairs, and indeed had virtually no experience of any kind behind him, apart from war service and a couple of years lecturing at the L.S.E. To be bracketed with Ramsay MacDonald as a possible Foreign Secretary was therefore a remarkable compliment. Henderson's comment was off the cuff, doubtless influenced by sharing a platform with Dalton in Cambridge a few days before. Yet it is a sign of Dalton's promise that the suggestion should have been made.

Dalton returned to London and the School, where his students burst into clapping and cheering as though he had won.[26] He immediately started to ask about other seats, and then on 24th March he and Ruth departed for a holiday in Oxted, near where their daughter Helen was living in a boarding establishment called Blue Lane House. Now, for the first time, Helen began to appear in Hugh's diary. Her appearance was tragically brief.

IX

Ruth and Helen

Why did Hugh and Ruth place their daughter in a residential home?
Blue Lane House still stands – a large, forbidding, Victorian edifice in
the Surrey village of Limpsfield.

Little is known about the establishment that operated there in the
1920s, except that it was small, private and for very young children.
Was Helen living there all the time? She was certainly at Blue Lane
House in the summer of 1921, and in the period surrounding the
Cambridge by-election in 1922. It is possible that she was placed there
for short visits; a reference by Hugh in his diary to educational facilities, however, suggests a more permanent arrangement.

If this was so – even, indeed, if she was left in Limpsfield only for
spells of a month or two at a time – why was she there? One possibility
is an illness or disability. Joyce Parker, a distant cousin, was taken as
a little girl to visit Helen at the home and recalls meeting an exceptionally pale-looking child. One friend of Hugh's, surprised by Ruth's
apparent lack of interest in Helen and reluctance to talk about her,
speculated about the possibility of some kind of handicap, mental or
physical. This theory, however, is not supported by anything Hugh
or Ruth ever said, or by any of the references to Helen in Hugh's diary,
which reveal no hint of anxiety about her before March 1922. One of
the few photographs of Helen that survive shows a plump, attractive
little girl, happily engaged with bucket and spade at the seaside with
her father, during one of the Daltons' rare, brief holidays *en famille*.

Perhaps, in their hectic pursuit of Hugh's political advancement,
the Daltons simply wished to avoid the encumbrance of a child. Yet
even this seems puzzling – for the normal middle-class solution, a
living-in nanny, was well within their means. Another possible explanation is that Hugh and Ruth were seeking to do the best for their
daughter by applying what they felt to be progressive principles of

child-rearing, believing that a child, especially an only child, would benefit from being taken away from its parents and placed in a community with other children. Ben Keeling would have approved of this kind of Fabian communalism; so would Edward Carpenter.

What seems clear is that neither of the parents minded long periods of separation from their daughter and that Helen did not have a high priority in their lives. How else to explain the two-month holiday in Italy in 1921 without her? To understand better, we need to look more closely at Ruth, whose own childhood was sufficiently disturbed to account for what she herself described as her lack of maternal feelings.

Most people who knew Ruth well in later years sensed that she was unhappy. If so, was her unhappiness a permanent state? Had there been better days? Little is known about her early life, except what she herself told others. What follows, therefore, is an exercise in oral history – pieced together from the recollections of friends.[1]

Ruth's own view of herself was that her problems derived from an isolated and affectionless childhood, the burden of which she was unable to shed. The dominating – perhaps crushing – influence in her life had been her mother, Valentine, born Valentine Ogilvie. Like Ruth, and like Helen, Valentine was an only child – orphaned as a young girl when her father had been killed fighting for the French in the Franco-Prussian War. Brought up by puritanical Scottish guardians, Valentine escaped into an unsuccessful marriage to Thomas Hamilton Fox, Ruth's father.

Despite her upbringing, or because of it, Valentine was a romantic: a fierce, adventurous, strong-willed woman whose extravagant tastes her husband was unable to indulge. Frustrated by the emotional and material limitations of her life, she became the close friend and probably the mistress of Arthur Peterson, a barrister who eventually became a High Court judge and a knight. Peterson was a bachelor, and might have married her. The scandal of being cited in a divorce case would, however, have wrecked his career. Hence he supported the entire Hamilton Fox family – Valentine, Ruth and the unfortunate Thomas – at his various homes, which included a large, Italianate mansion called Hurtwood Edge in Surrey, and a house at 39 Cheyne Walk, Chelsea. Proprieties were thus maintained. Ruth's father (derisively nick-named 'L'Ometto' – the little chap), weakly tolerating his own humiliation, turned to drink.

Ruth reacted differently. Instead of succumbing, she created a quite separate life. Later she recalled with bitterness the secrecies and hypocrisy of the arrangement – how she would have to take her father to concerts, with instructions not to return until a certain hour, in order to give Valentine and Peterson time together; how great parties would be held in Cheyne Walk, for which Valentine would make all preparations down to the flowers on the table and then discreetly retire, forcing upon Ruth the unwelcome role of hostess, to her mother's resentment and her own discomfiture. Hating this world of false respectability and feeling that her mother, preoccupied with her own grand passion, had rejected her, Ruth withdrew into a world of books, developing intellectual and cultural interests of her own.

She wanted desperately to go to Cambridge. Yet when she was offered a place to read Classics at Newnham, she turned it down and went to the L.S.E. to read for a social science degree instead. The reason for this change of plan is unclear. Her mother apparently influenced the decision not to go to Cambridge; her father may have pointed her towards the L.S.E. Ruth soon regretted her choice and felt uneasy at the School. Most students came from lower-middle or working class backgrounds, and she was conscious and ashamed of the opulence at Cheyne Walk. Embarrassment prevented her from taking friends home. Hugh was the exception – neither the wealth nor the irregularity bothered him.

This was Ruth's story. There was probably another side to it which we shall never know. Despite herself, Ruth was clearly fond of Peterson, and was much affected by his death. Peterson regarded her as an adopted daughter, and made her his heir. A large sum left in trust provided Ruth (and hence Hugh) with a comfortable private income. Hugh also seems to have respected his wife's benefactor and to have enjoyed visiting him and Valentine at Hurtwood Edge before the war.[2] Politically, Peterson was a liberal with a keen interest in international law, favouring the strict control of chemical weapons.[3] Hugh was sufficiently close to him to accept help with legal aspects of his book on inequality.[4]

Yet there seems little doubt that Ruth was permanently scarred by her early years. Later she displayed industry, integrity, generosity – but little warmth. People felt a barrier: a sense of frigidity, a private desolation. As one friend put it, 'she had an expectation of sadness'. Where Valentine had been selfish and extravagant, Ruth adopted a hard, self-punishing puritanism – as though doing penance for her mother's indulgence. 'Duty' was a concept which apparently meant little to Valentine and everything to Ruth. Even Ruth's enjoyment of the arts seemed intellectual and moral – culture for self-improvement rather than for its own sake. There was something remorseless about her socialism, in contrast to Hugh's exuberance. It was as though, having decided to be a Fabian, her attitudes and tastes were rigidly determined by that choice.

There was a curious twist to Valentine's relationship with her daughter and son-in-law. According to Ruth, Valentine's envy and possessiveness, combined with a sense of the tragedy of her own life, made her react against what she perceived as her daughter's marital fulfilment. Despairing of her relationship with Ruth, Valentine turned for friendship to Hugh's despised sister Georgie.

Here was an odd symmetry. While Ruth was in revolt against the elegance and sophistication of her own background, which seemed no more than a shell, Georgie, reacting against a dowdy, clerical up-bringing, craved the things her sister-in-law rejected. Such was the strength of this new relationship that before Valentine died she made Georgie her residual legatee. An inevitable effect was to worsen relations between Georgie and Ruth, who regarded Georgie as a 'social climbing snob' and 'a person of no consequence with dreadful politics'. Georgie, for her part, created the theory that Hugh only married Ruth because of his attraction towards older women – in this case Ruth's mother.

Were Hugh and Ruth ever in love? Most people who knew them late in their lives found it hard to believe that they ever were. There seemed to be a space between them, as though they had always lived in separate compartments. 'You didn't have to be perceptive to get the feeling that she bitterly regretted her marriage to Hugh and stayed with him only out of duty', commented one friend. Another felt that 'there had been an estrangement of a kind since the day they married'. Yet whatever impression Ruth may have given in old age, Hugh's diary and the few letters between them that survive suggest that for most of the first twenty-five years of their marriage they were close and affectionate. The impression between the wars is of an intimate and harmonious team – Hugh's ambitions neatly comple-mented by Ruth's ideals.

This team-work, which eventually broke down as Hugh pushed ahead, undoubtedly contained its strains. Friends joked that Hugh treated Ruth as though she were another man; some suggested that her own identity as a woman was hazy, and that Hugh had been drawn to her partly for that reason. Certainly there was little that was gentle or feminine in her appearance. Beatrice Webb described her at 36 as 'a buxom figure, perfect complexion and pretty hair but plain features and commonplace expression'.[5] She was striking to look at rather than handsome, with pale skin, dark eyes and an aquiline nose. Her strong black hair was cut short and she never wore make-up. Hugh once said that he married her 'because her profile reminded him of a Greek goddess on a coin', a remark which suggested that he could only conceive of physical relations in the context of classical mythology and an asexual ideal.

Dalton's image of Rupert Brooke, 'playing simple tunes on a pan pipe', had also been idealised and desexualised. It is not entirely fanciful to see a link, even a rivalry, between the god-like Rupert and Ruth with her Latin features and rejection of a conventional role. Ruth entered Hugh's life in 1911 just as Rupert was leaving it. 'You can shelve your wife', Rupert had written before his final meeting with Hugh, when Hugh and Ruth were just back from their honeymoon. Ruth was conscious of this rivalry, especially after Brooke's death. Sometimes she would hint at Hugh's romantic attachment: she told a friend that Hugh 'threw himself on his bed and sobbed like a child' when he heard that Rupert had died at Skyros. Later, Hugh turned to Rupert-like young men for social comfort, befriending them, helping them and guiding them, allowing himself to be teased by them, as though seeking to replicate in every way a relationship which remained the most precious of his life.

The sense of a conflict between Hugh's love for Rupert and his love for Ruth is most strongly conveyed by an unusual entry in Hugh's diary written in Italy during the summer of 1921, after Hugh and Ruth had spent several weeks together alone, without Helen. Hugh was not in the habit of writing down his dreams. It is therefore particularly significant that he should have chosen to record this one:

In the night a very vivid dream, in which Rupert came and talked to me in some house where I was living. R was also living there, but not in the conversation. Rupert and I both knew that he was dead, killed in the war, but the conversation was quite matter of fact. In the course of it I said, 'what good things have been published lately in your shop?' (meaning, in the way of literature) and he told me of two books, the names of which I forget, and added, 'But Shaw's last book is not worth reading', (meaning Bernard Shaw). I had a photograph of him in my room and he said 'I see you have a picture of me here' and apparently it had written below it some lines by one Cook, apparently a Rugby master, on which he commented as if he had seen them before. One was, I think, 'And we turned down our thumbs on them' (i.e. on the young men who died in the war). He talked about money, and the impossibility of living decently on a small income, and said he had been making some arrangement about [his brother] Alfred's money. Once in the course of our conversation he touched me, and felt quite corporeal, but I had a shrinking feeling, which prevented me from voluntarily touching him.

We agreed to dine together at a Restaurant in the town, with R who would arrive independently, and reserve two seats. Then Rupert vanished. I went alone to the restaurant, losing my way in the dark and forgetting its name. But at last I stumbled in and found it pretty full. Most of those who were sitting there were young men, who smiled rather sarcastically and knowingly at me as I came in. R had reserved two seats opposite to her. She said, 'Isn't Rupert coming?' I said, 'No, he's gone'. Then she smiled too, and said, 'What, has the expedition for Constantinople started so early?' Then I woke ... '[6]

Dalton went on to recall that he had just read that a Greek had written on Brooke's tomb at Skyros that he died in the war 'to free Constantinople from the Turk'.

Sex may not have played a large part in the Daltons' lives. In later years they always slept in separate rooms. Hugh liked beautiful and clever women, but those he knew best tended to be happily married and were seldom attracted to him. Women saw him as a good and loyal friend rather than as a lover. Some wondered whether his romantic interest in young men might not exclude heterosexual activity altogether.

Ruth was interested in sexual relations in the abstract. A leading pioneer of the Birth Control Movement, she was an ardent exponent of Marie Stopes's demand that sex in marriage should be enjoyed by women as well as by men. Yet men sensed in her an inhibition that made physical love-making hard to imagine. She also gave an impression to some women friends that the idea of sex with Hugh was, or had become, distasteful to her.

What were her feelings towards her own child, third in a line of daughters who for one reason or another were deprived of a mother's affection? Ruth always gave the impression that the appearance of Helen was both unexpected and undesired. Her account of the conception was typically disparaging. She told a friend that Hugh came home from the war and to her surprise 'one evening he felt like it – and Helen arrived'. The child was born during a Zeppelin raid in November 1917. Hugh was in Italy, so Ruth was left to face two kinds of fear alone. After the birth, she returned to work first as a government translator, and then (in 1918–19) as Assistant General Secretary of the W.E.A. A letter from Georgie before the end of the war suggests that, even in the first few months, mother and child were not inseparable.[7] Hugh saw his daughter only once, during a brief home leave, before she was thirteen months old.

According to one story Helen was first sent to a residential nursery because of Ruth's war work. What is clear is that the lives of both parents were so hectic between December 1918 and the summer of 1922 that their daughter cannot have filled a very big space in them; and that Ruth's role as confidante, collaborator and fellow-campaigner came before her role as mother.

When disaster struck, it was devastating for both of them. There was no warning until after the Cambridge by-election. Hugh wrote in his diary for 25th March 1922, following a visit to Blue Lane House:

> The atmosphere and arrangements of the place are very good for small children, but there is no education, except a rather mingy-looking governess for the older ones. H[elen] had an attack of asthma, as it was thought, the other day, with great difficulty in breathing. She was taken to a London doctor, who recommended dieting experiments. This seems rather rot, but she has not had any more attacks.

Asthma would not have worried Hugh unduly, because he had suffered from this as a child and made a complete recovery, so he may have regarded it almost as a normal childhood complaint. On 26th March, the three of them – Ruth, Hugh and Helen – went for a walk, climbing tree stumps and picking primroses. 'H[elen] is very perky', he noted. Hugh's main attention was still focussed on constituencies and he talked endlessly of alternative options with Ruth. On 27th March he lunched with the Webbs and Henderson – hoping that Henderson might address his mind to the question of seats. But nothing came of it. 'I aim to leave with him and talk walking to the House', Dalton wrote. 'But Beatrice (damn her!) engages me in pointless conversation and I miss the chance.' Over the next two months, negotiations with Egerton Wake, the National Agent, led to Dalton's adoption as candidate for Maidstone, as the best of a poor batch of possibilities for the general election.

On 12th May Ruth's mother's friend, Sir Arthur Peterson, died painfully and unpleasantly, after bursting a blood vessel while playing golf in the New Forest. Ruth was deeply upset. Dalton was ghoulishly fascinated by the details of the death:

> At the end he asked for Harrison [his doctor]. His eyes lit up when the latter came in and he seemed to recognise him. Then there came a great gush of blood and it was finished. Then they bound up his chin and at first his face, V[alentine] told R[uth], was beautifully peaceful and calm, with a rather sad smile. But then the blood kept coming, and then all his face fell in and he had a great swelling in his

stomach as though there was a cushion there. He had to be put quickly into a coffin and nailed down.

The next day – even before the funeral – serious problems began with Helen. She had shown signs of kidney trouble, with curious swellings on the stomach and in the face. Yet even now Hugh did not become greatly concerned. He had barely seen his daughter for six weeks and she was not in the forefront of his mind.

On 13th May he gave a party in Cambridge for members of the University Labour Club. 'They *are* a jolly crowd', he wrote. 'They matter tremendously to the world, the first of the new generation un-scarred by the war. Politics, if it means dedicating myself to their happiness and opportunities, is a trade worth following.' The next couple of days were devoted to the funeral and memorial service for Peterson. But there was more anxiety about Helen now. 'Helen has kidney disease and is very swollen, but in good spirits', Hugh wrote on the 16th. 'She will, probably, have to be in hospital for a month. Apparently there is not much danger of it getting really bad. But it is a nasty jar just at this time.' Next day, Ruth brought her up from Limpsfield to the Chelsea Children's Hospital, 'very swollen and weighing 4 stone instead of 3. But apparently without pain and quite unaware of what she looks like.'

Hugh was still too busy to give this much attention. He was adopted as candidate at Maidstone on 20th May. The next couple of days were spent negotiating with local Liberals, who wanted to be given reasons why they should back Dalton and not run a candidate of their own. The issue of nationalisation was raised. Dalton indicated that his own commitment did not go beyond coal, railways, land, liquor and arma-ments. Though a leading Liberal 'wore a hostile look', the meeting seemed to succeed in persuading the Liberals not to run. On 23rd May Dalton returned briefly to London, where Ruth had found rooms with a landlady who looked like 'a rather dirty prostitute'.

Helen seemed better. Hot air baths had reduced the swelling slightly. Dalton did not change his arrangements and went to Cambridge for the weekend, having tea with the Peases in Girton. Back in London, he found Helen's condition stable. 'A slow business', he wrote. Soon, it became clear that it was not a passing childhood malady. 'H[elen] is not making progress', he recorded a week later, 'and we are rather anxious about her.' Perhaps the anxiety was responsible for psycho-somatic ailments in Hugh. On 6th June he took to his own bed for several days with stomach pains diagnosed as colitis, which kept him awake during a series of stifling hot nights. After ten days he was still on an invalid diet and unable to walk more than a hundred yards, but he staggered to Cambridge for the Tripos Examiners' meeting – giving firsts in Part II to Maurice Dobb and Austin Robinson. 'On the whole the young Cambridge economists are not as good as they ought to be', he considered. 'The later stages of Pigou are, I think, rather beyond them, and they are encouraged to run before they can walk.' When he got home, Helen's crisis had begun.

15/6/22

Back to London. Helen has a cold. This is dangerous. R & I now go to the hospital every day, and sometimes more than once. She lies flat on her back now.

16/6/22

Helen's complications, on top of nephritis, have become a new peril. Her cold is bronchitis.

17/6/22

Helen tonight looked so bad, as she lay asleep, so unhealthily pale and swollen and breathing so hard, with her eyes not properly closed, even in sleep, that we felt the odds were very heavily against her. Her cough has been hurting her more than before that day.

18/6/22 (Sunday)

Helen seemed better in the morning, naturally perhaps, as it is normal to look worse at night. But there is a danger of further complications now – pneumonia, peritonitis, meningitis. In the afternoon and early evening she was less comfortable and, almost for the first time, looked frightened. She gave once a queer little sudden cry – that was meningitis striking at her brain – and then, as though to find a reason, pulled out a piece of chocolate from under the bedclothes and signed for it to be taken away. Several times she tried to speak, but we couldn't hear what she said. I read her a story which she knew about Peter Rabbit and showed her the pictures. R began to sing her a lullaby, but couldn't go on. Just before we left, she held out her arm to R and said 'Oh Mother, I want to go away with you'. The fear of something unknown had come to her, and she associated it with the hospital ward. These were the last words we heard her speak. We came back in the evening. I signed an authorisation for the doctor to perform an operation to draw liquid from her spine to ease the pressure. She was sleeping or unconscious, and we did not see her then. We left about 11 p.m., and they were to send for us if a crisis came.

19/6/22 (Monday)

At 1 a.m. there was a knock on the door at Wellington Square.

We went round to the hospital. They were giving her oxygen. She was unconscious and breathing with a terrible effort, a gasping, groaning sound.

At 2.55 she died, still unconscious. Her breathing had stopped suddenly. I waved the nurses away from the bed. R and I kissed her hair and little lips and forehead, still warm, and held her little hands, already cold. Then we went.

At 10 we went back and saw her lying in the mortuary, with her hair bound up with a piece of white ribbon and holding some white flowers in her hand. Beside her, under a sheet, was another little girl who had died in the same ward this morning. On the wall above them was written 'Of such are the Kingdom of Heaven'. R had never seen a dead body before ...

Then a hocus pocus with death certificate and undertaker. We had just moved that morning from Wellington Square to 19 Margaretta Terrace.

20/6/22

We took Helen's body to Golder's Green. It was cremated and her ashes were scattered on a bed of roses. Only Canon D was there then. L'Ometto [Ruth's father] and John [Forbes Watson, Georgie's husband] had come up with the body but had gone, at my request, at the end of the few prayers which Canon D very beautifully read. He came back to lunch at Margaretta Terrace. When he had gone, I went upstairs and wept alone for 3 hours.

...

As that little coffin slid out of sight, I wept and kissed my hand to her.

...

She is safe anyhow now. Safe from disappointment and dis-illusion, miseries and a broken heart and the next war and growing old. Safe too, from love and beauty and the sunshine.

The next day Hugh and Ruth fled north to Whitby in Yorkshire and the solace of wide open spaces 'to escape from London and all who know us and to be alone and face it out together'. On the surface, Hugh recovered rapidly. Within ten days he was working on his new book about Public Finance, which he finished the same summer in time to be published before Christmas. He very quickly decided not to withdraw his candidacy at Maidstone. Although he stayed away from London and the L.S.E. for most of the next four months, he began serious campaigning for the election at the start of August.

Helen is mentioned only once more in his diary, seven years later:

' ... of Her, for fear of tears, I never speak.' The misery was buried deep and the subject became taboo, even with close friends. With those they knew and liked best, Hugh and Ruth would mention it briefly and abruptly and say no more. Which was the more affected? Ruth told one friend that when Helen died Hugh cried for days. But Hugh was able to throw himself into his politics and his writing. For Ruth it was harder. Peggy Jay, who didn't meet the Daltons until the mid-1930s, felt that with Ruth the death 'hung like a shadow'. Fourteen years after the event it seemed so constant a presence that it was as though it had happened the day before yesterday. When her marriage was falling apart early in the Second World War, Ruth confessed in a rare moment of candour that Helen's death had utterly changed her life.

A conscious decision to have no more children fixed the tragedy as the central event in their marriage. Once a friend asked Ruth whether she had ever wanted another child. 'No, No!' she replied very emotionally. Whether or not Hugh shared her views, he adapted to them and found a political justification. When he visited Germany after Hitler came to power he wrote, contemplating the likelihood of another war, 'We were right not to go on breeding!'[8] But there was more than reason in the decision. There was also bitterness and reproach. 'I would never have another child', Ruth told Rachel Keeling, Ben's widow, who became a colleague on the L.C.C. 'It would come second to Hugh's political career.'

Were they right to feel responsible? Irrational feelings of guilt would have been a normal response in any circumstances. In Ruth's case, it is easy to see how her over-developed conscience could fix on reasons to blame herself, or her husband. Yet it is worth noting the persistence of rumours that, with better care, the tragedy might have been avoided. Hugh's sister believed that the ultimate cause was Ruth's spartan views on education and child-rearing. According to Georgie, Ruth would put Helen, even as a small baby, outside in the cold without enough blankets; and when Georgie visited the Limpsfield establishment she was appalled, so she said, to find that the children had been forced to dance with bare feet on a stone floor in icy winter weather. There was also a rumour that Helen developed an infected mastoid from sleeping in a draught and that this complaint was at first wrongly diagnosed. In reality, Helen's actual illness – nephritis and meningitis – could not have been caused or made fatal by exposure. Nevertheless, the allegation of a faulty diagnosis seems to be substantiated. Kidney disease was not detected until a month before the end, and even then there was a falsely optimistic prognosis.

Perhaps Helen would have received earlier and better medical attention if she had been with her parents, if – above all – there had been no Cambridge by-election. There were feelings of guilt associated with the Italian holiday the previous summer, when Helen had been left in England: more than forty years later, Ruth told a new friend about this trip, saying that she was sorry she had not seen more of her daughter. But the link with the by-election – the symbolic start to Dalton's political career – was the most disastrous in its implications. Here Ruth placed the blame squarely on Hugh. Once – in a moment of particular wretchedness – she told Rachel Keeling that Hugh insisted that she should help in the election and that Helen died as a result.

In addition to the guilt and the recriminations, there was the image of the death itself. One friend recalls a discussion of meningitis and deprivation at a meeting of the Children's Committee of the L.C.C. in the early 1950s. Ruth suddenly remarked: 'You can't imagine what it is like to nurse a child screaming itself to death in your arms.' A decade later she told another friend that 'the most terrible thing that can happen to a human being is to see a child die.'

After June 1922 there was no obvious change in the pattern of the Daltons' lives, in which Helen had never played a very prominent part. They picked themselves up and carried on. Inspecting them five years to the day after Helen's death, Beatrice Webb recorded that they seemed happily married.[9] Hugh thought so too. In 1930, as a member of a hard-pressed Labour Government, Dalton wrote on Ruth's fortieth birthday: 'There is, at any rate, a fine perfection in my *private* life!'[10] Yet a ghost walked with them both.

X

Class Traitor

There were two sides to Dalton. Beatrice Webb had noticed the duality when he was still an undergraduate – dedication and seriousness on the one hand, personal ambition and an impression of slyness on the other. Helen's death made both the seriousness and the ambition more pressing. Just as the forward sweep of the Allied armies had obliterated the pain of defeat after Caporetto, so a fast-moving political career was one way to deal with private sadness. Dalton was never more active or productive than in the two-and-a-half years that followed his bereavement.

His political style remained in a military mould – attacking, bombastic, triumphal, as though the revenge after the retreat had constantly to be repeated in civilian life. It was a style that won victories, but made enemies at the same time. Many came to see behind his dedication a vulgar careerism, and behind his ambition, cunning. Duality became duplicity – back-slapping heartiness appeared as evidence of a manipulative relationship with the world which made him a man not to be trusted.

Yet Dalton was also a man whose political training and beliefs were well suited to the mood of the expanding Labour Party. He might be open to the charge of having flirted with Liberalism before the War, but his Fabian youth provided him with an emotional and intellectual ace; he could feel part of the post-war Labour crusade in a way that others could not. It was not hard for him to recapture Cambridge romanticism about the working-class. Where men of Liberal background, despairing of the crumbling Asquithians and compromising Coalitionists, turned to Labour as a second best, Dalton was equipped with different instincts. Ex-Liberals tended to stick to traditional Liberal issues, to ignore socialist policies, and to keep their distance from the trade unions. Men like Sydney Arnold, H. B. Lees-Smith,

Col. L'Estrange Malone, Arthur Ponsonby, Joseph Kenworthy, Noel Buxton and Charles Roden Buxton could never fully convince themselves that they were Labour men. Dalton, by contrast, was a child of the Webbs: pragmatic, paternalist, collectivist, a pre-war critic of property rights. He disliked Liberal high-mindedness almost as much as he disliked the rich, and had no difficulty in identifying wholeheartedly with the trade union movement.

Nevertheless he did not find his road to Parliament an easy one. He fought three more contests – at Maidstone, Cardiff East and Holland-with-Boston – before eventually finding a seat he could win. Each time he went to the hustings with high hopes. Each time his hopes were dashed, and he discovered how unpredictable electoral politics had become, with three parties in the field, and the old Liberal Party taking its time a-dying.

As he had expected, Labour polled well in by-elections and local elections during the 1918 Parliament and seemed poised for a major breakthrough. The collapse of the Coalition provided the opportunity. In October 1922, a meeting of Conservative M.P.s at the Carlton Club voted to withdraw support from Lloyd George. The Prime Minister resigned forthwith, and was replaced by Bonar Law, who called an election for the following month.

The national press gave Dalton a good chance of winning in Maidstone – partly because an independent, fighting with Liberal support, seemed likely to split the anti-Labour vote. In his campaign, Dalton laid stress on Labour's proposal for a once-and-for-all tax on capital – his own speciality. At the same time he soft-pedalled on other aspects of socialism in an effort to woo Liberals, announcing that Labour did not propose 'to attack any legitimately conducted private enterprise'[1] (whatever that might mean). He found speaking and canvassing cathartic, and he believed that he was ahead. He was wrong. When the votes were counted he came third, though only 924 behind the winning Tory.

Almost as annoying as losing was the knowledge that rivals elsewhere had won. Labour had 75 M.P.s at the dissolution. Now it had 142, some of them middle-class men, including H. B. Lees-Smith and Clement Attlee, both colleagues at the School. With more seats than the Liberals, Labour took over as official Opposition, electing Ramsay MacDonald as Party Leader. It was frustrating not to be a Member of Parliament at such a time. Dalton ended 1922 in bad spirits, feeling his exclusion, and planning to keep out of politics for a year at least.[2]

With no likelihood of another election for some time he picked up the threads of his academic career, involving himself more fully at the L.S.E. He did not regard his professional life as other than a stepping-stone to active politics. Yet he had not neglected his obligations and had, indeed, helped to build up the reputation of the economics department at the School. Given the nature of his interests it had been possible to use his expertise as an economist to launch his political career. It is to this second world of academic economics, in which his political and economic ideas supported one another, that we now turn.

There were two reasons for Dalton's rapid rise at the School. The first was a post-war expansion of students and staff. The second was his talent as a teacher and writer in his field.

Dalton had come back to the L.S.E. at an ideal time – just as the School was about to become important.[3] The architect of change was William Beveridge, appointed Director in succession to the ailing and failing Pember Reeves.[4] When Beveridge and Dalton arrived in 1919 there were 17 full-time teachers; when Beveridge left eighteen years later, two years after Dalton's own final departure, there were 79 and the School had become the largest centre for the study of social science in Britain. The intervening years were the period of the L.S.E.'s greatest promise and prestige. Dalton found himself among the vanguard.

In the economics department, Dalton had quickly established himself as the dominant personality – younger, less remote and with more experience of the world than Edwin Cannan. A high proportion of students in the first post-war generation were demobilised servicemen. Dalton was particularly good at communicating with young men who shared his experience of war and his urgent desire to see that war should not happen again.[5] He was accessible and unstuffy. 'At the time relations among the different levels of the staff were rather formal and there was a clearly defined hierarchy', recalls Eveline Burns, a student and then an assistant who delivered Dalton's lectures when he was campaigning. 'Students were in awe of the faculty and never interrupted or asked questions in class, and the age gap between the two groups precluded close personal contacts. It was into this elderly and dignified staff group that Dalton burst like a breath of fresh air.'[6] Another former pupil remembered 'his vast resonant laugh and the general sense of relish in hard thinking, fun and mischief which diffused about him as he entered a party or appeared through the senior common room doors.'[7]

Dalton lectured to first year students, initially in a temporary building on the site of the present Bush House in the Aldwych – his voice competing successfully with the noise of cranes and excavators as construction work went on outside. His style – thunderous and theatrical, as he strode the platform, his gown swirling – recalled the

performances of John Dalton in St George's Chapel. Hugh's humour
was also reminiscent of the Canon. 'Now who are those who are
opposed to birth control?' he would demand, peering above the tops
of half-cut reading glasses, during his lecture on population. 'First we
have the *celibate* bishops of the Church of England'. Physically, too, he
was beginning to resemble his father: already bald, and with his height
emphasised by a stoop.[8] Mannerisms that were to be permanent were
well established: wrinkling up his nose and baring his teeth when he
laughed, and a continuing habit, which the admonitions of *Granta* had
failed to cure, of 'carrying his head slightly down and forward so that
it looked, as we students said, as if his eyes were upside down'.

Birth control (a political interest shared with Ruth, as well as a
matter for demographic debate) was one of his favourite topics, partly
because the subject was still considered rather shocking. Eveline Burns
recalls the following conversation after she had announced her impending marriage in 1921:

H.D. Well I hear you are going to marry Burns. I hope you aren't
going to start having babies right away.

E.B. (Greatly embarrassed, for in those days people did not discuss
such matters and my fiancé and I had only just brought ourselves rather furtively to exchange a copy of Marie Stopes's
Married Love, and I felt everyone would be hearing what H.D.
was saying) I hope not.

H.D. Hoping won't help you girl. Who is taking the precautions?
You or he?

E.B. (Timidly) I think he will.

H.D. Does he know where to get them? I'll give you an address, and
tell him to be sure to get the right size.[9]

Like his father, Hugh was the kind of teacher whose oddities gave
rise to anecdotes. In Hugh's case the theme was usually a combination
of eccentricity, explosive temperament, good nature, and a mocking
view of himself and the world. He was particularly mocking towards
female students whose presence in his lectures he liked to pretend was
purely ornamental. He called one group of girls 'the Beauty Chorus'.
('Will the Beauty Chorus give us their opinion on this?') An oft-
repeated story captured both his irascibility and his willingness to be
teased. At the beginning of one lecture, he bellowed angrily at some
late-comers. The following week, everybody was punctual except the
lecturer himself. When he eventually arrived, the students he had
chided stood and chanted in parrot-like imitation: 'You're late, you're
late, you're horribly late! Sit down! Sit down! Sit down!'[10]

He was patient and tolerant towards students in difficulties, especially those with language or cultural problems. After lectures, according to one former pupil, 'he would sit with a quizzical expression on his face, a leg over the arm of his chair, and listen with great attentiveness to endless and incomprehensible questions from earnest Indian students of whom there were many at the L.S.E.'[11] In addition to Indians, he took a particular interest in the many Jewish, and Zionist, students who passed through the School. One of the latter, having returned from a visit to Palestine in the mid-1920s greatly impressed, eagerly recounted his experiences to Dalton and to Harold Laski, by now on the staff. Laski was friendly but detached. Dalton immediately arranged a tea at the House of Commons with Josiah Wedgwood, a Labour proponent of the idea of Palestine as a Seventh Dominion under the British Crown.[12]

Because teaching was based on lectures with no system of tutorials, many who heard him lecture never met him personally. Some students, however, he got to know well, and a few became lifelong friends. One in this category was Robert (later Sir Robert) Fraser, who became first Director-General of the Independent Television Authority. Another was the economist Lionel (later Lord) Robbins. Robbins warmly recalled 'the breadth of Dalton's views, his feeling for arrangement, his simple yet elegant expository style'. Dalton was helpful towards his student protégés, especially those in whom he saw an exceptional talent. Almost every advancement in his own early career, Robbins wrote later, had been a product of Dalton's support.[13]

Dalton was a full-time member of staff at the L.S.E. between 1919 and 1924 and from 1931 to 1935 and a part-timer from 1924 to 1929. Including his period as a research student before the war, he spent seventeen of his most active years in close association with the School. How was he himself affected by this contact? In attitude and outlook, as in his ambitions, four years at King's influenced him more. Yet he valued his connection with the L.S.E., and seemed very much its product. His method of holding the attention of large audiences was acquired in the huge lecture halls of the School, where 300 or more would crowd together. So was a habit, which drove opponents to fury, of addressing hostile gatherings as though they were composed of students in need of instruction.

More important, however, than the School's function as a training ground in oratory was the professional training – mainly self-training – which it afforded him. After the war, as before it, Dalton used the L.S.E. as a seminary. King's had provided his values. It was at the School that he acquired and refined the doctrines which gave him direction and furnished his armoury for the rest of his career. This period, indeed, was the vital last stage in his preparation for political life.

By the spring of 1923, Dalton had published three books on economics – one a treatise, one a text-book and one a polemic. All three reflected his politics.

Dalton's best known work was *Principles of Public Finance*, first published in December 1922 and for many decades a basic text in a field where ideas and practices were constantly changing. Based on lectures delivered at the School, it was designed 'to excite the judgement briefly, rather than to inform it tediously'. It ran to four editions and a large number of printings, and by the time of the Second World War it had been translated into Arabic, Czech, Dutch, German, Japanese, Turkish and Urdu. Many who criticised Dalton as Chancellor of the Exchequer had been introduced to financial policy on the basis of it.

Though essentially for student courses, it was also a subtle work of propaganda. As the author baldly admitted, occasionally he 'turned aside to criticise certain current opinions on questions of taxation, public expenditure and public debts ... ' In particular, he took issue with 'a somewhat negative attitude towards public expenditure' common to most economists. [14] Many students who grew up regarding increases in state spending with a more open mind than their predecessors owed a debt to the restrained elegance of Dalton's advocacy.

Within the world of academic economists, however, Dalton's reputation did not primarily depend on *Principles of Public Finance*. He was much more highly regarded for his first book on economics, based on his doctoral thesis, which had been published in 1920 under the title *Some Aspects of the Inequality of Incomes in Modern Communities*. [15] Robbins, who disagreed fervently with Dalton on many economic and political matters, wrote of this book that it raised very fundamental issues and 'certainly influenced thought, both on the analytical and ethical plane.' [16] Hugh Gaitskell, another economist who became a friend and protégé, wrote that *Inequality of Incomes* 'immensely clarified socialist thinking', pointing it away from the sterile academicisms of earlier writers. [17] More recently Amartya Sen has described Dalton's work on measuring inequalities as 'a classic contribution'. Indeed, among economic theorists interested in equality, Dalton's ideas have been enjoying a posthumous vogue. [18]

Inequality of Incomes was a theoretical work. But it was theory with a practical, and an ethical, edge. It was, in sum, a neatly argued intellectual justification for what Dalton understood by the word socialism in its economic manifestation. Politically, the book was a consequence of Windsor, Eton, Ben Keeling and Beatrice Webb. Economically, it developed the ideas of Pigou and Cannan in a socialist direction. In the introduction, Dalton made clear that, all along, his interest in economics had been based on a desire to explain why some people were richer, and some poorer, than others:

> While studying economics at Cambridge in 1909–10, I became specially interested in those books, or parts of books, which set out to discuss the distribution of income. I gradually noticed, however, that most 'theories of distribution' were almost wholly concerned with distribution as between 'factors of production'. Distribution as between persons, a problem of more direct and obvious interest, was either left out of the textbooks altogether, or treated so briefly, as to suggest that it raised no question ... [19]

In pursuit of his quest, Dalton set out to examine the whole concept of the distribution of income, and at the same time to consider what determined the distribution of income between rent, wages, interest and profit. He concluded that the distribution of income from property was dependent on the distribution of property itself, which in turn was largely a product of inheritance. A work of theory thus became a tract, made the more persuasive by its scholarly caution. 'The attack is delightfully insidious', remarked one reviewer; 'each step proposed is so gentle, so plausible, so eminently reasonable that few could take offence: but the cumulative effect is immense.'[20]

Dalton began historically, surveying the theoretical literature on inequality since Adam Smith and J. S. Mill. Then, drawing heavily on Cannan, Pigou and Jevons, he examined the causes of modern inequality. He pointed, in particular, to the possession of large incomes from inherited wealth by a small number of individuals. He poured scorn on the view that inequalities coincided with merit or ability. He regarded it as extraordinary that there should still be many people who thought that Mr Rockefeller and the Duke of Westminster were not only the thriftiest men alive, but also that they were very wise.

What was the cause of unequal distribution? The Marxists, who blamed capitalism, had failed to take into account the great inequalities that existed in pre-capitalist societies. It was more fruitful, Dalton believed, to examine all the legal and customary bases of inheritance. Just as economists had neglected the problem of distribution between persons, so too they had ignored the problem of inherited wealth. Dalton noted with contempt Edmund Burke's remark to the Duke of Richmond, that the Duke was one of the great oaks shading the country, perpetuating their benefits from generation to generation:

For reason begins to suggest that all families are really equally old, though unequally notorious, and even that, the worthier a family may be of 'veneration', the less its members should need the economic prop of inherited wealth.

Dalton quoted with approval the American economist, Irving Fisher, who described the distribution of property as dependent on 'inheritance constantly modified by thrift, ability, industry, luck and fraud.' Nowhere did Dalton mention the British Royal Family. Yet the implication for one of the oldest and richest dynasties in the world, its privilege and fortune uniquely dependent on the principle of inheritance, pervaded every paragraph.

Inheritance, Dalton believed, was a fundamental cause of unfair distribution. Yet, given that distribution was unfair, why were great inequalities of wealth necessarily bad? His argument was utilitarian:

> Put broadly, and in the language of common-sense, the case against large inequalities of income is that the less urgent needs of the rich are satisfied, while the more urgent needs of the poor are left unsatisfied ... An unequal distribution of a given amount of purchasing power among a given amount of people is, therefore, likely to be a wasteful distribution from the point of view of economic welfare, and the more unequal the distribution, the greater the waste.[21]

Dalton was not in favour of absolute equality. An ideal distribution would be 'according to the capacity of individuals, or families, to make a good use of income'. To produce such a distribution, what was needed was reform of the law of inheritance.

Deriving his approach from the Marshall-Pigou school, he took an optimistic view of social progress, predicting that modern communities would gradually move towards the extinction of large fortunes, independently 'of larger changes of a socialistic character, though perhaps concurrently with them'. He believed, however, that what Sidney Webb later called 'the inevitability of gradualness' should be given a helping hand. The process of change, he argued, could be assisted by two kinds of death duty. The first was called the 'Rignano' tax, after the economist Eugenio Rignano, whose work Dalton had discovered in the course of his Italian reading. This tax would fall on that part of an estate which had been inherited, while making graduated distinctions between different 'stages' of inheritance (wealth inherited from a parent who directly accumulated it would be taxed less heavily than from a parent who inherited it from a grandparent, and so on). The second was a tax on the net estate, graduated so that it would be 100 per cent above a certain level – thereby fixing a maximum inheritance, and hence a limit to personal wealth beyond what could be accumulated in a single life-time.

In addition to new types of death duty, Dalton proposed a steeply progressive income tax, a steeply progressive graduated Capital Levy for the redemption of War Debt, discriminating prices against the rich, subsidies for the poor, and the nationalisation of private monopolies. He further proposed that, when tax was paid, the state should be willing to accept securities or land in lieu of cash.

If prices fell, a capital levy would be necessary to stop the holders of government securities getting richer through the increased real value of their holdings. On the other hand, falling prices were, in general, to be encouraged on redistributionist grounds:

> If this would be provided for, it would constitute a steady tendency towards a reduction of inequality, and would automatically transfer to wage-earners, salaried persons, and many of the poorer property owners, a portion of the increasing real income of the community, independently of any increase in their money income. Psychologically, a given rise in a man's standard of life, brought about by an increase in the purchasing power of a given money increase, is probably healthier than an equal rise brought about by an increase in money income, the purchasing power of money remaining unchanged.[22]

Most of Dalton's thinking on economics was rooted here. Later, the philosophical differences between Dalton and economist colleagues were often hidden or ignored. There was an assumption – which at times Dalton himself seemed to share – that the basic aims of economists were the same, and arguments were about devices. Yet it was a false assumption. While others sought to increase production or liberate the trading system, Dalton's passion – intellectual and emotional – remained the problem of inequality, and the question of how to reduce it.

As Chancellor of the Exchequer a quarter of a century later, he was to act on some of these ideas, conceived at Edwardian Cambridge and refined at the L.S.E. More immediately, his attitude on current policy was much influenced by his assessment of likely effects on inequality. When some economists advocated the raising of price levels through expansionist or fiscal measures as a means of tackling unemployment, Dalton at first resisted because of his commitment to greater equality which, he believed, could best be advanced through taxation and falling prices. Later, as the Depression deepened, he changed his mind about deflation. But he continued to approach the problem of unemployment, as he approached all economic questions, primarily from the point of view of distribution.

Inequality of wealth and income was the subject of Dalton's first purely polemical book, an essay entitled *The Capital Levy Explained*, published in March 1923:[23] the culmination of a campaign that linked one of the main themes of *Inequality of Incomes* to a fashionable socialist platform. Dalton did not invent the scheme for a once-and-for-all tax on private wealth. He did however play an important part in adapting it for use by the Labour Party as a central election issue.

Despite the socialist implications of the name, there was at first support, and even enthusiasm, for the levy across the political spectrum. The idea was largely Liberal in origin and arose from vague wartime proposals to tax capital in order to pay off the national debt.[24] Economists favoured it for technical reasons. Pigou wrote a book advocating a graduated levy of up to 40–80 per cent as a means to economic recovery;[25] Keynes declared capital levy policies 'an absolute prerequisite of sound finance in every one of the European belligerent countries'.[26] Internationalists favoured the capital levy because they opposed the alternative of exacting large reparations from Germany. Lord Beaverbrook campaigned vigorously for a levy to catch some of the windfall gains of war profiteers. Even Bonar Law showed a passing interest.

What was acceptable on patriotic grounds during the war and in its immediate aftermath lost its appeal in the tumultous conditions that followed. Pigou and Keynes rapidly ceased to see the levy as a means to boost production, and Bonar Law discarded it on the grounds that it would set a dangerous precedent.[27] Liberal and Tory advocates alike had seen the levy as a regulatory, occasionally as a corrective, device. The device no longer seemed appropriate. The period 1918–23 saw the proposal transformed from one with a broad basis of support to a policy which even the Labour Party, or at any rate its more cautious leaders, hesitated to adopt for fear of upsetting moderate opinion.

Early arguments in favour of the levy paid little attention to redistribution. The redistributionist element would, indeed, favour the middle class (which paid income tax and therefore bore the burden of War Debt) rather than the working class, which paid no tax directly.[28] On the other hand, the capital levy would cause considerable discomfort to the very wealthy. Partly for this reason, the levy began to acquire an emotive appeal in progressive circles at about the time that respectable opinion was abandoning it. F. W. Pethick Lawrence, a socialist economist, led the way in advocating the scheme as an attack on the rich.[29] Dalton had always seen this aspect as one of the levy's most attractive features.[30]

By the end of 1921, as we have seen, Dalton had begun to come to the attention of the Party leaders as a middle-class 'expert', particularly on economic matters. Now he made use of this new role in order to press an issue about which he had knowledge and strong feelings – and which offered the prospect of a wider popularity within the Movement.

His chance came at a lunch given by the Webbs in February 1922, on the eve of the Cambridge by-election. Apart from Beatrice, Sidney and Hugh, three of the Party's most prominent leaders were present – J. R. Clynes, Arthur Henderson and Philip Snowden. 'Conversation moved to the Capital Levy', Dalton recorded. 'I defended it supported by Webb. Snowden opposed, rather ignorantly, not understanding what is proposed ... Henderson said it was an important question. We must have a policy on it and push it. We had better form ourselves into a committee on it and meet again at the House of Commons.' Walking back to the House with Henderson, Dalton seized his moment and offered to draft a memorandum. Henderson agreed.[31]

A Sub-Committee of the N.E.C. was formed to discuss the matter, with Dalton and Pethick Lawrence co-opted on to it – two Old Etonian economists plotting a broadside against their contemporaries. The Labour capital levy policy that emerged was largely of their construction.[32] During the 1922 election campaign, the scheme was given a central importance. 'The only live question before the country during the General Election was the Capital Levy', a Liberal opponent of the plan declared just after the poll.[33]

Dalton's little book on the subject was an elaboration of the Party policy document of which he was joint, and principal, author. The policy was never implemented, discreetly buried by the first Labour Chancellor, Philip Snowden, shortly after he came to office. Alarmed by accusations of confiscation and bolshevism, MacDonald and Snowden had decided, for electoral reasons, to play it down.

Dalton, however, remained faithful to his own pet scheme – long after the purely economic case had lost its relevance. For him, the issue was one of distribution more than of economics and he retained his interest in what seemed a perfect method of disinheriting the wealthy. 'It is my personal opinion', he wrote in 1935, 'that once we have made good progress with socialisation, the policy of the capital levy should be brought to the fore again ... '[34] Successive generations of students reared on his *Public Finance* text-book were made familiar with the arguments – as were his own pupils at the L.S.E. (to whom he would first give the case for the capital levy, and then out of fairness, the case against). As Chancellor of the Exchequer in 1947, he considered imposing a once-and-for-all tax on large fortunes, shortly before his own removal from office took away the opportunity for him to do so. Even in 1954, he continued to maintain that the case for a levy was unanswerable on egalitarian grounds.[35]

More than any other single proposal, the levy scheme symbolised his domestic politics, tying together all his most important ideas on economics, distribution and equality. It also indicated the careful thought he was prepared to put into the job of attacking the Tory enemy in their area of greatest sensitivity: their pockets. Tories felt, and they may have been right, that for all the intellectual sophistication of Dalton's utilitarianism, emotionally he was less interested in helping the poor than in hurting the rich. This was one reason why Dalton was always hated with more fury than any other middle- or upper-class Labour M.P., and why, more than any other, he was regarded as (and feared as) a traitor to his class.

One advantage of the L.S.E. was its easygoing attitude towards the political activities of its staff. Dalton's frequent electoral forays were treated with friendly tolerance by colleagues and students – an attitude that owed something to the Fabian origins of the School, and rather more to William Beveridge, who himself had political aspirations and had made his own freedom to engage in politics a condition of accepting the Directorship.[36]

Nevertheless, there were occasions when Beveridge, who valued Dalton highly as a member of staff,[37] had to defend him from the Governing Body. One Governor complained that the bias in Dalton's *Public Finance* would 'do harm to the School', revealing as it did 'a red tie under a scarlet doctoral robe'.[38] Another took up the protests of a lady in Hampstead who had read *The Capital Levy Explained* and been told that 'the teaching is very socialistic and that particularly in the Welfare Workers' Department it turns out young people with revolutionary ideas'.[39]

The Director dismissed these complaints, just as he resisted attempts to restrain Harold Laski, another member of staff who paraded his socialist beliefs. Dalton was allowed to teach, write and campaign as he pleased, without interference. Nevertheless he was irritated by the objections, and the rows they engendered made him more determined than ever to find a parliamentary seat. 'I feel that politics and not anaemic academism is my spiritual homeland', he told Ruth after one skirmish.

Dalton might feel called to politics. Getting elected was another matter. Party Headquarters regarded his efforts sympathetically, and did what it could to help. The problem was finding a local party in a winnable constituency to adopt him, and – hardest of all – assessing which seats in the new, fluid electoral conditions were winnable and which were not. Luckily for Dalton, general elections were so frequent in the early 1920s that he could afford to make mistakes.

In May 1923 Bonar Law was replaced as Prime Minister by Stanley Baldwin. That autumn, Baldwin announced his wish to introduce Protection, and dissolved Parliament in the hope of obtaining a mandate for a policy which his predecessor had promised not to introduce. As an election became more likely, Dalton – who had planned a break from politics – found himself searching for a suitable candidature.

Since the summer, he had been quietly cultivating the safe mining constituency of Chesterfield, even – as we have seen – visiting the elderly Edward Carpenter in an attempt to add to his contacts. His hope had been that the sitting member, a miners' agent called Kenyon, would either stand down or be pushed out. Unfortunately the rapid approach of the election forestalled the possibility that Kenyon might be pushed; while Kenyon refused to make clear, right up to the announcement of the poll, whether he intended to stand down.

Dalton approached Sidney Webb for advice. Webb suggested seeing Kenyon in person. Frantic at the possibility of missing the boat, Dalton dashed off to Chesterfield, was advised against calling at Kenyon's house, and dashed back again. A few days later Kenyon explained that he needed to hang on to the seat because of the parliamentary salary. 'I decide that Chesterfield is off', wrote Dalton, 'and begin pulling wires for other seats.'

One promising constituency still without a Labour candidate was Leicester West, where the Liberal contender was Winston Churchill. Leaving nothing to chance, Dalton obtained a letter of recommendation from Arthur Greenwood, head of the Labour Party Research Department. Alas, this was trumped by Pethick Lawrence who was able to produce a letter from Ramsay MacDonald. In the end, Party Headquarters tossed Dalton Cardiff as a consolation prize. He could have East or South, he was told, whichever he preferred. He picked East. It turned out to be the wrong one.

At Cardiff East, Dalton fought his usual rough-and-tumble campaign. The Liberal M.P. for the neighbouring Swansea constituency was a Jewish manufacturer, Sir Alfred Mond. At one meeting, Dalton told his audience that his own policy was 'to carry out the old injunction "feed my lambs" '. Encouraged by applause, he added: 'Mond, of course, doesn't get beyond the Old Testament'. For electioneering purposes, he let himself be known as 'Doctor Dalton'. This led to misunderstandings. The porter in his hotel asked to speak to him privately. 'Doctor, I'm suffering from piles. What do you recommend?' Dalton wished that he had had the quickness to reply: 'Join the Labour Party, and vote for the Capital Levy, our sovereign cure for excessive piles.'[40]

Dalton lost by 7,812 to 8,536, an even narrower margin than at Maidstone. Nationally, the Labour Party made a further advance – increasing its representation in the House of Commons to 191. Labour stood poised to form its first ever administration. Dalton, however, felt depressed and bitter. 'East Cardiff was disheartening', he wrote to his friend C. P. Trevelyan, now a Labour M.P. and shortly to be a minister, ' – amazing meetings, with an atmosphere of religious revival, and people weeping readily at references to war and poverty, but this only an unhealthy façade. No organisation behind and personal disunities owing to the fact that the last candidate was an N.U.R. man who wanted to stand again.'[41]

On the way back to London, Dalton found himself sharing a compartment with Ramsay MacDonald, shortly to become Prime Minister. He could have hoped for a better companion. The Party Leader, with something less than tact, informed him that the capital levy policy had lost Labour fifty seats. 'J.R.M., in private conversation, very right-wing and hardly to be trusted among the rich', Dalton noted gloomily. Later Dalton told Josiah Wedgwood, patrician Labour M.P. for Newcastle-under-Lyme, that 'only gentlemen are proof against the blandishments of Court and Society'.[42]

The Court, meanwhile, had been taking some interest in Dalton's own activities. After the 1923 election, Labour and Liberal M.P.s outnumbered Conservatives, and Court advisers were faced with a serious constitutional dilemma. If Baldwin was defeated when the House met, should the King call on Labour as the bigger Opposition party to form a new government? George V was alarmed by the revolutionary views of the newly elected Clydeside I.L.P. members, and he was particularly unsettled by a speech in which one of their number, Campbell Stephen, had declared that if MacDonald was refused a dissolution after becoming Prime Minister, that would be the end of the Monarchy. As it happened, Hugh and Ruth were staying in the Cloisters at Windsor over Christmas. The King instructed his Private Secretary, Lord Stamfordham, to use the opportunity for discreet inquiries.

After a long conversation with Hugh, Stamfordham made a careful report which was read aloud by the Queen to the King. Dalton must have relished the twist of fate which had turned him into the Royal Household's best available link to the political party which it feared the most. Dalton described the Clydesiders as men who were not as violent as they seemed, but who had been brought up amidst extreme poverty and bad housing conditions. 'Mr MacDonald has the Party wholeheartedly at his back', he was recorded as saying, 'while no doubt the Left wing of the Liberal Party are not widely separated from the Labour Party, and as time goes on there probably will be movement towards a union between these sections of the two parties.'[43] Dalton made his own report and sent it to MacDonald, doubtless pleased to be able to demonstrate his personal access to the Court.

Dalton began 1924 'brainless and disillusioned' and increasingly angry at his continued failure to find a seat.[44] Labour was in office and contemporaries were in government. He was 36. His own high ambitions could scarcely be achieved if he remained for much longer one of a group of clever young men who, in Beatrice Webb's words, 'await their destiny on the threshold of Parliament.'[45] 'There is a danger that I may win the reputation of a Jonah, a sort of Masterman', he told Trevelyan. 'This is the price of having taken on two sheer propaganda fights for the Party at Cambridge and Maidstone, instead of hanging back and wangling for something better.'[46] As the new Government got into its stride, his depression deepened. It would not take much to make him chuck in politics altogether. 'I am wasting the energies of the best years of my life', he wrote.

But he went on trying. The I.L.P. nominated him for Belper and he had his first experience of a 'Singing Competition' – a competitive selection conference.[47] He was chosen, but withdrew supposedly because of the expense of working a scattered constituency. Then, in July, he allowed himself to be propelled into a by-election at Holland-with-Boston. It was an unwise decision. The seat had been Labour-held since 1918, but the M.P. had been a popular local man and it was widely felt that he had carried a large personal vote. Moreover, after eight months in office the national tide was against Labour.

The fight was vicious. One local newspaper developed a particularly venomous line of attack, calling Dalton 'an extremist', a 'deep-dyed socialist' and 'a menace to British unity, liberty and constitutional government' whose 'gang of howling yahoos' had allegedly broken up a Tory meeting.[48] The Liberals claimed that Dalton was anti-religious, a foreigner and a drunkard, and had written a text-book used in Communist Sunday Schools. Dalton countered bizarrely by getting his father to write a letter of endorsement for local publication. 'As a Churchman and the son of a Churchman', Hugh declared, 'I shall at all times do all in my power to maintain the highest moral standards in relation to marriage and shall oppose any attempt to diminish the sanctity of the marriage tie by multiplying facilities for divorce.'[49] Fearing defeat, Party Headquarters in London sent a stream of M.P.s into the constituency.[50]

Once again, Dalton was beaten by a few hundred votes (12,907 to 12,101). 'The Liberals in Holland were indescribably dirty', he wrote afterwards. 'There will be no health in our public life until they are exterminated as a Party.'[51] He claimed that the Liberals had hit him below the belt with their 'scurrilous garbage', and he listed 'wealth, privilege, motor cars and untrue statements' as the cause of his defeat.[52] It was almost the last straw – his fourth successive defeat in 28 months. 'I'm utterly sick of politics and feel a fool to have come on this adventure', he wrote.[53] 'I consider that, on my Parliamentary candidatures alone, I have now earned a safe seat,' he told Pethick Lawrence, now installed as Labour Member for Leicester West, 'and unless I get the offer of one, I shall not stand again'. Bruised, he retreated with Ruth for a long summer holiday in Sardinia. For the moment, politics had become a nightmare and Parliament 'that Chamber of Horrors, about the doors of which so many of us beat our wings in vain'.[54]

Dalton's luck was, however, about to turn. The Labour Government, precariously sustained by Liberal support, collapsed less than a year after taking office. A general election was called for 29th October. Dalton found himself on the eve of a national poll once again without a candidature. Then at the last moment he was offered the highly marginal seat of Camberwell, Peckham, in South London, which had been held in 1924 by a Tory with a majority of just 156 over an elderly Labour candidate, now forced to withdraw because of ill health. The constituency seemed vulnerable because the sitting M.P. had also stood down, and local Conservatives had been forced to put up another candidate, Colonel Sir Martin Archer-Shee, at the last minute.

Dalton had vowed not to stand again, except in a safe seat. He had already stood and lost four times in less than three years. He could hardly afford to lose a fifth time. On the other hand, there was no chance of anything better. He had to make a snap judgment. 'We are finally forced up against a decision in a taxi on the way to the London Labour Party Office, where a deputation is waiting,' he recalled a few months later. 'I decide to accept. For I should feel an awful fool, if I refused and then someone else won the seat!'[55]

On election night, Dalton was sure he had lost. Then more boxes were opened and he forged ahead. After the first count, with victory in his grasp, he asked the mayor if it was not normal at such a point to give the actual figure. The mayor replied that the election was not finished. 'There were some signs of unpleasantness', recorded the local paper, 'but the mayor successfully appealed for quietness to be maintained.'[56] 'The scene was very exciting, watching the bundles of votes piling up for Shee and then for Dalton', a local veteran recalls. 'At about 1 a.m., Shee called for a recount then challenged twice again. In the end Dalton was elected amid great excitement. Peckham's first ever Labour M.P. was led to the balcony of Wilson's Grammar School. The cheers were tremendous at 3.30 a.m.'[57]

Dalton had won with 13,361 votes against 12,414 for the Tory and 3,194 for the Liberal, a majority of 947. This was a big improvement on the previous Peckham result, and against the national trend: Labour lost 64 seats, and gained only 22. Afterwards, the newly-elected Member attributed his victory to women, the Irish, and the good sense of the people of Peckham who 'refused to be frightened by Russian bogies and antics of the Tory stunt press'.[58]

XI

Mosley and Keynes

The P.L.P. in the 1920s was a party of novices: an odd mixture of street-corner demagogues, socialist propagandists and trade union officials, supplemented by miscellaneous hangers-on and carpet-baggers of little knowledge or weight. 'Deficient in brains and starved of money, it is a miracle that the Labour Party steadily grows in voting power', wrote Beatrice Webb in 1927. 'The impression left on the observer's mind is of slow underground social upheaval, moving independently of leaders or organisation ... '[1] Dalton was one able recruit who quickly realised that, provided the Labour Party survived, it would not be hard to rise to the top of it.

Later he claimed that when he first entered Parliament, he did so as a left-winger.[2] It is true that he clashed with Party leaders over the capital levy. It is also true that, on arrival in the House of Commons, he briefly associated himself with some of the activities of the left-wing Clydesiders, led by Jimmy Maxton. Later he proudly recalled that he had once been suspended from the House of Commons for five days, for taking part in a Maxtonite protest against a government Economy Bill. In April 1926, he and a dozen other Labour M.P.s expressed their feelings by sitting down in the lobby during an all-night debate and refusing to move, singing songs of defiance.[3] He always regarded himself as an opponent of the MacDonald clique, and his diary for the end of 1927 reveals him deploring 'a great sense of caution and anti-Leftism in the Parliamentary Party'.

Yet he was scarcely a serious rebel. The shelving of his scheme for a capital levy by the P.L.P. leadership might have been used by him to make his feelings heard, and to establish himself as a sharp opponent of caution and half-heartedness. Instead he held back. 'I could have played the part of Casablanca, both honestly and with some political profit, probably on the left', he reflected. 'But I decided against this and in favour of co-operating to find an alternative.'[4] This was about as close – and it was not very close – as Dalton ever got to left-wing revolt in the 1920s.

One powerful disincentive was that, in matters of economics (and increasingly of foreign policy as well), Dalton had made himself so indispensable that he had rapidly gained election to Labour's front bench. At the end of his first parliamentary session, he tied with Arthur Ponsonby (another Court-raised old Etonian) for last place on the Executive of the Parliamentary Party (the Shadow Cabinet). The two men drew lots to decide between them. Dalton won, and thereafter held his place until his voluntary retirement in 1955. The following autumn, trade union support put him on to the Labour Party National Executive in the so-called Constituency and Central Labour Parties Division (membership of which was determined by the whole of Party Conference, and hence by the trade union block vote). In 1927 he lost his seat on the N.E.C., but he was re-elected in 1928 and in every subsequent contest until 1952.

In June 1927 Hugh and Ruth accepted an invitation to spend a weekend with Beatrice and Sidney Webb at Passfield Corner. Hugh had now been a Member of Parliament for two-and-a-half years. He was 40, twice as old as when the Webbs had first met him, 'straight from Eton and a home in the outer-Court-circle'. The Webbs had watched his progress ever since, and their initial assessment had barely altered. They regarded him as committed, ambitious, immensely able, yet in some intangible way, personally unappealing. Beatrice was now in retirement, but her pen portraits were as sharp as ever. Dalton was not popular with his colleagues at the L.S.E., she wrote:

They say that he is a 'careerist' considering all things by the light of his own security and promotion. He is even inclined to pose as such. In the Labour Party he *is* popular; the Right Wing trust his judgement and knowledge, the Left believe in his fervour for 'Socialism in our time'. He gives *us* the impression that he believes in the 'inevitability of gradualness'; that he is 'sound' in his conception of the way reconstruction will come – not from workers by 'workers' control' or 'proletarianism'! Dalton dislikes and distrusts J.R.M. [Ramsay MacDonald] and puts his faith in 'Uncle Arthur'. Henderson thinks him the most promising of the younger men; even suggests that when the old gang go off the stage, Dalton may be first favourite for the leadership of the party. And certainly he has knowledge, a good voice and admirable manner; he is a lucid and impressive speaker, and would, I think, prove to be an energetic and sane administrator. But he has no personal magnetism and though an intellectual and moral man, he has neither intellectual nor moral uniqueness or distinction. And in his curiously deferential and ingratiating method of address with persons who are likely to be useful to him, there is just a hint of insincerity; in his colourless face there is a trace of cunning ... I am inclined to agree with Henderson that if the Labour Government arrives during the next ten years Dalton will certainly attain Cabinet rank – just after William, Graham and before Mosley. I neither like the man nor do I dislike him; but as stuff for the Front Bench he is far above the average of his fellows. He is undoubtedly an asset to the Parliamentary Labour Party.[5]

Three points are of particular interest in this sketch. First, the persistence of the strange flaw in Dalton's personality that made some people dislike him, the *impression* of insincerity and shameless self-seeking which, as Beatrice shrewdly observed, was partly a pose. (We are reminded of John Dalton's remark, intended to shock the minor canons, that there were two things he had never had, 'nerves or a conscience'.) Second, the rapidity of Dalton's rise to prominence, so that within twenty months of entering the Commons he was already being tipped as a future Party Leader. Third, the linking of Dalton's name to that of another apparent class traitor, Sir Oswald Mosley. Dalton's rivalry with Mosley, hinted at by Beatrice Webb, is of considerable significance to our story.

Sir Oswald Mosley was a newcomer to the Labour Party, though not to the House of Commons. Elected as a Conservative in 1918, he became an Independent Member in 1922, joining the I.L.P. in 1924 and losing his seat in the election of the same year. In 1926 he returned to Parliament at a by-election, and immediately established himself not only as one of the Labour Party's most surprising, but also one of its most talented, representatives.

In a Parliamentary Labour Party largely composed of working- and lower-middle-class Members, Dalton and Mosley were often bracketed together. Fenner Brockway (then secretary of the I.L.P.) recalls the powerful presence of these two personalities at meetings of the I.L.P. Finance Committee in the late 1920s, Mosley 'tall, handsome, arrogant and compelling, and Hugh Dalton, also an extrovert, loud in speech, a little angular in body and in person, but full of ideas and self-confidence.'[6] Both came from Tory family backgrounds. Both were fine orators, though Mosley's skill lay in bewitching vast gatherings of the unsophisticated, whereas Dalton performed best before audiences who came to listen rather than to applaud. Both were former wartime officers, with a tendency to employ heavy military metaphors in speeches. Both gave an appearance of ambition and aggression, of treating politics as a battleground, without regard for injuries inflicted or received.

Here, however, the similarity ended, and from their first acquaintance Dalton disliked Mosley more intensely than anybody else in his entire political career. No doubt there was an element of jealousy. Mosley was ten years younger than Dalton, yet when he returned to the House in 1926 he already had a notable career behind him. But there was certainly something more. Dalton's feelings were also based on an assessment that Mosley was an adventurer whose socialism was skin-deep, and that a huge gap existed between his public rhetoric and private values. 'How the fellow stinks of money and insincerity!' Dalton wrote in his diary.[7] Although both men came from families closely linked to the Establishment, the links were of a different order. Mosley belonged to the landed aristocracy, the class Dalton had grown up to detest. Mosley himself later drew attention to this social distinction. Within the Labour Party (he wrote in his memoirs) aristocrats such as himself tended to be on the Left while 'middle class newcomers' like Dr Dalton were reliable supporters of the Party hierarchy.[8]

His bitterness is understandable: Dalton was one of the very few people to rumble the future Fascist at a time when most of the Labour Party was being dazzled and bamboozled by him. In addition to Mosley's chicanery and wealth, Dalton had two particular grievances. One involved Ramsay MacDonald. The other concerned economics.

Mosley got on well with MacDonald. Dalton did not. Dalton's poor relationship with the Party Leader went back to Cambridge Fabian days, when MacDonald had made a bad impression during a visit to the University. (Later, Dalton would recall Ben Keeling's comment: 'JRM would "bolt for the Treasury Bench like a rabbit for its hole" if he got the chance'.)[9] More recently Dalton had, somewhat unwisely, questioned MacDonald's credentials as an intellectual, and criticised him for woolly thinking, in both *Inequality of Incomes* and *Principles of Public Finance*. He had clashed with MacDonald over the capital levy; and he had found it hard to conceal his distaste for MacDonald's social aspirations.[10]

It was not surprising, therefore, that Mosley's success with MacDonald should feed Dalton's dislike for both. Dalton watched with a special loathing as Mosley exploited the Party Leader's social vulnerability, turning the lonely and susceptible old man into an intimate friend. When Mosley invited MacDonald and Dalton to his country house at Denham for tea and tennis, Dalton refused to come, feeling an intense irritation that MacDonald, on this as on other occasions, should swallow the bait.[11]

Mosley's manipulation of MacDonald was not, however, Dalton's most serious objection. What annoyed Dalton even more was Mosley's opportunism in matters of policy – in particular, his eagerness to seize on any panacea that might offer a political advantage. This was particularly evident in the field which Dalton had made his own, and which Mosley had only recently discovered. Mosley had spent his brief absence from Parliament in 1924–6 mugging up on economic policy and public finance. By the time of his return he had become a crusader for an employment programme that had every appearance of radicalism. Leading left-wingers in the I.L.P. were impressed. Dalton was not, and suspected Mosley's motives.

Dalton's contempt for Mosley was fully reciprocated. Mosley later described Dalton as a 'third-rate don' who owed his position to assiduity in the lobbies. 'Like all third-rate dons, he was determined not to unlearn what he had learnt with such pains, and was consequently a model of orthodoxy.'[12] Mosley regarded himself as boldly original in his economics, and his biographer, Robert Skidelsky, has defended this self-assessment. According to Skidelsky, Mosley was a 'fact man', a pragmatist single-mindedly concerned 'to solve the economic problem' and seeking the power to carry out this aim. 'By 1930 he had a firmer grasp of what was needed to be done than any other politician in Britain.' While others remained cautious and uncertain, Mosley was an expansionist and planner before his time, a 'Keynesian' when Keynes's own ideas were still tentative and half-formed.

It is possible, however, to look at Mosley's behaviour in another way. By Skidelsky's account, Mosley stumbled on 'progressive' economic ideas. Yet there is little evidence that he understood them. Where Dalton was an expert economist who could offer a sharply professional note in discussions of public finance, Mosley was an amateur who was undoubtedly a brilliant advocate, yet whose background in economic and monetary matters was non-existent. Significantly, the shrewdest foreign observer of Labour Party politics between the wars, Egon Wertheimer, was in no doubt about Dalton's greater depth and superior capacities. 'He is not flashy like Mosley', Wertheimer wrote in 1929, 'and in the Party his position is welded by closer bonds of affection and respect. Intellectually he is made of incomparably better stuff.'[13]

Mosley's newly discovered radicalism was the product of two influences. One was Keynes's *Tract for Monetary Reform*, published in

1923, which advocated stable or rising prices rather than deflation. The other (more direct) was the mercurial personality of John Strachey, synthesiser, populariser, and eclectic intellectual showman, whose hunger for fashionable ideas led him first to Keynes, then to Marx and Stalin, and finally back to Keynes within the space of a dozen years. No intellectual himself, Mosley encouraged Strachey to pick his way around the most controversial economic ideas of the moment. Keynes was an obvious candidate for scrutiny; he was concerned to reduce unemployment, he shared the Left's hostility to rentiers, and he supported corrective action by the state.

Skidelsky attributes Mosley's discovery of expansionist economics to 'sheer quickness of mind'.[14] A less charitable explanation is that Mosley and Strachey, knowing nothing about economics, were blind to the possible snags in a theory that so admirably suited their purposes. It is the job of the politician, especially the politician out of power, to have a bold opinion. It is not to Mosley's discredit that he should have taken up and embellished with socialist rhetoric the boldest opinions around. With hindsight it is arguable that his programme – however hastily considered – contained interesting features, though how workable such a programme would have been in practice, long before the imperatives of 1930s mass unemployment, remains a matter for debate. Equally, it is not to Dalton's discredit that he should have wished for more than elegant phrases and glib assurances before allowing himself to be persuaded by a man he had reason to distrust.

In 1926 Mosley and Strachey unveiled their proposals in a document called *Revolution by Reason*. Shortly afterwards, the I.L.P. published a rival report entitled *The Living Wage* which presented similar plans though with a more explicitly socialist slant, and more 'underconsumptionist' than Keynesian.[15] Each document suggested policies for reducing unemployment by expanding purchasing power. Dalton rejected both.

His objection was not to planning or public works programmes. On the contrary. In 1924 he had written that it was humiliating for Labour to be less bold than a 'Liberal' like Keynes, who had proposed spending a mere £100 million on constructional engineering in order to create jobs.[16] His criticism was directed at a more fundamental aspect of both schemes: their opposition to deflationary measures. On redistributive grounds he was strongly in favour of a stable or falling price level, and he refused to accept that unemployment was directly linked to a low level of prices. 'I am more afraid of inflation in the near future than, I think, you are', he wrote to Pethick Lawrence in March 1924. 'My belief (in opposition to that of others I know) is that you can stabilise any level of prices you choose, and that there is no causal relation between the level chosen – and the volume of unemployment.'[17] In a review of *Revolution by Reason* he argued that up to 1914 there had been little connection between price changes and the level of production, and so Keynes's case for the stabilisation of prices, and the Strachey-Mosley plan for a new issue of money, were seriously open to doubt.[18] He accused Strachey and Mosley of following Keynes in exaggerating the evil effects on production of falling prices.[19] Nationalisation of basic industries, he argued, would be a more than sufficient task for the next Labour government.

For Dalton, in this as in most other economic controversies, the key issue concerned inequalities of wealth and income, and the question of how disparities might most effectively be reduced. The aim of the capital levy was to reduce War Debt which enabled the rich to avoid taxation because total interest on War Loan (most of which was held by the part of the population which paid tax) was higher than the total yield of income tax and super tax put together. Servicing War Debt, he suggested, amounted to 'the operation of an enormous penny-in-the-slot machine, with certain people paying taxation in and drawing it out again in the form of interest'. Mosley, on the other hand, gave debt redemption through a capital levy a low priority.

Mosley spoke of creating markets by printing money.[20] Dalton regarded this kind of talk as 'arrant nonsense, bad arithmetic and bad economics', aimed at winning Mosley votes for the National Executive, which in 1927 it succeeded in doing, pushing Dalton off.[21] In Dalton's view, the problem of unemployment (still below one-and-a-half million in 1927) was not separable from the issue of distribution.

Hence on monetary matters he differed little from his front bench colleagues. He gave two cheers for free trade, attacked tariffs and demanded that budgets should be balanced. Budgetary policy only really interested him, however, when it related to the issue of inequality. He was quick to seize any chance in Parliament to castigate the rich. What had happened to Snowden's 1924 Budget Surplus? 'It was thrown to the wolves', he told the House triumphantly, 'namely the Super-tax payers, who crowd round the doors of the offices of the Conservative Party to see what they can get.' The slackness of the economy was a product of inefficiency and lack of incentive. Inefficiency and lack of incentive were caused by the accumulation of wealth through inheritance. Why had businessmen lost their drive? It was because they had inherited property into the third or fourth generation. As a result enterprises had passed into the hands of 'people who now spend most of their time in going to the Criterion and places like that, or perhaps in going to bogus night clubs'.[22] The solution, Dalton believed, lay not in monetary or fiscal tinkerings, but in the capital levy, high death duties, steeply progressive taxation, nationalisation and an end to the irrationality of the market.

There was, however, one further reason for Dalton's political differences with Mosley – that went beyond personal hostility, political rivalry, shrewd character assessment, or arguments about prices and the capital levy. This concerned Dalton's complicated, armslength relationship with the main source of the economic ideas of Mosley and Strachey – Maynard Keynes.

If the family backgrounds of Dalton and Mosley were sharply different, the origins, and early choices, of Dalton and of Keynes had much in common. Both came from families with strong traditions of scholarship and public service. Both were educated at Eton and King's. Both were active Cambridge Union politicians as undergraduates, and both moved to economics from mathematics. Both were emotionally interested in men as well as women, both were in revolt against conventional methods and ideas, both embraced the philosopher G. E. Moore as their guide and prophet. Both had been members of the same King's-based group, counting Francis Birrell, Rupert Brooke, Ben Keeling, Gerald Shove, James Strachey, Arthur Waley and Dudley Ward among their close friends. Both became dons, while remaining restlessly determined that their ideas should be instruments for use in the world. These ties, unusual even in the narrow academic world of Edwardian and inter-war England, were enough to ensure interlocking circles of friendship for the rest of their lives. But they were not enough to provide mutual affection, and none existed.

Keynes regarded Dalton (when he bothered to think about him at all) as over-eager, exhausting, and lacking in either subtlety or distinction. Beneath this attitude there lay an imperturbable sense of superiority. Where Keynes was best at whatever he turned his hand to, Dalton seemed to belong to the second division: not quite a scholar at Eton or King's, not quite a First, not Secretary or President of the Union. The essence of the exclusive Apostolic world was an inner, spiritual confidence. Dalton never had it. Other Kingsmen went into Labour politics – Philip Noel-Baker, for example, and Leonard Woolf. Neither, however, exhibited the indelicate ambition and noisy energy displayed by Dalton. Keynes did not particularly dislike his former pupil. He simply regarded him as of no account – irritating to associate with, the subject of dismissive jokes. It was Keynes who coined the nickname 'Daddy' Dalton, about which there was an element of derision.

Yet until the early 1920s Keynes and Dalton remained on superficially friendly terms. As an undergraduate, and later, Dalton shared
the general admiration for his tutor, four years his senior. 'We, in
those pre-war years, made a corner of his brilliance', Dalton recalled.[23]
Dalton was an irregular attender of Keynes's lectures on Money, and
in a practice exam only obtained an $\alpha-$ (compared with Gerald
Shove's $\alpha+$).[24] But Keynes had included Dalton in his small discussion group, and after Dalton went down they met at least twice
before 1914.[25] It was natural that Dalton should contact Keynes
when the war ended as somebody who might be able to help him. A
letter from Dalton to Keynes written from Italy immediately after
the European Armistice provides an interesting glimpse of their
relationship and of Dalton's uncertainties:

My dear Keynes,
     It is, or seems, infinitely long ago that you used to teach me
economics and, since that distant time, I have only seen you once
or twice, though I have heard a great deal of the operations of your
hidden hand.
     In the hope that you haven't quite forgotten me, I have given your
name as a reference in an application which I am making for an
immediate job in the Ministry of Labour and Reconstruction. I
hear that [Leonard] Woolf at the former wants a lot of additional
people. My chief reason for wanting a job of this kind is to get
demobilised as quickly as possible, though, if I got it, I should keep
it, till things got a little clearer as to the future. In any case I shan't
go back to the Bar. Having been in the Army since December 1914,
and out of England for $2\frac{1}{2}$ years, I feel damnably out of touch with
everything and everybody. But once I get back that should quickly
right itself. I have still in hand an unfinished book on Distribution,
'with special reference to inherited wealth', which I began years
before the war for the London School of Economics. Parts of it, I
think, are rather good. It will take about 3 months to finish if I am
doing not much else. Otherwise longer. Also I have half written a
book on my war experiences in Italy, where I have been now for 17
months. That will not take long to finish, once I get home. I have
read a lot of Italian economics out here. The average level strikes
me as higher than the modern French; Einandi and Nitti interest
me most. If you still control the Economic Journal, as I think you
do, I shall ask you to give me Italian books to review in future.
     If I get home on leave before Christmas, as I hope, I shall ask
you to come and have a meal with me. I shall feverishly seek out all
the desirable and surviving people whom I have ever known, and

put them all round me in an immense ring, and sit in the middle, looking and listening ...

Will you, please tell anyone who writes to you about me that in my childhood you knew me, and that then I was ingenuous and eager and for several hours daily pursued truth?

Yours ever

Hugh Dalton[26]

What, one wonders, did Keynes make of such a letter? Beatrice Webb's later comment about Dalton's 'curiously deferential and ingratiating method of address with persons who are likely to be useful to him' seems particularly apt. The letter adopts a style – whether consciously or not is unclear – that mimics the light, bantering whimsical, even slightly flirtatious, tones of Rupert Brooke. What was charming in Brooke, it may be surmised, was less charming in Dalton.

Dalton saw less of Keynes than of other former friends and acquaintances during his period as candidate in Cambridge. There were meetings for lunch in 1920 and 1921, and many of the names in Keynes's engagement books were also known to Dalton: Shove, Fay, Dent, Noel-Baker, Barbara Wootton, Clara Rackham, Petica Robertson (wife of Donald).[27] After the by-election, however, social contact virtually ceased.

One reason was politics. Keynes had little interest in the Labour Party and none in Dalton's political career. So far from encouraging Dalton, he publicly backed Dalton's Liberal opponent in the 1922 Cambridge by-election. Dalton found this hard to forgive, and thereafter referred to Keynes as 'the Liberal economist'. It was at this time that Dalton began to attack Keynes for 'inflationary' policies which would work against a possible capital levy and negate the good effects of falling prices. He dismissed as 'mere Lloyd George finance' Keynes's suggestion that the Sinking Fund should be raided to pay for constructional work.[28] Gradually, coolness turned to hostility, and admiration to resentment, as the views of the two men increasingly diverged. 'Dalton had a personal prejudice against him', an economist friend recalls. While Keynes referred disparagingly to 'Daddy' Dalton, Dalton resurrected an old Cambridge nickname for Keynes: 'Jeremiah Malthus'.[29]

The political difference was, of course, partly a difference of values: Dalton wanted equality, while Keynes did not.[30] But it stemmed also from an intellectual and academic difference, encouraged in Dalton's case by the influence of the L.S.E. Dalton was Edwin Cannan's protégé. Cannan was the most vociferous opponent of Keynes's views on the gold standard and monetary management, and supported the policy aim of a return to pre-war price levels. Keynes complained that Cannan was hostile towards almost everything worth reading on monetary theory in the previous ten years.[31] Writing in a *Festschrift* to Cannan in 1927, Dalton tried to steer a middle course, suggesting that neither Cannan's approach nor that of the Cambridge School was obviously better.[32] Nevertheless Dalton accepted many of Cannan's arguments, which accorded with his own deflationist views.

After Dalton entered the House of Commons in 1924 he ceased to follow the latest developments in economic theory, tending to rely on principles absorbed during his early years as an academic teacher. These served to reinforce his preference for stable or falling prices, his prejudices, political and personal, against Keynes and the Cambridge School, and his hostility towards what he regarded as the half-baked and opportunistic schemes of Mosley and Strachey.

It is a matter of historical interest that Labour came to Keynesian ideas comparatively late – some time after they had been successfully applied (for example) by social democratic governments in Sweden and New Zealand.[33] Dalton virtually wrote Labour economic and financial policy in the early 1930s, when the Keynesian theory was coming to fruition. If he had wished to make Keynesian expansionism and the multiplier a central plank, providing a possible bridge to Liberals and Tory Reformers against the classical economics of the Treasury, nobody was better placed to do so. That Labour policy and Dalton's writings contain only a few gestures of acknowledgment towards Keynes and his teachings until late in the decade may be attributed in part to the web of influences which had pushed Dalton away from his former tutor. Circumstances were to bring the two men together again in 1945, working in close proximity for a Labour Government. But the history of their relations produced at best a cool embrace.

If Dalton's attitude towards Cambridge economics remained distant, his relationship with L.S.E. economics after 1924 became increasingly tenuous and uneasy. Long before Dalton finally severed his connection with the School in 1935, he had ceased to have anything in common with the dominant political tendency in the L.S.E. economics department. Ironically, this was a result of an appointment of his own making. Yet he did not abandon important aspects of the School's economic philosophy.

When Lionel Robbins, most promising student of his generation at the L.S.E., graduated in 1923, it was Dalton who persuaded Beveridge to take him on for a year as a research assistant. Two years later

Dalton again intervened to arrange for Robbins's return to the School as a lecturer, this time on a permanent basis. After Edwin Cannan retired in 1926, responsibility for the general economics side of the School was shared between Robbins and Dalton, by now an M.P. but still working at the L.S.E. part-time.[34] Then Robbins left the School to take up a fellowship at Oxford, and an American from Harvard, Allyn Young, was appointed to Cannan's chair. The assignment was brief: Young died suddenly in his first year, forcing Dalton, although heavily preoccupied in Parliament, to take over as acting head of department.

Dalton decided, in this new situation, that the best solution was to appoint Robbins as Young's successor. 'Great jealousy of Lionel in the Ghetto', Dalton noted, 'but I think I shall succeed in getting him back'.[35] Largely through Dalton's influence, Robbins was chosen, and the new head of department quickly showed that he was master of his opportunities. Still only 30, industrious, brilliant, messianic, Robbins established an economics faculty at the L.S.E. to rival Cambridge, by building around himself a group of lecturers and research students who shared his own determination and commitment. Arnold Plant, Fritz Hayek, John Hicks, Frederic Benham, George Schwartz, Richard Sayers, R. D. G. Allen, Evan Durbin, Maurice Allen, Nicholas Kaldor, Abba Lerner, Brindley Thomas, Ursula Webb, Ronald Coase, Ronald Edwards, Arthur Lewis – they all passed through the School in the next few years, and the L.S.E. gained an influence in the field of economics far greater than ever before. But the orientation of the new, proselytising department was very different from what Dalton had envisaged.

Dalton remained on good terms with Robbins personally and retained his foothold at the School. His influence over the direction of economics teaching, however, completely disappeared. Though he privately objected to Robbins's tendency to become 'an addict to the Mises-Hayek anti-Socialist theme',[36] there was little he could do to counter it. Not all the new staff members and research students shared Robbins's fiercely anti-interventionist sentiments. But in the intensely competitive atmosphere of the Hayek-Robbins weekly seminar, alternative views had little place. Busy with parliamentary business, Dalton had neither the time nor the inclination to play a significant part. Instead he became an outside figure – avuncular and patronal, teasing Robbins in a friendly way but not seeking to argue with this fierce, crusading young autocrat, who had so firmly placed upon the department the imprint of his own passionate personality.

Yet Dalton's political differences with Robbins did not prevent him from taking Robbins's side in one of the most celebrated aca-

demic disputes of the inter-war period. It was from Robbins himself
that Dalton first learnt of a quarrel between Robbins (his former
student) and Keynes (his former tutor) on the Government's Economic
Advisory Council in October 1930. The clash, which precipitated
years of bitterness between L.S.E. and Cambridge economists, arose
because of Keynes's apostasy on the question of free trade. In response
to the mounting economic crisis that followed the Wall Street crash,
Keynes had advocated a 10 per cent tariff on all goods. Robbins, anti-
expansionist and anti-tariff, disagreed strenuously and demanded the
right on the economists' committee of the Council to submit his own
minority report expressing his reasons for rejecting the views of the
pro-tariff majority. Keynes, as chairman of the committee, refused.
Deeply upset, Robbins walked out.[37] 'In his wrath [Keynes] treated
me very roughly', Robbins claimed later. 'He denounced me before
the others and laid down that, as a minority of one, I was not entitled
to a separate report. This was very distressing to me.'[38]

Robbins dined alone with Dalton at the Reform Club the same
night and bitterly poured out his grievances. It is of interest that
Dalton, immediately and without hesitation, gave Robbins his full
backing. 'The tariff stuff is pitiable', he noted. 'I was taught to despise
Protectionists at Cambridge. Do so still. Lord Oswald [Dalton's
name for Mosley] is much with Keynes at present. But of course, he
can only take in the simpler arguments.'

Dalton was a member of the Labour Government in 1930, and no
longer teaching at the L.S.E. Was it chance that took Robbins to him
immediately after the crucial meeting? Or was it the hope that, as a
minister who was also an economist, Dalton might be able to use his
influence to circumvent Keynes and the committee? Whether Robbins
had this in mind or not, Dalton determined to plead Robbins's case
at the highest level – by speaking directly to Philip Snowden, the Chancellor of the Exchequer:

> I see Snowden and tell him of Lionel's experience. A very friendly
> interview. He has just read the report. He speaks with withering
> scorn of Keynes ... Snowden liked Lionel's report. He thought it 'a
> most trenchant reply'.[39]

When the political crisis broke the following August, splitting the
Labour Party and leading to the formation of the National Government, Dalton never hesitated about where he stood: with Arthur
Henderson and the other Cabinet ministers who opposed cuts in
unemployment benefit, and against Snowden's pursuit of economies
to meet the demands of foreign bankers. This was because of political

values and loyalties, because he had a principled objection on the key issue, and because he disliked MacDonald and Snowden. Yet up to this point his own background as a 'London' economist with a primary interest in increasing equality, and his complex personal, political and intellectual relations with Mosley, Keynes and Robbins, did not incline him to dispute the deflationist approach of the second Labour Government.

XII

Grass Roots

Dalton's talents as a performer before large audiences – his powerful delivery, his skilful arguments and measured sarcasm – were much appreciated by parliamentary colleagues, by Party Conference and in the Labour press. They counted for less in his constituency party at Peckham. Here his political career nearly came to an abrupt end almost as soon as it had begun. Those who imagine that local party pressure on M.P.s is something new or look back to a golden age of mass membership and the absence of caucuses will find Dalton's Peckham experience instructive. For Dalton achieved the remarkable feat during his first Parliament of gaining election to the Labour National Executive and Shadow Cabinet yet clashing so bitterly with his management committee that it became necessary to look for another seat.

Though the outcome was similar to that of disputes in the 1970s and 1980s, the cause was not quite the same. Recent local party troubles have most often occurred where traditional organisation has been in decline. In Peckham the problem was the opposite: a product of newness, premature success, the lack of a settled party establishment, and an excess of zeal on the part of an inexperienced M.P.

Peckham Labour Party was founded in 1919. 'We had a job working things up in Peckham', A. C. King, a local party veteran, recalls. 'Nobody was interested. We got hold of a register of trade unionists and got half a dozen people to work as ward secretaries and that was it.'[1] There followed a period of rapid advance. Labour received 24 per cent of the vote in the constituency in 1922 and 35 per cent a year later. When Dalton took the seat in 1924, members of the recently formed party felt an understandable sense of achievement. Yet this was partly based on an illusion. Despite the result organisation was weak, and Dalton found large areas of the constituency without any party workers at all. Victory probably had less to do with effective campaigning than with the 'underground social upheaval' identified by Beatrice Webb, which was producing Labour gains in working-class districts for reasons unconnected with local Labour activity.

Instead of concluding that local campaigning was unimportant, Dalton decided that he must improve organisation or risk losing the seat. He made a start with local government. Peckham's success at parliamentary level had run ahead of its performance in local elections. 'There were many people on the L.C.C., the Borough Council and the Board of Guardians who wanted shifting', he told a Labour meeting a month after he became M.P. One person who helped to do the shifting was Ruth. In the March 1925 local election, she captured one of the two Peckham L.C.C. seats, thereby launching herself on a long and distinguished career in London politics.

Meanwhile, Hugh busied himself as a constituency Member. At his selection he had promised to help set up a Labour Club. He was as good as his word: when he became M.P. he contacted a brewery, arranged a loan and saw that premises were obtained and a Club established. He took up many of the war pensions cases with which he was inundated, and he joined fellow M.P.s in pressing for a South London Tube.[2] He had a good eye for publicity. On one notable occasion, still remembered, he fought a three-round exhibition boxing match in Brunswick Park, Camberwell with the Rev. G. H. Potter, the 'fighting vicar' of St Chrysostom's, Peckham, in aid of hostels for homeless and wayward boys.[3]

In a poor inner London borough there were many problems involving housing. A letter written by a former constituent more than half a century later provides moving testimony of Dalton's effectiveness in this field:

I have a very big memory of him.
Year's ago in fact 1926 I was living in one room with a little girl 3 year's old and my Husband was out of work
You will recall they were bad time's
We were living over a shop in Old Kent Rd and at that time you had to get out when they were selling the shop.
I had one week to go with another baby. My Husband went to see Hugh Dalton for help.
He didn't hold much hope but told my Husband he would do his best.
He did just that he got us a house in Dagenham it was a long way from Old Kent Rd. But he did more than his best he gave me my first House.

My Baby was born the next week and we named the baby after him. But what with all the worry my baby died 7 weeks old.
I am now 72 and alone but I still tell people what Hugh Dalton done for me.
and I still Vote Labour.[4]

During the 1926 General Strike, Dalton arranged for Peckham Labour Party to turn Peckham Winter Gardens into a club for strikers and their families. Cheap meals were provided, paid for by the local party and by the M.P. personally.[5] At a rally on 9th May Dalton declared 'that he was sure the workers would shortly compel the Government to resume negotiations where they were broken off.'[6] Three days later the union leaders climbed down and the Strike ended in failure. However, there were benefits for Labour in Peckham. Party membership trebled between 1925 and 1926, and by 1928 the local party had 900 members, making it one of the biggest in the London area.[7]

Yet if in some ways Dalton was an exemplary constituency M.P., he was not a politically astute one. He wrote later that he had spent too much time in the constituency 'and had unwisely allowed myself to become too involved in the running of the Party organisation'. His mistake, he considered, was in allowing himself to be elected Chairman, as a result of which he became embroiled in 'personal difficulties and animosities' on the General Management Committee.[8] This was an understatement. The reality was a blazing row between the Member and his agent which split local activists into warring factions.

At first Dalton got on well with his agent, a milkman called Ernest Baldwyn. Ironically, Baldwyn's presence in the constituency had been one factor persuading him to stand. Very soon, however, friction began to develop. Within two weeks of his election Dalton was asking the trade union leader Arthur Creech Jones, who until recently had been secretary of Camberwell trades council, for a private talk to discuss local party problems. 'I hear rumours of personal difficulties', Dalton wrote cryptically, 'but I am satisfied that we are now in a strong position to overcome them.'[9] By the end of 1925 Dalton was noting privately that Baldwyn was admirable in many ways, 'but not in all'.[10]

Dalton's method of overcoming the 'personal difficulties' appears to have been heavy-handed to say the least. The precise nature of these difficulties is unclear, but they seem to have related to his anxieties about party organisation. Having decided that organisation needed a thorough overhaul, he arranged a purge of the whole machine, using his influence with the Labour Party National Agent,

Egerton Wake, to help bring this about. 'First Taylor to be got rid of from the Chairmanship of the Party, and replaced by myself', Dalton recorded when the heads had rolled. 'This is finally effected by bringing down Wake "to knock the chimney pots about"! Then Carter and the Goldsmith Ward. Finally he is removed by the Ward members themselves.'[11]

Not surprisingly a new M.P. who behaved in such a fashion made enemies. By 1926 Dalton was publicly on the defensive. A speech delivered at the Co-op Hall in Rye Lane in February included a strange and rather shrill passage that was meant as a reply to an attack. Somebody had apparently been accusing him of not doing his job. Plaintively, he declared that his record of attendance in the House was better than that of almost any other Member:

> He had voted in 428 out of 506 divisions ... He went through all the all-night sittings but one, and then he was away by agreement, when they were working in relays. He had nothing to apologise for. On the other hand, he had taken up a number of cases of war pensioners and housing, unemployment and so forth. He had not succeeded in getting the right thing done in all cases, but he had done his best and would go on trying. Another thing he had done was to take parties round the House of Commons. If anyone who had not done so liked to join such parties he would willingly arrange them.[12]

Who had been attacking him? It is clear that Dalton's strongest local critic was Baldwyn. According to King, the agent was motivated by an ambition to become M.P. for Peckham himself.[13] Whether or not this is correct Baldwyn's later behaviour suggests that he was a difficult and unstable character. Baldwyn, however, was not alone in his criticisms. Another veteran, J. H. Hopkins, gives a rather different explanation from that of King: some members of the Peckham constituency party apparently considered that Dalton had been foisted on them by Party headquarters. They also felt ill at ease with Dalton socially. 'He always smiled upon us benevolently', Hopkins recalls, 'in much the way a bishop smiles on his flock but we were left well aware that his father was a chaplain to Royalty.'[14]

A thrusting M.P. eager to knock chimney pots about; a disgruntled agent; a resentful and suspicious rank and file. It was an explosive mixture. Exactly what ignited it we do not know. All witnesses agree, however, that discontent was brought into the open by a violent altercation between Dalton and Baldwyn at a Labour Party Social Evening, involving a bottle of whisky and a raffle ticket. Dalton apparently showed his disapproval of the proceedings, and his agent reacted. Perhaps there was something in Dalton's tone or manner that grated; King, who liked Dalton, felt that the trouble might have arisen because the M.P. was 'a bit of a la-di-da'.[15] Whatever the precise cause, words were exchanged that could not be forgiven, and party members began to take sides.

By February 1928, two years after the first signs of serious trouble and with a new election on the horizon, Dalton was trying to get rid of his agent. 'This man is getting more and more impossible, but it is damned difficult to dislodge him', he noted. 'His reputation as a quarreller is well known in S.E. London.'[16] The Peckham party, though still growing rapidly, was now riven with feuds. The previous September two councillors and a member of the Board of Guardians had suddenly announced their resignation from the Labour Party and Club in what the local press described as a split among local members. 'Certain things have happened in the party', declared another councillor mysteriously, 'so those individuals have found it expedient to take the step mentioned.'[17] There was a crisis over the local elections, in which Ruth and the other Peckham Labour councillor were putting up again. Despite Hugh's eager efforts, local organisation was once again in disarray. Two wards were without secretaries, and canvassers were thin on the ground. Ruth came top of the poll with a greatly increased majority. But Dalton was full of recrimination against Baldwyn.

The agent, meanwhile, had taken steps to defend his own position. By mid-March, Ruth was picking up some extremely hostile rumours. 'R is very gloomy and thinks I may have to threaten resignation to get him out', Dalton noted. 'He has collected a clique round him, whose minds he is steadily poisoning against me.' Dalton countered by inviting a key party activist for lunch at the House of Commons, assailing him with food and geniality. 'I think he will be all right', the M.P. concluded, 'though he may be inclined to be timid if a row comes.'[18]

Dalton himself, however, was far from all right. He was becoming anxious and upset. At about this time he sent a local party member an extraordinary letter, later published in the local press, which indicates strongly that the problem of personalities revolved around the M.P.'s personality most of all. There was a note of hysteria, even a loss of balance:

Among the criticisms reported to me are that I am not a suitable representative for Peckham, that I neglect my Parliamentary duties, that (according to some) I go to the constituency too often and that (according to others) I do not go often enough, that my public speeches are 'nothing but cheap piffle', that 'I do not know what Socialism means', that I do not contribute enough money to the Party, that I have had £1,200 out of the workers since I have been in Parliament, that I waste the workers' money in luxury on the Riviera, that I pay for luncheons and teas for some members of the Party and not for others, that I 'listen to tittle-tattle', etc.

Some of these criticisms, and those who make them, are obviously beneath contempt. But if others, or even a small part of them, were justified, then the sooner the Party finds another representative the better.[19]

The climax came at two long sessions of the Peckham Executive on 26th and 27th April 1928. The first lasted until 1 a.m. 'For the first time in my life, almost, I don't sleep a wink', Dalton wrote afterwards. On the second night, hoping that the national leadership would step in on his side, he managed to get the affair referred to Party Headquarters. 'This is the beginning of the end of Baldwyn', he noted. He was now so obsessed with the problem that he could talk of little else. Button-holing the Co-op. leader W. H. Green, he announced over tea 'that unless Baldwyn goes, I shall go'.

This had now become his firm position. A small sub-committee of the N.E.C. Organisation committee – consisting of Herbert Morrison, Arthur Henderson and the railwaymen's leader C. T. Cramp – met Dalton, Baldwyn and two other local officers on 3rd May and again on 10th May to try to find a solution. Roundly denouncing Baldwyn as inefficient, disloyal, tactless and bad at handling Party members, Dalton declared that either he or his agent must depart. Baldwyn refused. The sub-committee suggested mildly that the two men should try to work together. But Dalton was adamant. So was Ruth. 'She loathes the prospect of continuance of a hairshirt', Hugh wrote.[20]

If Dalton believed that the National Executive would come to his rescue, he was disappointed. The sub-committee concluded that the agent had indeed been tactless and indiscreet. But it also blamed Dalton, suggesting that the M.P. 'in presiding at the Party meetings and becoming involved in local disputes had made himself far too accessible and had allowed himself to get involved too much in internal troubles and conflicts between the local people'.[21] Once again the sub-committee sought a reconciliation. Once more Dalton refused to budge. 'I told them my view', he recorded, 'that it was impossible to make a disloyal man loyal by talking to him, and that I had taken my political life in my hands before and could do so again, preferring to fight the enemy in the open rather than to be poisoned in a corner.'

As a last resort, Dalton offered cash: three months' salary, relief from any mortgage responsibility for the Club, and a testimonial. Baldwyn turned him down.

The issue was now clear-cut. Since no compromise had been achieved, it was a choice between the M.P. and his agent. 'My God, how it has dragged on and poisoned everything for months!' Dalton wrote on 14th June. 'I really wish, at times, that they would so vote and make my resignation inescapable!' A crucial meeting of the Peckham General Management Committee was held six days later, with 'packing and wangling on all sides'.[22] According to King, Baldwyn lobbied hard among the delegates, having arranged that the meeting should take place when many Daltonites were on holiday.[23]

The proceedings were formal and judicious, like a court of law. Dalton and Baldwyn each spoke in turn and left the room. Then, under the watchful eye of Cramp (for the N.E.C.), accompanied by the Labour Party London regional organiser, the G.M.C. considered its verdict. 'Dr. Dalton had made it quite clear in his address that the General Committee had that evening to decide whether they were going to retain Mr. Baldwyn as their agent or himself as their candidate', declared the official report. 'As far as he was concerned they certainly could not retain both.' Somebody moved the dismissal of Baldwyn. This was defeated by 22 votes to 19.[24] 'The meeting was unrepresentative, the R.A.C.S. [Royal Arsenal Co-operative Society] were one short, and several unions were not represented, who would have voted against B', Dalton observed. But the decision had been taken.

This was not quite the end. Dalton made no official announcement. The N.E.C., which had hitherto taken a studiously neutral line, tried to lean on Baldwyn. Even Sir Oswald Mosley spoke out against him, drawing attention to an allegedly nefarious past in the Birmingham area. It was suggested that the agent should once again be asked to resign. The Peckham G.M.C., however, refused to make such a request. By now Dalton was relieved. 'This anyhow frees me at last from an unwelcome mooring', he noted.[25] He waited until after the Shadow Cabinet election, lest the announcement should affect his vote, and then issued a press statement declaring his withdrawal at Peckham.

Dalton's decision to push the issue to a choice was in a way a brave one, and he never had cause to regret it. He very quickly acquired a new seat which he greatly preferred, and he was much better off without the 'hairshirt' of a troublesome local party. But it was a jolt to his self-confidence, involving a serious political risk. He might easily have found himself without a winnable constituency in time for the

1929 election, in which case he would almost certainly have been out of Parliament until 1935 if not permanently.

Peckham, indeed, revealed some of Dalton's most damaging political weaknesses – his impatience, his insensitivity, his over-reaction to criticism, his capacity for causing offence, and his real fear of people he identified as enemies. Later he acquired a reputation for intrigue. Peckham showed him at his conspiratorial worst: plotting coups, packing meetings, trying to buy off critics. By the end, he wanted to get out of Peckham. But the conditions that created this desire were partly of his own making.

The characteristics which Dalton displayed at Peckham reappeared in his subsequent career, especially after he became a minister. Baldwyn-figures cropped up repeatedly throughout his political life, becoming most irksome and threatening at times of new responsibility, high achievement, anxiety and overwork. What the Peckham episode showed most of all was a particular feature of Dalton's character that combined benefit and disadvantage: an over-abundance of energy. He was like a volcano erupting simultaneously through many seams. He tried to do too much. Peckham showed the limits of his stamina. To some extent his experience was bad luck, caused by a rotten apple. Dalton himself saw the problem entirely in these terms, repeatedly using the words 'poison' or 'poisoning' to describe Baldwyn's behaviour. Yet he was prone to suffer such accidents, generally against a background of exhilarating success.

If Dalton was the eventual winner, Peckham was the loser, as a result of the parting of ways. There was a bizarre sequel. Peckham Labour Party lurched from misfortune to disaster. Baldwyn was sacked as agent shortly afterwards. The candidacy which Dalton vacated went to John Beckett, already M.P. for Gateshead, a Maxtonite I.L.P.er. Beckett held Peckham for Labour in 1929, but stood for the rebellious I.L.P. against an official Labour candidate in 1931. Both lost, and Beckett joined Mosley in the British Union of Fascists. Meanwhile Baldwyn had joined the Conservative Party. A Peckham Labour Party rump, disaffiliated by the N.E.C., announced early in 1932 that it had decided to become a branch of the I.L.P.[26]

Dalton was not entirely forgotten in Peckham. 'Everyone was proud of him as he progressed', Hopkins recalled, 'and we boasted that Peckham gave him his first seat.'[27]

Dalton later recalled that Arthur Henderson had been doubtful about the wisdom of his move. 'I said I was fed up with Peckham and would risk it', Dalton had replied. In fact it was a gamble based on careful calculation. Before burning his boats, Dalton had already made inquiries about other constituencies. 'Nibbling towards Gateshead and Bishop Auckland', he had written. 'I think I prefer the former and also have more chance of getting it.'[28] Soon, he had settled his main attention on Bishop Auckland, in County Durham, where the sitting M.P., Ben Spoor, had announced his retirement in the middle of June. By the time that Dalton had declared his withdrawal at Peckham, his name was already being considered by the Bishop Auckland party. Meanwhile, Henderson wrote a letter of recommendation to the Durham Miners' leader Peter Lee, and encouraged the Chief Whip to use his influence on Dalton's behalf.[29]

In September, Dalton visited the constituency for a series of meetings and interviews, making the most of a distant local connection: in 1910 he had gone down the pit at Auckland Park colliery.[30] Having gained the crucial backing of the Durham miners, he was selected by the Bishop Auckland General Committee at the beginning of October. 'Clouds pass away', he wrote when he heard. 'My position, with a safe seat and a place on both Executives in this critical year, is a very strong one, come what may.'[31]

Yet Dalton very nearly lost the seat before he was elected. Two days after the House had risen for the Christmas recess, Ben Spoor died in mysterious circumstances at the Regent Palace Hotel in London. Dalton's whole political future was suddenly in jeopardy. A general election might not be held until the end of 1929. Dalton could only stand at a by-election in Bishop Auckland by resigning his seat at Peckham, thereby causing another contest. Since the prospective candidate in Peckham, John Beckett, was himself a refugee from another constituency where he was currently M.P., this would mean two extra by-elections. On the other hand, anybody else who took over as candidate in Bishop Auckland would scarcely want to give up the seat at a general election.

Fortunately the Bishop Auckland party, having picked a good and well known candidate, wanted to keep him. This was partly because Dalton's predecessor had been a considerable embarrassment. According to the pathologist at Spoor's inquest, the Bishop Auckland M.P. died of heart and liver disease, 'accelerated by chronic alcoholism'. Spoor's drink problem had become so severe that, suffering from delusions, he had been certified as insane and confined to a series of institutions.[32] During rational spells, he had caused dissension in the local party, precipitating his final departure.[33] Yet he had been much admired in earlier days.[34] Switching candidates had been distressing, and the Bishop Auckland party did not want to go through it again. It was against this background that constituency officers put forward a solution which Dalton, even at his most ingenious and artful, would never have dared to suggest. That it went through without a word of protest is a reminder of the discipline, and perhaps the deference, of delegates in mining constituencies in the 1920s.

Spoor died on 22nd December. Hugh and Ruth spent a tense and exhausting Christmas at Windsor with Hugh's parents. Hugh was in a state of turmoil. What steps could he take to forestall disaster? His mood was not helped by the Canon, deeply preoccupied and even tearful about the state of health of the King, who was recovering from a serious illness. On Boxing Day, Hugh and Ruth hurried back to London, and Hugh hastened north to attend Ben Spoor's funeral. As soon as the former M.P. was decently buried, local officials turned to the prospective candidate. It was true, they acknowledged, that various obstacles prevented Hugh Dalton from standing in the by-election. Nothing, however, prevented Ruth Dalton from doing so. Although they had only recently met Ruth, they liked and respected her, and she had sound credentials as a Labour L.C.C. councillor. More important, she could be relied upon to stand down as soon as Parliament was dissolved. 'They say they don't want any other warming-pan', Hugh wrote delightedly. 'They want to get people into the habit of voting Dalton.' Brushing aside a momentary hesitation about Ruth's health, which had recently been poor, he gave his enthusiastic assent. If Ruth herself had any doubts, a telephone call from Arthur Henderson urging her to stand helped to make up her mind.[35]

Two days later the whole matter was settled. Without Ruth even attending for interview, the seventy-strong General Committee in Bishop Auckland decided unanimously that she should become the by-election candidate. No other name was mentioned, and the 'selection' conference, according to the press, was 'marked by great enthusiasm and confidence'.[36] A weight was taken off Hugh's mind. His worst fears would not be realised. There would be no interruption in his career, and he could campaign for his wife happy in the knowledge that he would succeed her in a few months' time.

Ruth, tired and unwell at the start, soon recovered and fought a spirited campaign. With a general election pending, the by-election, held at the beginning of 1929, aroused much national interest, heightened by the presence of a woman candidate. The towns and villages that made up the Bishop Auckland division had been particularly hard hit by the gathering depression. The *Manchester Guardian* described the constituency as the most distressed in the Durham coalfield: 'Only the most stricken districts of South Wales can show a poverty more abject or more heartrending than you will find within a few miles radius of [the town of Bishop Auckland].'[37]

An I.L.P. reporter recorded evidence of malnutrition. 'Everywhere we saw children – poor pathetic little mites – with legs and arms like matchsticks, thin, white faces, and all their natural vitality sapped by a constant diet of bread and "marg".'[38] Others found communities of up to 7,000 inhabitants 'absolutely without earnings', and mines abandoned to flooding, with pit-top gear dismantled, thereby excluding the possibility of a colliery revival.[39]

Ruth toured the constituency, speaking in every village. At each meeting she covered one or two subjects closely and in depth. Philip Snowden, C. P. (who had become Sir Charles) Trevelyan and Arthur Henderson came to give support. Sir Oswald Mosley also made an appearance, lambasting the Government before an audience of 1,500 at the Shildon Hippodrome. At the meeting attended by Arthur Henderson, Ruth carefully explained party policy on child welfare and maternity.[40] The I.L.P. reporter was impressed by her manner, 'from which mushy sentiment and the clinging feminine touch are entirely absent'.[41]

Hugh, constantly by her side, provided a noisy accompaniment. 'There are two teams in the political cup final', he announced in response to rumours of a Tory–Liberal pact, 'Labour United and the Coalition Ramblers, and Labour United is going to win.' Labour, he proclaimed, intended to carry the Red Flag of Socialism to victory.[42] But Ruth did not always find him helpful. Once when she was asked a question at a meeting, Hugh rose to reply. 'You sit down', she told him sharply. 'I'm quite capable of answering it.'[43]

The result was not in doubt. Ruth increased the Labour share of the vote from 55 per cent in 1924 to 57 per cent and more than doubled the majority.[44] Afterwards she collapsed with fatigue and took several days to recover. 'That tooth treatment must really have done a lot, or she would have broken down simply!' Hugh noted. 'I am very proud of her.'[45]

Ruth's parliamentary career lasted barely three months. She was declared M.P. for Bishop Auckland on 8th February 1929, and the House was dissolved on 10th May. In between, she performed conscientiously and well. She had been deeply affected by what she had seen during the campaign. 'Everywhere we noticed women who looked haggard and ill,' Ruth wrote before her election, 'who were obviously facing semi-starvation themselves in order that their families might have, not enough (for no one has enough in the coalfields these days), but as much as possible, to eat.'[46] On 13th March she gave her maiden speech, describing her constituency 'where over 45 per cent of the miners are out of work, where many of the pits are not merely closed but dismantled, and where the despair and distress are appalling'. She called for boots, clothes and school meals for the children.[47] 'Listening to Eustace Percy's account of how no one was hungry, or ill clad, or depressed any more', Hugh noted, 'any nervousness she may have had turned to indignation.'[48] It was more than words and emotion: privately and anonymously Ruth sent parcels of clothing, blankets, books and shoes for distribution among her constituents.[49] But she did not like Parliament, did not want to stay there, had no desire to return, and was glad to leave as soon as her mission – as a stop-gap – had been accomplished.

Hugh's own election as M.P. for Bishop Auckland was an anti-climax. It was his sixth contest, and the first time that his victory had been assured. He won the seat with a majority of 8,203 over the Liberal.[50] Except in 1931–5 he held it for the rest of his political life and never wanted to move again.

Peckham was an amorphous London constituency with little identity. Bishop Auckland, by contrast, had strong local and regional loyalties, based on the pits. It did not take Dalton long to become passionately interested and involved in the life of an area of which he had previously known nothing. The spectacle of misery in the Durham coalfields fired his idealism and gave him the sense of a challenge.

The poverty of the small towns and villages of south-west Durham – communities like Shildon, Evenwood, Coundon, West Auckland – was more hopeless and depressing than further north, even in Gateshead and Jarrow. At least on Tyneside, with the river and the continuing trade which it provided, there was always the chance of a job. In the pit villages everybody except the vicar and the teacher depended on the colliery and when that closed there was nothing. It was not uncommon for mining families on the dole to live for long periods solely off the produce of their gardens, apart from tea and bread.[51] In 1936 when the worst of the Depression was over, Dalton reported in Parliament that nearly 50 per cent of the insured population in his constituency were unemployed; that 80 per cent of these had had no work for a year; and that in some areas 90 per cent were without jobs.

Dalton was never in doubt about the solution. From the beginning he saw the necessity of positive state action to bring in new industries. 'Private enterprise, left to itself', he declared, 'would let all these communities perish.'[52] It was a belief that guided him for the rest of his life. No other north-east M.P. since the introduction of universal suffrage has ever done more to remedy or mitigate the chronic economic blight of the region. When, in the 1940s, he became President of the Board of Trade and then Chancellor of the Exchequer he made full use of his powers to revitalise the economic structure of the pre-war Distressed Areas. His achievement as the architect of regional policy, based on direct experience as a County Durham M.P., is not often remembered today. Locally, however, there are many older members of the community who recall his success in bringing factories to an area that desperately needed them. 'I always said he deserved a monument as high as Nelson's column for what he did for this region', comments one former miners' agent in Bishop Auckland.[53] In the Bishop Auckland division itself the West Auckland and St Helen's Trading Estates, and a range of new light industries – Ernest and Henry, Lewins, Bond-Malding, Alligator, Westool – would never had been established without Dalton's direct intervention, as M.P. for the constituency before the Second World War, and later as a minister.

If the north-east benefited from Dalton, Dalton also gained much from his connection with the north-east. County Durham provided him with a powerful political base and one which allowed him to get on with the job. For a middle-class southerner, the backing of the miners and of the important northern group of Labour M.P.s was a vital source of strength. M.P.s and miners' leaders such as Will Lawther, Jack Lawson, Will Whiteley and Sam Watson became his friends and allies. His own presence at the Durham Miners' Gala became an annual attraction, reinforcing the support of one of the most influential trade unions in the Labour Movement.

Almost as important as the backing of the miners was the support of a constituency party which gave him no trouble and made few demands on his time. Dalton was always quick and efficient in dealing with local problems. He did not, however, believe in spending more time in his constituency than was absolutely necessary, and his visits were widely spaced. His normal practice was to arrive at the start of the parliamentary recess and work hard for about four weeks, addressing meetings. In between these visitations, his appearances were infrequent.[54] At no time did he either buy or rent accommodation in the constituency. After 1931 he spent spare weekends in a newly acquired house in Wiltshire – a habit which seems to have caused no complaint.

At first Dalton did not have an agent, preferring to work through the constituency secretary, Will Davis, an elementary schoolmaster, at whose homes (first in Bishop Auckland itself, and then in St Helen's), he usually stayed during his brief visits. Dalton found Davis loyal, reliable and efficient. An added virtue was that Davis accepted Dalton's principle, born of the Peckham experience, that a healthy party was an inactive one. As a former regional official put it, 'the less Will gathered the party together, the happier he was'.[55] The same applied

1 (*left*) Royal tutor. John Neale Dalton in 1882, the year of the return of H.M.S. *Bacchante*. 2 (*centre*) Hugh's mother, Kitty.
3 (*right*) The Canon at eighty.

4 Hugh's birthplace. The Gnoll, Glamorgan, photographed in 1908.

5 (*left*) The infant Hugh, with his father and Dalton grandmother.
6 (*centre*) Sailor boy.   7 (*right*) Off to prep school, aged eleven.

8 'Is dancing sexual?' Fabian School at Llanbedr in 1907. Far left, James Strachey; two to the right, Marjorie Olivier; leaning against the fireplace, Rupert Brooke.

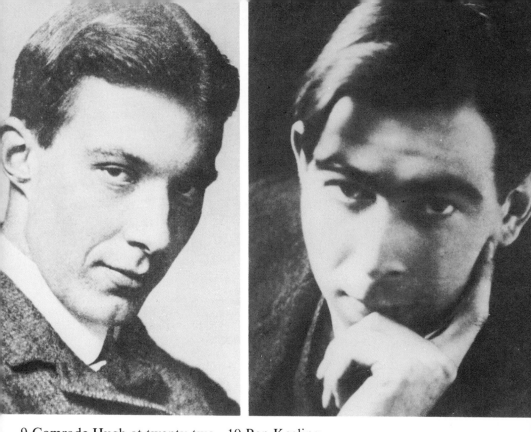

9 Comrade Hugh at twenty-two. 10 Ben Keeling.

11 Rupert Brooke with Brynhild Olivier in the New Forest, 1908.

12 (*left*) Hugh and Ruth at Virginia Water, April 1915.
13 (*right*) Newly weds. Hugh and Ruth (seated in chair) with
Georgie on 27th June 1914, the day before Sarajevo.

14 Ruth with Arthur Peterson's dog, in the garden at Hurtwood
Edge, April 1914.

Bombardiering: 15 (*above*) In Alpine uniform. 16 (*right*) With a fellow officer, 1917.

17 Dalton's gun (a 6-inch howitzer) and the men who fired and transported it.

TRENTINO

18 (*left*) Hugh and daughter, probably during the summer of 1919.
19 (*right*) Helen a month before her fourth birthday.

20 'How the fellow stinks of money and insincerity!' Sir Oswald
Mosley M.P. and supporters in his Smethwick constituency, just
before taking office in the 1929 Labour administration.

21 (*left*) Maynard Keynes and Lydia Lopokova on their wedding day in 1925. 22 (*right*) Stafford Cripps, K.C. in 1929.

23 Party Conference at the Dome, Brighton in September 1929. Dalton sits behind the table five from the right. Behind him, Lord and Lady Passfield (Sidney and Beatrice Webb), Beatrice in a beehive hat.

24 Colleagues. Dalton talks to Harold Laski at the Southport Party Conference in 1934.

to Dalton. 'I don't want a big party', he told one local officer, after Davis had ceased to be secretary. 'Too many members might upset the apple-cart and bring in militants.' Sometimes a year would pass without a single Executive meeting. Prodded by regional office in Newcastle, Davis would reply that the Executive did not need to meet because there was nothing to discuss.

That was in the 1930s; during the following decade meetings became less frequent still. In 1948 there were twenty active members of the Bishop Auckland constituency party at most. The entire individual membership could be listed on one sheet of foolscap, and only one local party, Shildon, was really functioning. The General Management Committee barely existed and never met. The Labour Party expanded nationally during the 1930s and 1940s, apart from a brief decline early in the war. In Bishop Auckland, membership contracted – a development which seems to have bothered Dalton very little.[56]

Will Davis acted as the M.P.'s eyes and ears, reporting gossip and relaying requests and instructions. People would contact Davis when they wanted Dalton to take something up, and Dalton would pass people on to Davis if they were interested in investing or setting up factories locally. During and after the Second World War a number of European Jewish refugees found their way into the Bishop Auckland business community through this connection.

Davis was not, however, the most powerful local personality. The dominating figure in Bishop Auckland was a station master and former train driver, J. R. S. Middlewood, who was for many years leader of the council. 'Uncle Bob' Middlewood's relationship to civic affairs was based on a mixture of paternalism and patronage that had long been the hallmark of County Durham politics. Feared and respected, Middlewood ruled Bishop Auckland council through a network of personal contacts and a system of favours given and received. 'If Uncle Bob recommended you for something, you got it', was an accepted local principle.[57] On the other hand, if Uncle Bob took seriously against you, life could be very hard indeed. One young Labour councillor for Escomb had the Labour Whip withdrawn because he left the room at a council meeting without permission from Middlewood in the Chair.[58]

Unfortunately Middlewood disliked and despised Will Davis, and the rivalry between the two was a factor with which Dalton had to contend. Middlewood accused Davis of being a covert Liberal, and (with some justice) of not earning his party secretary's £50 honorarium.[59] The real problem lay deeper: a difference of class and education, and a difference of temperament. Middlewood was strong-willed and forceful. Davis was subtle and persuasive. Middlewood was also jealous of Davis's special relationship with the M.P., which he felt was ill-deserved. Dalton's only open clashes with Middlewood were over the inadequacies, real or imagined, of Davis. Dalton always defended his friend loyally, but he also took care to placate Middlewood, establishing what one of Middlewood's associates called an 'armed truce', with clearly defined limits of power and influence.[60]

It was an odd, but effective arrangement. Meanwhile there were key areas of co-operation. On the one hand there was 'Mr Bishop Auckland', and on the other 'Huge' Dalton, or 'Hughie' as the miners called him, the olympian figure with the national reputation who fixed things in London and did not meddle in council affairs. The Dalton–Middlewood nexus was a vital link, of immense practical importance to the people of Bishop Auckland, tying together two political spheres. But it was never a personal friendship.

By contrast, the Davis household provided Dalton with emotional support as well as a constituency base – especially at the Davis's new home, the Manor House in St Helen's. Dalton stayed here regularly for twenty-one years and was treated as one of the family. He liked the feeling of space: he would stride up and down his large bedroom and throw the door open proudly declaiming 'This is *my* room!', much to Mrs Davis's delight. Mrs Davis became accustomed to his irregular and unpredictable habits. He would often turn up without warning, bringing several people with him and then sit round the table talking into the early hours. In the morning he would lie in and take his breakfast in bed. Sometimes he spent half the day in his pyjamas, rambling about the kitchen, and talking to the odd-job man and the cleaning lady. Mrs Davis became quite fond of him, though she always found his habits perplexing. 'He'd never been trained to behave in the house', she reflects. 'The eiderdown and blankets would be all over the place.' For some reason – never explained – the M.P. developed an almost phobic dislike of the Davises' dog, which he abused on sight and which always had to be removed from his presence.[61]

The hostility between Bob Middlewood and Will Davis was personal rather than political. Yet it was also a symptom of the rivalry that existed among three key groups within the local party: the railwaymen, the teachers, and the miners. As in most working-class constituency parties before the 1950s, the main divisions in the Bishop Auckland party were based on occupation and geography rather than on ideology. Will Davis, a miner's son who became a headmaster, had links with two groups, though he was generally associated with the teachers. The most important split, however, separated the working-class factions. Until after Dalton ceased to be M.P. the constituency was divided, sometimes bitterly, between the railwaymen of Shildon and the mining communities of Bishop Auckland town, West Auckland, Cockfield, Coundon and Evenwood.

Dalton rightly regarded the miners as most vital. The miners were more numerous than the railwaymen and better organised: they could swamp a local party meeting before a crucial vote and wipe out opposition. Each miners' lodge represented a separate fiefdom and Dalton took care to be on good terms with all of them. It was said that Jo Gordon of the Leasingthorpe Lodge, a devoted supporter of 'good old Hughie', could be relied on for a dozen votes on the constituency General Committee if ever the need arose. However, the power of Middlewood's railwaymen could not be neglected either. Dalton kept in touch with leading Shildon men like Charlie Gibson, Maurice Mason and Bill Walker, as well as Uncle Bob himself. When he was in the constituency, Dalton would make a regular practice of holding dinner-time meetings at the Shildon Railway Depot, drawing big crowds.

The teachers, of whom Will Davis was most prominent, were not a faction in the same sense, having no geographical base and little cohesion. Nevertheless they exercised an important influence. Ironically this was a product of the entrenched power in county affairs of men like Middlewood. The County Durham educational system was highly politicised, with key appointments in the hands of the Labour Party machine. Candidates for headships were allowed to canvass members of the education committee before an interview, and membership of the Labour Party was regarded as a prerequisite for any ambitious member of the profession. As a result, teachers formed a sizeable, though disunited, block within the local Labour Party – arousing jealousy and distrust among working-class members. It was often said that when you saw a teacher in the Party, you should beware. 'He was there until he got his headship, and then that was all you ever saw of him.'[62] Later on, hostility towards the teachers became political as well: in the Bevanite battles, teachers tended to be on the left (Davis was an exception), while most miners and railwaymen, though divided on other matters, sided with the right. As the mining domination was eroded in the early 1950s with the closure of local pits, so the teacher-led left wing grew in influence.

Until 1948 Dalton was resolutely opposed to having a paid agent, because of his experience in Peckham. Boundary changes proposed in that year, however, seemed to undermine the safety of the seat by turning a compact constituency into a larger and more rural one, including Teasdale and the town of Barnard Castle. Dalton was therefore persuaded to take on Tom Anderson, 'quiet, modest, very capable and loyal', a former rate collector who was currently agent for the nearby constituency of Blaydon.[63] The appointment was in one sense a success. Taking over a moribund party with no regular meetings, Anderson turned it into one of the most active in the region, lifting individual party membership to almost 2,000 in less than a year. By the time of the 1950 election, there were local parties functioning in every district, and ten women's sections.[64]

However, as in Peckham, expansion of the local party brought troubles in its wake. Improved organisation helped to produce a surprisingly good result in the 1950 election. But it also helped to create, for the first time, political differences between the M.P. and his party – coinciding as it did with the rise of the Left (later the Bevanites) nationally. Dalton's own position as M.P. was never in danger. But he found himself in the early 1950s facing a left-orientated Executive and needing, as never before, to take the opinions of his local party into account.

Anderson remembers Dalton with guarded affection. 'He was the shiftiest man I ever knew', the former agent maintains, 'but he was the best fellow to work with.' Dalton would take him to lunch with prominent people in the constituency or the county, saying, 'You know Tom, if you are present, you can see that everything is above board'. On this Anderson sometimes had private doubts. But he was amused by Dalton's platform tricks. One was to arrange to have a microphone in front of him before a speech, and then begin in a loud voice, 'Take this damned thing away, Tom. I don't need it.'[65] There was also another game:

> At any public meeting he would insist on me being at his side, and after he had made his speech, he would call me over – all 5 feet 5 inches of me against his 6 foot 4 inches – and say to the audience 'This is Tom Anderson – you all know him, don't you – well he's the fellow that bosses me about and tells me what I've got to do.'

Anderson found Dalton's method of running the constituency less endearing. There was a refusal to brook opposition, a strong paranoid streak, and temperamental outbursts, especially during election campaigns. Most trying, however, was an aspect which suggests that Dalton did not entirely learn his lesson at Peckham:

If there was any intrigue you could be sure Dalton would have a hand in it. He was always crafty enough to use other people. Even in his constituency he had his 'informers'. They were found jobs on New Town Development Boards – Personnel Managers on the Industrial Estates he had set up, and he made certain that they became the Constituency Party officers.[66]

This was a reference, in particular, to Will Davis, who would never have received the O.B.E. in 1947, gained a place on the Board of the Aycliffe Development Corporation, or acquired the somewhat surprising job of Welfare Officer for the West Auckland Clothing Company without Dalton's personal intervention.

Yet if some felt unsure about Dalton, in general he was regarded with a mixture of awe, affection, amusement, gratitude and pride. He was an alien and mysterious figure, big, loud, imposing and eccentric. But he had a genuine love for the area and warmth towards its people, and they enjoyed his company. He was also a man of national importance who took a practical interest in local problems and delivered on promises. Gentry were still powerful in semi-rural Durham, and traditional attitudes died hard. Although Dalton was unrestrained in attacks on Tories, his local style was more that of a patrician grandee than of a tribune of the people. His relations with his constituents, and with his constituency party, could be summed up in two words: mutual loyalty. He served them faithfully while remaining his own master. Edmund Burke, scorned by Dalton in *Inequality of Incomes*, would certainly have approved.

XIII

Towards the Peace
of Nations

Dalton's socialism came from within himself – from his own emotions and intellect – rather than from experience of the problems socialist policies were intended to solve. Windsor and King's had a greater impact upon him than any awareness of slums or malnutrition. Not until his mid-thirties did he acquire first-hand knowledge of working-class conditions, and then only from the standpoint of a candidate and M.P. By contrast, his interest in foreign affairs stemmed from direct involvement in the tragedy which he hoped that future foreign policy would prevent: the slaughter and suffering of war. The losses among friends, the privations of fighting men and civilian populations, the bigotry of senior officers, the callous arbitrariness of War Cabinet and High Command – these had a tangible reality, which provided the spur to Dalton's fiercest political feelings and hence to his most pressing ambition.

Dalton would later claim that he had had no strong preference between the fields of foreign and economic policy, and that he had viewed with equal enthusiasm the prospect of an appointment in either. We may disbelieve him. It is true that he acquired an expert knowledge in both fields which most politicians would have envied in just one of them. Yet there are many indications that his protestation was false: that – despite his interest in inequality and his training in public finance – his first hopes, from the moment he entered Parliament and perhaps ever since Caporetto, were directed at the Foreign Office.

We have seen how, as early as 1922, Arthur Henderson had tipped him as Foreign Secretary in a future Labour Government. During the 1924 Parliament, he was increasingly mentioned in the same connection. Examining alternative Labour candidates for the Foreign Secretaryship in the autumn of 1928, the writer on international affairs H. N. Brailsford mentioned four names: Henderson, Mosley, the N.U.R. leader J. H. Thomas, and Dalton. The front runners, in Brailsford's opinion, were Henderson and Dalton. Dalton, he wrote, 'would be an admirable choice, if any "intellectual" may aspire in the Labour Party to a post of this importance'.[1] Such an assessment was, indeed, no accident. Over the preceding three-and-a-half years, in his speeches and writings, Dalton had devoted more attention to the problems of defence and foreign policy than to any other topic.

During this period, he had made the currently fashionable subject of disarmament his speciality.[2] At first, he had appeared to follow a tradition which A. J. P. Taylor has since aptly labelled that of the 'Dissenters'. Dalton accepted much of the analysis of E. D. Morel and the old Union for Democratic Control, and he had been greatly influenced by his Cambridge mentor, Lowes Dickinson, whose book *War: Its Nature, Cause and Cure* placed equal blame for the First World War on belligerents of both sides.[3]

'They all clung to a simple proposition', Taylor has written of the inter-war Dissenters, 'if there were no armaments, there would be no war'.[4] Morel and Dickinson believed that a rational foreign policy should seek agreement to reduce and eventually abolish artillery weapons, military aircraft, tanks and battleships. So did Dalton, and at first there seemed no reason to hold any other view. Germany posed no immediate threat. It was hard to imagine the Soviet Union, pre-occupied with internal problems, as an aggressor. Yet the horror and the guilt of 1914–18 left a universal obsession with war and a lingering sense of foreboding. The lack of an identifiable foreign danger focussed attention on the danger within: the threat presented by the capitalist system, by arms dealers and manufacturers, by imperialist competition, above all by the inertia or hypocrisy of governments in their relations with neighbours.

During his first Parliament, most of Dalton's foreign policy speeches urged the more vigorous pursuit of disarmament. In 1926 Dalton argued that the size of the German Navy should be taken as a maximum for other nations, and as a starting point for further reductions 'verging towards complete and total disarmament which alone is the final solution of this problem'. In 1927 he deplored an apparent lack of Government initiative in not seeking to limit war materials directly. In 1928 he attacked 'the doctrine of what are called British requirements' for naval armaments (that is, a minimum size and strength for the Navy, below which no further reduction might be considered), and he criticised increased spending on the air force. In all his speeches he drew attention, following Morel, to the vested interests of capitalist arms manufacturers – a theme which he was able to link his attack on inherited wealth.[5]

Yet alongside these conventionally progressive views, there began to develop a streak of anti-Germanism that increasingly divided him from fellow disarmers. A major influence was a trip to Poland in the summer of 1926, which led him to write a powerful article calling for a new approach to the problem of eastern Europe. Dalton noticed, in particular, Polish fears of Germany. 'There is a much stronger case to be made for the present German–Polish frontier than progressive British opinion commonly recognises', he wrote.[6] It was this visit to Poland, he later recalled, 'which finally determined me to try to re-write the Foreign Policy of the Labour Party', in order to shift it away from its current anti-French, pro-German mould.[7] At the time, he declared that it was 'a false and futile line of approach to post-war problems' to suggest that a revision of the Polish frontier in Germany's favour was a necessary condition of future peace in Europe.[8]

Dalton's article was based on a sober analysis of the minority question. Yet it contained something more: a negative emotion towards Germany. We have seen how, as an officer in the war, Dalton had developed feelings of animosity towards Germans. The mood of the British Left in the 1920s required him to keep these feelings muted, but they helped to form his attitudes on key issues all the same. They also found expression in his private comments. When he visited Danzig, though he liked some of the Germans he met, he wrote disparagingly of German 'paunches and snouts'. 'How fat, ugly and badly got up these Germans are', he noted after one social event.[9] His impression of Germans as individuals reflected his views on Germans as a nation. Dalton blamed armaments for the slaughter of the First World War. But he also blamed Germany. In the course of his travels in central and eastern Europe during the 1920s, he acquired a sympathy for past and future victims of German expansionism which turned him into a pro-Latin, pro-Slav, anti-Teuton partisan to an extent that was to bewilder and offend other internationalists among his contemporaries.

The themes of disarmament, suspicion of arms manufacturers, and support for the 1919 frontier settlement, were combined in a book entitled *Towards the Peace of Nations* which Dalton finished writing at the end of 1927. Inspired by visits to Italy, Poland, Danzig, Dalmatia and particularly Geneva, home of the League of Nations, and drawing on the works of Keynes (with whom he disagreed about the Versailles Treaty), Dickinson, Laski, MacDonald, Noel-Baker, Alfred Zimmern and especially, Brailsford,[10] Dalton blamed commercial greed, poor statesmanship and lack of international organisation for the events of 1914. He also looked at ways in which a future war might be averted. His central demand was for a 'strong' League of Nations policy. He called for a League equipped with the economic and military weapons necessary to police the world and punish those who broke the rules.

This book was in sharp contrast to other radical works on war and peace written at the time. Superficially deferential to the liberal-minded, it was actually a blast against those who regarded the Treaty of Versailles as unfair to the Central Powers. It was also a blast against those who argued that the League existed only to 'stabilise capitalism', those who were more hostile towards France and Britain than towards Germany, and those who called for a general strike against war or for 'disarmament by example'. Taylor has suggested that the Labour Party condemned the Versailles settlement even before it was made.[11] Dalton did not condemn the Versailles settlement. On the contrary. In this scholarly but highly political book, he put forward a powerful case for a reprieve.

A strong theme was that the boundaries drawn at Versailles, bitterly criticised by liberal writers, needed to be defended. They were, the author suggested, 'very much less imperfect than the old', and reflected political and national realities. He took issue with 'certain peace-lovers' who spoke 'as though they would like to take a knife and re-partition Poland and hand back to a re-created Austria-Hungary all the Slavs and Rumanians who since 1918 have slipped away into their own national States ... ' Few countries would voluntarily relinquish territory. The attempt to force them to do so would itself lead to war. The root cause of international tensions was not the existence of unfair or unrealistic frontiers, but economic and other factors that cut across them. 'The only practical and wise starting point of immediate policy is to take existing frontiers for granted and to aim not towards their revision, but towards their obliteration.' It was important to avoid what Dalton called 'the cult of pet lambs': championing the impracticable demands of national minorities. Since the national minorities presenting the biggest problem were German, the implication was clear. There should be no territorial concessions to Germany.[12]

Dalton had returned from a trip to Geneva in the summer of 1925 a passionate advocate of the League. He now wrote that he saw the League as a tool, whose value depended on who used it. It was admittedly a poor tool. 'But it is the best we have, and the best the world has ever had, as an instrument of international co-operation.' Hence Britain should sign the so-called 'Optional Clause', pledging itself to submit all legal disputes to the International Court at the Hague. Hence too the League should be used as a means to disarmament all round and as an instrument for ensuring the security of smaller nations. National air forces should be abolished and replaced by an international air force under the control of the League's Council. The teeth should be kept well covered; but they were a necessary prerequisite of any serious move towards disarmament. [13]

Dalton paid lip-service to the view that Germany was less culpable or dangerous than sinister international capitalist forces. He advocated the nationalisation of arms manufacture in order to reduce capitalist resistance to disarmament. His position on immediate issues of foreign policy was not seriously at odds with that of other left-internationalists. Like them he believed in the urgent need to reduce arms and to achieve agreement through the League. But his opposition to frontier changes and his faith in the ultimate sanction of force made the step from disarmament by agreement to collective security through the League, and ultimately to rearmament, natural and logical once Hitler had come to power and the international situation had turned sharply for the worse.

Dalton received advance copies of *Towards the Peace of Nations* in January 1928, just as the Peckham crisis was entering its critical phase. He immediately distributed them to people he wished to impress – Arthur Henderson, Sir Charles Trevelyan, Ramsay MacDonald, Jimmy Clynes, C. T. Cramp (among the top Labour leadership), Philip Noel-Baker, Will Arnold-Forster, Goldie Lowes Dickinson and Arthur Ponsonby (representing the intellectual internationalists), Allyn Young, Theodore Gregory and Lionel Robbins (at the L.S.E.). The response was mixed. MacDonald, always made uneasy by expertise in others, was hostile. 'Can you tell me why Dalton wrote this book?' he asked Noel-Baker. 'It is to make the Party think that he is an authority on foreign policy. But he is not.' [14]

Despite the attitude of the Party Leader, the book succeeded in building Dalton's reputation as a spokesman on foreign affairs within the P.L.P. and helped him to achieve a key ambition: a Foreign Office portfolio, though not the Foreign Secretaryship, in the next Labour Government. The May 1929 general election brought Labour back to office with 288 seats in the House of Commons but no overall majority, once again under the premiership of Ramsay MacDonald. Dalton's appointment did not immediately follow this victory. After his own election in Bishop Auckland, he returned to London by train and sat impatiently by the telephone waiting for a call that did not come. Leading ministers were announced – Henderson at the Foreign Office, Snowden at the Treasury, Clynes as Home Secretary, J. H. Thomas as

Lord Privy Seal, even Mosley as Chancellor of the Duchy of Lancaster – but there was no mention of Dalton's name. 'To wirepull or not to wirepull?' he wrote. 'I decide not to wirepull.'[15] He quickly changed his mind, however, and began to angle for a post – in the end, almost any post – in the new administration. It was a busy and anxious week. 'One thing that amuses me is that the politicians are not very modest', Walter Citrine, General Secretary of the T.U.C., noted on 5th June. 'Dalton, I believe, has been living on the premises of the Labour Party Office since he returned from the country.'[16]

Among the new Government's 'Big Five', Dalton was backed for a place in the Cabinet by Clynes and Henderson – but opposed by the Prime Minister, Snowden and Thomas, which ruled him out. When it became clear that he could hope for only a second ranking post, he wrote to Henderson saying that the only two jobs that really attracted him were Financial Secretary at the Treasury and Under-Secretary at the Foreign Office, 'the latter especially under him'. Meanwhile, Dalton had written to Trevelyan saying that 'faute de mieux, I would be glad to serve under him at the Board [of Education]'. But he was spared this humiliation: at Henderson's insistence, MacDonald offered him the job which, after a post in the Cabinet, he most wanted. In a little ceremony at No. 10 Downing Street the Prime Minister, formally and rather dourly, asked him to take the Foreign Office Under-Secretaryship. Dalton, deeply relieved and almost grateful, replied that this was the field that interested him most. 'In other departments I have intellectual interests and social sympathy, but here a passion', he said.[17]

Henderson was in many ways an ideal Foreign Secretary. He could be difficult and cantankerous, and was at times bitterly resentful of his lifelong rival Ramsay MacDonald. Yet he was a powerful member of the Cabinet because of his strength within the Party, which he had helped to build and whose mood he seemed to embody. It was said that when he spoke of the Labour Movement you could hear the capital 'M'.[18] He had an iron will, he was a shrewd judge of men, and the workings of his mind were wholly mysterious to his officials. The nick-name 'Uncle' contained an element of wariness: his bear-like qualities inspired awe as well as affection. There was nobody in politics apart from Churchill whom Dalton ever admired so much.

Henderson seemed one of the few real successes in the doomed second Labour administration, and his stature rose by the month. Nevertheless his two years of office produced almost nothing of lasting importance. Nobody was to blame for this. In retrospect, the diplomacy that preceded the end of the Weimar Republic in Germany has a Chekhovian air – overshadowed by a future event which the actors

could scarcely have prevented even if they had foreseen it. The international deliberations of this twilight time seem neither sensible nor
foolish but sadly irrelevant.

Current preoccupations were with security, arbitration and disarmament. Dalton had long urged the previous Tory Government to
pursue disarmament. Now he was a member of a Government that
had made disarmament a primary objective. Was it really possible?
There has certainly never been as much agreement among the Great
Powers about its desirability. Yet with hindsight it is hard to see the
wholesale abandonment of navies and air forces by major powers as
other than fantasy. Arbitration and security were perhaps more
realistic aims. Henderson and Dalton were, indeed, confident of their
ability, through the League of Nations, to create both. Alas, they
failed to achieve either.

There was, however, an illusion of achievement, in which Dalton
for a time fervently believed. Early in 1931, he wrote in his diary that
the Government had done everything in the international policy
section of Labour's 1928 programme *Labour and the Nation* except
bring about disarmament.[19] After the Government fell, he published
an article in *Political Quarterly* which contrasted the dark days under
Henderson's Conservative predecessor, Austen Chamberlain, with the
progress he claimed had followed.

Labour's position before the 1929 election had been simple, Dalton
argued: the Party had been committed to pursuing disarmament and
supporting the League. 'Within five months of taking office', he
boasted, 'the Labour Government, by a series of bold strokes, had
changed the whole face of world politics.' In August 1929 Henderson
negotiated the complete evacuation of the Rhineland five years ahead
of schedule. In September Britain had sent the strongest delegation
ever to the League Assembly in Geneva. Meanwhile Henderson had
signed the Optional Clause, encouraging the dominions to do the
same, leaving only a small number of member states outside the ring
of those accepting compulsory arbitration. In October MacDonald
had visited the United States, helping to bring about the naval reductions eventually achieved at the London Conference. In November,
ambassadors had been exchanged with Moscow, improving Anglo-
Soviet relations.

These gains, Dalton continued, were consolidated over the next
twenty months. From the London Naval Conference at the beginning
of 1930 there had emerged the Three Power Treaty, which ended
competitive building between the three greatest Naval Powers for at
least five years. Later in the same year the Preparatory Commission
had been able with British encouragement to produce the framework

for a Disarmament Treaty which the Imperial Conference had subsequently approved. As a culmination, the date of the Disarmament Conference had been fixed for February 1932, with Arthur Henderson unanimously chosen by the League Council as President – clear evidence of the ability of the Labour Foreign Secretary to win the trust of foreign leaders.[20]

This was Dalton's picture: a two-year holiday from Tory muddle and short-sightedness, in which solid progress had been made. As things appeared at the time, there was some justification for it. The Government was, indeed, as lucky in its foreign relations, suffering no serious mishaps during its period of office, as it was unlucky at home. Labour had been fortunate to take power at a time when, in the words of one historian, 'the post-war peace settlement and international good will were at high tide'.[21] That the tide would shortly recede, obliterating all apparent advances, was not something that was predictable in 1931.

How much of the short-term progress, impressive on paper and in the eyes of contemporary statesmen, was due to Dalton? Henderson was without doubt greatly influenced by his Parliamentary Under-Secretary. Dalton was the leader of a team of middle- and upper-class intellectual experts who gave the inexpert Foreign Secretary crucial advice. Henderson had picked Noel-Baker, newly elected, as his Parliamentary Private Secretary, and a renegade Tory aristocrat with internationalist leanings, Lord Cecil, as an adviser on League of Nations questions. In addition, Will Arnold-Forster, an old friend of Dalton who was married to Rupert Brooke's one-time girlfriend Ka Cox, became Cecil's secretary. At a time when the strongest internationalist influences were liberal in origin or tradition, it was a peculiarity that three members of the team – Dalton, Cecil, Arnold-Forster – came from strongly Tory families. It was also an oddity that three – Dalton, Noel-Baker and (indirectly) Arnold-Forster – were linked to the pre-war Carbonari set at King's. Henderson worked closely with this team, and the combination of expert skills and political commonsense that resulted was a major reason for the smooth running of foreign policy during the two years of the administration.

The biggest burden of work fell on the shoulders of the junior minister, who had continuous access to the Foreign Secretary. An interesting assessment of Dalton's role was provided by Mary Agnes (Molly) Hamilton, a talented journalist and Labour M.P. who wrote a biography of Arthur Henderson. Dalton was a member of the British delegations to the League Assembly in 1929 and 1930, and it was during these visits that the Daltons and Mrs Hamilton became friends. Mrs Hamilton recalled Dalton at this time as a minister who played a major part in the shaping of foreign policy:

> No one could charge Hugh with having a thin skin; it is not a
> quality he admires or comprehends. He is the complete extrovert;
> he loves the political rough and tumble, the shouting and the fight.
> But ... I am sure that ambition is harnessed firmly to conviction; I
> have known him make great sacrifices for that. Moreover his real
> manners are much better than his superficial ones. There are not
> many under-secretaries who do not themselves suggest, or allow
> their wives to suggest, that the speeches of their chiefs were, in fact,
> written by him, and their better actions of his inspiration. Not so
> Hugh. Always he gave entire credit to Uncle Arthur for a success
> between 1929 and 1931 to which his own contribution was, actually,
> very important.[22]

According to Mrs Hamilton, the Foreign Secretary committed to
Dalton 'an unusually large share of responsibility over the detailed
working of the Office, and in the handling of papers'. Henderson had
no head for detail. Dalton supplied him with the facts and arguments
he needed. The Foreign Secretary was also an indifferent debater.
Dalton made up for this deficiency in the House.[23]

Dalton was, indeed, an increasingly impressive parliamentary
speaker. He was clear, confident and in complete command of his
brief. He had also perfected a style that aimed to infuriate Tories by
patronising them. 'As the son of the Canon of Windsor he thinks it is
enormous fun to treat the entire Tory party with the air of a super-
dowager glaring through high-powered lorgnettes', wrote Ellen
Wilkinson, a new Labour M.P. 'As a professor of economics at the
London School of that science he loves to answer questions from
obstreperous Tories like Earl Winterton, as though he were instructing his dullest and newest student in the first page of a primer. Nothing
delights him more as an old Etonian than to face a group of his ex-
schoolfellows on the warpath at question time, as though he were the
headmaster come down in wrath to deal with a Rag.'[24] A typical
performance was given in May 1930, when Dalton gave the Opposition a lecture on courtesy during an all-night sitting. When the Tories
bellowed with anger, the Parliamentary Under-Secretary responded
with taunts that made them bellow all the louder. 'Would not all this
trouble be obviated if the hon. Member dropped his superior tone?'
shouted one Conservative backbencher.[25] The hon. Member became
even more pedagogic, and it took 40 minutes to give answers to questions that should have taken ten. Dalton's skilful teasing – catching
Tories on sensitive nerves with a cool precision – did not increase his

reputation as a man of weight among members of his own front bench. But on the backbenches it was the source of great delight and he enjoyed himself immensely.

Yet there was another side to Dalton's ministerial personality. If his relations with the Foreign Secretary were generally excellent, his relations with permanent staff at the Foreign Office were often appalling. There were two aspects, hard to untangle: the determination of a forceful minister to push through his policies, and the inability of an insensitive minister to manage subordinates without upsetting them. Both aspects were present at Peckham. The conflict between them was to continue throughout his career, leaving a trail of unforgiven slights. At the Foreign Office, it earned him a thoroughly bad reputation which he was never able to repair.

As a determined and single-minded minister, who had helped to write Labour's programme, it was natural that he should seek to have that programme carried out. He wrote later that, having started with a concrete and detailed plan of action, the Labour Government did not 'need to ask either Civil Servants or any Commission of Enquiry containing a majority of its political opponents, to invent a policy on its behalf'.[26] Henderson's skills were at the personal level: he read little and seldom wrote. Dalton read and wrote copiously, and (as a Fabian) believed that details were inseparable from the realisation of great schemes. Part of the problem, therefore, was that Dalton knew and wanted to know more than his officials found comfortable.

Another part of the problem was social. Dalton's attitude may be contrasted with that of the Foreign Secretary. Henderson was abrupt and sometimes rude to officials who occasionally found him hard to handle. But personal feelings were not involved. Belonging to different social planets, the Foreign Secretary and his staff had no point of contact at which either could understand the other enough for emotions to become seriously engaged.

The same was not true of Dalton. He knew the world inhabited by diplomats all too well: a world that was full of a type that he had learnt at Eton to dislike and at Cambridge to goad. Was his behaviour, all these years later, incited by contempt, or fear, or perhaps envy? Or by the contempt and fear he sensed in the officials? His attitude seems, at any rate, to have been reinforced by a double prejudice: first that diplomats as a breed were ignorant, closed-minded, incompetent and directly responsible for the tragedy of 1914; second that they had a low opinion of politicians in general, with an additional snobbish element in their scorn for the Labour Party. Diplomats, he wrote, were people who 'sat up doing nothing in particular'. Abroad, he believed, they tended 'to move in rather narrow social circles, and so to give partial and incomplete accounts of political situations'. Some wanted to be 'not civil servants, but civil masters'.[27]

Dalton's prejudice, of course, contained a large element of truth. According to his private secretary Gladwyn Jebb (one of the few diplomats Dalton came to trust), the Parliamentary Under-Secretary regarded his officials as 'irredeemably bourgeois in their outlook on the world'.[28] That was a pretty accurate assessment. In style, as in composition, the Foreign Office remained the most socially élitist of the departments of state. It was not used to political interference, and it resisted, as an oyster resists a grain of sand, the attempts of a par-ticularly bumptious junior minister to challenge its hallowed prac-tices and traditions. The combination of ministerial abrasiveness and official non-cooperation produced some noisy rows. After one clash that rocked the building at the end of 1929, Dalton told his private secretary that he wished to avoid causing needless offence. Jebb replied that he had heard it said that Dalton was 'the first Parliament-ary U-Secy since Curzon' who had shown any capacity to get himself disliked in the office.[29]

Dalton's main bugbear and adversary was the Permanent Under-Secretary, Sir Ronald Lindsay. Lindsay had been forewarned about Dalton. 'Mr. Dalton had the reputation of being hard-headed and obstinate', one official told the Permanent Under-Secretary early in 1929.[30] Lindsay soon learnt the truth of this for himself. Shortly after Labour came to office, Lindsay and Dalton clashed during discussions on the Optional Clause, the signing of which was one of Labour's key objectives. Dalton, determined to push the matter through, insisted no fewer than six times at one meeting that officials should not seek to lead the Cabinet.[31] When Lindsay returned with new objections, Dalton told him bluntly that he was attempting to write the Govern-ment's policy himself.[32] With the aid of Cecil and Noel-Baker, Dalton managed to overcome official opposition, and the Cabinet eventually agreed that the Optional Clause should be signed. It was a considerable triumph, and other M.P.s were impressed. There was a theory in the Commons, wrote Ellen Wilkinson, 'that when these two awe-inspiring figures, Mr. Arthur Henderson and Dr. Dalton, marched through the corridors together, the Foreign Office staff, from the Ultra-Super-Important to the commissionaire, click their heels and say, "At your service, sirs!"'[33]

The battle over the Optional Clause was, however, only one reason for antagonism between Dalton and Lindsay. Another was a gaffe on Dalton's part that nearly caused a serious international incident. Just before going on holiday in Wiltshire with Ruth in August 1929, Dalton made a speech at an I.L.P. summer school in which he twice made in-discreet references to negotiations with Egypt, without realising that his remarks might cause embarrassment in Cairo.[34] The Egyptian Prime Minister was outraged and promptly threatened to resign. With Dalton out of the office, Lindsay was left to pick up the pieces. He sent Dalton a tart letter. 'The repercussions of my remark at Welwyn are very instructive', Dalton replied gaily. 'I am afraid I may have given some of you a hectic time explaining them away!' Lindsay answered sharply that the Parliamentary Under-Secretary had traded party capital at home for diplomatic damage in the Middle East.[35]

Dalton, feeling the snub, waited until he got back to the office before retaliating. Then he wrote privately to Henderson saying that he objected to Lindsay's method of approaching the Prime Minister 'with tendentious advice, which we know is contrary to S[ecretary] of S[tate]'s point of view'. Lindsay tried to smooth relations, inviting the Parliamentary Under-Secretary to dine privately at his house in Eaton Square. Dalton, still upset by the telling-off and sensitive on the issue of his own relative status, would not be appeased. 'A maid servant; a simple meal; everybody diplomatically adjusted to suit an Etonian Labour Under Secretary', he wrote. 'L[indsay] has an easy manner, which does not, however, conceal a certain quality of slyness without depth.'

Dalton was therefore delighted by a decision in the autumn of 1929 to send Lindsay to Washington as Ambassador and replace him with Sir Robert Vansittart. At first, Dalton was wary of Vansittart, whom he did not know. He wrote that the new Permanent Under-Secretary 'mustn't start running to J.R.M. behind Uncle's back, as Lindsay did'. Soon, however, Dalton discovered that Vansittart was a different kind of official from his predecessor. 'My first impressions are favour-able', he noted after they had met. 'Relations will undoubtedly be easier than with Lindsay. He is younger, has easier manners and is much more adaptable, and with fewer prejudices. His views on appointments are much more in line with mine. He is all for passing over duds, and wants to bring in commercial people occasionally, on their merits and in order to encourage consuls, etc.'[36] More important, Vansittart's views on foreign policy – anti-German and pro-French – were closely in line with Dalton's own. This was to become the basis of a close working relationship and, over the next decade, of an important political alliance. 'Hugh redeemed his little habit of breathing down our necks by an intuition of the German danger unusual in 1930', Vansittart wrote later. 'He had also sympathy for the doomed Poles, and it required courage in his party. I found him easy to work with and open to argument.'[37]

In November 1929, Dalton received an unexpected summons to No. 10 Downing Street. Would he be prepared, the Prime Minister wondered, to go to the House of Lords while retaining his present office? The reason for the offer, it soon transpired, was not a sudden burst of affection on MacDonald's part but the awkward discovery that the Government had exceeded the constitutional limit of six Parliamentary Under-Secretaries in the Commons. Taken aback, Dalton discussed the possibility with Henderson and with Ruth. Ruth was flat against. Hugh was briefly tempted. Though it would mean the loss of his parliamentary salary, there would be the compensation of freedom from constituency duties and hence more time for ministerial work, and for a private life. On the other hand, when Labour left office he would have to find a job, and it would be 'a trifle grotesque' for a peer to return to teaching economics.[38] So he refused, and Arthur Ponsonby, Under-Secretary at the Dominions Office, accepted instead. It was thirty-one years before an equivalent offer came Dalton's way again. In the meantime he had no regrets, despite the stress which ministerial life in a minority Government, subject to the whims of Liberals in the House of Commons, inevitably involved.

The political background to the whole of the second Labour administration was one of uncertainty from day to day. At any moment, ministerial influence might be replaced by oppositional impotence. Like other ministers, Dalton displayed an air of breezy self-confidence in public. In the autumn of 1929 he had told an interviewer that Labour would stay in power for at least two years. 'If we bring about disarmament, establish complete co-operation between the British people and other nations, and solve unemployment and other problems', he declared loftily, 'it might even be possible to defer the next election till 1934.'[39] In private, however, he was aware that the life of the Government hung by a thread, and the anxiety told on him. Just before Christmas Labour's majority fell to 8 on a key division, and there seemed a danger that the Government might soon fall. 'To me the emotional strain was very exhausting', he wrote.[40]

His moods were cyclical. There was a pattern: frenetic activity, high excitement, a feeling that everything was possible if only stuffed-shirts would not stand in his way, followed by tiredness, frustration, gloom, and a sense of all being for naught. When the Optional Clause issue was at its stickiest in August 1929, he thought – absurdly – about resigning. (Resignation fantasies at times of private depression were also, as we shall see, part of the pattern.) The following spring, as the economic deterioration became more evident and unemployment rose, a wider disillusionment with the Government set in. Much of his disappointment was directed against senior colleagues. 'A tired frightened snob, our great Prime Minister', he wrote in March 1930. 'One despairs of politics in such days as these. Cotton goes from bad to worse. In Mossley, Lancs., 80% of Gibson's constituents are out of work ... The Cabinet is full of overworked men, growing older, more tired and more timid with each passing week. Pressure from below and from without is utterly ineffectual ... We have forgotten our Programme, or been bamboozled out of it by the officials. One almost longs for an early and crushing defeat.'

At other times, when foreign affairs ran more smoothly, his mood would rise also. Yet his rejection of the Party leadership, Henderson apart, became steadily more bitter. Because he had nothing to do with home politics he could avoid taking the blame. At the same time, as an M.P. for a County Durham seat it was impossible not to be appalled by the deepening crisis. 'The gloom and sense of futility and exasperation have been awful', he wrote at the end of 1930. 'I am going to B[ishop] A[uckland] in the first days of January and hate the prospect of meeting my constituents again. It is all tragically different, so far as economic questions go, from what one had hoped and dreamed a Labour Government would be like.'[41]

1931 was a transitional year for Hugh and Ruth in ways unrelated to foreign policy or the economic crisis.

In the autumn of 1929 Ruth conceived the plan of buying a house far from London or Hugh's constituency and out of range of a telephone. The area she fixed on was Wiltshire, where they had spent their honeymoon. Just after Christmas she took Hugh back for a holiday and dropped the idea in his lap. 'R wants to buy a cottage or a farm ... !' Hugh recorded. 'She has been bottling this up for weeks!' The idea appealed to him and he immediately threw himself into the task of finding somewhere suitable. After looking at several possibilities and turning them down, they decided not to buy but to build a house instead. In April they discovered an ideal site – high up on the Ogbourne Road from Aldbourne with fine views to the south across the Marlborough Downs. They wandered around a muddy field in pouring rain, and then agreed on a price of £25 an acre for five acres. 'Rather a thrill', commented Hugh.[42]

Ruth handled the whole business of arranging for the design and erection of the house herself. 'Hugh has no taste at all in these matters', she told friends. Her own taste was decidedly advanced. An avid reader of architectural magazines, she was attracted by the work of Le Corbusier, who at this time was preoccupied with the emancipation of the house plan from its 'prison' of supporting walls and restrictive openings. She called in the architects Sir John Burnet and Partners to prepare plans which reflected the new style. As a result the house was of experimental design, one of the first of its kind in the country.[43] The Daltons paid £2,500 for the plans and construction.

Early in July building began, while Hugh sunbathed, swapped gossip with Beveridge in the Polly Tea Rooms at Marlborough, and monitored progress impatiently. 'Twelve months ago I little thought that I should be a Wiltshire landowner, building for the future in the narrower and more domestic sense, as well as in the national and international!', he wrote in August. In mid-November he noted 'a historic weekend': he and Ruth helped to plant 114 trees along the outer boundary of their new property. 'What a deep joy, spiritual and physical, comes from afforesting one's own lands!' They moved in at the beginning of 1931, Ruth having christened the house West Leaze. Hugh wrote: 'This is local, legitimate and apt for the westering sun and senile memories at the hour of sunset!'[44]

Thus began a thirty year love affair with a strange, box-like building high on the Marlborough Downs. Hugh and Ruth were seldom happier than when they were here – enjoying the isolation and the beauty of the rugged countryside, walking to Avebury, tramping through Savernake Forest, talking to local farmers, entertaining young friends, gardening, lying in the sun. At first there was no service of any kind – no electricity, gas or drainage. Rainwater was collected from the roof for drinking and washing, lighting was by oil lamp, heating and cooking were by paraffin burner. There was no telephone until a scrambler was installed in 1940. When the political crisis broke in August 1931, Hugh was out of range of all intrigue and gossip and had to be summoned to London by letter.

They visited West Leaze as often as they could, gradually shaping it to their needs. Ruth filled the inside of the house with Swedish pine furniture and Bauhaus design, placing in the middle of the dining-room a huge, circular glass table, which made Hugh's voice ring and echo. Outside, the garden belonged to Hugh. The leisure hours of William Ewart Gladstone at Hawarden were spent cutting down trees; Hugh Dalton's greatest private pleasure lay in planting them. Trees seemed to symbolise sturdy youth, hope for the future, the next generation. 'Perhaps I shall set up a body called Friends of Conifers', he told a friend. 'But the initials might shock people!'[45] The fruits of his industry are still to be seen, growing in irregular lines down the slope towards Aldbourne.

Many jokes were made about West Leaze. Friends regarded it as impracticable and ugly. With its rounded corners and odd geometric shapes it resembled the bridge on an ocean liner, or perhaps an early cubist sculpture. It was not a house a Conservative M.P., or a Bloomsbury intellectual, would ever have built; nor, for that matter, a run-of-the-mill Labour bourgeois. It bore the mark of its creators: inelegant yet at the same time bold and original. Some felt that it reflected Ruth's puritanism as well as Hugh's philistinism; inside it was cold and bare and the reverse of cosy. Today it looks and feels like a period piece, but not an unpleasing one. It seems to make a very personal statement, and if others felt startled or uncomfortable this may have been because it was a kind of statement they did not understand. For Hugh and Ruth, West Leaze was a substitute for a family, and they regarded it far more as home than their dull, drab Victorian flats in London, which they rented and never cared much about.

West Leaze was also a centre for plotting. Young friends were brought down and put through their paces; political allies, actual or potential, were invited to be bargained with or wooed. Molly Hamilton was one of the first guests; Stafford Cripps, recently drafted into the Government as Solicitor-General, was another. The Hendersons stayed for a weekend at the beginning of July. 'Very hard work, but very successful', Hugh wrote after this visit. 'I have taken them for two walks. And we have rested them and amused them very effectively. He is very pet. Asks what is the name of this style house. And which is the front.'[46] Others followed, and over the years there were few close friends who did not pay at least one visit. Molly Hamilton came four times. Other frequent visitors included the Noel-Bakers, Donald and Petica Robertson (from Cambridge), the Jebbs, the Robbinses, the Frasers, Eileen Power, Hugh Gaitskell and (later) John and Elsa Wilmot.[47] It was here, in 1935, that Dalton and Morrison laid plans for the succession to George Lansbury as Party Leader. Generally they came in ones and twos – to be walked and talked across the Wiltshire hills, and to be submitted to Ruth's terrible cooking.

In March 1931 Valentine Fox died after a short illness. Ruth had had a mixed relationship with her mother which did not improve as Valentine moved into an increasingly hostile and difficult old age. Valentine's final gesture – making Hugh's sister Georgie her residual legatee – was an added irritant, increasing the friction between brother and sister. The main significance of Valentine's death, however, was that it made Ruth a comparatively rich woman – with enough capital to ensure her own (and hence Hugh's) financial independence. Under the terms of Sir Arthur Peterson's will a capital sum had been set aside for Ruth and held in trust by Valentine. After duty had been paid, this sum produced an annual income of just under £800 – in addition to £300 which Ruth had been receiving from Peterson's estate since 1922. The total amounted to more than twice Hugh's parliamentary salary, and freed him from the money worries that were the common lot of most Labour M.P.s. It meant that – without children or extravagant tastes – personal financial considerations scarcely ever entered Hugh's political calculations. Valentine's death also left Ruth completely alone apart from Hugh. Both her parents were now dead, and without siblings or close cousins, her sense of isolation increased.

Canon Dalton died shortly afterwards. Hugh and Ruth had visited him assiduously but with declining enjoyment. 'Increasing evidence of the cumulative weight of age and weakening intelligence', Hugh observed on Christmas Eve 1929. The old man was becoming deaf, short-sighted, doddery, and more and more self-centred. He was also getting on everybody's nerves. 'I must write an essay', Hugh resolved, 'in a cool remote hour, for the guidance of my own declining years.'[48] The King, too, noticed how decrepit his friend had become. 'Dear old Dalton came to see me today', he wrote in his diary on 20th June 1931, 'he is ageing a good deal now.'

When the end came it was sudden. On 27th July Hugh made a speech in the Commons on the adjournment, and then had a drink with Gladwyn Jebb and some policemen and attendants in the House of Lords bar. The same night John Dalton made his own, final, peroration – reading the lesson in St George's Chapel with voice and vigour undiminished. He died in the early hours of the next morning. He had spent forty-six years in the same house, a legendary part of the Windsor establishment – the subject of humour, irritation, affection and dislike. Hugh was sorry at his passing. So was the King. 'Got the sad news that dear old Dalton passed away in the night', George V wrote. 'He was nearly ninety-two and came to Eddy and me as our tutor in 1871, just sixty years ago. I have always been devoted to him.'[49] The King's god-daughter seemed, to Hugh, rather less devoted. At the funeral Hugh noted the reaction of his sister 'who, egocentric as ever, weeps a little when she thinks that she has "never had a real father"'.

After a fortnight's holiday Hugh went back to the house at Windsor which his mother had to vacate to make way for a new canon. 'Three unbelievable days in the study', he recorded. There were piles of papers stuffed at random in drawers, mixed up with old bills, notes from Royalty, heaps of dust, even fleas. But what held his attention was an extraordinary collection of personal correspondence. 'Letters, all from men, except from members of the Dalton family', he noted. 'Some letters very affectionate. A strong homosexual strain is clear. Men fifty and sixty years younger than he called him "John". The more interesting we put aside.' The rest they burnt in a big bonfire in the Chapter garden.[50]

Having visited the Cloisters for the last time, Hugh and Ruth returned to West Leaze on 17th August, 'sleeping, digging, sunbathing, reviving'.[51] Their minds were scarcely on politics when the crisis broke a week later, and Hugh had been paying no attention to the growing domestic problems of the Government. The immediate cause of the collapse was a run on sterling, and a demand for economies (including a 10 per cent reduction in unemployment benefit) made by New York bankers as the condition for a loan. Faced with the likely resignation of nearly half his Cabinet if this condition was met, the Prime Minister had told the King that it was impossible to continue the Government in its present form. The King, anxious to maintain stability and (according to his official biographer) still 'in a mood of dejection' partly caused by Canon Dalton's death,[52] invited MacDonald to form a National Government. The result was a coalition in which only a handful of Labour ministers served, while the rest, and almost all Labour backbenchers, went into Opposition. Three months later MacDonald called an election.

Dalton was not offered a place in the National Government and did not seek one. His relations with the Prime Minister had not been good, and MacDonald's departure was far from unwelcome to him. Indeed by the spring of 1931 Dalton had come to the conclusion that his own promotion to the Cabinet could not be achieved unless Henderson became Party Leader. Nor was he particularly surprised by the Prime Minister's decision to seek Tory as well as Liberal support. It is likely that Ramsay MacDonald began to think seriously about a possible National Government in October 1930.[53] Dalton became aware of this as an actual possibility in mid-July 1931. Commenting on rumours among backbenchers of such a development, he noted that if the Tories were given a share of posts 'the sooner some of us come out and start to rebuild the Labour Party and its policy the better!'

On the issue itself, Dalton was uncompromising. Dalton had said little in public about domestic policies or the Government's economic strategy in recent months, and as a minister it was not possible for him to be openly critical, short of actual resignation, even if he had wished to be so. As we have seen, at least until the autumn of 1930, he did not seriously disagree with the Chancellor's approach in principle, and he was prepared to back Robbins against Keynes's demand for Protection. Yet he detested Snowden's vicarious masochism on behalf of the working class, and he opposed – as a matter of socialist conviction rather than of economics – proposals to cut benefits.

Resignation thoughts had never been far from his mind in the first half of 1931. Earlier, the idea of resigning had been related to his own frustrations at the Foreign Office. Now, more than eighteen months into the life of the Government, it was linked to a sense of the gap between Labour's socialist aspiration and its achievement. 'Snowden tried to persuade Cabinet to agree to reduce rates of unemployment benefit', he wrote in February. 'They declined ... so I needn't resign yet.' When the Prime Minister announced in June that there would be no cuts in benefit or increases in contribution – an undertaking that was shortly to be dishonoured – Dalton noted that the Cabinet 'had avoided the most obvious blunders for the moment'. There was therefore no division in his mind about the choice that faced senior ministers in August.

Dalton was summoned to London from Wiltshire for an N.E.C. meeting on 20th August. A long talk with Henderson convinced him that Labour was better off in Opposition. He returned briefly to West Leaze, only to receive an almost immediate summons to No. 10. 'The heartbreak would come if Uncle stayed in, while I felt that I must come out', he wrote. But when he reached London on 24th August the die was already cast: the King had asked MacDonald to form a National Government. MacDonald immediately accepted, taking Snowden, Thomas and Lord Sankey (the Lord Chancellor) with him into a small emergency Cabinet whose other five members included four Tories and a Liberal. On the afternoon of the 24th, the Prime Minister addressed a meeting of junior ministers and told them, with a great show of reluctance, that they were sacked. 'Christ crucified speaks from the Cross', Dalton wrote in disgust. But his main feeling was one of relief. 'What a change it is to have good, or in some cases even passable, relations with all the leaders of the Party', he wrote when it was all over. He calculated that a Labour Government under Henderson was likely within one or two years – with himself in the Cabinet.[54]

Publicly, he was one of the first to propagate the 'Bankers' Ramp' explanation of events, declaring that 'the first Labour Government was destroyed by a Red Letter and the second by a Bankers' Order'. At the beginning of September he gave his own version of events at a public meeting in Bishop Auckland:

This country should never have been led into such a bog of humiliation ... The plain truth was that the leaders who had not left them had been gradually losing their sense of direction. They had been keeping strange company and listening to strange counsellors. But the Labour Party, ever more loyal to principles than to persons, would go forward strengthened, united, and full of determination ...
They would not stand idly by and see our social services butchered

to make a bankers' holiday. But the root cause of our present economic troubles was the disastrous fall in prices for which the deflationist policies of banks and Governments were responsible.[55]

Dalton had, at last, abandoned his belief in the desirability of falling prices. But what was his solution? His answer had a familiar ring. The Government had failed because it lacked the resolve to attack the rich. This must not be allowed to happen again:

He recalled that when there was another crisis in August of 1914 the Government passed an Act, mobilising the foreign investments held by Englishmen ...
'If that had been done now it would have saved the flight from the pound and left a large measure to spare. We could have saved £50 million by the suspension of the Sinking Fund.
'So far as my personal position is concerned, I became a Socialist twenty-five years ago because I hated social inequality and was disgusted by the spectacle of the rich riding insolently on the backs of the poor. Because I have not changed my views in these respects I stand unhesitatingly and unrepentantly behind Arthur Henderson ... '[56]

In Parliament Dalton criticised the new Government's conception of equality of sacrifice. He also demanded an election. Snowden, who had stayed on as Chancellor of the Exchequer, replied that for Opposition members 'only a few weeks, possibly, remain before the place that knows them now will know them no more'.[57] For the Labour Party it was a time of transition, with new men rising up to replace the old. As it became evident that the break in the party was permanent, so it became clear that there were spaces to be filled. 'Alexander, Morrison, Dalton – in that order, are the most promising as possible leaders', a tired and disheartened Arthur Henderson told the Webbs on 20th September.[58] Margaret Bondfield, a former Labour Cabinet minister whose own career was about to end, noted the ascent of Dalton and Cripps during the last days of the Parliament.[59] In the economic sphere, Snowden's place was filled by Dalton, Graham and Pethick Lawrence. Dalton's position – with a place on the National Executive – was strongest. Moreover Dalton (unlike Graham, former President of the Board of Trade) did not suffer the embarrassment of having supported in Cabinet the policies which precipitated the crisis.

At the Scarborough Party Conference in October, Beatrice Webb noted the change. The smart set round MacDonald had departed. 'Henderson's bodyguard of intellectuals – Dalton, Noel-Baker, Laski,

Colin Clark', had replaced them.[60] As a result, Dalton was able to play a prominent part in shaping Labour's electoral programme. This included a plan to mobilise foreign investment as in wartime and to nationalise and control the banking and credit systems and basic industries. At the same time, it rejected tariffs.

But Dalton's rise to the front rank soon received a jolt. While delegates were still in session at Scarborough, the election was declared. Hugh travelled north, leaving Ruth to help his mother to clear out and vacate the house at Windsor. Though he missed Ruth, and – as usual – found his election agent ignorant and incompetent, he was not apprehensive about the results. The 1931 election was a confused affair. MacDonald, having promised not to hold a 'Coupon' election, was now holding one, and the electorate were faced with the spectacle of a Labour Prime Minister and Chancellor of the Exchequer at the head of a Tory-based alliance, with the Liberals facing three ways. The arithmetic was against Labour. Yet nobody foresaw the outcome. On the morning of the poll, the *Manchester Guardian* carried a prediction that Labour would hold 215 seats. In fact it held just 46, while supporters of the National Government took 554.

Defeat, when it came, was as big a shock to Dalton as to any of his colleagues. His own vote in Bishop Auckland fell enough to allow the National candidate, benefiting from the Liberal-Conservative pact, to slip in with a majority of 755 – the fourth occasion on which Dalton had been beaten by less than a thousand votes. It was a major setback, the worst break in the steady advance in his fortunes that had begun in 1918.

XIV

Practical Socialism

Before 1931 the history of the Labour Party had been one of rapid progress. Now it was easy to believe that the British attempt at parliamentary socialism had been finally crushed. Before the MacDonaldite defection there had already been two splits in Labour's ranks within the space of a few months: Sir Oswald Mosley and his 'New Party' followers had broken away on the economic issue, and there had been a growing breach with the left-wing I.L.P. Beaten, fragmented and discredited, the Labour Party after the election faced the most unbalanced House of Commons of modern times, with little hope of quick recovery.

For Labour's career politicians, the prospect of Government office seemed to fade beyond recall. Yet Dalton was luckier than most. Many colleagues who lost their seats were able to give only half their attention to politics. Others were forced to drop out altogether. Dalton was fortunate to be able to negotiate his return to the L.S.E. where, although notionally full-time, his duties were actually extremely light. The narrowness of his defeat meant that, once Labour began a modest revival nationally, his re-election in Bishop Auckland was assured. With a comfortable salary, Ruth's private means and a London academic base, he was able to regard the next few years as a time for regeneration and political stock-taking. Meanwhile his membership of the N.E.C. ensured the continued strength of his position within the Labour Movement.

Only three former ministers of any weight survived the 1931 election: George Lansbury, who became Chairman of the P.L.P. and in 1932 Party Leader;[1] Clement Attlee, who was made Lansbury's deputy; and Sir Stafford Cripps. At first, these three men virtually ran the tiny Parliamentary Party, speaking on every conceivable topic and trying to give the sense of being an Opposition. In the process, they sometimes led their colleagues in directions that displeased the Party establishment outside the House.

Here was a new problem. Partly because the election had removed almost all the links of dual membership that had previously bound together the N.E.C. and parliamentary leadership, there emerged in the early 1930s two Labour Parties: one in the House of Commons, left-leaning especially on foreign policy and defence issues; and the other at Transport House, cautious, intolerant of local indiscipline, and with its eye on the next election. Dalton belonged to the second. Over the next few years (and even after his return to Parliament in 1935) he was a 'Transport House man', on the side of working-class leaders against middle-class intellectuals, preferring pragmatism to doctrine. In return the trade unions gave him solid support. Before 1931 he had remained an outsider, disliked by and disliking the MacDonald clique. Now he became one of the rulers, a key figure at the very centre of the machine.

Part of Dalton's attitude towards the parliamentary leaders was personal. He resented the sudden increase in importance which the lucky survivors of 1931 had gained. For the defeated, he wrote, 'There is a risk of losing one's place, perhaps decisively, in the ever-shifting Parliamentary queue'. The two men who had most notably moved to the front, threatening his own position, were Clement Attlee and Sir Stafford Cripps. For the next twenty years a large part of Dalton's political life was to be determined by his relations with both of them.

Later Dalton speculated ruefully that if he had just won in 1931 instead of just losing, he rather than Attlee would have been made deputy chairman of the P.L.P., succeeding in due course to the Party Leadership when Lansbury resigned.[2] Certainly Dalton's standing before the election was far greater than that of Attlee, of whom few people had previously heard. Attlee had held minor posts in both Labour Governments, serving briefly in the second as Chancellor of the Duchy and then as Postmaster-General. His background in East End social work and local government gave him a better sense of the Party rank-and-file than that of other middle- or upper-class leaders. But there was little about him that seemed distinguished or inspired. Where others pushed themselves forward, he withdrew into the background. He was an indifferent speaker. On policy matters he followed the opinions of others rather than putting forward ideas of his own. 'I was never an intellectual', he told an interviewer after his retirement; 'they would never have allowed me as such.'[3] Dalton always under-estimated him.

By contrast Dalton's attitude towards Sir Stafford Cripps moved rapidly from wariness to exasperation and alarm. Like Attlee and

Dalton, Cripps came from an upper-middle-class background with strong Anglican Tory roots. Unlike either of them, religion played a very important part in his adult life. Cripps was also different in that his Tory family had close links with the Labour Party. Stafford's father, Lord Parmoor, became a Labour Cabinet minister having once been a Conservative M.P. His mother was a member of the Potter family, a sister of Beatrice Webb. Despite these unusual connections, Cripps showed little early interest in politics. Instead he concentrated on the Church and on a career at the Bar. Dalton and Attlee were failed barristers. Cripps was a brilliantly successful one, who gained a unique reputation in the field of scientific and patent law as a cross-examiner of technical witnesses.

Attlee and Dalton were both professional politicians. Cripps was initially an amateur, lighting on politics almost by chance and without any apprenticeship. Most ministers become Members of Parliament first. With Cripps it was the other way round. At the end of 1930 Ramsay MacDonald brought him into the Government as Solicitor-General, bestowing the knighthood that was by convention attached to this post. The appointment made it necessary for him to have a seat. Dalton played a key part in finding one.

As it happened a by-election was pending in the safe constituency of Bristol East. The Party managers decided that Cripps should fight it. However, there were difficulties: Cripps had joined the Labour Party only a year before and in Bristol there was fierce resistance 'to the Executive's method of dumping onto them a rich man, an aristocrat (*sic*) and a knight'.[4] The favourite for the candidature was Dalton's old Cambridge admirer, Leah Manning, who had become a prominent official in the National Union of Teachers. Arthur Henderson ordered her to step down. She refused. Shrewdly, Henderson sent Dalton to persuade her. Dalton played on past associations and the need to help the Labour Government in its hour of need. 'Uncle Arthur asks me to tell you that he will make this a test of your loyalty to the Party', he said. The technique worked. 'I can remember only a few times when I have given way to tears', recalled Mrs Manning; 'this was one of them.'[5] She withdrew, leaving an atmosphere of bitterness. After the National Agent had pleaded with the local party to accept the Transport House nominee, Cripps was chosen.

The Bristol East by-election took place in January 1931. Nine months later Cripps held the seat by a narrow majority, while Arthur Henderson and Hugh Dalton, who had worked to arrange this highly undemocratic selection, both lost theirs. Meanwhile Cripps, whose political views had hitherto been conventional or non-existent, had begun a spiral move to the left.

Dalton wrote later that his personal relations with Cripps after 1931 fell into three periods. From 1931 to 1939 there was much disharmony and disagreement. From 1939 to 1945 relations between them were 'tenuous but not unfriendly'. Thereafter, until Cripps's retirement, they were 'generally in harmony and agreement', working closely together and providing mutual support. As we shall see, this was not the whole story; but about the first period there can be no doubt. Cripps and Dalton were at loggerheads for most of the decade. 'I was at first astonished that so intelligent a man could talk such nonsense', Dalton recalled. 'He seemed to have no political wits and to leave his first-class brains inside his brief-case. Gradually ... my astonishment changed to vexation and impatience.' Later, when dealings between them became more cordial, the background of this conflict remained an unspoken but unforgotten constraint.

If 1931 produced in Sir Stafford Cripps what Dalton called 'an adolescent Marxist miasma',[6] Dalton's own response to the crisis and defeat was Fabian. Unlike Cripps, Dalton did not believe that socialism could only be achieved through constitutional dictatorship. Unlike John Strachey, he did not imagine that the crisis of capitalism was at hand. Unlike Ellen Wilkinson, he did not conclude that the best or only effective strategy was to march and demonstrate. Instead he believed that Labour needed better policies and better people. Now that the sudden removal of the old pioneers had turned him from an adjutant into a general, he set about trying to acquire both.

Over the next four years, the combination of a strong party position and freedom from parliamentary pressures enabled him to stimulate Labour's intellectual rebirth. Meanwhile, he abandoned his own pursuit of disarmament, moved even further away from the pacifistic attitudes of his contemporaries, and began to persuade the Labour Party that in the harsh new international climate of the 1930s the liberal doctrines of the 1920s were no longer appropriate. In many ways this was Dalton's zenith. It was certainly the period of his greatest influence within the Labour Party, and his impact upon its policy, philosophy, organisation and constitution during the 1930s was incalculable. Confident, energetic, without the distractions of office, he more than any other leader determined the direction in which the party should go.

After the election Dalton began to take an interest in a body called the New Fabian Research Bureau (N.F.R.B.), recently set up by an old rival, the Oxford historian and political philosopher, G. D. H. Cole. The aim of N.F.R.B. was to stimulate ideas and carry out research, which would then be fed to the Labour machine. Cole was concerned that his new organisation should have close links with the Party leadership. Hence, as his wife Margaret put it, 'respectworthy persons like Arthur Henderson and Hugh Dalton' were invited to join the Bureau's directing body.[7] Dalton agreed to be co-opted and at first gave N.F.R.B. his full encouragement.[8] Then his enthusiasm waned. This was not because of any revision in his own 'Fabian' outlook. Partly it was because the earnest, other-worldly attitude of some New Fabians, with their air of moral superiority towards practical politicians, irritated him. Partly it was because he continued to dislike the Coles, who embodied this attitude most of all. It was also because of two significant rows involving members of N.F.R.B., which highlighted the split that was developing between the National Executive and the leaders of the P.L.P.

The first row was over a paper called 'A Labour Programme of Action', drawn up by a New Fabian group of intellectuals that included a number of prominent left-wingers. Dalton, involved in early discussions about this Programme, found himself faced with a document which seemed dangerously anti-democratic. At the first drafting meeting in May 1932, he objected strongly to a suggestion by Harold Laski and William Mellor that socialists needed to arm themselves against the risk that 'capitalist' parties would prevent an electorally victorious Labour Party from taking office. 'Would any party which had just been defeated at a General Election dare to continue in office without summoning Parliament?' Dalton asked. 'Would it be able to collect any taxes, and would it not almost immediately bring itself into collision with the courts?'[9] Receiving no satisfactory reply he refused to sign the document. Attlee, much influenced by Cole at this time, agreed to circulate the Programme among Labour Members of Parliament. Dalton, on the other hand, encouraged the N.E.C. to ignore it.[10]

The second row was bigger and deeper. As well as warning against a possible capitalist coup, the Programme of Action demanded the takeover of the joint stock banks as a first step for an incoming Labour administration. This proposal had support which went far beyond left-wing intellectuals, or even the Labour Left in general – arousing interest among trade union leaders and rank and file members who felt bitter about the behaviour of the banks during the 1931 crisis. In 1932 the idea took a central place in Labour Party discussions about future policy.

Dalton considered the proposal economically irrelevant and politically disastrous. His objection was not to the radicalism of the proposal. Rather, that the proposal sounded radical while actually

promising nothing. It disgusted him that people who had been calling
for the Party to do some hard thinking should play to the gallery in so
crude a manner. 'Cole, who has been pressing upon me the case for
nationalising the Big 5, would like to have a talk with you about it ... ',
he warned Pethick Lawrence in May. 'I hope you will receive him
kindly, and give him some arguments to think over.'[11]

Dalton's own treatment of Cole was less than kindly. Abandoning
tact, he presented his own, post-crisis, political philosophy:

> Let us have no more MacDonaldite slush and general phrases
> meaning nothing definite. 'Taking over the Joint Stock Banks' may
> mean half a dozen different things! It is so easy to sound brave,
> and then to find one hasn't seen the real difficulties.[12]

Dalton lost the round. Unemployment had risen to record levels,
and the Labour Movement was in an angry mood. At the Party Conference in October 1932, an unusual alliance of trade unions and constituency parties rebelled against the N.E.C. and demanded that
'socialisation' of the banks should become official policy. This was
only a paper decision, easy to ignore in calmer times. Yet Dalton was
left feeling gloomy about the division in the Party, and especially the
growing rift between the P.L.P. and Transport House. 'The Parliamentary Party is a poor little affair, isolated from the National Executive whose only M.P. is George Lansbury', he wrote. 'Attlee is Deputy
Leader ... a "purely accidental position" as someone puts it – and he
and Cripps, who are in close touch with Cole, sit in Lansbury's room
at the House all day and all night and continuously influence the old
man.'[13]

Dalton remained a member of N.F.R.B., and several of his younger
friends were closely involved in its activities, producing discussion
papers and pamphlets. He decided, however, not to make Cole's
band of 'loyal grousers' (as the New Fabians called themselves) the
base for his own policy-making concerns.

Dalton's brief N.F.R.B. involvement did, however, have one very
important effect. More than any other event in his own life in the 1930s,
a visit to the Soviet Union under New Fabian auspices in the summer
of 1932 fundamentally altered his attitudes towards domestic policy.
Hitherto, his main interest, outside the field of foreign affairs, had
been the use of taxation – super tax, death duties, capital levy – to
reduce inequalities. He had given little serious thought to the possibility of re-structuring the economy. Now, mass unemployment, and

his own prominence within the Labour Party, provided new imperatives. In January 1932 unemployment in Britain had approached 3
million, 27 per cent of the insured labour force. The New Fabian visit
to Russia in July came at a time when Dalton was open to new
influences.

The trip was carefully prepared and organised. The aim was to
investigate and write about the Soviet experiment. Beatrice and Sidney
Webb (separately engaged on their own massive study of the Soviet
Union) noted that the plan was for each New Fabian to take a particular aspect of Soviet society and study it in depth, backed up by
researchers at home.[14] The party was mainly made up of socialists of
a Hampstead or Bloomsbury kind. Apart from Dalton, the travellers
included Margaret Cole and her brother Raymond Postgate, Dick
and Naomi Mitchison, D. N. Pritt, Graham Haldane and Pethick
Lawrence.

The New Fabians set out by Russian boat on 3rd July 1932. It was
a relaxing voyage. 'Act the part of God the Father in a series of Old
Testament charades', wrote Dalton. 'Much applause by the crew.
Three old ladies rather shocked.'[15] After a few days in Leningrad and
Moscow (where Dalton saw the Webbs) the party broke up into small
groups. Dalton journeyed east with two Oxford dons, travelling by
train with an interpreter to Sverdlovsk and Magnitorsk and back to
Kazan; by boat along the Volga to Stalingrad; and from there to
Rostov on the Don. Then he returned through Kiev to Moscow.[16]

He was an energetic traveller, rushing from official to official,
demanding documents and information. He was also an irascible one,
alternately annoying, and being annoyed by, his fellows. A British
architect called Geoffrey Ridley, with whom he shared a room, found
him boisterous and inconsiderate, behaving 'in a regrettably Englishman abroad attitude'. 'He is so dreadfully fussy,' Ridley wrote,
'grousing when anything goes wrong, even to the extent of rudeness.
He is a typical politician, all theories and nothing else.'[17] Margaret
Cole was irritated by his habit of seeking out important people rather
than talking to ordinary workers.[18] Dalton remained unaware of his
unpopularity, though he soon became bored by his British companions. Pethick Lawrence, he wrote, was rather like his own father
'but interested in finance rather than St George's Chapel'. Meanwhile
he took pride in his immunity from the dysentery and bed bugs that
afflicted other members of the party, and made magnanimous dona-
tions from his own stock of chlorodyne to the diarrhoea-stricken
Pethick.[19]

It was a glorious holiday, the more so for being political and educational. It was also Hugh's longest separation from Ruth since 1918.

He missed her deeply and wrote home several times a week. His letters show that ten years after Helen's death, and despite the strains of political life, they remained a far closer and more devoted couple than many friends realised. 'My Sweet Pet', began one letter, written shortly after his arrival in Russia. 'I think of you often as I go through these crowded days. *One* day I shall just stop and take a calm reflective rest. *One* day I shall hold you again in my arms, and tell you all about it.' He ended: 'All my love to my Little Goozle'. When he came back to Moscow after his long trip east, he picked up a letter from Ruth and wrote in reply: 'I love my Little Wife very, very much, and I want to kiss her eyes and have a nice hold.' As in his early days in France in 1916, sheets of careful notes, recording all his impressions, accompanied each missive. 'Let me know from time to time whether you have got all the diary', he wrote in mid-July. 'The pages are all numbered. I can then destroy the rather smudgy carbons.'[20]

He returned to England at the end of August, using the boat trip from Leningrad to reflect on the contradictions of Stalinist Russia. When he got back he wrote to Arthur Ponsonby, declaring himself 'rather torn between conflicting judgements and emotions':

It is a wonderful push. But it has some grim aspects, and they are short of food, and will, I fear, be still shorter in a month or two. And many of them are still incredibly inefficient, and impractical. And the lavatories – – – ! Far worse than anything in Spain or in pre-Fascist Italy. It became an obsession after a time ... I go North tomorrow to my unemployed constituents. In Russia at any rate everyone is working![21]

Margaret Cole admitted later that, though not uncritical, the New Fabian team had been prejudiced in favour of the Union of Soviet Socialist Republics. ' ... [W]e knew the men of the G.P.U., the secret police, as kindly souls who came to our rescue and found us seats on crowded trains.'[22] Dalton shared the sympathetic interest in the Soviet regime that was common to most progressive visitors. Yet he was certainly no innocent dupe. His view at the start of the Second Five Year Plan was set out in a chapter on the Soviet economy and Soviet planning in a book edited by Margaret Cole. Here he presented himself as a cautious convert not to Communism but to the concept of the Plan. He recognised that the problems were immense. But a rapid programme of industrialisation seemed a justifiable response to what Trotsky had called 'the slow tempo' of Russian development. Trial and error, he suggested, were better than error without trial. What he saw strengthened his belief that 'for a community as for an individual, bold and conscious planning of life is better than weak passivity and the tame acceptance of traditional disabilities'.

He was particularly interested in the redistribution of resources among localities as practised in the Soviet Union. There seemed to be a direct relevance for Britain, a country with huge disparities of industrial concentration and levels of unemployment. He observed that in the Soviet Union there was a conscious policy for the location of industry, involving the creation of a large number of medium-sized centres where previously there had been little industrialisation. Rejecting Communist theory, he concluded that the Russians were pragmatic rather than doctrinaire. 'The technique of planning has been developed empirically', he wrote. 'Planning, it was admitted in one conversation, is definitely post-Marxian. No direct guidance concerning this problem is to be found in any of the Marxian writings.' Yet was Soviet-style planning, which seemed to offer great economic benefits, compatible with Western freedoms? Dalton decided that it was. Large and beneficial results could be achieved 'even with a measure of social control far less extensive than that which prevails today in the Soviet Union'.[23]

These thoughts were more than casual observations. From now on, the word 'planning' took a central place in his political vocabulary. The objectives of planning in the Soviet Union, Dalton noted, were to avoid economic crises, maintain full employment, raise the standard of living, achieve a large measure of self-sufficiency and – of key importance – control inequalities. All these were desirable in Britain. A carefully prepared 'bold plan' on Fabian lines should therefore become the basis for Labour's electoral programme, taking the place of empty rhetoric and what he had denounced as 'MacDonaldite slush'.

Thus, while others were finding comfort in revolutionary-sounding slogans, Dalton adopted what he saw as policies of hard-headed radical realism, based on Soviet experience which he had examined firsthand. He was convinced, he wrote in a local Labour Party news-sheet just after the 1932 Labour Party Conference, that the only solution to economic troubles lay in emulating part at least of the Russian example:

It is my firm conviction that, unless we in this country also adopt the principle of economic planning on Socialist lines, we shall find no solution of our economic troubles.

And if the Russians can do it and can make much remarkable progress in so short a time how much more effectively could we in England do it! ...

Trade Unionism, illegal under the Tsars, is still in its infancy.

Political freedom, as we know it, they have never known. They have many difficulties still to conquer.

But they are moving onward, while we are standing still, or even going backward.[24]

Dalton continued to be an opponent of British Communism which he regarded as a dangerous distraction; much of his time during the 1930s was spent combating its influence. Yet he retained a powerful respect for the Soviet Union. Later this affected his attitudes on foreign affairs. More immediately, it had an impact on Labour Party domestic policy. This was partly because he returned from Russia just as serious preparations for Labour's electoral programme were about to begin.

At the end of 1931, the N.E.C. had set up an eight-man Policy Committee. Dalton was elected a member. 'This will be an important body', he observed.[25] He was right. Over the next few years the Policy Committee and its sub-committees created a policy-making machinery which the Party had previously lacked. The two most active participants and initiators were Herbert Morrison, who chaired the Local Government and Social Services Sub-Committee, and Dalton. Dalton became Chairman of the crucial Finance and Trade Sub-Committee; he also served as one of two N.E.C. representatives on the Economic Committee of the T.U.C. General Council, helping to provide a liaison between this body and the Policy Committee. As a result, more than any colleague, he was able to determine both the outlines and the detail of Labour's financial and economic programme. The strong theme of 'planning' that ran through the Party's official policy was largely of his making. 'At the moment he is the intellectual dynamo of the Party Executive', a leading journalist wrote in 1935.[26] Few at the time would have disagreed. Other leaders ran noisy campaigns, captured the headlines, and gained the adoration of the constituencies. But the Labour Party that entered the 1940 Coalition and formed a majority Government five years later had an unmistakably Daltonian stamp.

What was planning? Influenced by his Soviet experience, Dalton saw it as combining two key elements: freedom from market pressures and, in Britain's case, the means to overcome official caution and resistance. On his return from the New Fabian trip he presented ideas for the 'planned development' of industries that would be largely self-financing – creating funds for their own expansion; and proposals for phasing out the rich through a 'planned' attack on inherited wealth.

The method was to be classically Fabian, involving an élite corps of super-directors. In a memorandum submitted to the New Fabians, Dalton proposed 'some special machinery, analogous to the Soviet Gosplan, containing both intelligent and willing Civil Servants and Socialist "experts", engineers and others'. This machinery would be supra-departmental.[27] One immediate product of these ideas was the establishment by the N.E.C. of a 'Machinery of Government' Sub-Committee, to look into the problems raised.

A further element of planning in Dalton's mind was boldness: what he called 'a well-planned rush'. Without such a rush, socialist policies would founder. But boldness also entailed knowing where you were going. Boldness meant a specific, detailed, practical plan of action. In an important memorandum on finance and trade which became the basis of Labour's 1933 policy document *Socialism and the Condition of the People*, Dalton called for a fundamentally new approach. 'Speed at the outset is essential', he wrote. 'We must start off, as neither the first nor the second Labour Government did, with a rush.'[28]

The overriding aim of Labour policy was to overcome unemployment. The instruments were to be nationalisation and planning. But planning must be more than a statement of intent. It must involve a revision of the administrative structure, and an extension, through an Emergency Powers Act, of the power of a Labour Government to legislate quickly and effectively. Above all, Labour needed to know clearly, in advance, what it intended to do and how it intended to do it.

The Soviet Union provided Dalton with a sense of the capacity of government direction to alter economic destinies. Meanwhile, there were other influences on his thinking. Socialists had long discussed planning in a general way, as an alternative to the market. In the 1930s, many non-socialists also took up the cry, giving the idea more substance, and linking it to Keynesian expansionism. One of the writings that influenced Dalton most was a book by his friend Barbara Wootton, called *Plan or No Plan*, which compared aspects of capitalist and socialist systems, and came down on the side of the latter while incorporating much of the new expansionist doctrine. Like Dalton, Barbara Wootton had travelled to Russia and had been educated by the experience. She, too, argued that a condition of successful planning must be the creation of some body corresponding to the Russian Gosplan, and 'enjoying nation-wide authority'.[29] The notion that planning should involve physical control of resources by a central instrument of government became one of Dalton's strongest themes in the years that followed.

There was also a more surprising influence on his ideas – the product of yet another fact-finding tour. After the publication of *With British Guns*, Dalton's affection for Italy had remained, despite the Fascist takeover. He prided himself on his knowledge of Italian economic writing, which had influenced his own on the subject of inequality. But he knew little about the new, dictatorial and supposedly dynamic, Italian political system. In the autumn of 1932 he and Ruth decided to find out about it for themselves.

Hugh set out with a sentimental attachment to the country and its people, a prejudice against some aspects of the regime, but also a willingness to be impressed by any form of bold economic experimentation. 'I want to find out what the Fascists are really up to', he wrote to Ponsonby just before he and Ruth left England in December, 'and whether, as some say, the Corporate State is a new kind of semi-socialism, or as others think, just rhetorical verbiage.'[30] He met a number of Fascist and pro-Fascist intellectuals during the trip, including Filippo Marinetti. He was also able to renew his friendship with Gladwyn Jebb, whom he had placed in the British Embassy in Rome at Jebb's request, as a final gesture before relinquishing office as Parliamentary Under-Secretary in August 1931. The highpoint of the trip, however, was an audience with the Duce himself.

It was a strange encounter: Dalton, the ex-Foreign Office minister now reduced to the status of private citizen, and Mussolini, at the height of his success and power. The meeting took place at the Palazzo Venezia in Rome, without aides or interpreters. Mussolini put himself out to be charming and agreeable. The Italian dictator had had some practice in dealing with radically-minded British politicians: it was less than a year since Sir Oswald Mosley, rapidly moving from Socialism to Fascism, had also paid him a visit.

Where, asked the Duce, did Dalton learn to speak Italian? 'I learnt it at the Front (*"nella zona di guerra"*)', Dalton replied proudly. 'I am a soldier of the Unconquered Army.' This was a good start. Dalton praised the *slancio* and energy which he had observed in Italy – the draining of the Pontine Marshes, the afforestation, the public works. He wondered whether Britain might not acquire something of the same spirit of adventure. Mussolini seemed pleased. Fascism, he explained politely, was a form of socialism adapted to Italian needs. He, Mussolini, was an egalitarian and a seeker after peace and disarmament. He drew attention to a new law, currently in preparation, for the expropriation of private property. In the schools, he declared, the children of the poor and the children of the rich sat side by side and ate the same lunch.

After half an hour, Dalton withdrew. 'Be sure', said the Duce, walking him to the door, 'next time you are in Rome, to come and see me again'. Dalton returned to his hotel, star-struck. 'There is no other living man whom it would have thrilled me more to meet', he wrote in his diary. Then he added, 'R thinks he has conquered my susceptibilities too much'.[31] Unlike Mosley, Dalton did not return from Italy a Fascist. Nevertheless he was moved and invigorated by his visit, which reinforced his belief in the necessity of central economic direction as the essential tool for dealing with unemployment.

Here he was increasingly at odds with his colleagues at the L.S.E. At the School, Dalton lectured on Public Finance and Economic Planning. But he felt restless and disengaged. Whatever suspicions he might have had of Keynes were overtaken by the sharply reactionary direction in which L.S.E. economics seemed to be moving. 'The Robbins-Hayek tendency (and they have several echoes on the staff) is very retrograde', he wrote to a young friend at the end of 1932. 'It is curious that this movement should have set in at the London School, when both at Oxford and Cambridge there is a distinct movement among the younger teachers of economics in the opposite direction.'[32] Dalton's main academic energies in the early 1930s were focussed on a project funded by the Acland Trust, involving research into the public finance of selected countries. Dalton was responsible for supervising the detailed work of a number of research students scattered through the capital cities of the Western world. The final result of the project was a collection of essays by the participants entitled *Unbalanced Budgets: A Study of the Financial Crisis in Fifteen Countries*. This was completed in the autumn of 1933 and published in May the following year.

In his own contribution to the book, Dalton showed himself a passionate planner, but more a socialist than a Keynesian one. He was not against unbalanced budgets, pointing out that most countries had them without dire effects. He did not, however, recommend deficit financing as a matter of deliberate policy. Instead he suggested that budgets should be balanced over a period of years rather than in each year separately (an idea which he resurrected as Chancellor after the Second World War). His discussion of the new expansionist doctrine was brief and almost grudging. He argued that the expansionists now had the better case. However, to be effective their policy needed to be taken much further than most of them were willing to go. The only true solution, in his view, lay in physical planning of industry and resources. 'I believe that freedom from the plague of recurrent booms and slumps can only be found in a Planned Economy.'

He cited approvingly the example of Mussolini's Italy. It was possible to speculate about whether Italy was moving towards Socialism as well as Economic Planning. 'This suggestion is repugnant both

to most Italian Fascists and to many Socialists including Italian
emigrés, outside Italy', he admitted. 'Yet it is not to be ruled out as
unthinkable, nor even as exceedingly improbable.' No doubt recalling
his own private interview with the Duce, he pointed to recent Italian
arguments that the Corporate State must move towards a classless
society, ridding itself of the 'classical dualism' of employers and
employed; he also pointed to the suggestion that both the state and
workers' organisations should be represented on the boards of all
large companies, with increasing amounts of profit-sharing. Nor, he
concluded, was this mere verbiage. It was possible to observe the very
extensive state control of banking in Italy since 1926.[33]

Dalton's Italian phase was short-lived. Within three years, he had
lost all his respect for Mussolini. Yet for a brief period the influence
was real; and it remains a curious fact that the policy on which Labour
fought the 1935 general election owed some of its inspiration to
Italian Fascism and Mussolini's Corporate State.

Labour's new policy, embodied in a document called *For Socialism
and Peace*, was ratified by Party Conference in 1934. This was the
most comprehensive Labour programme of the inter-war period,
marking an important change of direction – with policies on nationalisation and planning that were far more specific than in the past. Dalton
was one of the main authors, having used his Finance and Trade Sub-
Committee to tie together the proposals of other Sub-Committees into
a coherent package. The proposals were closely examined in a wide-
ranging study, *Practical Socialism for Britain*, published by Dalton
the following spring.

If *For Socialism and Peace* was a more considered policy document
than the Labour Party had hitherto produced, *Practical Socialism*
was undoubtedly a path-breaking political book. The title accurately
described what it was about: not visions of a joyful future, but the
actual steps which a new Labour Government might take in office.
No previous study in the history of the Labour Party had provided
such a balanced appraisal, or one with such careful attention to
administrative obstacles or wider economic implications. One later
admirer described it as 'the first swallow of the post-1935 summer' of
socialist reformism, marking a return to self-confidence after the
1931 débâcle.[34] It also represented an entirely new way of looking at
policy.

Socialism, Dalton wrote, was a quantitative thing:

It is a question, not of all or nothing, but of less or more ... I make
no apology for not presenting an elaborate theoretical study of an

ideal society. That is stimulating but a different kind of exercise, which does not lack exponents. But, if our concern is with practical politics, we do better to decide the direction of advance than to debate the detail of Utopia. We must see clearly the next stretch of the journey. But we need not spend time now in arguing whether, beyond the horizon, the road swerves left or right.

The book began with Labour's promises, and set out to show how these could be carried out. Its tone was measured, scholarly and non-polemical. Reflecting Dalton's own passion, the heaviest emphasis was on planning. Seven chapters devoted to this subject drew on the writings of Sir Basil Blackett, Walther Rathenau and Sir Arthur Salter, among others. There were special words of praise for the 'admirable discussion' in Barbara Wootton's *Plan or No Plan* and for a book called *Reconstruction: a Plan for a National Recovery* by Harold Macmillan, a young Tory M.P. out of sympathy with the National Government's economic policies. Italy was barely mentioned. The Soviet experiment, on the other hand, was noted briefly but approvingly. Dalton quoted the findings of Graham Haldane, one of the New Fabian tourists, that the First Five Year Plan of electrification had been fully achieved. Britain, Dalton concluded, also needed intensive electrification and a socialised electricity industry. 'The Electrical Plan must dovetail into, and facilitate, the National Plan as a whole', he wrote. ' ... Here we can learn a lesson from Soviet Russia. Lenin's formula, Electrification plus Soviet Power equals Socialism, has become classical. He taught the Russians to plan electrification on a gigantic scale.'

Against those who said that planning under capitalism was impossible, Dalton declared that modest beginnings could accelerate the process of transition. He referred also, though with little elaboration, to the American New Deal and Roosevelt's Tennessee Valley Authority. 'Other similar schemes are to follow', he wrote. 'Each is designed to be a focus of economic and social planning in the surrounding area.' Keynes was, on the whole, relegated to footnotes. However, citing Keynes's *Essays in Persuasion* and the writings of Colin Clark, Dalton presented the expansionist argument in general terms:

The money to pay for all these things [in the National Plan] will come, partly from the money which is now being paid to the unemployed, who will be reabsorbed in useful work; partly from the savings which are now running to waste, financing losses instead of new investment; partly from the new money which will be created, in the form of additional currency and additional bank credits, in pursuance of the monetary policy ... whereby the general level of prices is kept steady and purchasing power expanded in proportion as production expands.

Dalton was opposed to those who argued in favour of a steadily rising price level, so that the burden of public debts and other fixed money charges should be steadily reduced. He believed, however, that because of the precipitous fall in prices in recent years, it might be desirable to raise the price level before stabilisation, both to reduce the burden of fixed money charges on the state and to boost production. 'Such reflation, or controlled inflation', he wrote, 'designed to cancel part of the ruinous deflation to which we have been subjected, is wholly different from uncontrolled inflation, with which some timid minds confuse it. Control is the essence of the policy.'

Sections on Planning and on Finance were kept in separate compartments, and the Keynesian multiplier – which made a brief appearance in the Labour policy document *For Socialism and Peace* – was not mentioned at all. However, a proposal for a Keynes-inspired National Investment Board to control the quantity and direction of long-term investment was given an important role. 'Such a board will, I believe, be one of our most effective instruments of Socialist planning and national development', Dalton wrote, 'a powerful agency for dealing with unemployment and, even so, only the germ of what, if it succeeds, is likely to become one of the central financial institutions of a Socialist community.' The emphasis was on the nationalisation of basic industries, and the use of power thus acquired to control and direct industrial development, to raise investment and carry out geographical planning. Equality was to be increased by extending the social services, and by disinheriting the rich. Planning for the Location of Industry was given a high priority. 'Such a policy', he wrote, 'should guide new industries away from London and its outskirts, and away from the larger cities, to selected smaller towns, to garden cities, both new and old, and into the depressed areas. And it should check the present drift from North to South.' There were also discussions of other pet schemes, such as National Parks and afforestation. The Party's commitment to take over the joint stock banks, which Dalton had always personally rejected, was quietly shelved.[35]

Practical Socialism was roughly treated on the intellectual Labour Left, partly because Dalton's own treatment of left-wing intellectuals had scarcely been gentle. A young Oxford don called Frank Pakenham (later Lord Longford), recently converted to left-wing ideas, criticised the author for being 'very tender towards the susceptibilities of capitalists'.[36] Yet the gap between Dalton and the Labour Left in actual policy, as distinct from rhetoric and style, was not wide. *Practical Socialism* may be compared with *The First Workers' Government* published a few months earlier by G. R. Mitchison, Treasurer of the left-wing Socialist League. Measures put forward by Mitchison as the basis for a Classless Society followed closely policies which Dalton had already inserted in Labour documents, and had refined in his book.[37]

Even more striking than the links with the Labour Left, were links with the ideas of 'non-socialist' planners whose writings Dalton had plundered extensively in writing his *Practical Socialism*. As it happened, many of the authors quoted approvingly by Dalton were joining forces in a new, loosely-knit body called the Next Five Years Group, which put forward a recovery plan that aimed to unite progressive opinion. The kinship between *Practical Socialism* and this plan (published in the same year under the title *The Next Five Years – An Essay in Political Agreement*) was so close that many sections were virtually interchangeable. Like *Practical Socialism*, *The Next Five Years* advocated the 'complete socialisation' of transport, electricity supply, arms manufacture, and some forms of insurance, with measures of control short of nationalisation for the joint stock banks.[38] It also called for a small Government Planning Committee including the Prime Minister and several ministers without portfolio 'of the highest rank'.

An anonymous review of *Practical Socialism* published in *The Economist* (probably written by the editor, Geoffrey Crowther, who was one of the main *Next Five Years* writers), drew attention to these similarities and suggested that Dalton's 'able and interesting book' contained hardly anything that would not be supported by progressive Liberals and Tories. The moral seemed to be that the word 'Socialism' in the context of British politics had become void of meaning, and remained 'only as a hindrance to the re-alignment of political parties in accordance with the real division of opinion in this country'.[39]

Why (we may now ask) did Dalton shun the political activities of non-Labour politicians and intellectuals who shared his belief in the need for interventionist policies? Why did he not encourage the 'Next Five Years' initiative, which aimed to broaden the anti-Government front and bring together men and women 'of all parties and of none'?[40]

At first Dalton did give a measure of support, backing the earliest stages of the Next Five Years venture. In February 1934 he even agreed to sign a manifesto inspired by Harold Macmillan (one of the Next Five Years initiators), Lord Cecil (his own former associate under Henderson at the Foreign Office) and the Liberal leader, Herbert

Samuel, calling for planning on the basis of 'scientific schemes of a far-sighted and far-reaching order'. Having taken this initial step, however, he was prepared to go no further. The next step – the discussions that led to the 1935 Next Five Years Group manifesto and book – went ahead without him.[41]

One reason was party political. Along with other Labour leaders, Dalton was under pressure from colleagues for whom the MacDonaldite betrayal was a recent, bitter reminder of the dangers of fraternising too closely with outsiders. In addition, Dalton could see little advantage in Labour joining up with a small group whose distinguished members were, as he put it, 'like officers without a rank and file, better known to each other than to the general public, moving in select and narrow circles, carrying almost no electoral weight'.[42] Dalton was writing for a Labour Party audience; the Next Five Years Group seemed to aim its message at dons, bishops, civil servants, and newspaper editors.

Yet there was also an important difference of philosophy. The Next Five Years Group agreed with Dalton that the present economic system was 'in many respects very unsatisfactory', that government intervention was bound to increase, and that what was needed was the planning of economic policy as a whole. Agreement on short-term policy, however, concealed a divergence of basic aims. Dalton was a socialist because he was an egalitarian. The Next Five Years authors avoided the word socialism (declaring that 'The historic controversy between individualism and socialism ... appears largely beside the mark') because equality was not their objective. Their aim was to shore up the capitalist system rather than to replace it. 'Stubborn resistance to the economic and social changes which this situation demands', they warned the Government, 'or even a negative attitude of inertia or timidity, would produce, sooner or later, the inevitable revolt against reactionary complacency.'[43]

Dalton, on the other hand, saw planning only as the first stage on a longer path, with equality as the goal. He did not reject what he called the 'plans, part private and part social' of the Next Five Years people. He endorsed them and stressed their links with the 'social planning' which he himself was advocating. For him, however, social planning was a means to an end far beyond immediate economic adjustments. 'Planning is not the same thing as Socialism', he wrote. 'Socialism is primarily a question of ownership, planning a question of control or direction.' His own aim was a transition to a 'better social order' of a kind that would have gained the approval of Karl Marx, though not perhaps of contemporary Marxists. For Dalton, death duties were a vital instrument 'for the progressive achievement of Social Equality'.[44]

This was a topic on which the Next Five Years Group was notably silent.

Dalton's attitude towards non-socialist planners was similar to his general attitude towards the new expansionist economics: they were moving in the right direction, but they did not go far enough. He denounced Lloyd George's ideas for a British 'New Deal' as 'wishy-washy' proposals, which a Labour Government would leave far behind. 'We are out for much bigger and more fundamental changes.'[45]

The Next Five Years Group did not last long. However its message continued to have a strong appeal in all parties, among academic economists, and especially in the civil service. During the wartime Coalition and under the Labour Government that followed there were many public servants, temporary and permanent, who were inspired by the Next Five Years approach, the 'mixed economy' mentality that led naturally to 1950s Butskellism, with an emphasis on maximising production and growth, minimising inflation and maintaining political and economic stability. Increased government intervention, according to this view, was neither right nor wrong in principle but simply inevitable. Gradually the Group's view 'that our actual system will in any case be a mixed one for many years to come'[46] was absorbed by a large section of the political and administrative establishment. Dalton welcomed the change of attitude and made use of it. But his belief in greater equality, not just as a technique but as an objective, his belief in the redistribution of wealth as a good in itself, helped to keep him significantly apart.

During the 1930s Dalton's circle of political friends moved away from his own generation. This was partly because there were few leading Labour contemporaries whose company he enjoyed; partly because of his emotional preference for young men; and partly because, early in the decade, he encountered a group of particularly able and stimulating political aspirants who looked to him for guidance.

Among existing leaders, his relations seemed worst with contemporaries of his own class. This may have been because of feelings of rivalry. Harold Laski described Dalton to Beatrice Webb as 'the Devil in the British Labour Party', alleging that he was considered by L.S.E. colleagues as 'an ambitious and unscrupulous self-seeker'. Susan Lawrence, a middle-class N.E.C. member representing the old (and largely defunct) Fabian Society, claimed that Dalton was the manipulator of a trade union-dominated group on the Executive which she labelled 'the nitwits and the drunkards'.[47] Dalton got on best with the more proletarian members of the N.E.C. – Joe Compton, Arthur Jenkins (father of Roy) and George Dallas in particular. None of these, however, provided real companionship, and so he looked elsewhere. Linking his private feelings to a political aim, he made a hobby and a crusade of seeking out, encouraging and nurturing the socialist leaders of the future.

Over the years this developed into a fixed habit. His motives were entirely altruistic: there was no intention, as some believed, of building a private political army. His satisfaction came from a sense of pride in the accomplishments of those he helped and in his enjoyment of their company. At the centre of his group were Hugh Gaitskell and Evan Durbin, economics dons at University College, London and the L.S.E. respectively; Colin Clark, another economist; Robert Fraser and Douglas Jay, both journalists on the *Daily Herald*; John Wilmot, Labour victor at the 1933 East Fulham by-election; and Nicholas Davenport, a young financial writer ('Toreador') on the *New Statesman*. To these and others Dalton gave friendship, advice and practical assistance, channelling them into appropriate posts and on to appropriate committees, and finding them candidatures. In return, they fed him with new ideas and kept him entertained.

Gaitskell and Durbin, mutual friends since Oxford undergraduate days, were Dalton's closest companions among his younger protégés. Durbin was the better economist and philosopher, writing a series of important works that related political and economic thought to socialist objectives. Gaitskell had the more practical intelligence, better suited to problems of administration.

Dalton influenced and helped Gaitskell most. The two Hughs had first met in 1928, renewing their acquaintance later through Dalton's student contemporary, the historian Eileen Power. By the early 1930s Gaitskell had joined a growing circle of Oxford socialists who had abandoned the *salon* of G. D. H. Cole and adopted Dalton as a mentor instead. Dalton had the advantage over Cole that he was interested in obtaining power and using it. In 1936, Beatrice Webb noted that Gaitskell and Durbin were now working closely with Dalton, and also with Morrison. 'Gaitskell considers that Cole, Laski and Tawney "have lost their grip over the workers"', she observed.[48] A few months later, Dalton provided the crucial contact that led to Gaitskell's adoption in 1937 as candidate for South Leeds, and hence, after the Second World War, to a career in Parliament.[49]

Unlike Gaitskell and Durbin, Nicholas Davenport was not a socialist. He was, however, an ardent reformer, with an iconoclastic view of the financial world and its inefficiencies. Dalton first met him in September 1931. Their encounter was not accidental. Dalton was trying to meet 'as many City blokes as possible', in the hope of providing the battered Labour Party and its sub-committees with information and ideas in a field about which it was embarrassingly ignorant.[50]

Early in 1932 Davenport helped to found an unusual group known as the XYZ Club – a 'cell' of Labour sympathisers in the City which aimed to educate the Labour Party in financial matters. The semi-secret Club met regularly above a pub, discussing such topics as 'the short term position of the merchant banks'. Papers were kept anonymous to protect authors. Among XYZ members there were City people (accountants, bankers, insurance men), economists and a few politicians. Gaitskell became secretary. Dalton played a key role as political patron, providing a link to the N.E.C. and its policy-making bodies. It was through Dalton that, at the first meeting of the N.E.C. Finance and Trade Sub-Committee, six members of XYZ were brought in to give their views.[51] Largely as a result of Dalton's skilfully directing hand, much of the financial policy in Labour's 1934 document, *For Socialism and Peace*, was a product of XYZ deliberations. The proposal for a National Investment Board, picked up by Davenport from Keynes, found its way into Labour's programme because of an XYZ paper prepared by Davenport and pushed through the N.E.C. Policy Committee by Dalton.[52]

Davenport has given a vivid description of how Dalton appeared at this time to the XYZ people:

> He towered over lesser mortals and in conversation he had the habit of turning up his eyes to heaven, so that they showed the whites. He was physically ungainly. His head was too large for his narrow shoulders. He had long legs but his arms were too short for his body, hanging like the fore-flappers of a dinosaur. When seated, his great bald dome dominated the table, and when he was plied with good wine his talk became lively and amusing, but he always boomed, and it was impossible to get a word in when his voice rang round the room.[53]

Dalton found XYZ much more congenial than N.F.R.B., even though some of his friends, including Gaitskell, took an active part in both. XYZ was social as well as political, more business-like, and more urbane; and Cole was not a member. It continued to exist after the Second World War, though as a dining club for Gaitskellites rather than as a ginger group or fifth column. Its greatest influence was in the 1930s, with Dalton tying its activities to Party programme making.

Through XYZ friends – Gaitskell and Davenport in particular – Dalton began to absorb and accept key features of the Cambridge

School economic doctrine. Dalton was not 'converted' to Keynesianism, and the differences between Keynes's liberalism and his own socialism remained. However, he came to see the force of the argument crystallised in Douglas Jay's *The Socialist Case* (published a few months after Keynes's *General Theory*) that Keynesian ideas could become the servant of socialist planning. Gradually, even hesitantly, this argument became a part of official Labour Party doctrine. Before the end of the decade, and unknown to the vast majority of its own members, the Labour Party had quietly adopted an expansionist approach to economic policy that was at least semi-Keynesian. 'By the outbreak of war the Labour Party had travelled light years in the depth and sophistication of its knowledge of British financial institutions and economic policy options since the dark days of 1931', the historian of Labour's financial policy has written. In this process 'Dalton's experts' – Gaitskell, Durbin, Davenport, Jay, Clark – played a crucial role.[54]

XV

Anti-Appeaser

In 1933 Labour was essentially a pacifist party. By the end of 1937 it had become a party that believed in armed deterrence, a party that urged collective security through the League of Nations and a party that bitterly opposed Neville Chamberlain's policy of appeasement. The architect of this remarkable change was Hugh Dalton.

Labour's official position in the aftermath of the 1931 election was the same as before it: the policy of Henderson and Dalton at the Foreign Office during the second Labour administration. Officially, the Labour Party stood for multilateral disarmament by negotiated agreement, and security on the basis of the League of Nations Covenant. Unofficially, large sections of Labour opinion were opposed to the use of force under any circumstances. Non-pacifists and pacifists could cautiously agree on the official formula, even though it held out the possibility of the use of force – so long as the danger that force might actually be used remained remote. When Hitler came to power, however, this fragile unity quickly collapsed. The threat of military sanctions by member nations against an aggressor, laid down in the League Charter, suddenly acquired a new importance, dividing those who supported it from those who did not.

Dalton had always believed in the necessity of the threat of sanctions, while pressing for disarmament all round. Even after the Nazi victory in Germany, he continued to take disarmament seriously. He remained, as he put it to friends in 1935, a 'bloody-minded pacifist', in favour of a strong League policy.[1] In *Practical Socialism for Britain*, written in 1934, he called for the 'all-round scrapping' of weapons legally forbidden to Germany under the Versailles Treaty, so that Germany should have no valid ground for alleging that it was still subject to differential treatment; for an international disarmament agreement based on strict inspection and control; for an 'international police force'; and for international control of civil aviation. But he also emphasised Article 16 of the League Covenant, which bound member nations to take necessary economic and financial measures against another member that resorted to war. 'In my opinion', he wrote, 'collective economic and financial pressure, or even the threat of it, if known to be seriously meant, would, in nearly all hypothetical cases, halt an intruding aggressor in his tracks.' He gave the Japanese aggression in Manchuria as a practical example. If Britain and the United States had acted firmly at the start, the outcome would have been very different. Always, in this discussion, Dalton referred only to *peaceful* sanctions. It was still indelicate in progressive circles even to mention the possibility of a British Government resorting to force. Nevertheless the implication of Dalton's stress on 'firm' and 'authoritative' action (and on such phrases as 'in nearly all hypothetical cases') was clear.[2]

As a Foreign Office minister in 1929–31, Dalton had pursued the triple aims of security, arbitration and disarmament. After 1933 his first priority became security. This was partly because his freedom from parliamentary duties made it possible to travel widely. In addition to his Russian and Italian trips in 1932–3, he visited Switzerland, Germany, Czechoslovakia, Austria, Belgium, Sweden and the United States, all between 1931 and 1935. Some visits were holidays, some were in response to invitations, some were related to the Acland 'Unbalanced Budgets' project. Each added a jigsaw piece to his picture of the unfolding crisis. Wherever he went, he cross-examined leaders of progressive opinion, carefully recording their comments and his own impressions.

One visit was of special importance, jolting him into a new perception of the European reality. If a trip to Stalinist Russia changed his view of practical socialism in Britain, a brief stay in Hitlerite Germany a few months later altered his view of foreign policy by giving him an acute sense of the Nazi danger.

When Hitler came to full power in Germany in March 1933, Dalton cancelled a planned lecture tour of German cities on the grounds that he did not want to claim privileges of free speech now denied to the Germans. He did not, however, cancel a plan to visit a young student called Brindley Thomas, one of the Acland scholars who was studying German public finance in Berlin as part of the 'Unbalanced Budgets' programme. He spent four days at the end of April in the German capital to 'make sure that it was safe, or at least tolerable' for Thomas to remain.

In the academic community Dalton found an atmosphere of tension and fear, and all his old anti-German feelings were re-awakened. He met Emil Lederer, Professor of Economics at Berlin, who had stayed with the Daltons at West Leaze. Lederer was an expert on the Theory of Planning. He was also a socialist and a Jew. Lederer told him that Nazis had ransacked his flat, stealing money, valuables and books. Lederer himself had been sacked from his university post. On the evening of 29th April, Dalton visited Lederer's flat a second time:

> Sit in a circle of the dismissed, several socialists, one of whom was in the Berlin Police, another a deputy for Hamburg ...
>
> 'Only those professors will be recognised', say the studenthoods, 'who are imbued with the spirit of the storm detachments.'
>
> Lederer gives me a list of 94 professors and other teachers who have been dismissed.
>
> In Bavaria children leaving school are no longer to be given a copy of the Weimar Constitution, but instead a selection of extracts from the Treaty of Versailles.
>
> B[rindley] T[homas] says that since June 30th we have been living in this world, where we are always working up to an ever-receding climax in an insane symphony.

Dalton was told about the seven-year-old daughter of a Professor at Marburg, branded by two Nazis with a swastika on her leg. He spent a day with the educationalist Kurt Hahn who told him that people were kept awake by the screams of the Nazis' victims in their barracks at night. He learnt of suicides, private executions and concentration camps. Rapidly, over these four hectic days, he acquired an overpowering sense of a vulgar abandonment of reason. Returning to England felt like an escape. 'Germany is horrible', he wrote. 'A European war must be counted now among the probabilities of the next ten years.'[3]

After the Berlin visit, there was no change in the logic of Dalton's attitude to international affairs. But there was a major shift in emphasis: hypothetical dangers became immediate ones. In the past, Dalton had seen the League as a court and a forum; now he saw it as a means for European defence. 'There are some ugly beasts prowling today in the international jungle', he told a Bishop Auckland audience. 'Britain should give clear warning that she will not hesitate to apply the full weight of economic and financial boycott against any nation that, in violation of solemn covenants which all have signed, resorts to war.'[4] If economic sanctions failed, it might be necessary for the League to resort to military sanctions as well.[5]

At first, Dalton trod carefully. His own views might have moved rapidly in response to international events. Those of the Labour

Movement had not. With more expediency than courage, he accepted on behalf of the N.E.C. a resolution advocating the 'general strike against war' at the October 1933 Party Conference.[6] 'My luck was in this year and I had a great success', he wrote after Conference had voted him top in his own section of the Executive. 'I was continually in the picture and scored particularly full marks, in the general judgement of the delegates, every time.'[7] Popularity was too sweet, for the moment, to be sacrificed on a point of principle.

Yet he soon allowed his better judgment to prevail. When, in December 1933, the young man who had presided at the Oxford Union in the famous 'King and Country' debate asked him to sign a declaration demanding that Germany should be allowed to rearm up to the British level, Dalton replied sharply that 'the bloody truth is that she has already rearmed to a dangerous extent, is rearming and will continue to rearm. And with equality of armaments even at zero, her war potential is terribly formidable, and her present rulers war minded to a terrible degree'.[8] Next summer Dalton pushed through the N.E.C. a document which declared in favour of 'the collective peace system' based on the League, emphasising the need to resist aggression while leaving open the means of such resistance. The 1934 Party Conference in Southport adopted this by a large majority.

It was the Italy–Abyssinia dispute a year later that brought to a head the issue of what resistance might, in practice, mean. The Labour Party and T.U.C. favoured economic sanctions against Italy in the event of an Italian attack, accepting that such sanctions might lead to war. Dalton, who had repented of his brief infatuation with Mussolini, strongly agreed. George Lansbury, the Labour Party Leader, was firmly opposed, on pacifist grounds. So too was Sir Stafford Cripps, for the rather different reason that he objected to capitalist sanctions imposed by imperialist governments.

Cripps showed the strength of his feelings by resigning from the Labour Executive, thereby adding to the embarrassment of Lansbury. Lansbury did not resign, but his stand on sanctions made his voluntary or forced departure seem probable. Two things were therefore at stake as the 1935 Conference approached: the future of Labour foreign policy and the succession to the Party Leadership. For the moment, Dalton stood back from the Leadership issue, leaving the business of disposing of Lansbury to the trade union leaders. Instead he concentrated on Labour's policy, and the threat presented by his most dangerous rival, Sir Stafford Cripps.

It was not their first clash. In the years since the 1931 election, Cripps had used his position as the possessor of a rare parliamentary seat to make speeches of Jacobin fervour that delighted constituency activists and infuriated leaders less fortunate than himself who had lost their seats and wished to regain them. In 1933 Cripps had been elected Chairman of the Socialist League, a body composed of left-wingers who decided to stay in the Labour Party when the I.L.P. broke away from it in 1932. Soon Cripps was repeating the arguments and rhetoric of the small but deeply committed League, propagating the defiant message that a newly elected Labour majority must pass an immediate Emergency Powers Act to forestall wrecking moves by capitalists. The right-wing national press presented this message as a demand for socialist dictatorship. The Labour establishment rounded angrily on Cripps for providing such explosive copy. After one speech by Cripps early in 1934 Dalton lost his temper at an N.E.C. meeting and bellowed abuse at the unrepentant Member for Bristol East. 'Cripps seems quite unable to see the argument that he is damaging the Party electorally', Dalton noted privately. ' ... He has become very vain and seems to think that only he and his cronies know what Socialism is, or how it should be preached.'[9] By the time of the 1935 battle over sanctions, Dalton and Cripps were already in bitterly opposed camps.

When Cripps resigned from the Party Executive, Dalton wrote to Kingsley Martin, editor of the *New Statesman*: '[Cripps] is naive, often to the point of sheer imbecility'.[10] Publicly, Dalton announced that Cripps's policy of opposing sanctions was in effect 'pro-Fascist and pro-War'.[11] The 1935 Brighton Conference focussed on the ritual martyrdom of George Lansbury. After Bevin had denounced him from the podium and delegates had voted against him from the floor, Lansbury gave up his office. Dalton, however, was much less interested in Lansbury than in Cripps.

'Transport House was set on steamrolling Stafford and his group', observed Beatrice Webb, 'and put up Dalton to do it with the help of trade union officials.'[12] Dalton had been deeply concerned lest Cripps, Lansbury's own preferred candidate, might succeed to the Leadership. He therefore did everything possible to prevent this coming about. He was much relieved when the unassuming, 'accidental' Deputy Leader, Clement Attlee, was asked by the P.L.P. to take over for the rest of the session. Such a temporary arrangement left open the question of who should become permanent Leader until after the expected general election, by which time other prominent politicians who might wish to compete would have returned to Parliament. Nevertheless the Leadership problem – carrying with it the Cripps danger, and the associated danger of a disastrous foreign policy – continued to dominate inner party conversations. Herbert Morrison suspected that Dalton was interested himself.[13] So did

Cripps. 'Dalton is being run by Transport House as leader in the next Parliament', Beatrice Webb was told by her nephew just before Conference.[14]

In reality this was not in Dalton's mind at all. As early as May 1935 Dalton had begun hinting that he would back Herbert Morrison in a possible contest. Dalton did not particularly like Morrison. Two factors however were crucial. First, Morrison was an able, determined, nuts-and-bolts politician who thought hard about policy, treated easy slogans with contempt, and shared his own outlook on many issues. Second, Morrison (who had just led the London Labour Party to its first ever London County Council election victory) looked like a winner – both against Cripps in the Labour Party, and against the Tories in the country.

Immediately after the autumn Party Conference, with the Leadership question still wide open, Dalton invited the Morrisons to West Leaze for a weekend of serious intrigue. Taking Herbert for a walk on the Marlborough Downs, he carefully explained how, by a process of elimination, he had made his choice. A. V. Alexander (the Co-op leader) and Sir Stafford Cripps were the two possible candidates against whom he would put all his influence. He himself was not a candidate though he might become one at some future date. As for the rest, 'Attlee is very small and [Arthur] Greenwood has hurt his mind by drinking'. That left Morrison. His own support, however, would have a price. 'I feel', he began, weighing his words, 'though it isn't a job one would hold out glad hands for in the present state of the world, that I could do the FO better than anyone else in the Party; if the external world was quiet, perhaps I could do something big on the Home Front.' Taken aback but not displeased, Morrison accepted the deal.[15]

Here the matter rested until after the general election six weeks later. Dalton had a troublesome campaign. Physical ailments often struck him at tense moments. On this occasion sciatica and lumbago, followed by a torn tendon, forced him to bed for the last week, leaving Ruth to address meetings and deal with the press.[16] Nevertheless he won back the Bishop Auckland seat decisively. His personal majority was 8,086. He was now firmly back in the House of Commons and his position was never again to be shaken during the remaining twenty-four years of his career. The national outcome, however, was disappointing. Dalton had not expected the Government to be defeated, but he had privately predicted a Labour total of more than 200 seats. The actual number was only 154. Most of Dalton's younger friends – John Wilmot, Robert Fraser, Hugh Gaitskell, Evan Durbin, in particular – who might have been expected to win, failed to do so. Though the P.L.P. trebled in size, it contained few new members who offered stimulus or real companionship, and Dalton viewed his return to the Commons bleakly. On the other hand, the small size and lack of talent of the P.L.P. ensured his own prominence within it.

As soon as the election was over Dalton put his earlier plans into operation. 'Now focus on (1) the Leadership (2) getting rid of this physical unfitness', he wrote immediately after his own count. 'As to (2) ionisation by Miss Wickstead. As to (1) many activities!'[17] Dalton's worst fear – that Cripps might win the Leadership – was removed when Cripps decided, after all, not to stand. With Cripps out of the way, Morrison's chances seemed excellent. There were only two other candidates: the diffident Clement Attlee, and the popular but often inebriated Arthur Greenwood, head of the Party research department, and Minister of Health in the 1929 administration. Morrison was the ablest of the three, and the most proletarian.

Dalton appointed himself, in effect, Morrison's campaign manager. This probably did Morrison more harm than good. A 'secret' canvassing meeting in Dalton's flat, leaked to the press, added to the reputations of both Dalton and Morrison for back-stage plotting; while Dalton's noisy declarations that apart from Morrison, the choice was between a nonentity and a drunk,[18] may have helped to bring the Attlee and Greenwood camps together. It was the first time that there had been any organised lobbying for the Party Leadership, and some M.P.s felt it improper.

The election went to two ballots. In the first, Attlee received 58 votes, Morrison 44 and Greenwood 33. In the second, Greenwood's supporters switched as a block to Attlee, whose vote rose to 88, while Morrison's vote only increased to 48. Morrison was bitterly disappointed and refused to take the Deputy Leadership, which therefore went to Greenwood. Afterwards, Attlee was quietly reassuring. He said that he had been elected for one session only, and if M.P.s wanted a change later he would not complain. Few of his listeners imagined that Attlee would in fact serve for two decades, longer than any other leader of a major British party in the twentieth century.

Dalton's failed attempt at king-making had important effects. It set a precedent for hard-fought Leadership contests which has been followed with increasing sophistication on every occasion since. At the time, it did Dalton some political damage. Though he re-entered the Parliamentary Executive in second place (ahead of Morrison) a week later, he had not endeared himself to senior colleagues. Morrison had gained no benefit from his support. Dalton had come out publicly against the new Leader and Deputy Leader, and privately against

Alexander (who, he had told Morrison, 'is incredibly vain, wants no big changes and has the outlook of a grocer who has once been to sea'.)[19] Meanwhile, there was no improvement in his relations with Cripps. 'Unfortunately, Dalton and Cripps are declared enemies', wrote Beatrice Webb early in the new Parliament.[20]

Dalton had asked Morrison for the Foreign Office in a future Labour Government as the price for his support. Attlee was under no such obligation – a difference which, as we shall see, was to have significance later. In the short run, however, Dalton's deal with Morrison seemed to have been unnecessary: Dalton got what he wanted from the candidate he had opposed. Recognising Dalton's interests and experience, Attlee made him Opposition spokesman on foreign affairs, a portfolio he continued to hold until the outbreak of war. This was a key appointment. Over the next four years its importance increased. As international tensions grew, Dalton used his position to attack any sign of weakness in the Government's attitude towards the Dictators, and to coax Labour opinion first towards a 'strong' League policy, and then towards the view that an armed alliance against Hitler would reduce the likelihood of war.

He was not able to achieve such a transformation on his own. For the moment, only a small minority in the P.L.P. agreed with his views. Hence he depended on the solid weight of trade union representatives on the National Executive and National Council of Labour and at Party Conference. Two key figures who shared his outlook were Ernest Bevin, of the Transport and General Workers' Union, and Walter Citrine of the T.U.C. The result was a political alliance called by one historian 'the Dalton-Bevin-Citrine block'[21] which succeeded in defeating not only the pacifists and the Crippsite anti-sanctions Left, but also the League of Nations traditionalists, who held back from the implications of a policy of peace-through-strength.

Dalton agreed with one 'appeasement' argument: that some of the things demanded by the Dictators might be ceded peacefully over a negotiating table. What he opposed, with a consistency shown by few others, was any sign of weakness in response to the threat of force. 'Italy would have had a case in equity if she had come into court with clean hands', he told the Commons just before the Christmas recess in 1935, 'but equity cannot be claimed by Mussolini when his hands are dripping with Abyssinian blood ... '[22] He pointed to British capitalist complicity – citing evidence of British oil fuelling Italian bombers – and used this as an argument for economic sanctions even at the risk of war. Over the next few months he provided a critique of Government foreign policy in the House of Commons that had previously been lacking. 'He is the perfect inquisitional type, the

Torquemada of the Socialist Party', commented the *Daily Telegraph*, with reluctant admiration. 'His eyes look upwards, and a faint, almost spiritual smile comes over his face as he applies another turn of the thumbscrews.'[23]

On his own side, however, Dalton's performances were not universally admired. Crippsites and pacifists found much in Dalton's fierce rhetoric that was objectionable. Beatrice Webb, voicing the opinions of her nephew, observed caustically that Dalton had become a 'dogmatic sanctionist', giving orders to the Party Leader.[24] Lord Ponsonby, a pacifist who had resigned from the Labour Leadership in the Lords on the sanctions issue, complained bitterly that Dalton's version of Party policy was 'to continue sanctions and strengthen sanctions – not to stop the war – but to punch somebody or other, to make the Italian people suffer and "to make a just peace" '.[25] Dalton did not worry unduly about opposition of this kind. Nevertheless it set limits to his own attack on the Government.

Labour opinion certainly helped to determine Dalton's position on the other major Fascist advance of early 1936: Hitler's reoccupation of the Rhineland. Winding up for the Opposition in the House, Dalton gave broad support to the Government, which had asked only for a formal condemnation by the League of Nations. There could be no question, he indicated, of any kind of resistance: public opinion drew a clear distinction between Mussolini's aggressive war beyond his own frontiers, 'and the actions, up-to-date at any rate, of Herr Hitler which, much as we regard them as reprehensible, have taken place within the frontiers of the German Reich'.[26]

Later Dalton admitted that he had been wrong. Hitler's entry into the Rhineland had been 'the greatest bluff of his life', opposed by Hitler's own military advisers. If the French army had moved against him, Hitler would have retreated. 'I over-estimated', Dalton recalled, 'in particular, relatively to other forces which could have been ranged against it, the immediate striking power of the German Air Force.'[27] Yet at the time nobody in the Labour Movement, and very few outside it, voiced a different opinion.

Dalton's attitude to Franco's rebellion in Spain, which began in the summer of 1936, was more complicated. Nothing in foreign or domestic politics between the wars aroused more passion and idealism on the British Left than the Spanish conflict. 'The issues are very simple', a young poet told Julian Symons, summing up the mood of a radical generation. 'This is a struggle between the forces of good in the world and the forces of evil.'[28] Almost all socialists, and many Liberals, agreed.

For Dalton the issues were not so simple. Unlike the Labour Left, he did not need Franco to remind him of the danger of Nazi Germany. Unlike most of the British Labour Party, he was not particularly impressed by the Spanish Republicans, believing that the Spanish Left shared responsibility with the Right for the breakdown of democracy. Most Labour leaders opposed the policy of 'non-intervention' adopted by the French and British Governments, arguing that Britain should give active support to the Republican regime. Dalton, by contrast, found himself 'far from enthusiastic for the slogan "Arms for Spain", if this means, as some of my friends eagerly thought it did, that *we* were to supply arms which otherwise we should keep for ourselves.'[29] He concluded that the Labour and Marxist Left seemed to care more about defending Spain from Fascism and Nazism than about defending Britain from the same enemies. Hence he was never very aroused by Spain, and said as little on the subject as he could.

This greatly affected his relations with the Labour Left, providing a far more serious quarrel than existed over domestic policy. Increasingly Dalton came to think of 'Spain' and 'Communism' as virtually synonymous, and to regard political action within the Labour Party in support of the Spanish Government with suspicion. When Laski tried to fix up a Labour Party emergency conference on Spain, he found Dalton 'the outstanding opponent of our plans'.[30]

Dalton thought in terms of election victories, not popular crusades. 'To *become the government*' was Dalton's supreme aim, Cripps complained to his aunt in April 1937.[31] Dalton would not have denied it. The next election was due in 1939 or 1940. What prospect was there of gaining enough seats to take power and adopt a new foreign policy if the Party fought under the slogan 'Arms for Spain, but no arms for Britain'? So long as the Labour Movement regarded Franco as a more serious threat than Hitler, Dalton could see little chance of a rational approach in international affairs. In such conditions, he told Leonard Woolf, the Opposition were 'as impotent as flies disapproving the approach of winter'.[32] The need to change Labour's outlook was therefore of the utmost urgency.

Shifting the Party was a task that called on all Dalton's manipulative skills. In contrast to Cripps and the Labour Left, Dalton saw no virtue in confrontations: he believed in winning. Hence it was necessary to move an inch at a time. In February 1936 the Government announced a £300 million rearmament plan. Dalton felt that this was a step in the right direction. So did Walter Citrine of the T.U.C. The Parliamentary Executive, however, decided that the plan was the beginning of a competitive arms race and moved a 'reasoned amendment' to the Government's White Paper. 'Awfully wearisome. We *are* unfit to govern!' Dalton wrote privately. 'Party won't face up to realities. Still much more anti-armament sentiment, and more agin our own Govt than agin Hitler. Pretty desperate.'[33] To have attacked the Party publicly, however, would have jeopardised his position on the front bench. So Dalton restricted his criticisms to private Party meetings.[34] When the P.L.P. followed the usual practice at the end of July of voting against all Service Estimates, he invoked the 'conscience clause' and abstained. Only Alexander and Dalton's old L.S.E. colleague Lees-Smith supported him among the leaders. There seemed a long way to go.

That summer, Hugh and Ruth escaped to Sweden, where Hugh spent instructive hours with the economist Gunnar Myrdal, learning about expansionist policies applied by the Social Democratic Government in Stockholm. At home, Dalton's failure to comment on events in another part of Europe did not go unnoticed. 'I am told, when I ring up, that Dalton is in Lapland', complained Kingsley Martin, as the Spanish War took a turn for the worse.[35] In September, Dalton travelled to Paris where he met Leon Blum, the socialist leader who had become Prime Minister at the head of the new *Front Populaire* Government. Blum convinced him of the merits of the non-intervention policy, presenting arguments which he could use against critics in England.[36] But his mind was not on Spain, which seemed a dangerous diversion. His main concern was rearmament.

'The Hitler Rearmament races on', he had noted in the spring. 'Few people in the Labour Party seem to know or care anything about it.'[37] At the Edinburgh Party Conference in October 1936, Dalton made his first major attempt to put this right by urging the Labour Party to abandon its earlier restraint and accept the necessity of armed deterrence. The N.E.C. put foward a carefully worded compromise resolution on rearmament, aimed at satisfying competing factions. Dalton, however, was exasperated by what he called an *'esprit de conciliation* in the drafting committee'.[38] At the N.E.C. drafting meeting on 18th September he pointed out the disastrous effects of the Party's present position and the need to strengthen Britain's defence.[39] Before he spoke he talked to J. T. Murphy, an ex-Communist who had become a staunch rearmer. 'How gravely he impressed upon David Davies and myself the seriousness of the growing power of Nazism', Murphy recalled, 'and that he intended to go all out for rearmament.' Yet Murphy was disappointed by Dalton's speech and felt that he pulled his punches.[40]

After the 1936 Conference Dalton's need for restraint became less, and his ability to influence policy greatly increased. Because of the 'Buggins' Turn' principle on the N.E.C. (whereby the Chairman was

chosen annually in rotation on the basis of length of service), Dalton
became Chairman of the Labour Party for the 1936–7 year. The Party
Chairmanship was not usually regarded as a powerful position.
Dalton decided to make it one. Few previous incumbents had also
been prominent parliamentary leaders – most had come from the
trade union section, where there was a tendency to leave politics to the
politicians. Yet the office of Chairman provided a unique opportunity
for anybody who chose to take it, carrying with it the joint Chairmanship (shared at this time with Ernest Bevin) of the powerful, union-
dominated National Council of Labour. In addition Dalton held the
Chairmanships of the Policy and International Sub-Committees of
the N.E.C. He was able to use these strategic posts to advantage.
Backed by the trade union leaders, outshining Attlee in energy and
platform presence, firmly in command at Transport House, he became
effective leader of the Labour Party for the next twelve months, pushing it with remarkable success along his chosen path.

He fought on five fronts. He was determined to make the Labour
Party electorally attractive, so as to win the next election. He wanted
to clarify the Party's position on rearmament. He wanted to highlight
the problem of unemployment. He wanted to beat down the rebellious,
left-wing Socialist League, and thereby spike the guns of Sir Stafford
Cripps. Finally he planned to steal the Labour Left's clothes by pushing through a major Labour Party constitutional change which would
greatly increase the power of the constituency organisations.

He turned first to unemployment. His most immediate concern was
an N.E.C. commitment given at Edinburgh to conduct a Labour Party
investigation into the problems of the Distressed Areas. Many on the
Left regarded this as insulting and hypocritical. 'Have we not had
enough reports?' Ellen Wilkinson declared. 'Is there a pore in the
body of an unemployed man that has not been card-indexed?'[41]
Dalton, however, took a Fabian view. Where Ellen Wilkinson
believed that the only practical policy was to 'rouse the people',
Dalton saw two possible gains from an inquiry: publicity and a chance
to work out a new policy. Dalton's arguments prevailed and a Distressed Areas Commission was set up with himself as Chairman.

After conducting a series of hearings in Scotland, South Wales, the
North East, Lancashire and West Cumberland, Dalton had two proposals. First, that production sites for the Government's new defence
programme should be placed in the Distressed Areas. Second, that a
Cabinet minister should be given responsibility for the condition of
the Special Areas, with power to require all new industries or factories to establish themselves where new employment was needed,
unless they could prove the need to set up elsewhere. 'We should

aim at the transfer of work into these areas', declared Dalton's Report, 'rather than the transfer of workers away from them.'

This was the basis for the Location of Industry scheme – father of all post-war regional policy – which Dalton introduced as war-time President of the Board of Trade. The idea had originated during Dalton's trip to Russia in 1932. It had found a place in Labour's policy document *For Socialism and Peace* and in Dalton's own *Practical Socialism for Britain*. Now it was reinforced by the evidence of massive imbalance between the boom-towns of the south and midlands and the ghost-towns of the north and west. 'We are impressed with the argument in favour of the development of light industries here in a town which in the past has specialised to an unhealthy extent on heavy industries', Dalton declared while visiting Sunderland, on the river Wear.[42] The steady replacement after the war of old industry in the areas of pre-war unemployment by new, light manufacture, owed much to Dalton's investigations as Labour Party Chairman.

Dalton's study of the Distressed Areas formed part of a wider initiative on domestic policy. His position as Party Chairman enabled him to make special use of his young economist friends, and he saw that Colin Clark, Evan Durbin, Hugh Gaitskell and Douglas Jay were co-opted onto the N.E.C.'s policy sub-committees and advisory panels.[43] Here they were able to inject some of the implications of Keynes's recently published *General Theory* into Labour policy-making.* They also played a part in shaping, under Dalton's overall direction, a short manifesto called *Labour's Immediate Programme* which was adopted by Party Conference in 1937..This document was based on a memorandum, submitted to the Policy Committee in January 1937, which presented Dalton's own evolving views on socialist planning, strongly influenced by Durbin, Gaitskell and other members of his intimate team.

Labour's Immediate Programme finally buried the 1932 Conference commitment to nationalise the joint stock banks. It was less extreme in tone than the dramatic 'confrontationist' demands of Party Conference at the beginning of the decade. But it was much more radical in substance because it described policies that could actually be carried out. There was for example a clear declaration of intent to 'command the main levers which will control the economic machine', namely Finance, Land, Transport, Coal and Power. There were commitments to set up a National Investment Board, nationalise the Bank of England and undertake large schemes of public development. There was also a section on the Distressed Areas, stressing the

* See pp. 222–4.

need for direct intervention. 'The State must accept responsibility for the location of industry', declared the *Programme*. 'Labour will bring new industries into these areas, will encourage existing industries, develop local resources and improve communications, assist Local Authorities and relieve the crushing burden of local rates.'

Specific commitments to the new Keynesian techniques were included in the original memorandum upon which the *Programme* was based. Dalton made little attempt, however, to retain these at a later stage, and they were excluded from the final version of the document.[44] The published statement reflected Dalton's own approach to the problems which would face an incoming socialist Government: the need, not just to provide financial or fiscal management, but to develop and re-direct industry in such a way as to benefit those sectors and regions most in need of help.

At the same time, Dalton was prepared to make concessions – to moderate the language of Labour's message (and drop irrelevant policies like the joint stock banks commitment) – in order to win votes. After the 1935 defeat he realised more than ever the need for Labour to gain support outside its working-class strongholds. He combined a mild and reasonable tone in the *Immediate Programme* with articles and speeches which emphasised the common interests of all wage and salary earners. 'We must not neglect the technicians and the salaried and professional classes, the "black-coated workers"', he wrote, 'among whom we have already more supporters than we sometimes realise.' He told an Upminster audience in November 1936 (repeating an argument he had first learnt from Bernard Shaw and H. G. Wells): 'You people who think you belong to the middle class are much nearer to those on the Means Test than to those who are millionaires.'[45]

Published in March 1937, *Labour's Immediate Programme* sold 300,000 copies before the annual Conference in October. A pictorial version sold more than 400,000.[46] More important, the Programme provided the Party's main policy theme – the basis for its self-image and its propaganda – until Labour came to power eight years later.

Meanwhile Dalton's conflict with Sir Stafford Cripps broke out into the open sooner than expected. In January 1937 Cripps and the Socialist League decided to act on their own, issuing a 'Unity Manifesto' in combination with the Communists and the I.L.P. and calling for a 'united front' campaign based on an alliance of 'proletarian' parties (Labour, the Communists and I.L.P.) against the Government. There followed a series of joint meetings and demonstrations involving members of the Socialist League and the two 'Outside Left' organisations.

The Unity Manifesto and the subsequent 'Unity Campaign' were in direct defiance of Labour Party edicts. Speaking for the N.E.C. at Edinburgh Dalton had denounced the united front demand as practically identical to a parallel demand for Communist affiliation to the Labour Party.[47] Conference had then rejected both proposals, endorsing a ban on joint activities with Communists. Hence the reaction of the Party Executive to the Unity Manifesto was predictable: the N.E.C. immediately disaffiliated the Socialist League from the Labour Party; two months later the Executive declared, in addition, that League members would be ineligible for Labour Party membership from 1st June. Attlee and Morrison both voted against this second decision. Dalton was in the majority, taking a tough line.[48]

Dalton's attitude to Cripps during the row combined irritation, perplexity, and an optimistic belief that his rival was destroying himself politically. Yet he did not entirely dislike Cripps, and in a way he was intrigued by him. Ernest Bevin saw Cripps as another Sir Oswald Mosley – an arrogant upper-class careerist with no loyalty to the Labour Movement or understanding of the working class. Dalton's view was less crude. He resented Cripps's prominence after so little work, much as he had resented Mosley's success in the late 1920s. But he did not regard Cripps as insincere, and he was – in spite of himself – impressed by Cripps as a parliamentary performer. Hence he adopted one of his favourite and most aggravating postures: the weary schoolmaster. 'Attlee says I am like a pedagogue addressing a pupil', Dalton noted on one occasion. 'I wish the pupil were a bit brighter!'[49]

The effect on Cripps himself is hard to estimate. Cripps, in this phase, seemed to regard political isolation as proof of his rightness. His apparent indifference to criticism may, however, be deceptive. Certainly Cripps's supporters reacted with fury at what one of them called Dalton's 'Cripps-baiting'.[50] Patricia Strauss, wife of Cripps's close friend and associate G. R. Strauss, accused Dalton of 'personal attacks and innuendoes that leave his opponents gasping'.[51]

One particular shaft caused great rage on the Labour Left largely because it was unanswerable. A new left-wing newspaper, *Tribune*, had been launched in January 1937 to provide encouragement and support to the Unity Campaign. This was an immediate financial failure, made worse when the Campaign fizzled out. Cripps and Strauss, both members of *Tribune*'s editorial board, put up £20,000 between them to save the paper.[52] In the meantime, the disintegrating Socialist League had also become increasingly dependent on handouts from Cripps.

The discovery that the Left's much publicised campaigns were being heavily subsidised by its own leaders was too much for Dalton.

BACK ROW RESERVED FOR TRADE UNION OFFICIALS AND OTHER GREAT STATESMEN

CRIPPS IS EXPELLED FROM THE LABOUR PARTY FOR BEING A SOCIALIST.

DESTROYING THE FABRIC OF CIVILIZATION, THAT'S WOT IT IS.

SHOOT 'EM ALL DOWN!

HE MUST BE ONE O' THEM PAID AGITATORS

UNION SEC.

EXIT

The League was 'little more than a rich man's toy', he declared. 'The so-called Unity Campaign was being financed by one or two rich members. If it were deprived of these plutocratic props, the whole agitation would speedily collapse.'[53] Cripps replied that the Unity Campaign itself was not being financed by rich men (without mentioning *Tribune* or the League) and asked Dalton why, in any case, there was any objection. 'The answer is that in any political movement financial dependence on one or two rich men is undemocratic and unhealthy', answered Dalton.[54] As far as the Socialist League was concerned, however, financial dependence did not long continue. In May 1937, bitter and divided, the League decided to disband itself, and Cripps's aim of 'proletarian' unity was shortly afterwards discarded.

The result of the Unity Campaign, as Fenner Brockway (Secretary of the I.L.P.) put it, 'was the destruction of the Socialist League, the loss of influence of Cripps, Bevan, Strauss and other "Lefts", the strengthening of the reactionary leaders, and the disillusionment of the rank and file'.[55] The isolation of Cripps and the fragmentation of the Crippsite Left also cleared Dalton's way for an important coup on defence policy.

In July 1936 Dalton had failed by a wide margin to persuade the P.L.P. to abstain on the Service Estimates, rather than follow the traditional practice of voting against. The issue was only a symbolic one, given the size of the Government's majority. But it was a potent symbol, of great significance for internal Party debates. Labour could scarcely claim to have a serious rearmament policy while opposing the Estimates. In 1937, therefore, Dalton canvassed hard among M.P.s, urging that an abstention would greatly strengthen his hand in debate. In so doing, he faced resistance from a group led by Arthur Greenwood, Deputy Leader of the Party.

On the eve of the P.L.P. decision, the *Daily Express* political correspondent, Guy Eden, reported that there had been a 'grim battle' between Greenwood and Dalton which had 'split the Parliamentary Party from top to bottom'. The Greenwood camp saw no justification for the rearmament programme and wanted to oppose all Government plans. By contrast, 'Dr. Dalton ... and his powerful group of "intellectuals" contend that while they are asking the Government to stand by collective security and to intervene in Spain, it is illogical to deny the country the forces to carry out this policy.' Dalton had the backing of Transport House, where it was believed that support for rearmament would win votes; and of the trade unions, which believed that rearmament would create employment. Eden concluded, none

Cartoon opposite. *Left to right, front row: Clynes, Greenwood, Morrison, Dalton, Susan Lawrence, Citrine, Attlee, Bevin. One of the men escorting a bowler-hatted Cripps bears the label 'UNION SEC'. Cripps's departure did not take place until 1939.*

the less, that Greenwood, supported by both Attlee and Morrison, was likely to win the contest.[56]

He was wrong. The 1936 decision was narrowly reversed: Dalton won by 45 votes to 39 with the rest not voting – a margin small enough to suggest that, without careful canvassing, the vote might have gone the other way. The P.L.P. stuck to its decision. When the vote on the Estimates was taken in the House the Party abstained. Only six Labour rebels voted with the noes – all pacifists.

'This was as skilful a piece of backstage intrigue as Dalton ever executed', Michael Foot wrote later.[57] *The Times* suggested that Dalton had greatly enhanced his parliamentary prestige, and the *Manchester Guardian* found it necessary to discount rumours that the decision marked the beginning of the end for Attlee and the arrival at the top of Dalton.[58] Well satisfied with his achievement, Dalton wrote to Kingsley Martin saying that he intended to keep quiet for the time being, and let tempers cool; but that he was confident of an overwhelming victory on the issue if it was raised at Conference.[59] His confidence was justified. The National Council of Labour, which spoke for the top leadership of the Labour Party and trade unions, approved a statement drafted by Dalton on *International Policy and Defence*, and this was endorsed both by the T.U.C. and by the October 1937 Party Conference.

It was a turning-point. With the help of the unions, Dalton had moved Labour's official defence policy away from the pacifism of 1933 to an uncompromising opposition to appeasement and firm support for rearmament. Care still had to be taken over phraseology. But by the end of 1937 Labour had clearly announced its belief in a strong League of Nations policy backed by a British military deterrent. This meant in practice an alliance of the three great powers within the League, Britain, France and the Soviet Union, against the possibility of German aggression – precisely the policy advocated by the Churchill and Amery groups among the Tory dissidents.[60] Dalton thought in terms of winning an election on the basis of Labour's policy. Left-wing and Communist tactics had made him hostile to talk of anti-Government fronts. Nevertheless – given the broad agreement that now existed between Tory rebels and the P.L.P. – the opportunity for co-operation across the floor of the House existed, should politicians on both sides have the will to pursue it.

One of the most important, and least noticed, controversies of Dalton's busy Chairman's year concerned the Party Constitution. The dispute (which has echoes in the 1980s) was a product of Labour's organisational growth since the First World War, and in particular of a great increase in the individual membership of constituency parties. This increase had been particularly rapid in the early 1930s. As recently as 1928 there had been fewer than 215,000 individual members, according to official figures; by 1936 the number had more than doubled to 431,000. One result, at a time when trade union membership had actually declined, was a demand among constituency activists for a greater say in the national affairs of the Party, and in particular for the direct representation of local parties on the N.E.C.

Hitherto the constituency parties had been virtually without any power at all, other than the power to select candidates. The so-called 'Constituency and Central Labour Parties' section of the Party Executive contained five members (of whom Dalton was one), *nominated* by local parties, but *elected* by the whole of Party Conference. In practice this meant that the fate of the entire Executive lay with the trade union bloc vote.

The nature of Labour's constitution caused little complaint when the local parties were in their infancy and Labour was gaining seats. It began to arouse resentment when the local parties became stronger and the Labour Party nationally had suffered two bad election defeats in a row. After the 1935 general election, constituency party protest developed into organised revolt. A constituency parties movement was launched, receiving wide support. At the Edinburgh Party Conference in 1936, more than 200 out of a total of 280 constituency delegates met and agreed to set up an unofficial Provisional Committee of Constituency Labour Parties. The aim was to turn the Labour Party Constitution into 'a great democratic instrument'. The secretary and organiser of this Committee was a young Labour candidate, much disliked at Transport House, called Ben Greene. The Chairman was the ubiquitous and munificent Sir Stafford Cripps.

Before Edinburgh, the N.E.C. had ignored the pressure for reform, treating the reformers as left-wing agitators in a new guise, lacking rank and file support. Evidence of support for the Provisional Committee, however, forced it to reconsider. The Executive faced a rebellion by the vast majority of those constituency parties which were strong enough to send delegates to Conference. It therefore decided on a strategic retreat. It would shelve the issue for the moment, but agree to discussions with local parties. On the last day of the Edinburgh Party Conference Dalton, as Chairman-elect, gave a public undertaking that the Executive would 'consider the matter in the most friendly and the most co-operative fashion' on the basis of 'friendly consultations with some, at any rate, of those who have proposals to put forward on this point ... '[61]

At the time, this seemed like another rejection. But Dalton kept his word. Over the next few months he held a series of Area Conferences with local representatives. The response he received was strong and clear: there was a universal desire for a directly elected constituency section on the N.E.C.[62] Dalton's own experience of constituency party politics, and power, had not been entirely happy. He was also a personal beneficiary of precisely the system of election to the Executive constituency parties section – by the union bloc vote – which the reformers wished to destroy. Nevertheless he allowed himself to be persuaded by the strength of local feeling and what seemed a legitimate demand. Having previously opposed constitutional change, he now swung over and became a keen advocate of reform. As such he was the best ally the activists could have had: better placed than any other member of the N.E.C. to win over or out-manoeuvre the trade union conservatives who regarded the constituency activists as dangerous upstarts.

Politically, Dalton was placing himself alongside his normal opponents. In the defence debate, he was allied to the trade unions against pacifists, the Labour Left and League of Nations traditionalists. In this simultaneous dispute, he was on the side of activists against some of the biggest unions. It was a difficult game. Open support for the constituency reformers might turn out to be self-defeating. He therefore faced both ways at once: publicly denouncing Ben Greene, the local parties' leader, while encouraging the N.E.C. Organisation Sub-Committee (of which he was Chairman) to give tacit recognition to the constituency parties movement. At the beginning of June, he interviewed Greene, who up to this point had regarded the Party Chairman as an arch-enemy. The constituencies' leader emerged from the meeting pleasantly surprised. 'Dalton has seen a little of the light and is rather dazed and dazzled by it', Greene wrote to a comrade, 'but apparently willing to learn more as he has invited me to an informal talk tomorrow.'[63]

Backed by the evidence of the Area Conferences, Dalton persuaded the Organisation Sub-Committee to accept the local parties' main demands. Then, despite strong opposition, he won over the full N.E.C. as well. Some of the major unions remained undecided, and upon their verdict the issue hung. At the October Party Conference in Bournemouth, Dalton lobbied vigorously. When the matter came up for debate, he exercised his authority as Chairman with shameless bias, carefully selecting speakers from the floor who would help the reformers' case. At first, the outcome seemed uncertain. Then the main opposition gave way. Some lunch-time bargaining with Ernest Bevin over the T.G.W.U. vote clinched the issue. The same afternoon, Conference voted by clear majorities that the constituencies' section should be directly elected by the local parties themselves and increased in size from five to seven. 'The Chairman, very happy, tried to look solemnly impassive', Dalton recalled.[64]

The change brought no immediate revolution. In the 1937 contest for the constituencies' section of the N.E.C., using the new rules, Morrison, Dalton and George Dallas were all re-elected; Arthur Jenkins stood down and Joseph Toole, fifth member of the retiring section elected under the old rules, was defeated. Philip Noel-Baker came on. So did three left-wingers: Sir Stafford Cripps, Harold Laski and D. N. Pritt. The old constituency parties' section had contained only one middle-class member out of five – Dalton. The new section contained three dons and two Wykehamist barristers, out of seven. Susan Lawrence (a middle-class member of the N.E.C. women's section) told Beatrice Webb just before Christmas 1937 that relations on the reformed Executive remained harmonious. 'Even Hugh Dalton was playing up to the new band, as he had done to the old one of nitwits and boozers.'[65]

Dalton wrote later that the new method of election 'worked, up to a point, rather conservatively'.[66] Yet it was not long before important differences were felt. Left-wingers on the N.E.C., though outnumbered, soon began to use the Executive as a platform to publicise their quarrels with official policy: disputes involving Cripps in 1939 and Pritt in 1940 would have caused far less stir if Cripps and Pritt had not been members of the Executive. The full impact of the change was seen after the war when the annual battle for places in the expanded constituency parties section became a recognised barometer of the relative strengths of competing factions.

In the end, Dalton was hoist by his own petard – defeated for the Executive in 1952 as a result of reforms which he himself had helped to bring about. Herbert Morrison, who was pushed off the N.E.C. in the same year and who had supported the 1937 changes, commented ruefully, 'We had innocently contrived our own downfall'.[67] The constitutional reformers had also contrived the eventual ascendancy of the Labour Left. In the 1970s the existence of a constituency parties section made up entirely of left-wingers helped to reverse the traditional relationship of mutual support that had existed between N.E.C. and parliamentary leadership, and prepared the way for the Labour Party upheavals which followed the 1979 election.

In his memoirs, Dalton took the credit for the reforms: 'I only got my way in the Executive by a very narrow margin, after I had made a pressing personal appeal ... ' he wrote. 'And we only got our way, after a hard tussle, at the Conference. If I had relaxed on this at all at any stage, the changes would not have gone through.'[68] Herbert

Morrison (who had first raised the issue in the early 1920s) maintained in his own autobiography that the reforms were produced by a 'joint agitation ... by Dalton and myself'.[69] Both chose to ignore the origins and basic cause – a spontaneous, grass roots campaign, led by the long-forgotten Ben Greene, and overwhelmingly backed by constituency activists. Nevertheless Dalton's claim had some foundation. With a different Chairman, less committed or less persistent, the main amendments might never have been accepted by a cautious N.E.C. and even more cautious trade union movement. After 1937, moreover, the Labour Party had more important issues to consider: if the changes had not been made that year they might not have come at least until after the war and perhaps not at all.

'I still feel very cock-a-hoop about Bournemouth', Dalton wrote to the President of the Oxford Union, Christopher Mayhew (his latest protégé) when the Conference was over. 'Things went as well as in the best dream.'[70] The N.E.C. pro-rearmament line had been endorsed by a majority of more than 8 to 1. Dalton's P.L.P. coup on the Services Estimates had been backed by an even bigger majority – despite angry clashes with the M.P. for Ebbw Vale Aneurin Bevan, who declared that collaboration with the Government would lead to 'a voluntary totalitarian State with ourselves creating the barbed wire around'.[71]

It had, indeed, been a fitting climax to what Dalton described to delegates as 'a wonderful year in my life'.[72] He had begun his Chairmanship with clear aims. All had been achieved. A domestic programme, largely of his authorship, had been promulgated, the Left had been routed, the Party's constitution had been reformed, foreign and defence policies had been knocked into shape. Dalton's personal prestige never stood so high. He was 'expected by many to be the next Socialist Leader', according to one paper; he might be asked to carry on as Party Chairman for another year, according to another.[73]

Yet how much did it all matter? In the long run, the constitutional changes greatly altered the Labour Party, and the domestic manifesto provided a framework for the 1945 administration. But what of foreign affairs and defence? Given the huge parliamentary majority of the National Government, it would be easy to believe that the Opposition was of little significance in the conduct of foreign policy. Moreover, the argument has been powerfully made that – even if Labour had been in a position to exert influence – its 'alternative' foreign policy was actually no alternative at all.

According to A. J. P. Taylor, whose book *The Trouble Makers* has influenced most later studies of this period, Labour remained firmly wedded to the view that the National Government could not be trusted with arms and therefore should not be given them. 'Even the most extreme Socialist believed that Hitler must be met by alliances and armaments', argues Taylor; 'even the most moderate admitted that this could not be done while the National Government was in power. The difference was only in emphasis.' Labour's demands were thus unreal. When Labour leaders called for an alliance with the Soviet Union, they did so in the sure knowledge that this was something that a Conservative Prime Minister would never contemplate.[74]

This argument is attractive: around the edges of mainstream Labour opinion in the late 1930s many contradictory and out-dated attitudes were to be found. It is, however, misleading because it looks only at the rhetoric, and does so selectively. Taylor displays, in particular, a notable amnesia on the subject of Hugh Dalton, and Dalton's role within the defence and foreign policy debate. Taylor suggests that Labour leaders remained slaves to the same tradition of 'Dissent' as Conservative appeasers. Ernest Bevin, he admits, was an exception, though 'unrepresentative' of the Movement.[75] He leaves Dalton almost entirely out of his account, giving no acknowledgment of the direction of Dalton's views, or of Dalton's standing in the field of international affairs. Yet Dalton was Labour spokesman on foreign policy, author of every Labour foreign policy document or statement of any importance, and by far the most powerful Labour politician on the foreign side for most of the 1935 to 1940 period. Bevin was an influential general secretary who could speak for a large section of trade union opinion. Dalton spoke for the Labour Party, even for the Movement as a whole. And by 1937 Dalton's declarations on foreign policy were as firm on the need for rearmament by the National Government as any that came from the Tory backbenches.

It is possible to find sentences or paragraphs which might seem to suggest that, even in its official pronouncements, Labour clung to an earlier, pacifistic, mentality. The politics of a major policy reversal required backward glances, with conciliatory gestures to defeated opponents and to waverers. There were also moments (the debate on conscription early in 1939 was one) when traditional attitudes reasserted themselves. Yet by October 1937 the official message of the Labour Party had become so clear as to leave no room for misinterpretation. Speaking in his capacity as Shadow Foreign Secretary, and on behalf of the two Executives, Dalton spelt out the Party's new position to delegates assembled at Bournemouth, who gave their overwhelming support:

In this most grim situation, not of the Labour Party's making, our country must be powerfully armed. Otherwise we run risks immediate and immeasurable. Otherwise, a British Labour Government, coming into power tomorrow, would be in danger of humiliation, intimidation and acts of foreign intervention in our national affairs, which it is not tolerable for Englishmen to contemplate.[76]

As the *New Statesman* put it at the time, this statement was little different from a preparation for an armed alliance against the Fascist Powers, and would give the electorate the impression 'that in the event of a war crisis the Labour Party would be at least as ready to co-operate with the National Government as Social Democracy everywhere proved ready to co-operate with capitalist Governments in 1914'.[77]

There was no uncertainty. As Dalton made clear to Oliver Harvey (private secretary to the Foreign Secretary, Anthony Eden) in March 1937, two months before Neville Chamberlain succeeded Baldwin as Prime Minister, if the Government was prepared to take seriously the job of deterrence and defence, it could count on the Opposition to back it up.

> Dalton said he fully supported re-armament but he would like us to undertake to defend Czechoslovakia. He thought clarity most important element in foreign affairs. I said I agreed but danger was that if we said as much as that we should split the country. There were, after all, the Londonderrys on one side and the Lansburys on the other who would not stand for this policy. Dalton said Lansbury was of no importance.[78]

If Dalton had once accepted some of the precepts of such 'Dissenters' as E. D. Morel and Goldsworthy Lowes Dickinson, he had long since moved on. Until 1933 he had believed in the possibility of achieving disarmament through international agreement, backed by a League of Nations peace-keeping force. When the situation altered, no major change of outlook was necessary to persuade him of the need for security against a rapidly rearming Germany. 'He was a fine, robust, and hearty fellow, who combined socialism and patriotism in a good old-fashioned way', wrote Harold Macmillan, another supporter of rearmament and opponent of the Government's schemes.[79] During the Labour Party foreign policy disputes of the mid and late 1930s, in which Dalton won almost every battle, the truth of this became increasingly apparent.

As to the importance of Labour opinion, this may be briefly stated. The Government had an overwhelming majority, but it was more vulnerable than it seemed – not least to the arguments (if never to the numbers) of critics on its own backbenches. The ability of these critics to be heard and to offer a serious challenge depended on the Opposition. It may be contended that criticism failed to stiffen the Government or alter its course. Yet this is only partly true. The gathering pace of British rearmament, the Polish guarantee, the September 1939 ultimatum, and the declaration of war, were all influenced – if not actually forced – by House of Commons pressure which the Labour Opposition helped to create. Most vital of all, the political combination which brought down the Government in May 1940 was as much a product of the hostility and tactics of the Parliamentary Labour Party as of disaffection on the Government benches. Neville Chamberlain fell from office because the Labour leadership refused to join a Government of which he was the head. The basis of that refusal had been laid long before the war began.

XVI

Towards War

After his year as Party Chairman, Dalton decided to take a break from Westminster and Labour Party duties. As soon as the Bournemouth Conference was over, he began to prepare for an extended working holiday in Australia and New Zealand. The pretext was the 150th anniversary of the foundation of Australia. Dalton was asked by Attlee to represent the Labour Party at the celebrations.

He set out a week before Christmas. 'I was *very* sad at leaving you this morning', he wrote to Ruth, as his train drew into Paris. 'Tomorrow you will be at W[est] L[eaze]', he wrote from Marseilles. 'I love to think of you there.' It was to be their longest ever peace-time separation. Hugh sent a steady stream of diary-letters, as from France and Italy during the war, and from Russia. Ruth replied with extracts from her own diary. Hugh was relieved at the freedom from responsibility, and glad at the chance to rest. Yet he missed Ruth greatly. 'I love having your diary ... ' he wrote at the end of the year. 'I can picture you walking the Downs and poddling about, if not too chilled, and lying on your couch reading.'

This time he was on his own, with no political companions to distract him. He enjoyed the sense of being an ordinary citizen, the loneliness in a crowd. On board ship through the Mediterranean, he sunbathed, played deck-quoits, and read books by Harold Nicolson and Leonard Woolf. He kept fit by putting on shorts every morning and running twelve times round the deck – until he strained an Achilles tendon, and had to switch to exercises on his bunk. The ship's company included businessmen, army officers and Indian civil servants. There was also – by odd coincidence – a lady from Adelaide whose mother had put up Canon Dalton at her house in Australia during the *Bacchante* trip fifty-five years before. 'So we go round in circles', he wrote, and the thought that he was following in his father's footsteps stayed with him throughout his travels. The boat passed through the Suez Canal, stopped at Bombay and Ceylon, and reached Sydney on 11th January 1938. As they approached their destination, Hugh remembered being told as a child how, while still far out to sea, his father and the young princes had been able to smell the Australian bush.

He spent a month in Australia and then a fortnight in New Zealand. Australia, in particular, fascinated him. As a young man he had shared his father's dream of emigration, and he often recalled that he had nearly taken up a post in Australia in 1910. He was attracted both by the inhabitants, and by the terrain. The people seemed outgoing, democratic, classless, and the country vast and untamed – especially the more rugged states of Western Australia and Queensland. 'These are the two still nearest to the early pioneering stage, least dominated by a great capital city', he wrote, 'with the richest undeveloped resources, and with the largest areas both stretching up into the Australian tropics.' Joe Chamberlainite, imperialist Dalton now came to the surface. So did the Dalton who had been stirred by Robert Service's *Songs of a Sourdough* and *Call of the Wild*.

The official purpose of the visit was to meet antipodean politicians. Dalton took this duty seriously, throwing himself with customary zeal into the task of making and renewing contacts. The Australians warmed to his vigorous style, and to his evident delight in their company. He was glad to find his own books in regular use in the economics departments of Australian universities, and he was much gratified to receive an honorary doctorate from the University of Sydney. In Queensland, he persuaded the Labour Prime Minister, Forgan Smith, to take on a young friend, Colin Clark, as Government Statistician and Adviser on Economic Planning.

He found the Australian Labour Movement friendly and robust, but short on ideas and anti-intellectual. There was a need, he believed, for a Fabian element. Still, lack of theory had its advantages:

Here they have too few intellectuals in the L[abour] P[arty]; at home we have too many and too talkative and too scribblish (Rowse, Cole, Laski). These semi-crocks, diabetics and undersized Semites would cut no ice with these Aussies. The last two would be more jealous of me than ever if they could see me in action with the local comrades!

If Australia was short on intellectuals, the New Zealand Labour Party included intellectual tendencies of dubious origin. 'Their minds seem to skid on the roadway of reality', wrote Dalton. 'I suspect that the Left Book Club[1] has had something to do with making the surface greasy.'

On the return voyage, across the Pacific and through the Panama Canal, Dalton jotted down impressions formed during his visit. A sheet of rough notes, no more than a series of headings, summarised his continuing domestic interests and priorities. As always, his theme was equality – social and economic:

Sturdy democracy.	Better than Europe!
Not ever socially cowed.	Nor proscribed, nor underground, nor in concentration camps.

No aristocratic embrace possible in Australia because no aristo-
crats ...
No tradition of a hereditary ruling class.
Some rich and some poor. But little social stratification.
But no servility and little snobbishness.
Social equality nearly achieved.
Economic equality much nearer than in Old World.
                              Plenty of air and space ...
High standards of health and physique.
Plenty of brains. Much discussion and reading.
But 'intellectuals' less desiccated, mentally and physically, and
                              fitter.

While Dalton had been away, the European crisis had entered a critical new phase. On 12th March 1938, German troops crossed into Austria. Next day the puppet Austrian Chancellor Seyss-Inquart proclaimed an *Anschluss*, and Austria was incorporated into the German Reich.

At home, the policy of appeasement had turned from a style into an official doctrine. Neville Chamberlain had made plain early in his premiership that, in contrast to his predecessor, he was determined to take a directing role in foreign affairs. In December, Sir Robert Van-sittart, an opponent of the Prime Minister's ideas, had been replaced as Permanent Under-Secretary by Sir Alexander Cadogan, and given instead the empty title of 'Chief Diplomatic Adviser'. In February, Anthony Eden had resigned as Foreign Secretary in protest at Chamberlain's personal diplomacy. Thus Dalton returned to a Europe in which the threat to peace had greatly sharpened, and the response notably weakened, since his departure.

During his final days of shipboard idleness, with his heaviest duty that of chairing the deck sports committee, Dalton turned his attention to these events. Soon he would have to throw himself into the task of

exposing the dangers of appeasement. An anxiety that had been close
to an obsession before he set out from England seeped back:

> When I left there was an unspoken question in my heart – but [to]
> whom would it have profited to speak it? – 'Will IT begin before I
> come back?' IT is the NEXT WAR, not some little War in a Corner, –
> China, Abyssinia and Spain. But War in the Open, all over Europe,
> perhaps all over the world.
>
> Well, it has not yet begun. But these have been bad months, even
> compared with the run of months for some time past.
>
> ...
>
> I ask myself these questions.
>
> Is there anywhere an equilibrium that could be reached by con-
> cessions to Germany? Or will she always hold out her plate,
> demanding a second helping, with her mouth still full? Can her
> present rulers comprehend the very idea of a reasonable discussion,
> on a basis of equality, leading to some compromise, or intermediate
> arrangement, between two initial sets of proposals?
>
> ...
>
> 'Time is on our side', some say. I doubt it, whether as to arms, or
> economic strength or allies.
>
> ...
>
> But if *we* go down, we shan't come up again. They will take care
> we don't. We shall be a small, starved, depopulated island on the
> edge of Europe, wholly and always at their mercy.
>
> ...
>
> No differences between victors and vanquished.
> A foolish fable. The Germans didn't believe it after 1918. We
> shouldn't have believed it if they had won. We shan't believe [it] if
> they win next time.[2]

This was extrovert Dalton in a depressive phase. It was also a sober
assessment of international realities. Dalton believed that it was vital
to seek by every possible means to avert war. Yet the issue was ceasing
to be whether there would be a major war, but when. Where, before,
all energy had been devoted to preventing a conflict, now there had to
be a concentration on avoiding the danger of defeat. Like the hard-line
Tory dissidents, Dalton believed that the Dictators would treat any
attempt at negotiation with contempt. He was also coming to believe
that, if there was to be a war, it was better sooner than later, and that
preparations should therefore be made to ensure that if war came it
was not lost.

In the remaining sixteen months of peace, Dalton pursued several parallel strategies – aimed at embarrassing the Government into re-arming more quickly, and at checking attempts to pacify Hitler through a diplomacy based on the making of concessions. He looked for the Government's weak points. He sought to lead and rally his political supporters. Finally, he made cautious attempts to link up with opponents of appeasement on the Government side.

First, he took care to see that he received accurate, up-to-date in-formation. He gleaned valuable items of diplomatic intelligence from strategically placed foreign friends, such as the French socialist, Leon Blum. He received a steady supply of anti-Government stories from journalistic allies, in particular Robert Fraser and Douglas Jay (on the *Daily Herald*) and Paul Einzig on the *Financial Times* (Einzig gave him information about British credits to Germany, and about various forms of economic appeasement).[3] He kept in touch with the Soviet ambassador, Ivan Maisky, the Czech ambassador, Jan Masaryk, and with diplomatic representatives of other threatened States. He ob-tained information unofficially and sometimes illicitly from within the British Air Ministry and Foreign Office.

Backed by these sources, he made bitter and incisive attacks on the Government in the Commons. He drew special attention to the desper-ate inadequacy of British air defences and Air Raid Precautions. Any lingering suspicion that the Opposition was not serious in its demand for rapid rearmament was demolished in a powerful speech at the end of May. Moving a Commons resolution that the Government should set up an independent inquiry into the state of Britain's air defences, Dalton first quoted *Labour's Immediate Programme* on the subject of rearmament:

> The Labour Government will unhesitatingly maintain such armed forces as are necessary to defend our country and to fulfil our obligations as a member of the British Commonwealth and of the League of Nations.

He went on to discuss what he called 'a most grim and most un-welcome relationship', namely: 'The relationship of the emphatic inferiority of British to German air power.' During 1935, he declared, Germany had passed Britain in the air. Since then, the gap had been widening:

> Ignorant optimists may say that time is on our side. That is not true; time is against us; it is working against us. The more time elapses, the greater becomes the superiority of the German air force to the British air force.

Using data supplied by a secret Air Ministry informant, he analysed, aircraft by aircraft, weapon by weapon, the shortfalls and the deficiencies. He indicted slowness and inefficiency in arms manufacturers. He demanded a reorganisation of the whole system of production. He called for the setting up of a Ministry of Supply. He complained about 'constant changes by the Air Ministry in the details of design' of Hawker Hurricanes, and of an order for hundreds of Spitfires in 1936, none of which had been delivered.[4] Speaking simply and coolly, he presented a mass of detail that deeply impressed the House. The *Spectator* described the speech as 'the most formidable attack made from the front Opposition bench in this Parliament'.[5] The *Daily Telegraph* called it 'possibly the best of his career'.[6] Aneurin Bevan, scarcely a Dalton apologist, wrote that the shadow Foreign Secretary's exposure of incompetence 'pervaded the House of Commons with a deep sense of uneasiness'.[7]

Though taking a strong line on rearmament, Dalton at first held back on the issue of Czechoslovakia. Was this not a case where a negotiated settlement might be reached? While still at sea, he had wondered, 'Should we privately advise the Czechs to give up their Germans?'[8] In May 1938 he expressed the hope that 'some accommodation' might be possible on the issue of the Sudeten Germans.[9] This, however, was not the same as a full-scale capitulation to Hitler's demands. Over the summer, while the Government's position softened, Dalton's own attitude hardened. One factor was the influence of an official close to the top of the generally pro-appeasement Foreign Office – Sir Robert Vansittart.

Dalton and Vansittart had kept in touch after their brief association at the Foreign Office in 1930–1. 'He was one of the first to sense the German danger at the beginning of the thirties, and the need to build the maximum strength of collective security against it', Dalton recalled.[10] Later Vansittart was to gain a reputation – and provide a name, 'Vansittartism' – for anti-German racialism, because of wartime writings and broadcasts which attacked German traditions and culture, suggested that Germans were inherently aggressive and made no distinction between the Nazis and the German people. In the 1930s, no senior official argued more strongly the case for negotiating from strength.

As Germany became more threatening, Vansittart began to use Dalton as an outlet for opinions which, as a civil servant, he himself was unable publicly to express. While still in charge at the Foreign Office, he gave Dalton secret briefings about the activities of his political masters. After his demotion, this habit became more frequent. Sore at what he regarded as a cruel injustice, more than ever at odds

with Foreign Office policy, ignored by his former lieutenants, and on
bad terms with both the Prime Minister and Cadogan, the Government's Chief Diplomatic Adviser repeatedly leaked information to
the main critic and opponent of the administration he was pledged to
serve. As tensions mounted over Czechoslovakia, and the Government's resolve became more doubtful, meetings between Vansittart
and the Shadow Foreign Secretary became a vital source for Labour's
critique of Government diplomacy. 'He did not think that he was
suspected by Ministers of contact with the Labour Party', Dalton
noted on 19th September. Vansittart urged discretion over the meetings, which continued. Between 5th and 24th September the two met
privately on at least five occasions for detailed discussions of the
crisis.

These talks made Dalton intimately aware of Foreign Office and
Downing Street uncertainties. As a result, he became convinced of
the need for Britain to indicate clearly its intention to resist German
aggression in Central Europe. 'There is certainly a strong war party in
Berlin', Vansittart told him on 5th September. 'They simply do not
believe that, if they attack the Czechs, we or the French or the Russians would do anything effective.'[11] When the crisis broke, Dalton
did everything in his power to ensure that, on the contrary, Czechoslovakia would be defended. 'War can be averted now only in one
way', he told a Labour demonstration in County Durham on 9th
September. 'Hitler must be warned in the clearest and most unmistakable language that if he commits this crime Britain will join
with France and Soviet Russia in armed resistance to his aggression.'[12]

On 15th September Chamberlain flew to Berchtesgaden. On the
17th, immediately after his return, Dalton, Citrine and Morrison saw
the Prime Minister in Downing Street. 'I don't believe that this will
be the last of Hitler's demands', Dalton told Chamberlain. 'I believe
that he intends to go on and on until he dominates first all Central and
South Eastern Europe, then all Europe, then the world. And at every
stage this situation may be repeated.'

Yet even Dalton hesitated for a moment, faced with the prospect of
a major European war. When he learnt that the French were divided
on the question of resistance, his confidence was briefly shaken.
Thoughts which had been in his mind a few months earlier came to the
fore. If Britain fought alone for the Czechs, might not the result be a
catastrophic defeat? Was there any point in making such a gesture?
On 19th September he visited Vansittart at home, and put a key
question. Had the time come 'for us privately to urge the Czechs to
give way rather than make a hopeless and heroic fight against overwhelming odds if they were to be deserted by all the great Powers?'

Vansittart was unequivocal, backing his case with inside knowledge. It was imperative, he argued, that Dalton and the Labour Party should continue to oppose the Prime Minister and the Foreign Secretary as hard as they could. Dalton was convinced, and did not waver again.

Meanwhile Hitler had raised the stakes, demanding an immediate occupation of the areas to be ceded to Germany. On 24th September, the French ordered a partial mobilisation. By the night of the 27th, almost everybody expected war within days. Dalton rang Masaryk to ask whether he felt the British and French Governments were getting a little more firm. 'Firm!' Masaryk exploded. 'About as firm as the erection of an old man of 70!'[13] Chamberlain flew to Munich on 29th September. He returned next day, having given Hitler everything he wanted and having destroyed the structure of European defence against Germany.[14]

As the tension and anxiety increased, Dalton sought out young friends. He was bitter and distressed at his inability to prevent Chamberlain's betrayal. He feared deeply that what he had foreseen on board ship – 'War in the Open' – was about to occur. 'If we are not at war in a few weeks' time', he wrote to Christopher Mayhew on 15th September, 'I will suggest a time and place where we could meet.'[15] When Chamberlain returned from Munich having surrendered on every important point, Dalton was filled with foreboding. In need of comfort, he visited Gladwyn Jebb, now at the Foreign Office. Together, the two men watched from Jebb's first floor room as the Prime Minister promised a cheering crowd outside No. 10 Downing Street 'Peace in Our Time'.[16]

It was one thing to attack the Government. It was another to take action which might succeed in forcing its hand. Given the size of the National majority, prospects for actually defeating Chamberlain were remote. However, an alliance of critics – Labour, Liberal and back-bench Tory – might conceivably persuade the Prime Minister to change his policies. This possibility – combined with the desperation of the times – persuaded anti-Government politicians of all parties in the last few months of 1938 to seek an arrangement which would make the most of their political resources.

Initially Dalton had been opposed to direct co-operation with members of other political parties. This attitude was partly a product of the 1931 legacy, partly a result of the various 'front' demands of Communists and the Labour Left which the N.E.C. and trade union leaders had always resisted. Having strenuously opposed leftist fronts, Dalton saw political difficulties in selling a centrist one to the Labour Movement. In any case, he had always argued that 'Democratic

Tories' were an illusion;[17] and only weeks before the Munich crisis broke, he had publicly declared that Labour decisively rejected 'all proposals for coalition with other party organisations, Liberal, Communist or Tory'.[18] Changing tack would be difficult. Hence he was inclined to resist new calls for close contacts with Tory dissidents, warning of the danger 'that we might upset a large number of our own Party and destroy our credit in our own home market'.[19]

The shock of Munich, however, created a new political mood. Dalton had never been against an alliance in principle: he had simply believed that it would be hard to bring one off. Now, very briefly, normal rules were suspended. In the immediate aftermath of the crisis there were two important initiatives, aimed at co-operation. One came from Tory backbenchers and the other from the Labour leadership. In both cases Dalton was asked to act as secret negotiator on Labour's behalf. He was cautious, but not unhopeful. The job as he saw it was for Labour to detach the Tory rebels from the Government and induce them to defy the Tory whip. If this could be done, great advances might be made. For a fleeting moment, he wrote later, 'it seemed possible that a large-scale Tory revolt against Chamberlain might change the whole scene'.[20]

The first initiative came from the Tory side. Winding up for the Opposition in the Munich debate, Dalton accused the Prime Minister of being 'unduly hurried, unduly intimidated, and even out-man-oeuvred' by the German Führer.[21] Sir Alexander Cadogan, who had helped to shape the Government's policy, admitted ruefully that Dalton's speech was 'extremely good and telling'.[22] Others thought the same. Dalton's words gave anti-Munich Tories the encouragement they needed. At the end of the day's business, Harold Macmillan (one of the most active of the younger Tory rebels) approached Dalton, and suggested a meeting with the Churchill group to discuss the terms of Labour's amendment to the Government motion on the Munich agreement. Dalton agreed.

That night, Dalton went to the North Street house of Brendan Bracken, Churchill's closest aide in the Commons. There he met Bracken, Churchill, Eden and others. The Tories were anxious that the Opposition amendment should not be too patently a vote of censure, lest it deter possible Tory abstainers. They discussed with Dalton a form of words to overcome this difficulty. Then they moved to a vital question. There was talk of a punitive 'Munich' election, to rally support around the Government and smash internal party opposition. If, as was feared, twenty or thirty of the rebels were victimised by the Government whips, what possibility was there of an agreement for mutual support in the constituencies?

Here was a chance to break the Tory ranks. What the rebels wanted
– constituency arrangements in the event of a 'coupon' election –
would be hard to supply, involving a dramatic reversal of Labour
policy on the subject of 'fronts'. Yet this was a quite different proposal
from the traditional 'united' and 'popular' front demands. To divide
the Government in the way suggested would be a major coup. So
would an agreement with Churchill. 'He is much more attractive than
the Edens and other gentlemanly wishy-washies', Dalton wrote. 'He
is a real tough and at the moment talking our language.'

Dalton was therefore discreetly helpful. He made no promise, but
indicated that if the rebels were victimised, they might talk again.
The Tories seemed satisfied. Next day the Labour Opposition tabled
an amendment which met their requirements, and on 6th October
between thirty and forty normal Government supporters abstained –
22 ostentatiously sitting in their seats as the vote was taken. The experiment in co-operation had been a success.[23]

The Tory move meanwhile received support from another, unexpected quarter: Sir Stafford Cripps. On the day of the vote (three
days after Macmillan's first approach) Cripps put to Dalton his own
suggestion for a parliamentary alliance across the floor of the House:
an agreement based on a limited joint programme for the preservation
of democratic liberties and for the establishment of an adequate
national defence.

Cripps's move was unexpected partly because he and Dalton had
for some time scarcely been on speaking terms; and partly because it
represented a sharp shift in his own opinions. Relations between
Cripps and Dalton had reached a low point at the end of 1937, after
the crushing of the Socialist League and the Unity Campaign. Thereafter there had been little contact between the two men. Shortly after
Dalton's return from Australia and New Zealand in April, Cripps
had left for the West Indies to convalesce after an illness.

Now Cripps reappeared, presenting a dramatic new plan. The aim
of the old 'united front' demand had been 'proletarian' unity: a
combination of socialist parties alone, with capitalist politicians
specifically excluded. In the revised plan, proletarian unity was
dropped. Whether or not Cripps was aware of the North Street talks
or of their nature, his own suggestion was in keeping with them. He
urged Dalton to arrange a meeting between Attlee, Morrison and
Dalton on the one side, and Churchill – perhaps accompanied by L. S.
Amery, Eden and (for the Liberals) Sir Archibald Sinclair – on the
other. Socialism, he declared, could be put aside for the moment.[24]

Dalton was taken aback by this somersault. It involved more than
just the abandonment of the 'proletarian unity' commitment. Only

three years had passed since Cripps had resigned from the N.E.C. on the issue of economic (never mind military) sanctions. He had repeatedly opposed rearmament. Now here was a completely different defence and foreign policy tune. Chamberlain could not be trusted with arms. Hence he must be removed at once, even if this meant compromise, so that rearmament and collective security could be conducted by a Government 'under the control of the common people'.[25]

Dalton was suspicious, but not uninterested. Support from Cripps would solve some of his own problems: it would help to guard his left flank, should any progress be made with the rebels. The major obstacle to an alliance lay not in the attitude of the P.L.P., but in the possible reaction of the Labour Movement outside Parliament. Here, Cripps's advocacy – carrying with it substantial support in the constituency parties – could be crucial. Dalton therefore obtained the agreement of Attlee and Morrison, and then saw Macmillan, suggesting a meeting on the lines of Cripps's suggestion.

The Tories, however, held back. The fears of the rebels had turned out to be premature: Chamberlain soon indicated that there would be no punitive election after all. Moreover, with the international crisis temporarily abated, unity among the rebels vanished – Eden and his followers were less inclined to pursue an alliance than some members of the Churchill group. Macmillan himself was eager for a '1931 in reverse' – a Tory dissident-Liberal-Labour combination aimed at forming a new National Government. However, though a wider meeting of leaders was planned, it never took place. The 'moderate' opponents of Chamberlain had lost interest, and there was no future in going ahead without them.

Why was Dalton unable to offer enough to clinch an agreement? One reason was the attitude of the trade unions, opposed to coalitions after MacDonald's defection, and slow to change an established opinion once it had been formed. Another reason, paradoxically, was a by-election win for a 'Popular Front' candidate, Vernon Bartlett, at Bridgwater on 17th November. This remarkable victory embarrassed the N.E.C., because the Party Executive had repeatedly condemned left-wing calls to back Bartlett's campaign. 'We of the National Executive did not shift our ground', Dalton recalled. Only 'a big Tory breakaway' would invalidate the argument which the N.E.C. had published in May condemning inter-party arrangements, 'and it would not be useful to say this publicly now'.[26] But a big Tory breakaway could only happen if Labour was willing to offer something substantial in return for the risks the Tories would have to take. Both sides waited in vain for the other to make the first move.

In a personal capacity, Dalton continued to do what he could to combine forces against the Government – even giving private support to local electoral arrangements where these seemed likely to defeat a pro-Chamberlain candidate. On one occasion he sent John Parker, a young Labour M.P., to discuss with Churchill's friend Professor Lindemann the possibility of an agreement in Epping, where some local Tories were opposing Churchill's candidacy; and he backed similar moves in Banbury and elsewhere.[27] Meanwhile he and Morrison quietly advocated 'greater elasticity' in handling cases where an electoral arrangement was proposed.[28] When his old friend Lord Cecil asked him why Labour rejected help from non-Party members who supported Labour foreign policy, he replied that it was worth considering the possibility of Labour backing anti-Chamberlain candidates who promised they would not vote against a Labour Government.[29]

For the moment, however, he preferred private understandings to public declarations, for which, he believed, the Labour Movement was not yet ready.[30] He kept in mind a remark made by Churchill at the North Street meeting: 'It is not enough to be brave. We must be victorious.'[31]

It was Sir Stafford Cripps who destroyed any chance that serious interest in an alliance might be revived. In October 1938 he had urged Dalton to seek a parliamentary deal with any Tory rebel who was prepared to listen. In practice, this meant an arrangement with Churchill, Amery and perhaps Eden. Cripps, however, was not a man of fixed opinions. When early negotiations with the Tories produced no dramatic result, he decided once again to strike out on his own.

First, he openly backed the Popular Front candidature of Vernon Bartlett at Bridgwater, in defiance of the N.E.C.[32] Then, in January 1939, he issued a personal declaration, which became known as the 'Cripps Memorandum', calling for 'a nation-wide campaign' and 'an immediate and special appeal to the Youth movement as a whole upon the basis of combined Youth activities and a special Youth programme'. In the memorandum, Cripps demanded a Popular Front that should include Liberals, Communists and I.L.P. but not, any longer, the Churchill group of Tory dissidents. Churchill was now presented as a warmonger, standing for 'reactionary imperialism'.[33] The proposal was quite different from Cripps's private suggestion to Dalton the previous October. Instead of an arrangement to beat the Government, Cripps was demanding a return to 'proletarian' unity, broadened to include some, but not all, capitalist opponents of the

Government. When the N.E.C. decided by 17 votes to 3 to reject the Memorandum, Cripps immediately dispatched copies to all Labour M.P.s, candidates and secretaries of affiliated organisations, including in each envelope a stamped, self-addressed postcard calling for support.

Dalton remained, for the moment, undecided between expelling Cripps at once and calling a special conference to give powers to expel him if he continued to agitate. He veered towards the second alternative. 'If we can manoeuvre him on to this ground', he noted, 'we shall, I think, avoid much of the outcry which would be raised if we now simply expelled him for his conduct up to date.' He observed, irritably, that the possibility of quiet local pacts had been removed. 'The man has the political judgement of a flea', he wrote.[34] In the vain hope of making Cripps see reason, he went to see him privately. 'I should have preferred a *tête-à-tête*', he recalled, 'but Lady Cripps remained knitting throughout our conversation, though she took no part in it. Her presence cramped my style and probably stiffened his.' After this, Dalton veered back to the first solution – expelling Cripps at once. On 25th January 1939, the N.E.C. asked Cripps formally to recant, and to promise good behaviour. Cripps refused. The Executive then expelled him from the Labour Party, only Ellen Wilkinson dissenting.

Cripps was undeterred by this decision. He immediately rallied his supporters for a highly personalised campaign which created the biggest rupture in the Labour Movement since 1931, and led to the most systematic purge of left-wingers since the Party's foundation. After it started, wrote Dalton, 'we were in a fight to the finish'.[35] Cripps's followers repeated the revivalist 'Unity' demonstrations of two years before. Big meetings were held supporting Cripps himself and others expelled with him, who included two prominent left-wing M.P.s, Aneurin Bevan and G. R. Strauss. The Party leaders responded with public denunciations, sometimes vicious in nature. Angry and bitter at such a misdirection of energy at so critical a time, Dalton accused Cripps of 'an indecent and blatant exploitation of private wealth', of a 'subtle form of Fascism', and of impersonating Hitler and Mussolini with a privately organised and financed campaign.[36]

It did not last long. By the time of the Annual Party Conference in Southport at Whitsun, Cripps's movement was dead and largely forgotten, its damage done. With the Nazis at the gates of Prague, the Labour Party, and the country, had more important things to think about. Cripps was allowed to make a speech appealing against his expulsion. He made a careful, legalistic case against the N.E.C., complaining about 'the somewhat unpleasant statements made about me by some members of the Executive', and hinting at the sums of money which he had donated to the Party out of his large income. He received little sympathy. 'He played the part not of the victim beside the block', wrote Richard Crossman, 'but of a pale ghost returning from Hades and arguing that he was still alive.'[37] Dalton replied for the Executive. Sir Stafford Cripps had not been expelled, he said, for expressing an opinion. He had been expelled for refusing to give the N.E.C. certain undertakings – namely to re-affirm his allegiance to the Party Constitution and to withdraw his Memorandum.

Dalton ended with an appeal to the common sense of the rank and file, and to principles of justice and equality. 'Little people would have grumbled that big people were getting off while little people were being disciplined, and demoralisation would have spread', he declared. 'Decent, loyal people would have packed up and got out ... '[38] Big people and little people among the Conference delegates appeared to agree. They combined to trounce Cripps on a card vote, confirming his expulsion by 2,100,000 votes to 402,000.

Outside the Labour Party, the episode was quickly forgotten. Within it, and for the leading actors, it had important repercussions. By a strange irony, the expulsion was eventually turned to Cripps's advantage: it enabled him to present himself, when war was declared, as a 'national' figure, above party politics. Cripps's private feelings at the time remain an enigma; though it is hard to believe that he easily forgave so humiliating and personal a defeat. Dalton's attitude was one of relief and righteous satisfaction. 'I astonished myself', he wrote, 'by my power of self-restraint ... and by the sense of regret at having to get rid of him which I think I managed to convey.'[39]

There was more to it than the issue. Since 1931, rivalry between Dalton and Cripps had been intense. Dalton had good grounds for fearing so dazzling, destructive and uncompromising a political personality. In any dispute on policy, in any contest for top jobs in a future Labour Government, Cripps was bound to be a strong competitor. More important in the fast-moving, passionate politics of the late 1930s, there was a real danger that Cripps might bid successfully for the highest Labour Party post of all.

Did Dalton himself have serious ambitions to become Party Leader? Attlee was regarded as little more than a figurehead, whose departure was frequently predicted. Morrison, the obvious successor, was spending most of his time on L.C.C. work, and was less and less to be seen across the river. After Dalton's spectacular success as Party Chairman, the possibility of succeeding Attlee must have been in his mind.

The Leadership was certainly in Cripps's mind when he approached Dalton with his suggestion for a parliamentary alliance. Could not Attlee be shifted, he asked, and replaced by Morrison? Might it not be possible to make a change the following month? Dalton had campaigned on Morrison's behalf in 1935, against Attlee. He had never disguised his belief that Morrison would make a better Leader. Yet he resisted Cripps's suggestion. It was quite out of the question, he replied. 'I should not be sure now of getting all the votes I got for him three years ago.'[40]

If Dalton had been contemplating a move against Attlee, Cripps would have been the last person to tell. In any case, Dalton's judgment was probably sound: only an earthquake could shift a Party Leader *in situ* whose sole offence was his inadequacy. Nevertheless, Dalton may have had a private reason for wishing to avoid an early contest with Morrison as front runner – namely, a hope that, if he waited, the Leadership might fall into his own lap.

Others certainly saw Dalton as a potential contender. According to one press report two months later, moves were afoot to oust Attlee and replace him with Dalton. Herbert Morrison would first be sidetracked into the Party Secretaryship and Arthur Greenwood would be asked to stand down 'in the interest of party unity'. Meanwhile, the report continued, 'Mr. Dalton is being "groomed for stardom", while a whispering campaign is being carried on inside the Labour Party Parliamentary ranks against Mr. Attlee.'[41] This story may have had no more basis than lobby gossip in a lean week: no indication was given about how so complex a putsch would actually be carried out. Nevertheless, the opinion that Dalton wanted to lead the Party continued to be voiced.[42]

Such an opinion, whether accurate or not, reflected an undoubted increase in Dalton's political strength. As war fears grew, so did Dalton's standing in the Party: on defence and foreign policy, events seemed rapidly to be proving him right. Hence the expulsion of Cripps had a special significance. Dalton offered a practical, authoritarian, directive, patriotic leadership. Cripps had offered an inspirational, crusading, morally-uplifting alternative. Beatrice Webb was in no doubt about Dalton's motive in the struggle. 'How could [Stafford] expect that his rivals for the leadership, Hugh Dalton more especially, should not succeed in getting rid of him?', she observed, adding: 'I doubt whether he will reappear in the inner counsels of the Labour Party.'[43] The same thought, or hope, must have occurred to Dalton as well.

When a threat to the Party Leader did come – in the early summer of 1939, after Cripps's expulsion – Dalton was torn between his growing desire to see Attlee replaced, and his concern to head off the main challenger. Attlee, ill and with an operation pending, was forced to be absent from much of the Whitsun Party Conference. This made him vulnerable. In the private session Ernest Bevin and the *Daily Herald* editor, Francis Williams, seized the chance to make pointed criticisms of his leadership. Meanwhile Ellen Wilkinson (a keen Morrison supporter) published two articles hinting strongly at the need for a replacement.

Dalton believed, more than anyone, that the Party urgently needed a full-time Leader capable of making a major political and electoral impact. ' ... I am prepared to go to all lengths to get the right sort of change', he told Francis Williams. But what was the right sort of change? Early in June, he wrote,

> To shift anybody from anywhere in this sheepishly loyal Movement of ours is a Herculean task. The fact remains that at Annual Conference, where H.M. and I are the principal performers, we can build up the self-confidence, unity and morale of the Party in a most surprising way ... and then, a few weeks later, others having resumed their feeble sway, down it all sags again![44]

The implication seemed to be that Dalton and Morrison were the real leaders of the Party, and that Attlee should be pushed out to make way for one of them. Attlee's most serious potential rival in June 1939, however, turned out to be neither Dalton nor Morrison. In her articles about the Leadership, Ellen Wilkinson had pointedly praised Morrison (and to a lesser extent Dalton). This had infuriated supporters of Arthur Greenwood, Acting Leader in Attlee's absence, who feared an attempt at a pro-Morrison putsch. Suddenly Greenwood's name began to be canvassed. Dalton was appalled. The previous autumn he had refused to back Morrison for the Leadership. Now he sided with Morrison in order to block a Greenwood challenge.

It turned out to be a false – or at any rate exaggerated – alarm. No formal attempt was made to have a contest. At a P.L.P. meeting on 14th June, with Greenwood in the chair, Ellen Wilkinson was rebuked, and Herbert Morrison was received coolly, for real or implied criticisms of the Party Leader. 'I was also the object of some organised suspicion and antagonism', wrote Dalton.[45] The Greenwood 'campaign' – if such there had been – was not mentioned.

The Leadership question did not die. It cropped up again in the autumn of 1939, after war had been declared. In the meantime, Dalton's attitude had shifted. If he had ever had serious Leadership hopes for himself, he set them aside. In the summer he had been more concerned to stop Greenwood than to move Attlee. By October, he regarded a change in the Leadership – almost any change – as his first aim. His preferences had also altered. In an important switch of alliances, he abandoned Morrison and put his weight behind Greenwood. The result was embarrassment and confusion. 'Greenwood was, as usual, dilatory in decision', Dalton reflected afterwards, 'and no-one else of any prominence in the P[arliamentary] P[arty] took any decisive attitude in his favour.'[46] A clumsy move by a backbench M.P. – who nominated the three most promising alternatives, Morrison, Greenwood and Dalton – backfired. At a P.L.P. meeting on 15th November, all three withdrew and there was no contest.[47] Afterwards in the Shadow Cabinet elections, Dalton's place slipped from third to tenth, reflecting P.L.P. distaste at his manoeuvrings.

In this way, Dalton succeeded in dissipating much of the political credit which he had built up. He remained a leading, almost dominant, figure on the front bench and on the N.E.C., but he was never fully trusted by his closest colleagues. By the end of the decade, for all his standing within the Labour Movement as a whole, he had allowed himself to become dangerously friendless at the top of it.

Throughout the middle months of 1939, Dalton maintained pressure on the government – urging improvements in defence and A.R.P. (Air Raid Precautions), demanding immediate, top level talks with the Soviet Union, and pointing to the danger of slipping back into the appeasement policies which the Prime Minister had at last abandoned, at least in theory, after Hitler's armies entered Prague.

There was one area of embarrassment: conscription. At the end of April, a limited form of compulsory National Service was introduced. The Shadow Cabinet and P.L.P., suspicious of Tory compulsion, opposed this move. Dalton was undecided. He believed that allies or potential allies would be impressed by a measure that went beyond material rearmament on its own. 'I was not happy about our line', he wrote later, 'and was also moved by the argument that France, Poland and Russia – as well as Germany and Italy – all had conscription and would not understand why we refused it.'[48] Yet he was not moved enough to make a stand. He did not publicly question the Labour Party decision; and the Opposition lost some of its credibility as a result. Soon, however, this episode became irrelevant. On 1st September the P.L.P. agreed overwhelmingly to back a Government Bill extending the age range of those to be conscripted.

Dalton filled the last, desperate summer of peace with frenetic, though sadly useless, activity. At the end of June, he led a National Council of Labour deputation to see the Prime Minister and Foreign

Secretary to protest at delays in completing an agreement with Russia. He told Chamberlain that 'information which he had received from Poland' indicated that the Poles had every intention of defending Danzig, and he urged that Britain should declare unequivocally that a move on Danzig would be resisted.[49] As possibilities of averting a German attack on Poland faded, he met, telephoned, and lobbied foreign diplomats and British officials endlessly, seeking to stiffen the Government. During the few days before war was declared, he buried his sense of impotence in an angry row involving the Foreign Secretary and the Director-General of the B.B.C. about an official message from the Labour Party to the German people. At stake was Labour's right of access to the airwaves, against B.B.C. or Government censorship. Dalton eventually won.[50]

If there was nothing he could do to stop the German invasion, he could at least help to prevent another Munich. German troops entered Poland early on 1st September. A British demand for a withdrawal, without time limit, was not issued until the evening. Dalton and other Labour leaders suspected that Chamberlain was about to welsh on the Polish guarantee. 'It seemed as though appeasement was once more in full swing', wrote Dalton. That night he went over to Gladwyn Jebb's room in the Foreign Office. Jebb blamed the French for delays. Leaving the building just before 1 a.m., Dalton ran into Sir Ivone Kirkpatrick, acting head of the Foreign Office Central Department. Kirkpatrick told him: 'If we rat on the Poles now, we are absolutely sunk, whatever the French do.' A few minutes later Dalton passed Halifax, coming in the door from Downing Street. 'I hope you have brought the French into line now', said Dalton. 'I warn you that, if the House of Commons meets again without our pledge having been fulfilled, there will be such an explosion as you in the House of Lords may find it difficult to imagine.' Halifax replied: 'I quite understand. It has been very difficult. But it will be all right tomorrow.' Dalton replied: 'Thank God.' When, next day, the Prime Minister announced the French ultimatum, Dalton wrote, 'I have not a shadow of doubt but that the House of Commons, and especially the Labour Party, have forced the British Government to force the French Government to do this.'[51]

XVII

Old Limpet

When hostilities began, Labour declared its full support for the war effort while retaining the right to criticise. In the spring, Dalton had approved the idea – put forward by Churchill, Eden and Duff Cooper – for a new National Government 'on the widest possible basis'. He had also made it clear, however, that 'the one necessary preliminary condition for national unity was the disappearance of the Prime Minister from office'.[1] This remained his own position until such a Government was eventually formed in May 1940. At the end of August 1939, with war imminent, he raised the issue at a Shadow Cabinet meeting, so as to strengthen the Party line against waverers who might be tempted to accept office under Chamberlain. 'My present feeling is that we should decline participation in Government if war comes – at least at the beginning', he noted. 'I remember how A[rthur] H[enderson] fared in the Great War, and it is not as if our present "leaders" were supermen capable of exercising vast influence though in a tiny minority.' The Parliamentary Executive agreed that nobody should accept office without specific authority. This decision was vitally important in ensuring Chamberlain's political isolation a few months later.

Nevertheless, the Labour leadership decided to maintain a special liaison with ministers. Attlee was still out of action, and Morrison was preoccupied with the L.C.C. and problems of the capital in wartime. So of Labour's top five, only Greenwood, Alexander and Dalton were initially involved – with Pethick Lawrence and Lees-Smith coming in as reserves. It was arranged that Greenwood, as Acting Leader, should keep in touch with the Prime Minister and Foreign Secretary, and Alexander with the Admiralty. Dalton, who had recently been concentrating on European financial dealings as well as air defence, agreed to liaise with the Minister of Economic Warfare

(Ronald Cross) and the Air Minister (Kingsley Wood).

Dalton had other contacts in M.E.W. apart from the Minister – in particular his young economist friend Hugh Gaitskell, recruited in a junior capacity and soon promoted to the post of Head of Intelligence for Enemy Countries. Gaitskell kept Dalton briefed on what to ask Cross at their regular meetings. 'H.G. suggests that with Cross I might converse as follows', Dalton noted early in October. 'Pre-emption. What is happening about Rumanian oil? Have we got it? And how about oil cake and oil seed from the Balkans?'[2] Dalton saw Cross every three weeks, and Wood once a fortnight. The arrangement worked well – partly because the Government wanted to be as co-operative as possible in the hope of bringing Labour into a coalition.[3] In the House, Dalton kept up his sharp criticisms of the Government. Only one minister impressed him – Winston Churchill, the new First Lord of the Admiralty. On 3rd October Dalton told M.P.s that he had listened to Churchill the previous night on the wireless. 'How much better he did this than some of his colleagues!' Dalton declared. Churchill, he concluded, would be of key importance in any bid to bring the Government down. The Parliamentary Executive discussed tactics once again on 19th September. 'Government can only be changed if there is a serious breakdown among their supporters, and if, as someone says to me privately, "Winston is ready to strike".' Dalton wrote. 'Not clear that we are here yet.'[4]

At the end of October Dalton visited France with an all-party group of M.P.s including David Grenfell, J. A. de Rothschild, Philip Noel-Baker, General Louis Spears, Leo Amery and Harold Nicolson. It was a welcome three-day break from restless ineffectiveness at home. The high point was a trip to the Maginot line at Sidon, near where there had been some fighting. Dalton spent two hours underground. 'We climbed into turrets, worked intricate range-finders', Spears recalled. 'Rothschild peered with myopic gaze at the instruments, Dalton's laugh boomed from high places ... '[5] Back in Paris, Dalton lunched with the Finance Minister, Paul Reynaud ('the pick of the present bunch of French ministers'), and later dined on the Île Saint Louis with Leon Blum, who expressed fears of a German attack on Holland.[6]

Meanwhile Dalton had returned to writing. At West Leaze he rapidly turned out a book called *Hitler's War: Before and After* which was published as a Penguin Special in March 1940. It was his sixth book and the last before the first volume of his memoirs appeared in 1953. It repeated with greater emphasis the message of *Towards the Peace of Nations*, written in a different world a dozen years before: peace could be maintained only on the basis of a well-equipped inter-

national peace-keeping force. A future international society or
regional society within Europe, he had told the Commons in November 1939, 'must be armed overwhelmingly against aggression'.[7] He
now argued for an organisation that anticipated and combined
features later to be found in NATO and the Common Market. In a
chapter on War Aims, he called for a post-war 'Federal Union' including the Allies, neutrals and even post-Nazi Germany, with power
over foreign policy, defence, economy, customs and major communications. In a chapter on 'Associations of States' he wrote:

> It must be a first principle of our action to dilute national sovereignty
> as much as possible over as wide an area as possible. Failing a great
> and wide dilution, and a contented acceptance of the consequences,
> Peace will not be firmly founded. We must do our best for a new
> Commonwealth of States and for new strong Federal Unions, as
> soon as men will take them.

He summed up his attitude to post-war international associations
in a slogan: 'Sovereignty or Security? Choose!'[8] Many years later,
when 'Federal Union' became a possibility and Dalton was himself
involved in early negotiations over European unity, he substantially
revised this opinion.

In Parliament and on public platforms, Dalton concentrated on
two themes: improving the blockade and taxing the rich to pay for
the war. Economic Warfare suited him well as a shadow responsibility; it allowed him to combine his economic and foreign expertises
and made it possible to point out the inadequacies of Government
policy without being accused of sabotage or defeatism. He also found
his friend Hugh Gaitskell an increasingly fruitful source of inside information – so much so that early in 1940 the Treasury became suspicious, and Gaitskell had to urge him to be more discreet. 'It will be
well therefore that I should make a parade of hearing my stuff from
Einzig, the City, etc,' Dalton recorded.

On the blockade, Dalton had a simple message: hit the enemy hard
and soon, and prosecute the economic war by all possible means.
Gaitskell complained: 'What can we do? The Foreign Office won't let
us bully any of the neutrals and the Treasury won't let us bribe them.'[9]
Dalton concluded that the appeasement mentality lived on. 'Our
economic warfare has been, and still is, waged half-heartedly', he
wrote in the *Daily Herald.* ' ... Some of our professional diplomats in
key posts are tired and elderly, too traditional and too gentlemanly
to be a match for Hitler's gangsters.'[10]

Dalton took a sharply socialist line on financing the war. He advocated 'drastic taxation, to whatever the amount required to supplement free loans and avoid inflation.' After the war, there should be a 'capital levy on a large scale' to clean up war debt. It was an old theme. He adopted the slogan 'No more five-figure incomes, either in peace or war', and told a conference in Preston that there should be a capital tax on all fortunes over £10,000.[11]

At the end of November 1939, Stalin invaded Finland. In England, this was widely regarded as an act of aggression comparable to the Nazi-Soviet assault on Poland. Labour's response was to back the British Government's offer of help to the Finns. Dalton disagreed but – as over conscription the previous spring – he was not prepared to cause a row or divide Labour's ranks on the issue. Privately he regarded the idea of an expeditionary force (strongly backed by some Labour leaders, including Noel-Baker) as lunacy.[12] In his view, it was absurd to embark on war with two major powers – Germany and the Soviet Union – at the same time. He still hoped that it might be possible to detach Stalin from his arrangement with the Nazis. He kept in touch with the Soviet ambassador, who told Beatrice Webb in April 1940 that Dalton 'had remained friendly with the Embassy and had never abused the U.S.S.R. in his speeches.'[13] On a visit to Brussels in February, he listened to Leon Blum urging the Labour and Socialist International that the Finns should be helped 'to the utmost and at all costs'. Dalton replied firmly: 'we have no mandate to go so far.'[14] Unlike leading colleagues, he did not join the hue and cry against the fellow-traveller D. N. Pritt, a Labour M.P. and member of the N.E.C., who was expelled from the Labour Party in March for writing a book in favour of the Russians and against the Finns.

By the spring of 1940 Dalton had regained some lost ground in the P.L.P., and he appeared to have been largely forgiven, at least on the backbenches, for his intrigues of the previous autumn. One reason was his ability to provide the leadership which seemed so sadly lacking elsewhere. Attlee had fully returned to active politics in November. His performances, however, remained lack-lustre, and comparisons continued to be made with other prominent colleagues – especially Dalton, who was delivering the most aggressive speeches from the Opposition front bench. There was also the continuing question of whether, or when, Labour should agree to enter the Government. According to one newspaper report in February 1940, Labour M.P.s were coming round to the view that a coalition was desirable, and Dalton was being mentioned as the leader to take them into it. Night and day, the report continued, 'in the lobbies of Westminster and the political clubs and pubs of the Labour movement, you hear a canvass of this man's claims for the reversion of Attlee's throne'.[15]

Dalton's own views on the relationship of the Labour Party to the Government, however, remained unchanged. He wanted a coalition, and he wanted to be a minister, but the departure of Chamberlain must be a precondition. The problem – the same problem as had existed since popular fronts and parliamentary alliances were first mooted – was how to bring the Prime Minister's departure about. How could one get a majority of the House to accept a new Government, or to reject the old? Dalton concluded that it was necessary to be patient, and wait for the Government to create its own unpopularity. 'The 1916 situation developed as a result of serious reverses in the field', he reminded a Fabian gathering, referring to the Cabinet putsch that had produced the war-winning Lloyd George Coalition.[16]

Dalton's firmness may not have been shared by all of his colleagues. At the end of March it was rumoured that Chamberlain had offered Labour three seats in the Cabinet, and that Alexander, Morrison and Greenwood were interested, while Attlee was opposed.[17] Even Attlee's opposition did not seem unshakeable. On 1st May, as the British initiative in Norway turned to disaster, Dalton noted that the Party Leader was wavering. 'C.R.A. tells me he thinks we shall have to face up to it', he observed. 'Clearly he is in favour of going in, on certain conditions. I say one must be that Chamberlain packs up.'[18] As rumours continued to circulate, nervousness at the top of the Labour Party became intense. Morrison indicated his own anxiety that Dalton might be picked for a coalition team rather than himself, by spreading a malicious story that Dalton was pro-Italian and 'had wanted Italy to have a mandate over Abyssinia'.[19]

Nobody could foresee at this stage the momentous event that was to occur a few days later. 'Looking back on the parliamentary crisis of May 1940 with the aid of hindsight', the historian Paul Addison has wisely written, 'we must remark how uninevitable the "inevitable" seemed to be at the time.'[20] On the Labour side, caution ruled. Dalton – who never for a moment doubted the necessity of a change of Government – was at first one of the most cautious of all. Then, when it became clear that the Government's position was weakening, he closed in rapidly and expertly for the kill. In the private discussions that led up to the fall of Chamberlain, he was able to capitalise on contacts with Tory dissidents established in the aftermath of Munich. His temperament was, moreover, well suited to the atmosphere of rumour-mongering and backstairs plotting which brought together the disparate, and mutually suspicious, elements that had in common only a desire to see the Prime Minister displaced.

On the first day of the crucial Norway debate, Dalton told Harold Macmillan that the Parliamentary Executive of the Labour Party would decide next morning whether or not to turn the issue into a vote on the Government's conduct of the war by demanding a division on the adjournment. Macmillan immediately passed this item of news on to the 'Salisbury group' of Tories opposed to Chamberlain.[21] Everything depended on how many Tories could be persuaded to vote with Labour or abstain: to divide the House without seriously splitting the Government ranks would merely strengthen the Prime Minister, by providing him with a vote of confidence.

Dalton was pessimistic: on the morning of the Executive decision, he calculated that the Opposition would be lucky to get more than a dozen or fifteen Government supporters to vote against the Government whip, though many might abstain. He was also concerned lest the Prime Minister might seize the opportunity to go to the country; if that happened, he feared a Tory victory on such a scale that Labour 'should be wiped further out than in 1931'.[22] Hence he opposed a division, arguing that a vote at this stage would consolidate the Government majority, and 'Chamberlain and Margesson would like us to have one'. Luckily, he was in a minority. The Parliamentary Executive decided to make this the moment to test the Government's strength.

When the House did divide, 41 members who normally supported the Government voted with the Opposition, and 65 were absent unpaired. Yet the Prime Minister was not defeated. The Government won the vote by 281 to 200, a majority of 81. The possibility remained that despite this massive blow to his prestige, Chamberlain might hold on to power by making changes to his administration. His opponents moved as quickly as they could to head off this danger. The day after the division, a meeting of Tory rebels chaired by Leo Amery agreed to support any Prime Minister 'who would form a truly National Government with a real War Cabinet based on personal merit and not just a Whips' coalition'.[23] Robert Boothby, one of the rebels, passed this on to Dalton. Dalton once again went out of his way to stress that 'no member of our Party would serve under Chamberlain'. At 6.30 the same night, Attlee and Greenwood conveyed the same message directly to Chamberlain, Halifax and Churchill. Attlee agreed, however, to consult the National Executive (assembling at Bournemouth for the Party Conference) for confirmation.

Before Attlee could do so there was a dramatic new twist. Early next morning (10th May), the Germans invaded Holland and Belgium. Chamberlain's reaction was that, in the new situation, he should stay on. The Labour leadership now faced a dilemma. Openly to attack the Government at this moment of acute crisis might appear un-patriotic, and might therefore rally support around the Prime Minister. Yet Labour leaders remained adamant about the need for Chamberlain's departure. Alexander rang Dalton to suggest that Parliament should meet. Dalton vigorously opposed, pointing out that it 'would give the cheer-leaders and crisis-exploiters a chance to rehabilitate the Old Man'. In response to Chamberlain's request for a message saying that Labour supported the Government in the crisis, Dalton drafted a declaration, issued over the signatures of Attlee and Greenwood, demanding a 'drastic reconstruction of the Government'. At 3.30 p.m. the N.E.C. in Bournemouth gave its decisive answer to the Prime Minister: the Labour Party would not serve under him, but would be prepared to serve in a coalition under somebody else. As soon as he received the news, Chamberlain resigned. Shortly afterwards, Winston Churchill drove to the Palace to kiss hands.

How important was Dalton in this rapid sequence of events? Many factors contributed to Chamberlain's eventual fall. Crucial, however, was the alliance, finally achieved, of Labour Opposition and Tory rebels. It was the conjunction of the rebels' insistence on a coalition involving Labour, and Labour's absolute refusal to serve under Chamberlain, which forced Chamberlain's hand.

In encouraging the Tory rebels, and in firming up Labour leaders, Dalton played a major part. His repeated insistence that Labour would not serve under Chamberlain helped to convince the rebels that a patched up administration, which some of them still hoped for, could not be achieved. It also helped to convince the Government. Before the critical division, Dalton told R. A. Butler, Parliamentary Under-Secretary at the Foreign Office, that Labour would be prepared to discuss a coalition – provided Chamberlain, Sir John Simon and Sir Samuel Hoare 'disappeared from the Government altogether'. Dalton made it clear that this was intended as more than mere gossip. 'I told Butler that I did not wish him to keep what I had said entirely to himself', he recorded, 'but should be glad if he would pass it on to H[ali]fax.'[24] This Butler did.[25]

As Dalton put it after the N.E.C. verdict had been delivered, 'the last blow which dislodged the old limpet was struck by us at Bournemouth this afternoon'.[26] But the Labour Party had no say in the choice of a new Prime Minister. This decision was made by Chamberlain, Halifax and Churchill in private conclave, with Captain Margesson, the Chief Whip, in attendance. Chamberlain's first choice, the King's first choice, and the first choice of most Conservatives, was Lord Halifax.

Churchill became Prime Minister only after Halifax had declined to take the job.

It has been widely believed that Halifax was also the man most desired by the Labour Party. Morrison's biographers have put it simply: 'The Labour leaders' choice for a successor to Chamberlain was Halifax.'[27] In fact the Labour leaders never made any formal decision or recommendation, and a number were uncertain. The reality seems to have been an assumption rather than a choice.

Alexander was in favour of Churchill, or so Dalton believed. Cripps wanted Halifax, but Cripps was no longer in the Labour Party.[28] Morrison seems to have taken a Halifax succession for granted, negotiating with R. A. Butler on this basis.[29] Attlee said contradictory things to different people at different times. It seems likely that his main expressed preference was for Halifax; later, however, he denied any such opinion, and also denied having told Brendan Bracken that Halifax was the preferred choice of the Labour Party.[30] Dalton's opinion was fluid. He was more concerned about getting rid of Chamberlain than with who might succeed, though (like Morrison) he was also anxious to back whoever came out on top.

After the Munich crisis, Dalton tended to regard Churchill as Labour's best hope – though not necessarily as alternative premier; until the spring of 1940 he continued to identify Halifax with the Government's appeasement team and appeasement mentality. He first mentioned Halifax as a potential successor in his diary on 1st May, and as his own preferred choice a day later. It is only on 8th May – two days before Chamberlain's resignation – that Dalton's private record gives a clear indication of a personal preference for Halifax over Churchill. In the course of his talk with Butler, Dalton said:

... if I was asked who should succeed Chamberlain as Prime Minister, my own view, which I thought was shared by a number of others, was that it should be H[ali]fax. In time of war I was not concerned with the fact that he was in the Lords. Indeed, this had some advantages in relieving the strain upon him. Some might think of Winston as P.M., but in my view he was better occupied in winning the war. If one passed beyond these two one arrived in the outer circles of Andersons, etc., and no-one there seemed to stand out.[31]

It is significant that these remarks were made to Halifax's deputy at the Foreign Office; and that Dalton's next recorded remark was a suggestion that Butler should tell Halifax what he had just said. In reporting Dalton's comments to Halifax, Butler (who had his own reasons for wishing to encourage the Foreign Secretary) wrote: 'Dalton said there was no other choice but you.'[32] Yet when, next day, Dalton and Attlee discussed alternatives and agreed that Halifax was preferable to Churchill, the two Labour leaders also agreed 'that either would be tolerable'.[33] One may guess that Dalton gave different emphases to suit the occasion.

Early on 10th May, following the invasion of the Low Countries, Labour opinion seemed to move in favour of Churchill. Shortly before resigning, Chamberlain revised his earlier belief that Labour M.P.s wanted Halifax: ' ... I heard that the Labour Party was veering towards Winston and I agreed with him and Halifax that I would put Winston's name to the King.'[34] Dalton's opinion seemed to shift too. 'Since that morning, with the new sharp twist in Hitler's offensive', he wrote later, 'all of us had felt, and most had said to one another, that it *must* be Churchill and not Halifax.'[35]

That Dalton was desperately keen for a post in the new Government was made clear by his behaviour over the next few days. It was like May 1929, when the second MacDonald Government was being formed, all over again. Then Dalton had been prepared to accept a second ranking appointment. Now he played for higher stakes. 'I should not be interested now in any job which had not got a very close relation to the waging of the war', he told Attlee in a taxi. 'Nor would I wash bottles for any one. I am through with that phase. I should prefer the Ministry of Economic Warfare. That is on the border line of economics and foreign policy. Those are the two fields I know best.'

After the N.E.C. had decided to join a Coalition under a new Prime Minister, Attlee and Greenwood returned from Bournemouth, where the Party Conference was about to be held, to negotiate with Churchill over posts. Dalton stayed with the Party Executive at the Highcliffe Hotel, liaising on the telephone between N.E.C. colleagues and the Party Leader in London. Attlee and Greenwood went back to Bournemouth on 12th May. The main terms of the Coalition had been settled: Labour would get two seats (to be filled by the Leader and Deputy Leader) in a five-man War Cabinet, one of the three Service Departments and a 'fair share' of other offices; Chamberlain was to be a member of the War Cabinet without a department, Simon was to go to the Woolsack, Hoare was to have nothing; and a number of Liberals and Tory rebels would also be included in the new ministry.

Dalton's own name, however, had not been mentioned. On 11th May, Attlee told him reassuringly on the telephone, 'We are getting several more very important offices and you are well in the picture'. Dalton was not so confident. Next day, he recorded anxiously that

Attlee had been told by Laski, 'that there is increasing concern because so far I have not been appointed to anything'. Attlee whispered in Dalton's ear: 'It is all right. I have told the new P.M. that you ought to be at M.E.W. and he is quite in favour. It is as good as settled.' Next morning, Attlee repeated this assurance. 'If it is as good as settled,' Dalton replied, 'why the devil isn't it announced?' Later, he told Attlee he would *only* take Economic Warfare. 'Failing this, I would stay outside.'

'The sun, and the sea are more than usually beautiful', Dalton wrote in his diary ' – tragic, tense, ironic beauty.' Party Conference opened next day, and the N.E.C. recommendations were passed by 2,450,000 to 170,000. 'The debate is a ragged affair with a lot of freaks talking pathetic rubbish', he noted. Still there was no news from London. He was becoming irritated at 'having to parry friendly questions'.[36] His nervousness became a talking-point, the subject of wry amusement.[37] The pacifist Vera Brittain recalled how 'under an incongruously cloudless sky Labour's leading personalities were awaiting their political fate beneath gaily-striped sun umbrellas, and Hugh Dalton paced like a caged panther beneath the lounges of the Highcliffe Hotel ... '[38]

Just before lunch on 14th May, Dalton's friend John Wilmot told him of a rumour that the Governor of the Bank of England, Montagu Norman, was trying to veto his appointment. The idea of an Establishment plot confirmed Dalton's worst suspicions, and he prepared for a fight. Labour colleagues began to discuss 'various forms of emergency action, e.g. a special meeting of the N[ational] E[xecutive] or a special message by a few of them to A[ttlee].'

But this was not necessary. At last a call came through, and Dalton spoke to the new Prime Minister at 6 o'clock. 'Your friends tell me that you have been making a considerable study of Economic Warfare', said Churchill. 'Will you take that Ministry?' Dalton replied: 'I should be very glad.' Immensely relieved, he rang through the news to Ruth, and returned to London by train.[39]

II

Daybreak

XVIII

Blockade

The Coalition rapidly found itself facing quite different tasks from those it had imagined at the outset: instead of looking for ways of taking the initiative in the war, ministers had to meet the danger of a catastrophic defeat. During five tense weeks in May and June, the entire structure of the Allied defence in Western Europe collapsed. Between 26th May and 4th June, 225,000 British and more than 100,000 French troops were forced to evacuate by sea from Dunkirk, leaving behind most of their equipment. By the middle of June France was suing for peace, and Britain was threatened with an imminent invasion. Against this background Dalton, placed in charge of a department whose objectives were offensive rather than defensive, needed to fight hard to give himself, and economic warfare, a role.

Dalton had asked for M.E.W. because he believed that economic weapons were capable of dealing the enemy a knockout blow. He recalled the conditions of 1918, when shortages crippled the German war economy and helped to foment revolution. He shared with Labour colleagues a hope that economic 'sanctions', in war as in peace, would bring ordinary Germans to their senses. 'Victory for democracy must be achieved', declared a Labour statement of war aims, which Dalton had helped to write the previous February, 'either by arms or economic pressure or – better still – by a victory of the German people over the Hitler regime, resulting in the birth of a new Germany'.[1] A lack of essentials, Dalton argued, would encourage both the Germans and those subject to German tyranny to hate their masters and seek to overthrow them.

Like Dalton, Tory ministers had also hoped during the 'phoney war' period for a German economic collapse. In their case, however, faith had been placed in economic weapons because of a reluctance to use military ones. Such was the naive optimism of some early claims by the first Minister of Economic Warfare, Ronald Cross, that the department earned a reputation as 'the Ministry of Wishful Thinking'.[2] Dalton did not quarrel with Cross's hopes; his objection was rather that fine words were not supported by brave action. 'We have dilly-dallied with the blockade', he accused the Government in April 1940. Prosecution of economic warfare had been 'hamstrung by antediluvian British conceptions of prize law'.[3]

When Dalton took over as Minister on 15th May, he brought his view of M.E.W. as a war-winning weapon with him. His motto became 'belligerency at all times' on the model of Clemenceau's *Je fais la guerre* in the First World War.[4] He also brought with him the view that economic warfare needed to be given a political dimension. Hence he sought, within the Government, to promote the idea of 'political' warfare linked to economic warfare as a fourth arm, which – if properly handled – could cause the collapse of the Nazi empire from within.

Such an idea depended for its success on an efficient blockade. Early in 1940 an efficient blockade was, at least, imaginable. Dalton's arrival at M.E.W. occurred at a time when it was ceasing to be so. 'I judged that my task was to strangle Hitler', Dalton wrote later.[5] Yet it seemed as though Hitler, rather than Dalton, was in possession of the noose: not only did the Germans now have the whole of Europe west of Soviet Poland and north of the Pyrenees at their disposal, until the middle of 1941 they had the active co-operation of Stalin as well, and the so-called 'trans-Siberian leak' was in practice unpluggable.

Nevertheless Dalton did not abandon his view of economic warfare as an instrument which could deprive the enemy of vital supplies and might eventually stir up revolution in the occupied territories. If his attitude contained a contradiction, it was arguably a necessary contradiction: the alternative to a belligerent policy was no serious policy at all. In the words of an M.E.W. memorandum in November 1940, without the application of economic weapons by the British Government, 'The Axis would be able to trade freely how and where she pleased, import and export goods without restriction, have access to the raw materials of the world, and obtain foreign exchange without interference'.[6] Such an eventuality could only be avoided by upholding the principle of the blockade, even when it was impossible to enforce the practice. The principle could only be upheld by making bold claims. Indeed, as the official historian of M.E.W., Professor W. N. Medlicott, later put it, 'in the summer of 1940 it needed some persistence and faith to maintain the blockade at all'.[7]

Economic warfare involved much more than physically stopping goods getting through. The key objective was to find weak spots in the enemy's economic system, and put pressure on them. Sometimes this meant the destruction of key installations within enemy territory (an aspect that became important later in the war); sometimes it meant putting diplomatic pressure on neutral governments. M.E.W. was thus heavily dependent on the co-operation of other departments. Bomber Command was called upon to carry out strategic bombing; the Admiralty was called upon to intercept blockade runners; the Foreign Office was brought in to help with the negotiation of war trade agreements with neutral countries, especially those adjacent to enemy territory. There was also a complex regulatory machinery for 'control at source', that involved both the Royal Navy and the Foreign Office. This machinery made use of compulsory 'navicerts' (any neutral ship not issued with a navicert, or with a cargo not navicerted, was liable to seizure), the refusal of facilities to shipping lines that disobeyed M.E.W. rules, the control of export licences, a Black List of 'neutral' firms that traded with the enemy, and financial pressures to stop the Germans gaining access to funds. Finally, there was 'pre-emption' – the buying up of strategically important materials, like wolfram or chrome, to prevent the Germans from getting them.[8] Essential to all these techniques was the gathering of information – the economic intelligence side of M.E.W.'s activities, aimed at discovering contraband evasion and at revealing the economic situation in Germany.

When, late in 1941, Dalton's old undergraduate friend Dudley Ward (temporarily employed by M.E.W.) congratulated Dalton on the success of the department and asked how this had been achieved, Dalton replied that he had a definite policy, and his officials knew what it was; and that he had 'a most efficient private office'.[9] His definite policy was to exploit every opportunity provided by M.E.W.'s web of interests and activities to the maximum possible advantage. This policy radiated from a private office, nerve centre of the whole enterprise, which the new Minister carefully constructed at the outset in accordance with his needs.

Dalton's very first appointment was that of Hugh Gaitskell, the socialist economist who had leaked secrets from the vantage point of a temporary post in the M.E.W. Intelligence section. Consulting nobody, Dalton asked Gaitskell to be his Principal Private Secretary and, in effect, 'Chef de Cabinet'. This invitation delighted Gaitskell but gravely displeased some of the career civil servants, traditionally hostile to outsiders. In an attempted blocking move, the Director-General of the Ministry, an old Treasury hand called Sir Frederick Leith-Ross, resorted to a classic Whitehall ploy. Leith-Ross summoned Noel Hall, head of the Intelligence section. 'You will get a minute from me saying that Gaitskell is to be appointed to Dalton's office', Leith-Ross told Hall. 'You will reply that, regrettably, he cannot be spared from his present duties.'[10] The ploy failed. Hall refused to co-operate and Dalton refused to budge. Leith-Ross later recalled 'some unnecessary shouting' at his first interview with the new Minister.[11] Dalton's diary suggests that the shouting was for a purpose. It was intended to show who was boss.[12]

Dalton picked as his P.P.S. John Wilmot, a personal friend and a shrewd grass-roots politician. Dingle Foot ('My Foot' Dalton called him), a young Liberal M.P. and barrister, became Parliamentary Secretary and ministerial No. 2, chosen by Churchill as part of the Coalition balancing act. Dalton saw less of Foot, however, than of Gaitskell and Wilmot, who became his key political advisers, complementing each other's talents: Gaitskell as intellectual stimulus, Wilmot as Labour Party antenna.

Eventually Dalton and the Director-General achieved a *modus vivendi*, and when Dalton moved to the Board of Trade in 1942, Leith-Ross agreed to come with him. Yet for a long time after their initial clash relations remained frosty. Dalton regarded 'Leethers' as over-cautious and insufficiently dynamic; Leith-Ross considered the Minister difficult, rude, rash and disloyal.[13] A crude anecdote summed up the tension that existed between them. Dalton, it was alleged, had issued a peremptory order for Leith-Ross to attend on him instantly. When a private secretary explained that Sir Frederick was not available, the Minister merely repeated the command. Tracking down the Director-General to the lavatory, the embarrassed secretary passed a note under the door. 'Tell him', came the reply, 'that I can only deal with one shit at a time.'[14]

Leith-Ross was a Treasury economic adviser, not by training an administrator. Dalton soon found that he preferred the Director-General in an advisory role. Such an arrangement was achieved by a bloodless coup carried out by Dalton a few weeks after his arrival, at a time when Whitehall – reeling under the double impact of a new Government and military disaster – was least able to resist. Towards the end of May a vacancy was created by the resignation, on health grounds, of Leith-Ross's second-in-command. Several Foreign Office officials, attached to M.E.W. since the beginning of the war, cast themselves as possible successors. Dalton ignored them. Instead he seized the opportunity to insert not one, but two, temporary civil servants, the Earl of Drogheda and Noel Hall, as Joint Directors, formally responsible to Leith-Ross but in practice taking control of most M.E.W. operations themselves. Power was thus removed from the Whitehall establishment and placed in the hands of determined administrators, 'live wires and war mongers' as Dalton described them,[15] who understood the Minister's 'definite policy', communicated well with his private office, and shared his hostility towards the appeasement mentality which lingered among some members of the permanent staff.

Later, Dalton described his unorthodox selection procedure:

Before deciding on these two appointments and others which were consequential, I had asked Hugh Gaitskell to arrange a series of conferences at one or other of which all the top dozen officials at the Ministry, and a few more, should attend and be made to talk, so that I might form quick judgements of my own about them to supplement the views of others. I offer this tip in political science to all newly installed Ministers.[16]

Drogheda and Hall were contrasting figures. Drogheda was the more surprising choice: an aristocrat and former diplomat who had left the Foreign Office to practise at the Bar, before returning to Whitehall at the outbreak of war, he came from a world for which Dalton had little affection. After his appointment, Dalton clashed with him as he did with all his officials. 'I *won't* see Drogheda!', the ministerial voice was once heard through the baize office door. 'Drogheda is a bugger!'[17] Nevertheless Dalton regarded Lord Drogheda more highly than any other member of the department and relied heavily on him for advice. Not only was Drogheda sound in judgment he also – crucially – commanded respect in the Foreign Office. Often, Dalton would end a long debate on paper with a simple minute: 'Act as proposed by Lord Drogheda.'[18]

If Drogheda came from a world which the Minister regarded as hostile, Hall was so much part of Dalton's own world that some people regarded his appointment – wrongly – as a political one. An economist still only 38 years of age (Drogheda was 56), Hall had held a chair in economics at University College, London (where he had given Gaitskell his first academic job), and then the directorship of the National Institute of Social and Economic Research. Drogheda provided a link to the Foreign Office; Hall's natural allies were the 'intellectual' temporaries, the dons and professional economists of whom there were a number in key positions at M.E.W. Like them (and unlike the patrician Lord Drogheda) Hall was never fully accepted by the permanent staff. This 'otherness' had its advantages: it placed him closer to the Minister, with whom he shared an impatience towards Whitehall ritual and obstruction.

Dalton's office revolution went beyond a mere storming of the citadel. Further changes followed swiftly. Some leading posts were filled by the Minister himself, following the conference organised by

Gaitskell. Other appointments Dalton made on the recommendation of Drogheda and Hall, after giving them four days in which to prepare a plan for reorganising the whole department. As a result, the vast majority of posts changed hands. Criteria for making new appointments were energy, ability, relevant skills and – above all – an aggressive attitude towards the economic war. Foreign Office officials were again chagrined to find academic and City experts in trade, finance and economics given precedence over themselves.[19]

'The very success of Hitler's *Blitzkrieg*', argued the editor of *The Economist*, Geoffrey Crowther, 'has made it easier to blockade him.'[20] It had certainly made it simpler: after the fall of France, there were fewer European neutrals through which goods could pass, and hence fewer governments to engage in difficult negotiations. Instead, most of the Continent of Europe could be regarded as hostile territory. The problems were finding the naval ships, properly equipped and free from other duties, to patrol and intercept at the perimeter; and ensuring that, when interceptions were possible, public and official opinion was not outraged on the other side of the Atlantic.

Dalton frequently clashed with the Admiralty, which regarded spot checks on possible blockade runners as a low priority; and with the Foreign Office, which was worried about diplomatic damage that might be caused by searching the cargoes of neutral shipping. In these battles, the Minister took a consistently tough line. 'What was needed by officials in a new department like M.E.W. was *support*', according to Hall. 'If you ran into trouble, you could put your foot down, in the knowledge that Dalton would back you up at the highest level. You didn't dare do that under Cross.'[21]

One of the new Minister's first forays, successfully concluded, concerned Italian cargoes. When an Italian declaration of war had become imminent, but had not yet been announced, Dalton wanted to take the precaution of intercepting ships heading for Italian ports. The Foreign Office, however, prevaricated. 'I cannot hope to do justice to the job which you have given me', Dalton wrote to the Prime Minister on 4th June, 'if this Ministry is to continue to live in the shadows to which it has apparently been relegated by past usage.'[22] Next day senior ministers considered the matter. 'Cabinet decided to stop Italian cargoes', noted Sir Alexander Cadogan, Permanent Under-Secretary at the Foreign Office. 'Dalton very offensive and got everyone's back up.'[23] It was a significant victory, establishing a double precedent: that M.E.W. should be consulted whenever blockade enforcement was involved, and that strict enforcement of the blockade should not in the normal way be subordinated to the requirements of diplomacy. A year later, Dalton was able to claim to Anthony Eden (by then Foreign Secretary), that he had 'always found the P.M. very much on the point where blockade was being discussed', and desirous of maintaining it as fully as possible.[24]

Spain presented another difficulty. Should Franco be given favourable treatment, despite his pro-Axis sympathies, on the grounds that economic pressure might push him into the war on Hitler's side? Dalton thought not. He was, however, strongly opposed by the British ambassador in Madrid, Sir Samuel Hoare. Dalton considered Hoare, former Foreign Secretary and architect of the notorious 1935 Hoare-Laval pact, an unrepentant appeaser. 'He asks for ship after ship to be let through', the Minister of Economic Warfare noted. 'If I left it to him there would soon be no blockade left.'[25] Dalton summed up his differences with Hoare: 'He wants to keep them sweet; I want to keep them short.' In Dalton's view, the Spaniards should be kept so short that they would not be able to re-export to the enemy, and would not be worth pillaging.[26] Embassy staff, who had to deal directly with the protests of the Spanish authorities, concluded that the Minister was motivated by a mixture of socialist prejudice and personal vindictiveness. One British diplomat later suggested that Dalton's 'antipathy to Franco's government unnecessarily soured Allied blockade enforcement', and complained bitterly about the Minister's alleged 'spiteful reaction to everything Spanish'.[27]

If pre-war politics and ideology provided a background to the dispute over Spain, these factors were an even bigger element in a parallel dispute over supplies to France. Here strategic, departmental and political considerations all came into play. Should occupied and unoccupied France be treated differently? Dalton wanted to treat the whole country as part of the enemy's sphere of influence, from which essential goods should be withheld. Other views, however, prevailed in the Foreign Office.

Dalton's knowledge of events on the other side of the Channel was derived from private meetings with exiled socialists. France, he was told by French comrades, had been betrayed by a handful of reactionaries after being *'menée par une classe depuis dix ans'*, and by people who preferred their private property to national liberty;[28] such people remained in positions of power within the Vichy regime, and they were not to be trusted. On the other hand some Foreign Office officials and Tory ministers felt that Vichy traditionalism had much to recommend it, that dealings with Pétain should if possible be encouraged, and that Vichy France was a neutral state which should be treated accordingly.

Churchill agreed with Dalton, at least on the issue in dispute, and

Cabinet authority was obtained on 25th June 1940 for a blockade of both occupied and unoccupied zones. Authority, however, was one thing, implementation another. Even when naval vessels were available to intercept ships bound for France, the Admiralty was reluctant to carry out interceptions for fear of provoking an armed clash with the French navy. Hence the blockade of French ports was at first little more than nominal: leaking, not like a sieve, but like a bottomless bucket. French naval officers at Casablanca boasted of having defeated the Royal Navy with one small trawler armed with a six-pounder, and were reputed to hold a regular sweepstake on the number of ships which would get through to Marseilles.[29] In the five months October 1940 to February 1941 the actual figure was more than 90 per cent: only 8 out of 108 French vessels passing through the Straits of Gibraltar were intercepted.[30]

Yet Admiralty resistance to the 25th June order was not the only obstacle to an effective blockade of France. Ironically, at a time when interceptions were at their most infrequent, Dalton had to answer the accusation that his policy would reduce the civilian populations of occupied Europe to starvation. The accusation came from former American President Herbert Hoover, reflecting an important body of American isolationist opinion. Such was the influence of the Hoover campaign that the State Department began to press for a concession on the basis of 'Milk for Babies' (supplies that would be of little use to the Germans).

The British Foreign Office saw no objection: such supplies were getting through in any case and it seemed better to make an apparently meaningless concession than risk damaging relations with the Roosevelt administration. Dalton, however, did not regard a 'Milk for Babies' concession as meaningless. He saw a principle at stake. In the first place, to accept a concession on the grounds that the blockade was in practice ineffective was tantamount to accepting the abandonment of the blockade. In the second place, there was the question of the purpose, in particular the political purpose, of economic warfare. The Americans argued that depriving civilian populations of food had nothing to do with the war. Dalton argued that a primary objective of economic warfare was to create shortages which would lower morale and stimulate opposition to the ruling power. 'Stubble will only easily burn', Dalton declared, 'after a dry spell.' However, to satisfy humanitarian American opinion he pointed out that in the case of France, starvation was a long way off. All that threatened was a monotonous diet. 'Even so, incidentally, have many British unemployed and their families lived for many years.'

Dalton therefore resisted pressure for an official relaxation of the blockade, and put forward a plan which would throw blame for any hardship back on to the Germans while also providing an inducement to revolt. He proposed the creation of a well-publicised food stock, to be 'held in trust for the Free Europe of tomorrow'. The existence of such a 'reserve', Dalton considered, would have propaganda value on both sides of the Atlantic.[31] He put this idea to the Prime Minister, who saw the strength of the argument, gave it his approval and announced the scheme in the House of Commons on 20th August. Dalton, working with the Foreign Secretary, Lord Halifax, drafted the relevant passage in Churchill's speech:

> Let Hitler bear his responsibilities to the full and let the peoples of Europe who groan beneath his yoke aid in every way the coming of the day when that yoke will be broken. Meanwhile, we can and we will arrange in advance for the speedy entry of food into any part of the enslaved area, when this part has been wholly cleared of German forces, and has genuinely regained its freedom. We shall do our best to encourage the building up of reserves of food all over the world, so that there will always be held up before the eyes of the people of Europe, including – I say it deliberately – the German and Austrian peoples, the certainty that the shattering of the Nazi power will bring to them all immediate food, freedom and peace.[32]

This statement was immensely important as an official declaration, at the highest level, of the principle of a tight blockade. It was even more important in giving official expression to another principle which Dalton had been pressing since the outbreak of war: that the withholding of foodstuffs from the 'enslaved area' had as a major purpose the encouragement of resistance – with 'food, freedom and peace' offered as the incentive.

The problem over demands for relief did not, however, end with this statement. The Hoover agitation continued to gather momentum, and American pressure for concessions grew in proportion. The Foreign Office, meanwhile, became increasingly impatient with what it regarded as Dalton's intransigence. Rejecting the argument that Vichy France was already in effect enemy territory, the British ambassador in Washington, Lord Lothian, called for an immediate capitulation to the Americans. In addition Lothian put forward a formula for relief to occupied territories other than France, urging that supplies of milk should be allowed through on certain conditions, namely:

1 That the German Government agrees to take no more food out

of Belgium, Holland, Norway and Poland, except in so far as it is
a barter arrangement necessary to balance the diet of the conquered countries, and that arrangements are made to give effect
to this agreement.

2 That Germany returns to these countries an equivalent of the
food supplies she has·taken out of them.

'Who will determine?' Dalton scribbled on this minute which he
regarded as an example of the appeasement mentality at its worst.
Quite apart from the naivety of contemplating negotiations which
depended on German good faith, there was the certainty that the
enemy would regard such a concession as evidence of weakness. So,
in Dalton's view, would the Americans. 'Once we began to discuss
allowing food through on any conditions', Dalton pointed out, 'we
were on a slippery slope and we might be forced to modify the conditions.'[33] The Americans, he believed, would respect tough-minded
obstinacy more than excessive readiness to please.

The Foreign Office already had a collective opinion of Dalton,
formed during the 1929–31 administration, as a brash and unrespon-
sive minister, a bull in a china shop liable to upset delicate negotiations. Now its worst fears appeared to be justified. Among embassy
staff in Washington, as in Madrid, Dalton's name became anathema.
Particular alarm was caused at the end of 1940 when news reached the
embassy of an arrangement for Dalton to broadcast to the American
people about the blockade. An embassy official immediately sent a
telegram to the Foreign Office in London urging in the most unflatter-
ing terms that the Minister of Economic Warfare should be kept off
the air. Mysteriously, this message found its way into the hands of the
M.E.W. Press Officer, David Bowes Lyon. Bowes Lyon passed it to
Dalton. There was a predictable explosion. Noel Hall was summoned
to the Minister, who waved a reply about Fascists and traitors in the
Washington embassy. With some difficulty Hall persuaded Dalton to
tear it up, and instead to insist, in less emotive terms, on making the
broadcast. Afterwards, Hall remained convinced that the Foreign
Office telegram did not reach Bowes Lyon by accident. 'It was a case
of FO sabotage', Hall maintained – a deliberate leak intended to
provoke a reaction harmful to M.E.W. interests which, indeed, it
nearly did.[34]

Dalton eventually won the battle over relief. A personal request,
direct from President Roosevelt, for medical supplies, milk and vitamin concentrates to be allowed through the blockade had to be granted
in January 1941. But this token relaxation was followed by an official
declaration that no further concessions would be made. Furthermore,

in March 1941, after a Vichy-German barter agreement had shown that the Pétain regime was in full collaboration with the Nazis in economic matters, the Prime Minister ordered that the blockade should be made even tighter.[35] Thereafter the principle of a strict blockade was maintained until the beginning of 1942, when another small relaxation was permitted, in the form of a relief shipment of wheat to Greece. 'This, then, is the first voluntary breach – apart from our few concessions to Roosevelt on unoccupied France – in the Blockade which has been agreed since I became Minister', Dalton noted. 'That is twenty months ago and, if I had followed the advice of many of my own officials, or yielded to the pressure of colleagues, the whole Blockade would be in ruins long ago.'[36]

In addition to stopping goods getting through to the enemy, M.E.W. was also concerned to destroy vital materials already in enemy hands. Most important of these was oil. Much attention was devoted at the Ministry, and in other departments closely concerned, to the problem of working out how the enemy's supplies of oil might be disrupted, on the grounds that, if such a disruption could be achieved, the German war economy would rapidly grind to a halt.

On this subject, Dalton was almost as guilty of naive optimism as his predecessor. Determined to find an Achilles heel in the German economy, and eager to make out as strong a case as possible for offensive operations, M.E.W. intelligence came up with some predictions which looked unconvincing and were indeed misleading. Basing himself on M.E.W. data, Dalton told Attlee a few weeks after taking office that Germany would begin to feel the effects of an oil shortage by the autumn of 1940 and would be dangerously short by the following spring.[37] To the Prime Minister, Dalton made the even more rash claim that, on assumptions favourable to Germany, 'the enemy will not be much above the dying-out figure of 1918 next April', a date which, he added, could be brought forward by strategic bombing.[38] 'Oil is the weakest link in the German war chain', Dalton urged Lord Hankey, Chairman of the committee dealing with the prevention of oil from reaching the enemy, ' ... oil targets are the most attractive from the point of view of the R.A.F. ... it is surely high time to cease being gentlemen, to become professionals and to do a little body-line bowling at the Hun.'[39]

Colleagues in the Government were unimpressed. So were senior officials. Cadogan summed up the somewhat weary attitude of Whitehall. 'Cabinet discussed eternal question of denying supplies of oil to Germany and got not much further', the Permanent Under-Secretary noted on 8th June 1940. 'I talked to Dalton after. He the "new broom", talking of "vigorous action". Due to ignorance and half to egotism.'[40]

Dalton imagined that one reason for the cool reception given to his plans for bombing oil installations was Tory snobbery: R.A.F. chiefs, more sympathetic than the heads of other services, carried less weight among Conservative ministers for social reasons. He took comfort from the remark of an air force officer that 'the Chief of the Air Staff was not at school with any one who mattered'.[41] The real explanation, however, was simpler. In the first place, Dalton's more extreme claims were rightly regarded as incredible. In the second place, the R.A.F. lacked the resources – given other priorities – to carry out attacks on the scale Dalton's schemes required. It was the same problem as over the naval blockade: economic warfare involved military weapons which were in short supply. Action to 'cut the jugular vein of oil', as Dalton put it,[42] could only succeed if bombing of synthetic oil plants was sufficiently massive and continuous to stop the Germans from making quick repairs. Yet, in 1940, as Sir Arthur ('Bomber') Harris put it after the war, 'The forces we were able to send against such targets were extremely small and their bomb loads negligible ... '[43] Daylight raids were hazardous, and by the beginning of 1941 it was widely felt by bomber crews that night bombing of economic targets was completely ineffective.[44] When the new Minister claimed in his first broadcast to the British public in June 1940 that the R.A.F. 'had been bombing with tremendous effect oil storage tanks and coal-oil plants in Germany',[45] his words bore little relation to reality.

Nevertheless, such strategic bombing as was carried out had long-term benefits. Cadogan accused Dalton of egotism. Egotism, however, had its place in wartime: as with the blockade by sea, enthusiasm and wildly exaggerated claims, even when greeted with scepticism, were necessary to establish a policy bridgehead. Militarily, the bombing raids aimed at economic targets helped to test the enemy's defences, providing experience the value of which became clear later, when air superiority was attained.[46] The broad economic impact of long-range Allied bombing, which did not develop as a major weapon of war until after Dalton had left M.E.W., remains a matter of controversy. The search for an Achilles heel in the German economy, however, was not misplaced: attacks on ball-bearing factories at Schweinfurt and elsewhere eventually had a crippling effect on German industrial production.[47]

As the war moved in the Allies' favour, so the effectiveness of all kinds of economic warfare – naval interceptions, 'control at source', financial pressures, strategic bombing – increased. The biggest changes, transforming the nature of the economic war, were brought about by the German attack on Russia in June 1941, and by the growing economic, and eventual military, involvement of the United States.

The full effects of the development of the war from a European to a world-wide conflict were not felt until after Dalton ceased to be Minister of Economic Warfare. Nevertheless, the achievements of his brief period of office were considerable. 'Control at source', largely established during Dalton's time, ensured that by the end of 1941 Germany was denied almost all ocean borne supplies except those carried in enemy or Vichy vessels. Moreover, by the summer of 1941 the control of imports to neutral countries in Europe was almost complete, and British naval action had become a serious threat to blockade runners.[48]

The most important effect of British economic warfare, however, may not have been in causing harm to the economy of German-controlled Europe in the short-term, but in persuading the enemy to devote manpower and military resources to circumventing current or anticipated economic pressures. As Professor Medlicott put it, 'fear of the blockade may have been more important than the blockade itself'. The prospect of shortages may have helped to bring about, or at least to hasten, the German attack on Russia. The prospect of shortages certainly encouraged Germany systematically to pillage the countries it invaded, thereby increasing the hostility of native populations. The mishandling of the occupation of the Ukraine ('liberated' Ukrainians might have been turned into allies against the Russians; instead the Ukraine was plundered and its people conscripted for forced labour) was one example of the deflection of strategy for economic ends. The diversion of forces from the main Stalingrad field in order to seize the Caucasian oil wells in 1942 was another. Arguably such errors were incited by the fear that food, oil and production, though still adequate for Germany's immediate needs, might be reduced in future by the Allied blockade.

If so, how much was directly due to Dalton? There is no doubt that Dalton made his presence felt, far more than either his predecessor or his successor. At no time in his life, except as Chancellor, did he work with such ferocious intensity as in his first months at M.E.W.: staying in his office until the small hours and sleeping, when he did sleep, in a bunk in the Ministry basement. Arriving at a key moment, he was able, in Medlicott's words, to place on all work at M.E.W. 'the stamp of his buoyancy, originality and courage'.[49] A weaker Minister might have been forced to live in the shadows cast by more powerful departments, better placed to compete in the desperate scramble over priorities – especially during the critical aftermath of the fall of France when the blockade seemed irrelevant and almost ridiculous. Instead, the combination which Dalton provided of energy, drive and a detailed grasp of the subject matter, together with an immense faith in the possibilities of economic warfare, gave M.E.W. a greatly increased importance; and from the principles and precedents which he established, major policies sprang, bearing fruit later in the war.

Yet there was a political cost. Dalton was not a man to see two sides of a question. In pressing the needs of his own department, he was apt to regard those who pressed the needs of other departments as fools or cowards or worse. This was particularly true of his attitude towards the Foreign Office, the one department of which he had direct experience, and towards whose officials he already had complex emotions. During his period at M.E.W., earlier prejudices were reinforced, on both sides. The Foreign Office, as we have seen, came to view him with distrust. Dalton reciprocated, concluding that British diplomacy remained in the hands of unreformed Municheers, some of whose fifth columnists were even to be found in M.E.W., holding key posts. As a result he tended to look coolly on those he called the 'Palsied Pansies of the F.O.',[50] regarding most diplomats as members of a freemasonry that was loyal only to its own kind.

Dalton's conflicts with the Foreign Office were not, however, solely or even mainly confined to his work at the Ministry of Economic Warfare. They also occurred in another field in which he was simultaneously involved, that of subversion and covert propaganda.

We have seen how, when Dalton first became a minister, he brought with him the idea of a political or psychological aim to economic warfare: an aim, not just of depriving the enemy of the means to fight the war, but also of stimulating discontent and revolt among civilians. Such an idea had two sides. For if economic pressures were meant to have a revolutionary purpose, it followed that such pressures should be supported by non-economic forms of encouragement. Such encouragement could take the form of propaganda, involving leaflets and broadcasts; or it could take the form of 'subversion', involving direct penetration by British agents. In the latter case, 'subversion' might be used to back up economic warfare directly: by attacking economic targets beyond the reach of bombing aeroplanes. Logic seemed to require, therefore, that 'economic' and 'political' warfare should be treated as a unity, housed under the same administrative roof, and made responsible to a single minister.

So Dalton reasoned. And so, too, he argued, through the embattled summer of 1940. For at the same time as pushing for a stricter enforcement of the blockade, he was also working – like a hunter who has caught a scent – to gain control of the various organisations which, when combined, were to be known as the Special Operations Executive (S.O.E.).

How did Dalton first find out about secret organisations such as the 'D' Section of the Secret Service, and MI(R), at the War Office? His source may have been Sir Robert Vansittart, still Chief Diplomatic Adviser, or, more probably, Gladwyn Jebb, who was working as private secretary to Sir Alexander Cadogan. Whoever told him, his diary reveals that, within a few days of becoming a minister, he was taking an active interest in the future of these bodies and was seeking to add them to his empire. 'The D plan is being concocted', he noted cryptically on 1st June. Other similarly mysterious references followed, suggesting strenuous wire-pulling. Jebb was a party to these man-oeuvrings, keeping Dalton closely informed about developments, while Dalton held out the carrot of a leading role in subversive warfare, should the prize come his way.[51]

What Dalton learned was that immediately after the fall of France Foreign Office and military authorities had decided to co-ordinate and strengthen the various organisations responsible for 'covert' operations. Armed with this knowledge, Dalton began to lobby those who would recommend who the co-ordinator should be. 'Dalton ringing up hourly to try to get a large finger in the Sabotage pie', Cadogan noted on 28th June.[52] One proposal was for Dalton to share responsibility with Anthony Eden, Secretary of State for War. Another, pressed by Cadogan, was to give extensive powers to the Director of Military Intelligence. Dalton opposed both plans strongly, especially the second. 'I concert counter-measures and invoke the aid of C.R.A. [Attlee]', he noted on 29th June.[53]

The matter was discussed at a meeting on 1st July attended by the Foreign Secretary and other leading ministers and officials concerned. Dalton made a vigorous case for the separation of subversive warfare from military operations, and hence for control outside the service departments. Political warfare, he maintained, should be political: there was 'a clear distinction between "war from without" and "war from within" and ... the latter was more likely to be better conducted by civilians than by soldiers.'[54] Subversion, he argued, involved agitators, trade unionists, socialists; the making of chaos and revolution was 'no more suitable for soldiers than fouling at football or throwing when bowling at cricket'.[55]

Dalton elaborated this view after the meeting in a letter to Halifax, which set out his own conception of subversive warfare, anticipating S.O.E.'s later self-image:

We have got to organise movements in enemy-occupied territory comparable to the Sinn Fein movement in Ireland, to the Chinese Guerillas now operating against Japan, to the Spanish Irregulars who played such a notable part in Wellington's campaign or – one might as well admit it – to the organisation which the Nazis themselves have developed so remarkably in almost every country in the world. This 'democratic international' must use many different methods, including industrial and military sabotage, labour agitation and strikes, continuous propaganda, terrorist acts against traitors and German leaders, boycotts and riots.

It is quite clear to me that an organisation on this scale and of this character is not something which can be handled by the ordinary departmental machinery of either the British Civil Service or the British military machine. What is needed is a new organisation to co-ordinate, inspire, control and assist the nationals of the oppressed countries who must themselves be the direct participants. We need absolute secrecy, a certain fanatical enthusiasm, willingness to work with people of different nationalities, complete political reliability. Some of these qualities are certainly to be found in some military officers and, if such men are available, they should undoubtedly be used. But the organisation should, in my view, be entirely independent of the War Office machine.[56]

To organise subversion it was necessary to have a subversive mentality – and this was not to be found among civil service chiefs or generals. Dalton noted, with approval, a remark by Lord Lloyd to Halifax – that the Foreign Secretary should not be consulted about subversion, because 'you will never make a gangster!' Yet the implication of Dalton's letter was not just that whoever controlled subversive warfare should be a civilian – it was also that he should be a socialist. Who else would understand labour agitation and strikes, really know about propaganda, or create a 'democratic international'? Fomenting revolt, Dalton urged Attlee to tell Churchill, needed to 'be done from the Left'.

Dalton's advocacy seemed to succeed. On 9th July, Attlee told him that it was settled that he was 'to do something in addition'. But he continued to hear nothing officially, and the Prime Minister was ominously silent. A rumour reached Dalton that Churchill was 'bothered and reluctant'; that the Chiefs of Staff Committee, the Director of Military Intelligence and Ismay all shared this attitude; and that moves were afoot to have Lord Swinton appointed instead.[57] It was a familiar routine: waiting anxiously for a call that seemed interminably delayed, and wondering who was standing in the way. Once again, Dalton sought to mobilise Labour influence behind him. A letter was quickly dispatched to A. V. Alexander, First Lord of the Admiralty, known to be the closest of the Labour ministers to the Prime Minister:

10th July 1940.

My dear Albert,

Clem tells me that yesterday morning at the Cabinet it was decided that I should take on some additional work, of great importance for winning the war.

I am confident that I could do it, and I know it is not being done at present. This evening an agitation has been started to reverse this Cabinet decision – I know by whom, but I won't commit the names to writing.

Clem says he will stand firm tomorrow, I hope you will back him up. Swinton has enough on his plate now.

So far as your Admirals are concerned, I think they have no doubt that I am a war monger! And, of course, I should always be in touch with you.

Yours ever,
H.D.[58]

What the First Lord made of this odd missive may only be guessed. But Dalton was right to be worried. The moves against him were real. At the War Cabinet next day, the Prime Minister opposed Dalton's appointment and indicated his preference for Swinton. Churchill's opinion would have triumphed had not Halifax and Attlee both dissented. Cadogan, who attended the meeting, also disagreed with the Prime Minister. '[W]e want to get someone to take a grip on Sabotage, etc. and put it into shape', the Permanent Under-Secretary wrote. '*I* think Dalton the best man.' Churchill bowed to pressure, and Dalton's name was finally accepted.[59]

What tipped the scales? One of Churchill's key aides at No. 10, Desmond Morton, told Dalton 'if C.R.A. digs his feet in he will win'. This seems to have been what happened. Not for the first, or last, time Dalton discovered that in the Coalition game, Attlee's support was what counted. 'It is all right', the Party Leader told him reassuringly on 12th July. 'You are to do it … I have told them that you will be quite tactful in dealing with the brasshats. The objections raised were not political at all. I think they came from someone in the P.M.'s entourage.'[60]

Who in the Prime Minister's entourage? Brendan Bracken? Lord Beaverbrook? Professor Lindemann? Even, perhaps, Desmond

Morton, until recently at M.E.W., and regarded up to now as a friend? Gradually, as the strains of office increased and it became clear that the Minister of Economic Warfare was not highly regarded in Downing Street, this question became an obsession. But for the time being, Dalton was too delighted by his new acquisition, and the opportunities it provided for 'body-line bowling at the Hun', to be much concerned about real or imagined enemies close to home.

His appointment was officially ratified by the War Cabinet on 22nd July. At last, Churchill made a formal offer. It was a proud and hopeful moment. 'I accepted the Prime Minister's invitation with great eagerness and satisfaction', Dalton recalled. '"And now", he exhorted me, "set Europe ablaze".'[61]

XIX

S.O.E.

In one sense, nothing quite like it had ever been tried before. Yet by the time S.O.E. was set up, most people in Britain probably believed that something of the kind already existed. For 'Special Operations' had a literary pedigree. The idea of secret government agents as a warrior caste, operating their own code outside normal military constraints, had been absorbed into the national consciousness through the writings of John Buchan and Dornford Yates, and of Sapper, whose novels Dalton had read avidly in Italian dugouts during the First World War. The notion of the Englishman as *agent provocateur* in a foreign land, leading the grateful inhabitants to revolt in the British interest, had been taken beyond popular fiction by the remarkable mixture of fact and fantasy, high strategy and boyish adventure that provided the subject matter of *Seven Pillars of Wisdom*. Indeed if S.O.E. created James Bond, then Lawrence of Arabia and Brigadier-General Sir Richard Hannay, K.C.B., D.S.O., *Légion d'Honneur* may be said to have created S.O.E. 'I spent a large portion of World War II working for S.O.E.', recalled one former member of the organisation. 'Practically every officer I met in that concern, at home and abroad, was like me, imagining himself as Hannay or Sandy Arbuthnot.'[1]

We should not be surprised to find, therefore, that throughout the twilight existence of S.O.E., as in the *genre* literature which S.O.E. has spawned (just under 200 books, excluding novels, according to one recent count),[2] the borderline between real and unreal was often blurred. S.O.E. met a psychological as much as a military need, even or especially among those with the firmest grasp of the true logistics of modern warfare, who later considered S.O.E. militarily irrelevant. In a war of rival technologies there was a particular need to believe that individual acts of guile and daring had a part to play.

Such a need was never greater than in the crisis following the fall of France, when by any rational assessment Britain was losing the war. One response was to regard defeats and stalemates as moral victories. Another was to put faith in the power of the human spirit and in the justice of the British cause. Dalton's extraordinary letter to the Foreign Secretary (quoted on page 296), presenting subversion in terms which suggested a sacred mission, fitted the mood. The letter is interesting for several reasons: first, because of its romanticism, open and unabashed; second because, as everybody knew, the nation's requirements were not exploding cigarette cases but ships, tanks and fighters. Third because the argument it contained was taken seriously at the highest level and swiftly given organisational expression.

Yet the setting up of S.O.E. was not attended by much optimism. If the Minister of Economic Warfare was enthusiastic, others were tentative. Was there a note of weariness, even of irony, in Churchill's injunction to Dalton on 16th July: 'Set Europe ablaze'?

The notion of a secret organisation holding a torch, so to speak, for democracy, igniting patriotic passions and creating an inferno of sabotage and revolt, was powerfully emotive. But as an actual command, the order to 'set Europe ablaze' bore as little relation to military reality as Hitler's directives to imaginary armies in the spring of 1945. Dalton's meeting with Churchill came less than a week after the Germans had launched the first of a series of massive air raids intended to destroy British defences. On the very day that the Prime Minister gave Dalton the S.O.E. assignment, the Führer was informing his generals: 'I have decided to begin to prepare for, and if necessary to carry out, an invasion of England.'[3] In July 1940 Britain, not Europe, was the most likely site for a conflagration.

Dalton's ideas on subversion involved politics as well as romanticism; or perhaps we should say that the romanticism was essentially political in nature. The idea of a 'democratic international' run by Englishmen who were to be filled with 'a certain fanatical enthusiasm' contained more than a faint echo of Ben Keeling's 'hundred really determined individuals' setting out to clear a space in the jungle of convention and shift public opinion. As one former aide put it, Dalton 'radiated energy throughout the organisation'.[4] The organisation bore the mark: Carbonari and members of the Fish and Chimney would have felt at home in the 'raffish, amateurish, disreputable'[5] atmosphere of S.O.E., with its ethos of egalitarian exclusiveness. If Edwardian King's provided one model of Fabian-style communalism – part of, yet in revolt against, the Establishment – S.O.E. was a wartime version of the same thing. Had S.O.E. existed in 1914–18, Arthur Waley, Francis Birrell, James Strachey and Amber Reeves would, no doubt, all have been members.

S.O.E. was apparently subjected to 'not infrequent slurs from outside that the organisation was infested by crackpots, communists and homosexuals'.[6] A few crackpots apart, the allegations were aimed at the wrong target: the Secret Service (S.I.S.) was infested, not S.O.E. Yet was there not about S.O.E. a touch of the homoerotic? The cult of intimate friendship with peasant-partisans would have gained the approval of T. E. Lawrence, and Edward Carpenter. S.O.E. recruited women as well as men. But these were plucky, outdoor, boy-women who enhanced the male camaraderie. We are reminded once more of Hannay, Leithen and their chums.[7]

Dalton's political romanticism had wider implications. S.O.E. was more than a secret society; it was also an instrument, based on a network of cells whose purpose was similar to that of the pre-war, Moscow-directed Comintern. It was indeed a paradox that a Tory-led Government should seek to achieve what its predecessors had hitherto actively, and on one occasion militarily, opposed: namely popular revolution all over the Continent of Europe. Such a revolution need not, of course, be socialist. But a 'democratic international', making use of labour agitation, strikes, propaganda, terrorism, boycotts and riots, directed against the Nazis but modelled on Nazi organisations as well as on the Sinn Fein and Chinese Guerrillas, was scarcely a recipe for restoring the *status quo ante bellum.*

Precisely for this reason, Dalton's vision proved hard to maintain. In 1940 there was a single aim: winning (or at any rate not losing) the war. Later, other aims emerged to complicate the picture. On the one hand there was a desire among S.O.E. controllers to support national groups that offered resistance to the occupier. On the other, there was a hesitation – partly a product of Foreign Office pressure, partly of the instincts of S.O.E.'s own senior officers – about embracing those groups with the most revolutionary intent. This dilemma became acute when resistance movements were strong enough to constitute a threat to the enemy. For the time being, however, the problem was not choosing among rival friends but becoming a body with any useful job at all.

How could S.O.E. be turned into an organisation large enough, efficient enough, sufficiently well connected abroad, to be given the equipment and the people it needed to operate effectively? This was the conundrum that faced S.O.E. in its first phase, providing Dalton with a challenge that called for the combined skills of politician, entrepreneur and strategist. By the end of 1940 solving it had become an obsession, and the Minister was pushing other tasks aside. The work of M.E.W. was relegated to a secondary role. Once the essential machinery of the blockade had been established, economic warfare required fewer direct political interventions. Dalton was able to rely on his Joint Directors, Drogheda and Hall, and leave the Ministry, for much of the time, to run itself. ' … M.E.W. is not now a full-time job', Dalton told Attlee in the autumn. Dudley Ward observed that the Minister was now 'largely concerned with other and engrossing duties.' [8]

As with all military commanders, Dalton's behaviour in the present war owed much to his perception of the previous one. Dalton attributed the slaughter of the First World War to the narrow assumptions of generals who sacrificed hundreds of thousands of lives in massive, immobile battles on the Western Front. Yet his direct experience was of a different kind of warfare, in which individual acts of courage and ingenuity had an important role: a war of defence and liberation, an adventure in a foreign land the very contemplation of whose beauty, he had written, 'sometimes brings one near to weeping'.[9] He had served in a small British contingent sent to stiffen the patriotic resistance of a beleaguered ally. His Dunkirk had been the retreat across the Tagliamento, after the Germans and Austrians had broken the Italian line.

Dalton entitled the section of his war-book which dealt with the re-building of Allied strength after Caporetto, 'A Year of Resistance and Preparation', words which would make an apt heading for an account of S.O.E. in its first stage. With Special Operations as his battery, he returned to the 'blasting and bombardiering' of a generation before, and over the next months crashed his way through the wires erected in Whitehall to frustrate him.

The Charter of the Special Operations Executive, endorsed by the War Cabinet on 22nd July, declared that the purpose of the new body was to 'co-ordinate all action by way of subversion and sabotage against the enemy overseas'.[10] The War Cabinet further laid down that the activities of S.O.E. should not be raised in Parliament, and that the Minister of Economic Warfare should be given absolute powers of direction, subject only to the Prime Minister. The essence of 'ungentlemanly warfare', as Churchill liked to call it, was breaking the rules, and it was felt unwise to admit officially that this was going on. Not only were the detailed activities of S.O.E. to be regarded as secret; so too was the very existence of the organisation itself.[11]

S.O.E. brought together a number of bodies which already had a shadowy existence in Whitehall, and fulfilled – in theory – Dalton's ambition of uniting economic and political warfare. In practice, not only were M.E.W. and S.O.E. administered separately, but S.O.E. itself was not a unitary establishment. From the outset, the work of

S.O.E. was divided between two sections: SO2, the 'cloak and dagger' unit, which had responsibility for the operational side (sabotage and the fomenting of revolt); and SO1, responsible for 'psychological' warfare, involving subversion through 'covert' or 'black' propaganda. Dalton continued to think of S.O.E. as a single entity, and sought to preserve his underlying idea of a combined economic and political campaign; but a variety of pressures – personal, practical, philosophical – pulled the two sections apart, and eventually SO1 was merged into another organisation, the Political Warfare Executive, set up in August 1941. Thereafter SO2 assumed the title Special Operations Executive, and it is with the SO2, operational, side that the initials S.O.E. have most often been associated.

SO2 was built from a marriage of a body hitherto controlled by the Foreign Office called Section D, the organisation which had first aroused Dalton's interest in the early summer of 1940, and MI(R), the military intelligence directorate of the War Office.[12] To help establish the new combined organisation Dalton brought in Gladwyn Jebb, who had guided the ministerial finger discreetly towards the sabotage pie. Jebb was given the title of Chief Executive Officer – supposedly in relation to the whole of S.O.E., but in practice with responsibilities relating only to SO2. His job was to watch over SO2's broad policy and to look after its interests in Whitehall.

He performed both tasks well. Clever, ambitious and resourceful, barely forty at the time of his appointment, Jebb was adept at negotiating his way around the minefield of civil service personalities. He was also, in Dalton's words, 'definitely bien vu by the Service blokes who matter'.[13] His special link with Cadogan, who thought highly of him, was an added advantage. Elsewhere in the Foreign Office there was fear of his sharpness, and dislike of his arrogance; also an uncomfortable awareness that he held many of his senior colleagues in private contempt. Yet there existed almost everywhere an acknowledgment of his formidable abilities. And if Jebb's radical (or at any rate critical) attitude towards many diplomatic assumptions created suspicion, it also strengthened his bond with Dalton – whose indispensable factotum he rapidly became.

Who was the real architect of SO2 policy? Each man considered, with about equal justification, that the organisation was his own creation. Yet so closely did Minister and official work together that it is hard to separate their individual influences. Dalton encouraged, pushed, shouted, stormed and paid careful attention to advice. Jebb entertained his Minister with a dry wit, fascinated him with acid appraisals of Whitehall personages, listened patiently to ministerial outpourings, and treated Dalton as one might a large and highly strung pet, dangerous if allowed to get out of control, but useful, if skilfully handled, for barking at hostile strangers. It was an unusual, though on the whole successful, arrangement.

Day-to-day running of SO2 was placed in the hands of an executive director, Sir Frank Nelson, a former Conservative M.P., older than Jebb, less ruthless and calculating and, in the end, more vulnerable. Like Dalton, Nelson lived for the job: having no family, he slept in a service flat close to Baker Street and was at his desk seven days a week from quarter to nine until midnight.[14] Most other senior staff were either inherited from the old Section D and MI(R) organisations, or picked by Jebb. Much recruiting, from outside the civil service, was done through an old boy network of City contacts. Dalton made a few appointments directly himself. One man who owed his job to the Minister's personal intervention was Colin Gubbins, a professional soldier who eventually became working head of S.O.E. Dalton had met Gubbins at a Polish Embassy dinner in 1939 and had been impressed by Gubbins's knowledge of Eastern Europe.[15] A reserved, ' "still waters running deep" sort of man',[16] Gubbins established the main S.O.E. networks abroad and master-minded the organisation's most effective operations (as well as some of its most outlandish schemes). Innumerable fictional undercover controllers were later modelled on him.

Occasionally, especially in the early days when S.O.E. was still a small organisation, Dalton was directly involved in choosing officers for more junior assignments. Julian Amery (son of the politician and political writer Leo Amery and himself a future Conservative minister) was still only twenty-one when, as Assistant Press Attaché in Belgrade, his name was put forward for some important S.O.E. work in the region. The suggestion was opposed by the Foreign Office. Dalton, hearing of the case, demanded to see the young man in question. Amery gives this account of his interview with the Minister of Economic Warfare in October 1940:

> At our first meeting he seemed rather larger than life. He was tall and broad. His head rose to a mighty bald dome. His voice boomed, and he accompanied his expansive gestures with an ominous rolling of the eyes. It was, indeed, the joke of the office that he would not have lasted long in the days of 'shoot when you see the whites of their eyes' ...
> Yet I have never known a kinder man or one prepared to take so much trouble to help his subordinates and young men generally. He cross-examined me for most of a morning beginning with my school days and making me relate the whole story of my life.

He asked about my political views and whether I had read certain books on economics. When I confessed to ignorance of the particular titles he mentioned, he boomed out: 'Aha! I see you are not very familiar with my works. I will send them to you tomorrow and then examine you upon them!'

Then, at last, he turned to the matter in hand and questioned me in detail about the Balkans. He seemed at first to be arguing the Foreign Office case but this was only to take my measure. Suddenly he brought his fist down on the desk and declared: 'Of course you are right and they are wrong. It is useless to expect any help from King Boris or Prince Palsy'. And he repeated the word 'Palsy' several times obviously relishing his own lampoon which Churchill would one day make famous. At the end of our talk he said: 'I want you to work for me in the Balkans; and, when I want something, I usually get it. You will be hearing from me'.[17]

Amery was duly appointed.

In addition to taking on new staff, Dalton disposed of some of the old. In M.E.W. he had trodden carefully, avoiding outright sackings. In S.O.E. he did not feel the same inhibition. His most influential victim was the original head of Section D, Major Lawrence Grand, who had been passed over for the directorship of SO2 and given the job of second-in-command. Grand was upset by his apparent demotion, and proved a restless subordinate. In addition, his mysterious and flamboyant style, more *Boys' Own Paper* than John Buchan, was not easy to accommodate in a body that had acquired practical ambitions.[18] Jebb found him impossible to handle and asked Dalton for his dismissal. The Minister complied, on the grounds of Grand's alleged disloyalty.[19]

This decision was less easy to execute than Dalton had envisaged. Grand fought back, arguing that the matter should be taken to the Cabinet, and boasting of powerful friends, including Anthony Eden and Churchill's aide, Desmond Morton. Dalton became anxious, fearing that Grand's noisy protests might cause a breach in the S.O.E. Charter, with outside ministers and officials interfering in internal S.O.E. business. Concerned to forestall this possibility, Dalton instructed Jebb to see Eden at once to 'rid me and yourself, of this lousy shirt quickly'[20] – a phrase which, like the situation itself, brings to mind the Peckham dispute of a dozen years before (when Ruth had used similar words about the Peckham Labour Party agent, Ernest Baldwyn). Fortunately Dalton possessed more authority as a minister than he had had as a constituency M.P. Grand's resistance crumbled, and the unlucky major was swiftly dispatched by sea for service in

India before he could cause more trouble.

Dalton took pride in his victory. At the end of 1940, Brendan Bracken, the Prime Minister's aide, greeted the Minister of Economic Warfare outside the Cabinet Room with a jocular rebuke: 'There is that great brute who, like his friend Mr. Bevin, tramples all opposition in the mud. He has no liberal sentiments at all!' A rumour had been going round, Bracken declared, that Dalton's treatment of Grand was an outrage, and Churchill should be told. Dalton never knew how to take Bracken, whose humour had a menacing quality. On this occasion he replied with as much aplomb as he could muster, 'Whatever I have been, I have never been a Liberal'. Yet he was not displeased to have been thus taunted. Privately he congratulated himself on 'scoring a little in the role of the "strong man"'.[21]

The role of the strong man was one which, for the sake of S.O.E. even more than M.E.W., Dalton needed to cultivate. M.E.W. was a new department, but at least it was recognised. S.O.E. was supposedly secret and had no official status at all. Secrecy, in the sense of being officially unacknowledged, had some advantages. It protected the Minister responsible from public criticism, and meant that Dalton needed only to worry about attitudes within the community of ministers, officials and military commanders who ran the war. On the other hand, secrecy made it harder to mobilise political support when S.O.E. got into trouble, or its demands were not met. Unable to publicise S.O.E. activities and successes, Dalton, Jebb and Nelson had to rely on Whitehall reputation, and the even less determinate factor of prime ministerial whim. Unlike the Secret Service, which was under the protection of the Foreign Office, S.O.E. had no powerful ministry behind it.

S.O.E. was also handicapped by its size. Estimates suggest that at its peak in 1944 its strength did not much exceed 13,000,[22] a tiny proportion of the total number directly involved in fighting the war. In Dalton's time, the establishment was much smaller. At the outset, apart from one man in prison in Stockholm, SO2 had no agents in Western Europe at all.[23]

Gubbins later gave an account of the problems of SO2 in its initial phase, indicating both the prejudices the organisation faced, and the frustration felt by S.O.E. officers at the contempt with which they were treated:

> ... [T]he creation of a new and secret organisation with such an all-embracing charter aroused suspicions and fear in Whitehall. At the best S.O.E. was looked upon as an organisation of harmless backroom lunatics which it was hoped, would not develop into an active

nuisance. At the worst, it was regarded as another confusing excrescence, protected from criticism by a veil of secrecy ... Finally there was the inbred fear that our actions in delicate political situations would create boundless friction, diplomatic embroilments and disastrous crossing of lines with our secret intelligence and political warfare organisations. So S.O.E.* went ahead rather on its own ...

Gubbins concluded that S.O.E., which took its Charter 'very literally and seriously', suffered the consistent obstruction of all in Whitehall and in the Services who might have helped it.[24] Not all senior officers agreed. George Taylor, head of the SO2 Balkan Section and then chief of staff to Sir Frank Nelson, felt that some of the clashes were unnecessary and unwise.[25] Yet there is no doubt that the organisation suffered badly from the conflicting interests of Whitehall rivals. The body which most feared 'disastrous crossing of lines' was S.I.S., whose head, Sir Stewart Menzies, was in daily touch with the Prime Minister. The needs of SO2 and S.I.S. often seemed to pull in diametrically opposite directions. S.I.S., concerned with intelligence, was afraid that SO2, dealing with agitation, would blow its cover. As a result, co-operation was only grudgingly provided, and SO2 was kept chronically short of special equipment, in particular the wireless transmitters that were vital for maintaining contact with agents in the field. It remained a matter of bitter resentment that because of S.I.S. hostility, there were no points of wireless contact in the Balkans when the Germans overran the area. In the end, SO2 was reduced to making its own secret wireless and forgery plants.[26]

Relations with the Foreign Office were scarcely better. The problem was essentially the same as over the blockade. Foreign Office officials felt that S.O.E. would harm relations with neutral countries. 'Whenever I try to destroy anything anywhere', Dalton complained to Halifax on one occasion, after a Balkan-based plan to blow up a Rumanian bridge had been vetoed, 'I am caught in some diplomatic trip-wire!'[27] The difference, as Jebb put it later, was that S.O.E. wanted to stir up trouble, whereas the Foreign Office wanted to damp it down.[28] The instincts of S.O.E. – like those of M.E.W. – were offensive; the instincts of the Foreign Office seemed to have changed little since peacetime. 'The impression in S.O.E. was that the Foreign Office wasn't really in the war', comments one former SO2 officer. 'They were carrying on being the FO, seeking to maintain pre-war diplomatic standards through the crisis with their convictions undisturbed.'[29]

* The political warfare organisation was SO1; 'S.O.E.' is here used to mean SO2 (i.e. the operational side of S.O.E.).

Hence a determined and influential minister was vital. Dalton's political weight ensured that his 'strongly worded papers' were seriously considered by the War Cabinet, and sometimes heeded. Part of Dalton's task was the paradoxical one of getting a secret organisation known among those upon whom its future depended. It was a job which might be labelled 'controlled publicity': spreading the word through unofficial channels at the highest level. 'His role was as champion and public relations man', according to Taylor. 'His constant preoccupation was "How can I claim something for Special Operations and so sell S.O.E." '.[30] Booming and bullying around the offices of leading ministers and civil servants, Dalton put the organisation on the map. 'It was under the régime of Mr. Dalton and Frank Nelson that the services and the government departments first became aware that our existence was sanctioned if not encouraged by the highest authority', recalled Bickham Sweet-Escott, Taylor's second-in-command in the Balkan Section.[31]

Dalton was equally energetic inside the organisation, earning the half-mocking, half-appreciative nickname 'Dr. Dynamo', a Jebb coinage. At the SO2 headquarters in 62–4 Baker Street, his influence was exercised by remote control: through Jebb, Nelson, Taylor, Gubbins and a few other senior officers. He rarely visited the establishment in person.[32] He made sure, however, that he was kept closely informed. 'People didn't like it when the Minister overrode them', recalls Sir Robin Brook, who had been Jebb's assistant at Berkeley Square House (where the Minister and his immediate entourage resided). 'But nobody could deny that he knew in detail (some felt in too much detail) what was going on.'[33] He met country section heads regularly, he saw secret coded traffic, he visited SO2 stations in the country, and he insisted on being briefed about major operations.

As in M.E.W., Dalton had a definite policy: he encouraged SO2's ambitions and pressed for continuous activity so that eventually the organisation created a job for itself. Above all, he generated a sense of urgency and importance. The principle was established that anything coming from the Minister had to be dealt with as soon as it was received. He was aggressively intolerant of inefficiency, loose thinking or disobedience (he sacked one country section head out of hand for disregarding an instruction). He was by no means universally popular in the organisation. But there was a general appreciation of his ability, drive and dedication. 'He drove himself and his leading figures in S.O.E. equally hard', recalled Gubbins, 'perhaps too hard in one or two cases.'[34]

What SO2 needed was a solid achievement to break the vicious circle whereby, as Sweet-Escott put it, 'without scarce facilities such as aircraft and wireless transmission communications we could not get results, but ... unless we did get results, we were hardly likely to get the facilities'.[35] Much of Dalton's effort, therefore, was directed towards producing a surprise victory to give the organisation a credential, and increase the standing of the Minister at the same time. Each operation became a gamble, carrying the risk of Whitehall derision, but also a chance of Whitehall reward.

In the spring of 1941, Dalton became closely interested in two projects, the outcome of which demonstrated both the improvement in 'covert' operations that had occurred since he took over (both owed their origins to the pre-S.O.E., Section D era) and the obstacles that continued to stand in the way. One was a scheme to engineer a *coup d'état* in Belgrade. The other was a plan to block the River Danube.

Churchill instigated the Belgrade operation at the end of 1940 with a direct instruction: SO2 contacts should be used to undermine the pro-Axis Yugoslav regime. Dalton threw himself eagerly into the task, delighted at a chance to show off S.O.E.'s capabilities. At first the aim was not a coup, but a change of policy. S.O.E. involvement in Yugoslavia was largely based on bribes to opposition politicians. S.O.E. sought, through these connections, to restrain the Yugoslav government from signing a treaty with Germany (the Tripartite Pact) which would entail full co-operation with Hitler. The attempt failed. S.O.E. agents were therefore told to use their influence to bring down the regime.

Before the operation was launched, the Minister took Sir Frank Nelson and George Taylor to dinner at Claridges. During the meal, Dalton indicated that Taylor was to be sent to Cairo in order to make preparations. 'This has got to be a success', declared the Minister. For once, resources were available to make success appear possible. Taylor received everything he needed – top level communications to General Wavell, rank, funds – to smooth the way. Opposition could be ignored because Dalton had the Prime Minister behind him.[36]

The Pact was signed by Yugoslavia on 25th March. Prince Paul and his government in Belgrade were ousted in a successful putsch two days later. Who was responsible? It now seems likely that it was not agents of S.O.E. but the British Air Attaché who induced General Simovič, the Yugoslav Air Force Chief, to make his decisive intervention.[37] Nevertheless S.O.E. cash and influence had prepared the ground. Dalton felt no qualms about claiming full credit, and the claim was not challenged. The Defence Committee of the War Cabinet graciously conveyed 'an expression of appreciation' to the Minister of Economic Warfare, who was deeply gratified. 'The money we have spent on the Serb Peasant Party and other opposition parties has given wonderful value', he noted.[38]

Dalton's Danube initiative followed shortly afterwards. The purpose of the Belgrade operation had been political and military: aiming to forestall a German threat to the region. The purpose of the Danube scheme was economic, linked to the aims of M.E.W., with the intention of tying together the 'economic' and 'ungentlemanly' wars. The Belgrade operation had involved subversion; the Danube scheme involved sabotage.

As we have seen, a major objective of M.E.W. had been to reduce Germany's access to oil. With this in mind, Dalton had spent much of his time in earlier months seeking to persuade Bomber Command to attack oil installations in Germany. SO2 offered an alternative approach.[39] By blocking the Danube, it was argued, huge supplies of Rumanian oil carried by river could be cut off at a stroke. An attempt to sink cement-filled barges in the Iron Gates had been foiled in April 1940. This time, SO2 worked through the Yugoslav authorities in the immediate aftermath of the Belgrade coup. Twelve barges were prepared for action, and on 3rd April a cable was sent to George Taylor in Belgrade: 'Minister and all high authorities know you realise fully that a successful blocking of Danube before it is too late would be the decisive factor for England in this War ... '[40] Three days later, half a dozen vessels were successfully sunk. Once again, there was rejoicing in Baker Street and Berkeley Square.

These two operations marked the high point of Dalton's period in charge of SO2. Yet both 'successes' soon appeared less substantial than they had seemed at first. The Simovič coup, so long in preparation, was swiftly nullified by the Nazi invasion of Yugoslavia which began on 6th April. The intervention had come too late; and in any case the new regime proved an uncertain ally during its brief existence. The most that could realistically be claimed was that the coup had delayed the Axis advance. Gains produced by the Danube venture also turned out to be smaller than originally envisaged. In mid-June, the Minister had to confess that the Danube was again clear. 'Never mind, you blocked it for two months', replied Churchill. 'That was good.'[41] In fact, the river was probably only impassable for three to five weeks and there was no significant drop in Rumanian oil supplies to Germany.[42]

As the historian David Stafford has observed, 'The S.O.E. Balkan operations had revealed the limits of what could be achieved even in favourable circumstances.'[43] Until after Dalton ceased to be the Minister responsible for its activities, S.O.E. did not again try anything so ambitious. 'Our operations are few and far between', Dalton was writing gloomily at the end of 1941. 'Our last reports have been most bare ... We are living on the past.'[44]

Yet the Balkan ventures were certainly not failures. They indicated that SO2 had a real operational capacity that could be developed. While neither project provided the kind of triumph which Dalton had sought, the modest achievements of both encouraged the military authorities to take S.O.E. more seriously. The range of SO2 activity, if not yet the scale of its operations, grew rapidly, and S.O.E. organisations and agents were established in an increasing number of countries. In September 1941 Dalton sent the Prime Minister a minute outlining progress to date. Twenty-one agents had been sent to France (S.O.E.'s strongest country) and 13 organisers had been recruited locally. In the Low Countries only a handful of agents had been infiltrated, and German advances in the Balkans had virtually wiped out S.O.E. networks; but useful sabotage was being carried out in Norway.[45]

Churchill responded encouragingly,[46] and over the next few months the expansion accelerated. In November, Gubbins was complaining that he was getting more arms from the War Office than he could use. By the end of the year S.O.E. had succeeded in infiltrating another 66 agents into Europe, 27 to France alone.[47]

As S.O.E. expanded, it became harder to control what was happening at the perimeter. Central direction of a far flung secret network had always been a problem. The problem turned into a crisis when, soon after the Balkan operations, S.O.E.'s office in Cairo was accused of internal feuding between members of SO1 and SO2, and of being inefficient, expensive, and unproductive.

The Minister Resident in the Middle East, Oliver Lyttelton, sent Dalton a brisk telegram. The Minister of Economic Warfare replied tartly that he was not accustomed to accept allegations against his staff unsupported by evidence.[48] Evidence that there was something seriously wrong in Cairo was, however, not long in coming, and Dalton soon agreed that an investigation was urgently required. But who should be sent to the Middle East to carry it out? Jebb put forward the name of a prominent merchant banker. This proposal turned out to be unfortunate. The banker invited Sweet-Escott, detailed to assist him on the Cairo mission, to dinner at his club, White's. Sweet-Escott was not impressed by his prospective boss.[49] Nor, a few days later, was the Minister. Dalton had not been averse to recruiting S.O.E. officers from the City of London and had, on the whole, accepted Jebb's recommendations on appointments. But this City character was one who quickly put the Minister's back up. Dalton's record of the interview illustrates his sharp prejudice, even in wartime, against

a particular type of Tory capitalist – and helps to explain why, in
capitalist circles, Dalton was so cordially disliked:

> He says 'I belong to a class for which I am afraid you have not much
> respect. I am a banker'. This seemed to me a most gauche gambit.
> I replied 'Most of you don't deserve much respect. But anyhow
> the mission we are going to discuss this morning is not a money-
> lending mission.' From this inauspicious start the conversation
> made no real recovery. [Nelson] said afterwards that the man had
> been very nervous. I said 'I don't want nervous people in my
> organisation. I want people of power and self-assurance'.[50]

Such incidents strengthened the widely held belief that Dalton ran
S.O.E. with a strong left-wing bias.

In the end Nelson himself went to Cairo, accompanied by Sweet-
Escott and another well-established S.O.E. officer. What they found
was 'an atmosphere of jealousy, suspicion and intrigue', with every
secret organisation seemingly set against every other secret organisation. Telegrams were sent to Dalton, who replied immediately,
approving plans to sack the local heads of both SO1 and SO2. A
general reorganisation followed.[51] There was no evidence of actual
illegality (which some had alleged) but the atmosphere of bungling
had already done serious damage to S.O.E.'s reputation with the
services – more so, perhaps, than either Nelson or Dalton realised
at the time. In August, General Auchinleck, the Commander-in-Chief
in the Middle East, and Air Marshal Portal, Chief of Air Staff,
roundly denounced SO2 to the Prime Minister as a 'bogus, irresponsible, corrupt show'.[52]

Organisational problems were not confined to distant outposts. In
London, too, internal strains had developed. A particular difficulty
arose in the autumn of 1941 over relations between M.E.W. headquarters at Berkeley Square House (where Dalton and Jebb were
based) and the Baker Street establishment. In particular, the direct
interference of the Minister in SO2 affairs became increasingly irksome to senior officials.

Part of the problem was the extremely close working relationship
between Dalton and Jebb, and their physical separation from SO2
staff. Ideally, Jebb would have been in Baker Street. But Dalton, as
Minister, had to stay in Berkeley Square. ' ... I could hardly leave the
immediate presence of the Minister', Jebb later maintained, 'more
especially since he was immensely interested in the SO2 side of the
work.'[53] As a result, Jebb lost touch with the SO2 machine, loyalties
crystallised instead around the ever-present Nelson, and Jebb gained

a (largely unjustified) reputation as a Foreign Office stooge, with a career diplomat's mentality.[54] The Minister defended his Chief Executive Officer against criticisms. 'He is damned good, this principal Officer of mine', Dalton wrote with feeling at the end of 1941. 'He creates in me not only confidence in him but renewed confidence in myself.'[55] But the Minister's passionate loyalty did not diminish, and may even have increased, ill-feeling within the Baker Street hierarchy.

Tensions that had been suppressed during the Cairo crisis produced an explosion soon after it. George Taylor had watched anxiously as Sir Frank Nelson, never robust in health, worked himself near to the point of collapse trying to cope with the problems that accompanied SO2's expansion.[56] Undoubtedly, Dalton's excessive demands were a factor. 'Sir Frank felt that Dalton was conducting affairs as if he, Dalton, were the Chief Executive with Gladwyn Jebb at his elbow, and interfering in the running of the show', Gubbins later recalled. 'There was considerable truth in Sir Frank's complaints on this score.'[57] At last, a particularly infuriating ministerial rebuke provoked Nelson into offering his resignation. Dalton had accused the executive director of 'concerting' behind his back. Nelson wrote angrily, 'I have been increasingly aware of late that you may perhaps be better served by someone who is not so adamant in his views as I am, as to the necessity of the "man in charge" of the office being allowed to deal himself with the staff, except in very senior and special instances.' Eventually, Dalton managed to persuade Nelson not to resign, but only after a bitter exchange in which the head of SO2 revealed his intense frustration at the Minister's interferences. Nelson's complaint was that 'he could never say yes or no, but must refer everything up'. He drew an analogy between his own position, and that of the head of the Secret Service, Sir Stewart Menzies, who never had to report his detailed proceedings to the Foreign Office.[58]

When Dalton spoke to Nelson's senior officers in a series of interviews over the next few days, almost all of them backed up their chief. The request that Dalton should stick to general policy, and not get too involved in operational details, was virtually unanimous. At the same time, there was a growl of complaint against the meddlings of Jebb, seen partly as Dalton's direct agent, and partly as the Minister's 'Foreign Office conscience'.

The outcome of this general airing of grievances was to produce a much clearer division of responsibility. Henceforth, Dalton and Jebb handled broad policy, and Nelson had sole charge of operations.[59] This arrangement proved satisfactory, and separation of ministerial and operational spheres was maintained long after Dalton, Jebb and Nelson had all left S.O.E.

Such organisational problems were teething pains: a product of rapid growth. Interventions that had been acceptable at the outset seemed petty and time-wasting when the responsibilities of staff had increased, and foreign involvements were more widespread. Yet Dalton's interest was not restricted to the job of developing SO2's structure, or to the details of operations. Grand designs which he had formed at the beginning remained much in his mind.

The chances of outright military victory never looked more remote than in the spring and early summer of 1941. The immediate threat of invasion had receded. Yet the tide of the war was still strongly in Hitler's favour, and it was harder than ever to imagine how Britain could become strong enough to reverse Nazi gains. Paradoxically, the very hopelessness of the military situation was an advantage to SO2. For, as in the summer of 1940, the failure of orthodox methods increased the attraction of unorthodox ones. According to Stafford, 'In this climate of gloom and desperation, the British Chiefs of Staff and the war-planning machinery were particularly receptive to plans which could promise victory with the limited resources available.'[60] SO2 was able to present itself as an alternative to military might: a catalyst that might release the hidden reserves of energy that were believed to exist beneath the surface of German-occupied Europe.

SO2's reputation had suffered severe knocks, and as yet there were no spectacular achievements to compensate. But a framework had been established where none existed before, and Dalton's vigorous pursuit of action in the field had begun to get the organisation noticed. It was partly a measure of despair, and partly a measure of SO2's increased strength, that in May and June 1941 the Chiefs of Staff actively considered some remarkable suggestions put forward by Dalton and his senior officers, aimed at turning subversion into a weapon which might directly win the war. These proposals involved the notion of a huge reallocation of resources in order to arm secret forces in Europe for eventual use against Hitler.

Dalton's new approach superseded his original belief that continuous sabotage should be employed in order to foment civil unrest and guerrilla warfare. He did not abandon his 'revolutionary' conception of S.O.E.'s role. On the contrary. But the shortage of aircraft for making parachute drops, the realisation that premature resistance would lead to massive reprisals, and the need to co-operate with exiled governments (who were generally opposed to such action) inclined him to take a long-term view.

Instead of continuous sabotage, he proposed that sabotage should be employed sparingly (as in the Danube operation) for tasks of immediate strategic importance only. Premature rebellions and guerrilla warfare were to be discouraged, in order to await the moment when uprisings and revolutions could succeed. Meanwhile, armies should be prepared in occupied countries in secret, 'ready to strike hard later when we give the signal'.[61]

The 'secret army' approach was fully expounded in a report prepared by the Future Operations Planning Section (FOPS) of the Joint Planning Staff, in co-operation with Major-General Gubbins and S.O.E. According to this document, the relative weakness of Britain's armed forces meant that 'we cannot hope to defeat the existing German Army in the field'. Instead of attempting the impossible, British strategy should concentrate on attacking German morale, and undermining the German economy, until eventually the enemy collapsed from within. The blockade and strategic bombing should be supplemented by subversion, including the organisation and arming of patriotic forces on a massive scale. Such a programme would help to prepare the ground for a once-and-for-all uprising through the whole of Europe, timed to coincide precisely with landings on the Continent.[62]

Behind this proposal (the 'detonator concept', involving the transformation of Europe into a powder keg, to be fired at a British signal), lay the ambitions of Dalton and Gubbins to place S.O.E. at the very centre of strategic planning. From the outset, Dalton had seen an almost unlimited potential in S.O.E. 'Detonator' was, indeed, a refinement of the scheme he had outlined in his letter to Halifax the previous year. Given adequate resources, the Minister now urged, it would be possible to create strikes, riots and boycotts in preparation for a general insurrection. 'We should be able overnight', declared the FOPS report, 'to produce the anarchy of Ireland in 1920 or Palestine in 1936 throughout the chosen theatres of operations.'[63] For an organisation which, as yet, counted its foreign agents in dozens rather than in scores, it was a sensational claim.

Was it realistic? Today, it is hard not to see it as a romantic absurdity. In the first place, it would have involved six months' full time effort by Bomber Command, a force which, in 1941, had other priorities. Secondly, it was based on assumptions about the ability of bombers to find their targets, and to undermine civilian morale, which now seem badly misplaced. Yet this is in retrospect. At the time, not only did Gubbins and Dalton stake their reputations on it; senior military strategists whose general attitude towards S.O.E. was far from sympathetic gave it serious and prolonged consideration.

Very quickly, however, the question became academic. Hitler's attack on the Soviet Union, which took place a few days after the FOPS plan had been presented to the Chiefs of Staff, altered the whole nature of the war and transformed the problem of fomenting resistance. In July, Dalton sent Churchill another memorandum, modifying the earlier proposal, yet still claiming that S.O.E. could, if so instructed, 'set in motion large-scale and long-term schemes for revolution in Europe'. This report laid out the S.O.E. requirements for a programme of three elements: sabotage, subversive propaganda and the building of secret armies. The number of aircraft sorties proposed was reduced to about 2,000, involving 50 aircraft only; the arming of secret forces in Czechoslovakia and Poland was now abandoned. Most effort was, instead, to be directed at France where an army of 24,000 was to be equipped by autumn 1942. Smaller forces in Belgium and Holland were also to receive supplies.[64]

But the moment had passed. 'Detonator' was already dead, and survived thereafter only as a rhetorical flourish in some of Churchill's speeches.

With Stalin in the War, S.O.E. had to revise all its previous views about subversion. Hitherto, agents infiltrated into occupied Europe had usually been on their own. S.O.E. activity had involved sabotage and meddling in the politics of supposedly neutral countries; there had been little contact with resistance or 'revolutionary' movements because few such movements yet existed. After the invasion of the Soviet Union, local Communists, and non-Communists as well, began to mobilise against the Germans independently of S.O.E. encouragement. This development provided Baker Street with new opportunities, and new headaches. In line with the 'secret army' approach, S.O.E. had tended to discourage guerrilla warfare, arguing that it was better to keep secret military resources in reserve. Now, especially in Yugoslavia and France, partisan attacks became a reality which S.O.E. was not in a position to prevent. Most difficult of all, S.O.E. faced embarrassing choices in the occupied zones.

Differentiating among anti-Nazi forces had not previously been a serious problem. The 'secret army' proposal, with its apocalyptic vision of a Europe-wide insurrection on the Day, had been based on a crude and Buchan-like lumping together of the anti-Axis foreigner, as though Albanian Moslems, French socialists and Polish Jews had aims that were identical and which, furthermore, accorded precisely with those of the British Government. The reality, of course, was more complex. Not only did British interests and the interests of national groups often conflict. Within each country, S.O.E. frequently had to deal, not with co-ordinated structures, but with rival and often fiercely competing factions, often divided within themselves.

Which group or faction in each country deserved S.O.E. backing?

This was a diplomatic issue as much as a military one and hence involved the Foreign Office; or so the Foreign Office argued. Nevertheless, Dalton had his own views. In the case of France, he was in no doubt. He agreed strongly with Admiral Louis Mountbatten, the new Chief of Combined Operations, that it was the political Left, and not de Gaulle, who deserved support. Dalton told Mountbatten in January 1942 that S.O.E. had a number of agents in France, and that these 'were in touch with the French workers, and that I myself strongly held the view that it was the French industrial working class on whom we must count'. When Mountbatten congratulated him on his opinion and expressed surprise that an important minister should hold it, Dalton declared that his own attitude 'was partly explained because I was a Member of the Labour Party and had had many acquaintances in French Left circles, both political and industrial'.[65]

Dalton did not remain at S.O.E. long enough for his preference for left-wing groups (and, by implication, Communist ones) to have much effect on policy; at the beginning of 1942, resistance was still in its infancy. Nevertheless it is interesting that he should have expressed this opinion so forcefully, showing once again that Tory suspicions of S.O.E.'s socialist inclinations had some basis. Dalton's attitude was in keeping with his original 'revolutionary' approach to subversion, and with his view that S.O.E. needed to be directed by a civilian politician drawn from the Left. It also linked closely with his consistent belief that political and economic warfare should be treated as a single entity. If the aim of blockade policy was to cause discontent and revolt, then those most likely to revolt would be on the Left, among the working-class.

There was, however, a contradiction in Dalton's attitude, or at any rate in his behaviour. Dalton wanted to make the working class of occupied Europe undergo deprivations, as a result of the blockade, to increase their anger against the Germans. Stubble would only easily burn, he argued, after a dry spell. A Marxist revolutionary could not have put it better: the oppressed must suffer to make them conscious of their oppression. Yet where were the experts on European labour movements, the Spanish War veterans, the union organisers and professional agitators, who knew about raising working-class consciousness? The answer is that those few who were employed in S.O.E. were not permitted to hold senior positions. Despite bold words about a 'democratic international', most temporaries recruited by Jebb, with Dalton's acquiescence, were solicitors, businessmen and bankers – the kind of person who had previously regarded social upheaval and subversion as matters for the police.[66]

In the view of one S.O.E. agent (who disagreed with many of the policies emanating from Baker Street), the choice of 'respectable grouse-shooting City men and squires to the work of helping poachers' was a subtle Establishment ploy to 'limit the damage' likely to be done to the social order of Europe.[67] In 1940, however, the Establishment was more concerned about its own survival. The reality seems to have been a significant failure on Dalton's part to question the action of the Chief Executive Officer, whose behaviour reflected the assumptions of his kind. On the other hand, had Dalton recruited people with a closer understanding of proletarian revolt he might have encountered political constraints. When a Tory M.P. accused him of 'organising a Gestapo of my own staffed with members of the Labour Party', he was able to rebuff the criticism by reciting to Anthony Eden, by then Foreign Secretary, the composition of his S.O.E. Council: 'a Foreign Office official, a Conservative M.P., a member of the Bank of England Board who is also Chairman of the G.W.R. [Great Western Railway], a regular soldier, an ex-Director of Air Intelligence, a Director of Courtaulds ... ! I ask him!'[68] If Dalton had not been able to make such a defence – if the accusation had contained some validity – dealings with the rest of Whitehall might have become impossibly strained.

As we have seen, Dalton's attitude towards S.O.E. was far from non-political: he expected the natural allies of the organisation to be found among the European Left. At Baker Street, he urged his staff to make use of pre-war international union networks; thus, one leading official of the World Federation of Trade Unions was attached to SO2, to help explore ways of arousing active opposition among conscripted workers.[69] However, such initiatives from within the Baker Street establishment were unusual. And it is, in retrospect, an irony that S.I.S. unwittingly employed upper-class Communists who later caused damage to Britain's interests, while S.O.E. scrupulously avoided taking on the kind of staff who could have best understood, and communicated with, the emergent partisan movements of Europe.

When Dalton left S.O.E. in February 1942, the organisation was entering a new phase of operational activity. There were agents in France, Norway and Belgium, contacts in Rumania, Yugoslavia and Greece, active missions in Cairo, Lagos, Durban, Delhi and New York, and representatives in Moscow, Stockholm, Lisbon, Madrid, Gibraltar, Tangier, Malta, Istanbul and throughout the Middle East. Yet the most remarkable phase in S.O.E.'s history was still to come.

What did the operational side of S.O.E. actually achieve? The debate continues between those who argue that S.O.E. remained, for the most part, a quaint side-show, and those who believe it was important in winning the war.[70] Few, however, would deny the organisation some notable victories. Possibly the most important, after Dalton had ceased to be in charge, resulted from an S.O.E. campaign of raids against heavy-water plants in Norway, which severely hindered German attempts to make an atom bomb. On the negative side, S.O.E. has the dubious distinction of having provided a model for the American Office of Strategic Services, forerunner of the C.I.A.

S.O.E.'s continued growth after 1941 was accompanied by a change of role and shift in the relationship of the organisation to the fighting services. From early in 1942, S.O.E. lost much of its early independence under the authority of a civilian minister; increasingly, it became a weapon of war, controlled by the Chiefs of Staff. Some early ideas were abandoned: in particular the hope of eventually tying together sabotage, propaganda and blockade in a combined strategy. There were two main reasons. One was the altered nature of strategic thinking, caused principally by the entry of the United States into the war. The other was the replacement of Dalton as the Minister responsible for S.O.E.

Dalton's move was not the product of any disagreement over the conduct of operational subversion. Rather, it was a consequence of personal and administrative problems in the far more troubled field of covert propaganda. It is to this side of Dalton's secret life – SO1 – that we now turn.

XX

Black Propaganda

For SO2 the shooting war was in the field. For SO1 it was in Whitehall. As we have seen, M.E.W. and SO2 had their problems in relation to other departments. Yet these were as nothing compared to the vicious fighting that took place over the administration of propaganda. The eventual outcome was the removal of Dalton from the whole field of economic and political warfare, and the complete separation of propaganda from the operational side of subversion. In the process Dalton, who had taken on 'black' propaganda so joyfully in July 1940, was driven close to nervous collapse. There are, indeed, few more striking instances of the sharp tension that existed beneath the public amity of the Coalition.

Much of the problem arose because of a failure, early on, to give propaganda a proper definition. As a result, propaganda – even more than sabotage in its early days – became a Whitehall orphan, nobody's child, drifting from department to department without a settled home. When SO1 was formed as part of a supposedly unitary subversive empire under the Minister of Economic Warfare, propaganda had just been through the hands of two other ministers within the space of a fortnight. A secret organisation had been set up in September 1938, disbanded, and then set up again – reporting first to the Minister of Information, then (from October 1939) to the Foreign Secretary, and then (at the beginning of June 1940) to the Minister of Information once again.[1]

Dalton did not take over all propaganda from the Minister of Information when SO1 was established. He became responsible only for the secret, unofficial side. As we shall see, uncertainty about what this meant, and about how and by whom the range of propaganda instruments should be controlled, remained a serious flaw in the new arrangement.

The first administrative problem facing SO1 was its relationship with SO2. In order that the notion of subversion as a single entity should work, it was vital that the activities of the two wings of S.O.E. should operate together in harmony. This never happened – partly because of a clash of official personalities.

Dalton's basic mistake was made at the outset. On the advice of Vansittart, his Chief Diplomatic Adviser, he appointed Reginald Leeper, currently head of the Foreign Office Political Intelligence Department, to take command of SO1. It was a decision soon regretted. Leeper turned out to be the kind of Foreign Office official Dalton had found particularly irksome during his spell as a Foreign Office minister a decade before. ' ... [T]all and spare with the thoughtful, concentrated face of some old-time papal secretary',[2] Leeper combined wide experience of diplomacy with contempt for most politicians (especially Labour ones), unshakeable conservatism, and a strong sense of his own importance. Dalton and Leeper rapidly discovered that they would be united only by a mutual antipathy. When Leeper moved SO1 headquarters from Electra House on the Embankment to Woburn Abbey in Bedfordshire (where many staff were already working), Dalton concluded that the new director of subversive propaganda was frightened by the bombing.[3] Leeper gave a different explanation. 'Dalton was driving him mad', he told the writer and journalist, Robert Bruce Lockhart, who became an SO1 employee as head of the Czech section.[4]

The real problem concerning Leeper, however, was not that Dalton did not get on with him. It was the tension that developed between Leeper and Jebb. The original plan had been for Jebb to provide a link between the Minister and both SO1 and SO2. Leeper was to be the opposite number to Sir Frank Nelson in SO2, with Jebb providing co-ordination between the wings. Unfortunately such a plan did not allow for comparative diplomatic statuses. In order to occupy his present job, Jebb, twelve years Leeper's junior, had received a double promotion. In vain, Dalton insisted that 'machines and hierarchies don't matter: it's men that count', and that 'you and Rex can work perfectly well together as equals: I will do the co-ordinating.'[5] In reality, however, hierarchies counted for a lot. Dalton recorded Gaitskell's comments on the subject a year after S.O.E. had been set up:

> R.L[eeper] is much too suspicious. He thinks that G[ladwyn] despises him and realises that G[ladwyn] always gets the best of any argument, having a much quicker and more incisive mind. Also he is jealous of the fact that G[ladwyn] sees much more of me [Dalton] than he does and he realises that I think much more of G[ladwyn]

than of him ... [Gaitskell] does not think G[ladwyn] realises that he sometimes antagonises people by his rather offhand manner and his apparent lack of interest in what they are saying.[6]

How was Jebb to make clear that he had a responsibility for SO1 as well as SO2? When SO2 was established, Jebb asserted his authority over SO2 by getting Dalton to sack Lawrence Grand, former head of Section D. With SO1 it was not so easy. Nevertheless he did his best – first by seeking to bargain with Leeper, and then by trying to get him shifted.

The attempted bargain is interesting because it had political implications. The issue concerned the left-wing journalist Richard Crossman whom Dalton had appointed head of the German Bureau at Woburn. Brilliant, forceful and unconventional, Crossman had no time for hallowed Foreign Office ways, and soon came into bitter conflict with the cold and inflexible Leeper. It was here that Jebb saw his chance. Jebb suggested that Crossman should be asked to resign in order to appease Leeper – but only if Leeper, in return, agreed to send papers intended for Dalton to him first. 'Only so can I see to it that propaganda is really linked to other activities, and that the machine functions as a whole', argued Jebb. In addition, as part of the deal, Leeper should be made to agree that senior officials must deal directly with Jebb 'on such matters as getting in touch with revolutionaries, sabotage etc.'[7] – thereby helping to link SO1 and SO2 together.

But the Minister, on this occasion, refused to play. Dalton was against sacking a talented political protégé just for failing to get on with an official. More important, he was scared that Crossman (who had been Assistant Editor of the *New Statesman*) would hit back in print with 'a violent attack on me and "Foreign Office officials" and a most unfortunate leakage of my new duties'.[8] Crossman stayed, and later had an enormous influence on wartime propaganda policy.[9] There was no package deal with Leeper.

Two further attempts were made to give Jebb control of SO1. In May 1941, Dalton sought – with an unfortunate excess of eagerness – to persuade Leeper to accept an offer of the ambassadorship in Rio. Leeper, who liked his present job, refused. In July, Jebb tried one final move. A Foreign Office official, Peter Loxley, had been placed as No. 2 at SO1, only to be recalled by the Foreign Office, without consultation, a few weeks later. Dalton complained angrily to Anthony Eden (who had succeeded Halifax as Foreign Secretary) about the 'theft of Loxley', which he regarded as brusque and high-handed. Eden replied that Loxley was needed for other important duties. Jebb thereupon made a suggestion: perhaps Leeper, not Loxley, might return to the Foreign Office, and Loxley might take over at Woburn? Dalton liked the idea. 'It would be an admirable solution', he considered, 'for almost every reason'.[10] But it did not happen. In September, the setting up of the Political Warfare Executive (as we shall see) altered the nature of the problem. Meanwhile, Leeper refused to be co-ordinated and there existed what Jebb called 'a perpetual *équivoque*' in relations between the two officials.[11]

As a result, though Jebb was technically Chief Executive Officer of the whole of S.O.E., his main involvement was with SO2. In November 1940, Bruce Lockhart recorded a 'huge battle' between SO1 and SO2 over control of propaganda in the field. 'Rex [Leeper] and Jebb are fighting', he noted. 'Whole thing is disgusting. Hours, days and weeks are wasted on these personal questions, and no work is done.'[12] Over the next few months, the two rapidly expanding organisations went their own, and often dangerously conflicting, ways.

Just as the blockade was intended to create opposition to the Nazis by making people feel hungry, and sabotage by making them feel insecure, black propaganda was meant to make them feel that they were badly led, or (in the case of enemy occupied countries) that the occupying force was weaker or more vulnerable than it seemed. The essence of 'black' or 'covert' propaganda was the undermining of morale by undercover and subtly dishonest means. White propaganda was the official voice of Britain. It aimed to disturb the enemy by telling the truth. According to Sir Hugh Greene, who ran official broadcasting to Germany, it was vital in this kind of psychological warfare never to play down a disaster. 'It would, for instance, be tempting from time to time within the limits of one news bulletin to give more prominence to a minor success than to a major defeat. This was a temptation to be avoided.'[13] Exactly the opposite was the case with black propaganda. Black propaganda disguised its source, told lies, and aimed to mislead, confuse and unsettle.[14]

Some aspects of propaganda caught Dalton's special attention. One was the manufacture of 'sibs' (from the Latin 'sibilare', meaning to hiss). These were false rumours spread by agents through the press in neutral countries, or beamed into enemy territory through the air waves. Ten thousand sibs were broadcast to Germany by the secret radio station G9 alone.[15] The idea was to combine plausibility and a sting in the tail. If those marked 'Approved' in October 1941 are any guide, plausibility seems to have mattered less than the sting. One sib (aimed at Germany) consisted of the rumour that, 'There have been 20 reported cases during the last week of German soldiers' genitals having to be amputated because of frost bite'; another, for

West Africa, suggested that, 'Green tea and sugar given you by the Germans will render you impotent and close the womb of your women'.[16]

Another aspect of black propaganda, developed later in the war, was the use of secret or fake 'freedom' radio stations, often operated behind enemy lines. A third was the invasion of enemy air waves. Early in 1941, a proposal was put foward for broadcasts to Germany on German wavelengths. According to a minute from Dalton to Churchill, the apparatus needed for this project 'would create a raiding Dreadnought of the ether, firing broadsides at unpredictable times at unpredictable objectives of the enemy's radio propaganda'.[17] The Prime Minister approved the idea, and the necessary transmitter, code-named 'Aspidistra', became fully operational in the autumn of 1942, greatly increasing the scope of 'black' broadcasting in Europe.

Dalton was less interested, however, in the technology of propaganda than in its ideological direction. With propaganda, as with fomenting revolt by 'operational' means, Dalton urged his employees to look to the European Left. Evidence was increasing, he wrote in a memorandum in December 1941, that the working class were Britain's best allies or prospective allies in Nazi-dominated countries. Positive propaganda should therefore be directed to the industrial workers, and should deal with the economic future:

> We must show that we seriously mean to satisfy the hopes of working people everywhere for a new and better social order after the war ... In the occupied countries the Left is, as a rule, more patriotic than the Right. And in the neutral countries the Left is, as a rule, more favourable to our cause than the Right ...

Developing this argument, Dalton concluded that Britain would only succeed in persuading the European working-class to help defeat the Nazis if, first, the British Government convinced the working class *in Britain* that 'social justice, more closely approached in war than in peace, will be maintained here, and even improved upon, after the defeat of the Germans ... ' Meanwhile, propaganda should use the results of post-war planning studies currently being conducted by various government departments, and proposals for post-war reconstruction.

These thoughts, which anticipated the use that was to be made, at home and abroad, of the Beveridge Report, received a cool response from successive Tory Ministers of Information. It was also received without enthusiasm by senior officials who were less convinced than Dalton that, 'Our best friends in occupied Europe are not the bourgeoisie, much less big business, or Generals, but the masses, and principally, the industrial workers'.[18]

Dalton often visited Woburn, where he enjoyed talking about such matters to the 'motley of University dons, advertising men, diplomats, motor salesmen, journalists and officers from the Services',[19] who inhabited SO1's 'country' Establishment. There was often a weekend house-party of selected staff in the Rectory, a large and comfortable house close to the Abbey, with a dinner on the Saturday night. Here, over brandy and cigars, Dalton or one of his officers would hold forth about propaganda policy and its role in the war. On the Sunday morning, Dalton would insist on taking his entourage on a strenuous walk in Woburn Park.[20]

Unlike the frosty Leeper, Dalton made a point of getting to know quite junior staff. One man he already knew well was George Wagner, a socialist refugee from Danzig, whom the Daltons had housed for several months in their Carlisle Mansions flat. Wagner had been working at Woburn for the old 'Electra House' propaganda organisa-tion for some time before SO1 was established. 'Hugh was the new broom', he recalls, 'and he didn't half sweep.' The story was the same as at M.E.W. Hitherto there had been a feeling (especially among the foreign exiles, who had first-hand experiences of the 'new' Germany) that policy was still in the hands of appeasers who failed to recognise either the brutality, or the unscrupulousness, of the Nazis. Dalton injected a spirit of realism, and an aggressive, war-winning mood. In the process (and this, again, was a familiar pattern) he upset people. Wagner remembers the Minister's deliberate rudeness, and the way senior officials would shudder at the enormous voice and the half-comic, half-frightening range of grimaces. He also remembers that among middle-ranking personnel (mainly temporaries, who did most of the creative work) Dalton's arrival was like a breath of fresh air, providing a chance to escape from the tram-lines of civil service thinking, and follow through new ideas.[21]

If Dalton's arrival caused a renaissance, his direct influence was exercised over a briefer period than in SO2. This was because of the unresolved status of black propaganda, and of a growing desire in the Ministry of Information to see 'white' and 'black' brought together. As a result, Dalton had less and less time to devote to internal projects and plans. Instead, he found himself embroiled in a mounting row over administrative control which had great importance both for propaganda policy, and for his own career as a wartime minister.

As we have seen, 'white' and 'black' propaganda were philosophic-ally distinct: one was truthful and officially acknowledged, the other false and officially denied. But there were practical difficulties. In the first place, there were varying shades of grey.[22] In the second place, overt and covert relied to a considerable extent on the same means of dissemination, the most important of which were leaflets and radio. These problems were tacitly acknowledged when SO1 was set up: it had originally been intended that white propaganda should follow black into the new organisation once SO1 had got off the ground. In fact, M.O.I. officials decided not to let official propaganda go. Hence the difficulties remained, becoming steadily worse as SO1 succeeded in establishing itself. Who was to decide what should be treated as overt and what as covert? Who was to provide co-ordination, to ensure that propaganda aims did not conflict?

Demarcation disputes between SO1 and M.O.I. continued until SO1 was absorbed into an overall propaganda body and then finally removed from the control of the Minister of Economic Warfare altogether. Meanwhile, the consequences of splitting propaganda were summed up in a civil service memorandum of August 1941 which stated that for twelve months the energy of the whole propaganda effort had largely been dissipated in inter-departmental intrigues and strife.[23]

At first there seemed to be two possible solutions. One was to re-unite propaganda under the Minister of Information, who had originally been responsible for all propaganda. The second was to re-unite propaganda under the Minister of Economic Warfare. Duff Cooper, the Minister of Information, favoured the first solution. Dalton favoured the second. Disagreement between the two ministers first became serious in November 1940, when Dalton accused Cooper of 'sheer poaching' and 'stealing leaflets', by discussing with Halifax, the Foreign Secretary, a plan to drop a leaflet in France – without first raising the matter with SO1.[24] Leaflets, however, mattered less than radio, generally acknowledged as the most vital propaganda instrument of all. It was in this field that Dalton made his bid. Was not broadcasting to the enemy intrinsically 'subversive', he reasoned, and should not SO1 therefore control the whole of it?

Cooper felt no less passionately than Dalton about radio. He agreed entirely with Dalton that divided control of broadcasting was illogical. He was not, however, persuaded by Dalton's solution. Desmond Morton, Churchill's personal aide, agreed with Cooper. On 13th December Morton advised the Prime Minister in the following terms:

Dr. Dalton suggests that he should take over all broadcasting to enemy countries, since he already controls *secret* broadcasts and leaflets.

In reply Mr. Duff Cooper points out that this would cause greater confusion than already exists. Broadcasting (whether open or secret) and leaflets are only a part of the propaganda machine. In his opinion all foreign propaganda whether directed to enemy or neutral countries and whether conducted by radio, leaflets, the Press or through any other means should be controlled by one Department only.

Mr. Duff Cooper therefore suggests that since he already controls the lion's share of foreign propaganda, leaflets and secret broadcasts should be taken away from Dr. Dalton and restored to M. of I., leaving Dr. Dalton to deal with 'projects' (bribery, sabotage, etc.) only.

The alternative, namely, to give all foreign propaganda to Dr. Dalton, would leave M. of I. with so little to do that it might well be abolished.

I submit that from the point of view of efficiency in administration there is much to be said for Mr. Duff Cooper's proposals.[25]

'Efficiency in administration' was not, however, the only criterion. Politics were also involved. Dalton strongly objected to giving up covert propaganda for a number of reasons. In the first place, it would be seen as a blow to the Labour element in the Government; S.O.E. had been given to him as part of Labour's apportionment, and it was not therefore negotiable.[26] Second, having recently acquired black propaganda, to lose it so quickly would seem like a personal defeat. Third, to take away SO1 would isolate SO2, and make much more likely the swift return of 'operational' subversion to the Foreign Office.

But there was also a more fundamental objection. The argument that propaganda needed unified control, if this meant unified control under M.O.I., could be countered by the argument that subversion, too, was a unitary concept. Furthermore, while the case for re-absorbing black propaganda into M.O.I. was largely based on administrative convenience, the case for linking black propaganda to operational subversion was strategic. How could discontent and potential revolt be fomented, if one of the major instruments for so doing was controlled by a separate department? It made no difference that S.O.E. was, in practice, scarcely a cohesive organisation, or that SO1 and SO2 were often at each other's throats. M.O.I.'s bid to control all propaganda threatened Dalton's theory of political warfare. Hence 'unity of subversion' became his battle cry.

In the short run, Dalton was successful. Churchill did not follow Morton's advice, and SO1 remained under the control of the Minister of Economic Warfare. It rapidly became clear, however, that the present anarchy could not continue, and that some form of co-ordination of propaganda was essential.

The result was the so-called 'Anderson Award' – a Solomon's judgment that gave neither unity of propaganda nor unity of sub-version, and added to the confusion it was intended to resolve. At a meeting in May 1941 chaired by Sir John Anderson, the Lord President, it was agreed that joint control of propaganda should be provided by a ministerial committee composed of the Ministers of Economic Warfare and Information, and the Foreign Secretary, with a supporting committee of three officials. But the degree of control, and the nature of ministerial responsibilities, remained unclear.

Whether this arrangement would have worked was never discovered. Before it had fully come into operation Duff Cooper, depressed by the constant rowing and by the lack of clarity over objectives, asked the Prime Minister to move him to another post. Churchill agreed, and in July Cooper changed offices to become Chancellor of the Duchy of Lancaster, leaving the Ministry of Information, as he later recalled, 'with a sigh of relief'.[27]

Dalton was taken aback, but considered that he had won a round. He was not pleased by the Anderson Award. Nevertheless, he had successfully resisted M.O.I. attempts at a takeover, and he had apparently hounded the Minister out of his job. The Ministry of Information, he concluded with some satisfaction, was 'a coffin' for any politician foolish enough to accept it.[28]

Dalton had barely formed this opinion when he was forced to revise it. On 15th July, he was disquieted to learn that Duff Cooper was to be replaced as Minister of Information by Brendan Bracken – a politician whose career to date gave no indication of a death wish. For Dalton, few appointments could have been less welcome. He told Attlee that the new Minister of Information 'has a reputation of being reactionary and anti-Labour'.[29] In fact it was worse than that. Bracken was a close, even intimate, friend of the Prime Minister. And he was definitely anti-Dalton. Dalton was no less anti-Bracken. 'To know Bracken was to like him', Beaverbrook once said; 'those who didn't know him did not like him.' What little Dalton did know about Bracken in July 1941, he definitely did not like.

In some respects, the two ministers were strangely similar in character – one reason, perhaps, why they got on so badly. Bracken was a genial bully, a bestower of cruel nicknames, a fixer, a climber (not a social but an 'important-person' climber, according to one friend), a man filled (as Churchill put it) with 'vital and vibrant energy'. Like Dalton, he was subject to occasional imputations of homosexuality, which (in the words of his biographer, Charles Lysaght), 'owed more to Bracken's apparent lack of interest in girls and to the fact that he numbered among his companions a number of noted homosexuals', than to any concrete evidence. He was also subject to accusations of hypocrisy, ruthlessness, and lack of scruple.

In other respects, Bracken and Dalton were mirror opposites. Bracken's physical appearance seemed to emphasise the difference. In contrast to Dalton's bald dome, there was Bracken's 'mass of red hair, the thickness, shape and density of a wire mop, fitted on top of his face like moss on a flat square stone ... ' It was said of Bracken that everything about him was phoney: even his hair, which looked like a wig, wasn't. The most bewildering aspect of Bracken, however, was his political outlook.

No Conservative Member of Parliament ever came from a more un-Conservative background. It was here that the contrast with Dalton was most extreme. Where Dalton had put his upper-class education behind him in order to make common cause with the workers, Bracken had clawed his way up to become part of the world of aristocracy and wealth which Dalton despised. If Dalton was a class traitor, Bracken was a traitor in the opposite direction. Deserting humble Fenian origins and renouncing his Catholic faith, Bracken had made his way in the world as an editor, publisher and newspaper proprietor. Meanwhile, as a very young man he had attached himself to Winston Churchill, by whom he stuck through all vicissitudes. In 1929 Bracken became M.P. for North Paddington. Ten years later 'Churchill's faithful chela', as Stanley Baldwin once called him, became P.P.S. to Churchill at the Admiralty. In 1940 the new Prime Minister took him into No. 10 Downing Street as a key adviser.

He had become, in Randolph Churchill's words, 'the fantasist whose fantasies had come true', helping to guide the Prime Minister in the nation's hour of peril. Later Evelyn Waugh satirised Bracken as the colonial adventurer Rex Mottram in *Brideshead Revisited*: ' ... [O]nly war could put Rex's fortunes right and carry him into power.'[30] Until July 1941 Brendan Bracken had exercised no real power. The M.O.I. appointment was his first ministerial post, and he intended to make the most of it. In view of the recent history of relations between M.O.I. and SO1, this was bound to be at Dalton's expense.

There was an unfortunate prelude. Dalton had long found it easier to deal with old-style Tory grandees, whose behaviour he understood, than with this robber baron of mysterious birth who played the game by his own quixotic rules. Oddly, their first direct clash was not the product of any personal contact between the two men. Rather it reflected Dalton's growing anxiety about attitudes at No. 10, and a fearful, almost obsessional belief that Churchill drew his opinions about ministers from his intimate circle.

In February 1941, Dalton became incensed by rumours that Bracken had been criticising him at semi-public gatherings. One of Bracken's alleged attacks so upset him that he took the remarkable step of drafting a statement to the effect that 'Bracken had been abusing me loudly in Carlton Grill at lunch'. He then obtained the signatures of two witnesses, and on the strength of this strange document, persuaded Attlee to complain to the Prime Minister. Not surprisingly, Dalton's action did more harm than good. Attlee reported back that Churchill was 'very angry' about the affair, and had given Bracken a ticking off.[31] Dalton, for the moment, was mollified. But Bruce Lockhart's diary, published many years later, suggests that, so far from being cowed by his conversation with the Prime Minister, Bracken dined out on the tale for months:

> W.S.C. sends for Brendan. 'Is it true that at dinner the other night, you attacked SO2 and Dalton's work?' 'What I said was that Dalton was the biggest bloodiest shit I've ever met!' Winston laughed.

Dalton had much to fear from Bracken.

The truth (though Dalton did not yet know it) was that Bracken was determined to succeed where Cooper had failed – and push the Minister of Economic Warfare out of propaganda once and for all. Three days after his appointment, Bracken explained to Bruce Lockhart the changes in personnel which, he said, would enable him to 'have SO1'. In the course of the conversation, the new Minister of Information, 'Made little attempt to conceal his desire to get rid of Dalton'.[32]

There followed a skilfully conducted war of nerves aimed at isolating and undermining the Minister of Economic Warfare by making him look foolish. Dalton was not scared of confrontations as such. What he did have – as Bracken discovered, with an unerring instinct for a psychological flaw – was a deep-seated fear of ridicule. Were there, perhaps, distant echoes of Eton? As we shall see, Dalton found himself ringed by people who regarded him privately with contempt. Bracken had on his side not only the friendship of the Prime Minister, an asset which, like a priceless gem, needed only to be displayed to exert its influence: he also belonged to the same social world as several of the other key figures involved. In the diaries of both Cadogan and Bruce Lockhart, Dalton is referred to by his surname. Bracken, however, appears as 'Brendan'.

Over the next few months, disagreement turned to hostility, and hostility to fury. Both men felt intensely frustrated at their inability to break through an administrative problem, not of their making, which hindered the conduct of the war. Each believed that, given proper powers, he could turn propaganda into an effective weapon. Each bitterly accused the other of obduracy. As the pressure mounted, 'the intransigence of Dalton', according to Andrew Boyle, another Bracken biographer, caused the Minister of Information to storm about his office 'hinting that he was "thinking of throwing in his hand"'.[33] Bracken, however, was the aggressor. Though he had less experience than Dalton he was younger, fresher and determined to win his spurs in this, his first engagement. By contrast, Dalton fought with a growing desperation, his anger reflecting a weary loneliness. Never in his public life did he feel so persecuted as during the winter of 1941–2, and never (except in the second half of 1947) so unhappy.

Bracken's first step – apparently innocuous but actually lethal – was to suggest what initially seemed like a variant on the 'Anderson Award'. The Minister of Information proposed a new department, to be called the Political Warfare Executive, which was to be responsible for all forms of propaganda to enemy-controlled countries. This would have its own head, who would be responsible to the two ministers and the Foreign Secretary jointly, working through officials. Dalton gave his cautious approval.[34] On 28th July the two ministers lunched together, Bracken giving the impression of being 'very friendly and co-operative'.[35] 'A grain of optimism regarding the final outcome is perhaps permissible', Bruce Lockhart (who had been switched from SO1 to become the Foreign Office official representative in the 'Anderson' set up) minuted to Eden the same afternoon.[36]

Bracken's olive branch was, however, merely a diplomatic preliminary. In reality, the Minister of Information's plan for an entirely independent political warfare department encompassing all overseas propaganda, and the determination of the Minister of Economic Warfare to hold on to control of SO1 as part of a 'unitary' subversive empire, were wholly incompatible. Furthermore, the proposed Executive would take effective control out of Dalton's hands. 'Joint' control was bound to be a misnomer: what Bracken had in mind was a body which, through his officials, he would be able to dominate.

A paper submitted by Bracken at the beginning of August made Dalton suspicious, but he remained off guard. 'I like it much less than what he said some days ago', the Minister of Economic Warfare wrote doubtfully, adding: 'We must maintain the essentials of the Anderson Award.'[37] But he accepted a watered down version of Bracken's proposal, apparently regarding it as an adequate compromise.[38] It was, however, a compromise in Bracken's favour. On 11th August, Bruce Lockhart minuted to Eden that in Bracken, 'forceful, sometimes pugnacious, sometimes impulsive, yet adroitly skilful in tactics', Dalton had met his match.[39]

Events soon proved this correct. Dalton's predicament was, indeed, not just a consequence of Bracken's manoeuvres. It was also a result of the attitudes of the Foreign Secretary and of the officials most closely involved. Eden had little interest in propaganda, did not want to be bothered with it, and was happy to delegate it to an official body. At the same time, the civil servants favoured P.W.E. as a device for reducing political interference.

Dalton thus found that not only did he have no allies on the ministerial committee; he had none on the supporting committee of officials either. The latter consisted of Bruce Lockhart, for a brief while his employee at SO1, but also an intimate friend of Bracken, with whom he was much in sympathy; Reginald Leeper, who wished to keep himself, and propaganda, as far away from Dalton as possible; and Brigadier Dallas Brooks (who had been running the Woburn establishment). Dalton's only possible supporter was Brooks. But Brooks's role on the official committee was to represent the Ministry of Information.

In mid-August, Dalton took a brief holiday at West Leaze. Before his departure, Bruce Lockhart gave Eden a vivid account of the plot that was being hatched against the Minister of Economic Warfare. The idea was to lull him into a false sense of security:

From the beginning, Dr. Dalton has been on the defensive and even today [11th August], when agreement has been reached, probably interprets 'joint ministerial control' in his own way. The scientific definition of daltonism is inability to distinguish between green and red, and I doubt very much if he has ever seen any danger signal to himself. He still relies on his charter from the Prime Minister, and this may have to be amended. On the other hand, Mr. Bracken is well pleased. He has enjoyed the contest.[40]

When Dalton returned, he found that Bracken and the official committee had been moving fast in his absence. On his desk lay a paper by the officials which, Dalton complained to Eden, 'reads as though SO1 was to be entirely abolished ... '[41] Next day, at a ministerial meeting, Bracken pressed home his advantage. The Minister of Economic Warfare, he demanded, should 'put the whole of SO1 personnel in the pot', while he, Bracken, did the same with B.B.C. and M.O.I. 'war zone' people.[42] Now at last Dalton saw the trap that had been set for him. The plan, which had the backing of all three officials and the other two ministers, would mean only the remote supervision of a pooled propaganda effort by a ministerial triumvirate on which he would always be outnumbered, two to one.

Faced with this challenge the Minister of Economic Warfare reacted aggressively – but too late. He refused Bracken's request. He made desperate, pointed visits to Woburn and the B.B.C. (already with a degree of joint control, under the original Anderson Award) in order to demonstrate his ministerial rights, infuriating officials by questioning them closely about their work.[43] He told Eden and Bracken (unwisely – for they were certain to pass it on to the civil servants concerned) that ministerial control and stimulus were needed because the officials were insufficiently dynamic. At this point Eden intervened with the carefully judged remark that, in his own view, the best solution would be to give ultimate responsibility to one minister – namely Bracken.

Dalton realised that he was cornered. If he continued to dig in his heels over P.W.E., there was a danger of an even bleaker alternative: loss of any say in propaganda at all. 'I apprehended', he noted, ' ... that I was faced with a combination of two Ministers and three officials who would be glad of an opportunity to say that I had been so difficult and obstructive that the proposals made to the P.M. would not work and we must think again.'[44] He was left with no choice but to permit the new body to come into existence. With his approval, therefore, the Political Warfare Executive was set up, and Bruce Lockhart was appointed Director-General.

It was, however, a retreat not a capitulation. Dalton calculated that, though the P.W.E. rules were to his disadvantage, they were open to different interpretations. He intended to interpret them in a way that made the most of his own influence in the areas in which he had an interest. Politically, he still had one important piece of ammunition – the Prime Minister's strong desire to avoid antagonising the Labour element in the Coalition. SO1 had been secret, and its significance for domestic party politics had therefore been limited. By contrast, the formation of P.W.E. was announced by the Prime Minister in Parliament. The new Executive, Churchill told the Commons on 11th September, 'will be responsible to the three Ministers sitting together'.[45] Dalton decided to use this declaration as a lever for claiming a major Labour stake in propaganda policy. The Labour Party, he determined, 'must be made to feel it a great advance that one of their number is now jointly responsible for this branch of the war effort'.[46]

To reinforce this position, Dalton turned once again to Attlee. His problems over P.W.E., he told the Party Leader, were part of a concerted attack, even a 'whispering campaign', by officials and Tory politicians against Labour ministers. 'The Labour Party ... are not in this Government as poor relations of the Tories', he stressed. 'Nor will our Party in Parliament or in the country tolerate our being so treated.'[47] He was not prepared to be a mere lay figure on the new P.W.E., he wrote, and he would be expected by the Party to take a keen interest in its affairs. Attlee, in reply, promised to complain to the Prime Minister if there was any trouble.[48]

Dalton combined building up his Labour Party defences with another tactic: pretending that P.W.E. did not exist. The Prime Minister's announcement about the setting up of the Executive, he concluded, need make little difference to the administration of black propaganda in practice, if officials on the 'covert' side continued to deal with him rather than with the impersonal joint committees. On 20th September, therefore, he summoned leading SO1 officials for an after-dinner discussion, and set about inciting them to mutiny. The P.W.E. arrangement, he declared, could only be justified if it provided a real gain in efficiency.[49] He then told bewildered staff, in effect, to disregard paper plans, ignore P.W.E., and keep control in their own hands.

Afterwards Gaitskell, who was present, suggested mildly that the Minister had 'barbed here and there a little too much'.[50] The feelings of the newly appointed Director-General of P.W.E. were much stronger. Bruce Lockhart felt that Dalton was seeking to deny him any influence whatsoever. 'Nothing has happened as a result of the changes except that SO1 has now control of everything ... ', Bruce Lockhart wrote. 'I have all the responsibility and no power. I shall have to resign before it is too late.'[51]

Dalton and Bracken were now on a collision course. Officially, the new Executive had come into being. Unofficially, the administration of propaganda continued much as before – with little co-ordination at the top. The crisis would come as soon as Bracken's 'integralist' interpretation of how P.W.E. should be run came into direct conflict with Dalton's 'federalist' one. This happened sooner than expected. The clash was precipitated, ironically, by a dinner party which had been arranged with the aim of easing relations between the two ministers.

Precisely what occurred is unclear. Dalton hoped – perhaps naively – for a reconciliation. Instead there was a terrible row. 'B.B. was rude, assertive, ignorant, inconsequent, stupid, angular and unreceptive ... ' Dalton noted. 'C.H. [Charles Hambro, an SO2 official] did his best and took this insufferable oaf away afterwards; I hope to some good purpose.'[52]

It was the turning point. Hitherto, Dalton and Bracken had treated each other with superficial cordiality. Now there was just a snarling ferocity, with Bracken goading Dalton into demonstrations of anger and distress in order to discredit him. According to Boyle, the Minister of Information relied on 'time, luck and sheer pressure to wear Dalton down'.[53] George Taylor, observing the conflict from the vantage point of Baker Street, felt that Bracken and Eden conspired together, aiming to bully Dalton into resigning. Dalton, Taylor considered, lacked an inner self-confidence; Bracken saw this, and exploited it. 'He treated Dalton badly. His language was brutal and his manner insulting.'[54]

'[Bracken] is in a state of violent excitement ... ' Dalton recorded, after receiving an abusive letter from the Minister of Information on 13th October, 'and seems convinced that I have been deliberately double-crossing him. What a fool and nuisance this man is!'[55] One issue concerned SO1 and M.O.I. representatives in South America. Bracken accused SO1 of having approached an Argentinian news agency with an offer to pay for the inclusion of articles – when the agency was, in fact, already owned by M.O.I. From Bracken's point of view, the case provided a perfect illustration of the need for an integrated propaganda department. Bracken made the most of it at a P.W.E. meeting on 21st October. 'This is Alice in Blunderland', he told Dalton, who sat there, 'white to the top of his bald head with rage'. As ministers and officials left, Cadogan said to Bruce Lockhart, 'I find myself moving in a very sinister jungle'.[56] That night, the Permanent Under-Secretary recorded: 'Dogfight between D and Brendan. Inconclusive.'[57]

If Bracken's aim was to wear Dalton down, he was succeeding. On 24th October 1941, Dalton recorded 'a fit of rather deep depression'.[58] The most obvious cause was the gathering crisis in his political life. There was also, however, a private dimension. It was, indeed, scarcely a coincidence that a period of bitter conflict with ministerial and official colleagues should have occurred during the greatest upheaval in his personal life since the death of Helen.

Dalton had been working with great intensity since joining the Government. The experience had been more fulfilling for him than for his wife. A once-equal partnership had become far from equal, and Ruth was increasingly burdened by feelings both of uselessness, and of being unwanted. In the summer of 1941, she decided to leave London and seek war work elsewhere. As a result, Hugh and Ruth lived apart for most of the remaining four-and-a-half years of the war.

It was twenty-seven years since Hugh and Ruth married, nineteen since they lost their daughter. After the single, terrible tragedy, there had been no major disturbances. Hugh had become increasingly absorbed by national politics. Ruth, without the diversion of children, had devoted her considerable energy and intellect to a routine of public service.

She remained, as she had always been, an intensely serious person. Josephine Smith, who knew Ruth through the National Birth Control Association, recalls that, unlike most members of the Association's national committee, she made her own, strongly socialist, political attitudes plain. Peggy Jay, befriended by Ruth on the London County Council in the late 1930s, remembers her as a fierce radical. 'Her attitude was: you didn't live for your own pleasure. You live for the underdog, for doing good by the state.' Ruth brought to this ethic a hard professionalism: cool, organised, non-polemical, non-passionate and well-researched. She was directly responsible for setting up the first birth control clinics in Walworth and in Durham; and, as a leading member of the L.C.C., she did much to improve opportunities for culture and recreation in London. Yet beneath the brisk, competent, busy exterior, there remained a sad and pessimistic core. Peggy Jay concluded that the 'inner hearth burnt low'.[59]

Before the First World War and in the early 1920s Hugh and Ruth had been inseparable, a political firm to be compared with the Webbs or the Coles. By the mid-1930s they were often apart, and independent. When Hugh went abroad, he increasingly travelled alone. At home, young, male political friends became his most frequent companions. Ruth had her own protégés – mainly younger women who, like herself, had few family ties. The war widened the gap.

George Wagner, the Daltons' young Danziger friend, and George's future wife Irene, also a refugee from the Nazis, saw much of both Hugh and Ruth in the early months of the war – George from the summer of 1939 when he moved into the Carlisle Mansions flat, and Irene from March 1940, after she had met George. The Daltons behaved towards them with characteristic generosity. Practical assistance was combined with good-humoured advice: the night before George started his first job, Hugh gave him a short lecture on all the Anglo-Saxon swear-words and their meanings.

George and Irene have happy memories of life in the strange Victorian flat, 'gloomy, stately, in good taste', as George recalls. There was a yellow-papered drawing-room, a study/dining room for Hugh's work, two bedrooms, a bathroom and a kitchen, with a tiny annex, where George slept. The Daltons treated it as a convenience rather than as a home. Ruth's life was filled with activity, yet she seemed lonely, and gave an impression of feeling neglected by Hugh.

Though she had many acquaintances, she appeared to have few close friends. There were no signs of tension in the marriage, only a 'very low temperature'. Hugh and Ruth were two people living together, yet never quite meeting. Hugh would sometimes peck at her cheek. Instead of responding, she would grimace.

Irene felt that, for all her protestations, Ruth desperately needed someone to mother. Since Hugh was seldom at home, Ruth decided to mother *her*. There seemed to be a link with Helen. Ruth once said curtly: 'You may wonder why we didn't have a child. We did, but it died.' Irene became aware (Anthony Crosland was to have the same experience years later) that her own age, 23 in 1940, was almost identical to the age Helen would have been had she lived. She felt that this thought was constantly in Ruth's mind. Ruth gave advice about British customs, and took her on sight-seeing trips to Greenwich and the National Gallery, and to see the sculptural and architectural works for which she was responsible in London parks (Ruth was Chairman of the L.C.C. Parks Committee). In Carlisle Mansions, she welcomed Irene's help with the cooking, having no interest in this activity herself. Hugh generally dined with friends in Soho restaurants, such as the Barcelona, the St George, or Josefs (now the Gay Hussar) in Greek Street.

Ruth helped George and Irene to decide on marriage. She announced that as George was working for the Foreign Office (in the German section of what was to become SO1) it 'wasn't done' for them to go on living in sin. So George proposed in the Dalton dining room. The wedding was planned for June 1940. Before the ceremony, Ruth gave Irene a solemn, clinical talk about birth control, explaining the evils of French letters and the benefits of Dutch caps. Irene recalls that it was all very matter of fact, 'like a farmer's wife discussing piglets'.

Because of George's job and the nationality of both bride and groom (Irene was an Austrian Jew) there was difficulty about getting permission to marry. Hugh used his ministerial status, newly acquired, to cut through red tape. The ceremony was fixed for 7th June, at Caxton Hall. Hugh was invited as witness. He arrived late, and found the Registrar trying to have George arrested as an enemy alien. 'My good man', he shouted at the bewildered functionary, 'the Prime Minister is waiting. Why don't you get on with it?'[60] The Wagners were duly wed, and Hugh rushed off to Downing Street for a Cabinet meeting. That afternoon Gaitskell and Dalton's Press Officer, David Bowes Lyon, had to ward off newspaper inquiries about the alleged presence of the Minister at the wedding of 'a German'.[61]

One effect of the Wagners' marriage was to increase Ruth's isolation. Hugh had joined the Government less than a month before. The war had entered its most critical phase. In the past, Hugh had taken a genuine interest in Ruth's public work. Now he no longer noticed it. Parks and contraception scarcely compared with the blockade and sabotage. At first they met quite often for meals, then less often. 'Lunch with Ruth', Hugh recorded on 25th January 1941. 'I tell her that we really are at last spending a weekend together!'[62] Increasingly, Hugh took to sleeping in a bed in the basement at Berkeley Square House, even though Carlisle Place, between Vauxhall Bridge Road and Victoria Street, was only a short walk away.

It was as though, Ruth felt, she had simply ceased to exist. Later she would complain of 'Hugh's complete self-absorption'.[63] What was the point of continuing to offer companionship to a man who seemed to have no need of it, who preferred the company of those he called his 'three sprites' – Jebb, Gaitskell and his P.P.S., John Wilmot – to her own? The crunch came during the blitz. Hugh, totally preoccupied with work, was scarcely aware of the bombing. In any case he was well protected from it in the M.E.W. basement. He gave little thought to Ruth, living alone in a fourth floor flat, and working as an air raid warden. Ruth's situation was no different from that of thousands of others. Yet the bombing had for her a special significance: awakening memories, best left dormant, of the night in November 1917 when Helen was born.

At the beginning of May 1941 the German Luftwaffe launched a series of heavy raids on London and other British cities. As it turned out, this was to be the last major assault on the capital until the V-1 campaign began three years later. In the air battle that accompanied it, the R.A.F. proved its superiority by shooting down 124 night raiders. For civilians, especially Londoners, the bombardment was the culmination of ten months of intermittent terror, a time of anxiety, sleeplessness, unpredictability and sudden death. The final raid took place on the night of 10th–11th May. It was the most devastating attack of the whole war. Three thousand people were killed or injured. Some of the worst damage occurred in the Westminster and Victoria areas of central London. The chamber of the House of Commons and the Deanery of Westminster were destroyed; Westminster Hall and Westminster Abbey were damaged.[64]

10th May was a Saturday. Hugh had been attending to SO1 business at Woburn in the afternoon; he spent the night at the Rectory, as was his custom. Next day he returned from Bedfordshire by car, accompanied by Gladwyn Jebb. As they entered the capital, the extent of the destruction became apparent. Hugh was fascinated by the awesome sights of devastation. Carlisle Mansions had been spared, though only just. Hugh's record of his home-coming does not mention Ruth:

> Before starting we had heard something of the damage done in last night's air-raid on London. As we come into London there are some signs of this, much smoke hanging in the air and the streets full of broken glass and charred bits of paper. We drive first to my flat and find that an incendiary bomb has burned out the top flat immediately opposite mine. This will improve my view and it is interesting to see that this old Victorian building, ugly though it is, is yet so solid that the incendiary burnt itself out without spreading either to right or left or downwards through the solid stone walls and floor to adjoining flats. No damage to my own.

Later, he inspected the awesome, smoking ruins of the House of Commons. Stepping through the rubble, he paid his last respects by urinating, symbolically, in the remains of the Members' lavatory.[65]

Ruth was able to regard the raid with less detachment. Unlike Hugh, she had been close to the centre of an inferno. By the morning, she was weak with fear and fatigue, and desperately in need of comfort. Perhaps Hugh offered it. If so, her resentment was such that she did not notice. She had hoped, she told her friend Josephine Smith, for some expression of interest in her welfare. Instead, Hugh's sole concern appeared to be with his own:

> He merely said 'Whew! What a relief to see that the flat is still standing! I must remember to take some suits to the office.'[66]

Those may not have been his precise words. Nicholas Davenport gives a slightly different version, presumably also derived directly or indirectly from Ruth. The main ingredient, however, is the same – Hugh's disregard for Ruth, her life, health or feelings, and his primary interest in himself:

> After the explosions, she heard the key turn in the front door of the flat. 'Ah!' she thought, 'Hugh has remembered me and has come home to see if I am safe.' 'Is that you Ruth?' he boomed. 'A terrible raid. I suddenly remembered that I had left my new suit in the flat. It would be a nuisance if that blew up.'[67]

In both accounts, Hugh reduces Ruth to something less, in his order of priorities, than the uniform of his official life. Was it the breaking-point? Ruth later told friends that this incident was the last straw, the final demonstration of his egotism and of how little she meant to him.

She determined, there and then, to give up pretending to provide him with a home, and to seek work outside London.[68]

She delayed doing anything about it. For the time being there was no change in their routine. Hugh's mind was immediately taken up with crises at SO1 and SO2, and by a report that on 10th May, the day of the raid on London, Rudolf Hess had landed in Scotland on a mysterious mission from the Reich. In late June, the Daltons managed to spend a sunny weekend together in Wiltshire. Perhaps Hugh was not wholly unaware of his wife's misery. 'Ruth much better for being here and for sun-bathing', he noted, not without sympathy, on the day that news came through of Hitler's attack on Russia. 'What she would really like to do would be to re-plan London.'[69]

In August, she told him what she had been feeling. She said that he hardly noticed whether she was there or not. 'I don't understand', he replied.[70] They decided to give up the flat in which they had spent most of their lives together. Hugh would make what he called his 'shelter bedroom' at Berkeley Square House his London home.

The move was completed in mid-September. Furniture, books and clothes were shifted from London to West Leaze, and to a nearby cottage, for storage. Ruth hoped to gain employment in the north or midlands. This could not be achieved immediately: even in wartime, opportunities for fifty-year-old women were limited. For the time being, therefore, she took a room in a hotel in Sloane Square. Hugh dined with her and the Noel-Bakers on 23rd October. 'She is now hoping to have an interview on Monday morning which may lead somewhere', he noted.

What were the implications for Hugh's office battles? Pressure at work led to the break up. At the same time, the separation and the uncertainties surrounding it exacerbated the tensions that had been building up at Baker Street and Berkeley Square House. During the weeks before Ruth left London, Hugh was particularly brittle and edgy. On 28th October, Hugh heard that Ruth's job interview had been postponed.[71] Next day, there occurred the uncontrolled outburst of rage that provoked Sir Frank Nelson to offer his resignation as head of SO2 and led to an important redefinition of responsibilities.[72] One strain added to the burden of another, reducing the Minister's ability to cope. Early in November, Bracken found Dalton in a greatly weakened condition as he closed in for the kill.

On 11th November, Dalton recorded, once again, 'a sense of deep depression'. All the optimism of eighteen months before had faded. Instead of body-line bowling at the Hun, there was the degradation of the Whitehall War. There seemed no limit to Bracken's aggressiveness, or his insults. 'I am rather tired of being told that I evade issues or am a liar', Dalton told Bracken during a gruelling meeting of P.W.E. ministers and top officials. 'I may have other qualities which are displeasing to the Minister of Information but I am not that sort.' Afterwards he wrote bitterly of Bracken's 'customary rudeness' and 'brainless bad manners'.

With nobody outside his office to turn to, Dalton unburdened himself to Gladwyn Jebb, a cool, philosophical listener. The Minister spoke, almost hopelessly, of the lives of politicians, 'embarrassed, transient, jealous, embittered phantoms', who drifted across the civil servant's skyline. 'We win our battles today and lose them tomorrow; we come in and go out, generally at quite short intervals', he reflected. 'To me, sometimes, the idea of going out has great attractions. I should regain my freedom of expression; I should regain full freedom of speech. I should declare in a loud voice that the P.M. was *très mal entouré*.' ('But what good would *that* do?' Jebb interjected.) It was the first time since Dalton had taken office that he had indulged in this particular reverie. Over the next few years – at the Board of Trade and then at the Treasury – thoughts about resignation became his favourite form of escape when the pressure was upon him.

Dalton's desire to declare publicly that Churchill was *'très mal entouré'* arose from his growing sense – part justified, part paranoia – that the prejudices of the Prime Minister's aides were doing him serious harm. For a long time, Bracken had kept his special link with Churchill in reserve. Now he brought it out, hinting or openly threatening that he would refer matters to Downing Street. ' ... [T]his is a vexatious little blighter and I am irritated by his constant attempt to play the P.M. card', Dalton wrote at the beginning of November.[73] Bracken also blackened Dalton's name by giving currency to luridly distorted accounts of their regular shouting matches. 'Doubtless Brendan tells these stories with gusto to his colleagues and friends', Bruce Lockhart noted, after discovering that Beaverbrook had been an eager listener to one of them. 'Max does *not* like Dr. Dalton who seems to have few friends.'[74]

It was time, Dalton decided, to mobilise Attlee once more. The Party Leader was visiting the United States. With increasing agitation, the Minister of Economic Warfare awaited his return. Meanwhile, Dalton haughtily informed Eden that Bracken was not the only P.W.E. minister with powerful allies. 'I summon up all my reserves of charm for this vain feminine creature', Dalton recorded after talking to the handsome young Foreign Secretary. 'I say that I shall pour out to C.R.A. the story of what I have had to put up with during his absence.'

When Attlee reappeared, Dalton opened his heart. As the Party Leader evidently saw, his colleague's need for support was as much emotional as political. He listened patiently, and sympathetically, making reassuring, assenting noises at the right moments. Dalton's own vivid account of the conversation between the two Labour ministers reveals much about the personality and style of both men, as well as about the politics of the Coalition:

> I ... showed C.R.A. all the correspondence between myself and B.B. He read it all through – though there is now a damned lot of it – snorting with indignation. He said 'This man is not fit to be a Minister in the middle of a war.' I said that he had clearly wanted to bring on a crisis, while C.R.A. was away, and to tell some cock and bull story to the P.M. and get him on his side. I had played for time and prevented this. I objected very strongly to B.B. continually running round to the P.M. and giving him an account of our affairs. It placed me in an intolerable position. C.R.A. said that he quite agreed, and that B.B. must be either a P.P.S. or a Minister conducting his business properly with his colleagues. I said that B.B. was always saying, when we were together 'As the P.M. said to me last night ... ', or 'I was lunching with the P.M. yesterday and he said ... ', or 'I have to be round at No. 10 in ten minutes' ... He said the M. of I. was the worst Ministry in Whitehall ... I said ... that A.E. [Eden] had hinted at one of our Ministers' meetings that all P.W.E. might be turned over to the M. of I. I said that I couldn't agree to this for a moment. I judged that it was important, other considerations apart, that one of the Labour Ministers should be in on propaganda. If the Party thought that an attempt was being made to edge us out of this, there would be a row. C.T.A. warmly agreed.

Thus unburdened, Dalton retreated to West Leaze, taking for company an assistant from his private office, Christopher Mayhew, a would-be Labour politician twenty-eight years his junior ('I'm making arrangements to see not everyone of competence is killed', he had written when he employed Mayhew – thinking, no doubt, of Rupert Brooke, Ben Keeling, and others of his own lost generation). In Wiltshire, Dalton put Mayhew through his physical and mental paces. It was a classic programme: walks and runs through the Marlborough Downs, chess and sleep in front of the fire, unrelenting intellectual debate. For the older man it was a tonic. Whitehall cares were briefly banished. 'He is still in some ways surprisingly young and immature and has not yet grown a very firm or worldly judgement', the Minister mused, 'but he is extremely nice.'

The following weekend Dalton returned to West Leaze, this time alone, his emotions still in turmoil. 'The Celt in me jumps up and down these days', he told Jebb. The bleak Wiltshire countryside in late autumn helped him to collect his thoughts. He read poems by Catullus and ran from Aldbourne to Woodsend in the moonlight. His career, recently so full of interest and promise, was whirling dangerously out of control and he no longer knew what he wanted or where he was going. How could he prevent his total exclusion from control of P.W.E.? How could he stop Bracken's humiliating attacks? Should he threaten to resign 'and blow a lot of gaffes'? There was a pattern: a swing in mood from bold exuberance to the brink of despair, under the weight of responsibility, overwork and the changing fortunes of office. It had happened before. It was to happen again, disastrously, when he became Chancellor.

Dalton spent Christmas apart from Ruth for the second year running. In late December 1940, he had visited Polish military camps in Scotland. This year, he toured S.O.E. training stations, taking Mayhew for company, as his A.D.C. In the course of one inspection on Christmas Day, he threw a bomb, which exploded satisfactorily. He was back in the office on Boxing Day. He saw in the New Year alone at West Leaze, digging in the garden, listening to the wireless and playing games of patience. On New Year's Day a long letter arrived from Ruth in Manchester. She had started a job as a liaison officer looking after hostels for women workers in the new Ordnance factories. Hugh scribbled in the margin of his diary, 'I miss her a lot'.

Back at Berkeley Square House early in January, Dalton conceived a new, desperate, strategy, to forestall the growing danger that he would be pushed out of the propaganda field altogether. As an alternative to a propaganda department, either under joint ministerial control or controlled by Bracken on his own, he proposed a Ministry of Economic and Political Warfare, under himself. This would fulfil his original dream of administering economic and political weapons as an integrated whole. Blockade policy, propaganda, subversion could thus be combined in all their interrelated aspects as a fourth fighting arm – a silent, unseen force that would have an important role to play alongside the three regular services.

For such a plan to stand any chance, Dalton needed to have the Foreign Secretary on his side. What made it a virtual non-starter was that Eden was considerably more sympathetic to Bracken than to himself. Eden's predecessor, Lord Halifax, had been a man to whom Dalton could relate – an austere, intellectual figure, who stood above inter-party strife. Dalton found dealing with Eden – ten years his junior, temperamental, ambitious and highly political – much harder.

Nevertheless Dalton clung to the hope that in the interests of solving the propaganda problem once and for all, the Foreign Secretary might be persuaded. He therefore sent Jebb to prepare the ground. Jebb was instructed to see Eden's private secretary, Oliver Harvey, and explain 'how much I admired A.E., how baseless, in the present political situation, would be any suspicion on his part that I was after his job, how like-minded we were on all large issues, and how eager I was to work with him … ' The tactic failed. Eden showed little interest in Dalton's proposal. Nor did he have any need of Dalton's political support. At the beginning of February, relations between the two ministers deteriorated sharply when Dalton received a memorandum from Cadogan which 'reduced me to the status of an Under-Secretary at the Foreign Office and was quite intolerable'.[75] The proposed Ministry of Economic and Political Warfare – rightly seen as a belated bid on Dalton's part for the whole propaganda empire – came to nothing.

The conflict with Bracken continued. At the beginning of February Bracken launched a new offensive, this time over the proposed Aspidistra transmitting station. Bruce Lockhart noted that Dalton became 'white to the gills' with anger at the Minister of Information.[76] Dalton commented on his adversary: 'He is, as G[ladwyn] says, simply a guttersnipe'. He was, however, a guttersnipe with influence. In the middle of the month, suddenly and unexpectedly, the propaganda issue was resolved – in Bracken's favour.

The occasion was a Government reshuffle. On 19th February, a new War Cabinet was announced. Like most ministers, Dalton wondered whether he would be affected by the changes lower down that were to follow. As it happened, he had arranged to make one of his rare visits to his constituency on the 20th. Should he cancel it? He asked Attlee whether he was likely to be moved. 'Certainly not', replied the Party Leader. Thus assured, Dalton travelled north. But Attlee was wrong. On 21st February, as Dalton was giving a speech at the Hippodrome in Shildon, he received a message to telephone the Prime Minister. When he did so, Churchill asked him to become President of the Board of Trade. For a moment, Dalton hesitated. 'I suppose the Board of Trade is a very full time job', he said – meaning, could he take sabotage and subversion with him? 'Yes, quite full-time', replied the Prime Minister.

So that was that. Dalton accepted, and the 'offensive' part of his war came to an end. Lord Wolmer (shortly afterwards the Earl of Selborne) replaced him as Minister of Economic Warfare, inheriting S.O.E. as well, but not the SO1 side, now fully absorbed into P.W.E. The Political Warfare Executive, with Bruce Lockhart as Director-General, became a two-minister affair – Eden handling foreign policy aspects, Bracken looking after administration.[77] Shortly afterwards, both Jebb and Nelson left S.O.E. – Jebb because he could not get on with Selborne, and Nelson for reasons of health. S.O.E. moved into a new phase, and the 'unitary' concept of subversion was finally discarded.

Almost certainly, Dalton was shifted because Bracken and Eden asked the Prime Minister to get him out of the propaganda field. No doubt an additional factor was Churchill's own irritation at repeated complaints by Attlee on Dalton's behalf, and by frequent reports from other sources of dissension at P.W.E. meetings. However, Oliver Harvey's diary entry for 20th February strongly suggests that the direct intervention of the Minister of Information and the Foreign Secretary was the crucial factor:

> A.E. saw P.M. again this morning when latter promised not to bring out the new list till Monday and not without consulting him about it. A.E. has also seen Bracken who is being helpful in urging P.M. to make drastic changes. A.E. has given Bracken his own list of changes and B. is going to take this to P.M. on Monday ... It is proposed to move Dalton from M.E.W. possibly to Health.[78]

Beaverbrook spoke of a 'triumph for Brendan and the removal of Dalton from P.W.E.',[79] and this is how it was seen. The P.M. card had trumped. The alternatives of sacking Dalton outright, or of leaving him at M.E.W. while squeezing him out of P.W.E., might have threatened the Coalition. So he was promoted instead.

It is unlikely that Churchill gave the problem much thought. Dalton's move came at the tail end of a series of ministerial changes that had a more fundamental cause. The war was not going well. On 12th February two German warships, the *Scharnhorst* and the *Gneisenau*, had slipped through the English Channel back to Germany, despite intensive efforts to stop them. Three days later, Singapore had fallen to the Japanese. In the opinion of many, it was the blackest week since Dunkirk.[80] The Prime Minister was reported to be in a state of great depression and anxiety.[81] Few matters concerned him less at such a time than propaganda. Faced with the problems of P.W.E., he dealt with them by a stroke of a pen.

The consequence, however, was major. Churchill's act rescued Dalton from a politically hazardous *impasse* and brought him back, with a bump, to the home front. It also ensured that, within a few months, his main interests would be directed, with massive effect, towards shaping the post-war world.

XXI

Coalition Poker

Surveying the ranks of M.P.s in the House of Commons shortly after he became a minister in May 1940, Dalton leant over to Captain Margesson, the Tory Chief Whip, and whispered to his political enemy of a few days before: 'Why don't you shut up this bloody monkey-house, or at any rate only open it one day a week?' Dalton gave little thought either to Parliament or to his party during his first months in office. Fascinated by the exercise of power, he was glad to be shot of the company of some of his older and more boring Labour comrades. He quickly developed a patrician contempt for M.P.s (like Shinwell) or members of the N.E.C. (like Laski) who behaved as though peacetime rules still prevailed. Before he would have enjoyed the sport of debunking them; now there were bigger fish to bludgeon. 'Long-winded, trivial and rather hysterical, but no damage done', was a typical comment on the proceedings of the Party Executive.[1]

For many years, Dalton's regular contacts had mainly been with radical intellectuals and people in the Labour Movement. Now, joining the Tory-dominated Coalition, he found himself part of a community that was dominated by a class and type which he had rejected as a young man. It was a kind of home-coming, a return to a distantly familiar world.

As Lord Gladwyn (formerly Gladwyn Jebb) has pointed out, on the foreign side it was an Old Etonian war:

Eden, Halifax, Cadogan, Vansittart, Neville Henderson (regrettably), Ronnie Campbell, Percy Loraine, Harold Macmillan, Duff Cooper, almost all the tops, had been at Eton. So were the two Ministers successively responsible for S.O.E., Dalton and Selborne, together with the Heads of the two Secret Services, Stewart Menzies and (after myself) Charlie Hambro. You might well throw in Edward Bridges, the Secretary of the Cabinet, as well ... I certainly would not pretend that there was a similarity in the process of thought or in the political affiliation of the characters mentioned. But I do think that the fact that they all had the same start did something to facilitate relationships and thus promote efficiency ... just as the *Polytechniciens* in France do somehow seem to form an inner group, or core, of the society, so the Etonians, in 1940, were a kind of inner fraternity.[2]

Such a concentration of Etonians was of course not coincidental. Like *Polytechniciens*, Etonians turned most naturally to their own kind. It is interesting that on foreign policy matters Dalton was no exception: his two closest friends (perhaps his only friends) among officials with a Foreign Office background, Vansittart and Jebb, both belonged to the fraternity.

Sharing the same culture, Dalton and Jebb were able to look at relationships within the Whitehall–Westminster village in a way which outsiders would have found incomprehensible:

Gladwyn makes the bright remark tonight that at Eton the Sixth Form are the Labour Party and Pop the Conservatives. The feud, in which I once took my share – the symbol of which was wearing pumps at early school! – has always, he thinks, gone on.[3]

And did so still. Dalton was not the victim of any aristocratic re-embrace. On the contrary. His relations with many of his prominent school-fellows were venomous. It was, however, a familial sort of venom. There were bonds that tied him to the Government's inner circle that did not exist for any of his Labour ministerial colleagues. He spoke the same language, had many of the same assumptions and had a sense of dealing with his own kind. He knew the rules of the club, even when he flouted them.

It is thus an irony that of all Labour ministers Dalton was the one who came to rely on the Labour Party most. The reason was simple. Where other Coalition ministers could expect to sink or swim on their merits, Dalton soon realised that without strong political support he would win few battles and would probably not even be a member of the Government.

Dalton felt a deep admiration, approaching awe, for Winston Churchill. Though he might criticise the Prime Minister's actions in detail and be hurt by rebuffs, his basic loyalty never wavered, even when Churchill's stock was at its lowest. Unfortunately, Churchill felt no affection for him in return.

The Prime Minister appreciated Dalton's pre-war record as a stalwart anti-appeaser. The problem was personal. Churchill had a distaste, almost a dread, for the unlucky Minister of Economic Warfare. 'Winston hates Dalton', it was said, 'calls him "an intolerable person".'[4] According to Sir John Colville (one of the Prime Minister's wartime private secretaries) Churchill also disliked Morrison, but he greatly preferred Morrison to Dalton.[5] 'Keep that man away from me', the Prime Minister would remark, 'I can't stand his booming voice and shifting eyes.'[6]

Dalton became aware of Churchill's hostility only gradually, and was too distressed by the discovery ever fully to believe it. He made clumsy attempts to ingratiate himself. He campaigned indignantly against prime ministerial aides who, he believed, had been spreading malicious gossip against him. At the same time, he adopted the more considered strategy of using the Labour Party, and Attlee as its spokesman, to protect himself.

In an effort to impress his virtues on the Prime Minister he befriended the chairman of Churchill's constituency Conservative Association, engaged Professor Lindemann in earnest conversations, and wrote letters to No. 10 Downing Street in a resonant and hyperbolic style that seemed to parody Churchill's own. The only effect was to cause embarrassment to his own advisers and amusement in the Prime Minister's office. Such was Dalton's nervousness about his relationship with Churchill that he had to be coaxed to make even the most essential calls to No. 10.[7]

Dalton's belief that his problems lay with Churchill's entourage began when he learnt that an unnamed aide had advised against giving him subversion in July 1940. He became even more wary of the staff at No. 10 when reports reached him in November of the same year of '"a prevalent opinion" that the P.M. did not like Dalton' – which he interpreted as a conspiracy of denigration, preferring to ignore the possibility that the opinion was right. Frustrations over SO1 and SO2 fed his anger against what he called the 'Camarilla' of detractors who, he believed, inhabited the Prime Minister's office and influenced the old man against him. A report that Desmond Morton, whom he had once regarded as a friend, had represented him, 'most amusingly, as a windbag, a careerist, and a witless fool who shouted contradictory objugations at his officials', upset him for days.

Morton was not Dalton's only imaginary or real enemy at No. 10. As we have seen, rumours that Brendan Bracken (at that time also a prime ministerial adviser, and not yet at M.O.I.) had been similarly abusive, led Dalton to complain to Attlee who took the matter up with

Churchill. Apart from providing Bracken and Churchill with some mild entertainment, this incident had the effect of securing Dalton a placatory invitation to Sunday lunch at the Prime Minister's official residence at Chequers.

The lunch took place on 2nd March 1941. It was a stiff, uneasy occasion which Dalton handled badly. The only other leading figure present was Robert Menzies, the Australian Prime Minister. Dalton used the opportunity to press for more aircraft for S.O.E. Less wisely, he aired his personal grievances. Questioned by Churchill about allegations that there were 'many left-wing elements' among SO1 staff at Woburn, Dalton replied:

> that I am accused by others of Fascist methods and getting rid of Reds and even Pinks at M.E.W. I say that our people are being sniped. I want him to be satisfied. He says, 'I am not dissatisfied. I know that you are a very able man.' (This would go all right in a headline, but not much warmth.)

Dalton went away with an uncomfortable feeling that Churchill was suspicious of him. 'It is not clear quite what he suspects me of', ruminated the Minister of Economic Warfare. 'Trying to get his job?'[8]

The real problem was that the Prime Minister preferred not to think about him at all. When Dalton did manage to bring issues involving M.E.W. and S.O.E. to Churchill's attention, he sometimes succeeded in getting the Prime Minister's support. In general, however, Churchill's dislike for the man encouraged a tendency to regard most of Dalton's work as unimportant. 'Winston did not believe much in sabotage', Morton told Bruce Lockhart in January 1941.[9] According to Colville Churchill was interested in the 'Ultra' intercepts of S.I.S., but in little else on the secret side:

> The Special Operations Executive and other clandestine organisations, however effective, did not attract his attention. He knew less than he should of the gallantry and initiative of British agents working in Europe under the direct threat of the Gestapo. This was partly because he saw as little as possible of Dalton, under whose broad authority most of them came, and there was no direct contact with No. 10 on these matters.[10]

On one occasion, after the Prime Minister had slipped up badly – through ignorance or oversight – in answering a Parliamentary Question relating to the work of SO1, Dalton complained bitterly to Attlee 'that the P.M. took no interest at all in this particular branch of my work and regarded it as a bloody bone which has been thrown to me in order to appease the Labour Party'.[11] This was probably a fair summary of Churchill's attitude to the whole of S.O.E.

The Prime Minister was scarcely more enthusiastic about the 'white' propaganda of M.O.I. For all Dalton's fears to the contrary, neither Cooper nor Bracken received much help from Downing Street. 'When I appealed for support to the Prime Minister I seldom got it', Cooper recalled. 'He was not interested in the subject. He knew that propaganda was not going to win the war ... '[12] Bracken made deadly use of 'the P.M. card' as a device to frighten Dalton and impress officials, but only at the very end was he able actually to play it. According to Lysaght, Churchill 'refused point blank to interest himself in the peripheral problems of propaganda'.[13]

The difference between Dalton's position and that of successive Ministers of Information was that neither Cooper nor Bracken had to cope with the Prime Minister's personal antipathy. Given Churchill's domination of the Government, the gap between being a prime ministerial favourite and being an unfavourite felt like a chasm. Churchill did not have to intervene against Dalton. Dalton's authority was weakened simply by the Whitehall rumour that the Prime Minister held him in low esteem.

Dalton learnt, therefore, that to survive he could not afford to neglect his political base. It was necessary to make maximum use of the Labour Party and its importance to the Coalition – even at the expense of arousing still further the hostility of Tories in the Government and on the backbenches. This had been true over P.W.E. It became even more true at the Board of Trade, where many of the President's concerns were of direct interest to M.P.s of both parties. During the remaining years of the Coalition, Dalton countered the P.M. card with the Labour Party card, with increasing skill and success.

Dalton's responsibilities for the blockade and subversion at M.E.W. and S.O.E. had kept him out of the public gaze. By contrast, the Board of Trade dealt with matters which were at the centre of public controversy. Dalton found himself at the head of a key department at a time when domestic politics were about to break out into the open, placing dangerous strains on the Coalition.

From the start, the style of the new President's administration was political. The House seems to have anticipated this: one colleague noted a sullen mood in the Commons on the day Dalton took office, with more party feeling than at any time since May 1940. When Dalton made his bow at the box, 'the Labour men, and only they, cheered'.[14] It was an omen. Dalton was soon to become the whipping-boy of the restless Tory backbenches.

The Board of Trade was a 'residuary ministry', looking after a rag-bag of problems with no connecting thread. Bankruptcy, company law, clothes rationing, films, utility furniture, concentration of industry, tobacco supply and price control, all came under the jurisdiction of the President who also had a general responsibility for trade and industry, imports and exports, and coal. There were three satellite ministers, each with the title of 'Secretary': D. R. Grenfell (a Labour M.P. and ex-miner) was in charges of the Mines Department, Geoffrey Lloyd (a Conservative) was in charge of the Petroleum Department, and Harcourt Johnstone (a Liberal) was responsible for the Department of Overseas Trade. Dalton soon learnt that although he could be called to account for the mistakes of these ministers, he had no effective means of controlling them.

Dalton took Hugh Gaitskell across from M.E.W. as his Personal Assistant, and then quickly promoted him out of his private office. More surprisingly, he also took Sir Frederick Leith-Ross, who was given the job of planning inter-Allied relief. Later, Leith-Ross worked on schemes for international financial co-operation, which culminated in the Bretton Woods agreement.[15] Wilmot continued as Dalton's P.P.S. The new President inherited Captain Charles Waterhouse, a Tory, as his Parliamentary Secretary. In September 1943 Dalton brought in Douglas Jay to work on Development Areas, and as a socialist stimulus.

The first storm Dalton had to face was over coal, and the problem of how to deal with an anticipated shortage. What initially seemed a purely administrative problem rapidly acquired dangerous political overtones.

There was never any actual shortage of coal – at no stage in the war was lack of fuel responsible for reducing vital war production. What caused anxiety was a sharp rise in consumption during 1941, and a consequent fear that a shortage might occur if measures were not taken to increase margins. There were several possible ways of tackling the problem: action to increase production with the same manpower; action to increase the size of the work-force, mainly by securing the release of face workers from the Armed Forces; and action to reduce consumption. Dalton pursued all three – and in doing so entered a snakepit of prejudice and special pleading.

The most desirable solution was to cut consumption. But how could this be done? Rationing, as Gaitskell minuted to the new President, was going to be the key issue:

It must be done for all fuel, and there is a conflict of views ... Can you ration fuel? This is the biggest question you will have to face, and you will have to go into it in great detail yourself.[16]

Dalton was quickly persuaded not only that rationing was necessary, but also that the best and most equitable method was a comprehensive scheme for all forms of fuel (coke, coal, gas and electricity). To do this, however, required a co-ordinated effort with the Mines Department.

Here the President's biggest problem was the Secretary for Mines himself. Dalton regarded Grenfell as stupid and incompetent, and wanted him sacked. 'If he stayed', Dalton told Attlee, 'it would mean that I should have to spend infinite time humouring him, and then do most of the job myself.' However, the Party Leader – now Deputy Prime Minister – refused to help. For all his faults Grenfell was popular with the mining M.P.s in the House of Commons, and Attlee was not prepared to face the political embarrassment of his dismissal.

So Grenfell stayed. Over the months that followed the President treated the Secretary for Mines with public solicitude and private scorn, as though dealing with a clumsy and backward child for whom all hope of genuine progress had been abandoned. 'He is my Calvary', Dalton wrote after the first few weeks of frustration.[17]

Dalton may not have been able to shake off the political head of the Mines Department; he was more successful in dealing with the administrative one. 'One of the real enemies of the war effort', Gaitskell commented on Sir Alfred Hurst, the Under-Secretary in charge of the Department. ' ... Regarded as quite untrustworthy from the point of view of a Labour Minister ... The most sinister figure in the Board of Trade, but very able.'[18] The President acted swiftly on this advice, and replaced Hurst with Lord Hyndley, the Commercial Adviser, who was fiercely critical of the existing set-up. The operation was carried out with a maximum of provocation and tactlessness. Dalton sent a message to the head of the civil service, Sir Horace Wilson, demanding that Hurst should leave his office within twenty-four hours. When Hurst made indignant protests, Dalton did not disguise his own sadistic pleasure.

Having thus imposed his will on a key part of his empire, the new President asked Sir William Beveridge (who had recently been appointed chairman of an interdepartmental committee on social insurance) to prepare a scheme for fuel rationing. Beveridge produced a report within five weeks, proposing 'a points system with interchangeable coupons'.[19] Dalton was enthusiastic. His gratitude was, however, somewhat cooled by Beveridge's stubborn refusal to modify the scheme in order to take account of political factors.[20]

'This inquiry was not one that I would have chosen, nor did it improve my reputation', Beveridge later recalled. 'I was not asked to say whether fuel should be rationed. That was settled before I began.'[21] Dalton had set his mind on introducing rationing: Beveridge was simply asked to show how it could best be done. The issue was not settled, however, as far as Tory backbenchers were concerned. To them, fuel rationing looked suspiciously like socialism by the backdoor. (R. A. Butler, the Minister of Education, put the backbench objection more crudely: Conservatives were opposed to rationing fuel, he told Dalton, 'because they are afraid that it will mean that they won't get enough for their country houses'.)[22] The strongest pressure came from the coal owners' lobby, which had powerful connections on the Tory side of the House. The coal owners suspected, from the start, that Dalton's real aim was to take over the mines for the duration.[23] Hence they sought, according to Gaitskell, 'to damage and, if possible, get rid of Dalton'.[24]

The coal owners were right: Dalton was well aware of the miners' desire for state control, and sympathised with it. The Tory M.P.s were also right to suspect Dalton of socialist motives. 'In advocating the rationing of fuel he was implementing Labour's policy of rationing necessities', the President told his Labour colleague, Chuter Ede.[25] Rationing, in Beveridge's words, was more concerned with distribution than with restriction. Hence it had a moral appeal to Dalton, the philosopher of equality. Nevertheless, the problem facing Dalton was not moral but practical: how to create the conditions which would produce a 'safe' margin between production and consumption. The main case for rationing, in Dalton's view, was one of administrative efficiency.

If Dalton was primarily concerned with a practical problem, what most influenced his opponents was a political mood that had little to do with coal rationing. Tory backbenchers had become increasingly resentful at what they saw as a growing Labour influence in the Coalition. Dalton was unlucky. The announcement of coal rationing coincided with a temporary lull in the war which permitted a return to traditional politics. Opposition to the scheme was a way of pointing out to the Government that it was the old-fashioned Tories of 1931 and 1935, former Chamberlainites, who kept the Prime Minister in office. 'The rationing plan became a sort of unacknowledged test of the relative strength of parties and interests within the Coalition and in Parliament', one historian has observed, 'behind a barrage of arguments about its administrative virtues and defects.'[26]

At first Dalton seemed to be making good progress. The Beveridge scheme was approved by Sir John Anderson's powerful Lord President's Committee (overlord on the domestic front). The Prime Minister, who disliked rationing in principle, but disliked the alternative of releasing 7,000 miners from the armed forces even more, gave his blessing.[27] Unperturbed by early indications of Tory unrest, Dalton told Jebb over dinner on 17th April 1942 that 'apart from not having him working for me, I find my present job much more interesting and exciting than my last'. The excitement, however, had barely begun. When, four days later, Dalton announced that the Government had decided to bring in a comprehensive rationing scheme in June, Tory backbenchers reacted so violently that lobby journalists became convinced that the plan would be dropped.[28]

Dalton was taken by surprise. To some extent he had brought his difficulties upon himself: on 17th March he had made the tactical error of giving the House notice of the intention to introduce rationing, and of the appointment of Beveridge. This unnecessary disclosure gave prospective critics time to marshal their forces.[29] The President, however, was not prepared to back down under pressure. He was convinced of the merits of the plan, which appeared to have strong popular support (70 per cent of the population were in favour of full-scale planning, according to one survey, and only 10 per cent were opposed).[30] He was also aware that to concede defeat would be taken as a sign of Labour's weakness. Defiantly, he published the Beveridge plan, and then sought to win his critics over by force of argument. It was a brave but hopeless mission. At a gathering of the Tory 1922 Committee, assembled at his request, one backbencher asked whether he would consider substituting 'restrictions' for rationing. Dalton replied that he would consider 'anything which gives me both economy and equity'. Such a remark did nothing to extinguish a growing Tory conviction that Dalton ran the Board of Trade with a socialist bias.[31]

There were, Dalton told John Wilmot as they shaved together in the ministerial bathroom, only three alternatives: 'victory, resignation or some kind of huggery-muggery which does not attract me at all.' Very soon, Dalton was forced to accept that, like it or not, huggery-muggery was the only way through. Early in May a group of Tories pressed a motion to cut the salary of the President of the Board of Trade, in order to force a vote on the scheme. It was a direct challenge. The problem, Dalton noted, was a mixture on the Tory side of dislike of miners and dislike of coupons, officialdom, Labour ministers and Dalton himself, 'a recognition that I am rather "clever" and a fear that I am trying to put through nationalisation of the mines by a sidewind'.[32] When the matter was debated in the Commons on 7th May, Sir Stafford Cripps, as Leader of the House, was forced to promise a further Government White Paper and yet another debate.

Any chance of carrying the rationing scheme in its original form now disappeared. There was also a new factor. In the first three weeks of May, a series of disruptive strikes occurred in the coal fields over wages and conditions, involving 58,000 men.[33]

Faced with the danger of a big Tory defection, Dalton had no choice but to retreat. He remained committed to the Beveridge scheme. Now, however, he adopted a wholly new tactic: he decided to wrap up the rationing issue in the wider question of the reorganisation of the mines. This would, he hoped, solve the problem of a possible coal shortage, satisfy the miners, meet Tory critics (who had been calling for more production) and please a number of Labour M.P.s (who suspected that rationing was a dodge to avoid putting the coal-owners' house in order). It would also enable him to save face.

Most ministers accepted this way out. One, however, did not: Churchill. The Prime Minister, who had early favoured rationing as an alternative to raiding the armed forces, now decided that the rationing plan must be killed altogether. Dalton observed with deep exasperation that as usual Churchill was not focussing his difficulties properly. 'I have never thought so ill of the P.M., nor been so vexed by him before', noted the President, after a wearisome Cabinet. ' ... He argues at immense length, almost alone, against a substantial majority of his colleagues ... The P.M.'s mind is nowhere near the merits of this problem, and he has been wholly swayed by Cherwell, who will have told him that on the figures rationing is not necessary, and by the Tory Party representations.'

Confronted by the Prime Minister's blanket opposition, Dalton retired alone to West Leaze to brood. Personal and political considerations mingled as he contemplated resignation – the siren which so often seemed to beckon at times of trouble:

17.5.42. I feel almost out of office. It's a mixed sensation. I should be free of routine, & responsibility for all things large & small in a Department, & of those long-drawn-out Committee meetings with colleagues, & even of the War Cab – how dreams fade when one wakes! – with desultory, uninstructed monologue, & suggestions that A.R.P. wardens should look in people's cellars to see whether they are burning or storing coal! I should be able to spend a week, or even weeks, on end down here in the summer. (But without R[uth], or other visitors for short spells, it would be very lonely. And arrangements about services & rations would be tiresome.)

I should be free to speak and write again, as I felt and not as I was constrained by ministerial prudence, & the perpetual pending of undecided, and therefore unmentionable, questions. If I went out the right way, I might greatly strengthen my position in the Labour Party.

On the other hand, I should miss, after a week or two, a great many things. The power to take decisions, a lot of which may make a bit of difference, – some inside knowledge of what is going on; the prestige, & the conveniences, including the salary, etc, of being a Minister. I should have to try to find, I suppose, a small service flat somewhere, preferably in Westminster, or a temporary abode with someone ...

And, on a longer view, I should miss the chance of having anything serious to do with the Settlement at the end of the War.[34]

The mood passed, and Dalton did not resign. For a time, however, other Labour ministers also considered leaving the Government on the coal issue, and there seemed a strong possibility that the Coalition might break up.[35] Meanwhile, interest shifted to proposals for the requisitioning of the mines.

The case for reorganisation (whether through state control or in some other way) had been strong enough to persuade the War Cabinet to set up a Committee to consider the question. On 20th April the Chairman of this Committee, Sir John Anderson, told colleagues that his aim was to consider 'objectively' the single question of how to increase output. The matter, however, was already too politically charged for objectivity. The miners were adamant: they wanted state control. 'Are we discussing this matter on the basis that the Govt. will requisition the industry for the period of the war?', demanded Arthur Horner, the miners' leader. 'If not they will get nowhere ... The men must feel that they are not working for the profit of the owners.' State control rapidly became the central issue.[36]

Dalton pushed hard for requisitioning. 'Our purpose is more coal', he told the Committee. 'This can only be got if we have the good will of the men. We must take this seriously into account.' There were arguments for state control which went beyond partisan politics, or even the long-held aspirations of the miners. The most powerful case was that direct government involvement would boost production by giving the miners, fearful of post-war unemployment, confidence in their own future. A number of leading Mines Department officials, including Lord Hyndley, held this view. To Dalton, however, requisitioning had an added, unspoken, advantage. As an M.P. for a mining constituency, he had witnessed at first hand the consequences of unmodified capitalism in the coalfields – the inefficiencies, the short-sighted flooding of the pits, the greedy indifference to miners' welfare. Like others on the Left, he regarded the coal-owners as 'a collection of hard-faced twisters'.[37] Together with Ernest Bevin, the Minister of Labour, Dalton believed that direct government control in wartime would be a step towards full nationalisation when the war was over. 'Both of us', Dalton recalled, 'were sure that, if the owners lost control of the pits now they would never get it back.'[38]

Yet the issue was complex. Backbench Tories and coal-owners were not the only people who resisted the plan to requisition. So did some of the miners' own leaders, who were divided among themselves. D. R. Grenfell, the Secretary for Mines, reflected the views of miners who felt that an attempt was being made to buy them off. Grenfell called for outright nationalisation on the lines of the London Passenger Transport Board, and doggedly fought anything that looked like a half-measure.[39] When, on 26th May, the Committee considered a paper by Dalton on 'Wartime Organisation of the Coal Industry' advocating requisitioning, Grenfell opposed. 'So this Welsh goat has now gone against Party policy both on requisition and rationing', Dalton wrote angrily. 'This should be let out.'[40]

Fortunately, Dalton had strong support elsewhere. Despite a divided view among the miners, most senior Labour ministers backed requisitioning. So did Sir Stafford Cripps, as Leader of the House. Nor were all leading Tories necessarily against. Hence it became possible to achieve a compromise, which gave substantial state control while stopping short of a complete take-over of the mines. The Committee accepted a scheme for Regional Controllers, with wide powers over the running of the mines, but without the financial implications of full requisitioning and without any interference with ownership. A White Paper issued at the beginning of June laid down the principle of 'dual control' – the state directing mining operations wherever necessary while the colliery owners continued to be responsible for the finance of the mines. Proposals put forward by Bevin for a National Coal Board and a National Wages Body were adopted. The Board was to include representatives of owners, miners, distributors and consumers, and was to be chaired by a minister in whom 'full control' of the industry would be vested. A Board of Investigation into Miners' Wages was set up (with a young statistician called Harold Wilson, a temporary civil servant in the Mines Department, as secretary). A fortnight later this Board recommended a flat-rate increase, a national minimum wage, and an output bonus. All were adopted.

The President considered that he had won on points. Under pressure from the 1922 Committee, and to satisfy Churchill who was himself influenced by Tory representations, Dalton gave up the struggle for fuel rationing. Rationing was relegated to an Annexe of the White Paper, postponed *sine die* and never introduced. The shelving of rationing was a victory for backbench Tories against the Government: the only occasion in the whole war that a Conservative revolt succeeded.[41] On the other hand, the sacrifice of one 'socialist' measure paved the way for the adoption of another. What had begun as a Whitehall debate about a hypothetical coal shortage ended with a significant move towards nationalisation of the mines. 'The state steps in', jeered Aneurin Bevan, 'not in substitution of private interests but as their guardian.'[42] Yet the measure of requisitioning introduced in 1942 greatly facilitated the transition to full state ownership a few years later. In addition, the miners obtained something they had been seeking for twenty years: the national minimum. Hence there was some justification for Dalton's claim that, in combination with Bevin, he had laid the foundation for a 'New Order in the Coalfields'.[43] At Party Conference in 1943, Will Lawther told delegates that Dalton and Bevin had done more for the mining industry than had any of their predecessors.[44]

Yet Dalton had been walking a tight-rope. Worries about 'miners' coal' and what Dalton called 'their traditional policy of "all or nowt"' had caused serious friction between the miners' leaders and Labour ministers during the negotiations. While Dalton pressed his Cabinet Committee colleagues to agree to direct state control, he knew that either the miners, or Tories within the Government, might harden their positions, that the miners might easily end up with nothing, that a fuel crisis might occur for which he would be held responsible, and that he might be forced by Labour pressure to resign. As it was, the miners only gradually came round to accepting the proposals, hoping until the last moment for something closer to full public ownership.

On 12th June a new Ministry of Fuel and Power was set up, replacing the Mines Department and taking coal away from the Board of Trade. Grenfell (who had taken an 'all or nowt' line) was dismissed, protesting, from the Government. Dalton was not sorry, either about what he regarded as a well-deserved punishment, or about his own loss of control of fuel. As Minister of Economic Warfare, he had bitterly resented moves to reduce his empire by taking away SO1. Now, his reaction at losing the Mines Department was one of intense relief. 'I wake today with no responsibility for coal', Dalton wrote. 'A most happy sensation!'[45]

What was the effect upon him of the coal dispute? Although at times he had felt deeply exasperated, the episode restored his belief in himself. It had been a fight in the open, in contrast to the narrow Whitehall battle over P.W.E. He emerged, despite his defeat over rationing, with his own standing both in the Government and in the Party enhanced.

Yet the dispute also left him with ambiguous feelings about fuel policy – and an impatient attitude towards the difficulties of fuel ministers. This was not the only occasion on which a fuel problem would assail him, as we shall see. In 1942 the problem was merely a risk. Five years later, as Chancellor of the Exchequer, he again had cause to draw attention to the danger of a fuel shortage. On that occasion, the threat would turn into a crippling reality.

Psychologically, the hiving-off of fuel in June 1942 was the major land-mark of Dalton's wartime career – dividing it even more sharply than his move to the Board of Trade in February. Hitherto, his life had been dominated by a series of overlapping crises. The incessant engagements of the Whitehall War had given him no chance to consider problems other than those of immediate interest to his department. After the summer of 1942 there was a change of pace, with more routine and hence greater opportunities for looking ahead. As a result, Dalton's remaining three years at the Board of Trade were in many ways the most influential and constructive that he spent in any office.

There were several reasons for the contrast. The most important was the changing nature of the war overseas (as distinct from the war in the corridors of power). The failure of Hitler to secure a quick victory over the Russians made an eventual Allied victory probable and a long war certain. Whitehall assumptions altered accordingly: short-run problems were no longer given the absolute priority which they had received while there was still a threat of invasion. A second reason was that most of Dalton's Board of Trade responsibilities related only indirectly to the conduct of the war. Hence Dalton was much less bothered than before by the interventions of the War Cabinet and Chiefs of Staff. A third reason was that Dalton no longer hoped for promotion within the Government. In his early, heady, days at M.E.W., he had imagined himself as head of a Service department, or even as Foreign Secretary. Now, given his unpopularity in the Conservative Party and his poor relationship with the Prime Minister, it was realistic to set aside such ambitions for the duration of the war. Consequently he worried less about his standing among colleagues, and concentrated on using his department as a base for unobtrusive forward planning.

The greatest advantage of the Board of Trade from the point of view of a President who wanted to exercise a wide influence was precisely the feature that made it bewildering to the outside observer – namely, its lack of coherence. 'I have now had just 8 months at B of T', Dalton noted in October 1942; '& have come to like, rather than resent, its infinite variety.'[46] His absolute powers were limited; few of his activities were not presided over by a watchful Cabinet Committee, dominated by suspicious Tories; the range of his responsibilities, furthermore, compelled a high degree of delegation. On the other hand, the breadth of his departmental interest gave him an excuse for involvement in almost every major domestic issue with an economic aspect. It was also, paradoxically, an advantage not to be in the War Cabinet: with a lighter administrative load, and fewer pressing commitments, he had more freedom of manoeuvre than was possible for some of his senior Labour colleagues.

Dalton received little credit for his most imaginative schemes. Although much of his work was well known to Parliament and the press, his most important activity was behind the scenes, receiving little or no publicity. His role in developing future policy was therefore ignored at the time, and the public saw him instead as the Minister of Controls – the man who gave and the man who took away.

'I was expected to provide more prams, more razor blades, more alarm clocks, more teacloths for pubs, more children's shoes', Dalton recalled; 'to prevent the prices of any of these being excessive; but not to issue too many Orders, or to have too many officials to enforce anything or to inspect anybody, lest this should seem to be "snooping" or "Gestapo".'[47] Backbench M.P.s constantly pursued him over shortages in their constituencies. Once he had to reply to a complaint that a lady constituent had tried in eight different shops to get an outsize corset. Gallantly, he responded with an order for an increase in the production of undergarments for the larger woman.[48]

Despite its contradictions, the job of controlling consumption fitted in well with Dalton's political beliefs. He approved of rationing everyday goods, just as he approved of rationing fuel. Distributing limited stocks fairly, and ensuring that the poor did not have to pay too much for them, seemed to the author of *The Inequality of Incomes* an excellent short-term alternative to the redistribution of wealth. 'If we had not rationing and controls', he explained to a union conference in 1943, 'the rich would have scooped the pool and there would be a lot of nakedness in Britain'.[49] Dalton's experience of rationing undoubtedly influenced him later as Chancellor – encouraging in him a belief not only in the practical advantages of running the economy on the basis of physical controls, but also in the moral desirability of doing so.

Remarks about preventing the rich from 'scooping the pool' did not, however, endear him either to the Tories or to the Tory-owned press. A myth developed (containing, indeed, an element of truth) that imposing controls was an activity which gave the President of the

Board of Trade perverse pleasure. As a result, Dalton became a scape-goat for those who most resented the red tape and bureaucracy which the war had created.

The belief that Dalton performed his duties with an excess of zeal was encouraged by a sharp increase in restrictions on consumer goods which immediately followed his appointment. In the spring of 1942 Dalton announced the reduction of the clothing ration by a quarter. In the summer, he ordered that the production of some items should cease altogether in order to save vital materials.[50] ('Umbrellas?' he wrote in a typical departmental minute. 'I never carry one. Why go on producing them?')[51] Meanwhile, he also introduced 'utility' models for furniture and household goods. The reason for these restrictions was the added economic strain imposed by the Japanese advance in the Far East. The minister whose duty it was to impose them, however, frequently got the blame.

One objection was that, while controls in general might be neces-sary, their location was often arbitrary. Here some of Dalton's public pronouncements did not help his cause. The decision which produced most uproar – because of its apparent pettiness – was an edict banning trouser turn-ups in order to save cloth. 'There can be no equality of sacrifice in this war', Dalton told a press conference, unwisely. 'Some must lose lives and limbs; others only the turn-ups on their trousers.'[52] There was an outburst of anger in the press, and one London magis-trate deliberately inflicted nominal penalties on people convicted of breaking what was widely regarded as an absurd regulation.[53] Other ministerial admonitions and slogans – revealing Dalton at his school-masterly worst – were also poorly received. On one occasion the President of the Board of Trade called for 'patches for patriotism',[54] on another he declared that 'More darns in your socks means more bombs on Germany'.[55] On yet another, displaying a surprising ignorance of the lives of ordinary citizens, he advised the public that 'it is wrong and out of date to be ashamed of wearing flannel trousers to the office, or wearing country clothes in town'.

Dalton's biggest public relations blunder occurred when he was opening a 'Count Your Coupons' Exhibition at Charing Cross Underground station in March 1943. In what was intended as a grand gesture of self-denial, he gave a pledge 'not to buy a new suit of clothes until the war is over'.[56] It was an undertaking he soon regretted. A member of the Chamber of Trade asked if he would be prepared to address the House of Commons without a collar and tie. 'Why not?', he defended himself. 'In warm weather, why not do without socks and collar and tie? A great number of women go without stockings in summer and even in winter. When they wear slacks they go without socks.' This was too much for the Beaverbrook-owned *Daily Express*. 'If Dr. Dalton will come to the House of Commons with a large red patch on the seat of his black pants', its political columnist declared, 'I will endeavour to have his picture published free in this newspaper – rear view only.'[57]

Perhaps the job of convincing the public of the moral virtue of austerity required an ascetic (such as Cripps) rather than an obvious hedonist like Dalton. Nevertheless, the attacks were caused by more than dislike of shortages or the President's own ill-judged remarks. They reflected a hotting up of the political war. If the fuel rationing battle marked the first major departure from the political truce, attacks on Dalton over the rationing of consumer goods became an anti-Labour guerrilla campaign, waged with increasing ferocity as military victory approached. Supposedly inessential controls were turned into a symbol of Labour's allegedly excessive influence in the Coalition. The view was widely held (and apparently shared by Churchill) that socialists at the Board of Trade were imposing more regulations than were absolutely necessary. At the end of 1943 the *New Statesman* condemned the Beaverbrook press for 'a vendetta against Hugh Dalton' on the issue.[58] Eighteen months later the *Daily Herald* pointed out that the President of the Board of Trade had had to suffer an unremitting flow of leading articles and cartoons all suggesting that 'while [Dalton] robs our women of their corsets, he strives without ceasing to imprison the world of commerce in a veritable strait-jacket of superfluous Orders and Regulations and Taboos'.[59]

To be the butt of Tory jibes probably did Dalton some good among Labour supporters. More widely, however, the attacks created a public image which he never entirely shook off. After the war he was often crudely presented in the popular press as a Chancellor who imposed unnecessary controls and taxation out of a kind of devilment. This reputation had its origins during his wartime period at the Board of Trade.

Dalton was not greatly bothered by press attacks. (Part of the trouble was that he seemed to relish them.) He was in any case much more interested in aspects of his work which were unrelated to short-term problems on the home front. Rationing, control over supplies, the concentration of industry to ease manpower shortages – these were routine matters at the Board of Trade. Sometimes they pressed upon the President, forcing him to attend to a mass of detail which, as he put it, blocked 'the vistas towards the brave new post-war world'. But it was these vistas which concerned him most, and he turned to them whenever he had the opportunity. He had discovered that, in hectic wartime conditions, it made sense to concentrate upon the future. It was hard to get concessions from powerful Conservative colleagues, influenced by a watchful 1922 Committee in a Tory-dominated House, on matters of immediate interest. Concessions made on tick were more easy to obtain.

Dalton's attitude was one of prudent determination. He was aware of both the opportunities and the constraints of the Coalition. He wanted Labour to seize its chance to the full, while avoiding self-destructive gestures. He never ceased to worry about the delicacy of Labour's position, and the danger that at any moment the Government might collapse. If this happened, he calculated, and a general election were held, an overwhelming Conservative victory and a one-party administration would follow. Hence he deplored pin-prick rebellions by the Labour Opposition in Parliament, and he sharply condemned talk of ending the Electoral Truce.

Emanuel Shinwell, leader of those on the Opposition benches who wished to make life hard for the Government, was his special bugbear. Dalton regarded the Member for Easington as a dangerous, destructive force. 'Master Shinwell has been rushing about with a maniacal glint in his eye', he wrote on one occasion. 'He reminds me of the chap who was determined to set fire to the house and burn it down for his own delight.' Shinwell's apparent desire for a conflagration carried the serious risk that all Labour influence within the Coalition might be removed.

Dalton's attitude was partly determined by a feeling that his own time in government was likely to be short. 'Attain the Elder Statesman-like age of 55', he wrote on his birthday in August 1942. Although he was fit and energetic, he knew that his political life could not go on for ever. Despite his thoughts of resignation in moments of frustration or despair, office remained dear to him. When Irene Noel-Baker told him that Philip was thinking of retiring to become a 'publicist', Dalton was dismissive. Only ministers, he said, counted for much. Both he and Noel-Baker would only be serious contenders for power at one more election. If that was lost, 'we should be too old, by the time the next one came, to do much.' The problem of how to stay in government, and to ensure that the next election, whenever it came, did not push Labour back into Opposition, was therefore a pressing one.

Dalton, however, was not only pessimistic about Labour's chances in a snap wartime election. He also took for granted that Churchill would sweep the country if a 'khaki' election were fought on party lines as soon as victory had been won. This was, at the time, a rational assumption (in view of the lack of credence given to opinion polls) and it was widely shared. Labour had never controlled the Commons. Its biggest ever percentage of the vote, in 1935, still left the Conservatives with a huge overall majority. Above all, it was reasonable to expect that Churchill's prestige when the war ended would be as great as Lloyd George's had been in 1918.

What was the answer? Dalton had no interest in joining a peacetime Coalition on 1918 or 1931 lines. He would not take a Tory 'coupon' even if such a thing were offered. However, a continuation of the wartime Coalition, fully backed by the Labour Party, might be another matter. The most serious danger was an election during the period of victory euphoria. As Dalton explained at a *New Statesman* lunch, Labour stood little chance if it 'merely arranged for a duel between itself and the present Prime Minister while he stood at or near the highest pinnacle of his fame.'

Hence Dalton backed the idea of an election at the end of the war in which the parties pulled their punches. 'Government' candidates from the Conservatives, Liberals and Labour would oppose each other in the same constituency, 'varying their emphasis upon one common programme'. Ministers would abstain from speaking, and be returned unopposed.[60] The Coalition would then re-form itself, presumably under Churchill's premiership, as soon as a new Parliament had been elected.

This idea had some currency in both Labour and Tory circles in 1943. Bevin showed interest. So did Morrison. Chuter Ede noted in May that Morrison had been creating perturbation among local party workers in the North East with remarks 'which seemed to fore-shadow a post-war coalition'.[61] Harvie Watt, Churchill's P.P.S., told Dalton that the Prime Minister wanted the Coalition to carry on so as to shape the post-war years. Lord Winterton indicated that Dalton's scheme had the support of the pro-planning Conservative Reform Committee. 'Tory and Socialist candidates would all support the Government', Winterton suggested, 'but the Tories would chide the Socialists with having voted against arms before the war, and Socialists would chide Tories as having been Men of Munich'. Yet another supporter on the Conservative side was Lord Halifax who had heard of the scheme from Morrison and liked it.

But the plan never got beyond the speculative stage. Early in 1944 it became clear that Labour rank-and-file pressure for a straight-forward inter-party fight could not be resisted. In October the N.E.C. felt compelled to issue a statement to this effect. Dalton therefore switched tack. He saw two possibilities. One (suggested by Morrison) was to urge that the election be delayed until after military victory in the Far East, in order to allow time for patriotic pro-Churchill fervour to calm down. The second was that Labour should rejoin the Coalition once the election, fought on traditional lines, was over. Dalton favoured a combination of both. After the D-Day landings (when a quick German collapse seemed likely), he agreed with Attlee that, if possible, the election should be postponed and that it would be best 'if then we could separate from the Tories without too fierce a quarrel'.

As the war dragged on longer than expected, chances of delaying the election or reconvening the Coalition faded. But Dalton still clung to the hope. In September 1944 he again pressed on Harvie Watt the case for 'a new Coalition', after an election; and in November he urged the Prime Minister personally to maintain the Coalition in its present form if, when the war ended, 'we were in mid-Session and Parliament was engaged in passing good Bills'. When, at the end of 1944, Party Conference came down firmly for fighting the next election as an independent party, Dalton expressed relief that no pledge was given against a Coalition once the election was over. Right to the end he continued to push for as long a gap before the election as possible, retaining to the day of the actual election result an unshaken belief that the Conservatives would win with a large majority.[62] 'Dalton was totally at one with Churchill in believing that the National interest required the continuation of the Coalition under Churchill into the period of post-war reconstruction', Thomas Fraser, Dalton's P.P.S. in the last months of the Government, recalled. 'He believed that the electors would rally behind Churchill in the coming election and the Labour Party would be cast into the wilderness for another generation.'[63]

The assumption that Labour would lose any inter-party electoral contest that took place either during the war or in its immediate aftermath provided a basis for all Dalton's wartime calculations. It was not a matter of regarding the Coalition as a second best: the Coalition offered Labour much more than it had ever had before (even in 1924 and 1929–31) or was likely to get when the war ended. The world was changing fast and such an opportunity might never come again. The task, therefore, was not to rock the Coalition boat but to seek, by skilful politicking, to push the Tories as far as they would go.

In the struggle between Labour and Conservative Coalition partners, both moved cautiously. It was a poker game. Who valued the Coalition most? Labour had put Churchill into office; he was still resented by some Tory M.P.s; if the Coalition broke up, he would be vulnerable. Labour ministers had to calculate their value to the Prime Minister against the Prime Minister's assessment of his own strength. At the same time both sides felt the pressure of their backbenches and grass roots – in favour of social reform or against it.[64]

In this game Dalton developed his own techniques. One was to route his demands through Labour members of the War Cabinet (especially Attlee). Another was to encourage the setting up of inno-cent-sounding interdepartmental committees; to get one of his (social-ist) temporaries to submit a well-researched paper outlining his plans; and then to rally sympathetic ministerial and official opinion in sup-port. A third technique was to galvanise the Labour Party outside the Government into action. Here the N.E.C. and its sub-committees played a part. Using his special access to official information, Dalton would write a policy document on a matter that concerned him and get it issued in the Party's name. Then he would point to this official Party declaration and claim, in the inner counsels of the Government, to be responding to a united Labour demand.

There were many Labour Party policies produced by N.E.C. com-mittees, supposedly providing a programme for an alternative Government after the war, which were actually meant as bargaining counters to strengthen the hands of Labour ministers in the Govern-ment that currently existed. Such policies took existing Government machinery for granted – and in so doing departed from pre-war Labour assumptions. After the 1931 débâcle the Party had started again from scratch. Policy documents in the early 1930s (and Dalton's *Practical Socialism* which was based upon them) assumed that to turn a laissez-faire economy into a socialist one the first step must be to refashion government itself. New committees must be set up, Cabinet business must be streamlined and 'planning' must be introduced. Now attitudes were different. Deep involvement in administration and a desire to retain the Coalition encouraged Labour ministers to think in terms not of smashing the system, but of using it.

As a result the Labour programme that emerged between 1943 and 1945, based on policies which Dalton had a major part in framing, bore the mark of the wartime administration and its requirements as much as of earlier Labour Party thinking. In theory, the election mani-festo that was eventually hammered out of this programme offered a fundamental alternative, a dramatic break with the past. In reality, the break with the past had already occurred: Labour's manifesto reflected no more than the official position of the progressive wing of an essentially harmonious Coalition, and differed more in emphasis than in substance from the approach accepted by the whole Govern-ment. The aim was not to antagonise or confront the Conservatives, so much as to influence and persuade them. Here, inevitably, there was a gulf between Labour M.P.s who were members of the Government, and those who were not. Dalton became increasingly impatient with the latter. In July 1943 he confronted angry backbenchers who wanted to stiffen the Labour element in the Coalition:

> PLP Meeting, at which much incredibly loose talk and rubbishy rhetoric is released on the need for planning – i.e., the setting up of one Minister to deal with everything. These fools have just no sense at all of what Government means, or what are either the inter-relations of Ministers or the proper limits of what any one Minister can do.[65]

Before the war, Dalton had spoken and written much on the subject of planning. He did not abandon his earlier ideas. His view of planning, however, did not greatly differ from the planning which already existed in the war economy – a kind of planning which he had come to understand and appreciate as one of the ministers most closely involved. He believed that such planning should be extended and given a more radical purpose. For the time being, however, he thought, not in terms of transforming the instruments of wartime control, but in terms of maintaining them. And while the war continued he discovered just how effectively they could be used.

In addition to Coalition poker, there was Labour rummy. The power game which had dominated and distracted the politics of the Left for most of the 1930s was dampened by the national crisis. But it did not disappear. After an initial dip, partly caused by conscription, a huge increase in individual party membership brought a new, sharper radicalism. Meanwhile there was a jockeying for position at the top.

Though the mood in the Labour Party was affected by rank-and-file revival, it was some time before the parliamentary leadership felt its direct impact. The pecking order in 1945 remained much as it had been in 1939. Ernest Bevin, brought into Parliament and Government from the trade union movement as Minister of Labour, immediately assumed a commanding role. Arthur Greenwood was dropped by Churchill in 1942 and never recovered his former standing. But the relative positions of Attlee (still with little of the aura of a 'Leader' about him) and of Dalton, Morrison and Alexander, were barely altered by the war. Sir Stafford Cripps, though outside the Labour Party, retained his hold on an important section of Labour opinion.

One reason for immobility among the top leadership was that there had been very few new recruits to the P.L.P. since 1929. Most of the seats regained in 1935 went to politicians who, like Dalton, had lost unexpectedly four years before: it was a small Party, and by the early 1940s an ageing one, set in its ways. Another reason was that Labour's involvement in the Coalition had a fossilising effect. Churchill had picked the Movement's most important political leaders in 1940 and there was little adjustment to the Labour contingent in the Government thereafter. With a few notable exceptions once-prominent people who remained on the backbenches were gradually eclipsed while those in office gained in prestige.

Though the hierarchy stayed the same, Labour leaders were greatly influenced by their experience of office – gaining a sense of what government, at its most flexible, could achieve and what it could not. No less important for the politics of the 1945 administration, their relations with each other were much affected by working together in the intense wartime conditions, and by the alliances and rivalries which a minority status in the Coalition encouraged.

At M.E.W., Dalton had had little contact with other Labour ministers, most of whom had domestic portfolios. At the Board of Trade, where his own interests were mainly on the home front, dealings were much closer. As a result, he came to revise some of his pre-war opinions. His respect for Bevin grew and his regard for Morrison diminished. He did not abandon his earlier contempt for Attlee, whose 'accidental' prominence he still resented; yet he found himself relying on the Party Leader, to an increasing degree, as a political shop steward. There was also a significant shift in his attitude towards Sir Stafford Cripps.

Dalton's wartime perception of Cripps had three components. One was a realisation of Cripps's bewitching effect on public opinion, and hence of the need to make a treaty; the second was resentment of Cripps's success and prominence; the third was a revived fear of his ambition. Cripps's political judgment in the past had been disastrously wrong; but it had also on occasion been brilliantly right. In June 1939, a few months after his expulsion from the Labour Party, Cripps made a prediction which showed how far he was ahead of his former colleagues. 'I don't think that "party politics" in the old sense will have any meaning in this country for a very long time to come', he wrote to his aunt, Beatrice Webb. 'They are discredited and useless as a means of directing policies in times like these.'[66] By removing Cripps from the Labour Party, Dalton and the Party establishment had believed that they were neutralising him as a political force. In fact they provided him with his opportunity. In the new conditions to be an outsider was a strength. Cripps ceased to be the spokesman of a Labour Party faction. He became the voice of national conscience – the Churchill of the Left.

Shortly after the Coalition was formed the new War Cabinet decided to send Cripps to Moscow on a special mission. Dalton was appalled, and made his views known. First he tried to kill the plan by questioning

25 Ruth in the garden at West Leaze, August 1935.

26 (*left*) Evan Durbin in 1937. 27 (*right*) Sir Robert Vansittart (P.U.S. at the Foreign Office) and Anthony Eden (Foreign Secretary) in March 1936.

28 'Hugh Dalton paced like a caged panther beneath the lounges of the Highcliffe Hotel.' Button-holing James Walker, a union member of the N.E.C., at Bournemouth in May 1940.

With exiled Poles in Scotland, December 1940:
29 (*above*) Christmas meal. Fourth from left, S.O.E. officer Colin Gubbins.
30 (*below*) Inspecting Polish troops with General Sikorski at Forfar on Christmas Eve.

31 (*left*) When Brendan Bracken said, 'Dalton was the biggest bloodiest shit I've ever met!' Churchill laughed. The Prime Minister with Bracken, 1940.

32 (*below*) Ruth, as Chairman of the L.C.C. Parks Committee, uses an oxy-acetylene cutter to remove iron railings in Lincoln's Inn Fields for scrap (February 1941).

33 'Trying Out the Dalton Plan.' Lampoon of Dalton's 'patches for patriotism' campaign, March 1943.

34 Speaking at Party Conference in Blackpool, May 1945.

35 (*left*) Attlee submits his list of Ministers to King George VI, August 1945.

36 (*below*) Ernest Bevin and Herbert Morrison compare notes at Blackpool, May 1945.

37 (*opposite above*) ' ... [B]y far the least attractive member of the Government, always looking round for someone to whom to pass the blame.' Emanuel Shinwell (Fuel and Power) inspects a model mine at a London exhibition in September 1947, accompanied by Lord Hyndley (Chairman of the National Coal Board), Aneurin Bevan (Health), George Isaacs (Labour) and a Motherwell miner.

38 (*opposite below*) 'Cripps is very much concerned about him, both as to health and as to capacity to tackle – or really to understand – this new Planning job.' The Lord President and the President of the Board of Trade greet each other after Sunday morning service at Margate Parish Church, May 1947.

39 'He lacked the gift of ultimate gravitas; or, alternatively, he was not a ruthless enough crook.'

Cripps's suitability. 'On purely legal issues he is first class', Dalton wrote to the War Cabinet on 18th May, 'but as soon as politics begin to colour any problem his judgment and his sense of proportion are apt to forsake him. Nor, as I have reason to know, in the light of considerable experience of him, is he a good worker in a team. Even if he were sent out with clearly defined instructions, I am inclined to think that he would return with some plan of his own which went far beyond them and, if this were not at once accepted by H.M.G., he would make heavy public trouble.'[67]

When this tactic failed, Dalton persuaded Lord Halifax, the Foreign Secretary, to deny Cripps the power to make a settlement of his own. ' ... [I]f it goes wrong', he told the Cabinet after the mission had been agreed, 'don't blame me.' From his own point of view he saw only one advantage: sending Cripps to Russia would keep him out of the way.[68]

Dalton's warning turned out to be justified. Cripps did little to improve Anglo-Soviet relations. However, through being ambassador-in-situ when the Germans invaded, he was widely credited with the Anglo-Soviet alliance of July 1941, and even with having brought Russia into the war. This gave him an importance in British domestic politics which he did not fail to exploit. Against a background of growing public acclaim, he urged the War Cabinet to give more whole-hearted support to the Soviets – even threatening to resign on the issue. 'Cripps is evidently preparing his case against us', Churchill commented to Eden.[69] On 23rd January 1942 the ambassador returned to Britain in evangelical mood and confronted the Government. It was a familiar pose: the man of principle, ready to sacrifice all. Churchill offered him the Ministry of Supply outside the War Cabinet. Cripps declined.

On 8th February Cripps delivered a radio talk in which he made a stinging attack on the feebleness of the British war effort by comparison with that of the Russians. Coming at a time when the war was going particularly badly, the impact was immense. Cripps's national standing, already great, was further enhanced. People began to talk of him as a possible successor to the Prime Minister. On 23rd February, Cripps was made a member of the War Cabinet as Lord Privy Seal in the reshuffle that shifted Dalton from M.E.W. to the Board of Trade.

Dalton regarded Cripps's progress sourly. When the returning ambassador turned down the offer of Supply, Dalton was cheered by Gaitskell's remark that 'it looks as though he is just as big a fool as ever in domestic politics'. Later Dalton tried to forestall plans to bring Cripps into the War Cabinet by telling Churchill's P.P.S. that there was a strong feeling against Cripps in trade union circles. When

Cripps was made Lord Privy Seal, Dalton noted evenly that 'if things go badly for a few months, his stock, now artificially inflated, will fall heavily and he will have to bear a large part of the responsibility.'[70]

Would Cripps be a help or a hindrance, now that he had been given such an influential position? Dalton rapidly discovered, much to his surprise, that Cripps was prepared to be helpful. Although Cripps was not in the Labour Party he needed allies. On matters ranging from India to domestic planning, his outlook remained progressive. Hence allies were more readily available on the Left than on the Right. During his first few months at the Board of Trade Dalton had reason to be grateful for Cripps's determined support over coal rationing and reorganisation. 'Stafford and I have been together on this', Dalton wrote to Beatrice Webb in June.[71] Gradually, Dalton began to view his old rival in a new light. 'I have the impression that [Attlee] is seeing less of the P.M., while C[ripps] is seeing more', he noted. It was an important consideration.

Meanwhile Cripps worked to establish himself as a War Leader to replace Churchill, whose reputation, as reverse followed reverse, was reaching its lowest point of the whole war. Some suspected that Cripps's interest in fuel rationing was motivated by a desire to find reasons for challenging the Prime Minister's authority. Bevin, who always distrusted Cripps, thought so. He told Dalton at the end of May 1942 that Cripps 'was very anxious to get an excuse to resign' and fuel seemed to be providing one. In August, when fuel was no longer a Board of Trade matter, Dalton's young protégé, Christopher Mayhew, who had known Cripps's son John at Oxford, spent an evening with the Cripps family. Afterwards Mayhew described the occasion to Dalton. Dalton concluded that Cripps might be a useful ally, but still needed to be watched:

[Mayhew] was the only outsider present. The rest were Cripps, his wife, son, Personal Assistant (David Owen) and some other hangers-on. The whole conversation was whether Cripps should resign or not and if, as Cripps appeared to take for granted, the P.M. fell, who should succeed him and what Cripps should do in that event. Should he or should he not serve under Eden? This was discussed at great length. I said to C.M[ayhew] that it all sounded a most nauseating, egoising performance, and quite remote, in nearly all its calculations, from probabilities ... There was no reason at all why the P.M. should fall; there was nobody to take his place; even if he met with an accident, I did not for a moment believe that either Eden or Cripps would be asked to replace him, but much more probably Anderson ...[72]

Beatrice Webb wrote in October: 'Stafford expects that he would succeed Churchill as Prime Minister.'[73] But the opportunity, if such it was, soon passed. Anglo-American landings in French North Africa and victory at Alamein marked the turning-point of the war. Fickle public opinion, which had moved away from Churchill a few months before, embraced him once again. Criticism of the Government's leadership faded away, much to Dalton's relief. ' ... Crazy Cripps will have to think again about the prospect of the P.M. falling from power', he noted, 'and find some new excuse for his own resignation from the Government.'

Cripps did not resign. Instead he was pushed ignominiously out of the War Cabinet and demoted to Minister of Air Production by a Prime Minister whose confidence was now restored. Dalton was delighted. His hopes had been fulfilled. 'Nearly all Cripps's "mystique" is now gone', he wrote, 'and he has missed all his chances – never really very good – of resigning with credit ... seldom has anyone's political stock, having been so outrageously and unjustifiably over-valued, fallen so fast and so far.'

Dalton did not discount Cripps. But for the time being Cripps mattered less. So Dalton switched his attention to Herbert Morrison, who had been moved into the War Cabinet in November 1942 to take Cripps's place. Dalton learnt from Ellen Wilkinson that Morrison was taking an interest in post-war problems. Morrison was Home Secretary and Minister for Home Security. Such was his standing in the government and in the Labour Party that it was essential to work with him.

Once again, there were fences to mend. Dalton had never been an enemy of Morrison, as he had been of Cripps. In the 1930s they had often been friends. Their relations had, however, been tarnished by a recent betrayal. Morrison resented Dalton's desertion to the Greenwood camp in 1939 when an attempt had been made to replace Attlee. To heal the wound, Dalton needed to show that his loyalty was restored. He calculated (correctly as it turned out) that Morrison intended to make a bid for the Party Leadership at the end of the war, if not sooner. He decided therefore to buy Morrison's support in the War Cabinet for his own post-war policies by giving the impression that such a bid would have his support.

Up to a point the tactic worked. In December 1942 Dalton asked Ellen Wilkinson to arrange a private dinner for himself and Morrison. All went well. 'We talk pretty frankly about persons in the Party', Dalton recorded, 'and I repeat, deliberately, though quite casually in the course of the conversation, that it is not part of my ambition to be the Leader of the Party.' This old ploy, first used before the Leadership contest in 1935, seemed to have its intended effect. In March 1943 Dalton noted that Morrison was now treating him as a close ally, which was all to the good.[74]

Morrison had a pressing reason for courting Dalton. Shortly after the 1942 Labour Party Conference, the Party Treasurer, George Lathan, had died – leaving a vacancy which was due to be filled in June 1943. The Treasurership had no importance in itself. The contest acquired a symbolic significance because Morrison chose to see it as a marker for another, more crucial, succession. Winning the Treasurership would be a logical step towards establishing his claim to Party Leadership when Attlee – whom many continued to regard as 'temporary' – eventually departed.

There were two other contenders for the Treasurership: William Glenvil Hall, nominated by the Miners; and Arthur Greenwood. Morrison was backed by a number of important unions but not by Ernest Bevin who was 'animated by a venomous hatred' against him.[75] Morrison, however, now had the support of Dalton who, as part of their unspoken deal, switched back again from Greenwood and put all his weight behind Morrison.

Before the 1943 Party Conference it became clear that because of Bevin's partisanship Greenwood would be ahead after the first ballot. Would there be a second vote? The Treasurership had never before been so hotly pursued and there was some uncertainty about the voting system. Was it first past the post, or exhaustive ballot? The question was crucial because there was a good chance that the Miners' vote might swing to Morrison if there was a run-off between him and Greenwood. Dalton plotted vigorously to bring this about. Unlike Bevin, however, Dalton did not have a large trade union vote in his pocket, and his attempt failed. Despite the lack of an overall majority, Greenwood's election was confirmed after only one ballot. Morrison was sore. This was the third time, he told Dalton, that the Party had turned him down, 'for the Leadership in 1935, for the Secretaryship, through imposing the ban on its being held by an M.P., and now this'.[76] Dalton also had reason to be sorry. The defeat meant that for the time being Morrison's need for Dalton's support was greatly reduced. Neither did Morrison have much reason to feel grateful. Dalton had helped to bring about one of his three Party defeats (over the Labour Party Secretaryship); and had failed, as his campaign manager, to prevent the other two. So talk of a close Morrison-Dalton alliance ceased.

Morrison's defeat was a reminder of where power really lay. Greenwood's election as Treasurer was a victory, not so much for Greenwood himself who did not count, as for Ernest Bevin. Bevin's tough directness and his ability to get his own way in union affairs had already earned him the respect of leading Tories, including the Prime Minister, making him Labour's most powerful representative in the War Cabinet. Now he had shown his ability to dominate a Labour Party election simply by instructing the T.G.W.U. delegates to vote for Greenwood.[77]

Dalton continued to need Morrison's co-operation. It was clear, however, that he needed to co-operate with Bevin, Morrison's arch-enemy, even more. As Dalton's interest in the location of industry increased, so his need to work with the Minister of Labour grew also. Hence in the months that followed Dalton set about courting the most influential and least tractable animal in Labour's political jungle.

Dalton and Bevin had been allies over rearmament before the war, but their relations had never been easy. Bevin was not accustomed to intimacy with middle-class politicians. Dalton found communication difficult. He was maddened by Bevin's habit of dominating meetings with rambling monologues ('the General Council's disease'). 'E.B. talks nearly all the time', he noted after one such session in the early days of the Government. 'He will have to learn to be snappier.'[78]

Yet Dalton was also fascinated by Bevin's style, impressed by his intellectual grasp, and rather afraid of him. Dalton behaved towards the Prime Minister and the Minister of Labour in strikingly similar ways. With both there was the same anxious deference and eagerness to please. Just as Dalton addressed Churchill in an heroic, mock-Churchillian style which he imagined the Prime Minister liked, so he approached Bevin in Labour Movementese. This was in contrast to his dealings with Cripps, Attlee or even Morrison, with all of whom (regardless of his private thoughts) he felt socially relaxed.

Bevin's attitude to Dalton combined suspicion of Dalton's ambitions, personal indifference and a high degree of agreement on domestic policy. To Dalton's great relief, Bevin turned out to be particularly helpful in the most important field in which their responsibilities overlapped: the location of industry. The Minister of Labour showed himself willing to discuss every problem in detail and instructed his officials to co-operate fully.[79] Dalton wooed and coaxed – but inducements were unnecessary. Bevin was entirely on his side. 'He is by far my best ally on Development Areas, as on a number of other things', Dalton recorded in July 1944. 'It is indispensable that he and I should play ball together, even if he is sometimes tiresome, long-winded and inattentive!'

Nevertheless, there was a price. The more Dalton played ball with Bevin, working with him to bring about the industrial location policies they both desired, the harder it was to play with Morrison, because of the intense hostility that existed between the two men. Bevin, consistently and ferociously, hated Morrison and regarded with suspicion anyone who supported him. This problem of personalities was difficult. Dalton, however, knew where his main interests lay. At a meeting of Labour's big four (Attlee, Bevin, Dalton and Morrison) in November 1944, Morrison proposed submitting to Coalition colleagues a paper on the Government's attitude to industry. Bevin poured cold water on the scheme and Dalton eagerly followed suit. 'This incident', Dalton wrote afterwards, 'I can see, helps my relations with E.B., and the reverse with H.M.; however, that can't be helped for the moment and E.B. is much more use than H.M. on all the things I care most about.'[80]

There was no breach with Morrison and no closeness to Bevin – just a shift in emphasis. By supporting Morrison over the Treasurership, Dalton had implicitly backed him as a successor to Attlee. Now he quietly pulled back. In May 1945 at Party Conference in Blackpool Ellen Wilkinson suggested to Dalton that Attlee should make way for Morrison before the election. Dalton replied that this was out of the question. For one thing, he said, the timing was impossible. For another, Morrison was no longer the inevitable successor. Many M.P.s, he now considered, would prefer Bevin.[81]

Dalton's alliance with Bevin paid immediate dividends. In Cabinet battles over the location of industry, the Minister of Labour was an invaluable supporter. The issue was only narrowly won, and without Bevin's help it might have been lost. Yet by the time the Coalition broke up, the old adage that there were no friends at the top was more true of Dalton's relations with senior colleagues than ever. Bevin remained an enigma: with a solid industrial base he needed no firm parliamentary allies and he continued to stand aloof from the career politicians. Suspicion clouded Dalton's dealings with his most natural associate, Morrison. Cripps had no reason to forgive or forget what Dalton had done to him in 1939. Attlee, who had fought many battles on Dalton's behalf, had received little evidence of gratitude or loyalty in return. None had any reason to feel friendship towards Dalton. All had grounds for believing that, if circumstances dictated, he would turn against them.

XXII

Pig

Dalton's moods related to his causes, his department and his career. When he was elated or upset, this was because of a triumph or reverse in his official life. At the same time, his 'loneliness in a crowd', his strange, bunker-like existence, took its toll. His relations with civil servants were never as bad as at the Board of Trade. It was as though, during the years apart from Ruth, a veil separated him from the emotions of subordinates.

At the Foreign Office in 1929–31, he had been known for his tirades.[1] More recently at M.E.W. and S.O.E., the rapid swings from exuberance to melancholy, the great thunderclaps of rage when he was crossed,[2] had caused some staff to dislike him. Most, however, had seen his bullying and aggression as necessary ingredients of a war-winning spirit. At the Board of Trade, by contrast, admirers were few and officials who were exasperated or offended were many.

An inability to gain civil service approval is not evidence of failure or inadequacy. It may be the reverse. Once again – as when Dalton served under Arthur Henderson – we need to distinguish between behaviour that was bad and possibly counter-productive, caused by private unhappiness or, as officials believed, by defects of character; and behaviour which was part of a political style that reaped results. More than in any other office, Dalton seems to have combined both at the Board of Trade. At no other time in his governmental career did he appear so irascible and self-centred, causing advisers who might have respected him to regard his Presidency as a penance to be suffered. Yet his remarkable success as a reforming President may have owed something, at least, to the abrasive style which many civil servants found objectionable.

Dalton's difficulties with Board of Trade staff began at the top. His relationship with the Permanent Secretary, Sir Arnold Overton, got off to a bad start and sharply deteriorated thereafter. 'Chemical antipathy', was how one civil servant described it. 'Overton was a caricature of a Wykehamist. Dalton was a caricature of an Etonian.'[3] The combination was explosive: the cautious and unbending mandarin with his armoury of precedent and procedure, and the volatile politician, no respecter of persons. Gaitskell summed up Overton at the beginning of 1942: ' ... [V]ery much inclined to keep things under his grasp and superficially at least, not very intelligent', adding damningly that the Permanent Secretary was 'by no means of the calibre required for a job of this character'.[4] 'Overton was not an initiator', recalls one former colleague.[5] 'He was negative', admits another.[6] 'No, No, No, said A.E.O.', satirised Douglas Jay.[7] Dalton never had reason to disagree. Before leaving the Board he urged for the sake of his successor that Overton should be transferred to another department.[8]

Dalton got on better with the Deputy Secretary, Sir Percivale Liesching. Where Overton withdrew into his shell, nursing a private resentment, Liesching stayed his ground. 'Dalton shouted at Liesching', the economist James Meade, temporarily employed at the Board, recalls: 'Liesching would argue back, sensing when the President had made up his mind. Then you would not hear another word – until the battle started again over the best way to carry the policy out.'[9] Liesching earned Dalton's grudging respect. 'A bit of a Tory no doubt and a little solemn', the President commented. 'But good brains and a good Whitehall reputation.'[10]

Dalton's image of his staff was, however, based more on the No. 1 than the No. 2. The President came to see his department as a bureaucratic mule, obstinately inert unless kicked and beaten into action. 'This morning I explode over the incident of the draft of the Location paper ... ', he wrote in a typical diary entry. 'I am very fed up with most of my officials on this subject. They give the impression of wanting to dodge future responsibilities. They have no "fire in their belly" over this.'[11]

Among Board of Trade staff, the main cause for resentment was the impression Dalton gave of insensitivity. There was also the common accusation – made at other times, but seldom with such passion – that he was a bully. 'He regarded the department as a machine', recalls one former official, ' – a collection of cogs – rather than a team of human beings, all anxious and working desperately hard to help him do his job.'[12] Another felt that he confused civil servants with domestic servants,[13] a proposition which neatly reversed Dalton's oft-expressed opinion that civil servants behaved like civil masters.

For G. C. Allen, a wartime temporary responsible for a study of areas of high unemployment, a subject that greatly concerned the President, the memory is still vivid:

> Of the four Ministers with whom I had close contact while I was a civil servant (Bevin, Lyttelton, Duncan and Dalton), Dalton was by far the worst. As a man, I held him in contempt. Lyttelton, though slow-witted and almost inarticulate, was a successful Minister and the Department under him did great things. But Dalton went far towards demoralising us. He was vain, arrogant and without any understanding of how to handle men.[14]

By contrast, junior officials found him friendly and approachable. One young principal was surprised to be taken by the President for luncheon at the Étoile and regaled over a bottle of burgundy with slanderous comments about Government colleagues.[15] Another former official, in charge of utility furniture (one of Dalton's pet projects), recalls that he saw the President once a week to report progress. On this occasion he was sometimes subjected to strong language. 'This never gave offence because one could feel Dalton's undoubted honesty and sincerity of purpose: indeed in my case this very much helped my confidence in persuading others to get on.'[16]

Dalton's problems were mainly with senior civil servants, who saw most of him. If he did not achieve an immediate *rapport* with an adviser, he became suspicious and rude. Advisers who were not his friends were regarded as his enemies. He had no sense of hierarchy, or of the importance officials attached to relative status. There was an impishness about the way he went round pricking pomposities, like a child puncturing balloons. A favourite trick was to give a senior official a dressing down in front of juniors. 'He took advantage of the civil service code of deference to the Minister', recalls a witness. 'The attitude of his staff was: if he was rude, it was just too bad. Everybody was trying to win the war, so they just bore that particular cross and carried on.'[17] According to his Tory Parliamentary Secretary, Captain Charles Waterhouse, who liked and admired him, the President was 'rough, ruthless, self-opinionated, definite in his views ... subject to violent likes and dislikes which many of the civil servants in his department found inexplicable.'[18] Dalton's personal secretary remembers his shouting. 'He did it on purpose', she recalls. 'There were lots of complaints.' Once a very senior official, a knight, shocked her by saying bitterly: 'I think Dalton's a pig.'[19]

Apart from the bullying, there was a lack of appreciation of what the civil servants regarded as the code of conduct governing relations between a minister and his officials. Dame Alix Meynell recalls writing a long minute for the President, and getting it back with the words 'Rubbish!' and 'Nonsense!' scribbled in red ink in the margin, as on a student essay. Furious, she stormed into his office. 'You can't treat a head of department like this!', she said, and demanded that he should erase his comments from the copy to go on file.[20]

Another problem was that Dalton's sense of humour left an area of uncertainty about whether he wanted to laugh with his officials or at them. Jokes that went down well with his private coterie grated on those who did not share his outlook. Eyebrows were raised after an official accompanying him on a train journey had commented politely on the President's ability to go to sleep and then to wake up completely alert twenty minutes later. 'Yes', replied Dalton. 'It's a rare gift. Few of us have it. Napoleon had it.'[21] Civil servants were outraged, not amused, when Dalton's response to a loud flying-bomb explosion near the offices of Sir Andrew Duncan, the Minister of Supply, was to rub his hands gleefully and say: 'Wouldn't it be fun if it has hit old Andy Duncan!'[22]

But there was an additional, sharper, accusation levelled against Dalton by some of his officials – that behind the aggressive manner there lay the familiar trait of the braggart and the bully: cowardice. One adviser recalls:

> I had no confidence in his ability or even willingness to stand up for his Department in the inevitable inter-departmental battles over scarce supplies or in the face of pressure of fellow-M.P.s or others in the outside world. He would thunder beforehand in the privacy of his own office and then meekly do a complete U-turn, subsequently explaining to his shocked officials 'One must be accommodating'. I remember with bitterness one such U-turn, in response to not very strong pressure in the House of Commons, which nearly wrecked the clothes rationing scheme, leaving even the T.U.C. flabbergasted![23]

Whenever Dalton got into trouble with his ministerial colleagues, so it was said, he would try to unload the blame on to his staff. G. C. Allen gives an example of an incident that followed an unwise order by the President that civil servants should be 'ruthless' in their administration of controls. 'When the less experienced of them obeyed this injunction and aroused storms of protest among M.P.s and industrialists, he ratted and accused his department of letting him down.'[24] There is also a striking contemporary account, by James Meade, of Dalton's exasperating habit of being 'accommodating' under pressure. Meade's diary for January 1945 records how, after reluctantly agreeing to a paper prepared by Sir Percivale Liesching, Dalton betrayed his adviser by writing to Lord Woolton, Chairman of the Reconstruction Committee, saying that the paper went further than he thought most of his ministerial colleagues would want to go.[25]

Was the accusation of cowardice justified? The answer depends on what the job of a minister is taken to be. For officials who found their carefully prepared schemes tossed cavalierly aside, Dalton's behaviour was disheartening. Yet Dalton's view of the role of the President of the Board of Trade was not the same as that of his civil servants or, indeed, of his own predecessors. Where in the past Presidents had tended to preside over a department whose responsibilities were largely regulatory, Dalton wanted to use the Board as an instrument for economic change. His aims were specific, and his energies were concentrated on achieving them. Sacrifices on tangential matters did not seem like sacrifices. What mattered was not the detail, or the labour of individual men, but victory on the central issue.

Before Dalton moved to the Board, he summed up his methods with the officials he was leaving behind: 'I have chased and hunted them and shouted at many of them, and written splenetic Minutes, but, faced with the possibility of a Minister who may be more inert, I think they were inclined to regret the change.'[26] In the case of the Ministry of Economic Warfare, he was probably right. The Board of Trade, however, was a very different kind of organisation. Unlike M.E.W. it was not a department thrown together hurriedly by the requirements of war, but one that was long established, with its own traditions. M.E.W. was an offensive department and so was S.O.E. Objectives were limited and relatively clear. At the Board, by contrast, there was no core area of policy; section heads, with wide-ranging responsibilities, were used to being left alone. 1942, moreover, was not 1940 – the adaptation to wartime conditions had already taken place. Hence Dalton's Dr Dynamo, bull-in-a-china-shop approach met much more concerted resistance.

The code of the department remained firmly in a laissez-faire, Adam Smith tradition – embodied by the Permanent Secretary, Sir Arnold Overton. ('Isn't he a bit *positive*?', Overton was heard to remark when Douglas Jay was brought in to look at the Development Areas.)[27] Against this background, Dalton was by far the most 'interventionist' President the Board of Trade had ever had. His Location crusade, in particular, had many opponents. One official, more sympathetic to Dalton than most, recalls: 'The amount of help given to the formation of the new areas by the permanent staff of the Department, apart from Watkinson's yeoman effort in getting the policy through the interdepartmental committee, was precisely nil.'[28]

The frequent complaint that Dalton resisted advice needs to be seen in this light. When is advice genuinely impartial? We need not doubt that the Board had, on the whole, an industrious and well-intended staff. But 'well-intended' and 'neutral' are not necessarily synonyms. 'Dalton was paranoiac', considers one adviser, 'in the sense that he suspected civil servants of having their own policies and not telling him things that were on his side of the argument.'[29] There may have been occasions when he was not paranoid, but right.

Yet there were personal as well as political or administrative reasons for the rough ride he gave his officials. Dalton had not wanted to transfer to the Board of Trade, and the change had been unsettling. 'Handing over S.O.E. twangs my heart strings', he wrote at the time, 'and I shall feel very desolate and unfriended if I lose the daily presence of those who have been for twenty-one months my trusted inner circle.'[30] His immediate reaction had been to take familiar faces with him, telling hostile Board of Trade staff that he could only work if he had friends by his side.[31] But it had not been possible to take Jebb, and Gaitskell was soon promoted out of his private office. The old comradeship of his three Berkeley House 'sprites' – Jebb, Gaitskell and Wilmot – was not repeated. Yet by far the biggest difference was the absence of Ruth. Until the autumn of 1941 Ruth had provided an emotional backstop – often disregarded and ignored, but available when he needed her. On 15th December, two months before Hugh changed jobs, Ruth made her move to Manchester, resigning as Chairman of the L.C.C. Parks Committee and shortly afterwards resigning from the L.C.C. altogether.[32] As a result, Hugh entered the loneliest period of his adult life.

At first they kept in touch. Ruth hated the north-west. 'It is frightfully black and sordid', she told Hugh, 'and the Lancashire people are all undersized and wizened, the offspring of our Industrial Revolution'.[33] Her only friends were the social historians J. L. and Barbara Hammond, authors of *The Village Labourer* and *The Town Labourer* ('Going to see them is my greatest treat in Manchester', she wrote).[34] She came to London as often as she could, dining with Hugh about once a month in 1942. They even managed several weekends together at West Leaze. In April, Hugh felt much brighter, and noted proudly a press report that Ruth had become 'a great factor in maintaining output in the North'.[35] Later, they met in Manchester when he was in the city for an official visit. But for the third year running they spent Christmas apart. Hugh toured R.A.F. stations, and Ruth visited a Co-operative Holidays Association hostel, inhabited by 500 factory workers.[36] In 1943 Ruth came to London less often and so the gaps between meetings widened.

Though she longed to leave the north, she had no thought of returning to Hugh. Instead her mind began to turn to the country for which she had always had a special feeling – France. She got in touch with Pierre Viénot, an old friend who was now de Gaulle's chargé d'affaires in London, and told him that she would like to help with the job of reconstruction after the return of Allied armies to Europe.[37] In October, she wrote that she had become a regular listener to the French service of the B.B.C.

Her plans now became more specific. Early in 1944, she set her sights on a job working for the United Nations Relief and Rehabilitation Administration (UNRRA) in France after the liberation. The problem was how to get selected. Ruth knew that competition for the kind of job she had in mind would be intense.[38] In March she saw Hugh and told him what she wanted and her difficulty. His response was characteristic: ' ... [S]he should let me and others pull strings to get her some special position.' She protested that she did not like this way of doing things.[39]

Hugh took no notice of her objections. The Deputy Director-General of UNRRA was Sir Frederick Leith-Ross. Hugh spoke to him. The response was swift. At the end of April, Leith-Ross informed his Minister that Ruth had been offered a job as an Administrative Officer Grade I in the organisation. Her release from the Ministry of Supply had been cleared with some difficulty, and she could start at UNRRA in June. Since she was specially interested in France, every effort would be made to fit her into the French section. Hugh wrote back that he knew Ruth wanted to get to France at the earliest possible moment:

> On the other hand, she would hate the thought that I was 'pulling strings' on her behalf. But, if you can, without mentioning me, do anything possible to facilitate this at the right moment, I should be most grateful.[40]

Unaware of what Hugh had been up to, Ruth accepted the job and left Manchester in May, staying for a few days with her friends Clifford and Josephine Smith before moving into a single room in a shared flat in Holly Mount, Hampstead. The possibility of living under the same roof as Hugh during her stay in London does not seem to have arisen.

Soon she was absorbed in her work as Personal Assistant to the Director of UNRRA's Displaced Persons Division, dealing with the problem of arranging the return of workers deported for forced labour.[41] When she dined with Hugh just after D-Day, she was in good spirits. She spoke eagerly of the prospects of going to France, and perhaps in due course to Berlin in order to help organise the repatriation of French conscript workers in Germany. Hugh gave her a book of poems as a present. But it was agreed that, until she went abroad, she should remain in Hampstead.[42]

After this they barely met until the war was over. The Allied advance was slower than expected and she did not get to France for many months. Pearl Jephcock, who shared the Holly Mount flat with Ruth during this period, recalled a quiet, reserved lady who kept herself to herself, had no visitors and cooked little meals of baked beans on a gas ring.[43] The death of Pierre Viénot in July brought Hugh and Ruth together briefly. Both attended the funeral in Brompton Oratory. 'R. was there, all alone, looking very sorrowful & strained', Hugh wrote. 'I made a little sign, as I went out, but she turned away.'[44]

In November 1944 Ruth had to leave Holly Mount because the house was being sold, and so she moved into the Norfolk Court Hotel in Belsize Park, which remained her London base until the beginning of 1946.

If Ruth's personal isolation in the second half of the war was acute, Hugh's was scarcely less so – disguised from others and perhaps from himself by the boarding school atmosphere of a wartime ministry. Here, having no other home in London, Dalton could be found at all hours.

The only close relative with whom he was in touch was his mother. She died in March 1944. 'The two Old Ladies seem quite changeless', he wrote after his final visit to see her and her companion at Datchet the previous August.[45]

Without any private life, Dalton turned more than ever to the company of young protégés, setting the pattern for his later years. He continued to see much of Hugh Gaitskell (even after Gaitskell's promotion), Douglas Jay and Evan Durbin. He also helped to launch a number of promising young men into politics. Kenneth Younger, Raymond Blackburn, Ivor Thomas, and John Freeman[46] were four Members of the 1945 Parliament who owed their seats in part to Dalton's intervention (Thomas won a wartime by-election). Harold Wilson was a fifth. Another discovery was a young army officer called Denis Healey. Impressed by a speech at Party Conference, Dalton told Healey to apply for the job of International Secretary at Transport House. With help from Dalton and Laski, Healey was appointed.[47]

Hugh saw his young men intermittently. But the relationship was scarcely equal. For all the joviality and gossip, he patronised them and they regarded him with awe, and ambition. In a rather different category were Bob and Betty Fraser, former students at the L.S.E., and protégés of an earlier generation. Fraser, an Australian, had been a *Daily Herald* journalist and was now Director of Publications at the Ministry of Information. Like most of Hugh's friends outside politics, he had political aspirations: yet it helped that their current jobs were in widely separated spheres. Starting in November 1943, when Bob asked Hugh to his Hampstead flat to discuss possible constituencies,[48] the Frasers provided a substitute family. Thereafter Hugh spent several weekends at their house at Sherrington in Norfolk, where he was able to get away from the war. 'He was affectionate, entertaining, simple and totally uncondescending', Betty (now Lady) Fraser recalls. He was more inclined to discuss the First World War than the Second. Once, out walking, they passed a detachment of Italian prisoners-of-war at work in a field. Hugh stopped and spoke to them in Italian about their families.

An important member of the Fraser household was the Frasers' only daughter, Rosalind (now Rosalind Gilmore) – aged six when Hugh encountered her in 1943. Hugh became an unofficial uncle. He would arrive, accompanied by a police escort, holding an Arthur Ransome book under his arm. 'I used to leave them playing together', Lady Fraser recalls. 'She was so pleased and content to be with him.'[49] According to Rosalind:

Outside the family, he was the most prominent adult in my life. I used to look forward to his visits. He seemed to have a lot of time for me, and talked to me on a rather clever level. He told me about going to see the King, and he described, in a story-book way, what he did in the government. I also remember him talking about flying bombs, and 'the stupid Germans'. Once we played a game involving drawing a pig while blindfolded. Mine was very crude. But his was a great big, bold pig, firmly signed 'Hugh Dalton – His Pig'. I kept it.

Rosalind attended a nearby convent and was unhappy there. So Hugh cheered her up with a fantasy, which she still remembers:

I would sit on his knee and tell him how much I hated the nuns. He invented a game about not giving the nuns coupons for blackout material, so that they would be taken in by the police because lights were showing, and I wouldn't have to go to school.[50]

Rosalind did not find out about Hugh's daughter until later in her childhood. To her parents, however, Hugh talked about Helen fondly and without reserve. Rosalind was a sickly child, and not much older than Helen had been when she died. 'I had a feeling that, to him, Rosalind and Helen were alike', Lady Fraser recalls. 'I used to think: I won't speak of Helen. I'll let him. I remember him saying once: "We all have our tears".'[51]

Towards the end of the war, Dalton began to suffer physical symptoms of a kind that commonly have psychological causes. These became particularly pronounced after Ruth had taken up her UNRRA job, when she was living apart from him in London and waiting to be posted abroad. In September 1944 bad rheumatism in his knee forced him to cancel engagements, see a specialist, and undergo regular massage. Shortly afterwards, an ugly boil – precursor of many over the next few years – appeared on a finger. He needed a general anaesthetic to have it removed. As he came round after the operation, he heard himself saying, in a tone of great indignation, 'Just like a bloody Cabinet Committee!'[52] Meanwhile he was affected by a lack of energy which was not the product of any particular exertion. 'I again feel damned tired!', he noted early in November. 'This is a great bore.' He wrote the Royal Physician, Lord Horder, a careful letter:

> Normally I am extremely fit; so much so that, for a number of years, I haven't had a regular doctor and have very seldom had resort, even on minor ailments, to medical advice. Hence this note.
>
> I have now done 4½ years as a Minister of the Crown in wartime, & most of it here, in this pretty laborious Department, working rather hard. Just lately I have been feeling a bit weary, and I don't want this to go on.
>
> I want all my strength & energy for the last lap of the War, &, not less, for the first post-war years. Could you advise me where to go to, for some sensible medical guidance?

After 'a bit weary', Dalton wrote the words 'and slower in reaction' and then crossed them out.[53]

Horder made a full medical examination and found nothing wrong. Commenting that the President was merely 'a bit stale', he prescribed vitamin and strychnine tablets.[54] Dalton became faddish about his food, sticking to a non-starch diet. But what he later called the 'Enemy Fatigue' remained.

XXIII

Planning for Post-War

Douglas Jay recalls that Dalton's sympathies during the war were very simple. 'He was in favour of miners, the young, white men, socialists, New Zealand, Australia and dwellers in Durham and Northumberland. He was against the Germans, reactionaries, the elderly and the rich.'[1] At the Board of Trade it was Dalton's hatred of Germans, and his liking for miners and north-easterners, that most influenced his actions. Politically, the two emotions made a useful mix. His advocacy of state intervention was the more successful for being combined with a jingoistic anti-Germanism that gave satisfaction to Tories who were critical of his ideas on social and economic reform.

There was nothing cynical or calculating about Dalton's attitude to Germany, which went back to his experiences after Caporetto and to his bitterness over the loss of friends on the Somme. It had continued during the period when pro-Germanism was fashionable on the Left, contributing to his fierce stand on rearmament and against appeasement. It had also contributed to, and had been fed by, his sympathy for the East European victims of Nazi aggression. Hostility to the Germans was a universal feeling in wartime. With Dalton, however, there was another element: a fervour, even an obsession.

From the beginning of the war, he had been interested in peace aims. In his book *Hitler's War*, published before he joined the Government, he had declared that 'the paradoxical conclusion that the aggressor should be free from all obligation to pay damages to his victims', must be avoided.[2] Now that he was in a position to exert influence he set about trying to give this view substance.

In August 1942 he wrote a long memorandum on Reparations, attacking the Treasury view that a 'clean slate' approach to the defeated nations was the best one. He was scornful of those who felt that it was dangerous or improper to 'interfere' with German economic

life, writing that, 'The sad results of insufficient interference were seen
last time'.[3] His initiative led to the setting up of an interdepartmental
Committee on Reparations and Economic Security (C.R.E.S.),
chaired by a Foreign Office official, Sir William Malkin. The Committee met 38 times between November 1942 and August 1943.[4]
' ... I feel so strongly on the matters to be discussed at C.R.E.S.',
Dalton told a civil servant before the first meeting, 'that, in certain
circumstances, though I am not by nature a Resigning Robert, I might
feel moved to take a very strong line.'[5] He was particularly concerned
that Germany should be made to pay for the devastation caused in the
East. But he also wanted to see Germany's hands tied strategically.
He told the Cabinet Reconstruction Committee at the beginning of
1943 that the defeated states should be forbidden to own civil, as well
as military, aircraft.[6]

Dalton watched closely the deliberations of C.R.E.S. He was glad
that members included his old pupil, Lionel Robbins, now head of
the Economic Section of the Cabinet Office, and that the Foreign
Office was represented by his former employee, Gladwyn Jebb. He
was less happy to find that another member was his former tutor,
Maynard Keynes, now advising the Treasury, and recently made
a Baron.

By this time, Keynes had become a major influence – even the
dominating one – on the Government's economic policies. Brought
into the Treasury as an adviser by the Chancellor, Kingsley Wood, in
1940, he had been mainly concerned with war finance. The first major
victory of the 'Keynesian Revolution' had been achieved in 1941, with
the institution of a new concept of budgetary policy.

The lionisation of Keynes by the civil service establishment was
not entirely pleasing to Dalton. A personal coolness which had existed
between the two men since the 1920s still remained. In June Gladwyn
Jebb passed on the rumour that the President of the Board of Trade
was 'not popular' with Keynes. 'It is because I have always refused to
sit at his feet', Dalton replied. When Keynes came to see him in August
to discuss cotton, Dalton noted that 'he and I both know that neither
of us much cares for the other'.[7] But there was also a political reason
for Dalton's cautious attitude towards his former tutor, particularly
in relation to reparations. Dalton regarded Keynes's *Economic Consequences of the Peace*, so admired by liberal internationalists in the
1920s, as one of the major causes of appeasement. Keynes had been
against punitive reparations in 1919, and might take the same line
again.[8] Dalton therefore did his best to keep Keynes off the new
Reparations Committee. When he was overruled, the President urged
the Chancellor of the Exchequer to 'rub into Keynes the need to

weaken Germany so much that she will be industrially unable to repeat her crimes in future'.[9]

In Dalton's opinion joining hands with Russia and the emasculation of Germany after the war should go hand in hand. Reparations would help to achieve both. Early in 1944 Dalton wrote to H. N. Brailsford explaining his attitude:

I count, as I have counted for many years – and repeatedly written and said publicly – on close Anglo-Soviet co-operation in Europe. I believe that we can get it. But it will not be easy. We shall have to let them do *most* of what they like in Eastern Europe and in Germany.

... I have no doubt that the Russians mean to make the Germans come and work for them, repairing the ruins ... I should hope that this forced labour will be drawn, not from the younger German generations, but from the miscreants of the Gestapo, the S.S., the S.A. and a large part of the Regular Armed Forces. The Russians are, in part, a most ruthless people, though, I think, they take things in their stride, callously, if you will, not noticing them. where many Germans take a perverted pleasure in similar acts. But if, as I hope, we and the Russians are to march arm in arm into the future, we must each get used to the ways of the other.[10]

In supporting the Soviet ally, Dalton was expressing the official view of the Government. His comments, however, went further than a willingness to compensate the Russians, or even a desire – widely shared on the Left – to remain friendly with the Soviet Union after the war. They amounted to an acceptance of all the brutalities of Stalinism as a necessary price for annihilating the German threat. The only qualification was that the 'younger German generations' should be exempt; though how 'younger generations' were to be distinguished from the 'miscreants' of the Regular Armed Forces, and why the Russians should be expected to preserve any such distinction, Dalton did not make clear. Before the war some right-wing appeasers had privately expressed the view that the Nazis should be used as a bulwark against Soviet Communism. Dalton stood this on its head and argued that Russia should be given a free hand to deal with Germany once and for all; and that, furthermore, the Western Allies should turn a blind eye ('get used to the ways of the other') to the cruelties which would inevitably result.

He saw one snag. If the Russians advanced too far, Stalin might try to absorb Germany as a Soviet Socialist Republic. Germans might then end up running the Soviet Union as well as Germany. 'This is the

greatest of all dangers in the background', he noted. Evan Durbin put
to him the possibility that the Russians might provide a more serious
danger to world peace than the Germans after the war, and that it
might therefore be sensible to keep Germany just strong enough to act
as a buffer. Dalton was not convinced.

The Reparations Committee came to nothing. When it reported in
the summer of 1943, Dalton was pleased with its proposals which
included the destruction of the German synthetic oil industry, a five
year period for 'very substantial deliveries in kind' and the payment
by Germany for international peace-keeping forces. 'It is not at all a
bad report', he noted, 'and the fact that Keynes is committed to it is
important.'[11] The report, however, was soon overtaken by events.
When the war ended, the problem was not how to cripple the German
economy, but how to resuscitate it; and the Russians did not need to
ask permission before exacting reparations.

Yet the episode helped to crystallise Dalton's own attitude, and
foreshadowed his bitter resentment as Chancellor after the war at the
huge cost of maintaining the British zone in Germany ('this most
intolerable imposition on our humane good nature', he called it)[12]
and his opposition in the 1950s to German rearmament. In the short
run, his close interest in reparations influenced the way in which he
was regarded in the Government and in Whitehall. On the one hand,
his *revanchisme* added to his reputation as the most warlike of Labour
ministers, balancing his reputation for socialism. On the other, it
strengthened the opinion, especially prevalent among senior diplomats, that his views on foreign policy were dangerously emotional.
When, at the end of the war, the prospect arose that Dalton might
become Foreign Secretary in a Labour Government, doubts about
Dalton's 'soundness' on Russia and Germany lent weight to the
Foreign Office view that Bevin would be a better bet.

Another reason why Foreign Office officials continued to distrust
Dalton was Dalton's attitude to Palestine. The Foreign Office wanted
to maintain the security of the British Mandate and protect British oil
interests while avoiding commitments that might destabilise the
Middle East. Dalton had no desire to add to British difficulties in the
region. On the other hand, his feelings for the victims of German
oppression encouraged him to become the firmest supporter of
Zionism within the Labour leadership.

At first, Dalton's Zionist sympathies were based on a mild interest
in politically-minded Jewish students at the L.S.E. in the 1920s. Later,
his assistance to Jewish refugees was more practical than political: in

the 1930s he helped Jewish families settle and establish factories on new trading estates in the north-east. He said little in public about a Jewish national home, and in *Hitler's War* his outline of the future world order contained no reference to Palestine. Only in the last phase of the war did the demand for a Jewish state become one of his personal causes.

Having made this commitment, Dalton did more than any other Labour politician to press the Jewish case. Although he had no influence on Government foreign policy, he was well placed to shape the programme of the Labour Party which the Coalition or its successor would eventually have to take into account. He was a member of the International Sub-Committee of the N.E.C., and the Chairman, George Dallas, was one of his supporters. It was not hard, therefore, to steer through a policy which more or less reflected his own views.

He did this by tying the Palestine problem to the whole of post-war foreign policy. In the spring of 1944, the N.E.C. issued a statement called *The International Post-War Settlement* of which Dalton was the instigator and principal author. This called for Anglo-American-Russian co-operation as the cornerstone of a new World Organisation. 'If we three hold together, all will be well', it declared; 'if we fall apart, all will be dark and uncertain.' There was one section on German war guilt, and another on Reparations and Restitution which demanded, 'Reparation by German labour ... if this is desired by any of the Governments concerned', and called for new German frontiers, with a strong hint (Noel-Baker, a member of the Sub-Committee, had reduced it from an actual commitment) that the transfer of large numbers of Germans living outside these frontiers would be involved. But the most important section – little noticed at the time – was a paragraph on Palestine. Here Dalton's words were unambiguous:

> ... [T]here is surely neither hope or meaning in a 'Jewish National Home', unless we are prepared to let Jews, if they wish, enter this tiny land in such numbers as to become a majority. There was a strong case for this before the War. There is an irresistible case now, after the unspeakable atrocities of the cold and calculated German Nazi plan to kill all Jews in Europe. Here, too, in Palestine surely is a case, on human grounds and to promote a stable settlement, for transfer of population. Let the Arabs be encouraged to move out, as the Jews move in. Let them be compensated handsomely for their land and let their settlement elsewhere be carefully organised and generously financed. The Arabs have many wide territories of their own; they must not claim to exclude the Jews from this small area of Palestine, less than the size of Wales. Indeed, we should re-examine

also the possibility of extending the present Palestinian boundaries, by agreement with Egypt, Syria or Transjordan.

At the December 1944 Party Conference, this extraordinary declaration aroused no interest. Delegates concentrated on the German sections which, many felt, smacked of 'Vansittartism' – a belief in the inherent wickedness of the German people. There was concern at proposals which seemed to imply the 'dismemberment' of Germany, and repetition of the errors of Versailles. Nobody raised Palestine, or the possible difficulties that disposing of 'this small area ... less than the size of Wales', might involve. In the end the whole document was accepted by Conference without a vote.[13]

Later Dalton argued that huge shifts in population were justified in the Middle East, as in Europe, in order to take advantage of a brief period of world-wide upheaval. In this way, it would be possible to 'telescope into a few years changes which otherwise would drag along, slowly, and painfully, through centuries'.[14] The truth was, however, that the paragraph ignored important problems. In particular it seemed to regard 'the Arabs' as a homogeneous people whose 'wide territories' could readily absorb displaced compatriots from Palestine.[15] There was much in the remark of Oliver Stanley, a Tory colleague, that the Labour commitment was 'Zionism plus plus'.[16] Yet it did not go as far as Dalton would have liked. In an earlier draft, toned down at the insistence of the International Sub-Committee, he had written: 'There is also something to be said for throwing open Libya or Eritrea to Jewish settlement, as satellites or colonies to Palestine.'[17]

What was the explanation for Dalton's casual indifference to the plight of Palestinians who, in his scheme, were to be transported, presumably by force, in order to make way for Jewish immigrants? One answer was that the extermination and torture of Jews in Europe gave the aspirations of survivors a special primacy. Another was that there were more Jewish than Palestinian lobbyists in the Labour Party. Labour policy had been opposed to the official British line on Palestine ever since the 1939 White Paper, which had limited Jewish immigration to 75,000 over a five year period. Although Dalton's paragraph expressed his own convictions, it was passed by the N.E.C. and Conference because it reflected views that were widely held. On the N.E.C., Dalton's strongest backer was Harold Laski; in Parliament proponents of an independent Jewish state included not only Shinwell (who, like Laski, was of Jewish origin), but Aneurin Bevan as well.

Dalton was also directly influenced by Jewish organisations. Dalton later claimed to have had little contact with Zionists during the war. In fact links were quite close, and Dalton's diary reveals a number of consultations with Zionist leaders. 'As you know', Dalton wrote to Herbert Morrison in October 1944, 'I keep in touch with Weizmann and his friends and have been pushing their barrow for them through the National Executive and into a paragraph, with which they were delighted, in the Executive's Declaration on the Post-War International Settlement.'[18]

In January 1945 Dalton became Chairman of the National Executive International Sub-Committee. Continued interest and support for the Zionist cause seemed assured. At this stage a Labour election victory still appeared unlikely, but Labour's uncompromising declaration encouraged a belief that within the Coalition there would be strong support for Jewish aims in Palestine. When in July the unexpected happened and a Labour Government was elected, there was dancing in the streets of Tel Aviv.

The euphoria was short-lived. Within a few days of taking office, Labour had abandoned its commitment. As Kenneth Harris puts it, 'There were many British ambassadors in Arab countries, and many Arab desks at the Foreign Office: the Jews had none'.[19] The new Foreign Secretary, Ernest Bevin, was quickly won over by his officials, and the 1939 White Paper became the Palestine policy of the new Government. Bevin had taken no part in the wartime discussions on Palestine. He was made rapidly aware of the strong resistance that would result in the Arab world, within Palestine and outside it, if Jewish immigration was not strictly controlled. In addition he had little sympathy for the aspirations of the Jews. Dalton believed that the new Foreign Secretary was inhibited by the belief which he often expressed that 'the Jews are a religion not a race or nation'.[20] This accorded completely with Foreign Office dogma.

Would Foreign Office counsels have prevailed if Dalton had become Foreign Secretary? Dalton would have discovered the absurdity of his plan for peacefully transferring Palestinians to the 'wide territories' beyond Palestine's borders. On the other hand, he would probably have been more receptive to demands to increase the rate of Jewish immigration, much more inclined towards Partition and much less willing to follow the advice of his officials. It is reasonable to assume, therefore, that if Dalton rather than Bevin had been in charge of the Palestine problem during the critical period following the Second World War, the subsequent history of the Middle East would have been very different.

Palestine was a political interest, not a departmental one. Dalton

could 'push the barrow' for Weizmann in the Labour Party, but there was no scope for doing so within the Government. The same was not true of Dalton's economic and industrial interests which related directly to his departmental brief. Here, politics and administration could be combined. In the autumn of 1942, Dalton established his own 'internal reconstruction' department, staffed with suitably qualified people.[21] By the end of the following year, his senior staff were directing their main attention towards plans for post-war production, commerce and the generation of employment.

An important channel for Dalton's ideas was the new Cabinet Committee on Reconstruction Priorities, which became the most important arbiter on domestic policy and social reform. Labour was well placed on this Committee, with four Labour ministers, Attlee, Bevin, Morrison and Jowitt out of the total of ten. Dalton was not himself a member (though he was on the key industry sub-committee) but he regularly attended meetings because so much of the business fell within his sphere. Through a mixture of bargaining, cajolery and argument, he greatly influenced the deliberations of this important body.

Dalton's manoeuvres in and around the Lord President's and Reconstruction Priorities Committees were backed up by a powerful policy-making drive within the Labour Party. The main areas in which the Reconstruction Priorities Committee developed a social policy were employment, social insurance and health. Dalton was mainly interested in the first. Believing that after the war steeply rising unemployment would be the chief domestic difficulty, he set about equipping the Government with the legislative and policy tools to deal with it – using his position on the Labour N.E.C. to make sure that he received Party backing.

Dalton was uniquely placed to provide such support. Not only was he one of the most senior members of the Executive; he had virtually founded the N.E.C. Policy Committee in 1931, served continuously as chairman from 1936 to 1944 and had long been regarded as the committee's guiding hand. Dalton's dominance of N.E.C. policy-making was, moreover, reinforced by the ambition and miscalculation of Herbert Morrison. As we have seen, in 1943 Morrison stood for the Party Treasurership but failed to get elected. As he could not stand simultaneously for the constituency parties section, this defeat cost Morrison his place on the Executive during the 1943–4 year. Apart from Attlee, who was fully occupied as Lord President (in succession to Anderson) and Deputy Prime Minister, Dalton was now the only departmental minister on the N.E.C. Without serious rivals, he was able to turn the Policy Committee into his personal instrument during the key period when post-war policy was being formed. After the 1943 Party Conference, the Policy Committee lurched into action, extending its consultations with the T.U.C. and preparing a programme for the next election. Dalton used it, skilfully, to demonstrate the direct support his ministerial policies currently received within the Labour Party.

N.E.C. policy-making was, however, more than a chorus: Dalton was as concerned with new ideas as with propaganda. To improve the quality of Executive proposals, he reorganised the structure of satellite committees. As chairman of the Finance Committee, he invited Hugh Gaitskell and Douglas Jay to prepare a joint paper on post-war employment and finance, and Evan Durbin to prepare one on post-war international arrangements.[22] All three men were original, individual voices, whose ideas had an independent influence on Labour thinking. Yet they were also Dalton's close friends, currently employed in Whitehall as temporary civil servants, and two (Gaitskell and Jay) were Dalton's own appointees. It was not surprising, therefore, that their views on Labour policy should have been close to Dalton's own, or that they should have proposed extensions of, rather than alternatives to, the work of the existing Government.

Labour's policy-making closely followed, and was strongly influenced by, the Beveridge Report. After presenting the scheme for fuel rationing in the spring of 1942, Sir William Beveridge had returned to his inquiry, begun the year before, into the social services. His conclusions, published in December, put forward a programme for a free national health service, family allowances, the maintenance of full employment and universal subsistence-level social insurance. The popular appeal of this blueprint for a welfare state was immense. Seventy thousand copies were sold immediately, and when a few days later Beveridge married his widowed cousin, Janet Mair, who had reigned at the L.S.E. in Dalton's lecturing days, the event was treated by the national press almost as though it were a royal wedding.[23]

The Labour Party was enthusiastic about Beveridge. Up to a point, Dalton shared the enthusiasm. He had no doubt that something of the kind was badly needed. Shortly after the publication of the Report he commented on a government survey which showed that 'a thinking minority' strongly favoured a wide range of social improvements: 'This is a most interesting and encouraging document, which should stimulate us all, Ministers and officials alike, to quicken our steps and leap over obstacles placed in our path by timid, short-sighted or sinister persons.'[24] Dalton's enthusiasm was, however, tempered by two factors: feelings about his former boss, and concern lest the Beveridge proposals should tear the Coalition asunder.

Just as Dalton's assessment of Keynesian economics was affected by distant recollections of Keynes as a tutor, so his response to the Beveridge Report was influenced by memories of Beveridge as an academic administrator. He had always got on well with Beveridge at the L.S.E. Yet he had also found him fussy, conceited and (at the Mines Department earlier in 1942) surprisingly naive about politics. Hence Dalton had difficulty in taking this oddly prophet-like figure with its 'straight white hair, sharp, bird-like profile and high-pitched, meticulous Oxford voice'[25] entirely seriously. He found it even harder to regard Beveridge as a national hero.

Dalton's personal reservation, however, was less important than his concern to stop pro-Beveridge populism getting out of hand. The Report brought into the open a conflict within the Labour Party which had hitherto been suppressed: between those who wished to make the adoption of radical policies the price for staying in the Government, and those who wanted to get as much as they could out of the Coalition even at the price of sacrificing a certain amount of radicalism. Dalton – who had already begun to discover that membership of the Government and behind-the-scenes radicalism were not incompatible – belonged to the second camp. There were reasons why a Labour politician might criticise the Beveridge Report: its assumptions were liberal, not socialist, and the provisions for children's allowances and workmen's compensation were strongly criticised by trade union leaders (Bevin in particular). Dalton, however, approved of the general direction of the Report. His concern was over the tactical mistake of going all out in support of it. He was afraid that a split in the Coalition on Beveridge might precipitate a general election – and a massive defeat for Labour.

Hence he was alarmed when backbench Labour M.P.s voted almost to a man against the Government after the Report had been debated in the Commons. He remained unconvinced by Morrison's argument that unequivocal support for the Beveridge programme would win Labour votes. When Jennie Lee was defeated as I.L.P. candidate at a by-election after campaigning on the slogan, 'I stand for every word, every letter and comma in the Beveridge Report', Dalton noted: 'This result casts some doubt on the readily accepted allegation that the whole country is hungering and thirsting after Beveridge.'[26]

Nevertheless, while seeking to calm pro-Beveridge hysteria, Dalton was able to use parts of the Report as an added weapon in his own campaign within the Government. Insurance and health, about which there was most hungering and thirsting, did not directly interest him. The suggestion in the Report that the powers of the state should be fully used to reduce unemployment, on the other hand, did. Beveridge's views accorded closely with his own, and were similar in origin. They owed much to the Webbs, and in particular to the approach advanced in the Webbs' pre-war book, *Soviet Communism*, which pointed to the advantages of state control of production and the detailed planning of the deployment of labour, rather than monetary and fiscal regulation of consumer demand.[27] Dalton's views, like those of the Webbs, had been derived from observations of Soviet planning in the early 1930s.[28] Hence the essentially pre-Keynesian employment sections of the Report strongly appealed to him.

Commissioned by the Government, and supported by the Labour Party, the Beveridge Report provided Dalton with a springboard for initiatives aimed at preventing a recurrence of pre-war levels and concentrations of unemployment. Dalton's main initiative was at the Board of Trade. At the same time, starting from assumptions that were already half-accepted within the Government, he shaped Labour policy so as to provide a political buttress to his activities in Whitehall. His principal agents were the young men he called his 'post-warriors', Durbin, Gaitskell and Jay, who completed the process, begun before the war, of welding the new Keynesian analysis to pre-war Fabianism.

Despite reservations about some of Keynes's views, Dalton was naturally in sympathy with the Cambridge belief that, by carefully managing the economy, full employment would be maintained after the war. Experience of government had reinforced his pre-war view that Keynes's ideas needed to be combined with a high degree of state control and direction of resources. He therefore gave full support to efforts to produce a Labour policy based on a Fabian-Keynesian amalgam.

Having let his post-warriors do the spade-work, Dalton produced the final version of Labour's economic programme. In January 1944 an informal meeting of the nucleus of the XYZ Club (the group of City radicals and socialist economists who had developed Labour's financial ideas before the war) met at the Reform Club to discuss a paper prepared for the Party's Financial Committee on Post-War Employment. Apart from Dalton, the company consisted of Vaughan Berry, Evan Durbin, Hugh Gaitskell, Douglas Jay, William Piercy and John Wilmot. 'A good paper and a good evening', Dalton noted, 'but it is left to me, as usual, to knock it about a bit before putting it up to its next hurdle.' After the Policy Committee, Dalton undertook to write the appropriate declaration for Conference, and in March, using the drafts of Jay, Gaitskell and Durbin, he produced a full statement. 'We all know pretty well what we want to say on F[ull] E[mployment]', he noted; 'the trick is to say it well.'[29] He said it well

enough for the Policy Committee, and then the full N.E.C., to accept
what were (in essence) the ideas of his young post-warriors, with his
own modifications added.

'It was largely Keynesian', he wrote later.[30] In reality, Labour's
new policy *Full Employment and Financial Policy* was a mixture of
Keynesianism and physical control socialist planning – pretty much
the combination that provided the economic ethic of the post-war
Attlee administration. In Dalton's view, as we have seen, physical
controls had great advantages in terms of equity. Moreover the
directing powers of Whitehall had already been used successfully to
create full employment. A major part of the task after the war, Dalton
believed, must be to hang on to wartime gains. He had been arguing
this case since 1942. 'Many of our war-time controls have come to
stay, though their post-war shape may change', he told a Nottingham
Labour Party meeting in the autumn of that year. 'Pre-war social
inequality must never return. The interest of the community must
unquestionably override all sectional interests.'[31] A couple of months
later he explained to the N.E.C. Central Reconstruction Committee
that the Bank of England had become a mere branch of the Treasury,
with the Joint Stock Banks acting as collecting agencies for Government finance. 'The Treasury Deposit Receipt is a wartime invention of
great value', he declared, 'and we must seek, after the war, to be most
conservative as regards financial institutions and to hold fast to what
we have won.'[32]

Thus what had *actually* happened in wartime provided the basis
for a 'socialist' strategy once the war was over. 'I should define
Economic Planning, in its widest sense, as the deliberate direction, by
persons in control of large resources, of economic activities towards
chosen ends', Dalton had written in *Practical Socialism* in 1935.[33]
What better description could there be of the activities of the wartime
President of the Board of Trade, the wartime Minister of Labour and
the wartime Lord President? Dalton's Labour Party document made
the point explicit – more or less equating socialism with physical
controls by central government over industry, finance and the supply
of goods. Wartime necessity was to be transformed into peacetime
virtue. The Bank of England, which Dalton had described in 1942 as
already an agency of the Treasury, must become 'in effect, no more
than a section of the Treasury, subject to the direction of the Chancellor of the Exchequer', while the wartime power of the Chancellor to
require banks to lend him money on his own terms should be maintained. Tight controls over industry should be continued after the war
through nationalisation. Wartime levels of employment should be kept
up by maintaining purchasing power, dispensing with the need to

balance the Budget year by year, and calling for international agreements to stabilise rates of exchange. There should also be a continuation of existing Board of Trade policy on industrial location.

These plans were the culmination of a dozen years of work by Dalton and his associates on the N.E.C. Policy Committee and its sub-committees, and of innumerable papers and discussions by XYZ and the New Fabians. The lineage from *Practical Socialism* was direct. Yet the most immediate influence was not socialist theory or university economics, but Whitehall. Gaitskell and Jay, on whose drafts the domestic passages were based, had become in the course of the war senior administrators, increasingly sharing the perspectives of their civil service colleagues whom they so closely resembled in background and training. Gaitskell's promotion at the Board of Trade had taken him away from the political influences of the private office; Jay did not begin seriously to consider a political career until 1945. It is a curious irony that *Full Employment and Financial Policy*, the basis of Labour's election manifesto *Let Us Face the Future*, the platform for Labour's most radical Government ever, should actually have been a coalitionist document which drew heavily on drafts by two Wykehamist officials who were both thinking seriously about staying in the civil service after the war.

'Socialist' was certainly a legitimate word to describe the 1944 proposals. But it would also be possible to describe them as the product of wartime Whitehall in an imperial and reformist mood. In 1942 Evan Durbin, the third in Dalton's trio of post-warriors, and himself a temporary civil servant, published a book called *What Have We to Defend?* in which he declared his belief in 'a planned economy' for the purpose of improving the efficiency of industry and finance, and in 'the substitution of conscious foresight for the instinctive adjustments of the competitive system'. There were many civil servants, especially young ones, who privately agreed. Except for nationalisation (and there were some who believed in that) there was little in Durbin's prescription for an open and meritocratic society, efficiently directed by an enlightened élite, that did not have wide support among those who had been recruited by competitive entry to the administrative class.

One requirement of an efficiently planned economy, Durbin considered, was 'unity of command and the power to enforce the execution of a general strategy'. The achievement of efficient planning, combined with fairer distribution, would be the beginning of a new social order. Unemployment could thereby be abolished and the social services extended. But above all there would be equality of opportunity:

We can then throw open the gates of knowledge and insist that every
child shall receive the training of hand or eye or brain to which his
inherited abilities suit him and see to it that the subsequent entry of
young men and women into the occupations of lawyer and doctor,
university teacher and industrial manager, becomes as easy as it
now is difficult. By the same token the calling of the miner and the
factory hand, the shop-girl and the railway porter will take on their
full dignity: the equal in social honour of any useful service to the
economy of a free state.[34]

Here was a charter to unite Fabians, Beveridge enthusiasts, White
Paper Keynesians and other reform-minded members of the professional middle-class. Dalton was so delighted that he sent copies to
the Prime Minister and Deputy Prime Minister. 'Your book is *bloody
good*!', he wrote to Durbin.

> ... I've read nothing more satisfying, nor more moving in some of
> the more personal passages, since this war started ... You and I, I
> know, are apt to like each other's thoughts on politics. I liked very
> much your *Politics of Democratic Socialism* ... And I remember your
> very nice review of my *Practical Socialism for Britain*. Some
> thoughts from the first four chapters of that book of mine peep
> through this most outstanding book of yours.

There was, indeed, a strong similarity of approach – with the same
emphases on equality as the end, planning as the means and common
sense as the style. There was none of what Dalton called the 'thin,
theoretical, tinny tintinnabulations' of a Harold Laski.[35] Socialism
would come, not through an apocalyptic upheaval, but by applying in
an old-fashioned British and Fabian way lessons drawn from administrative experience. Implicit in this view was the discovery of the enormous powers of the state. It was this discovery – epitomised in
Douglas Jay's famous remark after the war that 'the Gentleman in
Whitehall is usually right' – that found expression in Labour's
election programme.

The N.E.C. Policy Committee passed Dalton's paper on *Full Employment and Financial Policy* on 17th April 1944. Next day the International Committee passed his draft on *The International Post-War
Settlement*. Both events – and the deliberations that preceded them –
took place against a background of intense governmental activity in
the field of post-war planning. It was no coincidence that Labour's
Employment document preceded the Government's Employment

Policy White Paper by a month. Dalton had been involved in the preparation of both of them.

Meanwhile the President of the Board of Trade played an important part in another aspect of planning for the transition. This concerned international commercial policy – and arose from Keynes's scheme for a Clearing Union. By early 1942 Keynes had become convinced that Britain's best option was to take part in a multilateral world economy. He therefore sought to create a monetary order that was not dependent on the vagaries of American politics, putting forward a plan for an overdraft facility that would grant credit to deficit countries automatically when they ran payments deficits.[36] In 1944 a compromise scheme (which owed more to a parallel American plan than to Keynes's own clearing union) was referred to an international conference at Bretton Woods. From this conference there eventually emerged the International Monetary Fund and the International Bank for Reconstruction and Development.

Alongside Keynes's Clearing Union plan, James Meade, employed in the Economic Section of the Cabinet Office, had been drafting a complementary scheme for commercial policy. Meade's 'Commercial Union' plan stressed the political and economic importance of liberal trade policies, called for a convention to reduce tariffs, and provided for an international body which would have the power to interpret this convention and settle disputes between member nations.[37] Meade first convinced Keynes that his scheme would work. Then he looked for Whitehall and ministerial backers. In particular he needed the support of the Board of Trade. So he set about winning over Dalton.

Meade did not approach the President directly. Instead he turned to Gaitskell, a friend from before the war. Gaitskell read Meade's memorandum, discussed it at length with its author and redrafted it for Dalton. 'There is nothing very original in it, except, perhaps, the section dealing with State trading', Gaitskell wrote in an accompanying note. Dalton scribbled in reply:

This is a good paper. I agree generally with the policy proposed, though many points of detail are of first-class importance – and first-class controversial value ... I should like this paper circulated for comment here, – and also, of course, in the D.O.T. [Department of Overseas Trade] – , with a view to the Board of Trade taking the initiative, within, say, a month from now – or early in October – in putting up a considered proposal on Commercial Union to other Departments.[38]

Meade recalls: 'From then on, the Board of Trade bought it.'[39] Having seen a useful idea, Dalton pursued it with customary vigour. The memorandum was circulated. At Dalton's request an inter-departmental Committee on Commercial Policy was set up. Meade was seconded to the Board of Trade (while retaining a desk in the Cabinet Office), and placed on the Committee as one of the Board's representatives along with Sir Percivale Liesching, a senior official.

Thereafter Dalton gave Meade full support. 'He seemed less gawky than of old ... ', Dalton wrote at the start of the new arrangement. 'He will be an acquisition ... I was very right to prefer this economist to Harrod.'[40] The Commercial Union policy was developed in con-junction with Board of Trade officials, and by the following year it had reached a stage at which it could be used as a basis for inter-national negotiations. Sir Frederick Leith-Ross was instructed by Dalton to draft an international economic agreement. He did so with 'very little hope that anything useful could be realised in this field'; later, however, he admitted that he had been wrong.[41]

In addition to Dalton, another member of the Government interested in the plan was Richard Law, the Minister of State. 'Dalton and Law were strong supporters of Meade's Commercial Union', the historian of the currency and trade negotiations, R. N. Gardner, has written. The eventual outcome was the Charter of the International Trade Organisation, and the General Agreement on Tariffs and Trade (GATT), negotiated after the war.[42]

Full Employment and Financial Policy and Dalton's interest in Com-mercial Union were both related to his central reconstruction aim: the prevention of a post-war slump. 'Planning' was the key word – socialist planning of resources, Keynesian 'macro' planning of the economy as a whole. In the short-run, there was little that Dalton could do to advance this policy beyond injecting ideas and promoting discussion – at most, planning future planning, rather than giving it practical effect. In one field, however, he was able to use his powers in a very direct way. As minister jointly responsible (with Ernest Bevin at Labour) for concentrating and locating industry, his job was to create maximum efficiency in order to boost production. Such an objective, and the means to bring it about, could be interpreted in different ways. Dalton chose to see it as a device for placing industry in the pre-war Distressed Areas. Through a series of well-judged initiatives, he was able to use his 'location' responsibility to give a post-war employment cushion to communities whose need was likely to be the greatest.

Dalton had special reasons for undertaking this task. He sat for a constituency which had suffered one of the highest levels of un-employment in the country. He had led a Labour investigation into the Distressed Areas as Chairman of the N.E.C. in 1936–7. And in the first half of 1942 he had been forcefully reminded of the miners' fears that the end of the war would bring back all the miseries of the hungry 1930s, with mass unemployment concentrated in the same regions as before.

In turning to the problem of 'distributing' industry he drew on his own pre-war experience – his observations of Soviet planning in 1932, and his own Distressed Areas Report, and he made use of the Report of the Royal Commission on Distribution of the Industrial Popula-tion (the Barlow Report), published in January 1940, and immediately forgotten. His case was simple. Laissez-faire in industrial location should be abandoned. Work should be taken to areas that needed it and pushed out of areas that did not. 'Both to secure full employment in the depressed areas, and for other social reasons, I regard some national control of industrial location as essential,' he told Recon-struction Committee colleagues in May 1943.[43] This was a major advance on pre-war government objectives. Some small steps in the same direction had already been taken: in 1934 the Special Areas (Development and Improvement) Act had introduced measures of 'positive external assistance', and in 1936 the first publicly sponsored industrial estates had been established. Such measures were, however, little more than token. It was the Barlow Report (primarily concerned with urban overcrowding), and its call for 'some form of national planning of industry',[44] which provided an opening. Dalton made the Barlow Report his text and gave it a radically new meaning.

He set himself two aims: to persuade the Cabinet of the need for legislation to establish permanent post-war control of the location of industry by central government; and, meanwhile, to do as much as he could by selectively allocating building licences, by providing indus-trial estates, and by re-allocating ordnance factories for peace-time use, to ensure that as much new industry as possible went to areas where it would be most needed after the war.[45]

In the spring of 1943, he took up the matter with the Reconstruction Committee, and started to rally political support. Morrison was hesi-tant; Cripps was concerned lest factories in his Bristol constituency would have to be shifted. But Ellen Wilkinson (like Dalton, a north-east M.P.) was enthusiastic and so, crucially, was Bevin. Others added their backing. Soon a solid front among Labour ministers had been established. Initial resistance from the Treasury decreased after the sudden death of Kingsley Wood late in September, and Wood's replacement as Chancellor by Sir John Anderson.

Having secured a base, Dalton moved into action. First, he brought in Douglas Jay, currently working in the Ministry of Supply, 'to be in effect my P.A. for post-war', with the rank of Assistant Secretary.[46] Jay's job was to persuade Whitehall that the Distressed Areas (renamed by Dalton 'Development' Areas) must be rejuvenated as soon as the war ended. There were three stages: first came the task of inserting in the projected Employment Policy White Paper a passage authorising an ambitious scheme for the location of industry; the second stage was to establish in the Board of Trade the necessary machinery to carry it out; the third was to draft and help steer through Parliament a Bill giving the Board requisite legal powers (in addition to those over building licences). The 'ambitious scheme' involved enlarging and increasing the number of industrial estates in the former Distressed Areas, building 'advance factories' for sale or let, converting wartime factories to peacetime production, taking powers for increased government lending, and controlling new industrial building in the congested midlands and south-east. For the first half of the war Jay had helped to mobilise the labour force for the war production machine. 'Dalton knew clearly what he wanted, but he did not know how to get it', Jay recalls, 'and thanks to the last three years at the Ministry of Supply, I believed I did.'[47]

But there were strong objections from a predictable quarter. Dalton encountered immediate opposition from two old enemies: Beaverbrook and Bracken. Rumours reached Dalton that Beaverbrook – now Lord Privy Seal – was taking a particular interest in his plans. The ominous possibility suddenly arose that the wily press baron might be given the post of Minister of Reconstruction, 'a sort of Super-Minister on the Home Front, to boss us all'.[48]

Alarmed, Dalton turned to Labour colleagues for support. He told Attlee he would resign if Beaverbrook was put in charge of post-war plans, 'because I know, from three sources, that he has been doing his best to damage me personally and that he used to incite his staff, day by day, to "down that bugger Dalton again tomorrow".' It was like the old days at M.E.W. and P.W.E. Attlee was soothing, and helpful. The Deputy Prime Minister saw the Prime Minister and afterwards reported that they had had 'quite a row, as we usually do'. The upshot was that Beaverbrook was kept out of anything to do with post-war.[49] Dalton was much relieved. 'Sometimes I saw Max as a dwarf, whispering obscene secrets into the Emperor's ear', he wrote later.[50]

By beating off Beaverbrook, rallying his colleagues, finessing on the Reconstruction Priorities Committee and bullying his own civil servants, Dalton eventually succeeded in inserting a chapter on *The Balanced Distribution of Industry and Labour* in the crucial Employment Policy White Paper which the War Cabinet adopted on 19th May 1944. 'It will be an object of Government policy', the White Paper declared, 'to secure a balanced industrial development in areas which have in the past been unduly dependent on industries specially vulnerable to unemployment.'[51] This commitment was virtually a rephrasing of a sentence Dalton had inserted in Labour's 1937 programme: 'Labour will take steps to bring new industries into [the Distressed] areas, will encourage existing industries, develop local resources and improve communications ... '[52]

Dalton now set about using his powers relating to location and concentration directly. With the Location chapter in the Employment White Paper as his excuse, he set up a new department to give effect to the White Paper commitment in anticipation of a change in the law. Once again he turned to temporary officials to provide the drive and commitment for what he wanted to do – appointing as joint heads of his new crusading section a businessman, Sir Philip Warter, and the socialist economist, Douglas Jay. The wartime building licence system, which channelled all applications for post-war industrial building sites to the Board of Trade, was their tool. The plan was to make positive use of what had been designed as a negative instrument.

The Jay-Warter axis was effective, and a number of major location decisions were made as a result of their activities. A huge new strip mill was placed at Margam in South Wales; petrochemicals and car manufacture were established at Linwood and Grangemouth, and synthetic fibres were established in Pontypool, all as a result of Board of Trade pressure. Such matters were often settled arbitrarily. A hint, or a gentlemen's agreement, was often enough to produce the decision the Board wanted. This was true of the siting of a petro-chemicals plant by I.C.I. on Teeside. Dalton noted on 12th May 1944:

> Warter and Jay to see me with very good news. I.C.I. want to build a large new Works, to employ 5,000 people, south of the Tees and a few miles east of Middlesbrough. This would be a perfect location from the point of view of Cleveland, where the ironstone mines seem bound to go completely dead within a few years after the war.

Having formed this opinion, Dalton told Sir Philip Warter to give the Deputy Chairman of I.C.I., Sir John Nicholson, every encouragement, and inform him that for such a project I.C.I. would have 'as good industrial priority as the Development Areas'. As a result, a major complex was established at Wilton, becoming and remaining the biggest employer on Teesside, taking over from the ironstone mines which had ceased to operate completely by the early 1960s. Douglas Jay recalls how this came about:

> Sir John had a map, and said he would put his finger on the proposed location if we would say 'yes' or 'no' verbally, and keep the secret to ourselves until the land was bought. We agreed. Sir John put his finger on the south bank of the Tees near to the mouth and I said: 'Yes'. That was the origin of I.C.I. Wilton, and that was how such matters were settled between the Government and industry in 1944–5.[53]

One of the new department's most important openings was provided by the existence of millions of square feet which had been allocated to ordnance factories in the pre-war Distressed Areas, as part of a policy of strategic dispersal aimed at reducing bombing risks. In September 1943 Dalton had urged the Cabinet Reconstruction Committee that post-war arms production should be kept in these areas and, where such production was discontinued, an ordnance factory should be adapted to a suitable form of civilian production.[54] The Board acted on this recommendation, and immediately after the break-up of the Coalition, thirty-five such factories were released from munitions work and reallocated for civilian use.[55]

In addition Dalton put great emphasis on the building of 'standard' or 'advance' factories on new industrial estates. One of the latter in which he took particular interest was Aycliffe in County Durham, close to his own constituency. When a geography professor at Durham University who was a member of the Board of Trade's regional advisory body objected, Jay appealed to the President. Dalton exploded with rage and 'directed in stentorian tones that Board of Trade officials in London and Newcastle should push Aycliffe forward with all speed'.[56] The industrial estate was established, and after the war a new town was built at Aycliffe to house the workers this expanding centre needed to employ. Meanwhile Dalton appointed as Regional Controller in the north-east, his most favoured region, S. A. Sadler-Forster, a Middlesbrough accountant who was to play a major part in industrial and new town development in County Durham and Northumberland.

In his own constituency Dalton worked through his friend Will Davis to set up the West Auckland Trading Estate. He gave so much help to one particular newcomer, the West Auckland Clothing Company, run by a family of refugee German Jews, that anti-semitic rumours developed, especially among competitors in the trade. On a trip to Bishop Auckland at the beginning of 1945, Dalton pressed on

Sadler-Forster 'the importance of having only gentile firms hence-forth at St Helen's', in order to placate his critics.[57] Nevertheless, one particularly malicious story – that the President of the Board of Trade received free, uncouponed suits in return for favours – continued to circulate and returned to haunt him in the ugly aftermath of the Lynskey Tribunal hearings on corruption several years later.[58]

It was not surprising, indeed, that Dalton's new policy should arouse opposition from people who did not benefit from it. Building licences and the control of scarce building materials gave the President a power over civilian employment that was wholly new. Dalton's use of this power involved a degree of intervention in the market which no previous government had even considered.

Piecemeal intervention, however, was not enough for Dalton: he wanted the new policy to be strengthened and legitimised by an Act of Parliament. He was convinced of the need to make control of location permanent. His last few months in office were, therefore, devoted to the task of getting a Distribution of Industry Bill on to the statute books.[59] This was Coalition poker at its most nail-biting. It involved a piece of legislation, and a principle, that mattered more to him than anything in domestic politics since the start of his career.

Suspecting that the Distribution Bill might be dropped from the King's Speech at the end of 1944, Dalton wrote a letter to the Prime Minister on 21st November, making his most impassioned plea of the war. 'I know these Areas and their people well', he·wrote.

Through no fault of their own, they had a very raw deal between the wars. They are some of the pick of our industrial workers and of our fighting men, and I should feel, if we cannot get effective legislation next session, that we should be letting these fine people down, who will have contributed so much to victory.[60]

Before sending the letter, Dalton rehearsed it with Jay – declaring that if it was not accepted he would resign and publish it as a political creed.[61] In fact pressure succeeded and the Bill was mentioned in the King's Speech.

A new problem now arose. 'Coalition poker' involved the well-judged use of resignation threats. But party politics was beginning to break out everywhere. In December the Labour Party Conference decided conclusively to fight the next election as an independent party. Tory ministers in the War Cabinet – no longer having anything to gain by placating Labour – dragged their feet. Dalton began seriously to contemplate resignation if he could not get his way – not to force the Government's hand, but to leave the Government in a blaze of socialist glory on a good issue just before the election.[62] Once again the Prime Minister yielded. On 13th December the War Cabinet took Dalton's paper first and Distribution of Industry was put into the top sixteen Reconstruction Bills for the new legislative programme. Beaverbrook objected, but Ernest Bevin's intervention on Dalton's behalf was decisive.[63]

The Bill was published in February 1945, and received its Second Reading on 21st March. 'It is the first instalment of a debt of honour which we owe to some of the best and bravest of our fighting men, from Scotland, from Tyneside, from County Durham and from elsewhere', Dalton told the House.[64] The Bill gave the President of the Board of Trade extensive powers to build factories, make grants and acquire land in specified Development Areas, and it required industrialists to notify the department of their intentions to build a new factory ('compulsory consultation'). Clause 9 of the Bill, which aroused most controversy, enabled the Board to declare any area a Restricted Area, within which permission would be needed to build or extend an industrial building.[65]

There was no division, but Tory backbenchers were hostile.[66] The *Daily Herald* predicted that there would be 'a calculated attempt, as the Bill goes along to its further stages, to wreck it',[67] and this proved correct. The Bill started in Standing Committee on V.E. Day – 8th May. But it was still in limbo when the Coalition broke up on 23rd May. Fortunately, however, Dalton's successor at the Board of Trade, Oliver Lyttelton, and the Parliamentary Secretary, Captain Waterhouse, who continued to hold office in the Caretaker Government, supported the Bill. A concession was needed: Dalton readily offered one. Clause 9 was dropped. This had been put into the Bill as a 'pious hoax' – so that it could be surrendered at the right moment. At last, the Bill passed into law – receiving the Royal Assent on 15th June, the day Parliament was dissolved. It was a close run thing. Jay wrote later, 'Without Dalton and Bevin we should have had no post-war Development Area policy. But the prime credit must of course go to Dalton.'

This was not the end of the matter. The Distribution of Industry Act had been conceived in the expectation that a Conservative (or at best a Coalition) Government would be in power to administer it. Labour's election victory and Dalton's appointment as Chancellor provided an unexpected opportunity to see it put fully into effect. In co-operation with Cripps (first post-war President of the Board of Trade), Dalton ensured that the Act was interpreted in a vigorously interventionist manner. Grants were provided, industrial estates developed, new towns built. Unemployment in the north-east had been 38 per cent in 1932. By 1948–9 it was down to 3 per cent, falling to 1·5 per cent in June 1951. The economic climate would have ensured a drop in unemployment even without the Act. Arguably, however, laissez-faire in industrial location would have produced intense congestion and an acute labour shortage in London and the midlands, and, as soon as war production ceased, a big upsurge in unemployment elsewhere.[68] In particular, the use of Industrial Development Certificates as a prerequisite for planning permission by the Labour Government helped to ensure that in the 1945–7 period the Development Areas gained their greatest ever share of total new industrial development: 51·3 per cent of total national development (by area). 'This success was visible', writes a recent historian of regional planning, 'and it implanted in many minds the idea that regional problems could effectively be tackled by government policy.'[69] Dalton explained to a journalist in 1944: 'I see no reason why a variety of light industries – and some of the industries using the newer processes on which we must rely more and more – should not establish themselves in Scotland, on the North East Coast, and in South Wales.'[70] The Act remained the basis of all regional policy until 1960, and the reference point of policy that followed.

'I got away with a good deal more Socialism in the Act than I ever expected', Dalton boasted during the election.[71] Few successes in the Coalition poker game were more dramatic. None indicated so clearly the shape of things to come.[72] For Dalton, too, the achievement was important. Nothing could have had a more powerful effect in reinforcing his own belief in 'socialist planning' based on physical controls, as a practical accompaniment to the new-fangled techniques of demand management. 'Every extension of Socialism makes it easier to plan employment as a whole', declared Labour's 1944 document, *Full Employment and Financial Policy*, which Dalton had written.[73] His experience at the Board, especially over Location, strongly reinforced this opinion.

XXIV

The Switch

Apart from watching the final stages of his Distribution of Industry Bill, Dalton took little interest in the dying phase of the rump Parliament. The war in Europe had been won. An election was shortly to take place, and the result was still widely expected to be a 'khaki' victory for Churchill. Among the Labour ministers, after five years in office, there was a sense of a task complete. With a resumption of the Coalition increasingly unlikely, it was natural to assume that Labour would be out of government for several years at least.

All that remained was the ceremonial, and the campaign. Dalton found the ritual of handing over the seals of office at Buckingham Palace stiff, and he recorded his irritation with the King in a significantly sharp diary note:

> The King has very little to say and doesn't seem to have focussed any B. of T. problem ... I don't suppose he has ever seen a coupon, either for clothes or food. Anyway he really had nothing to say, and made no personal impact on me whatever. As nearly inanimate as an animate Monarch could be!

Saying goodbye to Churchill was better. Dalton thanked the Prime Minister for what he had done. 'You and all the others have always been exceedingly kind to me, and I should like to thank *you* for all you have done', Churchill replied. Later Dalton was moved by the sight of tears running down Churchill's cheeks as the premier addressed the ministerial gathering.[1] At the Board of Trade the retiring President assembled his senior officials and made a little speech, with a special word for each of them.[2]

In the run-up to the election, Dalton spoke for thirty-two candidates, including among non-M.P.s Evan Durbin, John Freeman, Roy

Jenkins, Hugh Gaitskell, Christopher Mayhew, George Wigg, Fred Willey and Kenneth Younger. He picked them because he liked them and thought they stood a chance of winning. Many had been selected through his intervention. Against the name of each he recorded an estimate of the likely outcome ('Freeman – Very attractive and glamorous Candidate, even so odds slightly against, but might win', and so on). He predicted victory for 20, defeat for 8, with 4 too close to call. 'We have certainly never had a better team in the field than this time', he wrote.

The campaign in Bishop Auckland was quiet. His opponent was an inexperienced Liberal National, who went round the constituency asking through a loudspeaker: 'What about Dalton in 1938?' but nobody knew what it meant.[3] Dalton fought on Labour's programme *Let Us Face the Future*, much of which he had written. A major theme was nationalisation of the mines. At the Miners' Conference in Blackpool at the end of June he told delegates that public ownership must involve 'miners themselves taking a full share of responsibility for the conduct of the industry'. He lambasted the Tories for their pre-war record, but praised the Coalition and avoided criticising the Prime Minister – until the night before the poll. Then he urged electors to distinguish between Churchill the war leader and Churchill the politician, declaring that during the campaign the Prime Minister had 'surrendered to the worst of his advisers' and allowed himself to be degraded into a petty party boss.[4] In Bishop Auckland, the big issues were pensions, housing and fear of a return to pre-war unemployment; there were also disturbing signs of hostility towards the Jewish owners of new factories. Socialism – either in the form of state planning or greater equality – was barely discussed.[5]

Polling Day was on 5th July. Because of the need to collect the service vote, counting was delayed until 25th July. Dalton went to West Leaze in the meantime to recover. Evan Durbin came to stay for three days and wrote in the visitors' book: 'Are we M.P.s?'[6]

Dalton's private hope was to increase his own Bishop Auckland majority to 10,000. He failed to do so, holding the seat by only 8,860, less than a thousand up on 1935. It was scarcely a serious disappointment. By the time of the announcement of his own result the national verdict was already known. There had been a huge movement of opinion in favour of Labour. Friends were unexpectedly elected – 30 not 20 of Dalton's chosen 32 won – and enemies were unexpectedly knocked out. 'The defeat of Bracken, coming early, gave me a very keen thrill!' Dalton later recalled.[7] By lunch-time on 26th July a Labour Government had become certain.

The same evening Dalton boarded an overnight train at Darlington.

It was his ninth contest and his fifth victory. He had been an M.P. for a total of sixteen years and had served as a minister for more than seven. He was almost 58. Before the election he had planned for a Labour defeat, the end of his ministerial career, an indefinite period in Opposition, perhaps even a literary retirement. Suddenly the future looked very different.

In spite of his own predictions, Dalton had never discounted the possibility of a Labour majority. Leaving nothing to chance, he had made clear to Attlee, well in advance, where his ambition lay if the unexpected should occur. On 16th May, a week before the Coalition broke up, he told the Party Leader firmly that he wanted to be Foreign Secretary. 'I thought that probably I could come as near to understanding and dealing with [the Russians] as anybody', he explained. 'I was sure they had to be met both with strength and with understanding and I said that I was not quite confident that this combination was being applied now, either on the political or official planes.' Attlee did not say either yes or no.[8] In mid-July, however, after Bevin had indicated that he was 'not in the running' for the Foreign Office, the Party Leader gave Dalton a strong affirmative hint. He wrote to Dalton agreeing that, as far as Bevin was concerned, 'the Home Front is his sphere'.[9]

When Dalton saw Attlee shortly before lunch on 27th July and was told by the new Prime Minister that 'almost certainly' he would be Foreign Secretary he took the news in his stride. Such an appointment had been widely predicted and would have been greeted with approval by the new P.L.P. and by the Labour Movement. The matter seemed settled when Attlee advised him to pack his bag for the journey to Potsdam next day:

> I asked whether we needed evening dress. [Attlee] said, No, Stalin didn't dress, but it was hot and I had better take a thin suit. He said they made one very comfortable at Potsdam. I asked him when this would be definite. He said: 'After this afternoon's meeting. I will ring you up as soon as I can'.

But the appointment was never made. Dalton and Attlee both attended a meeting of prominent parliamentarians at Transport House at 3 p.m. The meeting passed off smoothly without 'any word spoken by anyone of who might hold what office', and then dispersed. Around 4 p.m. Attlee rang Dalton, as he had promised, and asked to see him again. Dalton went immediately to the Cabinet Office in

Great George Street. The Prime Minister now declared that he had had second thoughts. He wanted Bevin to be Foreign Secretary and Dalton to be Chancellor of the Exchequer. Dalton was taken aback. 'I said I was much less confident that I could do a good job at the Treasury than at the F.O.', he recorded. Attlee replied: 'Of course you will, and we will all help you.' One reason for the change, the Prime Minister explained, was that Morrison and Bevin needed to be kept apart. 'If they were both on the home front they would quarrel all the time.' Dalton accepted this explanation, and the post offered him, and they moved on to discuss other appointments.[10]

It was a major decision, Attlee's first as Prime Minister. Financial and international arrangements of great importance for the post-war world remained to be settled, and in each of the two key departments the man in charge had a wide discretion. How might Bevin have handled the American Loan negotiations or, had it arisen, the financial crisis of 1947? What line would Dalton have taken on Palestine? Would Dalton have been less or more inclined to seek an understanding with the Russians? Seldom have the political ideas, prejudices and personalities of individual ministers mattered more. We need therefore to consider closely why the switch was made.

There are two distinct questions. First, did anything happen in the period between Dalton's two interviews with Attlee on 27th July to influence the Prime Minister, causing him abruptly to reverse a decision apparently reached earlier in the same day? Second – whatever the answer to the first question – what reasons persuaded Attlee not to allocate the two offices as most people expected, as Dalton and Bevin themselves wished, and as Attlee himself originally intended?

'With whom did C.R.A. lunch?' Dalton scribbled in the margin of his own diary entry,[11] believing that anybody who influenced the Prime Minister must have seen him over luncheon. Attlee denied one story that he lunched with Churchill.[12] Another suggestion was that the Cabinet Secretary, Sir Edward Bridges, intervened.[13] Yet another was that Attlee allowed himself to be influenced by several members of the parliamentary leadership at Transport House in the early afternoon. Herbert Morrison (whose own machinations at the time make him a less than reliable witness) claimed that he himself had warned the Prime Minister about Dalton's uncontrollable temper, saying that it would be a handicap in diplomacy. 'Whiteley [the Chief Whip] agreed; then Attlee agreed', Morrison wrote later; 'and so the appointments were made ... '[14]

Yet the first question – the 'mystery' of what if anything moved Attlee between lunch and tea – need not exercise us greatly. Contrary to common belief, Attlee was often dilatory in making key decisions. Forced up against one of such fundamental importance it is not a cause for great surprise that, being in two minds on the morning of 27th July, he should have leant first one way and then the other before making a final choice.

The more interesting question is what factor or factors, in general and over a longer period, induced him to make a choice which was not expected nor, apparently, envisaged earlier by Attlee himself. The Prime Minister's own explanation to Dalton (the need for harmony on the home front) is convincing as one reason, though scarcely as the only one. If it had been the only reason, it is unclear why Attlee should not have thought of it sooner, when he had agreed that Bevin belonged at home. Moreover, despite the strong mutual dislike of Bevin and Morrison, the two men had worked together satisfactorily as home front ministers for five years, without damage either to Labour unity or to the war effort.

If, as Attlee himself later conceded, other considerations were also involved, one may have been a belief that Dalton, who knew about public finance, was better suited to a department whose problems were often highly technical. Dalton himself was attracted by this idea, and by a rumour that Bridges had pressed the point on Attlee. 'I might have done either', he reflected, 'but Ernie couldn't have done the Treasury.'[15]

It is equally – perhaps more – likely that the new Prime Minister was persuaded that Bevin would be better, or more acceptable, as Foreign Secretary. Here there is evidence, both that Attlee had such a thought in his mind, and that his Foreign Office advisers were anxious that it should be put there.

Despite what Attlee said to Dalton on 27th July, he later told Bevin's biographer that he had been influenced by a feeling that the trade union leader would be better at standing up to the Russians. 'I thought affairs were going to be pretty difficult and a heavy tank was what was going to be required rather than a sniper.'[16] Attlee was given to *post hoc* rationalisations and we need not take this remark at its face value. What gives it significance, however, is that it coincides with a widely expressed view among senior diplomats immediately after the Labour victory had been announced.

In the Foreign Office, feelings were stronger about the sniper than about the tank. Officials knew little of Bevin. They knew enough of Dalton to dislike and fear him. Dalton's ambition to be Foreign Secretary had always contained an odd, though not irrational, ambivalence. His fascination with foreign policy had been combined with a fierce hostility towards many of those responsible for carrying it out. This hostility had been reciprocated. During the war, Dalton himself had been conscious of what he called 'strange apprehensions' about him within the diplomatic corps. 'It was apparently believed by some that I was building up a Foreign Service of my own', he recalled, 'and that my S.O.E. personnel were in training to take over a number of key posts from the regular diplomats on the fateful day when, as some feared, I became Foreign Secretary in a Labour Government after the war, or even, as a few feared, in some reshuffle of the Coalition.'[17] Anthony Eden, the retiring Foreign Secretary, undoubtedly expressed the views of many of his advisers when he wrote, on hearing that Dalton might succeed him, 'This would be very bad; it should be Bevin'.[18]

After Bevin's appointment, it was rumoured that Bridges had warned the Prime Minister not to appoint Dalton because several senior Foreign Office men would resign if he did so.[19] Gladwyn Jebb, who had served both Dalton and the head of the Foreign Office, Sir Alexander Cadogan, formed an impression that Cadogan had advised Attlee against Dalton.[20] Cadogan had recently been in Attlee's company in Potsdam, and was privately rooting for Bevin. 'I think we may do better with Bevin than with any other of the Labourites', the Permanent Under-Secretary wrote in his diary on 28th July. 'I think he's broad-minded and sensible, honest and courageous ... He's the heavyweight of the Cabinet and will get his own way with them, so if he can be put on the right line, that may be all right.'[21]

It was natural that, other factors apart, leading officials should want to have the 'heavyweight of the Cabinet' to fight their battles in preference to a man they had found difficult to handle as a junior minister and as minister responsible for the blockade and S.O.E. But there were also policy reasons. Bevin came to foreign affairs without knowledge, and hence without preconceptions. Dalton by contrast was regarded as 'viewy' because of his pro-Zionist stance on Palestine, and his sympathy towards Russian claims against the defeated Reich. It was feared that, on such matters, he might be reluctant to take advice. Cadogan's suggestion that Bevin was more 'sensible' and 'broad-minded' than any alternative should be seen in this light. The trade union leader's later reputation among diplomats as a great Foreign Secretary owed much to his readiness to be 'put on the right line'. We may imagine that, through Cadogan or Bridges directly, or as a result of an impression more generally acquired, Attlee came to believe that Dalton's appointment to the Foreign Office would cause serious trouble within the service. It is also possible that the full passion of anti-Dalton feeling in the Foreign Office only became apparent after Labour's victory.

There we might leave it, but for one other intriguing and much-debated factor: the King. On 26th July, the day before the two interviews with Dalton, Attlee had visited Buckingham Palace to accept office as Prime Minister. During a discussion about the shape of the future Government, King George VI expressed himself forcefully on the subject of one office: the Foreign Secretaryship. He was against Dalton and in favour of Bevin. Thereafter, the King always claimed to have been responsible for the choice of Bevin.

Was Attlee influenced by the King's advice? The account in the King's own diary seems to leave little doubt:

> I then saw Mr. Attlee & asked him to form a government. He accepted & became my new Prime Minister. I told him he would have to appoint a Foreign Secy. & take him to Berlin. I found he was very surprised his Party had won & had had no time to meet or discuss with his colleagues any of the Offices of State. I asked him whom he would make Foreign Secy. & he suggested Dr Hugh Dalton. I disagreed with him & said that Foreign Affairs was the most important subject at the moment & I hoped he would make Mr. Bevin take it. He said he would but he could not return to Berlin till Saturday at the earliest. I told him I could hold a Council on Saturday to swear in the new Secy. of State.

As this interview took place *before* Attlee's semi-offer of the Foreign Secretaryship to Dalton, we must assume either that the King misunderstood the Prime Minister's reply (Attlee had a habit of grunting in a way that might be taken for assent when he was actually reserving judgment) or that he changed his mind not once, but three times, within the space of twenty-four hours. Both possibilities indicate a high degree of uncertainty on Attlee's part, which is indeed suggested by the whole paragraph.

The most important feature of the King's record, however, is the clear evidence it provides of Attlee's initial preference for Dalton, and the King's strong objection. A memorandum written immediately afterwards by Sir Alan Lascelles, the King's Private Secretary (who was not present at the actual discussion and recorded what the King told him) provides confirmation:

> Mr Attlee mentioned to the King that he was thinking of appointing Mr. Dalton to be his Foreign Secretary. His Majesty begged him to think carefully about this, and suggested that Mr. Bevin would be a better choice.[22]

It should be stressed that the occasion for this conversation was not a general or informal exploration of possibilities. Having invited Attlee to form a Government, the King was asking the new Prime Minister whom he intended to place in it. It is inconceivable that Attlee was not prepared for the question, even if he had not yet reached a firm conclusion.

It is also improbable that Attlee would have ignored the King's comment. J. W. Wheeler-Bennett, the King's biographer, pointed out that George VI did not 'insist' on Bevin rather than Dalton. Indeed the King had no right or power to do so. But his remark certainly amounted to pressure. 'His Majesty begged him to think carefully' is strong language for a royal private secretary and suggests something close to the constitutional limits of royal advice. When a Sovereign 'begs', even Labour Prime Ministers, it is reasonable to suppose, pause before refusing.

Attlee later denied that the King's words altered his own opinion. 'I naturally took into account the King's view which was very sound', he wrote in 1959, 'but it was not a decisive factor in my arrival at my decision.'[23] Yet if the King's advice was 'very sound', why had Attlee put Dalton's name forward in the first place? As his own auto-biography shows, Attlee had a selective memory. While we need not disbelieve Attlee's statement that 'various reasons' impelled him, we may wonder whether Attlee's recollection, which contradicted the King's firm impression, was accurate. It is impossible to know what was 'decisive': but it is reasonable to suppose that the King's advice was an important factor. If that supposition is correct, we need then to consider why George VI, least political of British monarchs and seldom given to advising Prime Ministers on any matter, should have held such passionate views on this one.

Dalton, who was much engaged by this question, suggested that his own hostility to Neville Chamberlain and desire for a Soviet alliance before the war were partly responsible for the King's objection. He considered 'not unlikely' a story that at Churchill's final audience the retiring Prime Minister had told the King that Bevin would be Labour's best choice for Foreign Secretary. He also speculated that the King might have been influenced by having known the former Minister of Labour, who had been a member of the War Cabinet, better than the former President of the Board of Trade, who had not. Dalton's most interesting suggestion, however, was that his family connection with Royalty, so far from helping, counted against him:

My relations, as a Minister, with the King, though perfectly correct, were quite cold and formal. Nor did he show any inclination to make them less so.

Nor, I suspect, had I a good name at Court ... I had become a socialist at the University, and in due course had been elected to Parliament as a Labour M.P. and held junior office in a Labour Government. This was at best eccentric, maybe worse. 'Letting the side down', with an expletive, I can hear someone say.

Dalton recalled that, when offered the chance of being presented at Court to King George V by his father, he had declined. ' ... I am sure that this omission was chalked up against me, by some Court Recorder.'[24] He may have been right. It is hard to know precisely what the Royal Family thought of him. There is evidence to suggest, however, an attitude of extreme distaste.

The Duke of Windsor confirmed Dalton's own impression that his unpopularity at Court began with George V. 'Hugh Dalton was no favourite of my father', the Duke wrote in 1960. The reason, apparently, was Hugh's left-wing views.[25] The Duke once told a journalist from Bishop Auckland a story which lends weight to Hugh's own belief that he was blamed for 'letting the side down'. The Royal Family was surprised and hurt when Hugh came home from Cambridge 'full of hot-headed politics'. The Canon took him to see Prince George. 'But afterwards', recalled the Duke, 'my father told Canon Dalton "Don't ever bring that anarchist son of yours to see me again. I don't care for his ideas". We never understood why he turned against us.'[26] The Duke told Harold Nicolson a similar tale in 1949, when Nicolson was collecting material for his biography of George V. Having described the intimacy that existed between his father and the Canon, the Duke added: 'The only thing King George would not stand was what he called "your anarchist son" '.[27]

Did George VI feel the same? Modern British monarchs do not usually reveal their personal views about subjects, especially if those views are hostile. In the case of Hugh Dalton, however, George VI made a rare exception. That he felt towards Canon Dalton's 'anarchist son' a definite and powerful emotion is indicated by a remarkable entry in the diary of a later Chancellor of the Exchequer, Hugh Gaitskell, following an audience in May 1951, a few months before George VI's death:

[The King] spoke unusually frankly and said, 'There is really only one of your people that I cannot abide. You can probably guess who that is.' I said, 'Is it Bevan?' He said, 'No, I can manage him. It is your predecessor but one.' So we then talked about Hugh Dalton.

I explained that he was a personal friend of mine, and he was really much nicer than people supposed. I gathered that the King's dislike of him (I found this was shared by the Queen as well afterwards) really goes back to the Windsor days when Hugh Dalton's father was tutor to King George V, and apparently very like HD in having a loud voice and bullying manner.[28]

Three points are clear from this passage. First, that the King's dislike of Hugh Dalton was strong. Second that it was long-standing. Third, that it was personal more than political.

Why? We do not know. Hugh's contact with the King had been slight. Perhaps resentment against Canon Dalton, whose closeness to George V had been in contrast to George V's distant relationship with his own children, was carried over to the Canon's clever, opinionated, disloyal, mocking son who resembled the Canon physically and mentally in so many ways. Perhaps royal dislike of Hugh had been fed by the nature of Hugh's assault on the rich: his tauntings of the land-owning class and attack on the principle of inheritance. Royal Families have long memories. It may be that a prejudice had lain dormant, gradually brought to life by Hugh's growing prominence.

What is notable about Gaitskell's diary entry, however, is the intensity of feeling it reveals: Dalton was singled out as the object of a special hatred. Can this be explained simply by Hugh's treachery in 'letting the side down'? Or was there a particular slight? Hugh himself mentioned his refusal to be presented at Court; but this gesture of defiance had occurred in the days of George VI's father. Was there, perhaps, a more recent event which might have excited royal feelings against him? Again, we do not know. There is, however, evidence of one incident, a few months or a year before the election of the Labour Government, which may help to explain why, when faced with the prospect of Hugh as his Foreign Secretary, the King was so adamantly opposed. The cause was a particularly unpleasant Dalton family quarrel, with echoes of early Windsor days. The manifestation was – allegedly – a display of contempt by Hugh for his family's royal connection which the King, learning of it, found insulting.

When Kitty Dalton died on 25th March 1944 Hugh's distress was little more than dutiful. She had not been close to her children. During her short final illness, Hugh kept in touch by telephone with her companion Mrs Battye in Datchet, Berkshire, but made no attempt to see her. On the afternoon of her death he dealt with the funeral arrangements quickly, efficiently and on his own.

Domestic matters were seldom at the front of his mind. When he had to take note of them they were generally a source of irritation. His mother's death jolted him suddenly back into emotions he preferred to forget. Depressed and lonely rather than grieving, his thoughts turned to his despised and long ignored sibling:

> It is very odd that my sister Georgie has taken no notice at all of the letter Mrs B. wrote to her a week ago saying that my mother was very ill and queer. She has neither written, telephoned nor offered to come down. She would have done no good here anyhow; she would only have got in the way.

Having arranged a cremation for the following Tuesday, Hugh wrote Georgie a letter the same night, Saturday 25th. Assuming that Georgie's silence was deliberate, he apparently made no attempt to contact his sister by telephone. Next day he delivered to *The Times* a death notice which was printed on Monday, 27th March:[29]

> DALTON – On March 25, 1944. Catherine Alicia, widow of Canon J. N. Dalton K.C.V.O., C.M.G. Funeral at St George's Chapel, Windsor, at 3 p.m. on Thursday March 30, when her ashes will be laid beside those of her husband. The service will be private, but friends of the family will be welcome. Memorial service at Parish Church, Datchet at 2.30 p.m. on Friday March 31st.[30]

Here was the basis for a disastrous misunderstanding. For Mrs Battye's letter, if it was ever sent, was never received. Despite a difficult relationship, Georgie had kept in touch with her mother, writing weekly letters. Yet she knew nothing of the sudden deterioration, and learnt of the death when she read the notice, wholly unexpected, in the newspaper on Monday morning.[31] Hugh's letter arrived shortly afterwards. Georgie's shock at discovering the loss of a parent was now compounded by anger at her brother's apparently cavalier and presumptuous behaviour. With help from her husband, Sir John Forbes Watson, she composed a reply.

The involvement of Sir John may not have been intended as an aggravation; that, however, was its effect. As President of the Board of Trade, Hugh had had dealings with his brother-in-law, the Director of the Confederation of British Employers. The two men had never liked each other. Personal antipathy had recently been reinforced by political disagreement. Where Hugh wanted the war to produce socialist change, socialist change was precisely what Sir John sought to prevent. Sir John's views were made plain in his own comment to the Beveridge Committee. Urging Beveridge, in effect, to abandon his

investigation, he bluntly presented the position of the Tory industrialists. Britain, he said, had entered the war against Germany to preserve
freedom, not to improve social services.[32] When, as happened several
times after 1942, Hugh encountered his brother-in-law on Board of
Trade matters, he endeavoured to have as little social contact as
possible.

Studying the letter which he now received from Georgie and Sir
John, Hugh was much displeased by what he read. The unhappy row,
which a little explaining might have avoided, escalated:

> On my return tonight I write a careful letter to my brother-in-law,
> replying to lucubrations from him and G. The latter is still living
> on old grievances of having been 'completely ignored' some
> twelve years ago when R. and I had to tidy up, quite unaided by her,
> my father's affairs and my mother's future arrangements. It would
> be sad, were it less silly. My first inclination is to write a rather
> sharp letter, but I finally tone this down into a more 'dignified'
> allocution.

Meanwhile, without consulting Georgie, Hugh had asked the
Public Trustee to handle all the details of his mother's estate. On the
Tuesday, after attending a meeting of the Central Prices Regulation
Committee in the morning, Hugh cremated his mother in the after-
noon, having travelled down to Datchet and thence to Woking for the
purpose. No other member of the family was present.

Hugh took a lugubrious interest in the technical details:

> The process takes two hours. Now they use gas burners, two rows of
> them, one on each side of the coffin containing the body. Before the
> war they used solid fuel. From the burned remains pieces of wood
> forming part of the coffin are first picked out and then the pieces of
> bone are passed through a special machine which grinds them to a
> powder. The resulting ash is quite heavy. Today, when the small
> casket was brought out, quite full and still warm, it weighed, we
> estimated, 7 or 8 lbs. Oh, how quick and clean and final!

Catherine Dalton's ashes were laid beside those of her husband in
St George's Chapel, Windsor, at a funeral service two days later.
Ruth came down from Manchester. Georgie and her husband were
also there. It was the first meeting of brother and sister for several
years:

> R. and I call at the Deanery about a quarter of an hour before the

service and walk in immediately behind the Dean, who carries the casket. We find Georgie and John already established in their stalls next to ours. I suppose it will be a new grievance that they were not also invited to the Deanery and to join in the procession. When it is finished, we are just going off when G. comes rushing after me, having shown no particular warmth, or, indeed, emotion, at any stage in the proceedings, to ask whether it is clear that she will be able, whenever she likes, to go down to Datchet and stick a label on anything she wants, and buy it at the probate value. I say 'Oh yes, of course'. She then begins to complain that she has not yet received a copy of the Will. I say I am sure the Public Trustee will send her one before long. She then goes on to complain several times over that she has been left completely in the dark about everything for many years.

Hugh finished: 'I really don't feel I want to see her again.'[33] But it was not the end of the quarrel which now acquired a new, more dangerous, dimension.

Neither Hugh nor Georgie was poor or acquisitive. Hugh had a ministerial salary and no dependants, Georgie a successful husband. The battle that took place was emotional rather than material – as though their mother's death, breaking the last remaining bond between them, re-awakened a nursery contest.

Central to this sudden outbreak of sibling animosity was the connection with Royalty which had dominated their childhood. Georgie, god-daughter of a former King and bearer of his pet-name, always treasured her link with the Royal Family. Hugh, godson of the reprobate Duke of Clarence, scorned it. Uncertainty about the disposal of gifts from members of the Royal Family gave scope for a demonstration of this difference.

Hugh and Georgie each had an equal claim to all their mother's personal possessions other than ornaments and jewellery, which were left to Georgie, and private papers, which were left to Hugh. According to Catherine Dalton's will, the Public Trustee was required to sell to the two children such furniture, plate and other household effects as they wished to buy at probate value (less than market value), the purchase money to be added to the residuary estate which was to be divided equally between them. The will did not, however, specify who should have first claim on particular objects.[34]

According to Georgie's children (whose account came from their parents), the climax of the row occurred at a meeting between brother and sister held in the arbitrating presence of a representative of the Public Trustee. Asked to declare his own preferences Hugh indicated a royal item of obvious financial value, which he loudly proclaimed could easily be re-sold because it lacked the royal cipher. He then waved a contemptuous hand over the rest and boomed at Georgie: 'You can have the bloody lot!'[35]

This story, though told from a point of view hostile to Hugh, is not out of character. We may imagine that Hugh, angry (as his diary reveals) at his sister's distrust, used the occasion to attack Georgie. Dalton's diary also shows that he had little interest in his mother's possessions and was willing to let his sister take what she wanted.

There was a sequel. Georgie's daughter Heather was at boarding-school in 1944. She recalls, in the autumn of that year, receiving a letter from her mother which intrigued her so much that she missed her mid-morning bun and cocoa. According to the letter, her father had received word from a Court official that Hugh Dalton had sold a gift or gifts originally presented by members of the Royal Family. The King had been so displeased that he had asked for any royal gifts in the possession of the Forbes Watson family to be returned.[36]

We should treat the detail of this recollection cautiously. It seems odd, to say the least, that Georgie should have been punished for Hugh's misdemeanour. Nevertheless there is a core to the story which, though it cannot be proved, is believable. No royal items, apart from letters, are mentioned in Hugh's will and none were found among his or Ruth's effects, suggesting that if any passed to him he disposed of them in his lifetime. Hugh gave his refugee friends the Wagners a tea service presented by Queen Victoria:[37] another indication that royal objects had no special significance for him. If he did, indeed, sell recently inherited royal gifts, it is possible that a dealer or collector, puzzled by a sign of origin, informed the Palace.

If this is what happened, if Heather's recollection is essentially correct, then it is easy to see that any latent dislike of Hugh within the Royal Family might have been inflamed. Hugh's cool reception in May 1945 when he handed over the seals of office as President of the Board of Trade (the King seemed 'nearly as inanimate as an animate Monarch could be') becomes more explicable. And so does the King's readiness to speak against Dalton to Attlee on 26th July.

When George VI died in 1952 a flurry of newspaper reports revived earlier rumours that the King had demanded Bevin's appointment. Attlee, who was still Leader of the Labour Party, firmly rejected the suggestion that he had bowed to royal pressure. Dalton, however, continued to wonder. After the publication in 1958 of Wheeler-Bennett's biography of George VI, which included the royal diary extract quoted earlier in this chapter, Dalton's suspicions increased. In the final volume of his memoirs, Dalton commented that no objection could be taken to the King offering advice to the Prime Minister on Cabinet appointments or to the Prime Minister taking such advice. No constitutional issue was therefore involved. But, he added,

> there are two questions which, I confess, have interested me a good deal. First, why did the King advise Attlee to put Bevin, and not me, at the Foreign Office, and second, why did Attlee follow the King's advice?[38]

The answers to both questions remain uncertain. If, however, the King did change Attlee's mind, then his advice was undoubtedly the most important exercise of the royal prerogative of the reign. In which case it is a curious reflection that such an act, with its world-wide repercussions, may have occurred because of an emotion that derived in part from the turmoils of the Dalton nursery and the Saxe-Coburg-Gotha schoolroom, and from the strange interlocking of the two dynasties, more than half a century before.

XXV

Behold the Dawn Appear

So we went, each of us to his battle station, and I to the Treasury, to encounter most grave problems, wide opportunities, heavy strains, hard choices. But through it all I was to be sustained by the strength and comradeship and understanding of our great Parliamentary majority. And we all knew that, within us, and because of us, and around us, something had suddenly changed.

England arise, the long, long night is over:
Faint in the East behold the dawn appear.

Edward Carpenter's Socialist hymn at last had found fulfilment.

After the long storm of war, after the short storm of election, we saw the sunrise. As we had sung in the shadows, so now in the light,

England is risen and the day is here.

Hugh Dalton The Fateful Years (1956), pp. 482–3.

'When told that I was not to be Foreign Secretary, but Chancellor of the Exchequer, I was not unhappy, or disappointed, for more than half an hour. I swallowed my fate in one gulp.' So Dalton wrote, more than fifteen years later. We have encountered the phrase 'not unhappy' before: we may guess that, at least briefly, he was bitterly disappointed. Certainly he did not lose his desire one day to go back to the Foreign Office. But his new job swept him up so quickly that he had little time for reflection or regret.

Between 1945 and 1947, five men formed an inner core within the government, guiding its main decisions: Attlee, Bevin, Dalton, Morrison and Cripps. Morrison became Lord President, assuming the wide powers over the domestic economy which this office had acquired during the war, and taking charge of the nationalisation programme. Cripps, who had re-joined the Labour Party in time for the election, took over from Dalton at the Board of Trade. Other key posts were filled by Aneurin Bevan (Health), Chuter Ede (Home Office), Pethick-Lawrence, elevated to the Lords (India Office), George Isaacs (Labour and National Service), Emanuel Shinwell (Fuel and Power) and Ellen Wilkinson (Education).

At the Treasury, William Glenvil Hall became Financial Secretary and Evan Durbin the Chancellor's first P.P.S. On the official side Dalton was advised by Sir Edward Bridges, Permanent Secretary at the Treasury, Official Head of the Civil Service and until 1946 Secretary of the Cabinet. Beneath Bridges were six Treasury knights: three Second Secretaries – Sir Alan Barlow, Sir Wilfrid Eady and Sir Bernard Gilbert; and three Third Secretaries – Sir David Waley, Sir Herbert Brittain and Sir Henry Wilson Smith.[1] The new Chancellor appointed (or rather re-appointed) two economic advisers: Lord Keynes and Sir Richard Hopkins. Dalton's Principal Private Secretary, for most of his Chancellorship, was Burke Trend (later Lord Trend), a future Cabinet Secretary.

This official team was complemented by friends in the Labour Party: unlike some ministers, Dalton took care not to cut himself off from political influences. In addition to Durbin, he remained close to his other two 'post-warriors', Gaitskell (like Durbin a new M.P. and soon to become a junior minister) and Jay, who moved into No. 10 Downing Street as a prime ministerial adviser, before entering the House at a by-election in 1946. There were also other 'Class of '45' M.P.s, many of whom Dalton had helped to find seats. Some – like George Brown, Jim Callaghan and Christopher Mayhew – were members of his Finance Group in the P.L.P. At the same time, Dalton kept a private list of young politicians who were to be given automatic access to him whenever he was not at a meeting or in conference. Names included Raymond Blackburn, Arthur Bottomley, Barbara Castle, Aidan Crawley, John Freeman, Alfred Robens, Maurice Webb, and (in the Lords) Frank Pakenham.[2] There were later additions. Lord Trend remembers the Chancellor returning from a visit to the Oxford Union early in the summer of 1946: 'Make a note! Make a note! Name's Crosland! I want him here!' Shortly afterwards the young Anthony Crosland, still an undergraduate, visited No. 11 Downing Street and his name was put on the list.

Dalton aroused less hostility at the Treasury than at the Board of Trade. This was not because he had reformed but because of the difference of environment. At the Board, he had been a middle-ranking minister whose political philosophy was not that of the Coalition majority, or of most of his officials. At the Treasury, he was a powerful member of a reforming Cabinet, surrounded by civil servants who had a sharp appreciation of the change of epoch.

Nevertheless, there were problems. Trend recalls that the new Chancellor gave due warning:

'Would you like to be my Private Secretary?' he asked. 'Before you answer, there are two things you should know. First, unlike my predecessor [Sir John Anderson], I am a politician and a machine politician. Second, I am a man of ungovernable temper. There will certainly be occasions when I will use rough words. But I promise you one thing: I will never embarrass you in public.'

The pledge was fulfilled. So was the prophecy. 'He had a violence of anger, thrashing around like a wounded beast', according to Trend. 'If you were close to him, which was the best place to be at such times, you learnt how to deal with it. If you weren't so close, you found it alarming or offensive.'[3] The complaints were familiar: rudeness, lack of consideration, insensitivity. 'His forceful technique arouses hurt feelings or sycophantic agreement among the well-bred bureaucrats', wrote a well-informed journalist at the end of 1946. 'The failure to achieve a very harmonious relationship with his staff may prove to be Dalton's Achilles heel.'[4] Some felt that, in placing enormous burdens on his advisers, he had little notion of how the department operated. There was a story about Dalton wandering along the corridor peering at doors. 'What do all these people do', he asked, 'when they aren't talking to me?'[5]

At No. 11 Downing Street the Chancellor's office and staff were on the ground floor. As in his wartime ministries Dalton lived on the job: the Lord President occupied the first floor, and the Chancellor had his private quarters on the second. This caused difficulties for civil servants who had homes in the suburbs, and were used to working to a routine. 'He would spend hours chatting and putting things off, and then find he hadn't got very far', recalls Sir Thomas Padmore, briefly private secretary before Trend. 'He then had to stay up late to catch up.'[6] Trend remembers his own ingenious attempts to persuade the Chancellor to mount the stairs to bed. Just as he thought he had succeeded in time to catch the last train, Dalton would come running down with some new suggestion or request.[7]

In the end, however, there was a toughness about the Treasury, an ethos of unflappability, that made accommodation possible. There was also an element, generally lacking at the Board of Trade, of respect. Even the most exasperated Treasury officials appreciated Dalton's intellectual power, while the Chancellor came to make use of advice in a way that had seldom been true at Millbank House. 'He began with the assumption that a bloody official was a bloody official', says Padmore. 'But he found himself liking and getting on with people with whom he started badly.'[8]

One of these was Sir Edward Bridges – fellow Etonian, son of a Poet Laureate, coolest and most powerful of the super-officials. The two men started cautiously, then began to value each other's qualities. While Dalton found reassurance in the Cabinet Secretary's calm reliability, Bridges came to believe that on many matters (as Trend puts it) 'what Dalton wanted was right in the circumstances'. It is indeed a notable fact, relevant to the theory that the civil service will always try to sabotage or impede a socialist government, that in Labour's two most socialist years there was never any serious clash on policy between the Chancellor and the Treasury. (Relations with economists outside the Treasury, however, were another matter.)

Elsewhere at the top of his department, Dalton was impressed by the high standards of professionalism and expertise: there was no need for the sackings or transfers which he had engineered elsewhere. He had occasional difficulties with Barlow, and more frequent battles with Brittain, who bored him with legislative details. ('Why does this little man go on raising clause after clause?') His relations with Eady, Hopkins and Waley, however, were generally good. Sir Bernard Gilbert, whose special talent was for translating technical jargon into plain English, he would describe as 'the wisest of my advisers'. 'When the Chancellor got into a tangle on, say, compensation, there would be a brief note on a single page from Gilbert saying, very simply, do this or that', recalls Trend. 'Dalton would sigh with relief and put his initials at the bottom.'

Dalton's tantrums were sparked off by any irritant or frustration, and occurred with almost every senior official. An exception was Lord Keynes. According to Trend:

Dalton was wary of Keynes. Keynes was a strange, brilliant, powerful animal. He had sharp teeth and claws and crashed through life in a brilliant way. Dalton realised that he wasn't one of his buddies out hunting in the jungle; but he also realised that you didn't offend that sort of animal unnecessarily.[9]

Dalton's complex relationship with Keynes was to be vitally important during the first few months of his Chancellorship.

Later, Dalton wrote that he faced six urgent problems at the Treasury: first the reconversion to peaceful purposes of industry, manpower and expenditure; second, a smooth transition, maintaining full employment and avoiding industrial unrest or inflation; third, honouring the pledge to extend social services; fourth, changing taxation in order to cut the total and also reduce the gap between richest and poorest; fifth, carrying out nationalisation pledges; and sixth, finding a way to pay for the imports necessary to prevent mass unemployment and starvation. The last, he recalled, was 'more immediate and difficult than the rest'.[10] It was also the necessary condition for tackling the others.

The cause of Dalton's most pressing problem was a huge burden of international debt acquired during the war, which made Britain heavily dependent on the 'Lend-Lease' Agreement with the United States. So great was this dependence that it seemed inconceivable that any change would be made to the arrangement without careful consultation and long advance warning.

There were good grounds for confidence in the summer of 1945, even though the terms of the Agreement specified that Lend-Lease must end as soon as the war was over. Fighting in the Far East was expected to last another eighteen months or two years, which was felt to be ample time to work out a scheme for extending the Agreement. No consideration was given to the possibility that the Japanese might very soon be forced to surrender, or that, when hostilities ceased, the Americans would offer no extension.

In retrospect the view taken by Treasury officials, guided by Keynes, seems naively rational. Having convinced themselves that an end to Lend-Lease or its equivalent would have catastrophic effects internationally and do the United States immense harm, they concluded that the Americans would not be so foolish as to let such a thing occur. 'America will be on her knees to us in Whitehall when the war finally ends', Dalton told Noel Hall, a week after becoming Chancellor.[11] His remark echoed the assumptions of his advisers. What none of them allowed for was American law, American politics and the atomic bomb. Instead of dragging on for months or years, permitting leisurely negotiations, the Japanese war ended abruptly on 14th August, barely three weeks after Labour came to office. One week later, President Truman ordered the end of Lend-Lease, directing that all outstanding contracts should be cancelled.

Truman's decision was conveyed by Will Clayton, the American Assistant Secretary of State for Economic Affairs, to the British Chancellor and Foreign Secretary. On receiving the news, Dalton and Bevin 'looked very downcast'.[12] Well they might. British diplomatic intelligence had neglected to consider the legal nature of the Agreement, or to take into account opinion on Capitol Hill. By law, the Agreement ceased to apply when the war ended. Any decision to renew it required a vote of Congress; but Congress, economically unlettered and suspicious of British intentions, reflected the attitudes of grass roots Americans who believed that the time had come for their gallant ally to stand on its own feet.

At the Treasury, Dalton found that nobody knew what to expect, or what to do. He had inherited a wholly unprepared situation. 'A strange occurrence this week, when Bridges sent for me urgently', James Meade, employed by the Economic Section of the Cabinet Secretariat, wrote in his diary on 1st September. 'He showed me a copy of a minute by Bevin, Dalton and Cripps to the P.M. saying that in effect no work had been done on the possible effects of the end of Lend/Lease on our economy, and suggesting that the Cabinet Offices (i.e. the Economic Section) should be asked to do something ... '[13]

What might those effects be? In assessing them, Dalton leant heavily on his two advisers, appointed at the beginning of August: Sir Richard Hopkins and Lord Keynes. Hopkins, a Treasury official, was the acknowledged master of the subject of government finance. Keynes had in the course of the war acquired a god-like reputation among economists, officials and politicians alike; and, as the architect of the Bretton Woods system,* he had gained a world stature which seemed to place him above and outside the interests of individual nations. For the first few months of the Labour Government, Keynes's influence was pervasive. 'Keynes has been the Treasury over the last few years', wrote Otto (later Sir Richard) Clarke, a senior official in the Overseas Finance Division, when Keynes died in April 1946; 'he has determined policy, spurred on the officials by criticism and help, conducted the major negotiations ... He has been the brains and the conscience.'[14]

Arguably, the Chancellor could not have been better served. Yet Keynes's dominance at the Treasury did Dalton harm as well as good. Though the Chancellor greatly admired Keynes, he was made uneasily aware of the tutor-student relationship, established at Cambridge nearly forty years before. He also knew that he was not regarded as a star pupil. More important, his advisers knew it too. In private Keynes would refer to Dalton disparagingly as 'the dirty doctor', and give the impression of having written him off.[15] Civil servants were aware of the lack of intimacy, even of friendship, and that Dalton and Keynes were never comfortable together socially.[16] If Keynes's reputation

---

* Forty-four nations had sent representatives to an international conference at Bretton Woods, New Hampshire in 1944 to discuss ways of preventing a recurrence of pre-war financial crises and depression. The eventual outcome was the establishment in 1945 of the International Monetary Fund and the International Bank for Reconstruction and Development. The aim of the Fund was to provide reserves to meet balance of payments deficits; that of the Bank to advance loans to boost the development of member states.

had not shone so brightly, none of this would have mattered. As it was, Dalton found himself in the strange position of needing his chief economic adviser's good opinion rather than the other way round. A non-economist Chancellor might have felt less upstaged.

All the same Dalton listened closely to what Keynes had to say. Nobody in the Treasury had anticipated the rapid end of the Japanese war, or the sudden cessation of Lend-Lease. However, while the final stage of the European war (the period known to government economists as 'Stage I') still continued, work was being done on the problems not only of 'Stage II' (the period in which the war was against Japan alone), but also of 'Stage III' (the period after Japan had been defeated). In March 1945, when the Coalition was still in power and Stage III seemed far away, Keynes produced an important paper called 'Overseas Financial Policy in Stage III'. In the unexpected emergency, Keynes's paper became the basis for a British attempt to obtain financial help from the United States.

In September 1945, negotiations began in Washington to replace Lend-Lease with a new financial arrangement. At this point, the main difference between Keynes and Dalton was in degrees of optimism and pessimism. Keynes was both Cassandra and Micawber. He predicted dire consequences if the British deficit was not met, yet he was confident that something would turn up – believing that a new act of imaginative benevolence on the part of the Americans, like Lend-Lease, would save the day. Departing for the United States to lead the British team of negotiators, he mentioned to the Cabinet a figure of $6 billion and talked in terms of a grant-in-aid with few strings. 'His plan was to ask for £1,500 million as a free gift, or failing that, as an interest-free loan', wrote Sir Roy Harrod, Keynes's official biographer. 'This was surely within reason.' Sceptical ministers, including Dalton, were soon persuaded by Keynes's 'winged words'.[17]

As Marshall Aid later showed, Keynes's case was indeed 'within reason'. On logical grounds, American self-interest would have been best served by American altruism. Unfortunately economic rationality and political reality did not coincide. What seemed self-evident to a British liberal economist was regarded with suspicion by the Truman administration's advisers. Nor did Keynes's negotiating style help: resembling that of a university seminar or common room debate, it was particularly ill-suited to the temperament of the American chief negotiator, Treasury Secretary Fred Vinson, 'a conscientious conservative, border-state Democrat',[18] who had no knowledge of, or interest in, economic theory. 'Keynes brought out ideas too soon', believes one member of the British delegation. 'The Americans were frightened by ideas. Their reaction was to send for lawyers and politicians.'[19]

Keynes and Lord Halifax, the British Ambassador, began their talks with Vinson and Will Clayton, the U.S. Assistant Treasury Secretary, on 11th September. Keynes, concerned to avoid any sense of seeking charity, based his case on the mutual interest of the two countries in a multilateral regime. Financial aid, he argued, would speed up a return to normal trade practices 'without discrimination', and the resulting general expansion in world trade would benefit all countries far more than if wartime controls were retained and bilateral trade techniques were developed. American public opinion remained unconvinced, and so did the American delegation. On 10th October, Gallup recorded that 60 per cent of American citizens were against a Loan to Britain, and only 27 per cent were in favour. Vinson reflected this mood. 'His main objective remained what it had been during his career in elective politics', the historian of the negotiations has written, ' – to discover the popular will and translate that will into government policy.'[20] Populism and technical economic argument made a poor mix.

As a result, a gap developed between the British delegation, faced with the realities of the negotiations, and the ministerial team of Dalton, Bevin and Cripps, together with Attlee and Morrison (backed by official advisers) in London – whose expectations had been buoyed by Keynes's 'winged words' at the outset. Keynes's steady retreat from optimism was regarded in London with incomprehension.

By 26th September, Keynes had abandoned hopes of a grant-in-aid for the full amount desired.[21] A few days later, however, he wrote to the Chancellor that he did not 'at present take seriously [the Americans'] equally categorical refusal to consider a non-interest bearing loan'. The problem from the American point of view, he considered, was 'essentially a question of dressing it all up ... Meanwhile there is a good deal of play acting, slow motion and poker playing.'[22] At this stage, Dalton regarded the prospect even of an interest-free loan as too burdensome. 'I am doubtful whether we could undertake to repay that loan', he told Cabinet colleagues, 'especially as I do not know what conditions for trade the Americans might attach to it.'[23] To Keynes he wrote: 'My present inclination is to decline any loan which carries interest, however it is dressed up, because I do not believe that that principle is appropriate to the circumstances'.[24] It quickly became clear, however, that the Americans had in mind, not as Keynes had hoped, an interest-free loan, but an interest-bearing one. 'If best American offer is large loan at 2 per cent interest we would not accept it', Dalton telegrammed to Halifax in Washington on 8th October.

'We remain firm that we will not accept obligations which we do not see reasonable certainty of discharging.'[25] On 12th October, the Chancellor again stressed that the 'test' to be applied to any offer was that, barring some unforeseen economic catastrophe, 'we should see a reasonable certainty of being able to discharge any obligation entered upon'.[26]

According to Harrod, 'there was reluctance to allow [Keynes] to make the necessary concessions, and mutual vexation was the consequence'. Dalton added a footnote in his own memoirs, 'It was indeed'. Dalton's account of the negotiations reveals a process of grudging withdrawal on the British side,

> slowly and with a bad grace and with increasing irritation, from a free gift to an interest-free loan, and from this again to a loan bearing interest; from a larger to a smaller total of aid; and from the prospect of loose strings, some of which would be only general declarations of intention, to the most unwilling acceptance of strings so tight that they might strangle our trade and, indeed, our whole economic life.[27]

Dalton was gradually forced to acknowledge that the British case was based, not on any real bargaining position, but on a logic which the Americans did not accept. The Americans, it seemed, were arguing that aid to Britain 'would either be wasted or employed to further policies incompatible with American principles of private enterprise.'[28] Keynes used this aspect to put pressure on the British Cabinet. 'There is no way out remotely compatible with the present domestic policy of the Government except on the basis of substantial American aid', he wrote to Dalton on 28th October. 'Indeed, the fact that some Americans are becoming aware of this is one of the hidden, unmentioned snags in our path.'[29] The Americans had Britain over a barrel, and they knew it: this, at any rate, was how it appeared to leading actors at the time.

A number of ministers (Shinwell, Bevan and Alexander) stood out against concessions, more as a matter of principle than on the basis of knowledge. Lionel Robbins, who as Director of the Economic Section was part of Keynes's team, played the part of an intermediary between London and Washington. Later he recalled the difficulties encountered with politicians at home. '[We] had to negotiate, as it were, on two fronts simultaneously: with the Americans for terms which were not doctrinaire and exacting, and with the Cabinet for a descent from cloud-cuckoo-land and an understanding of the realities of the situation and the choices which they had to make.'[30]

Dalton found himself facing pressures that were equally contradictory. On the one hand, he was trying to stiffen Robbins ('whom I
regard as having played a poor and hysterical part in these proceedings'), and on the other to defend in Cabinet proposals which
some colleagues found too weak. Meanwhile the Cabinet Sub-
Committee of Dalton, Bevin and Cripps was drowned in a flood of
elegant and witty, but not always helpful, telegrams from Keynes.
The issue dragged on throughout the autumn, overshadowing domestic events. 'The Washington talks are moving – I wonder – to their
final climax', Dalton noted on 6th November.[31] Three weeks later,
key issues were still unresolved. Douglas Jay, employed as the Prime
Minister's Personal Assistant, recalls how discussions about the
Washington negotiations dominated Downing Street agenda:

> For virtually every weekday evening at No. 10 from mid-September
> to mid-December, Attlee, Bevin, Dalton, Morrison and Cripps met
> in the Cabinet Room from 9 p.m. until about midnight with
> Edward Bridges, Wilfrid Eady of the Treasury Overseas Finance
> Section and myself ... shoals of telegrams passed to and fro daily
> which I sought to sift and summarize for Attlee and add my com-
> ments, as Bridges and Eady did for Dalton. The plethora of tele-
> grams did not always make for clarity. On one occasion quoting
> from one of them, Dalton said peremptorily to Bevin: 'Foreign
> Secretary, have you got the telegram?' 'I've got 'undreds', replied
> Bevin, and Bridges trotted round the table to reshuffle the cards
> for him.[32]

Relations between London and the negotiators eventually became
so strained that Dalton sent Sir Edward Bridges to Washington 'to
pull things together'.[33] Bridges's mission was intended to toughen the
negotiators. Instead, the negotiators convinced him – and through him
Cabinet – that all that could be done had been done. As a result, the
British Government was finally persuaded to authorise the signing of
an Agreement on 6th December which bore no relation to the hopes of
three months before. It had been a long process of climb-down and
capitulation. The telegram announcing the conclusion of the negotiations reached the private office at No. 11 Downing Street early one
morning, while Dalton was upstairs in the bath. Trend, summoned
into the Chancellor's presence and ordered to sit on the lavatory, read
the details aloud through clouds of steam. Dalton waved, tossed and
splashed a large sponge, to express his mixed emotions.[34]

There was much in the eventual settlement that was to Britain's
advantage. The Loan was for $3,750 million, plus $650 million granted

in final settlement of Lend-Lease. Interest was at 2 per cent, and repayment was to be over 50 years. But neither repayment nor interest were to start until the end of 1951, and interest could be cancelled whenever exports were insufficient to pay for the pre-war volume of imports.[35] Given the delay, the interest payment was really only 1.6 per cent, and the grant for the cancellation of all Lend-Lease indebtedness was a major, and insufficiently appreciated, release. 'We had obtained a loan greatly inferior to what we would have wished', wrote Robbins, 'but it was thought perhaps just adequate, with careful husbandry and rigid control of the capital account, to see us through the ardours of the transition.'[36] Taken together with a parallel Canadian Loan of $1,500 million which came later, the main features of the Loan itself gave the British Government grounds, if not for satisfaction, at least for a degree of relief. The snag lay in the conditions attached. It was these which turned the Loan into a time bomb.

First, it was stipulated that there should be an immediate acceptance of the Bretton Woods proposals for the International Monetary Fund and the International Bank; and second, there was a requirement that Britain should restore convertibility for current transactions (the free exchange of sterling and dollars) after a period of just a year, as opposed to the five year transition period of exchange controls insisted on in the original Bretton Woods negotiations. In practice (since the final legislation authorising the Loan was not signed until 15th July 1946) the second condition meant that convertibility would come into force in July 1947. This had not been the Government's wish. 'We were most anxious to keep a somewhat longer period', Dalton told the Commons; 'it looked at one stage as though, on this point, negotiations might break down.'[37] But they did not break down, and instead the British yielded.[38] According to Dalton later:

> Narrowed to this point, the dispute between us, though on a most important point, seemed small against the spacious background of a 4.4 billion dollar credit and Anglo-American agreement, all of which, if we broke on this, would be lost. Troublesome though this would be in Parliament, none of our Inner Circle felt that we could make this the breaking-point.[39]

The British Government sacrificed little as a result of the Bretton Woods requirement. It is likely that the new monetary and commercial system would have been accepted anyway, if less abruptly.[40] But convertibility was another matter, and all on the British side regarded this condition as a hostage to fortune. 'Virtually none of us in London believed that convertibility would be possible at any rate for five years', Douglas Jay recalls; 'and we thought that to accept it meant a sterling crisis when it came into force.'[41]

The leading Opposition spokesmen, Sir John Anderson and Oliver Lyttelton, made precisely the same point in the Commons debate. Yet neither doubted that it was necessary to take the Loan even on the available terms. Dalton's simple question, 'What is your alternative?' seemed unanswerable. There was a general acceptance of Dalton's hypothetical portrait of a Britain without dollars:

> Our people would be driven down, once more, deeper into the dark valley of anxiety from which we thought we were beginning to struggle out ... [W]e should have to undergo greater hardships and privations than even during the war; and all those hopes of better times, to follow in the wake of victory, would be dissipated in despair and disillusion.[42]

Dalton put it even more strongly in his memoirs. Without massive aid, he argued, there would have been no hope of escaping a 'financial Dunkirk'. This would have taken the form of a sudden withdrawal from all overseas responsibilities, with great loss of prestige, 'and our acceptance in the world of the position of a second-class power, like that of France on the morrow of the German surrender'. It would have been necessary to seek charity from the Dominions, and 'an indefinite postponement of the best hopes, and the social and economic programme, of the new Government.' There would have been shortages, heavy and growing unemployment, and 'worst of all, from the point of view of public morale, practically no smokes ... ' The eventual result would have been defeat at the next election.[43]

Few disagreed. The Americans had driven a hard bargain, fraught with dangers for the British economy. Politicians of all parties, and economists of all persuasions, knew there would be difficulties; but most felt that the alternative of no Loan was too terrible to contemplate. Bevan and Shinwell opposed the decision in Cabinet. But the Commons passed it by 347 to 100, with most Conservatives abstaining.[44]

There were, however, important differences of emphasis. Keynes (whose opinion received more attention than anyone else's) also had a vision of the chaos and despair that would afflict Britain without the Loan. But it was not the same vision as that of Dalton, still less of the Labour Party which reluctantly fell in behind the Chancellor. Sir Roy Harrod (a bitter critic of Dalton) revealed in his biography of Keynes the extent to which Keynes's underlying values differed from those of the Labour Movement. According to Harrod, a number of considerations were running through Keynes's mind at the time of the Loan negotiations:

> If [Keynes's] negotiation was not successful, rations would have to be drastically cut; the factories would stand idle for lack of materials; there would certainly be inflation. Would there also be labour troubles and even civil strife? ... There might be violence of a kind unknown in the fair island for many generations. Its consequences could not be foreseen; many precious features of our civilisation might be lost. There would have to be a long period of grinding poverty and mendicancy ... Was this to be a turning point in history? Would the Britain of Shakespeare and Newton lapse into being a Secondary Power, a slum of squalid living and loutish ways? He thought of the amiable life of the Sussex countryside and the labourers whom he loved, he thought of the millions of Londoners on their tubes and buses whose perils he had shared, he thought of the universities, still in the vanguard of science and humanity, with their precious modes of life, philosophy, civilised discussion; he thought of talks with Lytton by the fireside, he thought of cultivated gentle people all over England, living modestly, loving books and music, disseminating sweetness and light. Were all these to be ground down by harsh distress and social strife? The next few weeks mattered much.[45]

Did Keynes really think like this? Perhaps Harrod was being unfair to his subject; perhaps he was attributing to the Government's chief negotiator thoughts and motives which were, or would have been, his own. All the same, it is worth considering how far the negotiations were based on Bloomsbury patriotism, which identified the standards and 'modes of life' of 'cultivated gentle people' with those of the nation as a whole, and on other values or aspirations which were not identical with those of the Labour majority.

As we have seen, the basis for British policy on the Loan was Keynes's paper of March 1945, written before the circumstances that arose in the summer could be foreseen. In this paper, Keynes had put three basic choices – 'Austerity', 'Temptation' and 'Justice'. 'Temptation' was a possible American course for providing Britain with large amounts of credit in return for the acceptance of all the American doctrines – free convertibility of sterling balances; major reduction in imperial preference; convertibility and non-discrimination. Keynes thought that some Americans would suggest this course (in fact few did so); he opposed it on the grounds that it would turn Britain into an economic and financial chattel of the United States. 'Justice' was (with modifications) what Keynes sought at the beginning of the negotiations: a general reconsideration of the proper division of the costs of the war, as part of a move towards a world-wide multilateral financial system based on North American loans and grants; the cancellation, freeing and funding of sterling area balances; and the British acceptance of *de facto* convertibility within a relatively short period.

The third choice outlined by Keynes, 'Austerity', meant complete financial independence of the United States. At the very best, Keynes had concluded, this would involve:

(a) the continuance of war rationing and war controls more stringent than in 1945 for three to five years after the war.

(b) the national planning and direction of foreign trade, both imports and exports, 'somewhat on the Russian model'.

(c) a serious retardation of Colonial development and Far Eastern rehabilitation and a strict limiting of all overseas activities that cost money – military, diplomatic or commercial.

Having thus set up 'Austerity' as an exceedingly unappealing option, Keynes rejected it as a serious possibility. It should be remembered, however, that Keynes was writing in March 1945. A year later, when the possibility existed that Congress might reject the Loan Agreement, a far less terrifying picture was painted by another Treasury official, Otto Clarke. In a minute dated 12th February 1946 Clarke concluded that, if the Loan was not forthcoming, 'I think we could pull through without having to embark upon such austerity as would reduce the British economy to a standstill'. Keynes himself now conceded much the same:

> ... [I]t comes out in the wash that the American Loan is primarily required to meet the political and military expenditure overseas. If it were not for that, we could scrape through without excessive interruption of our domestic programme if necessary by drawing largely on our reserves. The interruption of our domestic programme which is politically and economically possible so long as the military and political expenditure goes on on its present scale is strictly limited. The main consequence of the failure of the loan must, therefore, be a large-scale withdrawal on our part from international responsibilities.[46]

Circumstances had, of course, rapidly changed: not only since March 1945, but since October. That it would have been the Americans pulling out, not the British, made a difference. Keynes wrote to Bridges

with the United States as the capstone of the great constructive effort on which he embarked in 1941 to create a world-wide multilateral financial system.' While the British Cabinet were thinking mainly in domestic terms – how to get through the crisis, how to avoid the catastrophe which (so Keynes told them) threatened to engulf the country, how to make possible the programme of social reform in order to benefit the working-class, Keynes's ambition soared higher, towards the creation of a new world economic order. Having travelled so far, and having overcome so much, he could not bear to see the edifice collapse.[56]

With hindsight, many of Dalton's arguments, as well as Keynes's, appear specious. Dalton's concern that Britain would be forced to accept 'the position of a second-class power' reveals much about the post-war Labour Government's illusions. The 'nightmare' alternative put forward by both Dalton and Keynes looks particularly unreal. The danger of unemployment was probably exaggerated. Austerity would have been severe without the Loan, perhaps even more severe than in the war. Yet even the worst austerity of the war and post-war periods gave a better standard of living, and a better diet, to the British working-class than had ever been known before 1940.

Nevertheless, Dalton and the socialists were not so much the dupes of Keynes and the liberals as their accomplices. Both the Chancellor and his chief negotiator wanted to believe their own visions of disaster, and wanted others to share their belief, for reasons that were in reality quite distinct. If Keynes was able to use Labour's desire for socialism as a lever for gaining acceptance for Bretton Woods, Labour ministers were not unwilling to be so manoeuvred. 'Austerity' might not have meant chaos or starvation, but it would certainly have restricted or halted Labour's most ambitious plans. The arguments of Keynes were welcome to socialists, used to being accused of profligacy, who could now point out that the American Loan had to be accepted on almost any conditions to prevent economic collapse, and that the advantages outweighed the long-term snags. Dalton had little interest in multilateralism or Bretton Woods, which some Labour M.P.s saw as a dangerous surrender to international finance. He was prepared, however, to accept both for the sake of domestic reform.

Indeed if negotiations had not been resumed and there had been no dollar credit the Labour Government would have had the worst of both worlds. Austerity would have been blamed on 'socialism' while lack of dollars would seriously have curtailed the Government's socialist programme. What the Loan provided was an opportunity for Labour to do the things it had always wanted, and which it had promised in its manifesto. Would social security, the National Health Service, extensive nationalisation, have been possible without it? The next eighteen months were the most crucial of the whole administration. Adequate foreign exchange, and the maintenance of living standards, were necessary to sustain this period of change. Thus the risky terms of the Loan Agreement – regarded by some both as a means of avoiding social unrest and as a stepping stone to a new economic order – may also be seen as a decision to buy time for a radical programme that could not have been achieved without it. The price was the convertibility crisis of 1947, and its consequences. Leo Amery, who opposed acceptance of the terms, wrote that taking the Loan on the stated conditions would give, at most, 'some temporary easement for, perhaps, two years, at the end of which we shall face the same, or even a worse situation ... '[57] That turned out to be an accurate prediction. The 'temporary easement', however, was essential for Labour's socialist programme.

The Loan Agreement was Keynes's last major undertaking. '[T]his is what killed him', Clarke wrote in his diary, 'and he did it with great brilliance, but badly, over-complicating and finessing against London and against himself.'[58] After the end of the negotiations, Dalton sent his former tutor a letter of measured warmth – still containing the sense that every phrase had been chosen with excessive care. 'Even those colleagues who least like some details of the Agreement are loud in praise of your skill, resource and patience', wrote the Chancellor. 'And now come home and rest. I look forward very much to seeing you again, and shaking your hand.'[59]

Keynes, sick and exhausted, returned from America by sea. When he arrived, Dalton gave a private dinner at the Savoy for the Washington and Whitehall negotiators. Keynes attended, but was so ill that he had to lie on a sofa.[60] He died a few weeks later. Dalton wrote to J. T. Sheppard, Provost of King's: 'Of course I shall miss him terribly, both on public and personal grounds ... he taught me to unite Reason with Hope, as did few others.'[61] Some believed Keynes's death was much more than a personal or even an intellectual loss, removing a vital voice of caution, which might have restrained the headstrong Chancellor in his wilder schemes.[62] That is a matter of opinion. What may also be said is that Keynes's final legacy made possible his pupil's period of greatest fulfilment; and, in the end, destroyed him.

During the autumn of 1945, while the negotiating team was in Washington, politics at home did not stand still. The attempt to secure a Loan took place against the background of the first, triumphant session of the new Parliament. In these opening months, sustained, as he said, by the strength and comradeship and understanding of the great Labour majority, Dalton set the pace.

Later, he claimed that it had been 'one of my constant aims to radiate confidence all through the Labour Party, to rid it of inferiority complexes, and to keep the parliamentary troops behind me in good heart.'[63] He succeeded to a remarkable degree. The Chancellor gave the Government its style: winning the intellectual argument, generating the mood of 'We are the masters now'.[64] This was a Government that faced problems. But it was a Labour Government, and it was equal to the task of overcoming them.

'He bestrode the world', recalls Jim Callaghan.[65] His stature 'was increased by every speech he made', wrote Michael Foot in February 1946.[66] Foot later gave a vivid description of the first post-war Chancellor:

Dalton on the crest of the wave – and in the first two years after 1945 he rode higher than any other Minister – had the panache which the Government so much needed. His spirit of aggression against the Tories satisfied the most exacting standards ... Dalton at the Treasury provided the resources and no small part of the drive behind Labour's great reforming measures. It is the achievement that can never be taken from him.[67]

Foot remembers Dalton's speeches during the Budget debates of 1945–7 as among the best he ever heard. 'They were great socialist expositions', he recalls, 'in which Dalton showed how to put the ideas in his books into practice. His speeches completely held the House and helped to make him virtually the dominant figure in the Government.'[68]

Dalton combined lucid explanation and brisk repartee, the latter designed to delight his own backbenchers by rubbing the Tories' most sensitive wounds. He would adopt the manner of the teacher, 'patting the head of the House, like a pedagogue saying "There, there, dear boys ... It is all as simple as I tell you. Elementary, elementary!"'[69] Sometimes his tone would provoke the Opposition beyond endurance. Once, early in 1947, Churchill was unable to contain his rage. 'You are always trying to make a joke by turning a personal point against me', the Opposition Leader snarled; 'I have the utmost contempt for your taunts.'[70] Trend recalls the attention which Dalton would devote to his major speeches, composing and rehearsing as for a carefully scripted play: 'I never knew a Chancellor so conscious of the need for aesthetic completeness in a Budget speech. He would spend hours on

"The maddening thing about Dalton is his shining dome, seemingly impervious to reasonable irrationality."—
AN ENRAGED BLIMP

BUDGET SPORTS RUN

individual paragraphs, going through phrase by phrase and changing commas.'[71]

Dramatically, there were echoes of the Canon. One newspaper carried the following report at the end of March 1947:

> He curves his towering, six-foot-three inch frame far over the Dispatch Box, screws his bald domed head sideways and upwards and, from time to time, rolls his pale blue eyes so that the whites blaze and flash with an almost Mephistophelian effect. For his famous 'smile-on-the-face-of-the-tiger' act, he brings this stance, plus the Dispatch Box, into effective use. Not since Gladstone has there been a Minister who thumped the Dispatch Box with such vigour and frequency.[72]

Such orations moved one American commentator to write in June 1946 that Dalton was the 'outstanding success in the Cabinet'.[73] Even the hostile *Sunday Express* acknowledged in the same month that 'Mr. Morrison on the descending escalator passes Dr. Dalton going up', and described Dalton as the heir apparent to Attlee.[74]

Yet the most remarkable appreciation came from the radical wing of the Labour Party. Before the war, no leading Labour politician had been more hated by the Labour Left than Dalton. After the war, earlier battles were never entirely forgotten. Gradually, however, the confidence of the Left in Sir Stafford Cripps began to wane, as it became clear that experience of office had dulled his socialist ardour; while Dalton showed in his speeches and Budgets that he was the member of the Big Five most determined to turn socialist conviction into action. Some of those who had been most critical of Dalton in the 1930s changed their tune. In addition to Michael Foot, left-wing editor of *Tribune*, there was Richard Crossman, soon to become one of the Labour Government's sharpest critics on the backbenches. 'Dr. Dalton is always the master of his Bill, his brief, his Party and the House', wrote Crossman in the summer of 1946, 'dominating less by wit than by sheer intellectual and physical power, and a concentration of purpose which is increased by popularity and success.'[75]

Outside the Chamber, Dalton had other ways of radiating confidence. When Attlee grumbled about Dalton's supposed deviousness, Geoffrey de Freitas, the Prime Minister's P.P.S., reminded him that the Chancellor was a great encourager of the young. 'Grant that!' Attlee replied. 'Willing to grant that!'[76] According to Lord George-Brown: 'It would be hard to find any young Labour M.P. of talent in the 1945 Parliament who didn't get help from Dalton.' A very large number of new Members had reason to be grateful to the Chancellor – for pushing them forward, giving advice, providing introductions, recommending them for jobs. 'Encouraging the young' had long been Dalton's hobby. The conditions of the 1945 Parliament provided opportunities, as never before, to indulge it.

Dalton did not bestow his favours indiscriminately. Anybody young and vigorous could expect support, if the Chancellor did not have a particular reason for hostility or suspicion. But some received more attention than others. Later, Dalton's closest parliamentary friends were most often associated with the Labour Right. In the 1945 Parliament, Dalton's criteria for selecting young friends had more to do with intellectual interest than with ideology, and several members of his circle (for example John Freeman, Bill Mallalieu and Barbara Castle) were future Bevanites. Intellectual interest reflected education which, in turn, reflected class. As Lord George-Brown puts it, the Dalton Boys were 'mainly university socialites'. Significantly the exceptions – men like Brown himself, Alf Robens, Jim Callaghan –

mention as one of Dalton's most important influences that he widened their social horizons, providing links with people of a kind they had not previously encountered. 'Class mattered more then', says Callaghan. 'I entered a whole new circle', recalls Lord George-Brown. Robens talks of contact with 'the academic, Hampstead set'.

Dalton treated the trade union M.P.s among his protégés like clever proletarian students at the L.S.E. He drew them out, lectured, flattered, criticised, guided them. There were frequent notes passed during debates: 'Good speech, but too quick', and so on. 'He would come up to you at any time', recalls Robens, 'put his arm around your shoulder and talk to you for half an hour about anything of interest.' Brown remembers small dinner parties at which 'I met a rather special elitist group that lived quite a different style of life from people I knew'. 'Hugh took me into an international world', recalls Callaghan. 'Nobody else advised me', says Robens. 'It was like having a personal tutor.'[77]

Yet even at the height of his powers there was something about Dalton that made his closest followers stop short of hero-worship. He never attracted the devotion which Cripps, Bevan and Gaitskell were able, at various times, to arouse in their disciples. The reason is hard to define: it had nothing to do with practical achievement or honesty of purpose. It was more that the art in his performance was not well hidden. 'Sincerity' in politics is a strange concept. Dalton was more passionately 'sincere' in his aims than in his means: he lacked (unlike, for example, Sir Stafford Cripps) the vital political talent of convincing himself of the absolute morality of all his actions, the knack of equating expediency with right.

There was also a clown-like element, later tragi-comic, which made those who admired him despise him at the same time. 'You can't talk candidly about Dalton', says one friend, 'without describing him as, in a sense, a monstrous figure.' If in some of his characteristics he was a model for young politicians, in others he was the subject of caricature and mimicry. Physically he was becoming odder: his body ever more top heavy and pear shaped, with an increasing tendency to stoop, his bald dome more gleamingly polished, his voice more thunderous, his eyes more disconcerting.

Part of the problem was that he suffered from a sense of the ridiculousness of power and of those who possessed it, including himself. The view of politics as a college jape never entirely left him, and his delight in the discomfiture of the pompous of all parties helped to separate him from more dignified colleagues. Sir Geoffrey de Freitas told the following, illustrative, story:

On one occasion there had been talk in the House about Greece and the accusation had been made that people had been flayed and their skin used for leather. Sir Stafford Cripps, who was rather cranky about his appearance, happened to be wearing some rather unusual heels, and I noticed him looking at them. 'Do you like my shoes?' he asked me. 'Been to Greece recently?' I replied. He went rigid. Clem, who overheard, was appalled, and said so. Later I told Hugh about it, and the reaction of Cripps and Attlee. He couldn't stop laughing: 'Ho! ho! ho! ho!'

Dalton saw himself as Robin Hood in a fuddy-duddy world: the enemy of the old, the established and the stick-in-the-muds and the champion of the young, adventurous and handsome. 'All at the top agreed that Dalton wasn't one of them', suggests John Freeman. 'Although they had suspicions of one another, they were united in their feeling that Dalton was a different kind of animal.'

Dalton's most vulgar insults were reserved for Tories. De Freitas saw him as 'the first of the upper class renegades', who liked nothing better than the shocked faces of those who kept the old social code. He took pleasure in being a bounder and a cad, the kind of chap you itched to duck in the school pond or blackball from the club. Once, dining at the House, he interrupted his own monologue to boom in the direction of a Conservative M.P.: 'What's that suburbanite looking at me for!' The M.P. looked unhappy. 'Come on, let's show him how we in the Labour Party behave!' Dalton started to shovel peas into his mouth with a knife.

Freeman sees it in terms of loyalties. Dalton was an apostate. 'Having detached himself from the class and society in which he had grown up, he grafted himself onto the Labour Party instead.' The father's devotion to the Monarchy had become the son's loyalty, even love, for the Labour Movement, and hatred of its enemies.[78]

Within his group, he enjoyed the role of the arch-conspirator, the 'machine politician'. A story about Dalton entering the Cabinet Room, 'his eyes blazing with insincerity' was widely told. So was an anecdote describing Dalton's supposed technique with obscure M.P.s whose votes he needed: he had a reputation as 'the man who slaps you on the back in the lobbies and calls you by somebody else's Christian name'. Roy Jenkins, who entered the House in 1948, gives this account:

Once as we were entering the Chamber, Hugh called cheerfully to a working-class member: 'Hello, Fred!' Turning to me, he said, 'You know Roy, you'll never get on in politics until you learn to call

that chap Fred.' I pointed out gently that in fact the man's name
was Bert.[79]

All Dalton's friends told a version of this tale, usually with themselves
cast as confidant. In Robens's version, the trade unionist M.P. becomes unwitting victim:

> Hugh put his arm across my shoulder one night as we were going
> through the Lobby during a division. 'You see that man over
> there?' he said. 'What's his name?' I replied that it was Edgar
> Grierson, M.P. for Carlisle. Hugh removed his arm from my
> shoulder, went across and put it round Grierson. 'Well Edgar!', he
> said. 'How are things in Carlisle?' After the vote, I saw Grierson
> in the Tea Room. 'What do you think of that Alf?' he said with real
> pride in his voice. 'Did you see Hugh Dalton? He knaared me!'[80]

Such stories had a mythic quality: in one form or another they had
been around since Dalton first entered the House. Mosley, remembering the 1920s, described how Dalton was to be seen in the lobbies 'in
search of trade union quarry round whose shoulders the avuncular
arm would be placed with the query, "How's the family?" '[81] Perhaps
such incidents really happened. Even if they did not, the legend was a
key ingredient of Dalton's parliamentary image: as a man who, as
Harold Wilson puts it, was apt to meet himself coming back.[82]

Dalton undoubtedly believed that popularity could be acquired by
jollying people along. Even during his heyday as Chancellor, he was
an assiduous socialiser both in the Tea Room, abode of the loyalist
working-class M.P.s, and in the Smoking Room, meeting place for
the intellectuals and theorisers. 'If he was not entirely trusted it was
because he wasn't really at home in either', considers Robens. 'He was
a bit too cordial with both. Each lot didn't know whether he was with
them or with the others.'[83] An enemy puts it more crudely. 'He was
always fawning and arse-crawling around. He would sit in the
Smoking Room and summon people to him.'

Others did the same, but not so obviously. Dalton, as Beatrice
Webb had observed decades before, carried with him an impression
of slyness: as though expecting not to be trusted, even relishing his
reputation as a manoeuvrer. Here was an irony. However much
Dalton might pretend, like his father, to have neither nerves nor a
conscience, the reality was that among leading ministers no man was
more disinterestedly loyal to his friends or more clear-headed and
consistent in his principles; and in the harsh world of serious political
manipulation, most of his senior colleagues left him standing.

Could he ever have become Party Leader? Callaghan thinks that, if the cards had fallen differently, he might have made it. Freeman disagrees. 'He lacked the gift of ultimate gravitas; or, alternatively, he was not a ruthless enough crook.'[84]

By his own account, Dalton was 'happy' and 'gay' at the Treasury as never before. To the cartoonists he was always 'the laughing cavalier', the Chancellor who handled the nation's problems with extrovert good cheer. Few lives were fuller, few politicians better able to enjoy friends, audiences, the job in hand. Yet those who knew him best sensed beneath the surface a personal void. It was as though public triumphs were a drug, shots of exhilaration that needed constantly to be renewed, hiding a private failure.

After the war, the edge was taken off his loneliness by Ruth, who came home and moved back in with him. But it was an incomplete reunion. There was no restoration of the close companionship that had once been his sustenance.

Politically, Hugh had had a good war. Ruth had had a bad one which improved towards the end. She had been miserable in London and Manchester. Her UNRRA job, by contrast, had made her feel usefully employed for the first time, and she became so involved in the work that she had no wish to return to England.[85] On 16th August 1945 (three weeks after Hugh became Chancellor) she wrote from the UNRRA Mobilisation Base in France to a schoolteacher friend, Hilde Auerbach, saying that her job would soon be over and her own movements were unclear, but she had met many delightful and inspiring French people, 'and I shall be more than ever sorry if I have to leave France'. There was no mention of Hugh. When she came back to London that autumn, she moved into the Norfolk Court Hotel in Belsize Park.[86]

At this stage, she apparently still contemplated a permanent break. What persuaded her to change her mind? She may have found the alternative, as a childless, career-less woman in her mid-fifties, uninviting: she belonged to a generation in which divorced or separated wives were viewed askance. She had no close relatives. Life in Downing Street certainly had some advantages over a frugal existence in North London lodgings or hotel rooms. Perhaps there was an element of duty. Politics had been their joint mission; a busy Chancellor needed a wife. Possibly – though remarks to friends did not betray it – there was a surviving affection.

Hugh had been at the Treasury several months before she decided. There was a preliminary negotiation. At Ruth's request Josephine Smith, her friend from the Birth Control Movement, arranged a meeting in the flat of a mutual friend. Josephine made tea and withdrew. When she returned Hugh and Ruth had agreed to share a home together at Downing Street. Josephine asked Ruth if she was pleased. Ruth grunted. 'He bought me a book of French verse', she replied. 'He'd forgotten I'd already had it for years.' Later she claimed that she agreed to the reconciliation because she 'couldn't resist the house', making clear that there would be none of the 'other thing', meaning sex.[87]

First there was a joint holiday in Wiltshire. 'I am spending Xmas at West Leaze with Hugh', Ruth wrote to Hilde on Christmas Day, 'and shall be back [at the hotel in Belsize Park] on the 31st. As you can imagine, I am delighted to be there [i.e. West Leaze] again, and it will be fun getting the house and garden in order after years of neglect.'[88] Together Ruth and Hugh planned an extension to the main building. Hugh dug, slept and read, and viewed the future with a new optimism. 'I come back to London on New Year's Eve', he wrote to Evan Durbin. 'I shall be as full of bright ideas as a squirrel of fleas! ... Don't hasten back to London, but tell me when you're coming. Ruth will have your bedroom ready!'[89] In January Ruth began commuting to Downing Street, planning to take up residence there in the middle of the month. 'Now I am longing to move into our lovely flat, so as to start on all the schemes that I have been meditating', she wrote.[90]

In the spring Ruth re-joined the L.C.C. as an Alderman and became Vice-Chairman of the Housing Committee, re-establishing a place in London politics that she had abandoned in the war. She began to act out the part of Chancellor's wife conscientiously and with dignity, drawing on memories of entertaining in Cheyne Walk for her mother's friend, Sir Arthur Peterson, before her marriage. She took pleasure in showing off the elegant grandeur of No. 11 Downing Street to friends. Anglo-French understanding and cultural links became her special interest. A typical event at No. 11 during Dalton's Chancellorship was a soirée in support of the restoration of a castle in the Loire.[91]

Hugh took no part in such activities. Four years of unshared experience stood between them. The change was most noticeable in Ruth. Those who knew her in the 1930s remember a forceful, positive woman of vigorous opinions, who could also be light-hearted and amusing. Those who only knew her after the war recall her forcefulness; the sense of humour seemed lacking. Some people found her less easy to talk to. Irene Wagner, who had felt like an adopted child when she lived with the Daltons at Carlisle Mansions in 1940, took her two-year-old daughter for a visit to No. 11 in 1946. It was not a success. The younger woman felt that she had outgrown the relationship, and they did not meet again.[92]

Hugh and Ruth now had different habits. They seldom accompanied each other on visits, official or private. Ruth, though better informed than many political wives, took little interest in the great events around which her husband's life revolved. Her letters, oddly childish, presented the hectic round of high politics as though it was an exhausting and less than enjoyable holiday, through which it was necessary to keep up an appearance of having a good time. 'The Budget was exciting', she wrote to Hilde, typically, in April 1946. 'If you see the news reels this week, you may see us and the crowd in Downing Street!'[93]

Before the war Hugh and Ruth had non-political enthusiasms in common (walking, Wiltshire, foreign travel). After the war recreations divided rather than united them. Developing her own interest in the visual arts, ballet and literature, Ruth regarded Hugh with a defensive cultural snobbery. Their circles seldom overlapped. Hugh's political companions saw Ruth, when they saw her at all, as tight-lipped, school-marmish and lacking in warmth. Ruth's aesthetically-minded friends felt that Hugh failed to consider her emotional needs. People were puzzled by the combination of formal courtesy and lack of affection that characterised their relations. 'If they seemed uncomfortably distant and strained', recalls one who knew them both, 'this was because he no longer treated her as an equal. When he wasn't ignoring her completely, his attitude was one of polite condescension.' Others blamed Ruth's hardness and lack of sympathy.

Political life makes unusual demands. Husbands disappear into a tunnel of work, wives feel neglected. A degree of single-minded obsession, pushing private relationships aside, may sometimes be necessary. Even so, the gap between Dalton's public persona and what those close to him perceived as his inner self was dangerously wide – leaving him vulnerable and unprotected when the stimulant of success was suddenly withdrawn.

XXVI

Socialist Chancellor

Like 'sincerity', 'success' is a difficult word in politics. The features of momentary success – victory on an issue, acclaim – are recognisable enough. Success at the bar of history, on the other hand, depends on the judge.

Was Dalton a 'successful' Chancellor? Later, he looked back at the period July 1945 to January 1947 as the high-water mark of his career: the peak, he claimed, of his happiness, power, repute and achievement. 'During these months I was gay, confident, tireless, influential and on the whole successful.'[1] By mid-1947 there were many who, while acknowledging the Chancellor's gaiety and influence, disagreed profoundly about his success.

It is impossible, however, to separate a verdict on Dalton's Chancellorship from an assessment of the Attlee administration as a whole. Here, we should note a coincidence of dates. Dalton was at the Treasury for twenty-eight months, leaving office in November 1947. According to the economic writer Andrew Shonfield, a decade later:

> The Labour Party's creative period of office was over by 1948. By then the major acts of nationalisation had taken place, the state had acquired a commanding position in a crucial sector of industry and the post-war advance in social welfare had reached its climax.

This 'period of effective social revolution and spiritual certainty' stood in sharp contrast, Shonfield maintained, to Labour's remaining years of office.[2]

It was certainly a time of intense activity. In November 1945 Dalton announced his intention to push through Parliament, and find money to finance, a series of 'streamlined Socialist statutes'.[3] The statutes were not long in coming. By the autumn of 1947 the Government had provided most of the legislation needed to implement its pledges on social security. It had passed major National Insurance and Industrial Injuries Acts, and a National Health Act which became the basis for the National Health Service. Children's allowances had been introduced, and the demolition of the old Poor Law system had begun. Meanwhile, employment had been maintained (with one brief interlude) at a higher level than at any time between the wars. Rapid progress had been made with domestic and industrial reconstruction. Changes in taxation and death duties had helped to reduce the gap between rich and poor. The Bank of England, coal, civil aviation, electricity and railways had been brought into public ownership. These developments had occurred despite a crippling international debt, a huge military commitment of men and materials in Germany and the Middle East, an unprecedented process of decolonisation, and (early in 1947) an unexpected collapse of production, caused by freak weather conditions.

The value of the achievement may be debated. There is no doubt, however, that the most radical reform programme of the century was carried out in these crucial months; or that a society and a political system emerged by the late 1940s with very different assumptions from those that would have prevailed if the electors had behaved at the end of the Second World War as they had behaved just after the First.

The Left remained dissatisfied. Later, the fashionable question became: 'Where did it all go wrong?'[4] Marxists, in particular, alleged that 'power had not shifted between classes'.[5] Against this it may be said that, in view of international constraints, to have gone much further would have put the whole experiment at risk without probable gain.

From the opposite standpoint, the Right and Centre complained that Labour over-reached itself. Contemporary opponents echoed Sir Clive Baillieu, President of the Federation of British Industries, who urged the Government in April 1947 'not to rush their programme and to place production and prosperity above party plans and policies'.[6] When the path to prosperity proved less smooth than some had hoped, critics pointed to the 'doctrinaire' approach of the Labour Government, and of Dalton in particular. 'Many have tried to find a personal scapegoat in Hugh Dalton', observed the American historian Samuel Beer in 1965, reviewing the literature of a generation.[7] Yet those who blamed the Labour Chancellor for the nation's difficulties were also paying him a compliment, indicating the extent of his contribution – greater perhaps than that of any other minister – to the social revolution that occurred.

Here we enter the treacherous terrain of values: the question of what Labour's aims should have been, and the level of sacrifice that was acceptable to attain them. The most insidious and persistent accusations have been couched in 'scientific' terms, as though all concerned were involved in a common endeavour. The vilification of Dalton at the time, however, indicates how far the so-called post-war consensus was from realisation.

There have been seven Labour Chancellors of the Exchequer. Dalton stands apart from the rest in one respect at least: the degree of animosity he aroused among opponents. His predecessor and five successors were sometimes attacked and occasionally scorned by the financial world. None, however, was ever felt to be seriously threatening. By contrast Dalton was the subject of such angry, emotional dislike that the mere uttering of his name became a kind of curse. Since the war only two other Labour ministers, Aneurin Bevan and Tony Benn, have been attacked so viciously.

Partly this was deliberate choice. Like Bevan and Benn, Dalton actively sought to enrage his enemies. He wanted, he told Durbin just after the election, to be like Sir William Harcourt, who 'hated rich Right-Wingers'.[8] According to Einzig, resentment was 'enhanced by the obvious enjoyment Dalton derived from adopting measures unpopular in the business world and among the upper income groups'.[9] The basis of resentment, however, was solid enough. Dalton was hated by Tories and capitalists because in domestic politics he aimed, first and foremost, to reduce inequality.

Concern about inequality was common to all Labour Chancellors. The difference was one of commitment. Others thought of reducing inequality as a long-term aim, but were prepared, with varying degrees of reluctance, to postpone it under the pressure of competing priorities. Facing the same or fiercer pressures, Dalton was also eventually compelled to pull back. What makes him the most controversial Chancellor of the Exchequer of recent times is the consistently strong emphasis he placed on redistribution, giving it at least equal weight to 'production and prosperity'; and the determination with which he fought to preserve it as his own, and the Government's, main purpose.

Dalton introduced four Budgets – in October 1945, April 1946, April and November 1947. Despite the limitations imposed by balance of payments and other external forces, these contained measures which justify describing him as the most socialist Chancellor of the Exchequer Britain has ever had.

Dalton did not follow the new practice, developed in the war, of relating Budget proposals to a detailed survey of the economy. Instead he compromised between old and new (as had the 1944 White Paper) by announcing his intention to balance budgets over a period of years. Hence his budgetary approach, which has been described as 'Gladstonian' in style, was only in a broad sense Keynesian. 'At the Treasury I tried ... to apply the principles which I had learned, taught and published more than twenty years earlier', he wrote.[10] Nevertheless Dalton was Keynesian to the extent that he accepted the principle that fiscal policy could be used without qualms as a long-run full-employment weapon. His first aim was that of the 1944 White Paper: 'the maintenance of a high and stable level of employment.'[11] His so-called 'inflationary' Budgets should be seen in this light. Dalton's reply to those who complained of a 'suppressed inflationary potential' in the economy is one for which modern readers may have sympathy:

> Before the war we had deflation which was not suppressed, and which was not potential but actual, and if we must choose between a slight – and I emphasise that word slight – between a slight inflationary flush and a slight deflationary pallor, I prefer the slight inflationary flush.[12]

All the same, Dalton was conscious of the danger that, if inflation got out of hand, it might lead to a slump. The 1945–6 Budgets had to balance, on the one hand, the need to stimulate more production, and on the other, the need to hold back purchasing power 'from too precipitate and premature a release'[13] For this reason, tax changes were influenced by 'Keynesian' considerations of demand management. In the first post-war Budget, presented to the House in October 1945, Dalton reduced total taxation by £400 million (mostly income tax, which had been raised to high levels to pay for the war), cutting wartime Excess Profits Tax (E.P.T.) from 100 to 60 per cent. The following April there were further tax and other reliefs and E.P.T. was abolished completely, while death duties were raised.[14] Dalton's third Budget in April 1947, following the fuel crisis, was presented 'in a defiant mood, conscious of all my difficulties and of many enemies, but determined to surrender no important ground and to tell the story at full length, evading nothing.'[15] To counter the pressure of a rapidly growing dollar deficit, Dalton increased tobacco duty by 50 per cent.[16] His last Budget in November 1947, after the forced suspension of convertibility, had the simple aim of countering inflation: profits tax was doubled, taxes were imposed on betting, and there were increases in purchase tax and alcohol taxes.

These measures were essentially regulatory, reflecting the advice of officials and advisers including, for the first two Budgets, Lord Keynes.

Two skeletons have just been dug up in excavations under the House of Commons—
NEWS ITEM.

TUESDAY, APRIL 9, 1946

ALAS, POOR YORICK

(Copyright in All Countries)

The redistributive aim was disguised because Dalton reduced the total burden of taxation as compared with high wartime levels, added nothing to income tax, and showed a preference for indirect over direct taxation. ('One old teacher of mine, Professor Edwin Cannan, likened taxes on commodities to the medicines of our childhood which were wrapped up in jam!', he told appreciative Fabians.)[17] However, tax cuts were heavily in favour of the worst off. Dalton's first two Budgets took two and a half million people in the lower income groups out of tax altogether (by raising personal allowances and earned income relief) and substantially increased surtax. Dalton also revealed his socialism by what he deliberately neglected to do. He did not dismantle the tax structure that had been erected to meet wartime needs. As Anthony Crosland put it later, 'he maintained, and even extended, the great advance towards income-equality that was made during the war'.[18] For those paying tax, the effect was 'to steepen the slope of graduation, and to make [all tax on income] more sharply progressive than before.'[19] At its highest level, taxation on income reached 19*s.* 6*d.* in the pound.[20] In 1945–6, fewer than 1,000 people had spendable incomes over £4,000, and spendable income left in the hands of surtax payers was reduced to 3·3 per cent of the national income, compared with 7·2 per cent before the war. 'It is probable that the differences in spendable incomes in this country are already less than those which the Russians consider necessary to provide economic incentives', noted one sympathetic expert, a few months after Dalton left office.[21]

Meanwhile Dalton launched a broadside against wealth. His career both as an economist and as a politician had begun with a series of tightly-argued attacks on the owners of property, urging that taxes on capital should be used as a tool of redistribution. He did not forget these early campaigns now. There were many causes of inequality, he explained in November 1946:

Twenty-six years ago I published a book, in which I tried to list them all. One of the most important of all the causes of great inequality of income is the inheritance of great fortunes by a small minority ...

As Chancellor he was 'harking back to those early thoughts'.[22] One early idea, however, he abandoned, at least for the moment – the capital levy.[23] This was because of a calculation that the losses resulting from the reductions in the taxable capacity of persons paying such a levy would come so near to the total of the levy itself as to make it scarcely worthwhile.[24] Instead, he relied on death duties. Recalling H. G. Wells's description of inheritance as 'a fatty degeneration of property', he increased the maximum estate duty on big fortunes by 10 per cent to 75 per cent, while removing all duty on estates of £2,000 and less.[25]

The most creative aspect of Dalton's attack on large estates was also inspired by memories of earlier days. At the end of 1945 Dalton scribbled a note to Bridges to set 'the experts' to work on a proposal for:

Payment of all proceeds of sale of War stores into a special National Estate Fund – to be spent on real estate only, e.g.
   in providing National Parks
   in aiding National Trust
   in making good Death Duty Revenue when payment of this is in land.[26]

Bridges and the experts obliged. In his second Budget in April 1946, the Chancellor resurrected a provision in Lloyd George's 1909 Finance Bill which permitted the handing over of land to the community in payment of death duties. Dalton set aside £50 million, secured from the sale of war stores, for a special National Land Fund. This Fund was to be used to reimburse the Inland Revenue for land offered by executors to meet the obligations of the deceased owners. Dalton envisaged that the Fund should stand as a memorial to those killed in the war. 'As you know, I am a most empirical Socialist ... ', he wrote to the Earl of Crawford, Chairman of the National Trust. 'I once described the Trust in a book I wrote as a typically British "example of Practical Socialism in action". I added "It has behind it a fine record of public service and commands a widespread public goodwill. A Labour Government should give it every encouragement greatly to extend its activities." This is all I am trying to do.'[27]

In practice, the difference between probate valuations and market values generally discouraged the kind of transaction Dalton envisaged. Post-1951 Tory Governments, moreover, raided the Fund for other purposes – in 1957 Peter Thorneycroft, as Chancellor, reduced the capital in the Fund, which had grown to £53 million, to £10 million. Nevertheless many important houses and lands passed to the Trust, and the range of estates, stately homes and gardens open to the public is,to a great extent, a product of Dalton's measure. As Lionel Robbins (one of Dalton's fiercest critics on economic matters) later put it, 'the creation of the National Land Fund was one of the few forward-looking and imaginative acts of Government in this century in relation to general culture'.[28]

The National Land Fund scheme was one of the items that led Dalton to describe his second Budget as 'the most satisfying of the four for which I was responsible'. Faced with a smaller deficit and better prospects in the short-term than expected, the stage was set for the Government to indicate its social priorities. Other features were a substantial increase in spending on education, including the provision of free school milk; £4 million for universities; £38 million for the start, from August 1946, of family allowances; and £10 million more for Development Areas.

This last provision gave Dalton particular pleasure. Since he first became M.P. for a north-east constituency in 1929, one of his main aims had been to help the areas which had suffered high levels of unemployment. Now he was able to use direct government investment and the carrot-and-stick incentives of his own Distribution of Industry Act to complement tax changes as a means of reallocating income and wealth in favour of the poorest communities. In his Budget Speech, the Chancellor proudly declared:

... [N]o task lies nearer to my heart than this ... One of the first instructions I gave, when I became Chancellor of the Exchequer last July, was that, as regards constructive plans for the Development Areas, the Treasury was henceforth to be no longer a curb but a spur. I have told my colleagues that I will find, and find with a song in my heart, whatever money is necessary to finance useful and practical proposals for developing these areas, and bringing them to a condition which they never had in the past, of full and efficient and diversified activity. I pledge my word that this job shall not fall down for lack of incentives.[29]

In *With British Guns in Italy*, Dalton had used the phrase, 'with a song in my heart' to describe his emotions during the final Allied advance across the Piave. Now it became the signature tune of his triumphant assault on joblessness. 'Twice in our lifetime we have banished unemployment in wartime', he told an audience in Neath in July 1946. 'Now we must banish it in peace. I will find, with a song in my heart, all the money necessary for sound constructive schemes.'[30]

It was not long before Dalton's defiant rejection of traditional Exchequer attitudes was turned against him. Enthusiasm for projects to prevent a recurrence of unemployment was presented by opponents as an irrepressible urge to spend the taxpayers' money. Correspondents to the *Daily Telegraph* in October suggested 'I'm forever blowing bubbles', 'Beyond the Blue Horizon' or 'I can't give you anything but love' as the Chancellor's refrain.[31] By the following spring, the mood had become less light-hearted. The state was still borrowing money faster than ever, and money was being created for the purpose, complained *The Economist* in March. 'The song in Mr. Dalton's heart', it added, 'is wind on the nation's stomach.'[32]

Practical socialism meant pragmatic socialism. Dalton's first major enactment, taking the Bank of England into public ownership, was typically pragmatic. Although superficially ideological it was carried out in such a manner that it met little resistance in the House and was oddly uncontroversial. Indeed in retrospect it has aroused more criticism on the Left than on the Right.

'We're going to nationalise the Bank', the new Chancellor told his private secretary on the Monday after his appointment. 'We don't know how, but we're going to do it. Get the appropriate fellow to draw up the plans.'[33] Sir Herbert Brittain was set to work. Dalton's Bank of England Bill received its Second Reading in October 1945 and was passed early in the New Year, with a vesting date for 1st March. 'There is not the slightest ground for regarding the Bill as neces-

sary', declared the Tory *Spectator*, 'but not the slightest either for
regarding it as a calamity.'[34] Some socialists expressed disappointment that a calamity – for Tory capitalists – did not occur. Dalton,
however, was delighted: not at having saved the skins of capitalists,
but at having got through a potentially tricky piece of legislation with
a minimum of fuss. He saw the Act as a cleaning-up operation, adding
to the efficiency of a socialist state, rather than as a storming of the
citadel. Nevertheless he seems to have believed that he had achieved
more than was in fact the case.

As the economic historian Sidney Pollard has observed, the desire
to nationalise banks is a consistent Labour predilection, though justified in Labour policy documents in a variety of inconsistent and often
contradictory ways.[35] In 1945 Labour opinion was moved by three
considerations. First, there was an identification of all financial
institutions with capitalism; the Bank, as the supreme financial
institution, was therefore seen as the key target for an anti-capitalist
Government. Second, there was a fear, based on the 'Bankers' Ramp'
interpretation of the 1931 crisis, lest the Bank might sabotage a
Labour administration. Third, there was a proposal, which Dalton
had eagerly supported, to turn the Bank into the dynamo of a socialist
plan.

The main reason for nationalising the Bank in 1945 was that Labour
had promised to do so, largely on the basis of the first two reasons.
At the same time, Dalton continued to believe, somewhat abstractly,
in the third: seeing a nationalised Bank as a potential instrument of
socialist *dirigisme*. Here was a contradiction. The Bank of England
had little significance for Labour planning as actually organised.
Critics claimed that this was because of the form that nationalisation
took; such a view, however, ignored the economic conditions that
prevailed in 1945.

Confusion arose because of the centrality of the Bank of England in
pre-war Labour plans. In the 1930s, Dalton had taken up Nicholas
Davenport's scheme for linking the nationalised Bank to a proposed
National Investment Board. Such a Board, Davenport argued, should
seek 'to mobilise our financial resources and guide them into the right
channels'; the Bank, meanwhile, would be given power to issue and
enforce directives to the directors of other banks.[36] 'It is through the
Bank that control of other financial institutions can most effectively
be operated', Dalton wrote in *Practical Socialism*. 'Such control is
already exercised to a considerable extent, both through financial
pressure and through tacit agreement; it should be strengthened and
regularised.'[37] Dalton's intention had been to bring about a major
change in the function of the Bank.

In the Bank of England Act, this intention was reduced to an aspiration: or rather an aspiration wrapped up as an intention. For a change such as Dalton had proposed to come about, the first requirement would have been to give the Bank of England effective control over other banks. The Act provided control in theory. The fourth clause of the Act laid down that the Bank 'might request information from and make recommendations to bankers, and may, if so authorised by the Treasury, issue directives to any banker for the purpose of securing that effect is given to any such request or recommendation'.[38] Dalton imagined that this provision gave the Bank the ability to exercise a wide-ranging control.[39] But because the Act did not include legal sanctions against non-compliance, no control was provided in practice.

Dalton also decided not to pursue earlier plans to set up a National Investment Board. Instead of the proposed Board 'to determine social priorities', he established a National Investment Council, whose functions were advisory and not executive. 'In this respect it would differ from the National Investment Board which had for long formed part of the Labour Party programme', he told Cabinet in November 1945; 'but the position was different now that a Government was in power which was ready itself to take positive action to plan the use of the nation's economic resources'.[40]

Davenport believed that his scheme had been shelved because of Bridges's fear of a planned economy directed by 'independent experts' outside the Treasury, and that Dalton's failure to turn the Bank into an instrument of national planning was evidence of an inability to understand how the City establishment operated.[41] In fact the structure of early post-war 'planning' made an Investment Board inappropriate; while nationalising the Bank became a matter of peripheral concern. Certainly, nationalisation as carried out had little effect on policy, or on the activities of the City.[42] The Act formalised an existing relationship. In the words of the Chancellor, it provided that 'the Old Man of the Treasury and the Old Lady of Threadneedle Street should be legally married', to avoid any danger of their living in sin.[43] Arguably, the existence of formal powers added to the Government's authority over the Bank, even though such authority continued to be exercised in informal ways.[44] Together with the Borrowing (Control and Guarantee) Act, which became law in July 1946 (making permanent the Government's wartime power to regulate new capital issues), and the Exchange Control Act, which became law the following March (making permanent the wartime controls over foreign exchange transactions), the Bank of England Act was seen by the Chancellor as one of the 'short, simple and strong' pieces of legislation needed to create a new statutory framework for all

PUTTING UP THE BANNS *(Copyright in All Countries)*

private operations in the field of finance.[45] But the emphasis was on continuity, on not rocking the boat, rather than on changing the role of the Bank. To this end, Dalton worked closely and harmoniously with Lord Catto, the Bank's Governor.

Should the Chancellor have insisted on taking more powers? Not only would the Government have gained little by doing so: there were strong inhibiting factors. Remembering 1931, Dalton was anxious to avoid unnecessary action that might cause financial panic. He was particularly concerned in the winter of 1945–6 not to do anything to jeopardise the American Loan, or to encourage the U.S. negotiators to insist on stiffer conditions.

The Loan depended on Congress. Yet Congress was suspicious of socialism. Returning to Washington in the spring of 1946, Keynes reported back to the Chancellor that 'canvassing against the Loan in certain British quarters' was having a serious effect on the American delegation. Attention was being given to 'the argument against lending to a Socialist Government'.[46] Such an argument would have been strengthened by a fiercely contested fight over the nationalisation of the Bank. Dalton was greatly relieved, therefore, to be able to settle the matter over 'tea for two'.

If Dalton's handling of the Bank of England legislation aroused little opposition in the financial world, the same was not true of the policy which came to be most closely linked with his name. More than any nationalisation or budgetary measure, Dalton's reputation in the City as an exuberant profligate, gleefully frittering the nation's resources in pursuit of easy popularity, was a product of his campaign to reduce interest rates.

Dalton did not introduce 'cheap money'. As a policy, it had originated in the Treasury in 1932, and had been pursued with varying degrees of intensity ever since.[47] At the beginning of the war there had been a brief flirtation with the First World War method of boosting saving through high interest rates. Such a policy was, however, quickly abandoned, under the influence of Keynes. In the early 1930s, the aim had been to stimulate demand in order to create employment. Now the problem was to restrict demand so as to prevent inflation resulting from shortages, while at the same time encouraging saving to help finance the war. To achieve these objectives, it was argued that – instead of high interest rates – controls and rationing would encourage lending to the government *faute de mieux*, by removing opportunities for a better return. If this did not work, credit creation would make up the difference – with inflation kept in check by controls.

This was the situation inherited by the Labour Government, and in the immediate post-war period the case for following cheap money with even cheaper money seemed compelling. First, as we have seen, there was a fear of deflation and unemployment – against which the danger of inflation seemed much less serious. The war years had encouraged a belief that monetary policy had little effect on demand for goods and services, especially when backed by controls, and hence that cheap money would not, in itself, be inflationary: rather, it would provide a reserve of pent-up investment demand in the private sector, ready to burst out and mop up unemployment when the time came for lifting controls. Meanwhile, specific controls could regulate and direct private investment. At the same time, there was a hope that low interest rates would speed reconstruction, through increased local authority borrowing. There were the added advantages of avoiding the budgetary deficits which might result from high interest rates; and improving the balance of payments, given the large quantity of sterling balances held in London by foreigners in the form of Treasury Bills. For these reasons, Dalton was strongly advised by leading Bank and Treasury officials – including Keynes – to seek to reduce rates of interest.

Cheap money was thus a strategy which might have been followed by any post-war Government. It was, however, particularly attractive to a Government committed to an immense amount of investment in housing, schools and hospitals, and an extensive programme of nationalisation. Later, Dalton argued that the aims of cheaper money were:

> to save public expenditure on interest, to improve the distribution of income, to encourage investment and to make sure of full employment ... to help the local authorities to keep down the cost of housing programmes, and thus to keep down rents. I wished, most of all, to help the local authorities in the 'blitzed cities', both by special grants and by cheap loans. And I wished to prepare the way for the series of nationalisation Bills which, during this Parliament, we intended to pass. The higher the national credit, the lower the rate of interest, the less the annual compensation corresponding to a given capital value.[48]

Low interest rates could take the place of the abandoned capital levy scheme as a means of reducing the burden of War Debt on the taxpayer by 'conscripting wealth'. 'So long as the National Debt endures', Dalton told the House of Commons, ' – and that may be for a long time yet – the Chancellor of the Exchequer must be on the side of the active producer as against the passive *rentier*.'[49] Cheaper money had the attraction that it was (or seemed to be) an attack on the rich, who would suffer because of lower rates of interest on their capital. At the June 1946 Party Conference, Dalton reminded delegates that Keynes had spoken of 'the Euthanasia of the Rentier' in the context of ever falling interest rates. 'That is Lord Keynes's phrase and not mine', he declared. 'But all who are concerned with the effects of our financial policy on the distribution of wealth, should bear that phrase in mind.'[50]

What appealed to some economists and officials as a purely technical device thus became for the Chancellor something closer to a crusade, arousing – in the end – fierce resistance. Yet at first it caused little comment. There was no reaction from the Conservative benches to Dalton's announcement in October 1945 that the Government had reduced the rate on Treasury Bills from 1 per cent to $\frac{1}{2}$ per cent, and the rate on Treasury Deposit Receipts from $1\frac{1}{8}$ per cent to $\frac{5}{8}$ per cent, thereby cutting the interest charge on the Floating Debt by nearly a half. 'On balance', *The Times* noted, 'the Budget is well in line with the general principles of the White Paper issued by the Coalition.'[51] Nor was there any reaction when Dalton moved against the medium and long-term rates – with the aim of reducing these from 3 per cent to $2\frac{1}{2}$ per cent. As Davenport put it, Dalton was seeking to 'out-Goschen Goschen' – the Chancellor who had converted $2\frac{3}{4}$ per cent Consols to $2\frac{1}{2}$ per cent Consols. Dalton's methods included the rigid control of new issues, the restriction of trustee funds to a limited list of gilt-edged securities, the use on a vast scale of physical and price controls, and the use of government money in support of the market. These were regarded by some in the City as 'worthy of a "bucket" shop which usually supports its dubious issues in the market by manipulating buying'.[52] Nevertheless, they worked. By April 1946, Dalton was writing that 'as for cheaper money, things are moving perfectly just now'.[53]

It was the next stage which went wrong, bringing a sharp change of attitude in the City. In October Dalton made his fatal gambler's throw – carried out on the basis of the most reputable Treasury and Bank of England advice. On 16th October, he told the Commons that he was making an offer, in exchange for 3 per cent Local Loan Stock, of $2\frac{1}{2}$ per cent Treasury stock, 1975 or after, at par. 'A landmark has been reached', he declared.[54] 'Never before, in a cash issue', he claimed, 'have H.M. Government borrowed so much for so little for so long.'[55] The new stock – soon to be known, notoriously, as 'Daltons' – was floated on the market in January 1947. The price held only briefly. On 13th January it touched 100.22 and on 4th February it stood at $99\frac{3}{8}$. Then came the fuel crisis, with widespread stoppages and a sudden increase in unemployment. Gilt-edged prices fell, rallied, fell again in May and collapsed in the late summer and autumn, following the convertibility crisis. Faced with 'a gigantic bear raid' of institutional sellers,[56] the Chancellor's efforts to provide support from public funds failed. By the end of November, Daltons were down to 84, yielding almost 3 per cent. Cheaper money had foundered, and many purchasers of the undated stock suffered sharp losses as a result.

'The forces against me, in the City and elsewhere, were very powerful and determined', Dalton wrote later. 'I felt I could not count on a good chance of victory. I was not well armed. So I retreated.'[57] To succeed, cheaper money needed to carry conviction. This, in its later phase, it failed to do. Even people who supported it in principle felt that it should have ended sooner. Gaitskell wrote later 'that Hugh was absolutely right to go out for cheap money, that he went too far but that was definitely on the advice of the Treasury experts'.[58] There was a game of bluff, and the Chancellor lost. The buying of bonds by speculators who hoped to make capital gains gave way to selling because of fears that lower rates could not be maintained.

These fears were caused partly by the crises of 1947, and partly by a general climate of hostility towards, and lack of confidence in, the Chancellor among those who determined market levels by buying or selling stock. A key factor was the attitude of the banks. In January 1947 the chairmen of the 'Big Five' came out publicly against the Government's interest rate policy.

The most frequently voiced view was that, contrary to earlier expectations, low interest rates were inflationary, generating an excessive amount of borrowing and expenditure on capital pro- grammes, especially local authority capital projects, and diverting funds away from productive enterprise. Yet the extent of the inflation- ary impact in reality was probably low, and it remains a matter of debate whether there was any appreciable aggravation of inflationary pressures at all.[59] Arguably, indeed, cheap money failed, not because it was unsound in principle, but because it outraged the susceptibili- ties of the City.[60] There was a two-way process: prejudice in the City against the Chancellor and his policy leading to condemnation in the press; and press condemnation further undermining the confidence of the speculators. Interest rates, as Dalton remarked, could be talked up as well as down. A key figure was Geoffrey Crowther, editor of *The Economist*. Dalton dubbed *The Economist* 'the Prig's Weekly' because of its pessimistic forecasts.[61] If, in the end, Crowther got the better of the argument, this was partly because his prophecies were self- fulfilling.

There remained a strong case in favour of cheap money, even if the 'inflationary' indictment could be sustained. According to a report by Political and Economic Planning shortly after Labour left office:

> There is considerable truth in the argument that a loose credit policy contains inflationary elements, and so may be thought unsuitable for a generally inflationary situation. But the main conclusion reached ... is that, even in the conditions which have obtained since 1945, it was probably better to make borrowing easy in order to encourage the greatest possible industrial expansion at reasonable cost; had borrowing been more difficult, the volume of investment might have been somewhat reduced but the projects held up would very frequently have been the wrong ones.[62]

After the failure of cheap money in its final stage, the Government settled down to a 'neutral' monetary policy. Short-term rates were to be kept low as before, but the yields on government securities were to be left alone. Cheap money fell into disrepute. The collapse of Dal- ton's campaign had ensured that, in the gilt-edged market, 'the growling of the bears turns to joyous yelps of "I told you so" and the expected future bond rate is so much the higher for ever after.'[63]

Yet it was scarcely a catastrophe. The main impact was political and the chief victim was Dalton himself. The Chancellor had chosen to identify his name closely with a particular policy. His inability to sustain it was a bad dent in his armour, at a time when other problems were closing in upon him.

Cheap money did not falter until February 1947. Meanwhile, the Chancellor had already begun to encounter serious criticism from members of his own former profession. While bankers complained that Dalton was ignorant of the City, economists attacked him – more surprisingly, and hence more damagingly – on the grounds that he was ignorant of economics. Since Dalton was the most economically literate of modern Chancellors apart from his protégé Hugh Gaitskell, this view needs to be examined.

On the surface, the dispute was technical: about the methods the Government employed in its financial policy and planning. Beneath the surface there lay a significant disagreement about the proper objectives of a Labour administration. The background was the legacy of the war, and the nature of the 'planning' that emerged from it.

In the 1930s, Labour had imagined coming to office in prevailing conditions of laissez-faire, and establishing the machinery for socialist planning from scratch. Instead, the incoming Government inherited a wide range of controls and a powerful administrative machine geared to an economy mobilised for total war. So far from wishing to demolish or replace the existing structure, the new regime welcomed a system which, in the words of Aneurin Bevan, 'could not have been realised in normal conditions without something approaching a revolution'.[64] Encouraged by a belief that existing government arrangements were ideally suited to their purposes, Labour ministers slipped into the positions, and took over the powers, of their predecessors. 'Most of the controlling departments, agencies and committees had been established during the war, and were retained afterwards', commented one observer. 'Similarly the system of controls, or methods by which the controls were operated, originated, to a considerable extent, with the Coalition Government.'[65] Such a development had, indeed, been anticipated by Dalton in Labour's 1944 paper, *Full Employment and Financial Policy*, which owed much to his own experience, and that of his post-warriors at the Board of Trade.

In the Coalition, the Lord President of the Council had been given wide powers on the home front.[66] The office of Lord President retained the function of domestic overlord in peacetime. Herbert Morrison took responsibility for co-ordinating national economic planning and development through the Lord President's Committee, which remained the Government's key planning body. Under this Committee came the Industrial Sub-Committee, which included a nuclear group of four ministers (Morrison, Dalton, Cripps and Isaacs) who were authorised to report both to the Lord President's Committee and to the full Cabinet. Two other committees completed the planning structure: the Ministerial Economic Planning Committee, and the Official Steering Committee on Economic Development, made up of representatives of the key economic Departments together with the Economic Section of the Cabinet Office and the Central Statistical Office.[67]

In *Practical Socialism*, Dalton had envisaged a Supreme Economic Authority 'based, I think, upon an Economic Committee, or Planning Committee, of the Cabinet, consisting of a small permanent nucleus of Ministers ... ' The Lord President's Committee, with both Dalton and Cripps as members, seemed to occupy just such a role. In other ways too, 1930s Labour thinking had anticipated the machinery actually created by wartime conditions. In 1933, Morrison had advocated the separation of economic and financial spheres in socialist planning. 'A Minister of Public Economy', he suggested, 'would be responsible for presenting to Parliament the economic Budget of the State, just as the Chancellor of the Exchequer is responsible for presenting the financial Budget.'[68] Dalton made a similar distinction two years later, suggesting that the 'Supreme Economic Authority' should stand apart from the Treasury and financial institutions. The notion that the minister in charge of socialised industries should also be in charge of 'socialised financial institutions' he wrote, would be 'an unworkable addition to responsibilities which in any case would be in danger of becoming excessive for efficient discharge by one man'.[69]

The pre-war blueprints of Morrison and Dalton had an important influence during the first phase of the Attlee Government. In 1950, Bridges was able to remark that the Treasury had two main functions, namely 'prudent housekeeping and the newer function of general co-ordination in the economic field'.[70] Five years earlier, these two functions had been kept firmly apart. Reliance on physical controls during the war had reduced the importance of the Treasury relative to the Lord President's Office – a decline reflected in the exclusion of the Chancellor from the War Cabinet.[71] A degree of policy integration had been achieved, through the influence of Sir John Anderson, as

Lord President, and Bridges and Hopkins at the Treasury.[72] When Labour came to power, however, finance and economics were placed in separate compartments. Significantly, the press referred to Herbert Morrison as the 'economic' Chancellor of the Exchequer to distinguish him from Dalton as the 'financial' Chancellor.[73]

The relationship between the two ministers was not a happy one. Personally, Dalton and Morrison had already drifted apart. Departmentally there were strong pressures to distance them still further. 'The Treasury was always uneasy about other departments trespassing its territory', comments Lord Trend. 'In the end the Treasury will always clobber or absorb them.'[74] Absorption eventually took place. Meanwhile, senior Treasury officials were particularly suspicious of Max Nicholson, head of Morrison's economic co-ordination team.[75] 'Until economic planning was absorbed into the Treasury organisation', Morrison wrote later, not without bitterness, 'it was a matter of some doubt how far the Treasury was subject to the machinery of economic co-ordination.'[76]

Yet the problem was not just one of interdepartmental rivalry. It also concerned the whole approach to planning favoured by the Government: an approach that was increasingly criticised by the Government's own economic advisers. Ministers saw planning primarily as a matter of mobilising the nation's resources to create order out of confusion and to regulate fairness. 'Unemployment and destitution were, in the main, the products of letting things drift', declared Morrison in the autumn of 1946.[77] The aim of planning was to replace drift with central direction. Economists, inside and outside government, on the other hand, were acquiring wider and bolder ambitions. 'The glowing hope which the idea of planning arouses in so many breasts', observed Sir Hubert Henderson, a former Treasury economist, in May 1947, 'is that it will prove an efficient instrument of expansion.'[78] Lessons (some of them deceptive) derived from wartime experience, and excitement about new 'Keynesian' techniques, encouraged a new generation of experts to believe in the capacity of the right kind of planning to stimulate economic growth. Here we need to review developments in economic management since the beginning of the war, and to consider the role which academic economists had recently acquired in Whitehall, together with the theoretical assumptions which helped to motivate them.

The war had produced a number of major advances in the 'Keynesian Revolution'. Kingsley Wood's first 'Keynesian' Budget in 1941 had extended the purpose of budgetary policy so that it had ceased simply to aim, in Bridges's words, at producing 'a happy ending for one hero – a cash surplus for the coming year.'[79] Henceforth, government financial arrangements were no longer framed merely to meet the Government's financial needs. Instead, the Budget Speech became a comprehensive survey of the national economy. The 1944 White Paper on Employment Policy had provided another step forward, committing future administrations to policies aimed at full employment, by means of the maintenance of total expenditure, and involving official measurements of national income.[80]

Yet these changes, brought about by the war, had also been held back by wartime requirements. With direct controls used as the main means of restraining demand, budgetary policy assumed a comparatively minor role: a fact reflected in Dalton's 'Gladstonian' Budgets. 'Early post-war discussions', J. C. R. Dow observes, 'seemed at times to assume that since controls were there, no budgetary measures were necessary.'[81] When, eventually, controls were removed, the importance of budgetary policy became more evident. In the meantime, one reason why the Government did not remove controls in a hurry was a fear lest the pattern of boom followed by slump that occurred after the First World War might be repeated after the Second. The idea was to use direct controls – as in wartime – to hold down prices, while manpower was built up to the point at which production would be able to fill the gap between supply and demand. Dalton, in particular, was happy to see maintained a planning machinery that was essentially a system of rationing scarce resources, placing directive power in the hands of ministers. Such a system accorded well with his views on distribution.

Where Dalton cherished controls as a vital socialist instrument, some of the Government's own economists were envisaging the erosion of controls, and their replacement by budgetary policy as the central ingredient of a national economic plan of a far more comprehensive nature than the *ad hoc* allocations which passed for planning under Herbert Morrison. Such a vision of a properly planned future involved, however, a close co-ordination between economic and financial functions within the Government.

Keynes died in April 1946. 'Keynesian' passion never burnt so fiercely, nor so purely, as in the months that followed. One reason was the extraordinary position of influence his disciples – pre-war lecturers and professors – had gained in the corridors of power. Later, Bridges described how, several years earlier, these Jacobins of the economic revolution had taken Whitehall by storm:

First, it so happened that the outbreak of the war coincided – very broadly – with a time when economists generally were beginning to come to a far greater degree of unanimity than before about economic policies. Secondly, the war brought into being many difficult and novel questions which could only be settled with the advice and help of economists. Thirdly, many economists, who would otherwise have been engaged in academic work, were able and willing to give up that work, and to join the staffs of Government Departments where they rendered the most notable service, not only in helping to guide the country's war effort, but later in shaping our post-war policies and organisation. Finally, means were found of employing economists in positions in Government Departments in which they could exercise a real influence on the Government's economic policy.

Where the permanent civil servants inclined to administrative conservatism, the revolutionaries sought, from the start, to innovate. One early result was the Central Statistical Office, which (under Keynes's influence) initiated the preparation of statistics of the national income. Another was the Economic Section of the Cabinet Secretariat, charged with presenting 'a co-ordinated and objective picture of the economic situation as a whole and the economic aspects of projected Government policies.'[82]

The latter body was built up during the war by Dalton's former pupil and protégé, Lionel Robbins, himself one of the leading recruits, and now converted to many aspects of the Keynesian doctrine. The influence of the Economic Section depended on reasoned argument and tact, rather than on formal powers. 'Originally it was rather despised by Whitehall', a leading member recalls. 'Then it became known that the Lord President, Sir John Anderson, read its briefs; so its members were put on all economic committees.'[83] Armed with the authority of the Lord President and guided by the key Whitehall figures of Norman Brook and Sir Edward Bridges, Robbins established mutual confidence and trust. As a result, the Section played a central part in wartime economic planning.

Robbins returned to the L.S.E. at the end of 1945. Meanwhile, he had been replaced as Economic Section Director by James Meade, already working in the Section. Robbins now believed that 'the fluctuations of aggregate demand must not be left to look after themselves'.[84] His successor was one of Keynes's most dedicated followers and a fervent proselytiser of the new faith, having written the memorandum that inspired the 1944 Employment White Paper.

Here was a difficulty. The new Director believed strongly in the need for 'macro' economic planning. Yet he found himself straddling the separate financial and economic spheres, which he was unable to unite. As head of the Economic Section, he was under the jurisdiction of the Lord President, advising Morrison on economic planning. As a member of the Budget Committee, he advised the Chancellor of the Exchequer. As a member of the Official Steering Committee, he was part of the central economic team 'responsible for gathering and assessing economic intelligence, preparing forecasts, framing economic plans, advising Ministers on the advantages and disadvantages of these plans, and keeping under review the execution of plans when authorised and put into operation'.[85] Yet, to his intense frustration, he found that he was not allowed to reveal Budget details to the Lord President.[86]

Morrison relied more on his own staff – in particular Max Nicholson, Alexander Johnstone, and his principal private secretary, J. A. R. Pimlott – than on the Economic Section.[87] Nevertheless, Meade found him open to influence: with no knowledge of economics, the Lord President was prepared to listen to the professionals. Dalton was less receptive. On administrative matters and finance, he turned to officials at the Treasury or at the Bank. On details of planning, he was willing and even eager to be briefed by Meade and the Economic Section. On wider economic policy, however, he did not feel the need for instruction. Meade believed that Bridges wanted 'to muddle up the Cabinet Office and the Treasury' in order to produce co-ordinated planning. But the Chancellor could not be persuaded.

Meade had known Dalton slightly in the 1930s. He had encountered him again during the war, forming an impression of the then President of the Board of Trade as a 'paranoid bully' who shouted at his civil servants.[88] At the Board, however, Dalton had taken up Meade's suggestions. Now he ignored them. In June 1946 Meade gloomily recorded a discussion at the Lord President's Ministerial Committee on Economic Planning. The subject was the timing of the publication of the Economic Survey. The Chancellor seemed impervious to the 'macro' ideas advanced by the Economic Section:

> On this, the Chancellor of the Exchequer argues that he was in favour of the survey for the calendar year being published and debated in, say, November of the previous year. He was clearly thinking very much in terms of a division of labour between himself and the Lord President, he having his publicity in April on Central Government finance, and the Lord President having his innings on the Economic Plan in November. To one who, like myself, believes that the main instrument in a Liberal-Socialist state for carrying out any plan must be fiscal policy, and who therefore believes that budgetary policy and the economic plan must be as closely linked as possible, this was terrifying. Greatly daring, I intervened in the

discussion ... I suggested ... that we should prepare by November or December each year the first draft of a survey for the following calendar year, that during January to March this would be available for the Chancellor to consider in connection with his budget and for the Steering Committee and the Lord President in connection with the general aspects of economic policy, and that after the budget a final survey should be prepared without any gaps between demands and supplies, and should be published for a general debate on economic affairs in the light of the budget and of the other decisions which had been taken. The Chancellor misunderstood me to be suggesting that he should discuss his budget secrets with the Lord President, etc., and took me severely to task. I attempted to explain that this had not been my intention at all.[89]

This was not the only occasion on which the Chancellor refused to be educated about the need, pressed so fervently by the economists, to view the economy as a whole. Lord Trend recalls that certain words were anathema to Dalton. One was 'overall'. 'If you mean total, say total!' the Chancellor would declaim. 'An overall is a garment you wear.'[90] Unaware of this foible, Meade wrote a paper shortly after his appointment dealing with overall demand. When this was discussed at a meeting of leading officials, Dalton took no interest in the proceedings. According to Meade, 'All he did was make jokes about overalls and aprons.'

Part of the problem was that Dalton disagreed with Meade about the Section's proper role. The academic economists looked to Whitehall, rather than to Government ministers, for direction: continuing to believe that their influence depended on the degree to which permanent officials were prepared to accept them. Dalton, on the other hand, liked to envisage the Section as part of Labour's socialist vanguard which, in the case of many Section members, was far from the reality. Meade was greatly incensed on one occasion when Dalton introduced him at a dinner as one of the young Labour economists. 'I am nothing of the sort', Meade wrote indignantly. 'I am a Civil Servant.' Key to the whole planning effort, in Meade's view, was the co-operation that existed between himself and Sir Edward Bridges. He was appalled when Dalton seemed to suggest that he should spy on Bridges, his own superior in the Cabinet Office. After one encounter, Meade wrote of his dilemma:

In the course of his conversation the Chancellor told me that I must take the initiative and brief him or visit him whenever I thought that there was anything on which I should advise him. This raises very difficult issues for me a) as regards the Lord President as it may be awkward to be briefing both these Ministers simultaneously on the same issue, and b) more particularly as regards Treasury officials, since my relations with them might become very difficult if I was briefing the Chancellor independently on their subjects, without being a part of the Treasury machine.

Having reported the conversation to Bridges, who passed it off smoothly, Meade concluded that it was the good opinion of civil servants that mattered. 'I am inclined to believe that, however attractive is the immediate prospect of briefing the Chancellor when one wants to do so, in the long run the influence of the Section in the Treasury depends rather upon relations with Treasury officials than with the Chancellor.'[91] Thus Dalton, maintaining the separation of finance and economics, relied for advice on career civil servants (Bridges, Hopkins, Eady) and bankers (Lord Catto and C. F. Cobbold of the Bank of England, Clarence Sadd of the Midland), rather than on the economists.

Why was Dalton apparently so difficult? One reason was his concern to avoid fighting Morrison over spheres of influence. Another was the scepticism about Keynesian techniques that continued to exist among non-economist Treasury officials responsible for advising the Chancellor, despite the advocacy of Meade and his colleagues.[92] In the view of the economists, however, the most damning explanation was that Dalton himself – although trained in the discipline – failed to grasp the full implications of Keynesian theory. The Chancellor seemed to be guilty of the sin of 'orthodoxy'; men who had been brought up on his books now scorned him as a member of the *ancien régime*. Contrasts were drawn with Sir Stafford Cripps. 'Whereas Cripps didn't have pretensions as an economist and would listen', suggests Sir Austin Robinson, economic adviser to the Board of Trade and later a member of the Economic Planning Staff, 'Dalton did and wouldn't.'[93] Robbins wrote in retrospect that Dalton's 'infatuation with politics had by then long outlasted any great interest in, or perception of, the problems of economic policy'.[94] This view (including the prejudice against an 'infatuation' with politics) was widely held among the crusading Keynesians.

Yet more was involved than intellectual obduracy on the part of the Chancellor. The economists might consider that politics should take second place to economics: Dalton was equally certain that political aims should take precedence. Physical controls and physical planning appealed to him more than budgetary methods because they enabled the Government to allocate resources, and maintain the push towards redistribution. Nor was such a view without its supporters. Examining Labour's controls shortly after the Government left office, G. D. N. Worswick commented:

> Direct controls ... are by no means perfect. They require administration and may involve waste. On the other hand, they allow employment and output to be kept at very high levels. The exact point where the waste and costs of direct controls overtake the gains from higher employment cannot be found from any general reasoning. It depends on the economic situation, especially the likely developments in international trade. It also depends on a value judgment involving the intrinsic merits of a high level of unemployment, the distribution of income, and the intrinsic merits of free enterprise.[95]

Much of the criticism levelled at Dalton, while appearing dispassionate and value-free, was indeed highly political. 'If we wonder why a Socialist did not take up wholeheartedly the national income approach', writes Samuel Beer, 'it may be instructive to recall that Keynesian theory, from which this approach derived, was intended by its author to save capitalism.'[96] The proposition may be turned around. If we wonder why the economists were so adamant in their opposition to what Beer calls 'the ancient Socialist faith in public administration' rather than the market, it was because redistribution did not always rank high among their priorities.

In the end, the new doctrine triumphed, establishing its own orthodoxy which all non-Marxist Labourites, including Dalton, would eventually accept as unquestioned dogma. Even in the mid-1940s, some socialists were Keynesians, and many Keynesians regarded themselves as socialists. Nevertheless, there remained a difference of philosophy between those who placed the ethical claims of socialism first, and those who saw themselves primarily as technicians, tuning the engine in order to increase prosperity. Not until Crosland published *The Future of Socialism* in 1956 were the two outlooks partially reconciled.

In the immediate aftermath of the war, the instincts of Webbian socialists and of non-socialist Keynesians were often sharply in conflict, despite agreement on the need for government action to maintain full employment. Where socialists preferred a state-controlled economy to the market as a matter of principle, Keynesians longed for a return to the market and the abandonment of controls; where Dalton saw physical controls as a tool for reducing inequality, many Keynesians regarded the pursuit of greater equality for its own sake as a distraction from the main purpose of pursuing prosperity. 'There was for once almost complete unanimity between professional economists about the remedies which must be applied', claimed the writer T. E. Utley in 1949, discussing the crises of two years before. These remedies, he suggested, came close to 'the main sting' of the attack on Radical egalitarianism throughout the nineteenth and early twentieth centuries.[97] Many economists, newly converted, regarded socialism as an out-of-date economic theory, ignoring its ethical claims. The Keynesian system was presented as a modern, more serviceable alternative. It was widely believed that Keynesian economics, as Robert Skidelsky has put it, 'had to make its way against rival panaceas, particularly socialism, which laid chief emphasis on public ownership and the redistribution of wealth'.[98]

It was the attacks of economists outside government service, starting early in 1947, which first began seriously to undermine Dalton's reputation: urging the 'disinflationary' case that Britain suffered from 'suppressed inflation' (impeding the movement of labour, and diverting resources from export manufacture), that controls should be removed, that there should be a greater reliance on the market, and that there should be a heavy emphasis on fiscal policy. These attacks, reflecting common criticisms within the Economic Section, began with a letter from Hubert Henderson to *The Times* on 26th February 1947 which declared that Britain was suffering not from a shortage but from a maldistribution of manpower, arising from an excess of purchasing power. The criticism was taken up by *The Economist*, whose editor, Geoffrey Crowther, was a long-standing opponent of Dalton. The theme was followed through by others who had recently left Whitehall, in particular Roy Harrod and Lionel Robbins. According to Beer:

> The sequence in which this analysis arose and spread through the political community seems to have been: academic economists; then economic journalists; then Members of Parliament, especially the Opposition; and finally the Government.[99]

As we shall see, Dalton was squeezed during 1947 by a powerful combination: economic disaster, the rival priorities of ministerial colleagues, the restless ambition of Sir Stafford Cripps, and the tide of professional opinion. The most important factor was economic disaster. Yet adverse professional opinion counted strongly against him, not only in the press (which, being largely anti-socialist, eagerly embraced supposedly 'objective' reasons for attacking a socialist

Chancellor) but also within Whitehall and in the Cabinet itself.

The objective reasons masked a liberal passion. A professedly socialist Government was in power. Few men could have been less inclined to socialism than Crowther, Robbins and Harrod, highly respected figures in the economic and financial worlds. Crowther had helped to lead 'middle way' Keynesians before the war; Robbins, until his reconciliation with Keynes, had been a fierce anti-interventionist; Harrod, joint editor of the influential *Economic Journal*, believed that 'the substitution of central control for contract and enterprise' was 'the substitution of a crude, clumsy method of adjustment for a fine one, of a schoolboy's notion for the subtly organized product of a long evolution', and that by yielding to the 'plausibilities' of high death duties 'and abandoning the age-old institution of inheritable property, we may find that we have destroyed the race'.[100] Even Meade, who had once been a New Fabian and believed in a degree of redistribution, saw himself in 1945 as a liberal, and liked to think of the Labour Government as 'Liberal-Socialist', a label which his political masters would certainly have resisted.[101]

By wearing his prejudices on his sleeve, while the economists' prejudices were largely unacknowledged, Dalton encouraged a belief that he was the prisoner of an outmoded ideology. That he was an economist, and so could be expected to share the economists' world view, made his refusal to do so seem, to the economists, all the more perverse. We need not doubt that Dalton made errors of judgment, in particular in under-estimating the dangers of inflation (despite repeated warnings by Meade, before the situation became critical).[102] Yet we should pause before endorsing too readily Robbins's contempt for his former tutor's 'infatuation with politics', and bear in mind Harrod's concern for the welfare of 'cultivated gentle people'. In weighing the criticisms which began to spread from the academic community just as Labour's extraordinary programme of reform reached its peak (and just as the administration encountered its first serious difficulty) we should consider how far the ideal society sought by the elected Government and the vision of Dalton's most expert critics coincided, and whether indeed they were compatible.

XXVII

Crisis

1946 was a heady year. Labour's programme was in full swing: it was the year of nationalisations, of socialist Budgets, of legislation on national insurance and the health service. It was the year, too, of full employment. 'Annus Mirabilis', Dalton called it at the end of his life, 'the best British parliamentary year since the war'. The Chancellor's own personal popularity was at its peak. Attending Party Conference in Bournemouth at the end of June, he wrote: 'I am riding just now on a high tide of success. I must, therefore, cautiously watch my step!'

In August he took Ruth to Scotland to look at trees. Trees were like young men: sturdy, straight and growing tall, offering hope for future generations. Hugh had given the Forestry Commission £20 million for use over five years, twice as much as was spent altogether between the wars: 'A Socialist investment', he claimed, ' ... Real practical Socialism!' Now he wanted to see the early results. Each day he toured forests with Ruth and the Chairman of the Forestry Commission, Sir Roy Robinson. After a week, Ruth retreated. Hugh stayed for five days walking in Border Country. Then he returned to London, refreshed, his mind full of afforestation schemes.[1]

In mid-September he flew to Ottawa and then to Washington for the first business meeting of the Board of Governors of the International Bank and the I.M.F. At a press conference in the British Embassy in Washington, American reporters, addressing him as 'Sir Hugh', assailed him with questions about Britain's finances. He responded with non-committal good humour. 'On the American line of credit', asked one interrogator, 'is it likely that the full amount may not be drawn, or can you say anything about that?' 'Oh', replied the Chancellor, 'we must see how we go, must we not?'[2] Lord Catto, who also travelled to Washington for the inaugural meeting, faced a similar inquiry as he got off the plane. 'Let me ask you a question', the

Governor of the Bank of England parried. 'Do I look depressed?'[3]

Dalton's ebullience and the confidence of his advisers lasted until the New Year. Then 'Annus Mirabilis' became 'Annus Horrendus'. 1947 began badly and rapidly got worse. Dalton later recalled the seven months from mid-April to mid-November as the unhappiest of his public life.[4] In this period he was broken politically, suffering blows to his public image and, more important, to his self-esteem from which he never recovered.

How did it happen? The jury is still out on the convertibility crisis of 1947. An excess of imports over exports; a world-wide dollar shortage; high levels of overseas spending, especially military; a problem over sterling balances; the approach of a Faustian deadline, the date when the 'convertibility' clause of the Loan Agreement came into effect. These were some of the ingredients of the emergency that ended Labour's reforming phase, and brought a period of sharp austerity.

At the beginning of 1947 the most obvious strain on the British economy was the weather: 'the worst winter of the century, which chose the worst possible year in which to arrive.'[5] In 1942, as President of the Board of Trade, Dalton had taken steps to avert a fuel crisis. Five years later, triggered by a period of exceptional cold, the fuel crisis arrived.

Production was never held up for want of fuel during the war, despite the failure to introduce rationing. Nevertheless the danger that supply might not meet demand remained. For five successive winters, margins were perilously low. With a post-war boost in consumption, the likelihood of a shortfall increased. As some senior ministers were aware, disaster might strike at any time. 'This matter is much too urgent in the national interest to wait for further discussion', Dalton warned Attlee in November 1946.[6] The Prime Minister responded by setting up a Cabinet Coal Committee, under Dalton's chairmanship, with the Ministers of Labour, Transport and Fuel and Power as members.[7]

Unfortunately the Coal Committee lacked executive power. More unfortunate still, the member of the Committee least worried about the supply of coal was the minister responsible for ensuring that stocks were adequate. The previous August, Emanuel Shinwell, Minister of Fuel and Power, had announced publicly that there would be no fuel crisis. Privately, he warned Attlee against being taken in by pessimistic statistics. 'As an administrator ... S. is hardly a starter', noted Shinwell's deputy, Hugh Gaitskell, before this truth had become self-evident. 'He has no conception at all of either organisation or planning or following up ... He will always try and evade an unpopular decision, procrastinate, find a way round, etc.' Yet Shinwell was not wholly to blame for the shortages that occurred. To be effective, precautions would have meant restrictions, industrial shutdowns and unemployment which, in a year of export drive, would almost certainly have been so unpopular and economically damaging as to be unacceptable.[8]

As it was, the Government seemed completely unprepared for the severe cold spell which began at the end of January. At midnight on 28th January, Big Ben struck once and then, symbolically, fell silent. Next day the Thames froze at Windsor and ice-floes formed in Folkestone harbour. By 5th February, pits were blocked by snow and colliers were unable to leave port. In Birmingham alone, 60,000 workers were idle for lack of fuel. Two days later Shinwell confronted the Cabinet, and then the House, with a stark announcement: because of the coal shortage, all electricity must be cut off from industry in London, the south-east, the midlands and the north-west, and from all domestic consumers for five hours a day.

In the Commons, the statement was greeted with low whistles;[9] in the Cabinet, by disbelief. The Chancellor, who should have been the first to be informed, had received no advance notice. On 6th February, Dalton had expressed concern about getting through March. He had not considered that the Government would not even get through February.[10] Small wonder that when he wound up the Commons debate on 10th February, he failed to counter, in the words of *The Times*, 'the main charge that the Government had been surprised by the emergency with no plan ready to meet it.' There was indeed no answer.

Shinwell's measures amounted to 'the most drastic restriction of industry ever known in this country'. The Prime Minister was forced to announce a major military operation, with heavy penalties, including imprisonment, for disobeying restrictive orders.[11] 'Starve with Strachey, Shiver with Shinwell' was the Tory slogan. While blizzards raged, families went without heating. Even in government offices, politicians and civil servants wore overcoats, scarves and several pairs of socks.[12] Unemployment rose to $2\frac{1}{4}$ million, and there was a big loss of production for export. Harm to the prestige of the Government, whose 'planning' appeared fatally flawed, was permanent. Not until mid-March did the wind change, and daily life return to normal.

On 14th February, Lionel Robbins fired a warning shot at his old tutor, in the form of a letter, widely quoted, to *The Times*. According to the former head of the Economic Section:

The worst aspect of the coal shortage is not its bearing on domestic comfort and domestic employment but its effect on the external balance. If we do not succeed in increasing our overall exports by at least 75 per cent before the dollar credits run out we shall be faced with external bankruptcy. We shall not be able to get the food and materials we need. We shall not be able to meet our external commitments. Yet our export drive is being throttled for want of the other scarce materials, particularly steel and timber, which we could procure from abroad if only we had coal for export.

If nothing had been done by the end of 1947, Robbins continued, the hope of getting into some sort of equilibrium before the American Loan was exhausted would have almost faded. 'We shall be confronted with the prospects later on of external difficulties beside which our present troubles will seem insignificant.' Here was a vicious circle. Only exports could ease the strain. But coal was the key to manufacture for export. In Robbins's view, the answer was to increase coal production, which meant more miners. He therefore called for 100,000 men, 'native and foreign', for the mines. But where, Thomas Balogh asked a few days later, were 100,000 men to be found?[13]

Apart from sermons from economists, Dalton had to face the anger of public and press. As gilt-edged tumbled and the term 'Daltons' was added to the language of the City to refer to the Chancellor's ill-fated stock, a rumour spread that Dalton was to blame for the lack of coal and that the Minister of Fuel and Power was loyally covering up for him. 'Will Mr. Shinwell Speak?' asked a trade magazine.[14] The question, which Mr. Shinwell had himself deliberately inspired, was echoed in the national press.

The Chancellor's full fury now descended on his flustered, shaken colleague. 'He is by far the least attractive member of the Government', Dalton wrote on 10th February, 'always looking round for someone to whom to pass the blame.'[15] Dalton wanted Shinwell sacked. So did Cripps. The difference was that Dalton's reasons had become personal. 'If only there was a decent Minister in that job – Gaitskell or any other – I could talk to him as I do to my other colleagues frankly and constructively', Dalton wrote to the Prime Minister. 'But with Shinwell all this is impossible.'[16] At meetings, the Chancellor poured forth his bitter contempt. Once, discussing how to make better use of national manpower, Shinwell suggested that more effective use could be made of prison labour and recalled that 'when I was inside in World War I, I used to spend all my day riddling ashes'. 'A very suitable occupation for the future Minister of Fuel and Power', responded Dalton.[17]

Dalton's grievances were real. Yet, as in the past, obsessive hatred of a colleague was also a symptom, marking the moment when the smooth surface of success had begun to crack. There were other, physical, signs. After the election of the Labour Government, the boils which afflicted Dalton during the final months of the Coalition had mysteriously vanished. During 1946 they began to return. In the summer the Chancellor noted that 'the enemy Fatigue' had established some 'Advance Points', namely a carbuncle in his right ear and a boil on his right forefinger.[18] The winter brought a series of staphylococcal outbreaks, which Dalton's medical adviser, Dr. Urwick, attempted to treat with an autogenous vaccine.[19] But the affliction spread painfully to his buttocks during the harsh weather. Like the prophet Job, he was smitten 'with sore boils from the sole of his foot unto his crown'. In April, after three hours' emphatic banging on the despatch box during the Budget Speech, his finger went septic. As a result he had to undergo another minor operation, similar to the one in 1945, combined with penicillin treatment, and was forced to wear his arm in a sling.[20]

Like his outbursts against colleagues, Dalton's ailments seemed to be linked to stress: caused, in the spring of 1947, by more than the fuel crisis. The Chancellor did not need Robbins to remind him of the desperate balance of payments situation, exacerbated, but not caused, by the shortage of coal. When fuel restrictions were removed on 12th March, the problem remained, getting rapidly worse.

Dalton had long been concerned about the rate of drawings on the American and Canadian credits. His difficulty had been in persuading colleagues to feel equally alarmed. In January 1947, before the damage to exports caused by the weather, he had reacted in fury at the rejection of all the main proposals put forward by the Economic Planning Committee (composed of himself, Morrison, Cripps and Isaacs). These proposals were aimed at 'closing the gap' in the so-called manpower budget – that is, reducing the excess of labour requirements over labour resources and hence increasing production. After a Cabinet meeting on 16th January, the Chancellor wrote of 'easy-going, muddle-headed irresponsibility' among ministers, the premier included, who failed to appreciate the urgency of the situation. After a 'first class row' about military requirements with the Minister of Defence on the 17th, Dalton withdrew to Wiltshire to plan a counter-attack.[21]

His response took the form of a careful 'Note on a Difference of Opinion' setting out a demand for manpower and spending cuts. This he sent, accompanied by a resignation threat, to the Prime Minister. 'I had sooner be out of it all', he informed Attlee, 'if all my arguments are to be swept aside like flies.'[22] In his Note, Dalton told the Prime Minister what critics were soon to be saying in the press and in Parliament, in the mistaken belief that they were telling the Chancellor something he did not already know:

We are, I am afraid, drifting in a state of semi-animation, towards the rapids. We have started our course, since the last election, wonderfully well. But we look like finishing wonderfully badly – worse, perhaps, than in 1931.[23]

A week later Cabinet agreed, grudgingly, to reduce military expenditure by 5 per cent (£40 million) only half the amount Dalton had sought.[24] The shutdown of much of British industry because of the fuel shortage greatly increased the pressure. Meanwhile, the date ringed in red on the Chancellor's calendar – 15th July, when, under the terms of the Loan Agreement, pounds became freely convertible into dollars – drew ominously near. 'Very often during these months, I lay awake at night doing mental arithmetic', Dalton recalled. 'We had so many dollars; last month we spent so many; if we spend the same next month, we shall only have so many left. But we mustn't let our dollar reserves fall below so much, or we shall be sunk.'[25] In March, as drawings on the Loan gathered pace, he wrote a 'scorching paper' to frighten colleagues.[26] Senior ministers, each defending a departmental corner, were not frightened enough and little action was taken.

The Chancellor made what adjustments he could in his April Budget. At the beginning of the year, he had asked officials to investigate the possibility of raising tobacco duty to save dollars.[27] In the Budget – described by the generally hostile *Economist* as 'an acceptable, almost a good one' designed 'to disguise the fact that he is proposing to move in exactly the direction that his "deflationist" critics have urged upon him'[28] – a massive increase in duty was imposed. Further dollar savings were made by the Chancellor's insistence that, from April, American rather than British money should be used to resist Communists in Greece: an important change in policy which pushed the United States one step closer to accepting a world role.[29] But the dollar drain continued.

'In eleven months we had drawn more than half the United States credit', Dalton told Cabinet, bleakly, on 5th June, 'and if the present rate of drawing continued the credit would be exhausted as early as the end of 1947.'[30] The Chancellor accompanied this warning by yet another request for reductions in spending on defence and on the food programme. On 13th June he noted that the dollar shortage was getting worse all over the world. 'The rush of the Gadarine Swine towards the precipice is quickening', he wrote, 'and I am anxious that we should not lead the charge.'[31] But Cabinet once again refused drastic cuts. After some minor reductions, the volume of imports contained in the new import programme was actually higher than in the preceding twelve months.[32]

The crisis brought to the surface old emotions and prejudices. During the war Dalton had tried to ensure that Germany would be made to pay reparations. After the war, it seemed as though Germany's victims were doing the paying. A sizeable part of Britain's deficit consisted of the cost of maintaining an army and an administration in the British zone of the defeated Reich. It was quite intolerable, Dalton wrote in May, that former enemies should have practically no external debts while Britain bore such a burden. The Americans should be told that 'we can't spare any more dollars for the Germans'.[33] Trend recalls the Chancellor's sense of injustice that 'his dollars' should be squandered on 'Strachey's food, Shinwell's fuel and Bevin's Huns'. Other, deeper, feelings were also revived. To his Cambridge friends the Peases, Dalton spoke of 'watching drops of blood',[34] and he told another friend, more poignantly, that to observe the seepage of reserves was 'like watching a child bleed to death and being unable to stop it'.[35] The boils on his skin became red, wound-like blotches. 'Why can't life get better?' he demanded, striding round his office, as though railing against an unkind Fate. All sense of triumph had vanished, replaced by disillusion and a wretched sense of betrayal. According to Trend, 'his body and his mind had turned inward on themselves.'[36]

Publicly he put on a bold face. He told the House on 8th July, relaying the advice he had received from the Treasury: 'in large measure, 15th July has already been discounted and the additional burden of assuming these new obligations ... will be noticeably less than many people may suppose.'[37] At first it seemed as though it might be true; 15th July came and went with no immediate impact. On 27th July the Chancellor talked 'rather airily, rather buoyantly' over dinner at No. 11 with Kenneth Younger and Harold Nicolson about the Government's difficulties. 'Even when the dollar-loans run out, there are "reserves"', he told his guests. 'We could live on these reserves for quite a bit.'[38] But next day he presented a paper at a meeting of the Big Five stating the precise opposite, namely that 'if we are not to be completely defenceless against all American demands, we must not run far into our final reserves'.[39]

A brief moment of optimism following 15th July had, indeed, been quickly dispelled. During the first half of 1947 the dollar drain was a

serious cause for concern at $315 million a month. In the week
beginning 20th July, the rate reached $106 million a week, then $126
million in the next week and $127 million in the week after that.[40] On
24th July Dalton told Cabinet that at the present rate of drawing, the
credit would not last beyond November at best and might be exhausted
by late September.[41] On 30th July, he issued an even sharper warning.
He now predicted, not only that the U.S. credit would be exhausted by
the autumn, but that Britain's final reserves of gold and dollars would
last only a few months longer. In view of uncertainty about Marshall
Aid, immediate action was imperative. He proposed troop reductions
of 150,000 men and cuts in imports which would mean 'a loss of
amenities and some austerity if not hardship'. Such measures, he
declared, were the only alternative to a much worse fate later on.[42]

Yet, throughout, he took care to make a distinction: between cuts
which the crisis made essential, and cuts aimed at satisfying critics by
emasculating the Government's domestic programme. In Cabinet, he
stressed the need to concentrate on reducing overseas expenditure.
He took a similar message to a meeting of the P.L.P. the same day.
Angrily, he rejected rumours of an impending National Government
on 1931 lines. There would be no coalition, he assured M.P.s, no
election, no 'May Committee' to recommend cuts, of the kind that
had been set up by the second Labour Government. There was a need
to 'rephase' some of the building programme. The dollar drain and
Labour's social spending were, however, unconnected.[43]

Dalton put the last point even more forcefully to the Prime Minister.
Cuts in overseas spending, cuts in expenditure on troops and food,
were desperately needed. But the Labour Government must not allow
its domestic socialism to be sacrificed:

> Attempts are being made by our opponents to blame our external
> difficulties on what we have done at home in the past two years.
> We must firmly reject this argument. If we had done *nothing* good
> at home, our external difficulties would be no less; indeed they would
> be greater. But our capital programme must be more selective, and
> we must concentrate on completions, rather than on new beginnings,
> and on quick results.[44]

Dalton was determined, above all, not to be another Philip Snowden. In 1931 MacDonald and Snowden had yielded to pressure for
domestic cuts, escaping political difficulties by allying with the centre
and the right. Dalton, instead, turned the other way, taking comfort
from the support of the newly formed 'Keep Left' group within the
P.L.P. This left-wing faction, led by Crossman, Foot and Mikardo,

agitated loudly for a reduction in the armed forces and in military spending.[45] Over and over, Dalton urged the same case: the need for defence cuts. 'We *must* come out of Palestine', he told Attlee, 'and heavily reduce our forces in Egypt.'[46]

Late in the evening of 30th July, after a tiring day, the Big Five met, with Bridges and Eady in attendance, and failed to agree. 'C.R.A. shows no power of gripping or guiding the talk', the Chancellor recorded. Bevin appeared drunk, and Morrison was petulant. The Chancellor's sole supporter, on the issue of cuts in overseas spending, was Cripps. When no decisions of the kind he sought were made, Dalton once again considered resignation. Cripps urged caution. Gradually, the Chancellor recovered his composure.[47]

At Cabinet on 1st August, the Chancellor still hoped that it might be possible to reduce drawings for the month to $300 million.[48] On the 5th, he seemed to take comfort from a belief that the rate of drawings had not increased.[49] In the State of the Nation Debate on the 7th, he told M.P.s that he had 'good reason for hoping that the August figures will be substantially less than the July figures'.[50] But by now he knew that collapse was imminent. On 8th August he recorded his bitter sense of defeat, and his resentment of those who, he believed, had let him down:

> ... [T]he Prime Minister in particular and certain others are so afflicted, some with indecision, some with indefinite powers of loquacity and repetition, and nearly all with so complete a lack of any sense of the value of time – so that what astonishes me most is that a substantial number of my colleagues do not simply drop in their tracks. What a good thing if some of them did! We are, indeed, all very tired ... But *I* have seen it coming, and said so, publicly and privately on innumerable occasions. I am asking Trend to collect together into one folder all my successive warnings. The trouble is that so many have not heeded until now.

On Monday, 11th August, the Foreign Secretary, the Prime Minister and the Chancellor of the Exchequer agreed to send an official Mission, led by Sir Wilfrid Eady, to Washington 'to put very bluntly to the Americans the various possibilities before us'.[51] The Mission was instructed to give the U.S. Government warning of the impending need to suspend convertibility; Dalton urged Eady to emphasise, in particular, that once the Credit was used up the British Government could spend no more dollars on Germany.[52]

On 12th August, Hugh Gaitskell noted 'the pale exhaustion' of the Chancellor, disguised by boisterous indiscretion.[53] Next day, Dalton lunched with Robert Fraser ('very sensible and understanding') and retreated to West Leaze. 'I was looking forward passionately', Dalton recalled, 'to a good break.'[54] He did not get one. On 15th August, before Eady had even left London, Bridges and Trend drove down to Wiltshire to tell the Chancellor that the suspension of convertibility could no longer be delayed.

Rapid negotiations followed in Washington. In the week ending 16th August, the dollar drain had leapt to $183 million – with only $850 million of the American Loan now remaining.[55] At first the Americans insisted that Britain should designate suspension as purely temporary. After two days, compromise was reached. Working in the *Daily Herald* office, Douglas Jay heard rumours on 19th August of an impending decision and rang the Chancellor in Downing Street. Dalton, sounding 'tired, tense and near exhaustion', indicated that he would make a statement next day.[56] On the 20th, the Chancellor formally announced the suspension of convertibility, while reaffirming that the 'full and free convertibility of sterling' was still a 'long-run objective'.[57]

The suspension of convertibility marked a turning-point for the administration, and a staging-post in the acceptance, on both sides of the Atlantic, of Britain's decline as a world power. Dalton felt it deeply. 'This seemed to me at the time, a personal humiliation and a bad set-back to the Government', he wrote later.[58] The press, especially the Tory press, agreed. 'No Chancellor in history has seen a more disastrous end to his financial policy than Mr. Dalton', one paper declared.[59]

Yet no catastrophe ensued, of the kind that had filled Dalton's sleepless nights with dread. 'I saw spectres of mass unemployment, mass starvation, mass imprecations', Dalton wrote.[60] The spectres never took material form. After the suspension of convertibility, there was a sharp change of direction in British economic policy. A hurried series of import cuts in the late summer and early autumn virtually eliminated imports of many North American commodities. Dalton's fourth Budget in November, which reduced investment and sought to contain inflation, heralded the Cripps era of limits and controls. There were shortages, and a brief period of harsh austerity. But there was no starvation. Unemployment, which had reached a pre-fuel crisis peak of 408,000 in January 1946, fell to 262,000 in September 1947 and remained below half a million until 1958.[61]

The picture would certainly have been different if Marshall Aid, first mentioned as a possibility in June, had not been forthcoming. Cuts in U.S. imports might have brought a decay of industrial activity and, in Otto Clarke's phrase, 'a downward spiral' towards the plight of Germany. Such a development might have required a national mobilisation on the scale of 1940.[62] These possibilities were real. On the other hand, American intervention of some kind was always a reasonable expectation in view of the likely impact on the American economy of a British collapse. We may wonder, therefore, whether Dalton's sense of 'personal humiliation' was not excessive.

Both Dalton and Keynes, it will be recalled, had conjured up 'spectres' when contemplating the possible breakdown of the Loan negotiations. We do not know whether, if the Loan or an alternative arrangement had not been obtained, such fears would have been realised. Yet 1947 was undoubtedly a better time for a financial crisis than the end of 1945 or early 1946. Dalton made this point, perhaps with insufficient conviction, in the Debate on the State of the Nation on 7th August. Answering critics who suggested that, in view of the 'convertibility' clause that had led the Government to its present predicament, the Loan should never have been taken, he declared:

> We should have run into this same storm in which we are, and we should have run into it more than a year sooner ... We delayed this storm by just over a year by taking the loan then ... And I submit that more than a year ago we were less strong to face the storm than we are now.

Attlee took the same view. 'The U.S. and Canadian loans were essentially measures to buy time', the Prime Minister told the House on 6th August.[63] Because of the convertibility clause the loans had presented a Hobson's choice: as Douglas Jay points out, the Government would have been blamed for economic difficulties whether it had taken the money or not. However, the blow to industrial recovery, exports, investment and full employment resulting from non-acceptance of the Loan would in the end have been far worse 'than our having to undertake – under *force majeure* – a commitment we probably could not honour'.[64]

By such an argument, convertibility was almost bound to fail. Yet, given that the U.S. Loan had been accepted and hence the storm delayed, was there a serious possibility of averting the storm altogether? Most of Dalton's accusers concentrated, not on his decision to take the Loan, but on the measures, and lack of measures, which in their view brought about an avoidable crisis. The problem here is in assessing the price worth paying to avoid the collapse of August 1947 and its aftermath.

Dalton, as we have seen, was prepared to pay any price provided this did not involve abandoning Labour's domestic programme which, in his view, was the main justification for having a Labour Government. Nobody in the Cabinet pressed harder for drastic measures to close the gap in the manpower budget and reduce overseas expenditure than Dalton. No Minister complained more loudly when the case for major cuts was ignored. Though such reductions might have been inadequate on their own, they were certainly an important part of any effective attempt to slow the rate of drawings on the Loan. The failure to impose them was, however, not for lack of advocacy on the part of the Chancellor.

If dealing with overseas spending was only a partial solution; if, indeed, for strategic reasons such reductions were unacceptable (a debatable proposition); what of the argument that Dalton's obstinacy was misplaced and that a major candidate for cuts should have been Labour's domestic programme? This case was put strongly and openly by political opponents, who objected both to excessive government spending and to Dalton's 'inflationary' budgetary policies and cheap money drive. It was put more obliquely by 'neutral' economists and financial commentators, who linked their attack on Government profligacy to a wider accusation of mismanagement. After the view that the Government's home policies were a major culprit had passed into the conventional wisdom, the argument was given a harder analytic edge by R. N. Gardner, American author of the classic study of financial diplomacy in this period.

Gardner's carefully researched account is of particular interest, partly because most subsequent writers have accepted its verdict,[65] but also because it shows how a supposedly objective, technical assessment can conceal a political, or philosophical, critique. Gardner's approach was liberal: he was a fervent believer in the 'multilateralist' world order which the post-war American administration sought to set up. Multilateralism required the 'convertibility' of currencies. Thus, from Gardner's point of view, the most serious casualty of the convertibility crisis was multilateralism; against this, the long-standing objectives of the British Labour Party were of little consequence.

Like other commentators, Gardner pointed to a variety of causes for the deterioration in the balance of visible trade which precipitated the crisis. The bad harvest of 1946; the fuel crisis; a sharp rise in American prices and a 10 per cent deterioration in the terms of trade, neither of which had been accounted for in the 1945 Washington negotiations: these unpredictable developments, he suggested, all played a part. Nevertheless, according to Gardner, convertibility might have been maintained but for the irresponsibility of socialist politicians in putting ideology and electoral advantage before public duty:

> It was clear from the outset that the terms of the Financial Agreement could only be fulfilled by a heroic effort of self-denial on the part of the British people. Their Government would have to restrain inflation, proceed cautiously with expenditure on investment and social services, and take drastic measures to increase the output of such critical commodities as coal. This was a formidable and austere programme to offer the British people after the ambitious promises that had been made them in the course of the war. And, unfortunately, it was not the programme undertaken in the early post-war years by Britain's Labour Government. The British leadership in 1946–7 sponsored an inflationary monetary and budget policy, a large volume of capital investment, and substantial expenditure on food subsidies and social services. These led to an excessive demand for imports and left inadequate resources free to produce the required recovery in British exports.

There was also a further allegation. Not only had Britain been living beyond its means; the Government had hidden this uncomfortable truth from the British people. 'The emphasis on full employment, easy money, and social services', accused Gardner, 'created an unreal atmosphere that insulated the average British citizen from the deteriorating external position.'[66] Special blame lay with the Chancellor of the Exchequer. Dalton had ignored, and had persuaded others to ignore, the relation between his own domestic policies and the worsening balance of payments. Thus, in July 1947, the Chancellor even contrasted 'the great difficulty of the overseas position' with 'the relative ease of the purely domestic financial position, in which things are very much better and easier than we would have had any reason to expect two years ago'.[67]

Gardner's indictment echoed that of other American writers. More significantly, in terms of a long-term assessment of the episode, it also reflected views held within the British academic community. Even the Treasury, which had done nothing to discourage some of Dalton's misjudgments – for example, during the final stages of the cheap money drive, or over the 'discounting' of convertibility before 15th July – harboured similar opinions. According to a report prepared for Sir Edward Bridges in October 1947, after the damage had been done, the basic problem was 'an artificially high standard of living' maintained by the misuse of the American and Canadian Loans. A policy of borrowing from abroad combined with a policy of low interest rates plus high direct marginal taxation had encouraged excessive consumption and had diminished production. At the same time, 'productive resources have been directed to certain forms of Governmental expenditure which will not come back in increased productivity'.[68] The British Government had thus been satisfying its supporters and buying popularity with the aid of money it did not possess.

Yet – and here we return to a political question, disguised by technicalities – would it necessarily have been better, as the critics suggested, to sacrifice 'certain forms of Governmental expenditure which will not come back in increased productivity', in order to fulfil the terms of a badly drafted Agreement? Some parts of that expenditure, certainly, might have been curbed. Dalton believed that it was necessary to cut military spending and the food programme. He was also persuaded, too late, that the building programme should be delayed. Arguably, however, 'self-denial' on a scale necessary to avert a crisis would have meant postponing Labour's social programme *sine die*.

Gardner argued that the British Government 'insulated' itself from the deteriorating external position. This was probably true. 'You will have heard by now that we shall, this year, balance our Budget ... ', Dalton telegrammed to John Snyder, the American Treasury Secretary, in April 1947. 'I know you will share my pleasure at this achievement, which, as I said in the House of Commons this afternoon, is a clear sign of our internal financial strength.'[69] 'He wilfully shut his eyes to the relation between internal and external finance', according to Lord Trend. 'He was very much an internal man.'[70] Yet, without an 'internal man' the Labour Government might have proceeded with such caution as to render radical reform impossible. As Sir Stafford Cripps put it in a notable speech on 7th August: 'In times of economic crisis and difficulty it is essential to have a policy, and not to wait for it ... The one thing that would be fatal would be for all parties to abandon all their policies today, and so arrive at an amorphous negative attitude which would never get us anywhere.'[71] A social revolution was undertaken between 1945 and 1947. Such a revolution required, not only courage and determination, but an element of blind faith.

Dalton was certainly guilty of an excess of optimism. The impact of convertibility was seriously underrated (by the Treasury, as much as by the Chancellor). Convertibility had not been viewed lightly, either at the time of the negotiations, or after the Agreement had been ratified; as early as November 1946, Dalton urged Snyder to ease the burden of British expenditure in Germany, partly on the grounds of the added pressure of convertibility.[72] Yet the main anxiety through the first half of 1947 was not convertibility as such, but the larger long-term balance of payments problem which at the beginning of the year was expected by the Treasury to lead to an exhaustion of the Loan in 1949.

However, as Gardner himself showed, the obligation to make sterling convertible for current transactions was not in itself a major cause of the summer crisis. What mattered was that residents of a number of Transferable Account countries, noting Britain's adverse balance in visible trade and drawings on the Loan, decided what the British Government had not: that convertibility could not be maintained. Hence capital transfers, in the guise of current transactions, took place well in advance of 15th July.[73] As the Chancellor put it to the Cabinet on 18th August, the dollar drain had been 'far greater than anything that could possibly be attributed to the normal flow of current transactions'.[74] This development was something that had not been envisaged during the Washington negotiations. It had then been assumed both that convertibility would be confined to current transactions and that the bulk of the old sterling balances would be segregated and brought under control. Neither condition was realised.

Why was it not clear that convertibility could not be maintained, and why did the British Government not make strenuous attempts to have the 15th July date postponed? According to Gardner, the explanation was a combination of British pride and inadequate statistics, which laid excessive blame for the dollar drain on the fuel crisis. The Treasury and the Bank 'could not believe that, given the choice, a vast number of Britain's customers would choose to hold dollars instead of sterling, or that they would help themselves greedily in flagrant violation of their "gentlemen's agreements".'[75] The British therefore felt that they could do without a postponement. Meanwhile the Americans gave no encouragement to any hope that postponement might be possible, indicating, on the contrary, that the Agreement must be fulfilled to the letter.

Gardner does not, however, take account of British anxiety about the likely effect of requesting postponement. In the Debate on the Nation on 6th August, Oliver Stanley, leading for the Conservatives, accused the Chancellor of being 'content to sit and wait for help from America, as one might have sat and waited in the old days for manna from Heaven'.[76] Yet, in a sense, the opposite was true: Dalton was concerned lest 'help' from America should entail unacceptable concessions. As we have seen, Keynes had noted in the spring of 1946 strong pressure in Washington 'against lending to a Socialist Government'. The pressure remained a year later. 'The Americans really thought that Britain under a socialist government had gone communist and mad', recalled Nicholas Davenport, who visited the United States as a member of Dalton's National Investment Council in March 1947. 'The bankers and businessmen were all shocked and dismayed.'[77] Dalton had reason to fear that the price of asking for American assistance would be measures to allay the shock and dismay of the U.S. financial community.

Later he wrote that the British Government decided not to seek postponement of the date of convertibility on the grounds that Congress would either have refused outright or would have taken so long discussing any British requests 'with so much publicity for all our most unfriendly critics' that it was better to carry on with the date unchanged:

> Much of the criticism, moreover, was not merely of Britain, but of the actual British Labour Government and its policies. There had been talk of 'pulling England through the wringer', by which was meant bringing heavy pressure on us to abandon our policy of nationalising selected industries, and the 'creeping Socialism', as some Americans described it, of our National Health Service and of our other social services. These suggested American interferences with our internal policies angered me and my colleagues, and made us still less inclined to risk further debate with Congress.[78]

Dalton used this argument to frighten M.P.s into accepting such cuts as the Government imposed. To start dipping into final resources was unthinkable, he told the P.L.P. on 30th July, 'because we should then be putting ourselves at the mercy of the U.S. to dictate to us what sort of Government and what sort of policy we should have'. Though he urged drastic reductions in defence spending and in the food programme, neither he nor his senior colleagues were willing to contemplate domestic cuts on the scale, or of the nature, that the British Government would have had to offer the Americans in return for a postponement. ' ... [W]e had done a wonderful job in the last two years', Dalton told Labour M.P.s, 'and there would be no going back upon this.'[79] That meant no capitulation to the kind of American pressure that had destroyed the previous Labour administration sixteen years before.

Political principles of a different kind were involved in Dalton's failure to act on sterling balances. During the Loan negotiations, there had been hopes of persuading some of the countries holding sterling balances to agree that such balances should be partially cancelled or blocked. In fact only Australia and New Zealand co-operated.[80]

Yet, despite the inability of the British Government to gain agreement with other sterling countries, no adequate corrective action was taken.

According to the Financial Agreement, accumulated sterling balances were to be divided into three categories. Some were to be written off, some funded, and some made available for spending in any currency area. The Americans had been led to believe that only a small part would be released immediately, and they had assumed that total release would be exactly balanced in the 1946–50 period by net contributions from the overseas sterling area to the central reserve. Yet the Agreement did not show how this was to be achieved, leaving it to Britain to make 'every endeavour' to solve the problem. In practice there was probably only one direct answer: a unilateral declaration by the British Government that the balances could not be considered as ordinary commercial debt. Outright cancellation, however, was strongly resisted by the Foreign Office and by several leading ministers (Bevin and Cripps in particular) on the grounds that such a drastic approach might jeopardise progress towards Indian independence; by the Board of Trade, which saw the balances as a means for expanding British exports; and by the Treasury and the Bank of England which regarded the balances as solemn obligations.[81] 'Did we really intend to be negotiating independence with India and Ceylon with one hand and holding out the begging bowl with the other?' one official put it later.[82]

The alternatives were an Anglo-American approach to creditors, using a combined economic power to compel cancellation; or an approach by the British alone. 'Among British Ministers, and in Whitehall, there was no doubt', Dalton wrote. 'We all favoured an approach on our own.'[83] But the major sterling creditors were not anxious to negotiate, and the attempt to scale down balances on the basis of gentlemen's agreements failed. In August 1947, the Chancellor revealed that balances – less than half of which were blocked – had reached an all-time high. More than £1,800m was still within the control of creditors. As the crisis deepened, so drawings on these free balances increased.[84]

Was the situation avoidable? Keynes had envisaged a tough policy – combining blocking and writing off the sterling balances in order to make the I.M.F.-G.A.T.T. structure 'a really workable system'.[85] Robbins shared Keynes's view, and pressed it on Dalton. Later, Robbins argued that 'the complete failure to deal adequately with the problem of the sterling balances concerning which so many promises had been given at Washington' was a major disaster which Keynes might have prevented had he lived.[86] Robbins believed that the

British Government ought to have offered the prospect of an accelerated rate of release of blocked balances in return for the consent of creditor countries to write off the rest. 'Our name would have been mud for six weeks, and then the matter would have been forgotten.'[87]

Dalton, however, was advised differently at the time. In the view of the Bank of England the benefits of blocking were by no means certain. Thus C. F. Cobbold, Deputy Governor of the Bank, held that 'even the most extreme measures to block sterling balances would only at best have prevented a part of [the] dollar expenditure, and that at the cost of a major dispute with the countries concerned'.[88]

'The fuel crisis and the convertibility crisis were both cases where a specific problem had been mismanaged', concludes J. C. R. Dow; 'neither need have been.'[89] The convertibility crisis left the Government's economic policy, for the moment, in ruins. Advice had been given to the Chancellor which turned out to be wrong. Yet for the Chancellor to have come through successfully would have involved sacrifices, in one direction or another, which he was either unwilling or unable to make.

What of Dalton's efforts to cut the food programme and military expenditure? On 8th August, he noted:

Not only the 'Keep Left Group' ... but also a wide section of the Party feel that we should run down our Armed Forces much faster. And they are certainly right. And I said so to the P.M. as long ago as last February and wrote it in a letter, almost threatening to resign then. And I have said it again these last days, but have been met with mulish resistance from [Bevin] and [Alexander] who have been half backed up by the P.M. himself. The simple point is, not so much the money as the number of people kept in uniform and out of production. I made the best play I could yesterday with all the cards in my hand and moved a number of chaps a bit, but the effort of getting these totals down is monumental ... [W]hy the hell all this struggle to get something done which sticks out a mile? The truth is we are all in this, as in other things, exhausting each other and wasting each other's time by stupid failures to give ground early which clearly must be given later.[90]

Dalton cannot be blamed for paying some attention to his advisers in the Treasury and the Bank.[91] He can, however, be blamed for being insufficiently persuasive in Cabinet. It is the job of a politician not only to know what needs doing but to carry it through. The Chancellor may have been right to accept the Loan ('buying time' for recovery and socialism), right to reject the blocking of balances, right to avoid cuts in the domestic programme. But his failure to force colleagues to 'give ground early which clearly must be given later' especially over military expenditure, reveals him as, by the end, a politically weak rather than a wrongheaded Chancellor. To understand the reasons for this weakness, we need to examine relationships in, and around, the Cabinet.

XXVIII

Insolence of Office

Before the war, Dalton had been an ally of Bevin on foreign affairs and defence and of Morrison on domestic policy. He had also been the hammer of the Labour Left. By 1947 a significant change had occurred. Dalton now clashed often with Bevin and Morrison, and was viewed with a new respect by leading left-wingers. Most remarkable of all, he worked closely with the two rising politicians he had helped expel from the Party in 1939: Aneurin Bevan and Sir Stafford Cripps.

Dalton saw little of Bevan, never a member of the Coalition, during the war. When the war was over, Bevan's work as Minister of Health, with responsibility for housing and national insurance, brought the two men into frequent contact and encouraged each to appreciate the other's qualities. Bevan knew that Treasury policies were designed to make possible the capital programmes necessary for post-war social welfare and reconstruction. Dalton, for his part, was impressed by Bevan's vitality and drive. Regarding Bevan's measures – including schemes for free medical care, national assistance, the repair of war damage, and help to local authorities to finance housing for low income families – as the essence of practical socialism, he gave help in crucial battles.[1] 'After Bevan', concludes Bevan's biographer, 'Dalton was the chief architect of the National Health Service.' The Minister of Health was often to be seen at No. 11 Downing St, and there developed 'an excellent understanding' between the two ministers.[2] 'A.B. and I are on very good terms just now', Dalton wrote in May 1946, 'and I find him much brighter than most of them.'[3]

The Chancellor's relations with Cripps also entered a new phase. As we have seen, Dalton's wartime dealings with Cripps – over coal in particular – had been co-operative. After the war, as economics ministers, they were brought closely together and they discovered, somewhat to Dalton's surprise, that politically they now had much in common.

As a minister and roving ambassador during the wartime Coalition, Cripps had gained an enviable reputation as a figure above party: as a man who, like Lord Keynes, moved on an international stage. In the Labour Government he was able to combine two apparently contradictory images, based on his recent and more distant past. He was seen by some as an austere radical, the Robespierre of Labour's revolution; by others, including many of Labour's opponents, as the only home front minister with the will and ability to resist the allegedly 'doctrinaire' policies of the Government. Though both images were distortions, both contained elements of truth. Cripps was certainly a 'radical': more, perhaps, than any other member of the administration he was prepared to discard old ideas and take on new ones. As minister responsible for boosting exports he became an inspired manager, dazzling Whitehall and Parliament with his grasp of complex technical problems. On the other hand (and this became a reason for growing Establishment support and left-wing suspicion), experience of government before and after the Labour victory turned him into a compromiser. For the time being, he remained one of the most socialist members of the administration. Earlier apocalyptic visions, however, had faded.

At the same time, he retained his pre-war style. Where Dalton exulted at the discomfiture of opponents, the President of the Board of Trade combined ruthlessness with an appearance of private suffering. There was a Roman fortitude about Cripps which Dalton seemed to lack. 'Nobody at that time could compare with him', recalled a friend, 'in his ability to force the House of Commons and the nation to listen to dry unpalatable economic facts and to be moved by his presentation of them ... '[4] The contrast between the two ministers fostered a legend that Dalton and Cripps were at loggerheads over economic and financial policy. In fact, Cripps shared all Dalton's main objectives, backing the Chancellor fully in Cabinet, especially during the crisis year of 1947. Dalton, in turn, supported Cripps's calls for greater austerity. 'He really is an intelligent man', the Chancellor would say of the President of the Board of Trade; 'he understands.'[5]

In addition to agreement on the main purposes of the Government, three areas of policy in particular brought Bevan, Cripps and Dalton together between 1945 and 1947: nationalisation of iron and steel, the British Mandate in Palestine, and the need for reductions in overseas, and especially military, spending.

Dalton had long been committed to the public ownership of the iron and steel industry. In *Practical Socialism*, published in 1935, he had endorsed the T.U.C.'s 1934 scheme for a public corporation.[6] Thereafter he continued to argue that the industry was inefficient because of a chronic tendency to monopolistic restriction, and the concentration of power in too few hands.[7] His advocacy was effective against strong opposition on the N.E.C.: he succeeded in putting into the 1945 election manifesto a clear promise that the industry would be nationalised.

Herbert Morrison, the minister in charge of post-war nationalisation, did not share Dalton's commitment. Outvoted on the Party Executive before the election, Morrison did his best as Lord President to bury the scheme, ensuring that his Future Legislation Committee gave it a low priority. But it was not forgotten. Feeling within the Government and the Party in favour of public ownership remained strong, and in the spring of 1946 a proposal for full nationalisation, put forward by John Wilmot (Minister of Supply) was placed before Cabinet. Here a combination of Bevan, Bevin, Cripps and Dalton squashed objections. For the Chancellor, nationalisation of the industry had become a matter of symbolism as well as of economic management:

I made a row [in Cabinet] and asked whether we were a Socialist Government or not and when we expected to have a better opportunity than this, and how we could defend going back on our pledge at the Election ... Practical Socialism, I said, only really began with Coal and Iron and Steel, and there was a strong political argument for breaking the power of a most dangerous body of capitalists.

Early in 1947, temporarily standing in as Chairman of the Lord President's Committee while Morrison was off sick, Dalton seized the opportunity to push the nationalisation measure along. 'Cripps and I have taken the lead in pressing for Iron and Steel', the Chancellor wrote in April. 'So we are assured of a jolly good Socialist scrap in the autumn.'[8] The Lord President's recovery, and the socialist scrap, came sooner than expected.[9] When Morrison resumed his duties in May he pressed for a compromise, involving a plan which meant public supervision without full nationalisation. Cabinet considered the revised proposal on 7th August. Once again, Dalton led the attack, pressing the case for full public ownership. He accepted that it would be hard to nationalise at once, but argued that it might well be possible to take over the industry in 1948–9. Cabinet agreed, and Morrison's proposal was shelved.[10]

One result was to sour relations, already difficult, between the Lord President's Office on the first floor at No. 11 Downing Street and the

Chancellor's Office on the ground floor. Another was to strengthen the Bevan-Cripps-Dalton axis.

If contention over iron and steel helped to alienate Morrison, the Palestine controversy added to Dalton's problems with Bevin. The Foreign Secretary had taken no interest in Palestine before 1945 and felt little sympathy for the Jews. Dalton on the other hand had drafted Labour's 1944 statement on the Post-War Settlement, which had become a kind of unofficial Balfour Declaration ('Let the Arabs be encouraged to move out', he had written on behalf of the Labour Party, 'as the Jews move in'). After the formation of the Labour Government, the Chancellor continued to feel a sense of personal responsibility towards the worst victims of Nazi atrocities.

At first Dalton made no protest as traditional Foreign Office attitudes prevailed over Labour election commitments. He accepted without protest Bevin's recommendation in September 1945 that President Truman's request for the issue of 10,000 certificates for Jewish immigration into Palestine should be refused. However as the problem of terrorism grew and the Jewish Question came no nearer to solution, he put his full weight behind proposals for Partition. 'There must be a Jewish State – it is no good boggling at this', he wrote in January 1947, ' – and even if it is quite small, at least they will be able to let lots of Jews into it – which is what they madly and murderously want.'[11] Others, especially on the Left, shared the Chancellor's views. Dalton's most passionate supporter in the Government was Aneurin Bevan, who privately threatened to resign unless Partition was proclaimed.

Palestine later caused a major backbench revolt. In 1947 it remained the subject of simmering discontent, reinforcing other cleavages in the Cabinet. Meanwhile, the most important division was over military expenditure. Here, more than on anything else, Bevan, Cripps and Dalton spoke in unison.

We have seen in the last chapter how, throughout 1947, Dalton's main target for retrenchment had been overseas expenditure, and especially expenditure on the armed forces, which were still maintained at almost wartime levels partly for occupation and policing duties (as in Germany and Palestine), and partly to meet the threat posed by the Soviet Union. In attacking the extent of Britain's commitment abroad the Chancellor was following the advice of Lord Keynes who had pointed out that the American Loan was primarily required to meet British military and political spending overseas.[12] Dalton's efforts to persuade colleagues were, however, stubbornly resisted.

The Chancellor's most vocal opponent was the Minister of Defence. Dalton considered 'Albert Victorious', as he called A. V. Alexander, 'pompous, unconvincing and incompetent'.[13] But Alexander on his own would not have been a problem. The real obstacle was Ernest Bevin. The battle between the Foreign Secretary and the Chancellor over military spending became the most important conflict within the Government – reflecting on the one hand, rival departmental interests; on the other, rival priorities.

Bevin had acquired, both from his official advisers and from his own trade union experience, a deep suspicion of the Soviet Union and a fierce hostility to Soviet Communism. He regarded the danger of Soviet aggression in Europe as serious and immediate. He believed that in order to keep American friendship, and maintain an American presence in Europe, the honouring of Britain's overseas commitments was essential. From the summer of 1947, he also believed that a high level of British involvement overseas was the necessary price for American financial aid through the Marshall Plan. What he called 'the abnormal conditions of the present time'[14] caused him, therefore, to support Alexander's insistent rejection of substantial cuts in military spending, despite the colossal strain on the economy which such spending entailed.

Dalton, on the other hand, considered the extent of Britain's overseas commitments wasteful and unsustainable in the long run. He regarded it as vital not only that expenditure should be cut, but that manpower should be redirected from the unproductive armed services into industry in order to save on imports.[15] He considered it absurd that the British economy, and the British socialist experiment, should be crippled in the name of the uncertain benefits of American friendship. He remained much more hostile towards Germany – whose eventual resurgence he continued to fear – than towards Russia. 'So far as could be foreseen', he told Cabinet on 28th January 1947, when there might still have been time to avert a financial collapse, 'there was no danger of a major war in the immediate future; but we were actually confronted at the moment with a very grave economic situation ...'[16]

Dalton's arguments had some effect, and limited reductions in the armed forces were made. However, in the first eight months of 1947 the Chancellor remained the undoubted loser. As late as August, his demands – though accompanied by the direst warnings – were still being deflected by Bevin and Alexander, who had the tacit support of the Prime Minister.

The more the Chancellor met resistance, the more he fell back on people whom, before the war, he had denounced. Not only Bevan, fighting to protect reconstruction and welfare programmes, and Cripps, pursuing export targets, gave support. So did leading left-wingers outside the Government. The Labour Left had other concerns apart from the balance of payments. It wanted to de-militarise more than it cared about saving dollars, and it was also glad of an excuse to attack Bevin's pro-American foreign policy. Nevertheless, left-wing suspicions that the Government was planning a sell-out were helpful to Dalton. According to Michael Foot, the new Keep Left group 'backed to the hilt the demand for a much swifter demobilisation on lines which almost paraphrased Dalton's remonstrance to Attlee'.[17] When, as early as November 1946, the *Daily Worker* suggested mischievously that Dalton and Bevan were encouraging the parliamentary rebels behind the scenes, the Chancellor noted: 'I am not guilty of this, though I am not at all unsympathetic to part of their case, but I have had to conceal this fact.'[18]

At the same time the Chancellor faced a dilemma. The more urgent became the need for retrenchment abroad, the harder it became to resist the case for rejecting measures which might cause offence in the United States and for imposing, instead, measures which would convince the Americans of British 'responsibility'. Left-wing protests were useful in reminding M.P.s, and some ministers, that there was an issue of principle as well as of expediency. ' ... [I]s appeasement of America, in the hope that a further loan of dollars may serve to ease austerity, still the dominant feature of Cabinet policy?' asked the *New Statesman* early in August.[19] In public the Chancellor continued to slap down the Government's critics. But in private, he put precisely the same question to colleagues.

Thus by August 1947 Dalton's position within the Labour spectrum had shifted perceptibly. He had become, in effect, the leader of opposition within the Cabinet to a fundamental part of Bevin's foreign policy. On the most urgent problems facing the Government he was at odds, not only with the Foreign Secretary, but also with Alexander, Morrison and, crucially, with the Prime Minister himself. 'Dalton was the most left-wing member of the Big Five', considers Lord Trend.[20] The gradual perception of this truth gained him some unexpected supporters; but at the cost of a dangerous division between himself and those with whom, in the past, he had most often collaborated.

Political events moved fast during 1947, and so did the fortunes of individuals. If Dalton had been on the upward escalator in 1946 he was so no more. By the summer of 1947 he was on the way down, facing his former enemy, present ally, Sir Stafford Cripps coming up. On both sides of the House, in Whitehall and in the press, the President of the Board of Trade was regarded as the most dynamic figure in the Government: not only brilliant, but scrupulous, courageous and unique in his readiness to place nation before party. He was seen, in short, as he had always seen himself: as a saviour.

One reason for Cripps's high reputation was that, where other ministers seemed tired, Cripps radiated energy and a sense of purpose. The most immediate factor, however, was the Government's pioneering *Economic Survey for 1947*, issued in March. This document included a long section on economic planning, written personally by the President of the Board of Trade, who had absorbed many of the ideas and attitudes of the Economic Section economists. In the *Survey*, Cripps called attention to the need for economic 'budgets', to compare the future resources of the economy with future claims upon it.[21] Cripps's authorship was officially secret. But his attitude to the need for co-ordinated planning, and his inspiration of, and keen backing for, the *Survey* were common knowledge.

Cripps's close interest in the Government's planning, and in the possibility of controlling it himself, was not new. Immediately after the election he had pressed in Cabinet for a 'National Plan', and even tried to seize control of the Economic Section of the Cabinet Office, which had been given, instead, to Herbert Morrison.[22] As pressure grew to reduce imports and increase exports, his desire to persuade leading colleagues of the need to create an effective planning machine intensified. In 1947 there was a clamour for the 'overall plan', what *The Economist* called 'real economic planning' with 'purposive direction' in place of 'the present hortatory, sloganised drifting'.[23] In the words of one contemporary opponent, 'the most robust believers in planning began to criticise the existing form of planning and to call for the introduction of their own particular ideas of planning.'[24] On one point, however, robust believers were increasingly agreed: the need for a new Ministry of Economic Affairs to make planning effective. Cripps took up the cry. Dalton, in favour of anything that might halt the slide towards the precipice, gave encouragement.

Thus it happened that Dalton became embroiled in a series of manoeuvres aimed at strengthening the Government's grip on the economy, and, at the same time, at altering the balance of power within the Cabinet. Cripps was a tactician, rather than a strategist. He cannot have anticipated the final outcome. Nevertheless it is hard not to admire the sheer audacity, the naive brilliance, of the President of the Board of Trade as Dalton advanced, step by ill-judged step, into a trap. To see how this came about we need to return, once again, to the early months of the year when a number of leading ministers were showing signs of strain after seven years in Government.

During the terrible winter the Chancellor had himself displayed annoying symptoms, similar to those that had troubled him towards the end of the war. Dalton's ailments, however, were trivial compared with those of the Lord President and Foreign Secretary, both of whom developed serious illnesses in the early part of 1947.

In mid-January, Morrison was suddenly afflicted by a thrombosis which moved from his leg to his lung, threatening his life. After a partial recovery, he suffered a relapse and in February his condition was judged to be critical. Miraculously, the crisis passed and he left hospital on 25th March. But he remained severely weakened, unable to return to active politics until the end of April.[25]

Simultaneously it became clear that all was not well with the Foreign Secretary. In July 1946 Bevin had collapsed in his room, needing oxygen. Shortly afterwards Ruth, while sitting next to him at the opera, noticed that his hand shook; and Gladwyn Jebb reported that in Paris he had seen the Foreign Secretary switch abruptly from whisky to soft drinks. 'I have for a long time thought that he would suddenly go flop', noted the Chancellor. A few months later, Bevin's physical problems became more severe. Exhausted and suffering from heart trouble, the Foreign Secretary took three weeks' complete rest on doctor's orders before embarking on a strenuous trip to Russia. He also announced that he might have to have an operation.

On 5th February, Dalton noted 'a strange uncertainty about the personal future of many Ministers'. Next day – the day of Shinwell's fuel announcement – Ellen Wilkinson died, creating a vacancy at Education. ' ... [W]ith all these casualties and near casualties among my colleagues', wrote the Chancellor, 'my personal position is becoming what is called "very strong".' What would be the impact on the allocation of top level responsibilities? Dalton calculated that Morrison would not resume his normal duties until after Easter, and might not fully recover at all. He also thought that Bevin might drop dead in Moscow. 'It is quite on the cards, I fear, that he may not come back', he observed. 'But it is terribly difficult to know what to do, since he won't think of giving up yet ... '[26] Meanwhile the country was lashed by a month-long blizzard, and the balance of payments rapidly worsened.

One effect of 'casualties and near-casualties' was to increase the Chancellor's already heavy administrative burden. In addition to the Lord President's Committee, Dalton also had to fill in for Morrison as Chairman of the Socialisation of Industry Committee and the Economic Planning Committee. At the end of February, Ruth wrote to a friend that 'the Chancellor is extremely over-worked as the result of Herbert Morrison's illness on top of the fuel crisis'.[27] Another

effect was to make Dalton think beyond the next few weeks and
months of intense pressure, and consider his own political future.
Here we come back to the interesting question of the Foreign Secretaryship.

Dalton had never lost his desire to go to the Foreign Office. He
did not expect, or by now particularly want, to become Prime Minister. But his ambition to crown his career by becoming Foreign Secretary never waned. Hence his concern about Bevin's health was more
than solicitous. Contemplating the Foreign Secretary's infirmities the
previous August, Dalton had written: 'it is not escaping my thought –
nor perhaps of some others – that, if he were to collapse, I might have
to go to the F.O.'[28] At that time Dalton was too absorbed in his
work at the Treasury to wish for an immediate move. Later, however,
the prospect of an honourable escape gained in appeal. In February,
he was being tipped in the press as a 'strong man', capable of taking
the Foreign Secretary's place.[29] Meanwhile he reflected on the inadequacies of Bevin and on the rumour of his own impending succession to Bevin's job.

The Chancellor's well-known desire one day to become Foreign
Secretary provided a key element in the calculation of another minister who was looking ahead: Sir Stafford Cripps. Shortly after the
Budget, his arm bandaged because of the operation to his septic
finger, Dalton planned a week in Wiltshire to help recover from his
own exhaustion. It was at this point that Cripps presented a new
political bromide. On the day of Dalton's intended departure, Cripps
burst into his room at No. 11 Downing Street and 'outlined a proposition.

By this time, the idea of a new planning department had been
widely canvassed in Whitehall and among members of the Government. Such a department, it was suggested, would include a large part
of the present functions of the Lord President's Office. The obvious
candidate to head it was Herbert Morrison. Morrison, indeed, con-
fidently expected the job. Cripps had other ideas. The Lord President,
Cripps told Dalton, was not up to the key task of sorting out domestic
planning, which required somebody really strong. The Chancellor
eagerly agreed. Cripps suggested Bevin.

It was a master stroke. If Bevin returned to the Home Front as
Planner, a vacancy would be created at the Foreign Office which
Morrison was scarcely fit enough to fill. In that case, who was there?
Cripps and Dalton discussed the matter. The two Cabinet ministers
did a coy dance around the subject of who should take what job.
The Chancellor noted:

I had hinted to S.C. that, in any shift, he might either take the Treasury or the F.O. He made no response to the latter point and on the former said that it was not his line of country. I said that he could soon pick it all up. He said that no doubt he would.

Did this mean that Cripps would not compete for the Foreign Office, but would not mind succeeding Dalton at the Treasury? Dalton clearly thought it did. Elated, he rushed along the corridor to the Prime Minister's office. 'For my part', he told Attlee, 'I did not now seek a change, but I thought that I knew more about Foreign Affairs than any of my colleagues.' In reply, the Prime Minister was cautious. Dalton, he said, was 'so completely on top of everything at the Treasury' that it would be serious if he moved. Moreover there remained the problem of having Morrison and Bevin, who hated each other, together on the Home Front.

Neither Cripps nor Dalton abandoned the view that planning was a responsibility that should be given to a strong minister. Both agreed that 'unless we can get our planning done right, we shall be sunk'. In Wiltshire, the Chancellor reflected on his conversation with the President of the Board of Trade and concluded that Cripps 'will certainly be very active on this matter during my absence'. Meanwhile, Dalton's revived interest in the Foreign Office fuelled his criticisms of Morrison. Morrison, Dalton now decided, had been a failure at Supply in the early part of the war; he had allowed a small group of cronies to dominate him at the Lord President's Office; and he had quarrelled unnecessarily with the Treasury.

In mid-May, Dalton noted that the Lord President still did not look fit, and that 'Cripps is very much concerned about him, both as to health and as to capacity to tackle – or really to understand – this new Planning job'.[30] But hopes that Bevin might take over planning, allowing Dalton to escape to foreign affairs, soon faded. When in July a new National Planning Board was set up under Edwin Plowden, it remained under the aegis of the Lord President's Office. No new planning ministry was announced.

Cripps and Dalton were disappointed. So too was Sir Edward Bridges, who wanted planning shifted to the Cabinet Office so that it could be drawn into the Treasury net. 'The Treasury was always uneasy about other departments trespassing its territory', recalls Lord Trend.[31] During the summer, a Whitehall battle secretly raged over the control of the Board. According to Morrison's biographers, 'Demotion, fragmentation, isolation and ultimately elimination were the stages by which the Lord President's independent economic powers were whittled away and the Treasury was re-established in its primacy'.[32] For the time being, however, finance and planning retained their separate compartments. One result was to exacerbate still further the already strained relations between the convalescing Lord President and the over-stretched Chancellor.

Meanwhile the Foreign Secretary had staged a remarkable recovery. He did not drop dead in Moscow. Nor did his health seem to require a home-based job, as Dalton had envisaged. Instead Bevin returned from Russia looking extremely fit. 'He is fascinated with, and not unhopeful about, the next phase in foreign policy ... ', Dalton noted ruefully. 'Moreover he and Mrs. B. like their new official quarters and wouldn't want to move.'[33] There the matter rested, until the thunderclouds burst in mid-summer.

So far, Dalton's plotting had been of a very mild kind. Hinting to Attlee about his own preferences could hardly be described as conspiracy. Now, as the financial crisis deepened and options narrowed, the Chancellor turned with growing desperation and a weakening grasp on reality to the game of serious intrigue. With his policies apparently in ruins, his reputation battered by press abuse, and with each day bringing even worse news, his inclination was to blame other people. If only stupid or obstructive ministers could be shifted! If only there could be firmer leadership at the top! If only an opening could be created at the Foreign Office, so that he could move without disgrace! As in the past – at Peckham, and at M.E.W. – his anxiety expressed itself in outbursts of anger and in personal attacks which turned imagined enemies into real ones, increased the distrust of colleagues and made him even lonelier than before. His emotional turmoil, his sense of the world against him, also made him susceptible to the wiles of others more securely placed.

In March, Dalton had persuaded Attlee to promote his P.P.S., Evan Durbin, to a junior ministerial post. 'I did my best to push you', the Chancellor wrote to his young friend, 'and I thought it was about time too and said so, and it came off this last shot.'[34] Dalton replaced Durbin with another protégé, George Brown, a trade unionist who could keep him informed about union sentiment in the House. Becoming parliamentary aide to the Chancellor of the Exchequer, whom he much admired, was Brown's first big break. Brown was able, energetic and fiercely ambitious. He soon discovered, however, that the genial public face of the Chancellor concealed a private anguish. 'It was already evident, by the time I got to him, that things were getting out of his control', he recalls. 'Nobody knew outside his close circle. But the physical and mental signs were clear.' Dalton would return from Party or Cabinet meetings angrily denouncing 'the incompetent little Prime Minister' and the 'rambling monologues of your friend Ernie Bevin'. The Chancellor would also listen, too eagerly, for any political gossip that his P.P.S. had been able to pick up.[35] It was in this way that Dalton became involved in what may be called, for convenience, 'the July Plot'.

In July, during the brief, uneasy period when dollars and sterling were convertible, George Brown joined forces with Morrison's P.P.S., Patrick Gordon Walker, in an ill-conceived attempt to get rid of Attlee as Prime Minister. The two newly elected M.P.s had everything to lose from the failure of such a bid, and they did not undertake it lightly. Today, Attlee is widely considered a great Prime Minister. Few people, least of all in the Parliamentary Labour Party, regarded him as such in 1947. Then, the criticisms which had been made ever since he first became Opposition Leader in 1935 were constantly voiced. He was said to be colourless, dilatory, inactive and unable to cope with the growing problems facing the nation.

In organising their revolt, Brown and Gordon Walker were responding to a rumbling discontent both on the backbenches and in Cabinet at Attlee's lack of leadership, and to a general sense that the Government had become rudderless. The young insurgents imagined that, if a resolution demanding a change were circulated, so many M.P.s would put their names to it that Attlee would have no choice but to resign. Bevin was the preferred successor. No Cabinet minister was directly involved in the initiating stages. Brown, however, felt obliged to consult the Chancellor, his new boss, before proceeding.

On 25th July, Brown told Dalton about the plan and sought his opinion. The Chancellor's most sensible reply would have been a firm prohibition. Instead, Dalton offered qualified approval, suggesting that if backbench M.P.s were dissatisfied they should bring their discontent out into the open. 'That is all right', he told his P.P.S., 'but let them come and talk freely and kick up a row, if they feel like it, at the Party meeting next Wednesday.' At a time when his own problems were at their very worst, the Chancellor's attitude seems to have been that any bomb that might stir the Big Five into action was worth exploding.

The following weekend Dalton spoke at the Durham Miners' Gala and shared a car with Bevin on the way back. In the course of a long talk *à deux* (the journey took several hours) the Foreign Secretary complained bitterly about Morrison, Cripps and, especially, Attlee who, he said, was very weak and indecisive. None of this was unusual, for Bevin was apt to speak ill of colleagues. It gave Dalton an opening, however, which, unwisely, he took. George Brown, he said, 'has been telling me that a large number of Members want E.B. to become P.M.' Bevin replied that he had been told the same thing by his own P.P.S., Percy Wells, but he did not want to do anyone out of a job. Dalton urged him not to put the possibility of becoming Prime Minister out of his mind. Bevin showed no signs of changing his views; but Dalton formed the impression that the Foreign Secretary had not excluded the idea altogether.

Meanwhile the Chancellor considered once again whether he should threaten to resign. One odd aspect was that, while pressing Bevin to allow himself to be made Prime Minister, Dalton was fighting a losing battle with the Foreign Secretary over military spending. 'E.B. is set against cuts ... ' the Chancellor recorded on Monday, 28th July. 'It would be a great bore if I were threatening to resign on some point on which I don't see eye to eye with him, while, at the same time, I were, even remotely, connected with some move to make him P.M.!' But the same evening Brown reported to Dalton that the movement to make Bevin Prime Minister had petered out. Dalton was not particularly surprised. 'It is one of the ever recurrent Parliamentary miracles', he noted, 'how great waves of opinion disperse themselves in broken spray!'

Perhaps, as Brown put it to Dalton, there had simply ceased to be 'any pressure left in the pipe'. What is clear is that, soon after his conversation with Dalton, the Foreign Secretary decided that he would not challenge Attlee. According to Brown at the time, Bevin had a reputation for being 'very unfaithful to his friends'.[36] On this occasion, however, the Foreign Secretary decided to parade his loyalty. 'Go and tell them Percy', Bevin instructed his P.P.S., 'that I have been in this movement 60 years. I have never betrayed a colleague yet, and I have no intention of starting with Clem; he is a great little chap.'[37] Then the Foreign Secretary summoned George Brown, a member of his union, for a dressing down. Brown later gave the following account of the interview:

> He saw me in his room next door to the Prime Minister and wanted to know what it was all about. I told him. He looked at me, said that he had never really trusted me, and added, 'And now you are acting as office boy for that bastard Dalton! I don't want to see you again.' ...
> ... As I went out of his room he came down the corridor after me and put his great hand on my shoulder. I thought that he was trying to make things up a little, but he gave me another ticking off about organising revolts and disloyalties, asked me to tell Dr. Dalton just what he could do with himself and assured me that he, Bevin, would see to it that Dalton was properly dealt with for organising such a

revolt. Nothing I could say would persuade him that it wasn't poor Dalton who was doing it at all.[38]

Lord George-Brown recalls that this took place *after* the Dalton-Bevin car journey.[39] In other words, the Foreign Secretary had decided to interpret the Chancellor's remarks as evidence of a Dalton-inspired plot. During the conversation in the car, however, Bevin had given no indication of righteous indignation. We may wonder, therefore, whether the Foreign Secretary's anger at 'that bastard Dalton' had anything to do with a particularly fierce row between the two ministers over cuts at a meeting of the Big Five on 30th July.

It was some time before the Chancellor realised that he had been set up, that Bevin had decided to use the car journey conversation (which Dalton naturally assumed was confidential) to discredit him. Only in October did he discover from John Wilmot the full extent of the Foreign Secretary's betrayal:

> Soon after my return from Durham with E.B. at the end of July, E.B. said to J.W., with every appearance of indignation, that it was 'a fine thing' that I had been suggesting to him that he should take C.R.A.'s place as P.M. And Arthur Moyle, C.R.A.'s P.P.S., had got the story a day or two later! 'It looks', said J.W., 'as though E.B. had double-crossed you!'

So much for the July plot, essentially a grass roots affair which Dalton had passively encouraged, and which fizzled out – having, no doubt, increased the Prime Minister's private suspicions of the Chancellor and feeling of dependence on the Foreign Secretary. The collapse of the Brown-Gordon Walker conspiracy did not, however, put an end to moves aimed at ousting Attlee. On the contrary. In September there was another, far more serious, attempt. This time the move came directly from the very top, with three members of the Big Five – Cripps, Dalton and Morrison – all agreeing on the need for a new Prime Minister, but divided on how this should be achieved.

By the end of July the Chancellor of the Exchequer was close to breaking point. 'I am amazed how we all keep going somehow', he recorded on 31st July. At night, bitterness at colleagues and anxiety about the future robbed him of sleep. During the day he continued to demand major cuts, and talked angrily about resignation when his demands were brushed aside. Meanwhile his public performances were dangerously sustained by drugs. Dalton's diary for 1st August

contains a rather frightening entry, raising the question of how far
artificial stimulants may have been affecting his health, and his judgment:

> Though my speech lasted over two hours and it had a mass of
> statistics and difficult argument in it I never felt for one moment in
> the least tired. This is due to some truly remarkable pills (Benze-
> drine which the German soldiers took before going into battle)
> which I have been taking for the last two days. Urwick has been
> giving me various things to drink and swallow, the net effect of
> which on my morale and efficiency has been tremendous! But one
> can't go on living for ever like this on pills and potions.[40]

Even with the help of Benzedrine, the pressures were hard to bear.
Convertibility was suspended on 20th August. Heavy with defeat,
Dalton escaped for ten days' holiday on the 25th. 'He has been desperately tired', Ruth wrote to Will Davis in Bishop Auckland.[41] He
celebrated his sixtieth birthday with the Davenports at Hinton
Manor. 'Dead to the world', he wrote in the visitors' book. 'As dead
as sterling into dollars!' After a few drinks, tears ran down his cheeks,
and Davenport feared a nervous collapse.[42]

The Chancellor's spirits were revived by the arrival of a visitor. At
Dalton's request, Davenport had asked Anthony Crosland, recently
elected a Fellow of Trinity College, Oxford, to join the party. Dalton
had first met Crosland the previous summer and wanted to become
better acquainted. The young don appeared in a bright red sports car,
wearing the scarlet beret of the Parachute Regiment. 'Master Tony
Crosland who happens to be in Oxford is brought across one evening
to dinner', the Chancellor noted. 'He is an attractive and promising
young man and in a year or two should be sufficiently experienced to
begin to be useful as a Socialist Economist.'[43] It was a successful
evening: Crosland was at his most mischievous and magnetic. 'As he
drove away', Davenport recalled, 'I could see in Hugh's eyes the re-
kindling of his romantic love for gallant and handsome young men.'[44]
Dalton returned to London on 4th September, feeling better.

Next day Sir Stafford Cripps came to see him with 'some very striking ideas, including a pilgrimage by three of us, on behalf of a fourth
to a fifth'.[45] These ideas provided the framework for the September
plot.[46]

Earlier in the year, Cripps's private discussions with Dalton had
turned on Cripps's proposals that Bevin should be brought home and
put into the planning job, thereby creating a vacancy at the Foreign
Office; if Dalton succeeded Bevin as Foreign Secretary, Cripps might

then succeed Dalton as Chancellor. Now the President of the Board
of Trade had a bigger, bolder scheme. In the spring, Morrison had
been his main target. This time the main (or at any rate, the preliminary) target was Attlee. Cripps proposed that he and Dalton should
persuade the Lord President to join the two of them in a united delegation to Attlee in order to force the beleaguered Prime Minister to
retire in favour of Bevin. If the plot failed, Cripps would resign on the
grounds, as he explained to Dalton, 'that C.R.A. was no use as P.M.
in this crisis'.

It was a novel approach – palace revolution, banana republic style –
and it startled Dalton. But there was a cold Crippsian logic to it. Cripps
was less worried about the premiership than about planning. In the
short term, he was anxious about his own Export Plan, due to come
before Cabinet, where he expected strong objections. In the longer
term, Cripps was concerned about the need to co-ordinate planning of
the economy as a whole. Though he envisaged enlisting the Lord
President to help bring about a change at No. 10, he was far more
critical of Morrison, the minister notionally in charge of planning,
than of Attlee. Morrison, Cripps declared, was 'quite out of his depth
and doesn't understand what planning means, nor how it should be
handled'. A major purpose of the scheme was thus to take planning
away from Morrison. Cripps's ingenious proposition was that
Morrison should be persuaded to help depose Attlee in order to instal
a premier who would immediately rob Morrison of the most important
part of his empire.

There was also another feature. In Cripps's earlier proposal, Bevin
had been ear-marked as chief planner. This was also part of the new
scheme. Bevin, Cripps suggested, should become Minister of Production as well as Prime Minister. But there was now an added twist.
Cripps proposed that he himself should become Bevin's Chief of
Staff as Lord President, taking Morrison's economic job, while
Morrison was pensioned off with impressive but empty titles – Deputy
Prime Minister, Leader of the House, and Lord Privy Seal. Shifting
Attlee was thus to be more than a means of getting a stronger man to
run the Government, or even of pushing Morrison out of planning. It
was a device to enable Cripps to control the planning powers whose
true importance, in his opinion, only he understood.

The Chancellor listened attentively. When Cripps spoke of Attlee's
lack of leadership and Morrison's ineffectiveness, Dalton did not
demur. He also listened closely while the President of the Board of
Trade spoke of other possible changes in the Government. If the main
objective of making Bevin Prime Minister was achieved, Cripps explained, Shinwell could be banished and Gaitskell promoted. But

above all, and from Dalton's point of view this remained the crux, there would be a vacancy at the Foreign Office.

What would be the fate of Attlee, as ex-premier? Cripps had considered this problem. He appreciated that the Prime Minister could not simply be dumped. The best solution, he concluded, would be to make Attlee Chancellor of the Exchequer. This left one candidate, and one candidate only, for the Foreign Secretaryship. With a flourish, Cripps produced his ace. 'No one else could do it', he declared triumphantly, apart from Dalton, who 'could, if need be, shout at Molotov and bang the table. C.R.A. couldn't.'

Dalton found all this interesting, entertaining, and more than a little tempting. But he was not entirely convinced. While the changes which Cripps described were much to his taste, he doubted the viability of the whole scheme. In the first place, a new Prime Minister – especially one as strong-willed as Bevin – would make his own appointments, and would not necessarily do what suited Cripps or Dalton. In the second place, Dalton thought it unlikely that Morrison would back a scheme out of which he stood to gain nothing, and which involved promoting Morrison's enemy Bevin to a position of authority over him. Nevertheless the Chancellor was not opposed in principle and agreed to give the plan his passive support. If Morrison agreed, he would join such a pilgrimage as Cripps proposed.

Dalton was right. Morrison did not agree. Like Dalton and Cripps, the Lord President was eager to depose Attlee. But he was not eager about Cripps's choice of a successor. Indeed he was deeply hurt. Morrison regarded himself as best fitted for this role. If there was to be a leadership contest, he declared, it must be an open one. There must be no *fait accompli* in favour of Bevin, whom he distrusted.

Faced with Morrison's refusal, Cripps shifted tactics. He abandoned the 'pilgrimage' and decided to see Attlee alone. Instead of three against one, it would be one against one. Cripps would demand Attlee's resignation. If Attlee said no, he would resign instead, declaring publicly his opinion that Bevin should be Prime Minister. Such a step, Cripps told Dalton on 8th September, would create a furore in the press, forcing a leadership election in which Bevin might stand and win.

These were brave words, and Dalton was impressed. 'S.C. at least has courage and clarity', he wrote. But Cripps had no sooner articulated his latest plan than he had begun to adjust it to changing circumstances. On 9th September Cabinet accepted the Board of Trade Export Plan, thereby removing Cripps's most pressing problem.[47] A threat of immediate resignation now seemed less appropriate and, from his own point of view, less necessary. All the same he still intended to confront the Prime Minister, proposing, as Dalton put it, 'to try to persuade the little man'.

The crucial meeting between Sir Stafford Cripps and 'the little man' took place the same evening. What it proved, once again, was the shrewdness of the prosaic, unprepossessing Prime Minister, surrounded by prima donnas. When Cripps declared that he thought Bevin should be premier and Minister of Production, that Dalton should go to the Foreign Office, and that Attlee should go to the Treasury, the Prime Minister took no offence and was 'most reasonable'.* Calmly, Attlee replied that he could not himself do the Treasury because he had no head for financial questions, that Bevin did not want to leave the Foreign Office, that the Party would not have Bevin as Leader and (an old point) that Bevin and Morrison would never get on in close proximity in the same Cabinet. The Prime Minister then trumped. Cripps had been pressing for a strong planning machine, presenting himself as the man to look after it, under Bevin's suzerainty. Now Attlee, with no appearance of defeat or concession, gave Cripps most of what he wanted. He offered him the job of Minister of Production. Alongside this, Attlee suggested, there should be a small committee of senior ministers (the Big Five plus Addison) to take much of the detail out of Cabinet.

When Cripps saw Dalton after the interview, he was sheepish. Instead of emerging with either Attlee's resignation or his own, the original alternatives, he had left the Prime Minister's office with a promotion. It was slightly embarrassing. In effect, he admitted, he was pinching most of Morrison's job. Morrison would suspect a deep-laid plot from the start.

Dalton was magnanimous. He had not expected much to come out of Cripps's challenge: certainly not the capitulation which Cripps had professedly been seeking. He regarded the actual outcome as being for the best. He shared Cripps's contempt for Morrison, and he admired the energy and single-mindedness of the President of the Board of Trade in a Cabinet where such qualities were in short supply.[48]

The potential obstacle was Herbert Morrison, required to accept a demotion in order to make way for Cripps. In the event, however, the Lord President (who kept his title) raised no serious difficulty about

* Did the Prime Minister, in Cripps's presence, also ring Bevin, who declared unequivocally that he had no intention of leaving the Foreign Office? Attlee told this tale later, and it has often been re-told as evidence of Attlee's matter-of-fact style and of Bevin's unquestioning loyalty. (See, for example, K. Harris, *Attlee*, p. 349). Yet it is surprising that Cripps failed to mention any such telephone call when he described his interview to Dalton immediately afterwards (HDD 9th September 1947).

losing his planning responsibilities. Having recently been ill, Morrison may even have felt relief at ridding himself of an insoluble administrative problem,[49] and at shedding the wearisome burden of 'brooding in ignorance' as a shadowy co-ordinator without full financial information or control.[50] Hence the central aim of Cripps's baroque conspiracy was achieved: cleanly and without bloodshed.

Thus presented, the September plot consisted only of a flurry of private conversations among the Big Five, a family affair in which nobody else was involved. In fact it was not so straightforward. In the first place, Cripps's solitary 'mission' to Attlee on 9th September cannot have taken the Prime Minister by surprise. The lobbies had been buzzing with rumours of some such move ever since the collapse of the Brown-Gordon Walker campaign in July.

Dalton had himself been talking freely, perhaps too freely, about the possibility of a 'pilgrimage' long before Cripps presented his striking ideas. Gaitskell's diary entry for 12th August records that Dalton had attended a dinner of close friends in a private room at the House the previous evening. Those present included Gaitskell, Jay, Durbin, Hall, Davenport and Bill Piercy. Dalton was at his most voluble, his indiscretions aided by Queensland Rum. 'Once a communist, always a crook!' he shouted in denunciation of John Strachey, so loudly that windows on to the terrace had to be shut to prevent his words being overheard. Conversation then turned to the abortive July plot. Gaitskell recorded:

> I asked HD how a change of this kind could *technically* be brought about. It seemed really out of the question for the Parliamentary Party to resolve to dismiss its leader in the middle of a Parliament. HD agreed. Then he said that if the other four of the 'Big 5' – Cripps, Bevin, Dalton and Morrison – all agreed that such a change was needed and all told CRA the latter would probably give way. There was, however, no prospect of this, since HM would never agree and EB was not at all keen to leave the F.O.[51]

These remarks were made more than a week before the suspension of convertibility, and three weeks before Cripps suggested that he, Dalton and Morrison should see Attlee. Evidently, therefore, the ideas which crystallised into the September plot had been fully considered long before the attempt to put them into operation. Neither was Dalton the only minister to have discussed coup possibilities with friends. Foot recalls that Cripps made soundings among the most 'loyal' members of the Party, and sought to enlist Aneurin

Bevan's support for a bid to get rid of Attlee to 'make way for Bevin or himself'.[52]*

What was happening among the leaders during the critical period, 17th to 25th August, when Dalton had broken his holiday in order to deal with the suspension of convertibility? We know more about Cabinet discussions than about top level plotting. Clearly, however, the Prime Minister was under strong pressure. On the very day that Dalton returned from the country – 17th August – there was a dress rehearsal for the September plot: a pilgrimage, not to Attlee, but to Bevin. In the afternoon Dalton and Cripps saw Bevin at the Foreign Office, and Cripps made a tentative approach to the Foreign Secretary to 'take over' from Attlee. Once again, Bevin refused.[53] 'It's all this intriguing I won't do', he told his Parliamentary Under-Secretary when the others had left. 'Dalton, Cripps, all of them. What happened to Lloyd George and Asquith? The public gets to know you're an intriguer.'[54]

The public, indeed, soon learnt that intriguing was in the air, though without discovering who was behind it. On 20th August the *Daily Mail* carried a banner headline declaring, without a question mark: 'ATTLEE RESIGNING SOON BEVIN TO BE PM'. The paper went on to tip Dalton for the Foreign Office, Cripps for the Exchequer and Bevan for Supply.

Eight months later the Royal Commission on the Press questioned the *Mail*'s editor, Frank Owen, about this scoop. Owen replied: 'The only matter about which we were completely sure (and in the event it shows we were wrong) was that Mr. Attlee was going to depart and Mr. Bevin was going to take over'. Pressed further, Owen maintained that the *Daily Mail* Lobby Correspondent, Wilson Broadbent, had come to him *at least a week* before he decided to print the story:

> *Chairman*: Did [Broadbent] give any indication of the evidence upon which he was basing it? – [*Owen*]: Yes, sir, he told me of personal conversations he had had with some of the Ministers whose names you have there, and further evidence of friends of theirs who had confirmed it. You will realise that we would not have published that kind of matter unless we were pretty sure it was going to happen ... I was completely assured, after a week's careful thought, that Broadbent was telling me the truth. It did not happen, and it did not happen because, when it was printed, the parties

* Foot maintains that Bevan refused, expressing dislike of palace revolutions. Others remembered differently. Eight years later, Alice Bacon embarrassed Bevan at a P.L.P. meeting by reminding him that he had walked her down a corridor 'saying that C.R.A. was hopelessly weak and that they must have Bevin as P.M.!' (HDD 16th March 1955).

agreed not to carry out what they had intended.[55]

Who, one wonders, had expounded the details of the conspiracy in such definite terms? Not Morrison (in Jersey at the time, and hostile to a Bevin premiership). Cripps had spoken to friends, and either he or they might have talked directly to the press. If Owen received the information a week in advance, this meant that Broadbent had it by 11th or 12th August, several days before the meeting between Cripps, Dalton and Bevin. Dalton, as we have seen, talked about the feasibility of getting rid of Attlee in company with strong Fleet Street connections on 11th August. The Chancellor himself may therefore have been one source.

The important point, however, is that somebody leaked. Broadbent was wrong in his prediction. But his account of what was intended was substantially correct. If you are planning a putsch, surprise is a help. By September 1947, there was virtually none. Attlee's coolness during his interview with Cripps on the 9th was therefore scarcely remarkable. The Prime Minister must have been expecting something of the kind for weeks, and may already have consulted Bevin to gain assurance of his support.

Thus it seems likely that Attlee's response, and in particular his decision to offer Cripps the planning job, had been well prepared. Yet the Prime Minister was badly shaken by the challenge, which reminded him of where his own interests lay. Throughout the summer, he had suffered fierce criticism from all sides. Only one powerful figure stood by him. 'Defence expenditure was a reflection of foreign policy', writes Michael Foot; 'foreign policy was in the hands of Ernest Bevin and in any dispute Attlee would infallibly side with Bevin and the Defence Ministers against all comers.'[56] We may wonder whether the Prime Minister's attitude towards Britain's overseas commitments owed something, at least, to his absolute political dependence on the Foreign Secretary.

There was another aspect. Cripps led the attack in September. But he had not been involved in the July plot. Dalton had been an accessory or a conspirator both in July and in September. The Chancellor's implication was known to the Prime Minister. The workings of Attlee's mind remain a mystery. But it would be strange if, by mid-September 1947, Attlee had not marked Dalton out as a serious threat to his position.

Cripps's new job was ratified at the end of September. The Minister of Economic Affairs was given control both of the home economic front and of overseas economic and trade policy, with an authority over five production ministries – Labour, Supply, the Board of Trade, Fuel and Power, and Works. Meanwhile the Economic Information Unit, the Economic Section of the Cabinet Secretariat and the new Central Economic Planning Staff were brought under his direct control. The creation of the planning department was part of a reconstruction of the Government which took some time to complete. Dalton threw his full weight behind Cripps's appointment as head of the new Ministry and against the main alternative, Morrison. He also urged, repeatedly, that Shinwell should be sacked.

His battles for retrenchment continued. So did his private battle against fatigue. Having pressed that a date for the withdrawal of the British administration and British troops from Palestine should be announced,[57] he retired for a few extra days' recuperation at West Leaze. Newspapers were told that the Chancellor was taking 'a brief rest on doctor's orders before the winter'.[58] When he returned at the beginning of October, he was only half-recovered.

The success of the September plot in solving the immediate planning problem did not diminish Dalton's desire to leave the Treasury. On the contrary: now that escape hatches were firmly shut, his longing for a change increased, and the thought of quitting seldom left him. After a wearisome Cabinet on 2nd October, during which cuts in the armed forces were discussed yet again,[59] the Chancellor wrote that he always seemed to get just enough to make it very difficult to threaten to resign. 'When alone now, I always want to resign', he added. 'But the company of my officials, and even of my colleagues, saps my will!'[60]

The new Government arrangements were finalised over the next few days and announced on 8th October. To the Chancellor's intense relief, Shinwell was shifted out of the Cabinet and replaced as Minister of Fuel and Power by Gaitskell. Harold Wilson, still only 31 years of age, had come into the Cabinet on 29th September to fill Cripps's place at the Board of Trade. Philip Noel-Baker was now also added to the Cabinet, taking over at the Commonwealth Office ('I never forget how much I owe you', he wrote to Dalton).[61] Robens, Callaghan, Younger and Freeman – four young Daltonites – entered the Government from the backbenches. So did George Brown, bought off with a junior post at Agriculture. 'May you be three times blessed!' he wrote to Dalton, who had pressed for this promotion.[62] Douglas Jay, who had won a seat at a by-election the previous year, took Brown's place as the Chancellor's P.P.S. John Wilmot, meanwhile, was sacrificed at the request of both Morrison and Cripps, as scapegoat for the confusion over steel nationalisation. Despite this loss, Dalton was pleased by the reshuffle. 'It is a much better govt', he wrote, '& a good

TOUGH LAMB

deal younger in the tail, as it should be. It's a bet which of these younger men do well, and which don't.'[63] As it happened, three of the promoted 'younger men' became Leaders of the Labour Party; two also serving as Prime Minister.

Cripps's appointment, attributed in the press to his 'astonishing rise in prestige', was particularly acclaimed. Even the left-wing *New Statesman* deprecated 'silly jokes about Sir (Austerity) Cripps, etc', recalling that Sir Stafford had first earned this soubriquet after his famous 'moral' broadcast in 1941. There was also a general recognition that Dalton as well as Morrison had been downgraded. According to the *Statesman*:

> In the new Cabinet, Sir Stafford Cripps and Mr. Bevin are charged with supreme responsibility, the one for economic policy, the other for foreign affairs and defence. Like Moses on the mountain, the P.M. stands with his hands held aloft by two faithful lieutenants. As long as these two agree, his leadership will remain secure.

The *Statesman*, however, struck one note of caution. Having observed that the essential issue was one of 'guns *versus* margarine' it expressed concern lest the Government should become one 'not only of economists but of *The Economist*'.[64]

'After many vicissitudes the Chancellor and Cripps are staunch allies and on the best of terms', Gaitskell wrote on 14th October.[65] Dalton bore no resentment towards his erstwhile opponent. It was, however, a fragile alliance. With Cripps at the Board of Trade, the interests of the two ministers had been virtually identical. With Cripps at the Ministry of Economic Affairs, this ceased to be the case. The Treasury regarded Cripps's dynamic new planning empire as a dangerous competitor. The demarcation disputes that had existed between the offices of the Chancellor and the Lord President soon began to re-surface. If the planning ministry had remained separate from the Treasury for long, a fierce rivalry between the two would doubtless have developed.

More important, however, than the prospect of interdepartmental clashes, was a curious reversing of political roles. Before the war, Dalton had been the 'responsible' Labour leader, and Cripps the *enfant terrible*. Now it was the other way round. Cripps, the man who had split the Labour Party from top to bottom in 1937 because it would not move fast enough in a socialist direction, had become a crusader for efficiency. 'Dalton was wary of Cripps', Lord Trend recalls. 'Cripps seemed to want to plan the economy without any concern about the domestic policy for which Dalton cared.'[66] Cripps's sober belief in the necessity for sacrifice commended itself to the Opposition and contrasted with the Chancellor's alleged extravagance and doctrinaire socialism. On the day of the Government reconstruction, Harold Nicolson recorded a conversation with a leading Tory, Leo Amery. 'He thinks there will be a conflict between Cripps and Dalton', Nicolson noted. 'The former will wish to tell the public the harsh truth; the latter will wish to soap them over with half-lies. It is extraordinary how much respect Cripps arouses. He is really the leading figure in the country today!'[67]

There was, in fact, no conflict. Both ministers agreed on the need for austerity measures, and they worked well together. But there was an important difference. While Cripps remained buoyant, Dalton was burdened by depression and guilt. Cripps felt no compunction about reducing domestic spending and demanding a tightening of belts. Untarnished by the crisis, he approached his task clinically. Dalton, on the other hand, regarded the deflationary measures he was forced to introduce as a personal defeat.

Weary and disillusioned, the Chancellor no longer believed in his own defiant rhetoric. 'I am still a bit below my optimum', he wrote at

West Leaze on 12th October. 'But I hope it will come back! ... I am haunted by the thought of a people starving, unemployed, and in revolt! And of the end of our Socialist experiment, and of all our Dreams!'[68] Danger signs were becoming apparent to colleagues. 'I wish to God we could get Hugh Dalton away for a bit', Jennie Lee recalled her husband, Aneurin Bevan, saying. 'You mark my words. Something pretty awful is going to happen.'[69]

'Shall we have an Autumn Budget?' the Chancellor wrote to the Prime Minister's press secretary, Francis Williams, on 26th September. 'For advice, please!'[70] Within a few days he had decided in favour because, as he explained to Cabinet on 9th October, 'inflationary pressures would inevitably be increased by the steps which were now being taken to reduce imports and increase exports, and he was satisfied that measures to relieve this pressure must be taken ... '[71] The next few weeks were spent in the company of officials, preparing details. Aid under the Marshall Plan was now likely, but not yet certain. Until it became certain, action was needed which, in the words of an official minute to the Prime Minister, 'will not only cause some hardship at home but will also inevitably be damaging to other countries ... '[72]

Such action was made the more urgent by a continued drain of gold and dollars. Reserves of foreign assets, including the undrawn amounts of the North American Credits, had stood at £1,614 million at the end of 1946. By the end of August 1947 they had fallen to £870 million.[73] On 20th October, the Chancellor warned Cabinet that by the end of 1947, even after drawings from the I.M.F., they would have dropped still further to £500 million plus £65 million of unused Canadian Credit.[74]

At last, Cabinet colleagues began to accept the necessity for drastic action. The Chancellor was encouraged by a meeting of the Big Five on 19th October, and by the Cabinet meeting next day. 'I feel a good deal happier after yesterday and this morning than for some time', Dalton noted. 'As usual, I had been thinking that, if I could not get a good deal of my own way, I should have to resign but, as usual, this possibility has faded out again for the moment.'[75]

On 23rd October, Cripps announced a package of measures aimed at halving the dollar gap by the end of 1948. 'We intend to rely mainly on our own resources', he told M.P.s. The price of self-reliance would be a severe cut in the standard of living. By now, even the Left was reconciled to increasing doses of austerity, and there seemed no better person to impose them than the unflinching, ascetic Minister of Economic Affairs. 'The Cripps speech brought home, much more clearly than anything that had been said before, the extreme gravity of Great Britain's international position', commented the *New Statesman*. 'It also conveyed the impression that the problem is at last being courageously and realistically handled.'[76]

On 24th October, Dalton explained his own policies to the House. He defended his decision not to seek American help before it became necessary to suspend convertibility; and he attacked the Tories for wanting more unemployment. He also poured scorn on 'old wives' tales which had recently circulated 'above the signatures of academic persons'. 'Such as Professor Robbins?' interjected a Member. 'Including my old pupil, Professor Robbins, a very talented economist but not fully informed ... ' he replied. At the same time, the Chancellor refused to lay blame for the crisis on his Treasury and Bank advisers.[77] 'This is something which we shall not forget, and for which we shall always be deeply grateful', Bridges wrote to him next day.[78] After the speech, his last before the Budget, Dalton retired to autumn sun and mist in Wiltshire. 'It was a crashing bore to make', he wrote. 'But now it's behind me!'[79]

The Government's popularity, damaged by the crisis, remained in mid-term recession. Since August, Gallup had shown (for the first time since 1942) an actual Tory lead. In the municipal elections at the beginning of November, Labour lost 640 seats compared with 200 gains the year before. There was a small grain of comfort: the two most speculative gilt-edged stocks – $2\frac{1}{2}$ per cent Consols and 'Dalton' $2\frac{1}{2}$ per cent stock – staged a mild recovery.[80]

All eyes turned to the Chancellor. 'I am now putting the final touches to my Supplementary Budget', he wrote to his agent, Will Davis, on 6th November.[81] There were pressures from every side. 'All four corners of the business compass', wrote one left-winger just afterwards, ' – the F.B.I., *The Times, The Economist* and the financial columns of the daily press – were blowing gales at the Chancellor intended to buffet him in the direction of a panic deflation.'[82] 'Few Chancellors have framed a Budget amid so much insistent advice from their enemies', commented the *New Statesman*, which offered its own warning: a huge dose of deflation would complete the disillusionment of the Labour Movement, and cause an electoral defeat.[83] Experts awaited Dalton's speech with particular interest because it seemed likely that, for the first time, the Budget would be used as a regulator of the economic machine.[84] Everybody – friend and enemy – agreed that the November 1947 Budget would be an historic landmark.

On 12th November, Dalton spent the morning polishing and refining the speeches he was to make in the House and on the wireless later the same day. Although the Budget was to be short, its preparation had been unusually arduous. It was therefore with a special feeling of relief that Burke Trend handed the Chancellor over to Douglas Jay, Dalton's P.P.S., just before luncheon.[85] Dalton and Jay ate alone at No. 11, discussing the proposals which, Jay discovered, were to be of 'calvinistic austerity' in their deflationary intent. When they had finished their meal, the two men drove the short distance from Downing Street to Parliament Square, where a queue for the public gallery had begun to form in the pouring rain. They continued their discussion in the Chancellor's room.

Dalton was due to speak at 3.30 p.m. The Commons was still meeting in the Lords Chamber, and so it was necessary to walk the whole length of the Library to the Inner Lobby – the Members' Lobby of the House of Lords. With a few minutes to spare, the Chancellor and his P.P.S. strolled along the Lords corridor. As they approached the Inner Lobby, Dalton turned to Jay and asked him to go in to the Chamber and arrange for a glass of water to be placed by the dispatch box. When Jay returned he found the Chancellor 'speaking in the Lobby to someone I did not know'.[86] He took Dalton by the arm and hurried him into the Chamber. The Chancellor began his speech a few minutes later.

Dalton's fourth Budget Speech was less dramatic than its predecessors. 'My reason today is that we must strengthen still further, and without delay, our budgetary defences against inflation', he began. The Budget, he explained, was intended to cut purchasing power, and hence to reduce demand in the home market relative to the reduction in supply that would result from steps to cut imports and increase exports. He spoke deliberately, almost testily. There was none of his usual jauntiness or bounce, no sarcastic taunting of the Opposition, scarcely any jokes. After speaking for almost half an hour, he glanced at the clock and said with what later appeared as a cruel unconscious irony: 'Now I will turn to the revenue, and to the increase in taxation which I propose. It is past four o'clock and the Stock Exchange will soon be shut.' A Tory M.P. called out: 'It closes at three o'clock.' Dalton continued: 'Then it is already closed, and it is safe for me to proceed with this part of what I have to say.'[87] The reason for the Chancellor's remark was that tax details were revealed unusually early because of the shortness of the Budget.[88]

At one minute past four, Dalton proceeded to list a number of indirect taxes.[89] There were no real surprises, and hence there were few interruptions. When he announced an increase in tax on whisky, two Scottish voices were raised in protest: the Communist, Willie Gallagher, shouted, 'Is that all?' and the ex-I.L.P. Member, David Kirkwood, cried, 'Not half enough'.[90] The Chancellor gave no final peroration. Just before 4.30 he folded his papers and sat down abruptly, after 57 minutes on his feet.[91]

If Dalton hoped to appease his critics, he was disappointed. The Budget was undoubtedly deflationary. But in the eyes of the Opposition and the press, it was not nearly deflationary enough. *The Economist* accused the Chancellor of shirking a public duty.[92] The *Financial Times* considered that the Budget conveyed a strong impression that the Treasury was not really worried about inflation at all,[93] and even the middle-of-the-road *Manchester Guardian* condemned it as indirect and inadequate.[94] All this was predictable and, as it happened, quite wrong.

So far from having overestimated the effects of the Budget, Dalton and the Treasury actually underrated them. Dalton estimated that his tax increases would bring in £208 million in a full year and £48 million in what remained of the current financial year, with a consequent effect on expenditure and inflationary pressure. In fact, the revenue effect was much greater, and so was the impact on inflation. The accusation that the additional taxation imposed would be inadequate to remove the excess of demand was misplaced. When Dalton's successor at the Treasury, Sir Stafford Cripps, introduced his first Budget the following April, he announced that the prospective surplus, entirely based on Dalton's taxation, was £319 million. The new Chancellor's own tax changes merely raised this by £11 million. Virtually the whole of Cripps's surplus was handed over to him by Dalton and was due to Dalton's taxation.[95]

It was an odd twist that Dalton's last Budget was the only one to draw the sort of criticism which was later assumed to be justified in respect of his whole tenure of office. Dalton's fourth Budget has since been regarded as a pioneering one, the decisive turning-point in the Government's economic and financial policies, and a model for the 'austerity' Budgets of Sir Stafford Cripps which (contrary to legend) were actually milder than Dalton's last Budget in their effects. 'It was [Dalton] who first directed budgetary policy towards disinflation', Dow has pointed out; 'while Sir Stafford Cripps was to show inflexible determination in not relaxing taxation, it was Dr. Dalton who accepted the heavy political onus of *increasing* it.'[96]

This may be put another way. Inflation appeared to be under tolerable control up to the end of 1946, and only became serious in 1947; by the beginning of 1948 it was again being brought under control. If Dalton had stayed on as Chancellor he would have received much of the credit which instead went to his successor for the remarkable improvement in economic affairs that followed his departure. The attacks upon him in 1947 would have been forgotten (just as the

WEDNESDAY, NOVEMBER 12, 1947   **BIG GAME HUNT**   (Copyright in All Countries)

Cartoon on Budget morning. The Chancellor's sack is labelled: 'curtail spending Budget'.

attacks on Attlee and Morrison were later forgotten). The legend that one Chancellor who squandered the nation's resources was replaced by another who guarded them thriftily, would never have been born.

After delivering his speech Dalton stayed in the House for Question Time. One Tory applauded him for resisting pressure from 'the great majority of economists in this country'. Dalton interjected, contemptuously, 'Financial scribes'.[97] He then returned to Downing Street, made the customary Budget Day broadcast, and went to bed. His conversation in the Lobby just before giving his speech had passed entirely from his mind, and he had, he later recalled, 'no faintest foreboding of tomorrow's earthquake'.[98] Yet Dalton's Chancellorship was to be ended, not by what he had said in the Chamber, but by what he had said outside it.

XXIX

A Single Sentence

The man talking to the Chancellor minutes before the Budget Speech was John Carvel, a Lobby Correspondent of eleven years standing who worked for the London evening *Star*. Though Jay had not recognised him, Carvel was well known to leading ministers. A large, amiable Scot, Carvel had been on close drinking, lunching and gossiping terms with Dalton since early in the war, and was regarded by the Chancellor as one of his two or three best friends in the Lobby.[1] It was not surprising, therefore, that the two men should stop to speak to one another outside the Chamber.

Nor was the Lobby a surprising place to find a journalist at such a time. Carvel knew the procedure well. The main pre-Budget stories had been written. Nothing more of substance was expected until the Chancellor announced his proposals for tax changes to the House. However, in the immediate run-up to the Speech any variation in the ritual became news. Over lunch, Carvel had told the financial journalist Paul Einzig that his office was anxious to publish a last-minute Budget story in the Stop Press section of the late edition.[2] It was in the vague hope of picking up what his editor called 'the latest tales and hints in the Lobby' that Carvel spent the interval before the Speech waiting by the entrance to the Chamber. Later Carvel maintained that he had no definite ideas about a story, 'although I was on the alert for news, and it was in my mind at least to provide my office with some Diary paragraphs about the general Budget Day atmosphere, as I had done on many former occasions'.[3]

John Carvel was accompanied by his son Robert,* a young reporter on the *Daily Express*; and by Willie Alison of the *Evening Standard*. Alison, a close friend, had a similar purpose. Like the Carvels, he was hoping for tit-bits of gossip to add colour to the dry arithmetic of

* Now Political Editor of the London *Standard*.

changes in taxation. He was particularly interested, on this occasion, in the Chancellor's Budget Day eccentricities. In addition to the vigorous arm movements and the famous box-tapping fore-finger, a traditional Daltonian feature was a silver coffee pot, from which the Chancellor would pour himself fortifying draughts of rum and milk. This was the kind of detail diary editors liked.

As Dalton and Jay approached the end of the Law Lords corridor, Alison turned to Carvel and said: 'All I want to know, John, is whether Dalton is drinking rum and milk like last time'. At that moment, the Chancellor entered the Lobby through the swing door. The three journalists were standing a few yards away, at the corner of the Lobby opposite the Law Lords corridor (next to the corridor to the Central Lobby). 'I'll find out for you, Bill', replied Carvel and walked the few strides that separated him from Dalton. 'That was my father's main motivation', Robert recalls. 'To help Willie Alison.'[4]

As Carvel approached, the Chancellor turned towards him. Then, linking arms, Dalton steered his friend back into the Law Lords corridor, where the two men stood in a corner. Carvel's opening remark – according to his son – was a conversational gambit, not seriously intended as an inquiry at all: 'Well what is the worst you have for us today?' (Dalton remembered slightly different words: 'How about the Budget?') Before Carvel could follow up on rum and milk, the Chancellor replied: 'You will soon hear all about it, and it will be quite a short speech this time – not more than an hour.' Apparently taking this answer as a cue, Carvel immediately asked about particular taxes, starting with tobacco.

Instead of brushing the questions aside, or replying evasively, Dalton cut Carvel short and told him in detail,

> in a single sentence, what the principal points would be – no more on tobacco; a penny on beer; something on dogs and pools but not on horses; increase in Purchase Tax, but only on articles now taxable; Profits Tax doubled.[5]

No embargo was placed on the use of this information, nor was the subject of its possible use raised. Yet the 'single sentence' was a clear breach of the hallowed principle that the contents of the Chancellor's red box should remain secret until the Chancellor revealed his proposals in his Speech to the House.

When Jay came back from his errand and hustled Dalton into the Chamber, Carvel returned to his companions. During the brief conversation the beverage question must have been asked, because

Carvel said to Alison 'It's rum and milk!', and Alison immediately set off to telephone his paper.[6] Late editions of the *Evening Standard* contained the information that the Chancellor stuck to his usual rum-and-milk, but had replaced the familiar coffee pot with a tankard.[7]

When Alison had gone, Carvel turned to his son and said that they were going to telephone through a new forecast of the Budget. 'My father was certainly excited by what he'd got', Robert Carvel recalls. 'He felt it was a scoop, though it was obviously going to be touch and go whether it would get into the paper. He was the only journalist in possession of details of the Budget, and he was now acting purely on a journalist's instinct to get the stuff into the office.'[8] A good turn to a friend had by chance landed a rich professional reward, if only he could reach the telephone in time. 'At that second I had only one thought', John Carvel told the subsequent inquiry, 'and that was to get the tip across into my paper, which would not be carrying the Speech.' Asked whether he thought he had a scoop, he evaded the question. 'Never for a moment did I imagine that I had more or less the bulk of Dalton's main proposals', he replied. 'I never thought of it.'[9]

Together the Carvels walked through the Lobby and along the corridor, before taking the lift to the emergency press gallery on the committee floor, where there were direct telephone lines to Fleet Street. 'My father was 52, and bulky', Robert recalls. 'But he was a hiker, like Dalton, and we moved nippily!'[10] The journey took about three minutes.[11] As they arrived, they saw Alison telephoning his own message to the *Evening Standard*.

The two Carvels entered another booth, and John rang through to the *Star*, dictating a message to a short-hand telephonist in the news receiving room. When he finished speaking, the telephonist noted: 'end message 3.17'.[12] Allowing for time taken in making the call, and in reaching the booth, the end of the Carvel-Dalton conversation may be estimated at not later than 3.12 p.m.[13] As we will see, the question of timing was to be important.

Carvel's crucial message to the *Star* was as follows:

I believe that when Mr. Dalton introduces his Budget today the following will be among the proposals. Penny a pint increase in the beer duty; no change in tobacco; Profits Tax to be doubled; Purchase Tax to be substantially increased but not to be applied to any new commodities.

Carvel then spoke (as was his normal practice) to the editor of the *Star*, A. L. Cranfield, referring to his 'latest forecast'. Cranfield asked if the information was reliable, and Carvel replied that it was. In accordance with Lobby convention, Carvel did not reveal the source, and Cranfield did not seek it.

According to Cranfield, Carvel was 'always very mysterious' about sources and it caused no surprise on this occasion that he said nothing about the origin of his story. Did a note of excitement in his voice convey the urgency? If Carvel felt that he had a scoop, he must have wished to make this clear to his editor. There was, however, nothing in Cranfield's treatment of the message which distinguished it from others of its kind.

Carvel's last minute call was, indeed, far from unique. Budget forecasting was a game, like tipping winners, played competitively among financial and political journalists. A variety of forecasts had been made over preceding weeks. Everybody knew that taxes were to be imposed. The only question was where they would fall. As Cranfield pointed out afterwards, most of the items in Dalton's fourth Budget had already been guessed correctly by one paper or another. The penny increase on beer had been suggested in the *Sunday Chronicle* and the *Sunday Dispatch*, the doubling of Profits Tax in the *Sunday Chronicle*, the increase in purchase tax in the *Evening Standard* and the tax on pools in the *Daily Mail*. The *Star* itself had been particularly keen on pre-Budget tips, and Carvel had prided himself on his ability to supply them. 'Carvel had been giving us forecasts almost I will not say every day', declared his editor, 'but in September he started forecasting the Budget.'[14] The telephone call at approximately 3.17 p.m. on 12th November was treated, therefore, as the last of a series based on 'the latest tales and hints in the Lobby'.

As Carvel put down the receiver, he saw Alison leaving an adjacent booth. Robert recalls: 'My father said, with the exultation only a journalist can feel, "There goes Willie! Rum and milk!"'[15] The Carvels then followed Alison down to the Press Gallery. As they took their seats, John suddenly realised that his message to the *Star* was incomplete. He had failed to report Dalton's comments about gambling taxes. He slipped out of the Gallery, this time on his own, and made another call to his paper.[16] On the way he met Paul Einzig, his companion at lunch. Einzig later recalled seeing his friend 'in a great hurry, hastening towards the telephone boxes, whispering to me with a triumphant and excited air as he was passing by: "I have got my Budget story!"'[17]

Carvel's second call was received by the editor's secretary, who took no note of the time; but Cranfield later estimated the lapse between the two calls as ten minutes – indicating that the second call began at 3.27. Carvel's dictated message read: 'There will be a tax on dogs and football pools but not on horse racing'. There then followed a second routine conversation between Carvel and Cranfield.[18] Dalton started speaking in the Chamber at 3.32.[19]

As Carvel knew well, the key edition of the *Star* was the Second Late Night, due to go to press at 3.20 p.m. If his first message had reached the office a few minutes earlier, the 'forecast' might have been blazoned as a headline on the front page. As it was, Carvel missed the main part of the paper but caught the Stop Press or 'fudge' section of the same edition because actual printing did not start until 3.40.

A message, subbed by the editor himself, beginning 'Star Correspondent writes: "It was expected Chancellor's proposals would include ... " ', was prepared on the basis of Carvel's first call. The detail in Carvel's second call was tacked on immediately afterwards. At proof stage, the phrasing of the last sentence ('There will also be a tax on dogs and football pools') was toned down to read: 'Also likely to be a tax on dogs and football pools', apparently on grounds of literary consistency. The correction was sent through to the *Star*'s printing offices at Commercial Wharf and Bouverie Street, but arrived too late for the first batch of printed copies. Hence some copies of the edition said 'will' and others 'likely'.

The full message, as it appeared in print, was as follows:

'PENNY ON BEER'

TAX ON POOLS AND DOGS LIKELY

'Star' Political Correspondent writes: It was expected Chancellor's proposals would include:

1 d. a pint increase in the beer duty.

No change in tobacco.

Profits tax to be doubled.

Also likely to be [*in a few thousand copies*, There will also be] a tax on dogs and football pools, but not on horse racing.

Purchase tax to be substantially increased but not to be applied to any new commodities.

The very first copies (without the correction) began printing at 3.40 at Bouverie Street, and at 3.46 at Commercial Wharf. After pulling up the machines for the race results (as usual) an item containing the opening remarks of the actual speech was added at the Wharf at 3.57, and at Bouverie Street at 4.08. At 4.21 (Bouverie Street) and 4.22 (Wharf) the first of the Chancellor's tax proposals as stated in the House were added, without removing the original Carvel story.

The margins therefore were tight. To recap: Dalton finished speaking to Carvel at 3.12, or just before. Carvel finished his first call at 3.17, and made his second at about 3.27. Printing of the story began at 3.40. At 4.21 and 4.22 – 41 or 42 minutes later – 'authorised' taxation news was placed on the machines. But *barely 21 minutes* separated the beginning of printing of the unauthorised disclosures and the start of Dalton's public announcement of his tax proposals in the Commons at one minute past four.

Approximately 272,000 copies (including a small amount of local 'printing-in' on an earlier edition) contained the Carvel fudge. A few of these drew attention, unintentionally, to the accuracy of the 'forecast' by also including some of Dalton's actual tax proposals as announced in the House. This happened because Dalton reached the tax part of his speech with unusual speed. 'I do not recall the taxation changes ever coming so early as on this occasion', Cranfield observed.

Only a very small number of copies with the incriminating fudge were on sale in advance of the actual announcement of the tax changes. First copies available to the public were a bundle of 260 handed to a roundsman at Bouverie Street at 3.45, reaching Fleet Street at 3.50 for delivery to sellers in the immediate neighbourhood. These were not available for sale to the public until 3.53 or 3.55 – in Fleet Street, in Middle Temple Lane and at a bus stop near Aldwych tube station, close to the London School of Economics. In a couple of country areas, a very small number were on sale at 3.55. No other copies were in the streets before the Chancellor's official announcement of tax changes began six minutes later.[20]

Although the Stock Exchange closed at 3 p.m., transactions took place between offices until about 4.30 p.m. If any well-placed *Star* reader had realised (what the *Star*'s own editor apparently did not) that the Stop Press item was more than a last minute guess, the handful of copies available shortly before 4 o'clock might have influenced dealings. In fact, nobody was sharp enough or fast enough to make the necessary deduction and no unusual movements of prices occurred on 12th November which could be attributed to the *Star* report.

If the edition had been held up for ten, or even five, minutes it would probably not have reached the streets until after Dalton had started to announce the tax changes. In that case, the disclosure might have seemed less serious. Yet the common belief that Dalton was the victim of an improbable series of technological coincidences has no foundation. According to one rumour, the message only got through because printing of the early edition was running late.[21] This is incorrect. Printing started punctually at the scheduled time of 3.40, five minutes after the Carvel story had reached both printing offices. Even if the story had arrived later, it would have been used. Five additional boxes were inserted in the fudge at Bouverie Street, and three at

Commercial Wharf, before the insertion of the box mentioning the
'authorised' tax proposals.[22]

It was also rumoured that the story got in because the Stop Press
section was held up to wait for a racing result. Douglas Jay heard this
from Walter Layton, Chairman of the *News Chronicle* and *Star*. 'It
was a million-to-one chance that a conversation at Westminster after
3.20 p.m. should be on sale in a newspaper at 3.45 p.m., and has probably seldom if ever happened before or since.'[23] But Jay is wrong about
both times. At least 41 minutes, not 25, separated the leak from its
publication in the streets; and Cranfield's detailed evidence shows
that the racing results (the 3.45) were not inserted until 3.56,[24] by
which time incriminating copies were already on sale. Layton's comment shows, indeed, how little a leading proprietor could know about
the technology of his own newspaper.[25]

Dalton declared afterwards that 'having regard to the time and the
subject matter of our talk, it certainly never entered my mind that
[Carvel] would telephone it to his paper, or that they would publish it,
or indeed, that they would have time to publish it before my speech
began to come through.' This was obviously the truth. Yet there was
nothing technically surprising about what happened. To use Cranfield's word at the inquiry, the Fleet Street organisation was extremely
'slick' – especially on Budget Day, when it was geared to precisely the
kind of rapid processing which caught the Chancellor out.

Who first discovered that there had been a leak and drew attention
to its significance? A casual newspaper reader would not necessarily
have concluded that anything untoward had happened. Only experts
in the techniques and procedures of Fleet Street would have guessed,
from the correctness of the forecast on every point and from the
timing of the edition, that the unlikeliest explanation was the true one.
Such experts existed in the offices of the *Evening Standard* and the
Evening News. It was not long after the publication of the authorised
details that the accuracy of the fudge came to the attention of the
editors of the *Star*'s two rivals. Both papers had recently been accused
of obtaining information from Labour M.P.s by illicit means, while
the *Star* had smugly enjoyed their discomfiture. One theory is that, in
deciding to draw attention to the item in the *Star*, the editors of the
Standard and the *News* were working off a grudge, not against Dalton,
but against Cranfield.

First intimation of trouble came from Willie Alison, the rum-and-
milk man. Alison had seen Carvel talking to the Chancellor. Hence,
when he heard from his own office about the *Star* fudge, he was immediately aware of two things – the source of the leak, and the dire
predicament in which his friend was placed. Quickly he sought out the

Carvels. John had gone home. About 6 p.m., he found Robert, and passed on what he had learnt: that the editors of the *Standard* and the *News* knew of the leak, and that at their instigation a Tory M.P. called Beverley Baxter (former editor of the Beaverbrook-owned *Express*) planned to ask a Question about it next day in the House.[26]

This was not quite correct. Baxter had been approached. He did not, however, relish the task of asking the Question himself. Perhaps he was unwilling to get involved too closely in Fleet Street's game of dog-eats-dog; or to be publicly associated with an attack on a fellow journalist. Whatever the reason, Baxter decided to keep in the background and find somebody else to perform the deed for him. After receiving the message about the leak, he went to the Smoking Room at the House to look for a suitable questioner. Starting at the top, he asked Anthony Eden. Eden refused. He then spoke to several other prominent Conservatives. Each in turn gave the same answer. Soon it became clear that his own reluctance was widely shared. Tory M.P.s were keen that the Question should be put so long as they themselves had nothing to do with putting it.

Baxter had almost given up when he saw his friend Victor Raikes, right-wing Conservative M.P. for Westminster. Raikes was not one of the best-known members of his party, but he was one of the most hostile to the Government. Baxter therefore put his request to Raikes. Raikes immediately undertook to do what his colleagues found so distasteful. Sir Victor Raikes recalls that the origin of the leak was by now known, or guessed, by Tory M.P.s. Why did he agree to point the finger? 'I didn't give a damn', he says. 'Besides, I felt it was my duty.' Today, he remains convinced that, but for his devotion to duty, the Parliamentary Question about the Budget Leak might never have been asked.[27]

Meanwhile Robert had alerted his father by telephone and had then sought the advice of Maurice Webb, the Chairman of the P.L.P. Webb was a former Lobby correspondent (on the *Herald*), a near neighbour of the Carvels in the suburb of Pinner Hill, and a family friend. At first Webb was against precipitate action, arguing that the whole affair might blow over. The two men continued to discuss it as Robert drove them both home. In the car, the implications and dangers became more apparent. Before the end of the journey, they had concluded that the Cabinet must be told. Back at Pinner, John took the same view.

Next morning (13th November) Robert and Maurice drove together to Downing Street. Maurice, whose leg had recently been amputated, moved from Robert's car to the door of No. 10 with the aid of a crutch.[28]

Cabinet was in session, discussing wages policy. The meeting was long and dull, with Cripps and Morrison arguing against Bevan, who angrily accused Bevin of leading the Government down the road to Fascism. Gaitskell noted afterwards: 'In the middle of all this I saw HD sitting rather silent and looking rather tired. I caught his eye and he smiled at me.'[29] The debate did not directly concern the Chancellor. His sole recorded contribution to the morning's deliberations concerned the Royal Family: he proposed that Parliament should be asked to make further financial provision for H.R.H. Princess Elizabeth on the occasion of her forthcoming marriage. Cabinet agreed.[30]

Dalton gave two different accounts of how he first learnt of Carvel's 'forecast'. According to one, he found out during the morning Cabinet. According to the other, he did not discover until afterwards. In his memoirs he wrote:

> Just before noon a messenger handed Morrison a note ... The note was from Maurice Webb. It said that a very serious situation had arisen. There had been a bad Budget leak yesterday evening in the *Star*. The Tories were in full cry and one of them had put down a Private Notice Question to me for this afternoon. Morrison passed the note to me and I wrote on it: 'Discuss when we adjourn'. And then, for the first time since yesterday afternoon, I remembered that, on my way to the Chamber to make my Budget speech, I had had a few words with John Carvel, the *Star*'s Lobby correspondent, about the contents of my Budget.[31]

This version, written many years later, differs significantly from Dalton's evidence to the Select Committee on the Budget Disclosures set up immediately after the event. According to Dalton's original account, it was not until 1 p.m. that he was first made aware of his indiscretion. 'As soon as I heard this', he told the Committee, 'I said to two colleagues who were with me "This means I must resign my office".'[32] What of Maurice Webb's note at the Cabinet meeting? The reference to 'a bad Budget leak' would not necessarily have made Dalton think of Carvel, until his attention was drawn to the connection later.

Lord Trend's recollection supports Dalton's original version, suggesting that the Chancellor did not realise his own implication until *after* the Cabinet. Trend remembers that Dalton had returned to his study at No. 11 when Morrison and Webb (two colleagues) arrived, demanding to see him. They emerged ten minutes later. Trend went back into the Chancellor's room. 'Hugh seemed calm, but he was swearing to himself quietly under his breath.' Dalton then explained what had happened.[33]

When the Prime Minister's office was contacted, Attlee was busy. News of the leak reached him in the form of a note from his principal private secretary, L. M. Helsby, explaining that a private notice question had been put down about an alleged Budget leakage in the previous day's *Star*. Helsby's message continued:

> The Chancellor of the Exch[r] would like to discuss urgently the terms of the reply to be given with you, the Lord President & the Chief Whip. Could you manage 2.15 here?
>
> (It is better in the circumstances that the meeting should not be in the House).
>
> Subject to your approval, the others are coming here at the time suggested.[34]

Attlee scribbled: 'Yes CRA' with a red pencil in the margin; and the meeting was duly held.* Before it took place, Dalton invited Cripps to join them. 'We five were alone in the Cabinet Room', Dalton wrote. 'We all agreed that I must make full and frank admission of my responsibility and express my deep regrets and apologies to the House.' A reply to the expected Question was drafted. The Chancellor repeated what he had said to Morrison and Webb: 'This means I must resign my office'. Later, he recalled that his words were brushed aside by the others, especially by Whiteley. He also recalled that he turned to Attlee and stated formally: 'Prime Minister, I now offer you my resignation.'

Immediately after the meeting Dalton went back to No. 11 and told Ruth. The two of them ate a late lunch together, alone, in their small dining-room on the third floor.[35]

When they had finished, the Chancellor went over to his room at the House. Douglas Jay, who had accompanied him through the Lobby the day before, joined him. Dalton pointed to Raikes's Private Notice Question, which referred to the accurate forecast in the *Star*. 'Here's a bit of fun', he said. He then explained, saying that he intended to give an honest answer. Jay was appalled and urged him to stop and think. 'One must always own up', Dalton replied.[36]

At first it looked as though the Chancellor's frankness would save him. In the House that afternoon, Raikes asked about the accuracy

---

* Why was this exchange between Helsby and Attlee, which must have occurred shortly after the Cabinet, in writing rather than by word of mouth? The reference to 'here' provides a clue. The consultation with Dalton was held in the Cabinet Room. Attlee may have attended a meeting in the Cabinet Room as soon as the morning Cabinet ended, in the course of which his secretary handed him a note.

of a forecast in a newspaper on sale at 3.45 p.m.* Dalton replied, speaking 'with gravity and emphasis, but with unfaltering coolness':[37]

> I very much regret to tell the House that the publication to which the Hon. Member refers arose out of an incident which occurred as I was entering the Chamber to make my speech yesterday. In reply to questions put to me by the Lobby correspondent of the *Star* newspaper, I indicated to him the subject-matter contained in the publication in question. I appreciate that this was a grave indiscretion on my part, for which I offer my deep apologies to the House.

There was then an odd exchange, in which the thrust of the Tory attack was apparently aimed at Carvel and the *Star*, rather than at Dalton himself.

Mr. Raikes: Will the Chancellor of the Exchequer convey to that newspaper, apart from any indiscretion on his part, the very grave breach of journalistic honour on the part of a newspaper receiving such information to publish in advance before it could properly appear?

Mr. Churchill: May I acknowledge on the part of the Opposition the very frank manner in which the Right Hon. Gentleman has expressed himself in the House and our sympathy with him at the misuse of his confidence which has occurred?

Mr. Beverley Baxter: May I ask the Chancellor, since this involves the professional honour of journalists in general, did the Lobby correspondent in question know that it was a friendly and private if, perhaps, ill-judged statement, or did he think that it was for immediate publication?

Mr. Dalton: I do not think that I should add to what I have said to the House. I take the blame for having committed an indiscretion in my relationship with this Lobby correspondent whom I have known, as we have known so many of the Lobby correspondents, over a period of years, and I do not think that it would be suitable for me to pass any judgment on him. I have apologised for my part in the matter. I would prefer to leave it there.[38]

Most people at the time felt that this was the end of the matter. The attack, if such it was, had scarcely been savage, and seemed to divert blame away from the Chancellor. Dalton had made a full confession –

---

* As we have seen, the actual time of first sales was 3.53 p.m. 3.45 was presumably an estimate made in the offices of the *Standard* and *News*.

there was not after all much to confess – and had done it well. Douglas Jay, in the row behind, noted with relief that 'the whole House murmured approval of Churchill and sympathy with Dalton'.[39] Gaitskell whispered to the Chancellor as he sat down: 'What's it all about?' Dalton passed a copy of the *Star* and said 'That bloody fool Carvel'. Gaitskell felt that Churchill's statement amounted to an exoneration. 'I thought it was irritating but all over and left the Chamber', he wrote next day.[40] Morrison formed the same impression.[41] Robert Carvel was much reassured when, later the same afternoon, Maurice Webb came up and told him that there was no longer any question of the Chancellor having to resign.[42] The *Daily Mail* correspondent, Wilson Broadbent, summed up the view of the Lobby when he wrote that, following Dalton's statement, 'it had been assumed that the incident was closed'.[43]

But it was not closed. After speaking, the Chancellor stayed on the Front Bench until about 5 o'clock, making notes with a pencil, and laughing at M.P.s' jokes. When Oliver Stanley called him 'St Hugh, the Benevolent Patron Saint of Spivs', he acknowledged the insult with a grin.[44] Then he returned to Downing Street for another interview with the Prime Minister.

'It was a sad and short conversation', Dalton recalled:

I began by reminding him that it was now nearly four hours[45] since I had offered him my resignation. I hoped that he would now accept it. He replied that he felt he must, but I was moved to see that he was much more deeply moved that [sic] I was at this moment. He said he hated – hated – he repeated this word several times – hated to lose me. He thanked me for what I had done as a Minister in several successive departments, and hoped that I should be able to rejoin the Government later, in some department, as an 'elder statesman'.

There was an exchange of official letters. The tone of each was warm. Dalton wrote of the Prime Minister's helpfulness, encouragement and kindness; Attlee of his own deep sympathy for an old and valued colleague. At the same time, the Prime Minister also stressed that 'the principle of the inviolability of the Budget is of the highest importance and the discretion of the Chancellor of the Exchequer, who necessarily receives many confidential communications, must be beyond question'.[46] Attlee said that the new Chancellor would be Sir Stafford Cripps. Dalton pledged his loyalty, returned to No. 11, and prepared for bed. Ruth, meanwhile, had summoned Hugh's physician, Dr Urwick, presumably to administer a sedative.[47]

It was only at this point that Dalton was handed a letter from Churchill, which declared that, in view of the precise and comprehensive form of the Chancellor's disclosure, and the fact that no obligation of secrecy had been placed upon the journalist, the Opposition intended to demand an inquiry by a Select Committee. Dalton claimed later that he did not receive this letter until after his resignation and Cripps's appointment had been broadcast by the B.B.C., and there is no reason to doubt him. Churchill's note was released to the press at 10 p.m.[48] – fifteen minutes before the resignation was officially announced,[49] though a full hour after Cripps had been asked by Attlee to become Chancellor.[50]

There are three puzzles. First, why did the Tories give the impression that they were not going to press the matter, and then change their minds? Second, why did Attlee accept Dalton's resignation? Third, why did Dalton offer it with such determined insistence?

Quite apart from the personal tragedy, the irretrievable setback to a distinguished career, Dalton's fall had a major effect on the Labour Government, changing the balance at the top and symbolising the end of the radical phase and the start of a period of compromise and consolidation. It is important to consider, therefore, whether the actual outcome of the leak was the only possible one. Afterwards, the resignation and Attlee's acceptance of it both seemed inevitable. Yet few would have been outraged if Dalton had carried on as Chancellor.

Herbert Morrison's account, though written much later, contains interesting clues. According to Morrison, Dalton withdrew from the early afternoon consultation of senior ministers having offered his resignation, leaving Attlee, Morrison, Cripps and Bevin (who appears in place of Whiteley in this version) to discuss what should be done:

> As tended to happen all too often the Prime Minister gave no definite lead and meticulously refrained from voicing his own opinion, obligingly murmuring 'yes, yes' or 'no, no' to much the same sort of question according to the answer the questioner seemed to be expecting. Inevitably the upshot of this fruitless meeting was that no decision was taken on Dalton's offer to resign, but I felt that I was the only one there who wished to save Dalton.[51]

The crux (according to Morrison) was the subsequent change in attitude of the Tories – rumours of which may, indeed, have preceded the actual sending of a letter by Churchill in the evening. Dalton's appointment to the Chancellorship had been preceded by prevarication and indecision on the part of Attlee; we should not be surprised, therefore, if his departure from the same office had a similar accompaniment. If, however, the Tory change of attitude was a factor in making up the Prime Minister's mind, how was this change to be explained?

Sir Victor Raikes recalls that a short time after Dalton's confession Churchill (whose initial intervention had been implicitly critical of the questioner) came up to him and apologised.[52] The aspect which Churchill stressed in his letter to Dalton was the lack of an 'obligation of secrecy'. The Leader of the Opposition had condemned Carvel in the House for betraying a confidence. Later it had been drawn to his attention that 'no obligation of secrecy' had been imposed.

Who made this point to Churchill? The answer seems to have been the Lobby, incensed by Churchill's slight on its professional honour. Paul Einzig recalled telling Dalton's old enemy Brendan Bracken that, since the Chancellor had not made it clear that his remarks were off the record, Carvel had every right to pass on the information for publication. According to Einzig, Bracken immediately told Churchill.[53]

Yet the 'obligation of secrecy' question was really a red herring. Carvel's mistake was understandable; but even Carvel admitted that he had broken the code. ' … [I]f you had stopped to think you would have known that it was not legitimate. That is right, is it not?' he was asked at the inquiry. 'Yes', replied Carvel.[54]

Churchill's letter had stated: 'I am told that no obligation of secrecy was imposed upon the journalist, though that certainly seems to me to have been implicit.'[55] This sentence contained a fundamental contradiction. According to the Lobby's own spokesman at the inquiry, 'implicit' obligations of secrecy had *exactly* the same status as those that had been specifically imposed. Speaking for the Lobby, the Secretary of the Parliamentary Lobby Journalists, Guy Eden, agreed that an embargo could be implied as well as explicit, and that an implicit embargo was no less binding than an explicit one.[56] Nobody ever challenged this judgment, which reflected the normally accepted practice of the Lobby as a whole. Indeed, as Sir Norman Brook, Secretary to the Cabinet, pointed out in notes to both Attlee and Morrison a few days later, if Dalton *had* given any explicit hint about not publishing, this would have made matters worse, by showing that he was conscious of what he was doing. The leak would then have appeared deliberate, not accidental.[57]

Thus the issue of an obligation to secrecy was an excuse, not a reason. The simplest explanation for the Tory change of tack is probably the right one. The Government was under serious pressure in the wake of the convertibility crisis and the Opposition relished an opportunity to extend its embarrassment. No Labour minister was more hated on the Tory side than Dalton. After years of suffering his taunts, the bloodlust was hard to contain. 'We had him', Sir Victor Raikes recalls with satisfaction, 'wriggling on the end of a hook'. This mood gathered force on the Tory backbenches after Dalton's confession. According to Harold Macmillan, 'a feeling in the party began to develop in the course of the evening in favour of exploiting our advantage'.[58] 'I go to Pratts', Harold Nicolson wrote the day after the resignation. 'Llewellyn is there and Harry Cruikshank. They discuss the Dalton case. The Tories or rather the 1922 Committee are going to squeeze out every drop of value from it. What a cruel thing is politics.'[59]

Yet there were divisions within the Opposition ranks. Harold Macmillan formed the impression that most Tory front benchers wanted to let the matter drop.[60] This was not because of any closet sympathy for the Chancellor (' ... Dalton's a swine', Churchill told his doctor a few weeks later. 'He spoke of him with violence', Lord Moran noted.)[61] Rather, it was because of a feeling that to press too hard on such a minor issue was unsporting, and might appear hypocritical. Afterwards, many leading Tories felt that the punishment of resignation or dismissal was altogether out of proportion;[62] having pushed Attlee, they were slightly embarrassed when he gave way. Churchill himself was heard to mutter to Eden as they walked out of the Chamber the day after Dalton's departure: 'I would never have accepted a resignation in those circumstances'.[63] The attitude of decent Tories in the immediate aftermath was best summed up by the exclamation of Nigel Birch: 'My God! They've shot our fox!'[64]

This brings us to the second puzzle. Why *did* Attlee shoot the Tories' fox?

Dalton's probity was never in doubt. No harm was done by the disclosure, and the Chancellor's reaction, once he knew what had happened, was honourable to a fault. Gaitskell wrote immediately afterwards: 'the Party view is that he did the right thing and probably his prestige there is higher than ever'.[65] The Tories were not able to force the resignation even if they had wanted to at such a time, and many did not. The inquiry, which Churchill had belatedly demanded, revealed nothing of substance. If Attlee had refused to accept the resignation, there would have been very little disquiet in Cabinet or Parliament, and it is unlikely that the reputation of the Government would have suffered. 'Had Mr. Attlee wished to retain Dalton in his Cabinet he could have done so', maintained the *Financial Times*, a paper generally hostile to the former Chancellor.[66] The generally accepted view that the Prime Minister·had no choice but to sack Dalton therefore needs to be examined.

The Prime Minister, so the story goes, was a man who maintained the highest standards of conduct himself and expected the same from all members of his Government. He therefore insisted on Dalton's departure as a matter of principle, *pour encourager les autres* and to maintain the inviolability of the Budget. This was Attlee's own explanation. 'If he hadn't resigned would you have fired him?' the former premier was asked many years later. 'I would have had to', Attlee replied. 'There was never any trouble over that. He realised.'[67] It was also the view that Dalton held, perhaps desperately needed to hold, for the rest of his life. Yet the necessity of Attlee's action is far from clear.

Dalton's offence was far less serious than that of Lloyd George and Sir Rufus Isaacs during the Marconi affair in 1913. After a scandal in which Lloyd George and Isaacs put themselves in a position in which their public duty might have clashed with an undisclosed private interest, and having treated the House of Commons with deliberate evasiveness, the career of neither was interrupted or done permanent damage. Isaacs went on to become Lord Chief Justice, and Lloyd George to be Prime Minister. Yet, according to Lord Blake, they had been guilty of

> a degree of indiscretion and subsequent disingenuousness which seem in retrospect almost incomprehensible ... The relatively harmless and trivial indiscretion for which Mr. Attlee so promptly dismissed Dr Dalton from the Chancellorship of the Exchequer does not begin to compare with the conduct of Isaacs and Lloyd George.[68]

Had standards of political conduct risen since Lloyd George's day? Perhaps. There was, however, a very recent case with which Dalton's offence could be directly compared. On 20th August, the day of the suspension of convertibility, A. V. Alexander, a senior Cabinet minister, had told the press that the Chancellor would broadcast the same evening on the subject of convertibility. Yet the Government's intentions at that moment were highly secret. 'This blazing indiscretion might have greatly profited Wall Street operators whose markets were still open', the *Financial Times* rightly pointed out.[69] As with Dalton's slip, no moral blame could be attached to Alexander's behaviour. Unlike Dalton, Alexander received no punishment.

Kingsley Martin, editor of the *New Statesman*, suggested that the Prime Minister might have been influenced by a recent scandal in which a Labour M.P. had been expelled from the House for writing an article accusing M.P.s of breaches of confidentiality for reward. Martin felt that this case made Attlee especially concerned 'to dispel any suspicion of shady personal behaviour'.[70] But Dalton's behaviour had not been shady. His resignation did not dispel suspicion; on the contrary, it aroused it. Wild rumours spread, based on the assumption that so severe a penalty must have involved a significant offence. For the same reason, the resignation caused bewilderment – and some scepticism – abroad. As one American commentator laconically observed, if similar standards of ethics were applied in Washington, there would not be enough members of Congress left to make a quorum.[71]

Finally, let us deal with the argument that the leak was a glaring example of Dalton's habitual inability to keep his mouth shut. This view was favoured by colleagues who often found themselves at the sharp end of Dalton's malicious wit. It also formed part of Attlee's retrospective explanation. 'Perfect ass', Attlee told an interviewer twenty years later. 'He always liked to have a secret to confide to somebody else to please him. He did it once too often.'[72] In fact, Dalton was keenly aware of the distinction between political gossip and classified information. As he pointed out in a letter to Louis Spears, he had carried the wartime secrets of S.O.E. with complete security.[73] 'No one, in my experience, was more cautious in talking to the Press', wrote the Political Correspondent of the *Observer*. 'He was the one man whom one never expected to winkle any news out of.'[74]

If there was no moral, constitutional or political necessity for Dalton's departure; if, indeed. such talk was largely humbug, what are we left with? Again, the simplest answer is the best one. The Prime Minister accepted Dalton's resignation because he wanted to be rid of him.

We have seen how, over preceding months, Dalton had battled unsuccessfully against his colleagues, and against Attlee in particular, for action in the crisis; we have seen how a hue and cry of press, City and academic economists had pursued Dalton, blaming him personally for the country's ills; we have seen how the Chancellor, desperately and foolishly, had backed successive attempts to bring about a change at No. 10. These were reasons enough for regarding Dalton's gaffe as a heaven-sent opportunity. Attlee could not, however, have acted without the support, or at least passive agreement, of senior colleagues. We need therefore to look once again at the Chancellor's position within the Government.

Morrison claimed to have fought against the acceptance of Dalton's resignation. But relations between the two men had not been such as to cause the Lord President to shed many tears when he was overruled. The two ministers had frequently been in conflict, in particular over steel nationalisation. More important, Dalton had made his own views on Morrison's capacity to run the Government's planning known, and he had strongly supported Attlee's decision to take planning away from him.

Ernest Bevin had even less cause to resist a change at the Treasury. Bevin and Dalton had been allies on appeasement and rearmament before the war, and on industrial location during it. Since 1945, however, they had differed on a number of issues – most recently on Palestine, and on overseas expenditure. Refusing to see the impact of his own policies, the Foreign Secretary unfairly blamed Dalton for the financial crisis. By 1947, Bevin regarded the Chancellor as a trouble-maker who was after his job. His vow the previous summer will be recalled: that Dalton would be 'properly dealt with' for taking part in the July plot. When Dalton offered his resignation, it is unlikely that Bevin pressed Attlee hard to refuse it. According to Gaitskell, the Foreign Secretary was cheerful and slightly drunk on the night of 13th November – and not at all upset at having lost a close colleague.[75]

What about the Minister of Economic Affairs? For some time, Dalton and Cripps had been working together – over steel nationalisation, over Palestine, over cuts in spending on the armed forces, and latterly over the failed attempts to shift Attlee and the successful attempt to give Cripps responsibility for planning. Even in retrospect, Dalton always denied that there had been any conflict between them. Later he wrote:

> As regards Cripps and myself, there was a great Press build-up of supposed disagreements and antagonisms between us. This was all quite baseless. He and I had had serious differences in the past, before the war, as was publicly known. But over the last twelve exceedingly difficult months, no two members of the Government had seen more closely eye to eye on *all* questions than Cripps and myself. I had wanted him to be Minister of Economic Affairs, and had told the Prime Minister so, before the appointment was made. Since it was made, there had been no friction between us; we had worked in the closest harmony.[76]

Yet we can only guess at the thoughts of the new planning minister. Cripps was a man of religion, a man of high ideals, a man of brilliant perceptions, a man of determination and zeal. He was a man who, as Michael Foot puts it, thought of himself as rectitude itself.[77] He was also a man with a high assessment of his own abilities and an unwavering belief that these should be put to the fullest possible use. As early as May, Cripps had been hinting at his interest in the Treasury. Having acquired Morrison's planning functions, the limitations which these imposed quickly became clear to him. He needed full financial control, as well as economic control, in order to do his job properly. Cripps knew that the departure of Dalton, towards whom he had no reason to feel personally loyal, would almost certainly deliver a coveted prize into his hands.

Like Bevin, Cripps showed no signs of sorrow or regret on the night of Dalton's resignation. Francis Williams noted Cripps's coolness and avoidance of Dalton's name immediately after hearing of his own appointment.[78] Gaitskell also formed the impression that Dalton's troubles were not exactly uppermost in the new Chancellor's mind. ' "No friends at the top". This is what Asquith is supposed to have said ... and it is certainly true', reflected the young minister. 'Cripps showed no remorse and I could not help feeling that he had satisfied one more ambition by becoming Chancellor.'[79]

Characteristically, the Prime Minister gave little away about his own private attitude at the time. Dalton laid great stress on the display of regret with which Attlee accepted his resignation. It was undoubtedly an emotional moment. But the Prime Minister's emotions may have been mixed – containing an element of relief at the elimination of a colleague who had actively participated in a series of discussions and plots whose central aim was to displace him; a colleague, moreover, who had backed his principal opponent in 1935 and had since then frequently spoken of him in derisive terms – as a nonentity, a little mouse, a rabbit, a little man. Sir Geoffrey de Freitas, P.P.S. to Attlee in 1945–6, and also a friend and protégé of Dalton, recalled that the Prime Minister never trusted the Chancellor, regarding him as devious, with an 'indirect' way of operating.[80] To those in the know, there must have seemed a touch of irony in Attlee's reference, in his official letter, to Dalton's 'loyal services' and 'friendship'.[81]

So much for the leaders. What of the P.L.P. as a whole? According to most newspapers, Dalton's resignation was accepted as a regrettable necessity. In fact, such a view was far from universal: as Wilson Broadbent, the *Daily Mail* reporter who had written the 20th August story predicting Attlee's imminent replacement by Bevin, pointed out. Two days after Dalton's departure, Broadbent reported that the Labour Party would insist on a private inquest into the whole affair. In particular, he claimed, Attlee would be criticised for not publicly expressing a view. 'Labour politicians' were apparently saying that the Prime Minister ought to have put forward an explanation which would have modified the importance of the offence. On 17th November, Broadbent repeated the story, maintaining once again that 'socialists' were intent on their own inquiry. 'They want to know why Mr. Dalton's resignation was accepted by Attlee', he wrote.[82]

Who were these 'Labour politicians' and 'socialists'? The answer was: left-wingers on the backbenches. In view of past associations, one might have imagined that the Labour Left would welcome Dalton's replacement by Cripps. In fact, the opposite was the case. The Left had come to feel that Dalton was the true guardian of the programme of 1945 within the Government.

According to *Tribune*, Dalton now had closer ties with and a more astute feeling for the mood of the Labour Movement than any of his colleagues among the Big Five. The ex-Chancellor stood for 'an expansionist, incentive-minded plan' as against 'dreary restrictionism coupled with a serious invasion of working-class standards'. By contrast, the other four members of the Big Five had 'failed to impress the Party or the country with their resolute determination to fight their way out of the crisis on a Socialist policy'.[83] There was something a bit too convenient about Dalton's departure at such a time. 'Perhaps', as the *New Statesman* put it, 'Attlee jumped at the chance of ending a Cripps-Dalton disagreement in the Cabinet!'[84] 'Attlee was cowed by the Tory attack', Michael Foot considers. 'It was typical of him to refuse to throw his mantle over his chaps in difficulties. One after another, when colleagues got into trouble – Nye, Shinwell, Morrison – he deserted them. This was another example. He certainly should not have accepted the resignation.'[85] However, while the Labour Left sympathised with Dalton, and disputed the Prime Minister's motives, it had no means by which to save him.

The right-wing press more or less agreed with the *Tribune* analysis of the distinction between Dalton and Cripps. It was widely believed that Cripps had been pressing for more drastic cuts than Dalton would permit, that the new Chancellor, unlike the old, was by temperament a deflationist.[86] For the City, there was the cheerful prospect of an end to the pursuit of cheaper money. But above all (and it is interesting how leader-writers disguised their political prejudice beneath supposedly detached analyses of Dalton's economics) there was a feeling that Cripps was less of an egalitarian, and would the more willingly sacrifice the Government's social programme. Dalton was presented as the Chancellor who refused to listen to warnings that the nation's resources were being over-stretched. 'New factories, modern machinery, all the houses that could be planned, new schools and other public improvements', commented the *Manchester Guardian*; ' – he had money for all good things.'[87] Cripps, on the other hand, never wavered in telling the country it was in trouble. 'Sir Stafford ... was insistent that drastic measures were necessary, and there can be little doubt that he found Mr. Dalton's proposals inadequate', announced the *Observer*. 'It can be taken for granted that the next Budget will make the present one look like a jollification.'[88]

Press denunciation of Dalton, and enthusiasm for Sir Stafford Cripps, may well have influenced Attlee. In an oddly masochistic way (for the new Chancellor had been even more disloyal than his predecessor) the Prime Minister had a soft spot for Cripps. This went back to the beleaguered 1931 Parliament, when Cripps and Attlee had shared the leadership of the P.L.P. with Lansbury, while Dalton and Morrison watched anxiously from outside. In 1933, at a time when Dalton was treating Attlee with the utmost disdain, Cripps had donated £500 to the Labour Party, specifically to pay Attlee's salary as Deputy Leader during Lansbury's illness. Without such help, Attlee would have resigned and would, therefore, never have become Prime Minister.[89] Perhaps this explains why machinations which were a cause for complaint when engaged in by Dalton, were forgivable in Cripps – whose lofty ideals seemed to soar above personal aggrandisement.[90] Moreover, while a change at the Treasury was not politically necessary, it made good political sense. With Morrison already downgraded, the Prime Minister could now base his own position far more securely on the twin pillars of the Foreign Secretary and the new Chancellor, whose respective talents were complementary, and whose mutual distrust minimised the possibility of an alliance against himself.

The truth was that by the autumn of 1947, the Government inner circle no longer needed Dalton, who had allowed himself to become fatally isolated. His popularity on the backbenches and in the Party outside was insufficient protection against the growing body of his detractors. For months, in his frustration and fear, he had been alienating one influential colleague after another. Now he had obligingly laid himself on a slab. The *Financial Times* archly reminded its readers that 'not long ago Dr Dalton privately expressed doubts as to whether Mr. Attlee could ride the storm'. This opinion had duly been reported to No. 10 Downing Street. As a result, the Prime Minister had shown that he possessed the quality 'of being what Mr. Asquith called "a good butcher" '.[91] The *New York Times* also inclined to the cynical view. According to its London correspondent, Dalton went because he had been so widely criticised in the financial press. The Budget leak gave the Prime Minister his chance, and he struck.[92]

Finally, we come to Dalton himself. The pressures on him had been relentless. He was exhausted, disillusioned and depressed, with a deep sense of failure and defeat. There had been a pattern in his life – furious activity and triumphant success, following by mounting anxiety and near-despair. The autumn of 1947 found him in the trough at the bottom of this cycle. It may not be fanciful to see a link with the private tragedy in his life, a quarter of a century before, which also followed a period of elated, brittle energy.

We have seen the violent psychological impact upon him of the dollar drain – the sleepless nights, the unreal spectres of mass starvation, the frightening images of drops of blood and of a child bleeding to death. 'He used to feel a pain in his chest, so he told me', Davenport recalled, 'whenever the official from the Bank of England came to announce another loss of gold.'[93] We have seen other physical symptoms – boils, carbuncles, septicaemia – directly related to stress. During his last months as Chancellor, Dalton was chronically constipated for the first time in his life.[94] The gruelling ministerial round that had once been a source of pleasure had become self-punishment, sustained by an explosive alternation of sleeping pills and Benzedrine.[95] His perilous reaction (as at earlier times of depression and personal crisis) was to lash out at real or imagined enemies: Shinwell, Strachey, Morrison and, disastrously, the Prime Minister himself.

Could Dalton have carried on? 'He was a prodigal spender of his own energy', Lord Trend recalls. 'He had the stamina to continue, but I doubt if his immense vitality could have been maintained.'[96] He had become noisier, more irascible, more sensitive to criticism and insensitive to the feelings of others. 'Anyone could see for some time that Dalton was under such strain that something was bound to happen', Aneurin Bevan remarked to Francis Williams. 'There is no immaculate conception of disaster.'[97]

'So odd was it that people began at once to construct explanations as bizarre as the event itself', wrote Kingsley Martin. ' "Did he do it on purpose?" I was asked, as if of a child who picks up a precious bit of crockery and throws it on the floor.'[98] We may dismiss the possibility of deliberate suicide. As *The Economist* put it, no more explanation was needed than that Dalton, keyed up for a great occasion, said too much to a friendly correspondent, 'a momentary example of badly suppressed inflation'.[99] Yet such behaviour may not have been unrelated to the pressure upon him. 'It was a Road Accident', Dalton wrote to Leonard Woolf. 'I was a very secure driver I thought ... till this moment's inattention, and over she goes!'[100] It was a revealing metaphor. For there had been ominous signs of carelessness and indifference to consequences before the accident occurred.

Stress may help account for the resignation, as well as for the incident that precipitated it. As Francis Williams remarked, it was undoubtedly 'one of the silliest indiscretions in recent political history'.[101] But it was also one of the most trivial: today, when central features of the Budget are floated months in advance, it would barely be noticed. Though Dalton had to offer his resignation, he did not have to press it. Here we come back to the suspicion that, in a large part of himself, Dalton wanted to go. ' ... [H]e really loathed it at the end', commented Durbin, his former P.P.S., early in 1948, 'in fact ever since the beginning of the year.'[102]

As we have seen, thoughts or fantasies of resignation had been an oft-repeated theme. Dalton wrote later that he had considered resigning in January over the failure to reduce the armed forces, over the 'manpower gap' when the Economic Survey was being prepared, and several times came near to resigning over the import programme.[103] Before the convertibility crisis, resignation or the threat of resignation had been seen as a weapon to force an issue. During the weeks before the Budget, resignation became the one remaining means of escape. 'My chances of resigning are always being snatched from me', he wrote on 20th September. The last, almost despairing, reference to resignation in his diary was on 20th October. Four days later, the diary mysteriously breaks off.

Perhaps the leak should be seen, not as a compelling reason for resigning, but as a cast iron alibi, something that could be presented to himself as inescapable. Nicholas Davenport, who saw Dalton privately just before and after he left the Treasury, felt that the Chancellor insisted on going because he knew in his heart that he was no longer capable of doing his job.[104] This was a cruel assessment, from a close friend who had become a stern critic. Yet it is striking that Dalton's immediate reaction was one of total concession: 'This means I must resign my office.' There was no pause to weigh the possible damage, or the likely reaction of friends and enemies. Dalton, and others, called it duty. Afterwards, Dalton adopted a new persona – the man of honour, not afraid to face the music, the socialist who obeyed the public school code. 'I was thought to have behaved well over the Budget incident and "added to my stature", particularly among my political opponents', he wrote with pathetic pride at the end of his life,[105] indicating that the good opinion of his Etonian peers mattered to him after all. We may admire Dalton for his example. Yet such a rigorous interpretation of duty without reflection or investigation,[106] suggests that his decision may not have been entirely reluctant.

While regretting the manner of his departure, Dalton soon ceased to regret the fact of it. A few months later, Durbin commented that he seemed much happier out of office.[107] Dalton himself admitted that the relief was immense.[108] Ruth told him that if it had not happened as it did, he would have gone on getting more exhausted and less efficient, and 'that the only good way out would have been for Urwick to insist that I should resign on grounds of health – with the chance of coming back to the Govt later when I was better.'[109] He did not disagree.

What was the effect of Dalton's departure? His keenest supporters were on the backbenches. Despite Broadbent's predictions, no revolt materialised. This was partly because Dalton went without protest, partly because a revolt after the event could achieve little, and partly because, in the eyes of most observers, the gravitas and asceticism of Cripps suited the times. 'Mr. Dalton would always yield to the call of popularity', proclaimed the *Manchester Guardian*, 'Sir Stafford Cripps will always listen to the call of conscience.'[110] This was the general opinion. Cripps, as David Marquand has put it, was pre-eminently a bishop. In November 1947 a bishop was just what was required.[111]

The myth was soon built up in the financial press (especially in the fiercely anti-Labour, anti-Dalton *Economist*) and handed from the financial to the political press, that in policy and competence, as in personality, Dalton and Cripps were polar opposites: the one vain, ebullient, expansive, heedless of advice; the other self-sacrificing, courageous, considering only the interests of the nation. As we have seen, this was to stand truth on its head. Far less courage was required for Cripps to follow the advice of financial columnists and the City, than for Dalton to struggle, for as long as he could, to preserve and develop the social revolution envisaged in *Practical Socialism*.

Dalton's departure altered the administrative structure of the Government. It ended the division between financial and economic functions, and restored the dominance of the Treasury: the new Chancellor retained his wide powers as planning minister while acquiring responsibility for finance. It was welcomed by the economists, who had long sought just such a combination; and by Treasury officials, whose relations, first with the Lord President's Office, and then the Ministry of Economic Affairs, had contained an element of rivalry.

Yet there was no sudden redirection of policy. Dalton had already accepted the end of what he bravely called the years of 'Hard High History',[112] over which he had presided, and his final Budget the day before his resignation heralded the new era. Cripps, and Cripps's successor Gaitskell, developed the policy that Dalton had begun: the replacement of physical control planning by 'macro' management of the economy. Dalton was the only Chancellor who had ever attempted to perform his duties in a distinctively socialist way. The experiment ended with the convertibility crisis; it was never tried again. Dalton's subdued oration to the House on 12th November marked the final abandonment of the attempt.

Against this background, Dalton's mishap seems strangely pre-ordained: not a ludicrous interruption, but a culmination, a ritual offering, a declaration that a different season had begun. There had been mistakes. The Government wanted to start afresh. For some time there had been a need for a victim. First Shinwell had been cast for the role, then Morrison, and then, through the summer and early autumn, Attlee. But both Shinwell and Morrison were too well entrenched and Attlee was able to play one personality off against another. Gradually, as Cripps pushed inexorably forward, the neatest, cleanest and most convenient sacrifice became that of the Chancellor of the Exchequer. The Budget leak was an accident. But its immediate consequence had about it a dramatic certainty, as though necessary to complete the plot.

XXX

Aftermath

The morning after his resignation, Hugh woke for the last time at No. 11 Downing Street. It was a ghastly day. First he had to confront a great pile of letters of sympathy. He turned them over child-like, saying 'It's rather like having a birthday!' Trend, watching him, felt that he had suddenly become an old man.[1]

Hugh and Ruth had given up their Victoria flat in 1941, when Ruth had gone north and Hugh had moved into the Ministry basement. Now they discovered the acute problem of accommodation in bomb-damaged post-war London. 'Everything's impossibly expensive!' Ruth told her friend Enid MacLeod on the telephone.[2] But the immediate difficulty was not finding something cheap or suitable, but finding anywhere to go at all. The new Chancellor had been appointed. It was necessary to move out of Downing Street without delay. Desperately, Ruth rang Nicholas Davenport's wife Olga, the film actress. Hugh could not sleep another night at No. 11. The Davenports had a flat in Hertford Street. Could Olga and Nicholas put him up? Olga offered their small spare room.[3]

That evening Hugh drove to Buckingham Palace to surrender the Seals of Office to the King.[4] There was a bleakly dignified ceremony with senior officials in Downing Street.[5] Then he left for good. Hoping to offer consolation, Nicholas Davenport and John Wilmot (also a recently sacked minister) took him off for dinner at Josefs in Greek Street, a familiar haunt. Afterwards, Hugh returned with Nicholas to the Hertford Street flat. Meanwhile Ruth had arranged to stay with friends of her own. She seldom stayed with the Davenports, and did not choose to now.

It would have been better if she had. In the middle of the night, Olga was woken by the sound of rushing water in the bathroom, then a crash. Running to investigate, she found Hugh lying full length on the tiled floor, unconscious. She wondered whether he had suffered a stroke. Together, Olga and Nicholas heaved him on to his bed. Nicholas went to the kitchen for some brandy. While he was gone, Hugh came round, rose to his feet and grasped Olga. 'Oh my darling! My darling!' he cried out. Overcome by this outburst of misery from the huge, broken man, Olga staggered back, half-fainting. Hugh called: 'Nicholas! Come quickly! Come and help Olga!' Eventually Hugh was helped back into bed. Next morning, he had recovered his composure. Later, reflecting on this sad, revealing incident, Davenport saw it as a sudden release of emotion following the tension and 'slow torture' of his office.[6]

After one night at the Davenports', Hugh stayed briefly at the Wilmots' flat in Kensington,[7] before retreating with Ruth to West Leaze 'like an animal in its hole' (as he put it). He remained in Wiltshire for the rest of the year, returning to London briefly to give evidence to the Select Committee set up to investigate the Budget disclosures, and making short visits north to his constituency, and to the New Forest to stay with friends.[8] 'We are spending December here, resting after the emotion of Hugh's resignation', Ruth wrote to Hilde Auerbach from West Leaze on 10th December, adding, with Ruthian bathos, 'You can imagine how sad I was at leaving No. 11.'[9]

During the London trip they found a flat in Ashley Gardens, off Victoria Street, close to their pre-war flat in Carlisle Mansions, but smaller. Ruth went with Josephine Smith to look it over. Josephine remembers that Ruth was cool and business-like. 'I can sit here and Hugh can have the other room', Ruth said, thinking aloud. 'If he wants I can always bring his meals in.' She seemed to be taking for granted that they would eat apart. 'I was reminded of a French novel', Josephine recalls. 'I wondered whether, from now on, the blinds would be permanently drawn. There was the sense of a final chapter. This was how it was going to be.'[10] Hugh and Ruth moved in with essential furniture early in January[11] and stayed for the rest of their lives.

They never parted again, except for holidays and official trips. She stuck by him loyally. It remained an ill-fitting arrangement – as one friend put it, not so much a marriage, more two people choosing to grow old together.[12] Ruth had been able to offer little comfort during the dreadful summer and autumn of 1947. A man with a firmer emotional base might, perhaps, have been saved from some of his worst midjudgments in dealing with colleagues, might have identified less personally with the changing fortunes of his office. Yet Hugh had been glad to have her at his side, and was genuinely upset at the impact upon her of his resignation. 'Her life was much more dislocated than

mine, by moving from No. 11, with its smooth, labour-saving ways',
he wrote. 'This was one of my worst regrets.'[13] His fall from office
brought them closer than they had been for many years. Suddenly he
needed her, and she was supportive, in a prickly, undemonstrative way.
If it was scarcely a rekindled love affair, letters and Hugh's diary for
their later years show a mutual regard of which outsiders were usually
unaware.

Hugh Dalton and John Carvel never spoke to each other again.
Carvel wrote from the Press Gallery on the day of the resignation,
'My Dear Hugh, I hope you have no feeling that I let you down.' His
son Robert helped compose the letter.[14] The ex-Chancellor scribbled
on the top, 'I did not reply', and passed it to the Select Committee.[15]
After a short voluntary absence Carvel returned to the Lobby, continuing to work for the *Star* until 1955 when illness forced his retirement. Occasionally Tories would slap him on the back and say, 'Good
old John! You did a fine job there!' His son recalls how much he hated
it.[16] Friends felt that the incident had knocked the stuffing out of him,
that he was broken by it and never the same man again.[17] Many years
later Carvel and Dalton were both changing trains at York on their
way to Labour Party Conference at Scarborough. A mutual acquaintance tried to bring them together but both turned away.[18]

Ministers who resign seldom return; ministers who resign because of a
personal error, almost never.[19] Dalton did return, and spent the last
three and a half years of the Labour administration as a senior member
of the Cabinet. Yet it was not the same. 'He was a shadow of what he
had been', considers John Freeman.[20] Most other friends agree. So,
later, did Dalton. 'Well, I had had it, my personal high tide, and I had
gone under', he recalled. 'All the rest, I thought, would now be anti-
climax; cross-currents in the shallows ... And I was not far wrong.'[21]
Before, he had been a history-maker, driven by ambition and a vision
of the future. Afterwards, he was a politician, exerting influence,
living the Westminster life. His appetite for real power – the fierce,
obsessive appetite that distinguishes statesmen and revolutionaries
from the rest – had vanished, never to reappear.

He had gone under. But he had not been disgraced. The general
feeling in the Party was one of sympathy and a sense of loss, the ex-
Chancellor's defects discounted much as one might discount the
defects of a friend.[22] Bishop Auckland Labour Party gave him a
unanimous vote of confidence, the House received him warmly on his
return on 17th November, and when he rose to speak at a meeting of
the P.L.P. two days later he was greeted with cheers.[23] Rumours that
he might retire from politics altogether were quickly dispelled, and it

was widely assumed that his ability and standing would ensure his speedy return to office.[24] He had for so long been a dominating presence that it was hard to imagine a Labour Government without him.

First, however, he had to find himself a role as an ordinary M.P. – a hard task after so many years on the front bench. For a time he was undecided between loyal Government supporter, and candid friend. After a while he decided on candid friend. 'He talks again of launching a great attack on the City', Gaitskell noted after dining with Dalton early in December. 'Alternatively of attacking some Minister. All rather crude. He must have an outlet for his aggression.'[25] The press had been convinced that Dalton was a far less enthusiastic deflationist than Cripps, and that there had existed 'a sultry under-current' in their relations. Now that Cripps was at the Treasury, Dalton was expected to lead a left-wing cave within the P.L.P. 'The left-wing of the Party has for some time believed that Mr. Dalton was more sympathetic to its views than was Sir Stafford Cripps', noted the *Observer*.[26] 'Stafford's socialist roots were shallow', explains Michael Foot, one of Cripps's keenest admirers in pre-war Socialist League days.[27] The new Chancellor was seen as a potential coalitionist, whose repeated national appeals would lead him to ally with Tories and Liberals.[28]

Dalton was careful not to be overtly disloyal, while making clear that he still carried weight. Some believed that he would play the part of Sir Austen Chamberlain to Attlee's Baldwin – remaining aloof from cliques, but ready to intervene in a crisis.[29] He made only two speeches in the House before rejoining the Government. The first, in February, attacked Chuter Ede, causing the Home Secretary to moderate proposals for re-drawing constituency boundaries. As a result, a number of seats were saved for Labour at the next election. The second, in April, was ostensibly in support of Cripps's first Budget. Dalton returned to an old theme, and one which pleased left-wingers: the need for a capital levy. Noting that Cripps's Special Contribution (a tax on investment incomes over and above income tax) was really a small levy on capital, Dalton asked the Chancellor 'to keep the idea of a larger capital levy on his list of "possibles", as I did when I was at the Treasury.'[30]

It was a mild thrust, but it was enough to cause speculation. The Tory Right fulminated and the Labour Left applauded. What was Dalton up to? 'His speech is held in some quarters to place him at the head of those on the Socialist back-benches who complain that realities have rendered the Socialism of Sir Stafford Cripps and others less Socialist than it was', noted the *Daily Telegraph*.[31] One right-wing critic even saw it as a Leadership bid, by 'a man with more guile than gumption'.[32] In fact, Dalton was merely signalling that he could not for long be ignored.

Superficially, he had recovered quickly. By February, he was back in full voice, apparently unabashed. After dealing expertly with hecklers at a by-election meeting in Croydon, he returned by train to Victoria with the Labour candidate, Harold Nicolson. 'I come back with Hugh Dalton who speaks freely (and totally disregarding the others in the compartment) of his own misfortunes', Nicolson noted.[33] Meanwhile he turned to journalism, writing for the *New Statesman* and contributing a series of articles on economic policy to the *Daily Herald*. Spring in Wiltshire with Ruth also helped to restore his spirits. 'The Easter sunshine was wonderful, and the peace I find here – and I hope and think she still does – is very deep', he wrote. But of one thing he still felt certain: ' ... I try to write this quite honestly, *I don't want to go back into the Govt yet*. I feel almost cowardly in saying this. But the sudden relief from responsibility was immense, and it is continuing.' For Ruth's sake, he wanted to return by August, though he thought this unlikely 'unless someone near the top cracks'.[34]

The call came sooner. The Prime Minister had been hinting at a possible job since December. '1947 has been a tragic year for you', Attlee wrote just before the New Year. 'I hope that in 1948 the opportunity will arise of bringing you back in the team, where we need your help.'[35] Dalton's speech in the Budget Debate seemed to stir the Prime Minister into action.[36] In the middle of April, Attlee offered him Civil Aviation. Dalton was not attracted, indicating his preference for a non-departmental post. They settled on the Chancellorship of the Duchy of Lancaster, agreeing that he should come back just before Party Conference at Whitsun. Dalton was pleased, clear in his own mind about the reason: Attlee and Morrison had agreed that it was safer to have him inside than out. 'Otherwise my popularity in the country may keep on growing, and I may say some awkward things.'[37]

By Whitsun, Dalton was still on the backbenches. The delay bothered him little. He enjoyed the Scarborough Conference, even though Shinwell was in the chair, and took pleasure in the company of Roy Jenkins, now an M.P., and Tony Crosland, who hoped to become one. In the poll for the constituency parties section of the N.E.C. Dalton came second after Aneurin Bevan: reflecting his new reputation as a left-winger, and proving that his resignation had not reduced his appeal to local activists.

After Conference, he set out on a walk along the Pennine Way with a group of Labour M.P.s and other friends – including Arthur Blenkinsop, George Chetwynd, Geoffrey de Freitas, Barbara Castle, Fred Willey and the Secretary of the Ramblers' Association, Tom Stephen-

son. He had just accepted the Presidency of the Ramblers, and this
was a characteristic way of performing his duties, advertising himself
and the joys of rambling at the same time. It was also a return to an
old pastime, harking back to pre-First War Fabian schools, Trevelyan
Man Hunts, and Dalton family traditions. He was now in cracking
form. 'Westwards across the sombre moors Arthur Blenkinsop, the
greyhound of the party, set a swinging pace', reported the walkers'
journal, *Out of Doors*. 'Even he was forced into a trot by the long legs
of Hugh Dalton in a neck-and-neck race on the last lap into Dufton.'[38]

The three-day expedition became an annual event, attracting carefully orchestrated publicity. The following year the party moved to the
Lake District, in 1950 to Northumbria and in 1951 to Pembrokeshire
and Brecon Beacon.[39] Members of the group changed little from year
to year – Barbara Castle taking part in every trip. 'National Parks, so
long talked about, must be brought into being', Dalton declared
when the first walk was over. 'The law regarding rights of way must
be clarified and strengthened ... '[40] It was typical of him to inject a
political aim into his pleasures – and equally typical that, within a
short time, the aim should have been achieved.

Refreshed by physical exercise, by Conference popularity and by
the sense of being back in the public eye, Dalton was in a jaunty mood
when he visited No. 10 Downing Street on 26th May for a meeting
with the Prime Minister. He felt less jaunty when he came out. The
interview was a chastening one. Dalton had not adjusted to his new
status. For a dozen years he had treated the Party Leader with barely
concealed contempt, as a temporary incumbent, an 'accidental' office
holder with little real standing in the Movement. Attlee had been
forced to put up with it. Now, the Prime Minister made clear that times
had changed. Dalton was chagrined to find himself cast in the role of
a schoolboy receiving one last chance from the head man:

[Attlee] is not quite so warm as last time, and this, I sense, is partly
due to someone having told him that I have been criticising Stafford.
He says that, with me back in the Govt, 'this might make things
difficult'. I say that it is completely untrue. As he will recall, when I
was in the Govt SC and I were steadily in agreement, often against
others. He says he remembers this. I say that nothing has changed
in my attitude since then. The enemy press, of course, have been
persistently trying to make trouble between SC and me, but any
statement that I have been criticising SC is quite untrue. Where does
it come from? He says it has been reaching him both through
Parliamentary and Party channels. I say it is [a] bloody lie and I
should like to know who told him. But he won't be drawn further.

Who had sneaked? Dalton suspected Morrison or Bevin, imagining that they wanted to keep him out of the Inner Circle. He was badly shaken, and his new, subservient, position was established. Over the next few days he became extremely concerned lest the Prime Minister should exclude him altogether.[41]

But the Prime Minister had been admonishing, not punishing. On 1st June Dalton returned to the Cabinet as Chancellor of the Duchy. He did not take on the German responsibilities of his predecessor, Lord Pakenham; instead it was decided that he would help the Cabinet in a general way and 'be available to undertake any special duties which may be allotted to him from time to time by the P.M.'[42] Back-benchers were pleased. Whitehall, on the other hand, was nervous. On the day of Dalton's appointment, Sir Norman Brook, the Cabinet Secretary, advised the Prime Minister against putting the newly-returned minister on many Standing Committees. 'If, however, you should think it necessary, or he should himself ask, that he should have some committee work', wrote Brook, 'you will want to avoid putting him on committees concerned with economic co-ordination.'[43]

Dalton's own view that Attlee had brought him back in because of the danger of leaving him outside was widely shared. 'At the Labour Party's Scarborough Conference, it was clear that endless difficulties would arise between the National Executive and the Cabinet if Dalton was not a member of both', wrote Richard Crossman. 'Whatever he said was interpreted as a criticism of the Government or a "split" between Transport House and 10 Downing Street.'[44] Right-wing newspapers agreed, though by saying that Dalton was still a powerful figure in the Labour Party they were also implicitly criticising the Government for not resisting his influence. Dalton was not displeased. 'I am still formidably popular', he wrote, meaning within the Labour Party, 'and this has been encouraged by the Tory hate!'[45] *Tribune* wrote of Dalton's ability and abiding loyalty to the Movement. 'Praise from such a sinister quarter as *Tribune*', it added, 'will no doubt be mysteriously interpreted in the Tory press, which has been busy for the past few months finding Hugh Dalton's hand at work in every plot, manoeuvre and intrigue which they have concocted in their own offices.'[46]

Dalton was given fifth place in the Cabinet's official pecking order, after Attlee, Bevin, Morrison and Cripps. However the actual importance of the Chancellorship of the Duchy, in itself virtually a sinecure,[47] depended on responsibilities defined by the Prime Minister. Attlee ignored Brook's advice about keeping Dalton away from economic co-ordination, and placed him on the Economic Policy, Lord President's, Future Legislation and Civil Aviation Committees of the Cabinet. Yet his duties remained limited and vague, and there were signs of his reduced importance. When he asked for Thomas Padmore, who had briefly served him as principal private secretary at the Treasury in 1945, to take the same post at the Duchy, Padmore turned down the offer. He did not like Dalton and the post seemed a dud one.[48]

At first people continued to speak of Dalton as one of the Big Five, imagining that his old influence would be restored. This soon ceased. The Big Five became the Big Four. As chairman of the committee of all ministers in charge of Production Departments, Cripps exercised a vast power. In the new structure Attlee, Bevin, Cripps and Morrison divided up the broad direction of policy at home and abroad between them. Describing the Government later the same year, Francis Williams placed Dalton in a group of four ministers with co-ordinating functions of 'an important but less major character' than those of Bevin, Cripps and Morrison. Others in the same category as Dalton were A. V. Alexander (Defence), Viscount Addison (Lord Privy Seal), and Chuter Ede (Home Secretary).[49]

There was some initial speculation that Dalton might fulfil the ambition of a life-time by succeeding Bevin at the Foreign Office.[50] Dalton himself clung to this hope. In September he had his first private meeting with Cripps since his resignation. It was a polite but strained conversation. Once again, Dalton was made to realise his drop in status. Cripps's old enthusiasm for changes at the top had gone. 'He still thought EB should be PM, but EB still said no', Dalton noted. ' ... SC said HM couldn't lead either the Cab., or the Party or the country. So there we left it!'[51] They did not return to the subject. Dalton had never been an initiator, and he was no longer important enough to have value as a front-rank ally.

Meanwhile, Cripps became the toast of the financial world. The balance of payments problem eased and inflationary pressure became less severe than expected. Marshall Aid, Washington's belated response to the onset of the Cold War, reduced the burden of European indebtedness. Cripps, evidently on top of his job, brimming with confidence and worshipped by his advisers, took credit for improvements in the domestic economy that owed much to the policies of Dalton and Bevin and to developments beyond the control of any politician. Cripps's refusal to make concessions to Labour Party sentiment was applauded, and so was his quick grasp of new economic techniques. Morals were drawn and contrasts made between the iron discipline of the new era, which was apparently succeeding, and the alleged willingness of the deposed Chancellor to pander to the masses.

Yet Dalton felt no jealousy of Cripps – just a continuing relief at not being in his shoes. Cripps's lucidity and mastery of detail even seemed to justify Dalton's withdrawal on patriotic grounds: if he had not gone, Hugh and Ruth reasoned, co-ordination of the Treasury and the Planning Machine could not have been achieved. 'But we agree that this [is] only possible', Hugh noted, ' ... because SC is so brilliantly on top of his form.'[52]

Though Dalton's public reputation was soon over-shadowed by that of his successor, his standing within the Labour Party, where he was still identified with left-wing causes, remained high, aided by the 'Tory hate'. As a member of a three-man team set up to prepare Labour's election programme, he was believed to be the keenest on extending nationalisation.[53] In November, perhaps to discourage him from causing trouble, Attlee made him head of the British delegation to the Committee of Western European Powers, a new body charged with examining ways to increase European unity. At last, Dalton's rehabilitation seemed complete. Though not as powerful as before, he was an important minister with a key job involving aspects of foreign policy that had always fascinated him, far from the world of finance. Then a new storm broke.

It was a scandal in the French sense: a flurry of accusations and rumours that reflected a social malaise. Early in the autumn, allegations made within the Board of Trade (and passed to the new President, Harold Wilson) that ministers and other public servants had been taking bribes led the Prime Minister to set up a Tribunal of Inquiry under Mr. Justice Lynskey. The Attorney-General, Sir Hartley Shawcross, presented the case and examined witnesses. The hearings lasted five weeks and aroused enormous public interest. 1948 was the year of the publication of *Nineteen Eighty-Four*; like Orwell's novel, the investigation captured a mood of restless frustration after three post-war years of rationing, unobtainable luxuries, bureaucracy everywhere, and no end in sight. Controls and shortages were justified by the Government on grounds of fairness. The suggestion that rules were being bent to ease the lives of the politicians and officials who were responsible for enforcing them stirred the embers of popular resentment.

The central character at the Lynskey hearings was a Polish-born confidence trickster known as Sydney Stanley, who had made money by representing himself as a friend of the powerful. Little actual corruption was proved. As a result of Stanley's evidence John Belcher, a junior minister at the Board of Trade, was forced out of public life; and George Gibson, a trade union director of the Bank of England, was mildly rebuked. Stanley himself was condemned as a liar – but not before his wild fabrications at the Tribunal, where he enjoyed legal immunity, had given the public an impression of seedy self-advancement in official circles.[54]

Serious allegations were made against a number of public servants apart from Belcher and Gibson, including several members of the Labour Government. The most prominent, and hence the one subjected to the fiercest publicity, was Dalton.

Dalton's name first cropped up on 6th December. In reply to a question, Stanley declared that the previous spring a possibility had arisen that Dalton might become a director of Great Universal Stores (G.U.S.), but that the chairman, Isaac Wolfson, had vetoed the appointment. 'You're not really saying that Mr. Dalton sought a directorship for £10,000?' asked Shawcross. 'I took [Dalton] up there and he left it to me', the witness replied. 'You can ask him, you can put him in the witness box.'[55] Stanley recalled having first met Dalton at a Grosvenor House dinner in honour of George Gibson and having said: 'Here, Dalton, I think I have a proposition for you. You are out of the Government now. I may be in a position to recommend you to one of my friends to join one of his boards.' According to Stanley, Dalton had later gone to his flat, and the two of them had visited G.U.S. together.

None of this, in itself, was very incriminating. What put Stanley's remarks about Dalton in a different light from his unsubstantiated stories about other ministers, and helped to fuel rumours, was a piece of documentary evidence. Stanley was able to produce a typed letter which read: 'Dear Stan, I am afraid I am engaged for the following evening. I shall not be able to see you.'[56] It was signed by a secretary and ended: 'pp. Hugh Dalton'. Stanley made no suggestion of bribery and contradicted himself by first saying that Wolfson offered a directorship and then that he refused to give one. However the 'Dear Stan' opening suggested an intimacy between a former Chancellor of the Exchequer and a shady financial operator which was surprising, to say the least.

Dalton had been told in October that his name might be mentioned. Coming so soon after his return to the Government, few pieces of news could have been less welcome. Determined to answer the accusation – such as it was – in full, he informed the Attorney-General that he wanted to give evidence on his own behalf. In vain, Shawcross tried to dissuade him, pointing out that nobody believed Stanley, and that to go into the witness-box would lend credence to what had been said.[57] Dalton rejected the advice and, at his own request, appeared before the Tribunal on 14th December.

Dalton's version of events agreed with Stanley's on some points.

He admitted meeting Stanley at the Grosvenor House dinner, being offered a G.U.S. directorship, and later going to Stanley's flat, where Stanley had offered a substantial fee in return for one attendance a month. He claimed, however, to have turned down the offer – agreeing to see Wolfson next day (16th April) solely on the grounds of a mutual interest in Development Areas. Dalton added that he had by now decided that Stanley was 'a contact man of low repute, and I wished to have nothing more to do with him'. The 'Dear Stan' form of address, he insisted, was simply a typing error, perhaps a result of dropping his voice in dictation.[58] Though the Tribunal accepted Dalton's account, its report refrained from comment on this final explanation, and Shawcross privately found it unconvincing.[59] Afterwards, there were many who felt that Dalton had done himself no good by appearing; and that, while he had done nothing either illegal or improper, he had taken some foolish risks.

When the Tribunal ended its hearings, there were jokes at the expense of ministers: 'All this would never have happened had Clem Attlee been alive', and 'Anyway we have got the best Government that money can buy.'[60] But Dalton had no cause for amusement. The same day it was announced that 500 letters offering information, stimulated by publicity surrounding the inquiry, were to be investigated by the Fraud Squad. At least one of these concerned Dalton's constituency. While Dalton was giving evidence to the Tribunal, two Scotland Yard detectives had already started an inquiry, of which the press were kept closely informed, into allegations concerning the issue of building licences in the Bishop Auckland and South West Durham areas.

The new allegations had been sent by the local Conservative Party to Lord Woolton who had passed them on to the Attorney-General, who, in turn, ordered an inquiry.[61] Dalton believed that the original source was the Tory agent in Bishop Auckland, as part of a dirty tricks campaign to boost the fortunes of the young Tory candidate, Lord Lambton.[62] Attention concentrated on a family of German Jewish refugee manufacturers, Leo Lewin and his two sons Ken and Ernest, whose West Auckland Clothing Company, now employing 1300 people, had been helped by Dalton. The investigation concerned alleged irregularities in the granting of licences for extensive alterations to the Lewins' large country house, the Grove, at Hamsterley, Co. Durham,[63] where Dalton had sometimes stayed.

The police were thorough. Local people were asked whether they knew Dalton, how often they saw him and for what purpose, and whether they had given him presents. Employees of the West Auckland Clothing Company and the Northern Clothing Company at

Shildon were asked whether they had ever given him, or cut for him, suits of clothes.[64] Nothing came of these investigations, and the Attorney-General was able to respond firmly to a Tory Question on the subject.[65] But the matter did not end there.

Early in the New Year, a right-wing journal called *The Review of World Affairs* claimed that a police dossier on a well-known Labour politician had given Downing Street a 'very miserable Christmas'. The 'editorial adviser' of this journal was Victor Raikes, the Tory M.P. whose Parliamentary Question about the Budget leak had led to Dalton's resignation. Dalton's attention was drawn to the report by Ken Lewin, who angrily protested that it was 'the most malicious and most slanderous article I have yet read in connection with this disgusting story'.[66] Dalton did not respond until the debate on the Tribunal Report on 3rd February.[67] In the course of the debate, in a phrase heavy with innuendo, Raikes described the Report as a 'salutary warning' to public men. Provoked beyond endurance, Dalton challenged him to comment on the offending passage in his magazine. Raikes refused to be drawn.[68]

Raikes also refused to comment on a story that, in addition to police inquiries, somebody (presumably somebody prepared to make a substantial financial investment in discrediting Dalton) had engaged a private detective to carry out independent investigations. This report was confirmed a couple of days later by the *Daily Mirror*, which identified a Mr. Mack, from Newcastle, as the source of the original letter which the police had followed up. The letter had been sent to Lord Woolton 'on authority'. Whose authority? The Tory agent in Bishop Auckland insisted that local Conservatives had nothing to do with 'any dirty matters like that'.[69]

Harrassed by police, press and private agents, Dalton hurried up to Bishop Auckland to organise unanimous confidence motions, and to try to contain gossip that showed no signs of abating.[70] 'I am well aware that there have been for some time past whispering campaigns designed to discredit and to damage both myself and the Labour Party', he told reporters. 'I do not like this kind of thing. It is not English and it is not straightforward.'[71] Meanwhile an ugly, tell-tale, boil appeared on his left cheek.[72]

At a stage-managed meeting in Bishop Auckland on 11th February, he rounded on his persecutors. Why had the police called on local Conservatives, he demanded, when they never visited the Labour Party office? If Lord Woolton had received an anonymous letter, what had he done with it? Dalton was at his melodramatic worst. When he asked whether the audience included any Tory representatives, or a private detective from Newcastle, there was a long, un-

40 The Chancellor of the Exchequer leaves No. 11 Downing Street for the House of Commons on 12th November 1947. Minutes later, he leaked the Budget. Half-hidden in the doorway: Douglas Jay, his P.P.S.

41 Nothing to hide: talking to the press in 1948.

VICKY'S NATIONAL GALLERY
(CLEANED PICTURE DEPT)

VICKY
AFTER
FRANS HALS

"THE LAUGHING CAVALIER" IS BACK

42 Return to the Cabinet, June 1948.

43 N.E.C. meeting in 1949. Left to right: Dalton, Foot, Morrison, Attlee, Morgan Phillips (Labour Party General Secretary), Jim Griffiths.

44 Playing ball with Herbert, Isle of Wight, 1949.

45 (*left*) Nye's dog. Harold Wilson at Margate for the Party Conference, October 1950

46 (*below*) Opening Shildon Industrial Estate, near Bishop Auckland, April 1949.

47 (*right*) 'The wild is calling
… let us go.' Walking up
Brecon Beacons in rain, mist
and wind, with Arthur
Blenkinsop and Barbara
Castle, May 1951.

48 (*below*) Dalton and Attlee
confer, 1951.

49 Fabian School at Beatrice Webb House, Easter 1953. Left to right, Jim Callaghan, Bill Rodgers, Tony Crosland, Hugh Dalton, Hilary Crosland and Audrey Callaghan.

50 Denis Healey, Harold Wilson and Hugh Gaitskell in Dreamland, Margate, October 1955.

51 Relaxing at the Davenports', mid 1950s. Left to right, Tony
Crosland, Nicholas Davenport, Dobs Little (wife of economist Ian
Little), Hugh Dalton.

52 In the study at West Leaze.

53 In the garden at West Leaze, August 1961.

54 Ruth (centre) among dignitaries. An opening ceremony in Lancashire, April 1963.

comfortable pause while he made a great play of waiting for somebody to stand up. If all this was intended to reduce press interest it was misjudged. The popular papers revelled in the spectacle of the wounded minister, like a bear in a ring, lungeing clumsily at the Tory dogs snapping at his heels. ' "Whispering led to Yard probe" – SAYS MINISTER', one headline announced next day.[73] 'Dalton over-reacted', says Lord Lambton (prospective Tory candidate for Bishop Auckland at the time). 'Beneath the surface, he was a tumult of nerves.'[74]

In March 1949, Dalton was still pursuing Lord Woolton on the subject of the private detective (whose employer was never established). On the other side, insinuations and snide comments continued to be made at Dalton's expense. Dalton, as Francis Williams had recently written, was bitterly disliked by many Tories who 'consistently accuse him of self-interest in his socialism'.[75] The Lynskey and post-Lynskey smears provided perfect ammunition, and could be linked with Labour's past economic and financial policies. When one Tory M.P. used parliamentary privilege to remark that 'Public opinion sees something sinister in association with Mr. Dalton, and members are relieved to know he no longer has the influence he used to have', Labour M.P.s rushed to Dalton's defence, condemning the Opposition campaign as scurrilous, scandalous and entirely unfair.[76] But some of the mud stuck.

Was there any substance to the allegations? The answer is virtually none. Nevertheless Dalton probably took more interest in Stanley's remarks than he was prepared to admit. At the Tribunal, Dalton claimed to have brushed aside Stanley's offer of a directorship saying that it was 'not in my line'.[77] His own record, however, shows that he was seriously tempted and only failed to take the matter further because he was about to rejoin the Government. One thing which never came out at the Tribunal was that Stanley's offer, on 15th April, was made immediately after Attlee had half-promised Dalton a post in the Cabinet.[78] Dalton had gone straight from the Prime Minister's office in Downing Street to Stanley's flat at Aldford House, Paul Lane. Here, the ex-Chancellor had listened carefully to Stanley's proposition.

'They would pay me a large "fee" ([Stanley] suggests £6,000 a year to begin with)', Dalton noted, 'and expect very little of my time, knowing how busy I am. One or two meetings a month.' If Dalton went back into the Government, Stanley indicated, he would leave the Board of Directors, but return if he left office again. While on the Board, he might like to make important trips on behalf of the firm.

Dalton wrote that it was 'all very amusingly timed!', presumably a reference to his interview with Attlee earlier the same day. He concluded: 'I find it difficult to evaluate this little man, but it is clearly an approach not to be too rudely repelled.'

At the Tribunal, Dalton maintained that his only reason for lunching with Wolfson next day (16th April) was because of a shared interest in Development Areas. Dalton's diary, however, tells a slightly different story:

No definite proposal is made to me, but a hint is made. W[olfson] would so like me to dine with him; he is in Manchester next week. S[tanley] is clearly to discuss details tentatively. S says when we are alone, (on two previous occasions), that he is paying Arthur Greenwood's hotel bill at Brighton, unknown to the latter, and is arranging to put him on one of his Boards. (It will be a test of his influence whether he does).[79]

And that was all. As Dalton's return to the Government became more certain, so his interest in the proposed directorship waned.

Of course there would have been nothing illegitimate about taking a substantial salary in return for adding respectability to a business organisation's notepaper. Tory politicians did it all the time. However Dalton was a socialist, known for his attacks on easy-money capitalists. To have linked himself to a firm in such a way would have encouraged entirely justified charges of hypocrisy. It would also have been out of character: financial greed was not, in general, one of Dalton's vices. At the same time we should keep it in proportion. If Dalton briefly allowed himself to be tempted by the prospect of rich rewards for prostituting his reputation (and in 1948 £6,000, for minimal effort, was a very large sum indeed), the important point is that he resisted the temptation.

To some extent, Dalton had himself to blame for the 'Dear Stan' furore. By contrast, the building licences allegations were scurrilous inventions that reflected his energy as a local M.P., and the envy, malice and opportunism of his opponents. Since he was first elected as Member for Bishop Auckland, Dalton had done everything in his power to bring investment and jobs to his constituents. In addition to policy-making on the N.E.C. and major legislation as a minister, he had encouraged individual entrepreneurs to set up factories on local trading estates, giving what further help he could once local employment had been created.

Favours to some members of the business community were, however, easily misinterpreted and resented by others – especially those who felt the pressure of outside competition. As we have seen, Dalton enjoyed his reputation as a string-puller. False rumours of backhanders and financial corruption were a result. According to one story, Dalton had used his wartime powers as President of the Board of Trade to benefit Courtaulds, which had factories in the locality, because he himself owned shares in the firm. According to another, Bishop Auckland factories fitted him out with suits of clothes free.

An ugly element of anti-semitism in many of the rumours was encouraged by the Lynskey hearings. Stanley was Jewish, and so were many of his business associates. Summing up at the Tribunal, Shawcross warned against the danger of gossip which might stir up racial animosities.[80] Such gossip was an undoubted influence in Bishop Auckland. Questioned by the police about Dalton, a local Board of Trade official replied that the main interest of the M.P. had been to get work back to the area. He added that there had been racial bitterness towards some of the newcomers. 'Folk complained from time to time about "B" Jews being able to get anything', he reported, ' – those factories on the Estate before the war were tenanted by ex-German Jews.'[81]

One such tenant was Leo Lewin, focus of the accusation about building licences. Local jealousy and suspicion of Lewin and his family expressed itself in the rumour that Dalton, while a minister, had evaded Government regulations to help a wealthy friend. In fact, the evidence shows that Dalton behaved with strict propriety.

After making one application for a licence for £3,000 worth of repairs to his house, Lewin had applied for a supplementary building licence for electrical work and decoration that would cost an additional £1,750. Impatient about delays, he had asked Will Davis, the local Labour Party Secretary, to seek Dalton's help. Davis passed on the message;[82] and Dalton – who was still Chancellor of the Exchequer – had conscientiously directed a complaint from a constituent to the appropriate minister. Nevertheless the witch-hunt atmosphere generated by the Lynskey hearings seriously damaged Dalton's image locally, and official denials failed to eliminate a belief that, in a county where petty political graft was a way of life, the M.P. for Bishop Auckland had been part of the system. Early in December, Dalton predicted that the police investigation would be the principal topic 'in every public house and workmen's club at Christmas and the New Year throughout the area'.[83] The rumours actually continued for much longer, and Dalton remained deeply concerned lest the repercussions might lose him the seat.[84]

What was the effect nationally? At a time when he was still on probation, Dalton's fragile reputation suffered a severe knock. Carelessness seemed to have become a dangerous habit: Dalton's description of his casual first encounter with Stanley outside Grosvenor

House contained a disturbing echo of the Carvel incident. 'The whole conversation in the street only lasted a few minutes', Dalton told the Tribunal.[85] It was almost a re-wording of his comment to the Select Committee on the Budget Disclosures. Though there was no link between the Budget leak, the 'Dear Stan' letter and the building licences investigation, an association between them in the public mind was inevitable. There may also have been an impact on Labour Party opinion. Dalton's post-resignation increase in popularity was not maintained in 1949, and at the beginning of June there was speculation that he might be pushed off the N.E.C. altogether.[86] In fact he held his seat, though only in fifth place, the start of a downward slide. Two years later Dalton noted that he had 'gained from resignation, and my marginal contact with the Lynskey Tribunal, a certain reputation for unreliability, and talking too freely'.[87]

The Lynskey inquiry also took a physical and emotional toll. 'It has been a wearisome end to the year with this bloody Tribunal', Dalton wrote after Christmas 1948. For six gruelling months, October to March, the allegations and investigations were a serious anxiety. At the end of it all, when the rumours seemed at last to be subsiding, Dalton sought advice about his health. 'I am often conscious – though not of pain – of the existence of my heart and that I have been feeling a bit weary lately', he recorded, 'even though having no Department.' A specialist revealed an irregular heartbeat. Dalton's doctor put it down to 'wear and tear following a period of heavy strain and severe worry'. He recommended drug treatment and ten days in a nursing home. Nevertheless Dalton found the report disquieting. He was 61. 'It casts shades of age upon me', he wrote. 'I don't feel I could run a Dept effectively now!'[88] The Prime Minister seemed to agree. At the end of November Morrison, consulted about Cabinet changes, had suggested Dalton as Minister of Health.[89] For the time being, Attlee preferred to keep him where he was.

XXXI

Duchy

All the same, the Prime Minister had given him an important job. As leader of the British negotiating team charged with examining proposals for European unity, and then of the British delegation to the Council of Europe, he was able to play a major part in shaping post-war European institutions. He was also one of the first Labour leaders to view such institutions cautiously.

In April 1948 the European beneficiaries of Marshall Aid signed the Convention for European Economic Co-operation with the ultimate aim of forming a large free trade area. The original purpose had been largely economic, but worsening East–West relations added a defensive aspect, reinforcing the Treaty of Brussels (the precursor of NATO) which had been signed by Britain, France and the Benelux countries a few weeks earlier.[1] Meanwhile an independent political movement had gained strength. In December 1947 a variety of groups and organisations had formed an International Committee of Movements for European Unity, which in turn organised a Congress of Europe at The Hague in May 1948. The Congress (of which Winston Churchill was President of Honour) declared its desire for 'a united Europe' expressing 'a common European opinion' on the problems of the day.

In October the Consultative Council of the Brussels Treaty decided to convene a five-power 'Committee for the study of European unity'. This met in Paris on 26th November 1948, ten days before Dalton's name was first mentioned in the Lynskey hearings. Apart from Dalton the six-man British team included Gladwyn (who had become Sir Gladwyn) Jebb, Lord Inverchapel and Sir Edward Bridges. Dalton was the only minister in any of the delegations. The Committee's first session lasted until just before Christmas, the British team making its headquarters at the Hotel Plaza Athénée. Despite his worries,

Dalton enjoyed the sense of being back in the swim. It was a relief to escape, if only briefly, from incestuous Westminster politics, and he revelled in the bustle and convivialities of international diplomacy. 'Inverchapel and Jebb, though belonging to widely separated age-groups, had for some time been two of my favourite diplomats', he recalled.[2]

Before the Committee was a Franco-Belgian proposal for a parliamentary European Assembly. The British countered with a proposal for a non-parliamentary consultative organ, with strictly defined terms of reference. Over Christmas, Dalton reported to Cabinet colleagues. When the British delegation returned to Paris in January, he presented a compromise proposal for a Council of Europe consisting of a committee of ministers and a conference of delegates appointed by Governments. The compromise, however, did not meet the objections of the French, who continued to demand that delegates be appointed by parliaments, that ministers be excluded from the conference, and that delegates should vote individually, not en bloc.

The difference reflected a fundamental divergence of view between the two Governments about aims. What was 'European unity', and what was it intended to achieve? Dalton himself was equivocal, greeting French aspirations with scepticism. For this reason, Churchill had strongly opposed his leadership, arguing that he only wanted 'socialist' collaboration, and that he had tried to wreck the Hague Congress.[3] Dalton, however, was not out of step with Government colleagues; as one newspaper put it, he had been chosen 'to state the British case of "go slow"'.[4] 'E.B. and I have been steadily in agreement on W[estern] U[nion] policy', Dalton noted before negotiations began, 'and I anticipate no difficulty in maintaining this agreement during the Paris talks.'[5]

The British attitude was based on what the Labour Party (guided by Dalton as Chairman of the N.E.C. International Policy Committee) called the 'functional' approach, which meant co-operation and consultation, but little else. Above all, the Labour Cabinet was opposed to federalism. Dalton was cautious about multiplying international agencies, believing that Britain should not merge its identity in that of Europe, 'if this means cutting ourselves off from our kinsmen in Australia, New Zealand, etc.' A European Assembly, in Dalton's view, should not be allowed to interfere with British social services or plunder British gold reserves. Such an Assembly as the French advocated would have made 'a wonderful platform for Churchill on the one hand and the Communists on the other'.[6] Always a passionate internationalist, Dalton remained a very sober European. Nevertheless, once the main features of an Assembly had been decided in principle, he was more flexible than Bevin on its proposed powers.[7]

The negotiations led eventually to the Statute of the Council of Europe, signed in London by ten foreign ministers on 5th May – a month after the end of the talks that set up NATO. The French abandoned the parliamentary appointment of delegations; the British accepted that delegates could vote individually. All accepted Dalton's proposal (originally made to Bevin by Jebb) that the new Assembly should be established in Strasbourg as a symbol of Franco-German amity. The Statute established a Committee of Ministers to provide intergovernmental co-operation, and a Consultative Assembly, consisting of members of parliament acting in an individual capacity, as 'a means through which the aspirations of the European peoples may be formulated and expressed, the governments thus being kept continually in touch with European public opinion.'[8] The Council of Europe was much less powerful than the French had hoped (largely because of the British insistence on the non-supranational principle)[9] and the ministerial committee had little importance in practice. The Assembly, on the other hand, became an influential and innovative body.[10]

If Dalton agreed with Cabinet colleagues on the main features of the Council, he had already taken a personal stand on one aspect of proposed European 'unity'. This concerned the position of Germany in the new Europe.

The Council of Europe was intended as part of a broad strategy to build up the Western democracies against what many believed was a Soviet ambition to dominate the whole continent. As such, it was warmly applauded by most Conservatives. Feelings on the Left were more mixed. The setting up of the new Council brought to the surface a long-standing division in the Labour Party between those who saw the Soviet Union as a socialist country to be copied and befriended, and those who saw it as a political and military threat. While the first, mainly left-wing, group looked for a 'Third Force' in world alignments, independent of both power blocs, the second was concerned to strengthen western defences – which came to mean the acceptance of a re-armed Germany.

Despite his involvement in the Paris talks, Dalton did not align himself fully with either group. Before the war he had taken an interest in Soviet planning and had sought an alliance with Russia; but he had no illusions about Communism as a political system and he was seriously concerned about the need for strong defences. On the other hand, he was worried about too heavy a dependence on the United

States. More important, he retained a deep fear of German revanchism and bitterly opposed German rearmament which, he believed, might lead directly to a Third World War. 'We'll gouge out their eyes', Dalton sang to Nicholas Davenport on the way to a Strasbourg function at which Germans were to be present. 'We'll stamp on their bellies, We'll tear out their livers!'[11] The hymn of hate was only half in jest. An unreformed Vansittartist, Dalton saw Germany as inherently aggressive and regarded attempts to rehabilitate the German people as a betrayal. He therefore stood midway between the 'Third Force' left-wingers and the pro-American Atlanticists. Politically, it was to become a lonely and precarious position.

Now he threw his full weight against bringing Germany back into the Western fold. At Cabinet just before Christmas, Cripps posed the problem: the Government must make up its mind whether Germany was still a danger, or a potential ally in building up Western Europe. Dalton, caught in a thunderous mood induced by press reports of police investigations in Bishop Auckland, spoke sharply of the German threat which, he declared, was greater than the Russian. 'We should *aim*, I said, at a strong Atlantic Pact – with strong US and Canadian contributions, a strong UK, a strong France, a strong Benelux and a weak Germany.'[12] There were angry reactions from colleagues. No immediate association was envisaged between the Council of Europe and West Germany, which did not yet have a government. Although Italy, Norway, Sweden, Denmark, Iceland, Eire, Greece and Turkey were invited to join the Council, Germany was not. But the problem, and the division of opinion, remained – crystallising later.

After his success in the negotiations, Dalton was tipped to lead the Labour delegation to the first meeting of the new Assembly in August.[13] It was a sign of his reduced standing that he was passed over. Morrison was appointed leader, with Dalton as deputy. Dalton felt the slight keenly. 'I had often been one of the Labour Party representatives at such conferences, but I doubt if Morrison had ever attended one of any importance before,' Dalton later complained. 'He showed no aptitude at all for handling foreigners, or for showing conventional civilities or performing simple functions such as fall to all political leaders.'[14] After the first fortnight in Strasbourg, Morrison left for a recuperative holiday in the South of France, telling the press that as Deputy Prime Minister he had a duty to the British people to take care of his health. Dalton replaced him and when Churchill, leading the Conservative delegation, also left, Harold Macmillan took over at the head of the Tories.

Morrison had quarrelled with Churchill. Dalton and Macmillan, two radical Etonian intellectuals, were on the best of terms and worked closely together. Macmillan recalled that in the general economic debate, Dalton spoke extraordinarily well.[15] At a press conference at the end of the session, Dalton declared that the Assembly 'had shown its collective sense of responsibility by refusing to go too deeply into embarrassing discussion of Germany and the devaluation of currency'. He also stressed that 'We could not approve any policy that took us further away from the Commonwealth'.[16] Later he wrote: 'In Europe, Bevin and Cripps and I were all definitely anti-Federal. Morrison was a bit woolly and wobbly.'[17] Thus were the foundations of Labour's anti-Europeanism laid.

In addition to the formal business of the Assembly, Dalton was able to enjoy the company of young Labour politicians within the British team. It was a talented group, including Maurice Edelman, Aidan Crawley, Fred Lee, Margaret Herbison and James Callaghan, with Denis Healey (the Labour Party International Secretary) providing Transport House backing. Edelman, a journalist, writer and *bon viveur*, was one of Dalton's favourite off-duty companions. 'Ah, Mr. Edelman!' Dalton called to him after a wearisome session. 'Mr. Edelman is rich. Let's have champagne!' When bottles and glasses were brought to the party of British delegates and reporters, Dalton declared: 'Now I'll show how we put up our feet in the House of Commons.' Up went his feet. Down came table, glasses, and Edelman's champagne on to the floor.[18]

Dalton also indulged one of his favourite pastimes: spotting winners among the younger generation. Afterwards he wrote careful reports for Attlee, like a tutor assessing the performance of boys in class. Callaghan, Dalton observed, was a very capable and self-confident young man, easy to handle and co-operative, and had learnt a great deal in a short time; but he had been greatly outdistanced within the Labour team by Crawley, Herbison and Healey. What of Morrison? Herbert, Dalton informed the Prime Minister, choosing his words carefully, had found the first stages rather worrying. 'I hope he ceased to worry about them when he got away to the South of France.'[19]

Dalton was not solely concerned with European and foreign policy questions. Despite Opposition and Whitehall hopes that he would be kept away from economics and finance, his membership of several Cabinet Committees – in particular the Economic Policy Committee, responsible for the Government's planning – gave him a bigger role in the broad strategy of the administration than the public were aware of at the time. Indeed, during the summer and autumn of 1949 his influence on key decisions affecting financial policy was greater than that of any other senior minister outside the Big Four.

In June 1949, Sir Stafford Cripps warned Cabinet colleagues of the danger that all resources would be exhausted within a year, causing a collapse of sterling. Attlee drew the analogy that was always in the minds of older leaders: '1931 over again'. For Dalton the parallel was more recent. 'It reminds me awfully of 1947', he said.[20] In many ways it was a re-run, with the same, desperate and insoluble shortage of dollars. There was another kind of parallel too. As in 1947 the immense physical and psychological burdens of the Chancellorship were too much for one man to bear. With Cripps's health collapsing under the strain, control of financial and economic policy shifted towards the ministers dubbed by Dalton 'the young economists': Hugh Gaitskell, Douglas Jay and Harold Wilson. None of these three men ranked high in the Party or the Government. Hence Dalton, the only senior minister apart from Cripps who understood economic questions, became a channel for the young economists when they wanted a point made at top level.

In one respect, 1949 was not like 1947. In 1947, Cripps and Dalton had agreed, against the majority of colleagues, on the necessity for strong measures to stop the dollar drain. While pushing himself forward, Cripps had supported Dalton in Cabinet. Rumours that Cripps and Dalton had been in conflict, Cripps demanding fiercer cuts than Dalton was prepared to contemplate, were untrue. Now, disagreement between the two ministers had become real. As the 1949 crisis deepened and Cripps yielded to pressures to cut back still further on public expenditure, Dalton argued that the Chancellor's domestic proposals were unnecessarily and harmfully draconian, reflecting the political prejudices of advisers, which were in opposition to the values of socialists and the Labour Party. The Budget, Dalton insisted, was not a factor in current economic troubles. In accepting the conventional view that Britain was overtaxed, the Chancellor was merely echoing the right-wing *Economist*. The Chancellor's apparent inclination to submit to City pressures and tighten monetary policy was to be deplored; so was his proposal to cut food subsidies by £100 million. 'This would cause the gravest political trouble in the Parliamentary Labour Party', Dalton urged, ' – and perhaps within the Government itself – and would completely dishearten our followers in the country.'

Dalton's pressure was effective. Denouncing the whole of Cripps's stringent recovery package, due to be presented to the House in July, as 'a conspiracy of Bridges, Plowden, Eady and the Bank' (Sir Edwin Plowden was head of the planning staff), Dalton did his best to isolate Cripps within the Cabinet. He succeeded. The Chancellor was forced to retreat. Instead of removing subsidies, Cripps announced measures to cut dollar imports.

On the controversial subject of devaluation, Dalton changed his mind. At first, he backed the Chancellor. 'Devaluation of sterling is no solution, nor even part of a solution of our present troubles', he told the Economic Policy Committee at the beginning of July. 'I welcomed S.C.'s clear line on this.'[21] But his opinion shifted crucially during the next few weeks, ahead of most colleagues, and he was able to play a decisive part in forcing the issue in the autumn.

Dalton's most important contribution to the devaluation debate occurred, paradoxically, before either he or the young economists had come round to the need for devaluation. Early in July Dalton persuaded the Chancellor to bring Douglas Jay, Economic Secretary at the Treasury, into relevant talks with American and Commonwealth finance ministers, as a political counterweight to official advice.[22] This led, in turn, to Gaitskell's involvement in key discussions as well.[23] Participation in talks at the highest level had a vital effect in shaping the ideas of the two young ministers during the weeks that followed, and gave them an influence which they would not otherwise have obtained.

On 19th July the Chancellor of the Exchequer – still firmly opposed to devaluation – left England for Zurich to receive health treatment. In his absence, Treasury policy was placed by the Prime Minister in the hands of Gaitskell, Wilson and Jay. By now Gaitskell and Jay, in contrast to Cripps, had been won over by the argument that devaluation was necessary in order to boost reserves.[24] They set about convincing Dalton. Both men knew Dalton closely as a friend, and both had worked with him as civil service advisers during the war. Confronted with the two young ministers on such an urgent mission, Dalton listened carefully, said he would think the matter over, did so, and came round to their point of view. 'We ... saw H.D. and persuaded him without difficulty', Gaitskell noted on 3rd August.[25]

With Dalton converted to devaluation, the problem of how to convince the Prime Minister and the Cabinet still remained. Dalton approached Attlee directly, telling him that Treasury and Bank warnings about the disastrous effects of high public expenditure should be disregarded. Attlee replied that he wanted to have it all out in Cabinet. 'I say I hope he will ask all the young economist Ministers to speak', Dalton wrote. 'He says he will.'[26]

It had become a familiar battle: Dalton against those in the Government and Whitehall who regarded Labour's socialist aims as ballast to be discharged when the economy hit rough waters. The dispute over devaluation was not just between pros and antis. Dalton found himself opposing, not only the die-hard anti-devaluationists (headed by Cripps, Bevin and leading Whitehall officials), but also an expanding group of pro-devaluationist official advisers (including Robert Hall, director of the Economic Section, and Sir Edwin Plowden),[27] who argued that devaluation without an accompanying austerity package would be worse than no devaluation at all. Dalton had been persuaded that what was needed was a devaluation with a reduction in investment programmes and personal bank loans. Freed from Treasury shackles, the former Chancellor of the Exchequer now argued without restraint against those who wished – either as a substitute for or as an accompaniment to devaluation – to sacrifice working-class living standards. The existence of a domestic surplus, he maintained, was sufficient justification for keeping a high level of social services. Bevan, Strachey and (more hesitantly) Morrison gave support.

The young economists won the day. Gaitskell and Jay – backed (on the official side) by Bridges – eventually galvanised the Prime Minister into ordering Cripps to accept devaluation.[28] On 18th September the Chancellor announced a devaluation from $4.03 to $2.80 – having resisted to the last. Cripps felt a sense of personal humiliation, much as Dalton had done over the suspension of convertibility. Dalton had no thought of revenge. Nevertheless, the irony of the situation did not escape him.

The Economist, which had previously contrasted Cripps's courage and clarity with Dalton's alleged willingness to shirk unpalatable duty, declared that the decision should have been taken months before. Yet devaluation itself was a mainly technical measured delayed, as David Marquand has pointed out, because Cripps and the Cabinet had been persuaded by the City and the Treasury to regard it 'as a sign of fiscal irresponsibility if not of downright moral turpitude.'[29] It was the controversy surrounding devaluation, rather than the act, that made it political. 'Montagu Norman walks again', Dalton had chided Cripps at the Economic Policy Committee on 1st July, implying the continued dominance of City orthodoxies. On this occasion, Dalton himself had been among the vanguard.

The change in exchange rate, however, was not the end of the matter. Those who had opposed devaluation altogether, and many (including most leading officials) who had come round to its necessity, were agreed on one point – the adoption of the new exchange rate must be followed by a package of public spending cuts of the kind which Dalton had helped to scupper in July. The row between the pro-austerity group, led by Cripps (now backed by Gaitskell), and those who felt that such measures were unnecessary, led by Dalton and Bevan and supported by Wilson and Jay, soon became bound up with two other issues – the coming election, and the succession to the Chancellorship.

Though Gaitskell accused Dalton of holding a 'very rosy view' and regarded Dalton's opposition to proposed economies of £300 million as 'rather dishonest',[30] the dispute between the two friends was not personal. Nor, at this stage, was the disagreement between Gaitskell and Bevan – which appears, in retrospect, as a dress rehearsal for the conflict that led to the resignation of Bevan and two other ministers over health charges eighteen months later. '[Bevan] thought SC would resign rather than give up his main proposals for economy', Dalton noted, after a conversation with the Minister of Health on 11th October. 'Others, including himself, would resign rather than agree.'

Dalton's sympathies were with Bevan. He was also critical of Gaitskell. 'I think Plowden has been working on HG', Dalton reflected, 'for he quotes him to the effect that, when he went to see his doctor the other day he found the waiting room full of women gossiping, with slight colds, coming for a chat and a free prescription.' Dalton's faith in his friend remained, however, unshaken.

On 13th October, the Cabinet decided against an election before 1950. Eight weeks later, Attlee held a conference of senior Cabinet ministers (apart from Bevin), together with the Chief Whip. Addison, Dalton and Bevan – the three regarded as most senior after the Big Four – were present, in addition to Cripps, Morrison and Whiteley. All except Morrison agreed that the best date was February.

Dalton saw Attlee alone on 27th January, for the last time before the campaign. They spoke of the years of Labour Government. Forgotten were the plots and jealousies, recalled instead, through a rosy haze, were the comradeship and team spirit. 'I said, looking back over 5 years, it was amazing how well Cab and Govt had work[ed] – a few personal antipathies, Herbert v. Ernie, and Nye v. Both – but bark worse than bite, and no real splits or resignation threats', recorded the Chancellor of the Duchy, having conveniently erased from his mind Hugh v. Ernie, Hugh v. Herbert, and Stafford plus Hugh v. Clem. ' ... Much of the credit, I said, was due to him.'[31]

What, the Prime Minister must have wondered, did Dalton want? The answer was Gaitskell's advancement. Dalton's ambitions had moved since his resignation to the careers of those he had helped to bring into politics. For himself, he did not care whether the coming election was won or lost. The prospect of a literary retirement to Wiltshire, to be spent writing memoirs and up-dating *Principles of Public Finance*, had definite attractions. However for the younger, rising men in the Party, the outcome of the election had a great im-

portance. If Labour won, there would be ministerial changes and
vacancies to fill. And at the very top, one vacancy in particular seemed
imminent.

Sir Stafford Cripps, 'driven to the last ounce of exhaustion',[32]
disappointed over devaluation and (as it transpired) mortally ill, had
finally played himself out. The question of who might follow was in
many minds. Dalton had two overriding interests: first, to stop
Morrison, and second – if possible – to clear the path for Gaitskell.
Dalton's hostility to Morrison, which had grown steadily since the
war, was part personal – based on envy and rivalry – and part political:
he considered Morrison fundamentally conservative, without clearly
defined aims. His championship of Gaitskell was based on a friendship
of twenty years' standing; and on an admiration for Gaitskell's
intellect, industry and clear-headed approach to practical problems.

A few days before Dalton's pre-election meeting with the Prime
Minister, Gaitskell had impressed the Economic Policy Committee
with a paper on Controls and Liberalisation – offering a view which
later characterised Gaitskell's own Chancellorship: 'always have a
bit of inflationary pressure, but use physical controls to prevent it
breaking through'. Dalton had been worried by the Minister of Fuel
and Power's earlier inclination to side with officials on the need for
spending cuts. He was therefore delighted by this slap in the face for
Cripps and the Treasury. 'A great score today for the "young economists"', he wrote.

Gaitskell had distinguished himself in the eyes of senior colleagues
because of his cool and skilful handling of the devaluation crisis.
After less than five years as an M.P., however, he was still relatively
unknown to the public or even to the Party outside Parliament. To
facilitate Gaitskell's succession to the Chancellorship, Dalton
reasoned, it was necessary to anticipate and to improve his qualifications *vis-à-vis* rivals who included – apart from Morrison – Wilson
and Jay.

When Dalton saw Attlee, Gaitskell was much in his thoughts:

> I said that SC was absolutely irreplaceable as Chancellor. No one
> else could do it, until, in due course, one came down the line to the
> 'young economists'. At Treasury one needed not only quick intelli-
> gence or bright ideas, or diligence or methodical admin, but power
> to resist high powered advice. One or two who were mentioned as
> possibles now would be quite impossible (I had HM in mind).

Dalton now expanded helpfully on this theme. Cripps had too much
on his plate. What was required, while Cripps remained in charge, was

a Minister of State to take over the 'old Treasury' aspects of the job; otherwise both the machine, and Cripps with it, would break under the strain. Who better for such a post than Hugh Gaitskell? When the Prime Minister indicated assent, Dalton went on to expatiate on Gaitskell's merits as a potential Chancellor.[33]

Having thus prepared the ground for a post-election carve-up of the ailing Chancellor's responsibilities, Dalton hastened to Gaitskell to tell him what to expect. The young minister was surprised, but pleased. 'HD wanted to be sure that if the P.M. offered me such a job I would take it', he noted.[34] Then the election engulfed them all.

At the start of the campaign, many commentators were predicting a Tory victory. Even in Bishop Auckland, the result seemed uncertain. Boundary changes,[35] and the scandal which had so recently touched him, made Dalton nervous and jumpy as polling day approached, and liable to lose his temper at the slightest provocation.[36] Although the danger of a national defeat bothered him little, to lose his own seat would be a bitter personal blow.

On merit as a constituency M.P., he should have had little to fear. Visits to his constituency had continued to be irregular. Sometimes a couple of months separated them, and it never occurred to him to spend free weekends in the north, rather than in Wiltshire. He once told Douglas Jay that it was not the job of an M.P. to be a social worker.[37] Yet few M.P.s have ever done more for their constituents. Dalton's Distribution of Industry Act, passed before Labour came to power but implemented by the Labour Government, had been a massive benefit to County Durham. In the first four years of the Act, over 800 factories had been completed in the county – more than in the whole of the 1918–39 period. As a result, there were more people employed in the north-east in 1949 than ever before, in peace or war.[35]

Dalton was not directly responsible for all of what amounted to a social and economic revolution in the region. Much was the product of the post-war boom which had created a full employment economy nationally. But serious regional pockets of unemployment would certainly have remained without Dalton's pioneering legislation, and without his concern to see it followed through. In addition, he had been closely involved with an ambitious programme of New Town development (presided over by Lewis Silkin, Minister of Town and Country Planning), as part of the post-war housing drive – with Washington, Aycliffe and Peterlee ear-marked for development in the north-east.[39]

Electorates, however, are not always grateful. Would such achievements be enough to save him? There were signs of his declining fame.

Speaking at Chelmsford, in Essex, before the start of his own campaign, he only half-filled a hall which John Strachey had packed a week before.[40] Fortunately, organisation had much improved in Bishop Auckland, and local Tories – so active during the Lynskey hearings – were inactive during the election, partly because their candidate, Lord Lambton, was confined to bed with 'flu. Dalton had little trouble at meetings. When he was reminded of his 'song in his heart' speech, he replied: 'I said that I would find, with a song in my heart, all the money that was needed to finance new productive work in these old, distressed areas, and I kept my word.'[41]

On election day, Dalton was more irascible than ever, and drank heavily.[42] His worries were unnecessary. He won Bishop Auckland with a majority of 11,370 – a sharp increase on his 1945 result; the effects of boundary changes had been miscalculated. Nationally, however, Labour lost many seats and retained power only by a whisker, with scarcely any minor party 'cushion' of the kind that kept Labour in office, despite narrow victory margins, in the 1970s. 'The thought of a small Labour majority depresses me deeply', Dalton had written the previous autumn, 'with all the economic difficulties ahead, and added strains on tired men, and an unpopular Budget, and the Govt at the mercy of any small disloyal clique.' Now it had happened, his view did not alter. Though he agreed with most colleagues that the Government should carry on, he expected that the new Parliament would only last a few months. 'Worst possible situation', he noted. ' ... As it is, we have office without authority or power, and it is difficult to see how we can improve our position.'

Dalton had been in two minds about taking a department if Labour won. Privately, he had wondered whether he was up to the physical strain; yet, when he saw Attlee just before the campaign, he made it clear that he would like one.[43] After the election, the Prime Minister offered him a combination of Housing (to be separated from Health, where Bevan had been Minister) and Town and Country Planning. Dalton agreed in principle, slept on it, then stated his price: Bevan must be shifted from Health to avoid 'possibilities of great friction and jealousies both on the ministerial and official levels'. Though he respected Bevan, he preferred to keep him at arm's length. Life would be much easier, he considered, with Jim Griffiths at Health, rather than Nye.[44] Attlee's response was swift. He summoned Dalton and told him that the Housing offer was withdrawn. Instead, Dalton might like the Colonial Office.

Dalton was appalled:

I had a horrid vision of pullulating, poverty stricken, diseased nigger communities, for whom one can do nothing in the short run, and who, the more one tries to help them, are querulous and ungrateful; of Malaya and a futile military campaign; of white settlers, reactionary and as troublesome in their way, as the niggers, of ineffective action at a distance, through telegrams to and from Governors, whom one has never seen; of all the silliness and emotion about the black man who married a white typist, and Dr Malan and the demand for Protectorate; of friction over trusteeship at UNO; of irritating personal relationships with Ernie, and Phil, and Shinwell; of continuing difficulties over groundnuts; of Parliamentary questions by pro-native cranks and anti-native capitalists – all this in a rush of a few seconds.[45]

So that was that. Dalton accepted Town and Country Planning as it stood, on the vague understanding that Housing might be brought in later. Instead of one or other of the important posts offered, he had chosen a minor one.[46] Yet he was perfectly happy with a responsibility which consisted of little except National Parks, New Towns and the job of speeding up planning procedures.[47] He retained his place of fifth in the Cabinet pecking order, and as he expected another election by the autumn, he felt that he had lost little.

What interested him far more than his own employment was the progress of his leading protégé. As he had suggested and hoped, Gaitskell was appointed Minister of State for Economic Affairs, with a place on the Economic Policy Committee, and, in effect, Vice-Chancellor of the Exchequer. 'It shows that my advice is sometimes taken', Dalton wrote.[48] For Gaitskell, it was a key promotion. Without it, he would never have become Chancellor when Cripps resigned; and if he had not become Chancellor, he would not have been in the running for the Party Leadership when Attlee retired five years later.

XXXII

Call of the Wild

'Politically, Town and Country Planning was a wretched little back-water', recalls Baroness (then Dame Evelyn) Sharp, Deputy-Secretary under Dalton. Nevertheless, Dalton enjoyed his new ministry and made the most of limited opportunities. New Towns had long interested him; National Parks were a passion. He now became the vocal and effective champion of both – showing how much difference a major politician in a minor department could make. He still carried guns in Cabinet. 'Dalton had a tremendous impact, with his bullying and shouting ways', Baroness Sharp remembers. She makes an interesting comparison between Dalton and Richard Crossman, whom she advised many years later:

Crossman could be dazzling in seminars in ways that Dalton couldn't. But Dalton was much more skilled at managing Cabinet. Also, he was a warm-hearted bully: if you told him he was being unfair or unkind, he was shocked. Crossman, on the other hand, was quite ruthless and enjoyed hurting people.[1]

Dalton got on better with Evelyn Sharp than with his Permanent Secretary, Sir Thomas Sheepshanks who, Dalton considered after a year, 'will never miss a catch and never hit a six'.[2] Dalton regarded Sheepshanks as another Overton of the Board of Trade. 'Minister, there are three reasons why you can't do this', Sheepshanks once told him. 'You go away and bring me one reason why I should', Dalton replied.[3] All three – Dalton, Sharp and Sheepshanks – happened to be the progeny of Anglican clerics; but Sheepshanks was the son of a bishop, and it showed.

Dalton, however, was not to be deterred by a negative official. Ignoring the awkward fact that the powers of the department provided little scope for initiating anything at all, Dalton badgered New Town chairmen (of whom his old boss, Sir William Beveridge, was one) to produce results. It was a characteristic approach. Fearing that if houses were not built, the New Town programme might be halted, Dalton was guided by a simple principle: 'You must show houses on the ground'. This brought friction with the Board of Trade (determined that the establishment of factories should precede the building of houses) and with the Treasury which was against spending money. 'He tended to roar and rant when houses weren't actually sprouting', recalls Baroness Sharp.[4] But the roaring was effective in drawing public attention to his aims, in stimulating recalcitrant local and national officials,[5] and in winning Cabinet battles.

Dalton inherited two major Acts, which he had helped to frame in Cabinet Committee: the 1947 Planning Act and the 1949 National Parks Act. His main job, as he saw it, was to see that these were implemented. He began with a flamboyant press conference, dressed as if for a wedding. 'Now look at me', he told his dour Permanent Secretary, as photographers adjusted their machines, 'and pretend we're planning something!' He announced the first three National Parks – the Peak District, the Lake District and Snowdonia – all to be designated later in the year. He declared his intention to establish 'long distance routes' of which the Pennine Way would probably be the first.

His appointment, as one journalist remarked, had acted on him 'like a summer shower on a parched and neglected flower',[6] and soon others were noticing the same. With personal ambition behind him, he could perform his duties with fewer signs of nervous strain. He still had a sense of mission, and he worked hard, expecting subordinates to do the same. 'Nobody could be more considerate if you were really busting a gut for him', Baroness Sharp recalls.[7] But his style was now less frantic, less self-punishing and less competitive, and his reputation gained as a result. Despite the roaring, there were no furious rows of the kind that had characterised his dealings with officials in the past.

Outside the Labour Party Dalton became known as the friend of the countryside. Even the highly conservative *Country Life*, whose usual concerns ranged from trout-streams to death watch beetle, praised him for a successful defence of the Pennine Way against the onslaughts of the War Office.[8] At Whitsun he was able to combine business with pleasure by taking his annual walk with a hand-picked group of Labour M.P.s along the northern part of the proposed new route.[9] The Pennine Way was eventually approved by Dalton in July 1951. It ran from Kirk Yetholm in Scotland to Edale in Derbyshire, passing through nine counties, and involved the creation of 70 additional miles of rights of way.[10] Created in close consultation with Dalton's friend and walking companion, Tom Stephenson, there could scarcely have been a better expression of the Minister's Fabian passion for the countryside and for long, wild walks.

In the Labour Party, too, Dalton was staging a recovery. In April, the *Observer* had noted that his political standing had been quietly going up,[11] and in June his old enemy the *Daily Telegraph* echoed this view, suggesting – what had not been said for some time – that he was widely tipped as a successor to Bevin at the Foreign Office.[12] It was an odd late blooming, a product partly of his unthreatening appointment, partly of the growing decrepitude of senior colleagues. But it was real. 'However much Mr. Attlee may turn away his head in order not to be hypnotised', wrote one commentator, 'the strange fact remains that the bulk of the Socialist Party is bewitched by Mr. Dalton.'[13]

This was important because of Labour's developing attitude towards European unity. The lightness of his formal duties enabled Dalton to take a close interest in general issues that came before Cabinet, and (as a member of the N.E.C.) to help shape Labour Party policy. One area in which he continued to be involved was Europe. When the European Assembly held its second meeting in Strasbourg in August, Morrison stayed at home, and Dalton led the Labour delegation. Meanwhile Dalton showed that he had not yet grown into a harmless and benevolent old man by making a statement on European policy that caused press and Opposition to explode with fury and indignation.

As Chairman of the N.E.C. International Committee, Dalton had helped to prepare Labour's answer to a plan put forward by the French foreign minister, Robert Schuman, for the pooling of French and German steel and coal production under a joint authority in an organisation open to other countries. The Schuman Plan had 'functionalist' features – it did not, for example, require any transfer of sovereignty. But its long-term goal was undoubtedly federalist, its author describing the scheme as 'a first step in the direction of European federation'. This federalist aspect led Labour's International Committee to produce a document called 'European Unity', which has since been regarded as a turning-point in relations with Europe, marking the beginning of Britain's exclusion from the E.E.C.[14]

'European Unity' was prepared in draft by Denis Healey, secretary of the Committee. It was accepted by the Committee in modified form, initialled by the Foreign Secretary without comment, and in the presence of the Prime Minister and other ministers, put to the full N.E.C. which approved it unanimously. It was then quickly printed, and Dalton accepted a Transport House request that he should take a press conference to launch it on 12th June, the day before a Government statement and White Paper on the Schuman Plan were due.

This was a mistake. The press assumed, incorrectly, that the timing of the anti-Schuman document had been deliberately fixed by Dalton to embarrass the Foreign Office. More important, the demeanour of the Minister of Town and Country Planning at the press conference seemed to lack the solemnity felt to be appropriate for such an occasion. Dalton was accused of dodging questions and employing his usual range of tricks – hearty laughter, academic reproach, boom and bounce.[15] 'He was aggressive and bombastic', complained A. J. Cummings of the pro-European *News Chronicle*, 'and behaved exactly like the offensive John Bull depicted by foreign cartoonists in the last century.'[16] 'It is a truly deplorable document', declared Harold Nicolson, despairing of his recent opportunistic decision to join the Labour Party. 'It means that Dalton, who sponsored it, cannot possibly succeed Bevin.'[17] Anthony Eden, Opposition spokesman on foreign affairs, advised the Prime Minister to keep Dalton 'in his Planning pen'.[18]

Behind such reactions lay anger over Labour's new policy. By appearing uncompromisingly anti-European, Dalton gave an impression of running an alternative foreign policy, and some commentators saw his behaviour as a blatant bid for Bevin's job.[19] But the supposed split in the Government was an illusion: both Bevin and Attlee had been fully aware of what 'European Unity' contained, and had raised no objection. Privately, the Prime Minister was consoling. 'CRA says Press has been monstrous and I need not worry', Dalton noted. Nevertheless, the whole business upset him, and he lost some of his sparkle. For the first time since his return to office in 1948, he began to fantasise about the possibility of resignation on one issue or another.[20]

When Dalton returned to Strasbourg for the European Assembly in August, he found that his reputation as a rogue elephant had preceded him. Before leaving England, he had strongly reaffirmed Labour opposition both to federalism and to the half-way house implied by a supranational authority for iron and steel.[21] Far more than in 1949, he was regarded as the major stumbling-block to proposals for greater unity. Churchill, again leader of the Tory delegation, treated him brusquely, and it was left to Macmillan, with the aid of some stiff drinks, to smooth things over.[22]

It was not so easy to smooth things over with the French. Nor did Dalton make much effort to try. Once again, the main division at Strasbourg was between the functionalists, led by Britain, and the federalists, led by France. Dalton's deliberate absence from one particular vote so angered the French delegation that Guy Mollet, the French foreign minister, threatened to resign from the position of *rapporteur* to the Assembly's General Affairs Committee. Meanwhile, relations with the German contingent were not helped by a rumour that Dalton had snubbed one of the German delegates, Dr Carlo Schmidt, because Schmidt had spent part of the war in Occupied France.[23] On 21st August, Dalton reported back to Bevin, pointing to 'the strength of the anti-British Labour feeling' that was evident in Strasbourg.[24] Few observers would have disputed the diagnosis, though the explanation was not hard to see. Afterwards, many European delegates believed, perhaps rightly, that the British Government was intent on sabotaging the whole experiment.[25]

Dalton found Strasbourg humid and irritating.[26] Fortunately, however, he had taken steps to ensure that his leisure hours would be enjoyable. As leader of the delegation he had picked his own team, including Jim Callaghan as his deputy, and Anthony Crosland, newly elected an M.P., as economic adviser, with Denis Healey again providing assistance on behalf of Transport House. The choice of 'three of the youngest, most intelligent, most amusing, and most physically fit of my team',[27] had been made for social as much as for political reasons: partly, as he later told Crosland, 'because I so much enjoy your company and your stimulus.'[28]

As soon as the session allowed, Hugh evaded the rest of the party and took his young friends off on an expedition to Le Donon in the Vosges mountains to the south-west of the city. They spent the night in the Hotel Velleda:

> On arrival we walked up a valley behind the hotel and, at the top, found Denis, seated like a sphinx, on top of a stone edifice called Le Musée. Then we turned and ran back down the valley, spurting in the last lap before reaching the hotel; we had a lovely sweat, an ardent thirst, a magnificent view; and now we had a wonderful dinner, after which we sat up talking till a late hour.
>
> After breakfast the next day, the four of us had a long, most amusing and quite uninhibited conversation for several hours. Then some photographs on the terrace, and then an admirable lunch. Then we plunged downwards through the forest along tracks broad and narrow, and past hidden lakes in the woods until, after another lovely sweat, we reached Raon-sur-Plaine, and thence drove back to Strasbourg.
>
> It had been a wonderful trip, which I shall long remember, in most

agreeable company, seasoned with wit and wisdom, walking and wine.[29]

'We went for a run', Jim Callaghan remembers. 'Hugh kept up remarkably well. Then we got very drunk.'[30] For Callaghan, it was a pleasant break from public duties. For Dalton it was something more. Suddenly he felt happier than for years past, and the future seemed more hopeful. The Le Donon weekend, with its 'uninhibited conversation' and echoes of comradely mountain hikes before the First World War, became a marker in his life, the moment when he decided to pass on the baton to the young.

Back in England, he withdrew to West Leaze for private contemplation. His mind turned to war, death, youth and senility:

Maybe Russian atom bombs will make an end of us, or most of us, within a few years. I think much of the younger people, those I know and am fond of, and the young in the mass, in this country and in others, especially in Scandinavia and France and Australia and New Zealand and Canada ... I hate the thought of growing old & feeble and to survive a Third War, in which so many of the young would have died or been maimed, would be unbearable.[31]

This train of thought was linked to a recent re-reading of letters from Rupert Brooke, which Maynard Keynes's younger brother Geoffrey (who was editing Brooke's papers) had borrowed and just returned. Dalton had written to Keynes, urging him to publish soon, and fully:

Too often I find myself trying, without much supporting evidence, to tell the Young how great and lovable he was ... It is, I feel, a shame to deprive the Young of today and yesterday – and of tomorrow – of the inspiration which, if you publish even now, they would eagerly absorb. Why let him, with the drift of time, become a mere Legend of the Past? He would have wished, I am sure, to be a Living Legend to the Present.[32]

Dalton decided to leave his Brooke letters to King's, to help perpetuate their author's memory. But what about his own Living Legend, once he was gone? '"To die will be an awfully big adventure" said Peter Pan', he wrote reflectively. All his political life he had kept a diary, first in neat long-hand, then dictated to a secretary and typed, and recently hand-written in smudgy red ink on loose sheets of austerity notepaper. Now his mind turned to this great unpublished work.

Two years earlier a reading of Churchill's *The Gathering Storm* had made him consider, not for the first time, the possibility of writing memoirs. Talk of publishing Brooke's ephemera re-kindled the idea.

But what if he should die before the project was complete? To guard against this risk, he decided to appoint literary executors. First, he thought of his old L.S.E. student and lifelong friend Robert (who had become Sir Robert) Fraser. He needed somebody else as well. Gaitskell perhaps? Ruth suggested Tony Crosland. She had barely met this young man. But having heard Hugh speak of him, and knowing her husband better perhaps than he realised, she felt such a choice would be ideal.

Hugh was delighted by the suggestion. He was even more delighted by the response. Crosland replied that he would love to be an executor, but he hoped it might never be necessary.

After the Le Donon weekend, Dalton became increasingly restless in office, and privately hoped for an early election. He recalled a recent comment by Crosland's brother-in-law, the historian A. J. P. Taylor, that 'all men are mad who devote themselves to the pursuit of Power, when they could be fishing or painting pictures, or sitting in the sun'.[33] He did not expect Labour to win. Looking ahead, he saw a period of Opposition followed by a victory which would take his young friends into, or close to, the Cabinet. As for himself, he told Crosland that he did not want another 'heavy' office:

> If I'm still reasonably fit, there's a lot to be said for pushing the Govt from behind to be brave and brainy, and for thinking up some new ideas, and for encouraging the next lot of young men who'll be snapping impatiently at your ministerial heels![34]

But would he still be 'reasonably fit' in four or five years' time? One reason for thinking about retirement was that his once-robust constitution, in which he had always taken such pride, could no longer be taken for granted. In September a bad gastric attack caused him to faint and fall in the middle of the night, cutting his face. A heart specialist was called. When Dalton insisted on voting in a crucial division on steel nationalisation, his doctor protested that he was seriously risking his life. 'I am a soldier ordered into battle', he replied haughtily; 'do you want to persuade me to be a deserter?' Ignoring warnings, he got his P.P.S., George Chetwynd, to drive him – scarred and very weak – to the House. He made his way to the Chief Whip's room, voted, and went straight back to the nursing home in Fitzroy Square where he was being treated.[35] Chetwynd recalled Dalton's anxiety, during this foray, not to draw attention to his condition.[36]

He spent eight days in bed, taking advantage of the break to begin his memoirs, starting with Eton.[37] Then he made an uncomfortable journey, heavily sedated, to Margate for Party Conference, where he pleased delegates by speaking vehemently against the European federalists. ('Malicious demagoguery', complained the *Manchester Guardian*.)[38] He was not too ill to help young men. His friend Sam Watson, the Miners' leader, was Conference Chairman. Dalton was able to see that Tony Crosland and Roy Jenkins were given opportunities to make speeches that were widely reported in the press. Then he returned to London and to bed.

Dalton remained ill for several weeks. His recovery coincided with the collapse of Sir Stafford Cripps. On 18th October, Cripps resigned as Chancellor of the Exchequer, his health finally broken. It was not unexpected, and the ground for Gaitskell's succession had been well prepared. In August, Dalton had urged Attlee once again to go for Gaitskell in preference either to anybody senior (that is, Morrison or Bevan), or one of the other two 'young economists', Harold Wilson and Douglas Jay. Now that Gaitskell had spent eight months as Minister of State for Economic Affairs, and for much of this time effectively standing in for the Chancellor, the case for choosing him had become much stronger.

With Cripps gone, Dalton determined to repeat his own earlier advice. But before he could get to the Prime Minister, Jay told him that the appointment of Gaitskell had already been made.[39] Dalton was overjoyed: pleased for his friend, and feeling it as a personal triumph. 'My dear Hugh', he wrote. ' ... I am very proud of, & confident in, this new young Chancellor of the Exchequer, whom I spotted years ago among the Colts ... [M]ay you do big things, & keep always, as the years advance, the fulsome valour of childhood! And I will always help all I can.'[40] 'I owe you such a lot', Gaitskell replied, ' – for having "spotted" me and backed me and trained me – entered me for the races, encouraged me, befriended me.' Dalton scribbled on this letter: 'If only a few of the young men I have picked and backed do only half as well as H.G., my political life will have been worth living.'[41] But he also wrote, shrewdly, 'Hugh will have a hard time and much jealousy to face.'[42]

For Dalton, with a sense of his own ministerial career past its peak, it was a vindication of his judgment and of a lifelong mission. 'Dalton's promotion of Gaitskell in the nasty, backbiting world of high politics was one of the most selfless things I have ever seen', comments Roy Jenkins.[43] Since first taking Gaitskell under his wing, Dalton had watched over the younger man's progress, grooming him for high office, much as the Canon had groomed the young princes. Now his confidence and efforts were rewarded.

Yet Gaitskell's politics, in style and purpose, were distinctively his own. Harold Macmillan noted the superficial effects of Dalton's tutelage – Gaitskell's gestures, smile and pedantic tendencies bore the mark of his master. On the other hand Macmillan also cannily observed, meaning it as a compliment to Gaitskell: 'if he is Daltonesque in manner, he is Crippsian in matter'.[44] The troubled course of Labour Party history over the next ten or a dozen years owed much to this difference.

Crucially, Gaitskell lacked Dalton's political roots. It was not just that Gaitskell had had less parliamentary experience than any Chancellor of the Exchequer for a century and a half.[45] It was more that, to use Bevan's dismissive and envious phrase, the new Chancellor was 'young in the Movement'. Dalton had been shaped by the passions of Webbian Fabianism at its most evangelical, by the scramble for a seat in the anarchic early 1920s, by the traumas of 1931, by wheeler-dealing on the N.E.C. – all before he became a senior minister. Gaitskell's public service career, by contrast, had a smooth upward trajectory, without any real background in the rough-and-tumble of Labour political life. As an economist and then as an official, he had acquired an imaginative understanding of the new thinking upon which Treasury policy had come to be based. But he did not have Dalton's intuition for Party feeling, nor the gift of political presentation.

There was also a deeper difference. Dalton, as we have seen, was a social outsider, actively – often passionately – disliked by members of his own class, a loner, an angry egalitarian who hated the rich, who hated him back. Nothing would have excited him more than to see carried out the massive appropriations of land and capital envisaged in *Inequality of Incomes* and *The Capital Levy Explained.* Gaitskell's politics reflected a less uneasy temperament. Gaitskell was hostile to great wealth and privilege and believed, as Dalton believed, in a limited redistribution. Yet what for Dalton was a matter of emotion, tempered and supported by reason, was for Gaitskell based on a disciplined intellectual conviction. Gaitskell might attack the privileges of the better off; but it was a measured attack, by a man who belonged, in a way that Dalton did not quite belong, with the middle classes. High-minded, clubbable and cliquish, Gaitskell was more liked and admired by Tory reformers and progressive mandarins than any other leading Labour politician before or since. In polite society it was almost eccentric to like or admire Dalton.

Gaitskell was primarily an 'economic' socialist; he saw socialist change in terms of the ability of a Labour Government to plan for prosperity and greater fairness. He lacked Dalton's wider vision of comradeship and fraternity, a product of Durham miners, the old I.L.P., and King's. For Gaitskell, the essential problem of socialism was technical. In a revealing conversation, he once told a civil servant that, with a greater equalisation of property, 'the philosophical differences between the parties would gradually diminish and their rivalry would turn increasingly – as in the United States, he said – into a competition in governmental competence.'[46] Like his predecessor in the first two Labour Governments, Philip Snowden, Gaitskell was a jam-tomorrow egalitarian. His main goal as Chancellor was administrative efficiency.

Gaitskell's outlook was certainly more modern, more in tune with the changing times, than that of his mentor. It was significant that both Cripps and Gaitskell eagerly embraced the full implications of the Keynesian managed economy, while Dalton had tended to hang back, prejudiced towards physical planning on the basis of an older, cruder socialist economics. The difference that existed between the intellectually inelegant, but morally distinct, Daltonian socialism with its odd ancestry of Webb and Cannan, and the civil-service Keynesian liberalism of Gaitskell and his later followers, marked the new age. It also had much to do with social attitude and instinct. In these, despite their friendship, Dalton and Gaitskell always stood far apart.

Gaitskell was much in Dalton's mind in the autumn of 1950. The new Chancellor took second place, however, to a rising Labour politician whose personality was to dominate Dalton's affections in his last years. Since August, Dalton had been restlessly conscious of his own growing attachment to the youngest and most glamorous of the Le Donon comrades, Tony Crosland.

Crosland had been an undergraduate, recently returned from war service in Italy, when Dalton first met him and began to take an interest in his fortunes. The friendship had been cemented during the desperate high summer of 1947 when Crosland had joined the Davenports' house party at Hinton Manor to celebrate Hugh's sixtieth birthday. Thereafter Hugh adopted Crosland as a special companion, the most interesting and beguiling of the young men he was bringing on. 'George Brown, Jim Callaghan, Barbara Castle, Denis Healey, Tony – all were encouraged by Dalton', records Crosland's widow, Susan. 'The protégé he loved best was Tony.'[47]

Dalton had used his considerable influence to help many other young men find Labour seats. Now he set about performing this vital service for Crosland. 'Keep me informed of your doings and plottings', he advised after a long talk with the National Agent in September 1948. There was hope, he wrote, of 'fixing up you and others'.[48] The chance came the following year. Roy Jenkins, also seat-hunting towards the end of the 1945 Parliament (in his case because of boundary changes) recalls discovering for himself Dalton's private pecking order of young men. Early in 1949 Jenkins mentioned, casually but hopefully, his own interest in South Gloucestershire. Dalton froze. 'No, No. That wouldn't suit you at all.' Jenkins was puzzled. 'South Gloucestershire', Dalton explained, 'would be a very good seat for Tony.'[49]

' ... [I]t is not a thing which one can easily or lightly forget', Crosland wrote, after Dalton had helped tie up the selection.[50] 'Tony Crosland might be Prime Minister of England one day', Dalton told a friend.[51] Introductions, fatherly advice, letters of encouragement followed. Shortly before the selection, Crosland had written an anonymous article in *Tribune* seeking, elegantly and ingeniously, to stand every criticism that had ever been made of Dalton's Chancellorship on its head.[52] Determined to bring the views of this young economist to the attention of the makers of economic policy, Dalton now persuaded Crosland to write a paper on 'Disinflation', so that he could send copies to Sir Stafford Cripps and Douglas Jay. Meanwhile he visited South Gloucestershire, speaking for the new candidate. The southern boundaries of Crosland's prospective constituency were only a short drive from West Leaze. Eagerly, the Cabinet minister suggested 'a run on the Downs' as part of the itinerary. 'My hide-out will not be tenanted that week-end', he pointed out, 'as my wife will not be going down.'[53]

Few men were less in need of patronage than Crosland, once he had a foot on the ladder. Few had more bestowed upon them. After the February election, Dalton – still a senior minister – was able to provide a direct line to the very top. In June 1951 Michael Foot was complaining that Dalton had become Crosland's and Callaghan's 'over-cover representative in the Cabinet'.[54] The same month, Dalton had written to Gaitskell about the novice Member of sixteen months' standing:

He is amazingly able and astringent, & is becoming as good a politician as he is an economist. I get much more mental stimulus out of him than out of any of the others. On sheer ability, & knowledge of the subject, and personality, he, of course, ought to be the next Treasury Junior Minister.[55]

Crosland did not get this promotion. But Gaitskell soon became a keen admirer.

'One owed so much of one's early career in politics to him', Crosland wrote of Dalton later.[56] At the time he liked to give the impression that he found Dalton's attentions amusing but exhausting. He enjoyed stories about Dalton's alleged jealousy of his girlfriends, such as Davenport's description of the time at Hinton when Tony's early departure with a female companion left Hugh so upset that he paced the room and would not eat his supper.[57] He would joke that if Hugh had married somebody more heterosexually inclined than Ruth, he might have overcome the effects of King's and Eton.[58]

Yet it was actually a complex relationship on both sides. Another friend wrote of Crosland: 'He was lovable because he did not mind whether he was loved or not.'[59] It was an unusual trait in a politician. Was it really true? There was a game Hugh and Tony played. Hugh was the doting, admonishing, over-attentive parent; Tony the wayward, ungrateful, irrepressible, enchantingly mischievous, always forgiven son. As Susan later remarked, Tony behaved towards Hugh much as he behaved towards his mother.[60] Roy Jenkins suggests a kind of sadomasochism. 'Tony was cruel to him, called him an old windbag to his face', Jenkins recalls. 'Hugh would take it and come back for more.'[61] ' ... [A]lways tell me just what you think', Dalton begged Crosland on one occasion, 'and answer – and kick – back whenever you feel like it!'[62]

Both men were competitive talkers. 'Tony's approach to people was a form of banter and knockabout, confronting them', according to Susan.[63] Hugh's approach was to try to argue people into the ground. With Tony, he varied his pace. Sometimes, in company, Hugh was measured and gentle, lobbing easy balls for the young champion to smash back, only for him to send them back up, high over the net. On other occasions there were quick-fire volleys. 'Tony often reminds me of Gladwyn', Hugh wrote after one contest. 'But Gladwyn is much colder and more cynical.'[64]

Most of the time the association was older and sharper: Rupert Brooke. There were, indeed, similarities. Like Rupert, Tony was beautiful, boyish, clever and narcissistic. Like Rupert, he was a hedonist with a controlling serious streak, on the run from a loving but claustrophobic background, and half-frightened by his own exceptional endowments. Like Rupert he was fascinated by fame, yet appalled by its pressures. As with Rupert, he seemed unable to form a lasting relationship with any of the women he attracted. Was there also in Tony, as there was undoubtedly in Brooke, an emotional ambivalence that enabled him to respond to the affection of another, especially an older, man? It may not be irrelevant that both Brooke and Crosland lost their fathers in early manhood; or that in his intimate Cambridge circle, Dalton had been known as 'Daddy'.

Hugh's affection for Tony reached a peak of intensity in the months following the Le Donon weekend. Susan found two yellowing pages from Hugh's diary, covered in red-ink scrawl, among her husband's papers:

(5/11/50) Tonight Tony is dining in King's with Kaldor. I don't think he's ever dined there before, where the ghosts of all my undergraduate friends walk. They are all dead; nearly all of them died in the First World War ...

Am thinking of Tony, with all his youth and beauty and gaiety and charm and energy and social success and good brains – and a better Economist & a better Socialist than Kaldor, & with his feet on the road of political success now, if he survives to middle age – I *weep*. I am more fond and more proud of that young man than I can put in words.[65]

Did Crosland see this entry at the time, or did he discover it, as a literary executor, after Dalton's death and prudently extract it? Susan assumes the former: that Dalton sent it to Tony, in a maudlin and perhaps intoxicated mood, as a kind of love letter. The question, however, is not of great significance because shortly afterwards Dalton left Crosland in no doubt about his feelings.

Late in November – the month of Caporetto and Helen's birth, of desperation over P.W.E. in 1941 and of the Budget leak in 1947 – something passed between them that brought their friendship to a crisis. Tony was a student of Freud.[66] Perhaps he presented Hugh with an uncomfortable interpretation. If so, the result was to jolt the older man into some unaccustomed introspection.

In his bedroom at the Nouvel Hotel in Strasbourg, the leader of the British delegation wrote the young M.P., thirty-one years his junior, a remarkable letter:

Saturday afternoon
25/11/50

Dear Tony,

Thank you for your message ... from the Railway station. I did not expect, or try, to see you this morning. I know how well you sleep!

And I shan't expect, or try, to see much of you when we are back in England. I have come to the conclusion that I have been fussing you too much since you came into Parliament and that this has bored you and made a setback, on your side, in our friendship, which was and is, very precious to me.

A year ago last August in this Hotel I had a letter from you telling me of your selection for S. Gloucester and saying some very nice things about my part in bringing that about. I shall keep that letter.

Six months later you were elected, but I sense that you have found the life of an M.P. disappointing, boring and narrowing ... If I have any responsibility for pushing you from Oxford into politics, I am partly responsible for this disillusion and decline. But I think I only pushed because you asked me to? ...

You are splendidly gifted – physically, mentally and socially – and you have been going through a period of great and varied successes, even in politics which you find so second rate and dreary.

I have told you last summer how I feel towards you – that I believe tremendously in you and your future, and admire immensely your wonderful diversity of gifts, and am *very* fond of you (but with no disturbing carnal thoughts about you), and get great stimulus from your company and from what you say and write, and would do anything any time, if you asked me, to help you.

But I am nearly twice your age, so that I tend to think of you, as when drunk I also told you, more as a beloved son – only a year younger than my little daughter Helen who died in 1922, or, when I am feeling a good deal younger than my age, as an adorably gay younger brother.

...

Well, you've stirred me up, damn you, more and more during the years I've known you! And your friendship stands very high on the list of things that matter to me.

But, being so keen on you, I've fussed and focussed you too much lately. I shall do it no more. I shall leave you alone. Any initiative must come from your side now, and I don't expect many, because your life, apart from politics, will be fuller and fuller. And I don't expect an answer to this letter. And I shall never write or say all this to you again. But my feelings towards you will never change.

So good luck always!

Hugh.[67]

On the top is scrawled in Hugh's hand: 'Written after a wakeful night, & discussed with Tony before delivery. 27/11.'

Before Dalton's promises could be put to the test, international politics briefly obtruded, and the threat of a Third World War blotted out all other considerations. In the same letter Hugh had told Tony

gloomily: 'If there's a war – & it's a fair risk – I don't want to survive it.
But I would like somehow, if it could be, to die having saved the lives
of you & others who are worth survival!' Five days later, the danger of
war became terrifyingly immediate. On 30th November, President
Truman, in an ill-considered statement, declared that the use of
nuclear weapons against the Chinese in the Korean conflict rested
with commanders in the field. There was serious alarm in London.
What should be done to stop the Americans from committing a
calamitous and lunatic act? Dalton, fresh back from the diplomatic
front in Strasbourg, moved swiftly. The Prime Minister, he decided,
must travel at once to convey in person the views of the British
Government to the American President.

Dalton spoke to Aneurin Bevan in the Commons. Bevan agreed.
Then Dalton passed a note along the front bench to Attlee:

> The latest events, so full of the gravest possibilities – including
> Truman's statement today on the atomic bomb – have convinced
> me that *you ought to fly out to Washington at once* – to confer with
> Truman.[68]

Attlee responded by calling an immediate Cabinet, which decided
to announce such a visit the same night. The Prime Minister flew to
Washington, and thereafter the President spoke with greater restraint.[69]

A few days after Attlee's flight, Dalton – barely recovered from his
illness in September – was struck down by another fever which caused
him to spend ten recuperative days at West Leaze, planting trees and
reading Boswell's *Journal* and his own old diaries. By late January,
when his health seemed restored, his emotions towards Tony had
subsided.

In November, Tony had apparently been trying to fend Hugh off.
Now he was more than ready to treat his friend as a personal as well
as political counsellor. Indeed if the fussing did not stop, this was
partly because Tony did nothing to discourage it. He, too, had been
in a state of private turmoil, and found Hugh a sympathetic listener.
Should he, or should he not, marry his girlfriend? More than half a
century before, Canon Dalton had cautioned the young Arthur Benson against the dangers of early matrimony. Hugh gave similar advice.
'You must be firm – to the point of ruthlessness – about marriage', he
declared. For a future statesman, choosing a wife was a serious part
of the political calculus.[70] For the time being, Tony remained single.
With Hugh, he returned to the bantering, teasing basis for their
friendship. The dangerous explicitness of Strasbourg exchanges was

forgotten. 'Hugh was very pure in his attitude towards Tony', Olga Davenport recalls. 'It was a crush which reminded me of my first crush on my headmistress.' She recalls Hugh and Tony at Hinton engaged in 'schoolboy horse-play', much to the delight of fellow guests.[71] Others remember Hugh's friend Catherine Walston scolding Tony at a Cambridgeshire house-party for leading Hugh on by draping himself languidly over a sofa.[72]

During the long overnight sittings caused by the Government's slender majority and the determination of the Opposition to press every advantage, Hugh and Tony were together, talking and arguing, more than ever. In February 1951 Hugh spent an enjoyable evening in the company of Tony Crosland, Aneurin Bevan, and Crosland's former pupil at Oxford, Tony Benn, who had succeeded Cripps as M.P. for Bristol East. As usual Crosland was on the offensive:

> My trouble, he said, was that all the people I admired, and who influenced me, at Cambridge were second rate – Rupert, Belloc, Pigou, Goldie, Moore – and Cannan after. I liked his frankness in saying this – he had had a few drinks – we have, I hope, achieved the Principle of Total Frankness even when sober. I said I wouldn't inquire on his second rate influences, beginning with Cole. He said Rupert came very badly out of the Keynes book ... He said he was the only person there who'd read my book 'With B[ritish] G[uns] in I[taly]'. He said he'd read it at Lords, during a dull spell of some match. His next door neighbour asked him what he was reading. 'A book by Dalton.' 'What Dalton? Not Devil Dalton?' I said the account of the Retreat was good. He said 'No. Only Fifth Form stuff.' I said Toscanini's climbing Monte Santo was even better. He didn't remember that.

Dalton's fascination with the working of his friend's mind encouraged him to pick up ideas which he would have taken from nobody else. Since 1945, Dalton had been resolutely wedded to the principle of cheap money. It was Crosland's advocacy in June 1951 which persuaded him that 'provided there was no increase in floating debt rates, and since there was no compulsory redemption of debt till 1953, it was all right to let gilt-edged prices slide, and not to intervene either by word or deed.'[73] Nor did Dalton forget Crosland's remarks about *With British Guns*. A few months later, he wrote in the first volume of his memoirs that 'Much of it, at this distance of time, reads rather schoolboyishly',[74] which was almost a direct quotation.

Dalton's influence on Crosland is harder to measure, but was undoubtedly profound. Crosland was on the way up, his ideas and his world expanding. Intellectually he was eclectic, drawing on friends, mainly outside politics, whose originality and radicalism impressed him. One close friend describes him as a 'vertical' thinker, 'who drilled down into a subject with unflagging force until he was at last able to come up with the ore of his own conclusions.'[75] Another writes that, having decided who were the best-informed people in a particular field, he 'put himself into a very demanding tutorial relationship with them'.[76] Dalton was not, or no longer, much use as a front-rank academic expert. Nevertheless, the tutorial aspect was continuously present. In their early dialogues, Crosland was able to benefit from Dalton's experience of high policy, about which Crosland could learn little from his own circle of contemporaries.

In their political values, Dalton and Crosland stood close together, both believing that socialism should entail the use of government to create a fairer society, and identifying class distinctions and the distribution of wealth as key obstacles. 'The real interest now', Dalton told his friend in December 1951, 'is to sketch the next stretch of road towards socialism.'[77] Crosland agreed, and during his first years in Parliament this task became his main preoccupation.

On 1st February 1951, Dalton became Minister of Local Government and Planning – combining his existing duties with all of those currently exercised by Aneurin Bevan (who moved to Labour) apart from Health, which was given to another minister, Hilary Marquand. Dalton's appointment was part of a long-expected reshuffle, and it seemed logical that the combination envisaged by Attlee immediately after the election – Town and Country Planning plus Housing – should now be brought about.

The decision followed several weeks of bargaining in which Dalton displayed a lack of concern about the extent of his own responsibilities. The previous October he had written to Attlee saying that he wanted more to do, both administratively and in the House.[78] By December, however, his desire for a heavier workload had diminished, and he told the Prime Minister that he would be happier just taking Local Government, leaving Housing to someone else.[79] Gaitskell noted that Dalton 'was not particularly keen to take housing ... '[80] It was Bridges's intervention, arguing that Housing and Local Government should not be separated, which persuaded Attlee that Dalton should get a greatly expanded department.[81]

As a result Dalton became, for the first time since his resignation, one of the most important administrative figures in the Government.[82] He moved into the old Ministry of Health headquarters in Whitehall, and took over half of the staff – increasing his employees from

1,300 to 3,000.[83] When the Conservatives took office a few months later, Harold Macmillan inherited Dalton's housing responsibilities. Later Macmillan acknowledged his debt to Dalton's energetic championing of New Towns, and was grateful for the legacy of the New Town Development Bill, which facilitated urban overfill schemes and the movement of industry out of cities.[84]

Given that a dissolution could not be long delayed, possibilities were limited. Dalton's working principle remained, 'Let something be done at once'. He planned 'to push Housing along' by cheapening and simplifying design, and to press ahead with New Towns and the designation of National Parks, in order to show maximum results before an election.[85] It was uphill work. As a condition of accepting Housing, he had insisted on taking Evelyn Sharp with him ('the best man I've got'),[86] but he was not pleased with all his newly acquired officials, regarding those on the Local Government side, in particular, as 'ageing duds'.[87] From the point of view of the officials, there was little incentive to pursue Dalton's schemes in view of the growing expectation of a Tory victory: civil service eyes were beginning to look elsewhere.[88] 'I can't pretend, in these conditions, to be able to get up a really driving interest in my new Department', Dalton wrote less than two months after taking over. ' ... [W]hat, in these conditions can I as Minister do?'

One thing he might have done was to angle for the Foreign Secretaryship, which was at long last coming free. He chose not to do so, doubtless perceiving that he would not be offered it. Late in February, Attlee saw him at No. 10 and hinted that Bevin's retirement was imminent. Without being asked, Dalton quickly excluded himself as a possible successor, partly on grounds of health. He could not afford to take on the Foreign Office, he said, and fall short 'physically and mentally'. A few weeks earlier, when John Freeman inquired whether he wanted to succeed Bevin, he had replied that at this stage he did not. 'I didn't want soiled bedclothes, only for an hour.' To others who approached him on this question he repeated the same oddly indelicate metaphor, as though the Foreign Office was a woman he had courted all his life, only to reject her in old age as a whore.

All the same, Dalton took a keen interest in other contenders, both for Bevin's job and for lesser appointments. He warned Attlee against Sir Hartley Shawcross ('Sir Peacock', he called him, or 'Sir Tartly Doublecross'. 'No lawyers at the FO!', he proclaimed). He urged the Prime Minister himself to double up as Foreign Secretary – as MacDonald had done in 1924. When Attlee brushed this aside, he proposed Jim Griffiths in preference to the most obvious choice, Herbert Morrison, against whom he warned in the strongest terms.

When, at a second meeting, the Prime Minister turned to junior posts, Dalton praised Jim Callaghan, John Freeman, Geoffrey de Freitas, Arthur Bottomley and Fred Peart. They agreed that Ian Mikardo and Austen Albu were unsuitable, Attlee apparently on racial grounds ('they both belonged to the Chosen People, and he didn't think he wanted any more of *them*'). At the very end, the Prime Minister said: 'Crosland. That's an able chap.' Dalton replied 'Yes, very', and eagerly gave an account of Crosland's performance in Strasbourg. 'But I think he'd better wait a bit', said Attlee. 'Yes, I think so too', said Dalton, a little sadly.

Attlee ignored Dalton's advice and gave Herbert Morrison the Foreign Secretaryship. Dalton immediately predicted that Morrison would make a mess of it, and damage his reputation.[89] Years later, Attlee admitted that Dalton had been right. 'Worst appointment I ever made. Jim Griffiths should have got the job.'[90]

Although Dalton knew he had no chance of becoming Foreign Secretary and had indicated that he was not even a bidder, the decision marked an important ending in his career. It was now certain that one ambition would never be fulfilled. He wrote to his old comrade, Sir Gladwyn Jebb:

> ... [E]ver since the election of 1945 and my after-lunch switch ... my desire for the F.O. has steadily weakened and, for a considerable time now, I have not wanted it at all. And this, to save any possible embarrassments, I have made known. To shape a policy yourself in an important field, from a fresh start, may be tremendous fun, especially with time in front of you and a majority behind you. To take over a policy already half-shaped by someone else, and half mis-shaped by events, with not much time to play with and not much majority – that is less attractive. A duty, perhaps, if pressed upon one; hardly, in my view, a prize to strive for.[91]

This may not have been the whole story. In the first draft of his letter, Dalton wrote 'not a prize to run after, or intrigue for'. Perhaps he had retained a lingering hope that without running, striving or intriguing the prize he had coveted all his life would finally come his way.

There was an uneasy feeling to the Government in 1951. Younger men were staking claims for the future; older men were looking anxiously over their shoulders. All had to submit to the heavy strain of lengthy sittings and lack of pairing, and to a nerve-racking uncertainty, from one week to the next, about the life of the Parliament.

Dalton spent more and more time in the company of young friends – mainly class-of-1945 M.P.s – and less and less with his contemporaries, for whom, these days, he seldom had a good word. His determination not to let age and responsibility make him stuffy or pompous, and his need for the affection of his young men, led him into parliamentary frolics reminiscent of his earliest days in Parliament, when he had been suspended for singing in the Lobby and refusing to move when ordered by the Speaker.

On one occasion Miss Florence Horsbrugh, a Tory Member, was making a speech just before 1 a.m. about sausages. 'It is important that people should know that some sausages are to have milk powder in them, and some are not', she declared. 'What I do feel strongly about is that the housewife should be able to know if the sausages she buys are of the one sort or the other.'[92] Dalton was sitting on the Government Front Bench, and the boredom was too much for him. 'What do we do with a sausage?' he boomed. 'The same as they do with bananas at Girton!'[93] Miss Horsbrugh chose to hear only one word. 'I hear someone saying "bananas"', she continued, 'and I should like to talk about the nutritional value of bananas, but that would be out of order.' *Hansard* recorded the reply, but not the interjection.[94]

Two nights later, Dalton took part in a lusty rag in the Smoking Room. Each new Labour arrival was loudly cheered, and each Tory departure was sung out to the tune of 'Good night Tories!' When Harold Macmillan rose to get a drink, a Labour M.P. at once sat in his seat. Labour M.P.s also sang 'We'll make Florence Horsbrugh go a'hiking with Dalton, when the Red Revolution comes!'

Such frivolities passed time during the long nights. They were a symptom of a growing tension in the P.L.P., reflected in a quarrel within the Government itself. This quarrel was about to produce the biggest Labour Party split since before the war, helping Labour to lose the next election and stay out of power until 1964.

On 22nd March there was a major battle in Cabinet over a proposal by the new Chancellor to impose charges for false teeth and glasses, and to put a ceiling on Health Service spending. Aneurin Bevan, architect of the National Health Service, reacted fiercely against this breach in the principle of free medical care, and threatened resignation. In the background were other causes for disquiet: in particular, the heavy cost of the rearmament programme, incurred because of the Korean war. Attlee, meanwhile, was in hospital undergoing treatment for an ulcer.

Dalton found himself delicately placed. He saw plainly that behind Bevan's anger lay jealousy and disappointment at having been passed over for the Treasury and the Foreign Office in quick succession.[95]

As an ex-Chancellor, he understood the pressures confronting Gaitskell.[96] Unlike Gaitskell, however, he also felt that if Bevan resigned,
it would be a serious loss to the Cabinet. He admired Bevan's courage,
clarity and vision. Recently, too, they had been agreed on many
things – on steel nationalisation, on the need to curb American belli-
cosity in the Far East, and on the danger to Europe of a survival, or
rebirth, of German militarism.

Hence Dalton was by no means an uncritical or wholehearted
Gaitskell supporter. He gave the Chancellor loyal backing when he
needed it. But he listened to both sides, in the hope of mediating
between them.[97] On the one hand, he told Harold Wilson (the only
Cabinet minister firmly behind Bevan) that the Minister of Labour
had things out of focus. On the other, he issued Gaitskell a stern warning, born of a long experience which the Chancellor lacked:

> ... I thought he seriously underestimated Nye and his potentialities
> for mischief. I thought that HG thought too little of the Party and
> too much, relatively, of the general body of the electorate.

On 6th April Dalton saw Bevan alone. They spoke at length.
Dalton's strongest impression was of Bevan's furious resentment of
Gaitskell. The Minister of Labour seemed bitterly angry about
Gaitskell's promotion as Chancellor, about Gaitskell's alleged hostility towards his Health Service, and about the rearmament programme which was being allowed to take precedence as a call on
expenditure. The Chancellor, he declared, was 'wildly pro-American
and anti-Russian'. Dalton urged restraint; but Bevan declared that
he would resign at the time of the Budget Speech unless the charges
were withdrawn.[98] Next day Dalton wrote to Bevan urging, 'Don't
do it now'.[99]

On 9th April there was a crucial Cabinet on the Budget. Bevan and
Wilson claimed that, if legislation was introduced imposing health
charges, there might be enough Labour abstentions in the House to
cause a Government defeat. 'In that event', they maintained, 'the
Government would face a General Election in circumstances which
would enable the Conservatives to pose as the champions of a free
Health Service.'[100]

Between Cabinet sessions, Dalton went to Bevan's room at the
House for a further talk. Bevan attacked the Cabinet. 'Who are they?'
he declared. 'I didn't choose them. The PM chooses them. They are
either old men or rootless men, like Gaitskell and Gordon Walker.
They are dismantling the welfare state.' Dalton was now filled with a
sense of doom, believing that the long-term future of the Labour Party

was at stake. Bevan was not so much to blame, he.concluded, as those who egged him on. He vented his feelings in angry denunciation of Bevan's entourage: Richard Crossman, Michael Foot, Ian Mikardo and Harold Wilson. Apart from George Tomlinson (the Minister of Education), who sought a postponement of a decision on the charges, Harold Wilson remained Bevan's only Cabinet supporter. 'Nye and the dog', Dalton called them.

Yet his feelings were confused. He was concerned about Gaitskell's stubbornness, and lack of finesse. He was conscious of the power and importance of Bevan within the Movement. At the same time, he was particularly saddened to see John Freeman, threatening to resign with Bevan, attach himself to the rebel camp. 'J.F. hopes that, if he and I are on opposite sides of the gulf, it won't end our friendship', Dalton wrote the same night. 'He expresses a great regard and affection for me. I say I feel the same for him.'[101]

Next day (10th April) Gaitskell announced the fateful prescription charges in his Budget Speech. While the Opposition replied, Dalton and Bevan were to be seen in animated conversation on the Government front bench.[102] Later the Minister of Local Government and Planning was observed 'wolfishly stalking through the corridors, on the prowl for any tender little sheep likely to let out a bleat on Mr. Bevan's behalf',[103] and button-holing any friend he saw coming out of the Tea Room in order to ask how the bulk of M.P.s had reacted to the Speech.

Before a meeting of the P.L.P. next day, Dalton was still somewhat wolf-like. 'Good morning, Mr. Dalton', Harold Wilson greeted him, politely. 'I hope we're still colleagues. I've been trying to persuade Nye not to resign.' Dalton growled back, 'I've heard different.' After the meeting he called across to John Strachey, a pro-Bevan waverer, 'If there was an election now you'd be down the pan good and proper, with some better men than you and some worse ones.' When Strachey replied, indignantly, 'You have got a simple and genteel way of putting things', Dalton barked back: 'well, you've been psycho-analysed, you should not find any difficulty in plain speech.'

For the moment the resignations were postponed, and Dalton retired to Wiltshire for a weekend of solitary digging. On Saturday night news came through of Ernest Bevin's death. Bevin was the first of the 1945 Big Five to die. He and Dalton had been ministerial colleagues for most of the time since May 1940, and allies before that. 'He did a lot of big things and, as F. Secy, made some big mistakes', Dalton reflected. 'But on balance, he did a lot of good in his life.'

Once again Dalton's thought turned to the future. Apart from his 'fibulating' heart, he himself had no immediate, or serious, physical worries. His aims, however, had ceased to focus on himself. 'I am 63. I have lost all hustling ambition, if I ever had it', he recorded. 'I want to hold the Party United, to encourage it to be bold and fresh, and to help on the best of the young.'[104] Helping the young had long been a favourite pursuit. Now it became his central purpose.

'Our average age is too high', he wrote to the Prime Minister in hospital. The Government was top heavy with ageing ministers past their best. Young talent needed to be brought forward. In particular Bevin's place in the Cabinet (in March, Bevin had become Lord Privy Seal) should be taken by Alf Robens, an up-and-coming trade unionist. Arthur Henderson and John Strachey should be ejected from their respective service departments and replaced by two Daltonian protégés, Geoffrey de Freitas and John Freeman. Richard Crossman, on the other hand, should *on no account* be given a junior post at the Foreign Office. With most of this, Attlee agreed.

On the crisis, Dalton wrote: 'As you know, we were once or twice very close to the precipice. But we just didn't go over and smash the Party at the bottom.'[105] He was wrong. The lull was only temporary, and over the next few days tensions increased. As often at times of high anxiety, Dalton began to strike out at random. He was so rude to James Meade at an XYZ meeting on 18th April that Crosland made him write a letter of apology.[106]

At Cabinet next day Bevan placed on record his firm intention to resign on the Third Reading of the Health Charges Bill.[107] Dalton now moved quickly. On 20th April he rushed first to the Prime Minister's bedside, where he followed up his letter and pressed Attlee to bring in Robens as Minister of Labour should Bevan resign; and then to the Chancellor, pressing the merits of Freeman, in a last ditch attempt to separate Freeman from the Bevan camp. Gaitskell was receptive. 'Hugh said he liked him very much, and knew that I did', Dalton noted. 'And Dora liked his wife.'

Dalton's mood was the same as in September 1939, when he had spent the last few days of peace in a series of frantic and fruitless errands, dashing from one actor to another. This time his excitement led to sleeplessness and an over-reliance on pills. 'I haven't felt so tired out', he wrote the same night, 'mentally and spiritually, for years.'[108]

His plan was to isolate Bevan. Accusations of anti-working-class bias would fall flat if a hole created by Bevan was immediately filled by somebody as 'rooted' in the Movement as Robens. At the same time the offer of a better job might tempt Freeman not to join the resigners.

On Saturday 21st April, eleven days after the Budget, Bevan sent the Prime Minister a long letter of resignation which extended the area of disagreement far beyond teeth and glasses.[109] On Sunday, Dalton took Freeman for a walk on Hampstead Heath, pulling out all the stops: Gaitskell's liking for him, Dora's liking for his wife, and the possibility of promotion.[110] 'Hugh was terribly hurt and anguished that I should be on the other side', Freeman recalls. 'He hated the idea that his little group of young men was being split apart.'[111]

The following day, Bevan's letter was published, and Harold Wilson's resignation was also announced. Freeman, unmoved by Dalton's attempted bribery, determined to follow them. 'Tempers will be high and cruel things said for a time, but our friendship will always mean much to me', he wrote to Dalton, when it was too late.[112] Bellowing with rage, Dalton went in search of Crosland. 'I shall never recommend any one to read *Tribune* again ... I'm through with you', was the worst thing he could think of to shout at Michael Foot. 'Within five minutes I could get Freeman promotion if I knew he would take it', Dalton told Crosland, missing the point. 'But what does he want?'

When Freeman was summoned to the Prime Minister's hospital bed that night, Dalton lent him his car. Patting the young minister on the shoulder, he said 'Think again. Be prepared to change your mind.' Freeman had already given his answer: a firm 'no' to a direct offer from the Chief Whip. Later, Freeman and Dalton met for a talk, no longer as colleagues in the Government. 'I said to John that he was a wonderful scalp for the uglies', Dalton noted sadly. 'I had heard Mikardo exulting over him in the entrance to a lavatory.'[113]

'It was a battle between us for power', Gaitskell later acknowledged; ' – he knew it and so did I.'[114] Bevan, with his plaintive cry 'Aren't I worth £23 million?' (referring to the cost of the health charges), clearly felt the same.[115] Yet more was involved than a struggle between the Cabinet's two most forceful personalities. As Attlee's biographer has pointed out, the conflict could be interpreted as a contest between 'consolidationism' and 'advance', between reformism and socialism, or between 'pragmatists' and 'realists'.[116] There was also another dimension. Gaitskell and Bevan were fundamentally opposed, not so much in policy, as in political style. Behind that difference lay divisions within the post-war Parliamentary Labour Party, reflecting, in turn, social class.

In 1945 the P.L.P. had been transformed. Suddenly it had become more confident, better educated and more heterogeneous than ever before. Previously, most Labour M.P.s had been proletarian and trade unionist; after 1945, all classes were strongly represented. So large was the post-war Party that there even emerged identifiable social groupings within the ranks of non-union, middle-class M.P.s. The most dominant was a kind of public school and Oxbridge club: the nucleus of the so-called Hampstead Set. Within this unacknowledged society's social walls, close friendships were forged and intimate rivalries developed.

These were substantial men, principled, industrious, well-informed, and filled with a desire not to preach or convert, but to rule. They agreed with Douglas Jay's dictum that the Gentleman from Whitehall was usually right. They applauded Gaitskell, whose whole case had become, according to his biographer, 'that Labour had to prove itself a responsible party of government.'[117] They found allies in the big unions and among the apolitical union M.P.s. Early on, many of them began to climb the promotional ladder. In October 1946, Dalton was told of a joke going the rounds that to get on in the Government it helped to have been at Eton or Haileybury (Attlee's old school) or in the Guards.[118] Not everybody was amused. The tight control of the Wykehamists (Cripps, Gaitskell, Jay) on economic affairs; the rapid preferment of an Etonian peer, Pakenham, of another Wykehamist, Kenneth Younger, and of a Wellingtonian, Gordon Walker; the rising fortunes of two Haileyburians, Mayhew and de Freitas – these, and other appointments, gave the impression of a network.

'How can you support a public school boy from Winchester against a man born in the back streets of Tredegar?' Aneurin Bevan is supposed to have asked Sam Watson, the Durham miners' leader, who was backing Gaitskell. A similar question might have been put to Bevan in the 1930s, when he had supported Cripps against working-class leaders like Morrison and Bevin. Several of Bevan's closest followers in the early 1950s came from public schools: Crossman, Foot, Driberg and Freeman, in particular. The mood of the Bevanites, however, differed significantly from that of the Hampstead Set. Crucially, Bevanites stood outside the new establishment: an odd alliance of bohemian intellectual flamboyance (Crossman, Driberg, Foot) and anti-upper class resentment (Wilson, Mikardo, Barbara Castle). After a time, it was the second element that came to dominate, with 'Nye's dog' as its most natural spokesman.

Superficially, Hugh Gaitskell and Harold Wilson had much in common. Both were Oxford P.P.E. men, who had come into politics from university senior common rooms and the wartime civil service. Yet there were vital differences in heritage, and hence in attitude. Gaitskell's middle class had been Tory, southern, Anglican and upper. Wilson's was Liberal, northern, non-conformist and lower. Despite his own rapid advancement, Wilson spoke the language of the restless local party activists, greatly expanded in number, who were instinctively suspicious of mandarin-manqué politicians like Gaitskell, and who found in Bevan's evangelism a mood and an ideal to share.

Socially Dalton was closer to the Hampstead Set, which included many of the young men he had brought forward, and ties of friendship were increasingly to pull him in their direction. Politically, however, he remained divided. On the health charges, he had found Gaitskell's position easy to support and he was exasperated by Bevan's egotism. Yet he differed from many of his young men, including Gaitskell, in his hostility to traditional authority. Like the Bevanite bohemians, he saw himself as the Gentleman from Whitehall's worst enemy. He also shared many Bevanite positions on foreign policy and especially Germany. And, though he developed a powerful dislike for some of Bevan's lieutenants, he continued to feel that Bevan himself stood for socialist values that were worth preserving.

Michael Foot accuses Dalton of cynicism, of seeking to save himself by keeping in with both sides. In reality, Dalton seems to have been a sincere, if ineffective, peace-maker genuinely concerned to bring enemies together, puzzled and upset by the Party's disarray. So far from helping him, his exertions did his own position serious harm. Hitherto, the Left had backed him because of his performance as Chancellor, and because he provided a radical critique of Government policy from within the Cabinet. Now, his loudly proclaimed loyalty to Gaitskell revived old memories on the Left. At the same time, his stance on German rearmament, and his hatred of Morrison, still the main champion of the Labour Right, made the old guard doubt his reliability. As the row escalated into civil war, compromisers were being squeezed out.

For the moment, Dalton's position within the Government, and his wide responsibilities, ensured his continued importance within the Party. Ministerially he was enjoying an Indian summer. Bevin was dead, Cripps and Bevan were out, Morrison was an embarrassing failure at the Foreign Office. Attlee, still weakened by illness, listened to Dalton more closely than at any time since 1947. One newspaper saw Dalton as the fast emerging power behind the Prime Minister,[119] another as the only 'thinker' in the Cabinet.[120] There were comments about Dalton's allegedly dominating influence over Hilary Marquand, Minister of Health, and Sir Hartley Shawcross, now at the Board of Trade.[121] Meanwhile, Dalton used his special link with the Chancellor to press the case for more attacks on the rich, urging his friend not to 'forget the Party' over the limitation of dividends.[122]

Dalton kept in touch with the Bevanites. At the beginning of July, one Sunday paper commented that Dalton's 'loving arms have been observed festively entwined around the shoulders of one mutineer after another'.[123] Dalton told Freeman that he wanted room for manoeuvre, 'between Nye's proposals some of which I might like, and others not, and the mark timers'. Though suspicious, the Bevanites were not discouraging. 'There was never a close-down of discussion between Dalton and us', according to Foot. 'On many things – German rearmament, hostility to Morrison, for instance – Dalton and Nye remained firm allies.' Dalton had little time for Wilson, less for Foot, none at all for Mikardo or Driberg. But he remained friendly with John Freeman and Barbara Castle and continued his old sparring relationship, based on aggressive gossip and the telling of home truths, with Richard Crossman. He enjoyed Crossman's scurrility and bodkin humour, but distrusted his motives and accused him of a personal jealousy towards Gaitskell derived from Winchester school-days. There was also a developing friendship between Dalton and Desmond Donnelly, a maverick Bevanite who, unknown to left-wing associates, leaked Bevanite secrets to Dalton who passed them on to Gaitskell.[124]

In the autumn, Freeman told Crosland that he was counting on Dalton himself becoming a Bevanite within a few months.[125] Yet Dalton was also prepared to slap the Left, especially the fellow travelling Left, when it seemed necessary. In June he alienated his old Cambridge comrade, Leah Manning, by sacking her friend Monica Felton as Chairman of the Stevenage Development Corporation, because of a visit to Communist North Korea which had not been cleared in advance.[126]

Dalton's public face retained its customary ebullience. In July a characteristic gaffe, of a kind that Cripps, Gaitskell or Morrison would never have committed, caused some satisfying eruptions in the City. A light-hearted comment at a village fête to the effect that throwing the Stock Exchange into disorder was 'good fun' led to a bout of Fleet Street blimpishness. 'A remark so cynical, so irresponsible, so devoid of any sense of the gravity of the times', frothed the *Daily Telegraph*.[127] It was the silly season. The Chairman of the Stock Exchange wrote a pompous letter, and Emrys Hughes entertained the Labour benches in the House by declaring that miners in his constituency could not sleep, so appalled were they by what the Minister for Planning and Local Government had said.[128] Another storm, almost equally pleasing, occurred a few weeks later. As part of a campaign for more vigorous price control, Dalton urged housewives to withhold purchases of clothing until prices fell.[129] The textile trade reeled, and *The Economist* called it an 'irresponsible piece of election-eering'.[130] Dalton was delighted to be so much in the public eye. The

Communist *Daily Worker* noted that he still drew more Tory fire than any other Labour politician.[131]

Publicity did not, however, save him from an alarming slide in the N.E.C. election in October. Skilfully led by Mikardo, the Left had organised a 'plumping' campaign so that Bevanite votes would be concentrated on Bevanite candidates. Those not firmly identified as rebels lost support as a result. Dalton fell to seventh place – bottom of those who were elected in the constituency parties section. The sole compensation was that Shinwell was pushed off altogether.

Dalton was now 64. Should he retire from the N.E.C. at 65? Faced with the possibility of defeat, he considered the question seriously. 'Only if I could be pretty sure I'd be succeeded by an *effective younger* chap', he concluded. 'And neither condition could be counted on.' The danger was that Shinwell (eighth) or Wilson (ninth) would fill his place. He wavered. He did not want to end a run of twenty-five years with an ignominious defeat, or an undignified 'counter-intrigued' victory. There was also his own, oft-repeated, principle that the old should make way for the young.[132]

Before he needed to make up his mind, there was a general election. Since May, he had consistently advocated October as the best time for a poll – expecting Labour to lose, but by a smaller margin than if the date were delayed. In this, Dalton was opposed by leading colleagues, including Morrison and Gaitskell.[133] The poll was fixed for 25th October. Dalton was a member of a small drafting committee responsible for the manifesto, which allowed him to slip in an old friend: the capital levy. The final wording contained a promise to 'take measures to prevent large capital gains', a phrase which pleased the Bevanites, without committing Gaitskell to anything specific.[134]

For Dalton personally there was nothing much at stake. His campaign in Bishop Auckland was far less anxious than in 1950. Staying as usual with the Davises, he spent the mornings in his dressing gown, rang his agent around noon, and made speeches in the evening.[135] 'Do you want to go back to mass unemployment, the Means Test and the gross social inequality which we had when the Tories were in power before the war?' he asked audiences.[136] As polling day approached, he worried more about Tony Crosland's battle than his own. In Bishop Auckland, the result was mildly disappointing – a drop in majority from 11,370 to 8,986. But he was happy about the national picture: Labour narrowly beaten, Crosland and Freeman, both on the margin, holding their seats. 'The election results are wonderful', he wrote. 'We are out just at the right moment and our casualties are wonderfully light.'

And so, without shedding a tear, he bid farewell to office for ever.

Harold Macmillan, his old friendly foe, took over Housing. 'He won't
be able to build many more, if as many as I', Dalton predicted, incorrectly. Two days after the poll, he lunched with Attlee at Chequers
for the last time and went on a trip to the ex-Prime Minister's modest
new home, Cherry Cottage. Together they reminisced:

> We've done all that now; written the first chapter of the Socialist
> story, in law and administration. What next? The younger people
> must write the second chapter.

It was the end of an era. None of the top leaders of 1945 – or even
of 1951 – was ever to be a minister again. Attlee, Cripps, Morrison,
Dalton, Bevan, Alexander, Gaitskell: their careers in government
were over. 'How wise we Octoberists were!' Dalton exulted when the
result was known, believing that Labour would sweep back after a
short rest. [137] But he was wrong. His remaining years in the Commons
were spent in Opposition, and there was no Labour Government
again before his death.

XXXIII

Sunset

Loss of office changed the pace. Dalton had been a minister, with two short breaks, for eleven and a half years. Now, he wrote, he was robbed of his slaves and released in an instant from the pressure of responsibility.[1] In the past, he had used political defeat as an opportunity to prepare for the next victory. The days of passionate castle-building were over. Politics remained his life. But it had become the politics of rooted belief, of gut reaction, of Westminster love and hate.

With less to do, he was more than ever at West Leaze, digging, planting and writing. Ruth came back into the picture and their very separate existences moved closer together. Early in 1952 Ruth decided to retire from the London County Council. Her Chairmanship of Parks had been productive: she had introduced tea gardens and sculptural exhibitions, and decorated Kenwood House, after its transfer to the L.C.C., reopening it for public viewing.[2] But she had lost her enthusiasm for the work and wanted to make way for someone younger.[3] She turned to other committees, and spent more time at home.[4]

Hugh was also aware of advancing years. Just after the election he took stock. 'I am slowed down, physically and mentally', he wrote on 10th November, in cruel self-analysis, 'conscious of having a heart and flabby tummy muscles, and tending (sometimes) to repeat myself, and of being well past my best in every way.'[5] Yet he could still hold his own in the toughest company. Two days later he dined with Richard Crossman at the House. They discussed planning for the next stage of socialism. 'Whatever his other failings, Dalton remains a first-rate talker, which means not anecdotes but relevant discussion of the subject', Crossman, not given to undeserved compliments, wrote in his own diary.[6]

Unlike most of his senior colleagues, Dalton decided that he was no longer interested in holding Government office. 'I shan't be a Minister again', he wrote firmly in November. He did not change his mind. But he decided after all to stand again for the N.E.C. The main reason was that, when it came to the crunch, he did not want to exclude himself from the Party's inner counsels. There were other factors too. If he retired his likely successor was Harold Wilson, whom he disliked; and to go now, after the drop in his vote in 1951, might seem like running away.[7] So he preferred to stay and fight, believing that he could hold off the Bevanite challenge because of his championship of left-wing causes.

One issue which he thought might help was German rearmament. On this, he and the Bevanites stood shoulder to shoulder, though their reasoning was somewhat different. The Left was anti-American, pro-pacifist and still afflicted by the 'Russia Complex' – seeing the Soviet Union less as a potential enemy than as a socialist country to be emulated; hence it tended to favour a 'Third Force' approach, and to be suspicious of plans to strengthen a united Western Alliance.[8] Dalton, on the other hand, was pro-NATO and vehemently anti-pacifist, regarding the Soviet Union as a serious military threat. His views were determined by his attitude to Germany, not Russia. In Cabinet he had urged that German armed forces would inevitably attract ex-Nazis and re-kindle old ambitions, and that a German army would be a provocation to the Soviet Union, making war more likely not less.[9] But his friends were under no illusions about his real feelings. As Gaitskell remarked, he was against rearming Germany because he hated Germans.[10]

There was a conflict of loyalties; as the rival clans formed up in preparation for open war, Dalton found himself facing two ways. In opposing German rearmament, the Bevanites were as much concerned to attack the Party establishment (in particular, Morrison and Gaitskell) as with the issue itself. Just before Christmas, Dalton made a broadcast in which, while cleverly keeping within the Party line, he delivered a furious attack on German rearmanent. Crossman was delighted. 'This broadcast has its importance in the internal Party dissension', he noted, 'since it very definitely swings the Party further towards the Left'.[11] Yet Dalton's agreement with the Bevanites on defence did not lead him to join them in the wider Party struggle. He deplored the disunity which they caused, and developed an increasingly bitter dislike for two of their number, Tom Driberg and Ian Mikardo.

On the other hand, he was also uneasy about the official leadership. For the first time since they had known each other, relations between Big Hugh (as Gaitskell's friends called Dalton) and Little Hugh

became strained. Dalton's private ambition had long been for Gaitskell to become Party Leader. In this he did not waver. Yet there was
much about Gaitskell's recent behaviour which bothered him. Gaitskell's position on German rearmament was not the only reason for
disquiet. Dalton noted, in addition, his friend's automatic tendency
to take right-wing positions, and greater readiness to attack the Left
than to criticise the Tories. ' ... I am a little chilled by his excess of
"responsibility",' Dalton wrote in February. 'I must try to stoke him
up. Otherwise the chaps just won't follow him.' An uncomfortable
awareness that Gaitskell had a style and aims very different from his
own, produced something close to a real quarrel in the summer.

Meanwhile Dalton was becoming conscious of a threat to his N.E.C.
seat. For a time, he had hoped that the Bevanites would keep him off
their death-list. In May, George Brown warned him to expect the
worst; Crossman had been denouncing him in the Smoking Room,
despite his stance on German rearmament, as one of the most obstinate of the anti-Bevanites. Dalton pretended not to mind. The Constituency Labour Parties, he argued, were a difficult electorate to
organise. 'Anyhow, I shan't break my neck if I'm beaten.' All the
same, he was deeply worried. On the train coming back from their
comradely Whitsun walk, Barbara Castle's husband Ted confirmed
Brown's warning, indicating that his own preferred slate did not
include Dalton. Dalton exploded with rage.[12]

For the Labour Party, according to Michael Foot, '1952 saw the
most fretful and foetid spring and summer which most of us could
recall'.[13] The battle had less to do with philosophy and ideology than
with political kinship and the distribution of power. In the new climate,
Dalton had become more and more an excluded middle. It made no
difference that Dalton's record was incomparably more socialist than
that of his Bevanite rival, Harold Wilson, or that his Labour background was a great deal firmer.[14] The Left needed a symbolic victory.
The toppling of Dalton – authoritarian member of the old guard –
would provide one.

At the same time, Dalton was undoubtedly losing touch. What he
himself called his 'Slave years of Ministerial self-importance'[15] had
left him with his instinct for rank and file feeling less certain. He
seriously underrated the canvassing sophistication of the Mikardo
machine. He had also failed to notice the revolution in the Party which
had occurred while he was a minister. Patiently, Roy Jenkins suggested
that possession of a safe County Durham seat 'which sends you
messages saying "we are behind you whatever you do"!' had shielded
him from new realities.[16] Individual membership of the Labour Party
had more than doubled since 1945, reaching its historic peak of

1,015,000 in 1952, more than four times what it had been when Dalton first became M.P. for Bishop Auckland. There was a new kind of member, better educated and less deferential. The old assumption that a good platform style, a hostile Tory press, official union backing, and the Party's inbred loyalty to a familiar face, were enough to secure re-election to the constituencies section of the N.E.C., no longer held.

Meanwhile, Dalton's feelings about German rearmament made him deaf to calls for tribal loyalty. He remained an 'issues man', making up his mind on the merits of a particular case, apparently unaware that in the new Left–Right conflict anybody who stepped out from behind his own stockade was liable to be accused of treachery.

In April he travelled with Morgan Phillips (the Party General Secretary) and Barbara Castle in a deputation to Bonn to confer with European socialists. On his return he was able to use the opposition of both the French and Germans to German rearmament as a means of persuading the N.E.C. not to give official support to a Government-backed scheme for a European Army. To his delight, he succeeded in getting the job of drafting an N.E.C. statement proposing that the Russians should be consulted and German elections held before any commitment was made. He was now able to base his own pronouncements on the authority of an official declaration of which he himself was author. For the moment it felt like a great personal success. Richard Crossman described it as a triumph for Dalton who had 'staged a comeback on this German issue, by uniting the contending factions'.[17] But the triumph was short-lived. Dalton soon found himself attacked in the P.L.P. as a 'near-Bevanite',[18] and the accusation that he was a trimmer, with 'a cloven hoof in both camps'[19] left him with fewer firm allies on either side.

Dalton now conceived a plan. Despite the N.E.C. declaration, the Shadow Cabinet (and hence the P.L.P.) still seemed unlikely to oppose the Government's decision to ratify the Paris Agreements (intended to provide the basis for a European Army). In the run-up to the N.E.C. election, Dalton was thus presented with an ideal issue on which to gain publicity of a kind that seemed certain to win him the sympathy of the Labour rank and file. Less than a year before, he had considered a gracious retirement from the N.E.C. Now, the N.E.C. was what really mattered to him. Why, therefore – since he had no desire to be a minister again – stay on in the Shadow Cabinet? His parliamentary colleagues, 'dingy little people' who had to be sucked up to, bored him, and he could not be bothered with Tea Room electioneering any more.[20] Friends, and the press, were insistent that German rearmament was doing him nothing but good.[21] This, surely, was his chance to pull out, make a splash, and win favour in the constituencies:

Large numbers of Parl^y Party are dunderheads, and my influence with them is small. I w^d sooner, if I have to choose, continue to have influence on N.E.C. than on Parl^y party. If I resign on *this* from Parl^y Ctee, & Front Bench, & follow up with speeches, I should make myself safe on N.E.C. Feeling is certainly *agst* German Rearm^t.

So he calculated. But his young friends did not agree. Crosland, just back from a lecture tour in West Germany, put it bluntly. Dalton had a neurosis about German rearmament, and his hatred for Morrison was a matter for psycho-analysis. He should heed the warning he had himself given to the young: never resign, never refuse the offer of a job. Dalton reacted with frustration and anger, not against Crosland, but against other, despised and hated colleagues. It was a familiar pattern – rage at his persecutors; self-pity; an inclination to throw in his hand. Brooding for a weekend at West Leaze, he wrote: 'I shall gradually disengage'. He would not stand again for the Shadow Cabinet and if defeated for the N.E.C. he would not stand again for that. He would only fight one more general election. He would turn away from active politics, write his memoirs and – ultimate fantasy – fly to Australia before he got too frail, and perhaps never come back. 'Don't overstay your welcome', he wrote mournfully, '& bore the young.'

The following week Crosland gathered a small group of young Daltonites to persuade him to change his mind – Jay, Callaghan, Jenkins. The whisky flowed in Crosland's flat, and Dalton began to stamp and flail like a wounded beast, all balance and judgment cast aside. 'I wasn't going to be hushed up by the twopenny halfpenny little people on the Parliamentary committee', he shouted. Carefully, the young men explained that, while his resignation would not affect the German rearmament issue, it would be a great boost to the Bevanites. Dalton became agitated, projecting his misery on to the hated foreign enemy:

I am very angry and worked up about it all. I see Europe going by default. Free economy Germany will be forging ahead; with all their gifts of efficiency displayed to the full. And we, in our mismanaged, mixed-economy overpopulated little island, shall become a second rate power, with no influence and continuing 'crisis'.

I said I hoped I shouldn't be here to see too much of this, and I should advise all younger people to emigrate to Canada or Australia.

Then he stumbled out into the road towards the House. On the way, he met John Freeman, with another Bevanite, J. P. W. Mallalieu. To Freeman's embarrassment, Dalton denounced Mallalieu loudly for smearing Tony Crosland and Roy Jenkins. Mallalieu told him he was drunk. Later the same night, lonely and miserable, Dalton persuaded Gaitskell to come home with him. Gaitskell led the old man back to Ashley Gardens. Dalton was now almost in tears. 'I stamped on the floor and was very indignant', he recorded. 'I said I loved him, but hated many of his backers ... I said he mustn't be too stiff.'

Early in July, Crosland rang Dalton and said that he had decided, after all, to marry his girlfriend, Hilary Sarson. Despite his reservations, Hugh was fond of Hilary, and he noted that Tony had been a playboy long enough. 'He keeps coming back to her', he wrote. He gave the engagement his blessing. But it upset him, adding to his isolation.

A few days later Dalton's opportunity to make a principled resignation passed, as so often before. The Shadow Cabinet decided, after all, to resist ratification of the Paris Agreements. Although this removed Dalton's excuse for martyrdom, he was pleased at a notable victory on an issue about which he cared passionately. But he remained hurt that Gaitskell, whom he had done so much to help, should continue to oppose him. Taking his friend aside, he castigated him for being 'bloody obstinate'. Then, adopting his most schoolmasterly tone and revealing the confusion in his own emotions, he declared: 'Don't fight me too hard over German Rearmament. And don't just become H.M.'s Jack in the Box'. Gaitskell, annoyed, snapped back: 'Well, if you're going to be offensive, I can be too. You sit on the fence. You used not to like people who sat on the fence.' Dalton noted:

I said that, as bet" H.M. & A.B., it was very difficult to sit any-where *but* on the fence. He said one must realise that there was a bitter struggle for Leadership going on. It might last several years. The B-ites might win. Then he'd have to consider whether he could go on in public life. I said there were a lot of people in the middle, who wanted these personal hatreds suppressed. He said this rested with the B-ites. He was very tense and unsmiling.

One grievance concerned Herbert Morrison, against whom Dalton's feelings had developed (as Crosland had observed) into a deeply personal obsession, made worse by Morrison's appointment at the end of the previous administration to the Foreign Office, the one job Dalton had always wanted, and by the dispute over German rearmament. There was now an added factor – the growing danger that

Attlee might soon retire and that Morrison would succeed him. Dalton was furious that Gaitskell, who did not yet rate his own chances, favoured just such an eventuality.

Here was a major source of conflict, and its effect was to leave Dalton lonelier than ever. As the Left–Right conflict intensified, the Right felt the need to build up Morrison in order to counter Bevan's challenge. Angrily, Dalton complained to George Brown of Morrison's 'terrible weaknesses'. But this was not how Brown, or many of his friends, saw it. Forced into organising their own slate of N.E.C. candidates in order to resist the tactics of the Bevanites, the Right began to regard loyalty to Morrison as a touchstone. Brown made the position plain. Some right-wingers were doubtful whether, in addition to canvassing on behalf of Gaitskell, Jim Griffiths and Alf Robens, they should also work for Dalton, because he seemed to be gunning for Morrison. Dalton was marooned in political no-man's land – attacked by the Left as a pro-Gaitskell anti-Bevanite representative of the *ancien régime*; yet also challenged on the Right as a compromiser, and an anti-Morrisonian. In this new-style politics, rough and vicious, Dalton and Gaitskell found themselves rivals, competitors for influential backers and for rank-and-file votes. Hence the edginess in their relations. Dalton, eager to think well of his friend, blamed Dora. 'Best a non-political wife', he told Brown, 'like Hilary for Tony, if you can't have, like me a *wise* political wife.'[22]

Dalton won the immediate battle on German rearmament. In bizarre alliance with Shinwell and Bevan, he manoeuvred the Party's higher committees towards opposition to the Government.[23] But the price of victory was high. Frank Pakenham, speaking for many of the Morrisonians, called him a Bevanite, 'I hope without offence'. Dalton replied, 'Without offence but without accuracy.' Retreating to West Leaze, Dalton nursed wounds and considered his new situation. 'The resistance, organised by Morrison, has been very persistent', he wrote. 'Much ill has been spoken of me by the Morrisonites, & many faces, which used to smile at me always when we passed, do so no longer.'[24] The omens were bad.

Through most of the summer of 1952 Dalton worked on his memoirs, lifting himself out of the present and into the past. It was the first August since 1939 he had not spent as a minister. When he surfaced briefly for a Fabian school, his chosen role was still that of honest broker. 'I intend to do my best to help to bridge differences and bring rival factions together', he declared.[25] The *Observer* saw this as a rather desperate bid for the support of both wings of the Party. 'One can envisage his arriving at Morecambe', it noted, 'fresh from a hike along the Pennines, gathering the boys round a camp fire and giving them a chat on the Honour of the Patrol.'[26]

By the time he got to Morecambe for Party Conference, he expected to lose.[27] The night before the result was announced Jim Callaghan rang to say, in effect, that defeat was a certainty.[28] Dalton believed that he would be squeezed out by both Left and Right: that he and Mikardo would lose their seats to Wilson and Gaitskell.[29] In fact the Bevanites almost swept the board – taking six out of seven places, leaving the mild and inoffensive Jim Griffiths as a solitary representative of the old guard. Mikardo stayed, and Wilson and Crossman replaced Morrison and Dalton. Crossman, the bottom Bevanite, got 620,000, and Morrison was runner-up with 584,000. Dalton – having suffered at the hands of both machines, but still with a solid body of personal support – followed with 437,000, while Gaitskell trailed with 330,000.

The defeat of Morrison, much more of a surprise than that of Dalton, and the annihilation of Shinwell, placed far down the list, softened the blow. 'H.M. still has senile ambitions to be P.M.', Dalton wrote to Jebb in October.[30] However, Dalton's result had a finality about it which Morrison's lacked. Morrison's vote remained fairly steady, while Dalton's slumped badly, for the second year running. Dalton showed no emotion as his political execution was announced, but later Tom Anderson, the Bishop Auckland agent, found him in his hotel bedroom, with tears in his eyes, taking consolation from a bottle of whisky.[31] Soon he evolved a standard reply to commiserators: 'I think you're sorrier than I am.'[32]

The Morecambe Conference was 'rowdy, convulsive, vulgar, splenetic'.[33] Jay recalled it as 'one of the most unpleasant experiences I ever suffered in the Labour Party'.[34] Dalton stuck it out on the platform for the rest of the week, putting his usual exuberant face to the world. During a speech by Crossman he was to be seen 'in uncontrollable spasms of Homeric laughter'.[35] He left early on Friday, before the rush, having avoided condoling with Morrison or congratulating the victors (apart from Crossman) and having caught a bad cold in the head.[36] Earlier, Harold Wilson, herald of the brave new world, had sharply twisted the knife. 'Nye's little dog has turned round and bitten Dalton where it hurts', the new Executive member was heard to remark after the result was known.[37]

Morecambe took away Dalton's main power base. The N.E.C. was much more important in the 1950s than it has since become – tying together, rather than separating, parliamentary and extra-parliamentary organisations, settling policy, meting out justice and discipline. For a quarter of a century, Dalton had taken his Executive responsibilities more seriously than any other member. In the 1930s, he had used his N.E.C. seat to fill the Party's policy vacuum, to revise the Party Constitution, to reverse Labour's stance on foreign affairs and defence. During the war, he had updated and re-written Labour's domestic and foreign plans in preparation for the 1945 election. In recent years, as Chairman of the International Committee, he had battled against Bevin over Palestine, led Labour opposition to European federalism, and turned the Party away from German rearmament. His huge influence in Labour Party affairs was now removed, and his career as a 'Transport House man', almost the embodiment of Party loyalty, was over. Morrison was to fight his way back, gaining a place on the Executive, ex-officio, as Deputy Leader. But not Dalton.

Dalton stayed on the Shadow Cabinet, no longer taking much interest in its affairs. German rearmament had ceased, for the time being, to be a central issue, and he had no stake in the other fights, which bored and distressed him. 'I suppose I must stand. I'm awfully allergic', he wrote when the question of the Shadow Cabinet elections arose. ' ... The hatreds in this Labour Party are so hateful and so harmful that one would almost prefer not to be here.'[38] He was re-elected in fifth place – after Griffiths, Ede, Gaitskell and Robens and just ahead of Callaghan – showing that he was still popular among M.P.s. But he was much more interested in writing what he called 'my not-wholly-unamusing-nor-uncontroversial-life',[39] and before the end of November 1952 he despatched the first volume to the printers.

Late the same autumn, Tony and Hilary married. Hugh had offered wedding presents to the value of a hundred guineas, suggesting that part of the money might be spent on return tickets to Marrakesh for their honeymoon. Alternatively, he wrote, they might like to go to West Leaze for a few days, and spend all the money on furniture. 'It is remote & peaceful & there is a spacious double bed', he pointed out. There was also a woman to cook, and 're-make the double bed, each day'.[40] Tony opted for furniture, but not for West Leaze. Instead, he and Hilary accompanied Nicholas and Clarissa Kaldor on a motor trip to southern Spain.[41]

After the wedding, and much in need of a break, Hugh took himself off for a two-week Christmas holiday on his own to Israel, as the guest of an appreciative Government.[42] He met old L.S.E. students, including Moshe Sharrett, the foreign minister, and David Hacohen, a member of the Knesset. 'Here is a closer approach to Social Equality than can be found in almost any other modern country', he wrote when he got back.[43] The trip, a blessed relief from P.L.P. quarrels, revived his taste for foreign travel. As soon as he returned he accepted another offical invitation – this time to visit Brazil in the late summer and early autumn, thereby missing Party Conference for the first time in thirty years. Politically, he was slackening off. His garden, always a source of relaxation, took up more of his attention. In February he planted a spinney – 200 beech, 100 Austrian pine, 800 hybrid larch – and contemplated, with deep satisfaction, this dependable legacy to the future. When Roy Jenkins asked whether he would like to be in the next Labour Government, perhaps as Lord President, he replied that nobody over sixty-five should be in the next Cabinet, except the Prime Minister.[44]

Early in 1953 Crosland published a short study called *Britain's Economic Problem*. After reading it, Dalton sent eight pages of detailed criticism, bringing practical experience to bear:

> p. 212. New Planning Staff. Depends on chaps you can get. 'All under the Chancellor.' I suppose so, but it is a killing job. I don't see a reasonable & efficient solution of this. Perhaps large devolution by Chancellor to at least 2 able Treasury Ministers.

At the end, he wrote: 'But you've done damned well with your first book, & now I expect you're making rapid progress with your second.'[45]

Dalton's own book was published in May 1953, taking his life up to the 1931 election. Entitled *Call Back Yesterday*, it was vivid, funny, honest and irreverent. The last section contains the best account of the confused second Labour Government that has been written. As political autobiography, it was pioneering, and started a fashion for frank confessions which others have followed since. It got a mixed reception. 'I evoke strong emotions both ways', Dalton wrote.[46] Bloomsbury was offended by the assertiveness, the enthusiasm for power. Harold Nicolson, once an eager supplicant for Dalton's favours, admonished him severely for his literary style, 'that eccentric combination of the declamatory with the secretive, of the dogmatic with the confidential'.[47] Inside the Labour Party attention focussed, with fascination or alarm, on the author's political revelations. Herbert Morrison, finding a copy in Jim Callaghan's lavatory, remarked sourly as he came out: 'I didn't know the bugger kept a diary like that.'[48] Dalton's closest friends used the book as an opportunity for the kind of tough judgments he encouraged them to make. Roy Jenkins accused him of cynicism and of treating politics as a game;[49] John Freeman suggested that he had no political philosophy, simply identifying uncritically with his adopted class; hence his friends had learned to look elsewhere for guidance.[50]

Both were really writing not about Dalton past, but Dalton present, watching him and each other from opposing battlements. But Dalton was now far more absorbed in his own personal history and in distant, happy, pre-parliamentary memories than he was concerned about contemporary events. Rupert Brooke was more than ever in his mind.[51] When a reader of his memoirs sent a photograph of Brooke's grave, Dalton replied: 'Some day, maybe, I shall make a pilgrimage myself to Skyros.'[52] He told a new friend, Catherine Walston, that he himself had been 'quiet and strangely secret as a child'. The phrase was derived (perhaps unconsciously) from lines written by Brooke in 1908: 'We found you pale and quiet, and strangely crowned with flowers / Lovely and secret as a child ... '[53]

In August and September he spent six weeks in Brazil – again without Ruth – returning with jewels for his favourite beautiful wives: amethysts for Hilary, and topazes for Olga Davenport and Dobs Little, wife of Crosland's economist friend Ian Little.[54] He had missed Conference, and now that he was back, he was often away from the House. His absence did not harm his reputation. Perhaps it even helped it. Standing again for the Shadow Cabinet, he retained fifth place – with his vote up from 140 to 159.

1953 was a marking-time, literary, recuperative year. In 1954, Dalton had a renewed burst of political activity. In December 1953, the American Secretary of State, John Foster Dulles, threatened Western Europe with an 'agonising reappraisal' of policy if the debate on the European Defence Community (E.D.C.) was not brought rapidly to a conclusion. Within the Labour Party the old row over Germany began again. 'No guns for the Huns', was Dalton's motto.[55] In January he warned that Adenauer might revert to 'the traditional German foreign policy we know so well',[56] and he demanded that the West should placate the Russians by at least postponing plans to rearm Germany.[57]

Dalton was galvanising himself for an all out fight with his opponents on the issue when he slipped a disc, immobilised himself, and missed a key meeting of the Shadow Cabinet, which decided that, because the Russians had proved themselves irreconcilable, outright opposition to E.D.C. should end. The N.E.C. swiftly agreed. The contrast with two years before was poignant. Then, what Crossman called 'a really clever piece of Daltonian politics'[58] had produced a tactical victory in the two key bodies of the Party. Now, Dalton was no longer a member of one and had been absent through ill health from the other. As a result the battle was lost.

By April he had recovered enough to take part in the Budget Debate – his first parliamentary speech of the year – but there were grim signs of growing frailty. 'I'd been apprehensive beforehand', he wrote, 'feared I might be terribly immobile at Box, not easily able to "give way" and get up again, might feel suddenly very tired and lose thread, and lose it suddenly through sudden pain.'[59] Parliament was more than ever distasteful. He thundered on against the Party's policy on German rearmament. German territorial ambitions in the East were one of the most likely causes of a Third World War,[60] he declaimed, and drew unreal parallels from the 1930s.[61] Nobody really listened: he spoke only for himself. The press still saw him as a middle-of-the-roader, standing between the factions.[62] 'I'd sooner sit on the fence than lie down in the shit on either side of it', he told someone, liked the remark, and repeated it.

As an elder statesman, he began to enjoy a career as a pundit on the new medium of television – taking part in the B.B.C.'s *In The News* programme, where he faced old comrades like Lord Vansittart, iller and even more removed from the real world than himself. The B.B.C. Archives have kept the film of one such programme, televised in April 1955 during a newspaper strike, and called 'A Week Without National Newspapers'. In a discussion chaired by Frank Byers, a Liberal, Dalton and Richard Crossman face two Conservatives, Walter Elliot and Sir Robert Boothby. Dalton appears older than his years, patrician and episcopal, with a voice – a mixture of cathedral closes and High Tables – of a kind that is today unknown in the Labour Party. His remarks are crisp, witty, donnish and wry. When he speaks, he cocks his head on one side or dips his chin, revealing, as he looks up, the whites of his eyes. The lips are tight, the nose hooked. The top lip draws up in a snarl when he chuckles. He seldom blinks. The skin is drawn tight over a huge, gleaming skull, giving the impression of an animated waxwork or cadaver.

In April 1954, Dalton completed a new edition of *Principles of Public Finance*, with the aid of Ian Little and Brian Abel-Smith, a social policy expert recently established at the L.S.E., whom he regarded as his best discovery since Crosland. That autumn he again missed Party Conference, this time without an excuse. 'I now enjoy *not* going as much as I used to enjoy *going*!' he wrote. He was more interested in arranging for a new staff cottage to be built at West Leaze, to ease his and Ruth's lives in their old age.[63] The idea was to install a couple, to attend to domestic needs. 'Now I shall be in luxury', Ruth wrote to Hilde Auerbach, 'with someone to cook and clean the house and a gardener to grow vegetables and do odd jobs.'[64] Evening was setting in.

There was one last fling on Germany. In the summer, much to Dalton's pleasure, the whole E.D.C. scheme was torpedoed when the

French Assembly rejected it. However, both P.L.P. and Shadow Cabinet seemed to be leaning towards acceptance of the recent Paris Agreements which paved the way, finally, to West German sovereignty. Dalton saw no chance of turning official Party opinion the other way, but he wanted to make a final gesture. He decided, therefore, that he could not and would not vote for the Paris Agreements at the Party meeting. If the Shadow Cabinet refused to let him vote and speak according to his conscience, he would resign from the front bench.

To support his demand for freedom of speech, he employed an unusual weapon: his diary. He informed his colleagues that at the P.L.P. meeting in 1937 on the issue of the Defence Estimates, members of the Shadow Cabinet had been allowed to speak and vote as they chose regardless of their previous collective decision. Herbert Morrison, Dalton's bitter opponent on German rearmament, immediately tried to give this point a bureaucratic burial. The relevant minutes had, regrettably, been destroyed in the war, he said. 'How lucky that, if there is no official record, I have kept an unofficial one', Dalton replied with a triumphant smile. Colleagues were unmoved. Dalton therefore issued his resignation threat, invoking the famous conscience clause of the Party's Standing Orders. Conscience, he boomed, should mean more than Temperance and Birth Control. 'Do you tell me that I may have a conscience about beer bottles and French letters, but not about the life and death of my generation?' In the end a compromise formula was reached. Dalton agreed not to resign. In return, he and three other dissidents – Callaghan, Wilson and Ede – were allowed to abstain, but not to speak.

This invigorating but fruitless tussle (the decision to support the Agreements was carried in the P.L.P. by 2 to 1) did Dalton no harm in the Parliamentary Party. A few days later, he was once again re-elected to the Shadow Cabinet, moving up to fourth place, with only Gaitskell, Griffiths and Soskice ahead of him. But defeat on German rearmament left him feeling bloody-minded, cantankerous, and more than ever contemptuous of his colleagues. 'I see no reason, except crass conservatism, for voting Labour now', he wrote afterwards. 'The Tories are doing well, Full Employment, Buy What You Like, More for all, Higher Pensions on the way, Growing Vision for Peace, and the Labour Party, like the Tories, wants to arm the Germans!' On 19th November, still tired, he withdrew to West Leaze for a rest.

Early next morning he was taken ill with stomach pains, having once again contracted gastric 'flu. After a week of groaning and sleeplessness, the onset of complications caused him to be admitted to the

London Clinic where he spent three weeks – coming out just before Christmas. While he was in bed he came to two firm conclusions. First, he would leave the Shadow Cabinet at the end of the session, and do so with a flourish. Second, he would try to bring about Gaitskell's succession to Attlee as Party Leader, without an interregnum.[65]

Hitherto Dalton had taken for granted that Attlee's successor would be chosen from among the older generation of parliamentary leaders – those who had been prominent before the war. His main concern had been to stop Morrison, generally regarded as heir apparent. Believing that Bevan, who in any case he regarded as unsuitable, stood no chance, Dalton canvassed the idea of Jim Griffiths, also a former miner.[66] With Griffiths's eventual succession to Attlee in mind, he had urged Griffiths to put up against Bevan and Morrison for the Deputy Leadership.

But Attlee repeatedly postponed his retirement, and the old guard got even older. Morrison's performances began to falter, and Gaitskell, with the experience of the Chancellorship behind him, acquired a growing band of followers. Both Morrison and Griffiths seemed to be losing ground. Dalton decided, therefore, that the prospects for Gaitskell had improved so much that he should make a bid.

This was in spite of a continued coolness in their personal relations. For some time Dalton had been conscious of 'a veil of reserve' when they met. As we have seen, Gaitskell's attitude to German rearmament, and his unwavering support for Morrison, were factors. But so too was an uncomfortable feeling that Gaitskell regarded the fight with the Bevanites as a kind of holy war; allied to a worrying suspicion, that went beyond particular battles and disagreements about style, that Gaitskell's instincts were not as radical as they should be. 'Does he really want to change British society?', Dalton mused. ' ... HG makes me stir uneasily in my loyalty.'

Nevertheless, the loyalty remained. There was much to admire in Gaitskell who, judged on intellectual ability, was the outstanding figure among the Party's leaders. Dalton's pride in his creation was undiminished, and he did not find it hard to set aside recent differences. In February 1955 the two men lunched together alone in Ashley Gardens, and a reconciliation was achieved. With German rearmament out of the way, Dalton hoped that it might be easier to relate politically to the Gaitskell camp. Eagerly, he supported measures to punish Bevan for a renewed, apparently gratuitous, attack on the leadership. 'Can't have one law for big fish & another for small', he told his G.M.C.,[67] repeating the words he had used to justify the expulsion of Cripps and Bevan from the Party in 1939. Gaitskell recorded that Dalton 'has been excellent throughout all this'.[68]

Their friendship was much repaired as a result.

At the end of March 1955, Dalton urged Attlee to stay on as Party Leader 'until HM is no longer an inevitable successor'. Attlee did not commit himself, but eagerly agreed about Morrison's inadequacies. The matter was then temporarily set aside by the general election.

In the last few weeks before the new Prime Minister, Anthony Eden, went to the country, Dalton was diverted by a campaign on behalf of his most favoured protégé. Tony Crosland's South Gloucestershire seat had fallen victim to the Boundary Commissioners. Since February, Dalton had been trying to get a peerage for the elderly Morgan Philips Price, Labour Member for West Gloucestershire, so as to create a suitable vacancy. Through flattery and other inducements he sought to persuade Price to announce his resignation before a peerage had actually been offered, on the basis of an assurance that Attlee, as Party Leader, would put his name to the Prime Minister. As time ran out, there was a round of frantic telephone calls and conspiratorial button-holings, reminiscent of Dalton's last-minute bids to fix himself up in the 1920s. At one point, in desperation, Dalton even spoke directly to Eden, whose offer of a peerage might have tipped the balance. In the end, however, the whole thing fell through. Price remained unconvinced about the peerage (rightly, as it turned out) and insisted on standing again.

As Ruth put it, Hugh had been like an elephant going through the jungle, 'clumsy, trumpeting but sly'. He was bitterly disappointed, furious with the cautious Price ('silly, selfish deaf old blockhead!')[69] and deeply apologetic towards Crosland. 'I'm very grieved that the cards have fallen so badly for you in *this* game', he wrote.[70] To Abel-Smith he said, quoting Robert Service, the Canadian poet he had once recommended to Rupert Brooke, 'Well at least I've deserved the cowboy epitaph

> "He done his damnedest,
> Angels can do no more".'[71]

When it was clear that Crosland would not be in the new House, Dalton lost all interest in the election. He was bored by the campaign, his twelfth, 'the most tedious, apathetic, uninteresting and, I think, worst organised of them all'. Polling day was on 26th May. As expected, there was a small shift of opinion in favour of the Tories. Dalton's own majority fell to 5,845. After the count, Hugh told Ruth and Will Davis that he would not stand again. When he had become M.P. for Bishop Auckland, most men were unemployed, and many families were close to starvation. Now there was work for everybody and the miners wore dinner jackets for evening events. He had lost interest in his constituents. 'I felt I had had just about enough of *them*', he wrote, '& just couldn't bear to think of fighting another election there.'[72]

He now put into effect his earlier decision not to stand again for the Shadow Cabinet. For most politicians this would have meant a quiet and dignified retirement, with speeches, hand-shakings and votes of thanks. Dalton liked to do things differently. All his political life he had thought about and even threatened a principled resignation – but circumstances, or his own prudence, had held him back. His moment had come, not exactly for martyrdom, but for a grand, political departure. Helping the young had been his crusade. Age would be the issue of his final campaign. He would use his own retirement to launch 'Operation Avalanche', aimed at dislodging other long-serving members of the Shadow Cabinet, nine of whom were over 65. In addition, he would draw attention to Morrison's own advanced years at a time when this was likely to cause maximum embarrassment.

'My first job is to break the log-jam of ancients on the Parliamentary Ctee', he explained to Gaitskell. 'I am writing a letter to C.R.A. to be published in the Press a few days before Parliament meets ... I want to see at least 6 vacancies on the Parl[ly] Committee.'[73] Everything went like clockwork. 'I must now blow a bugle', he told Attlee, who replied, 'I will try to work out an echo'.[74] He then gave his letter to Desmond Donnelly, intending that it should be leaked. Donnelly obliged – passing it to Crossman, who arranged for advance publication in the *Daily Mirror*.[75] 'I myself have decided not to be a candidate for our Shadow Cabinet in the new Parliament', Dalton declared in the letter, 'and I hope that a number of my fellow-veterans will decide likewise.' Attlee, he carefully added, was the exception. The Leader should stay on in the interests of Party unity.[76]

'There is an engaging naivety about it; and at the same time a mischievous shrewdness', commented the *Manchester Guardian*.[77] Several of the ancients were indignant. 'We have all recognised Dalton's failing physical powers and can sympathise with him. Fortunately these signs of senility are not infectious', Chuter Ede told the press.[78] To a friend, Dalton recalled the Slav proverb, 'When the sun rises, owls feel uncomfortable'.[79] Nevertheless, Ede, Shinwell, Hall, Soskice and Whiteley decided to stand down. Three weeks later, Dalton proudly announced that Operation Avalanche had been a success – it had reduced the average age of the Parliamentary Committee by five years.[80]

Above all, Morrison's chances had been dealt a serious blow. Morrison did not retire. But he was now one of the oldest on the Committee.

On 9th June, Attlee agreed to set no date for his own departure. 'This is almost certainly the end of H.M. as possible future leader', Dalton wrote triumphantly. 'He'll be 68 next Jan, 69 in Jan 1957. Too old to succeed Attlee now.'[81] Dalton told the Oxford University Labour Club in October that, if Attlee was forced to retire because of ill-health, the P.L.P. would do well to choose somebody able to carry on for some years. 'You do not want to have a caretaker who is approaching 70.'[82]

After a talk with George Brown at the end of the same month, Dalton concluded that, barring accidents, 'H.G. has the Leadership in the Bag, if it comes loose in the next four months.'[83] He was right. The feeling that Morrison was unsuitable because of his age steadily gathered force. By lingering for six months after the election (as Dalton had urged him to do) Attlee reinforced the impact of Dalton's 'avalanche of ancients', allowing support for Morrison to melt away. Bevan's record of rebellion made him unacceptable as Leader to a majority of Labour M.P.s. Griffiths, the compromise possibility, no longer carried enough weight.

When Attlee finally announced his retirement early in December, Dalton led the canvassing campaign in favour of Gaitskell and against Morrison, whose campaign for the same post he had organised twenty years before. This time he was on the winning side. 'We've got it all sewn up for Hugh', John Parker heard Big Hugh tell Arthur Moyle, Attlee's P.P.S.[84] So it proved. Gaitskell won on the first ballot by 157 votes to Bevan's 70. Morrison came a humiliating third, with only 40. Morrison thereupon retired from the Deputy Leadership, the Shadow Cabinet and the N.E.C. His political career was over. Dalton felt no compunction or sympathy – only exultation. 'I was the small stone which deliberately started it, and all the rest followed', he gloated. 'I feel a little like a Creator now rested and beheld his handwork after much labour and saw that it was good.'[85]

Operation Avalanche and Gaitskell's election were Dalton's last serious forays. He was sliding away from politics and into other kinds of life, literary and social. Much of his time was now spent on the second volume of his autobiography, to be called *The Fateful Years*. Encouraged by this undertaking and the memories it evoked, he struck up an odd friendship with an old enemy, Lord Beaverbrook. In September 1955 he had broken an ankle while touring forests in Scotland.[86] This accident stimulated a letter of sympathy from the man he had once accused of poisoning Churchill's mind against him, and an invitation to Cherkeley.[87] The visit was a success, and thereafter he took a series of protégés along for Beaverbrook's inspection. Other weekends were spent with Harry Walston, a landowning

Labour candidate with whom he had Eton and King's in common, at Walston's large Cambridgeshire country house, Newton Hall. To Catherine Walston, Dalton described his three main interests: Parliament, his memoirs and planting trees.[88] It was no longer clear that Parliament came first.

One reason why Dalton became so bored by the 1955 Parliament was that Crosland was not a member of it. For Crosland, however, defeat provided an opportunity. Without the distraction of political duties, he had spent the months following the election putting together the fruits of several years' reading, talking and writing in order to sketch – as Dalton had urged – the next stage of social equality. The result was a book whose lucidity, range and synthesising brilliance make it the most influential essay on British socialism that has appeared since the war.

Crosland's *The Future of Socialism* contained much of Dalton, whose name appeared more often in the text than that of any other individual, with the exceptions of G. D. H. Cole and Karl Marx. Indirectly, there was the influence of works like Evan Durbin's *The Politics of Democratic Socialism*,[89] which had developed Dalton's pre-war ideas. Directly there was the impact of Dalton's personal tutelage. Significantly, Dalton was one of only four people (and the only politician) to read and criticise the full manuscript in draft.

Dalton's *Practical Socialism for Britain* had anticipated the great changes that occurred in the role of the state during and after the war. Durbin had given the ideas of Dalton and other friends a firmer theoretical base. Now Crosland drew attention to the changes which Dalton had predicted, while noting capitalist successes. He was revisionist in that he believed that the altered economic reality required a revised approach. He declared that 'today traditional capitalism has been reformed and modified almost out of existence, and it is with a quite different form of society that socialists must now concern themselves'. It was necessary, Crosland believed, to take account of the rapidly rising living standards of manual workers. Echoing Dalton's comment about miners in dinner jackets, he noted that the first miners' Car Rally had recently been held in Yorkshire, and that half the population now had at least a week's annual holiday.

His conclusion, however, was neither complacent nor defeatist. So far from announcing the irrelevance of the socialist dream, his book concentrated on the main, historic socialist purpose: the achievement of greater equality. The social and economic case for removing inequalities was, he contended, as powerful as ever. Nearly half his text consisted of a section on 'The Search for Equality', in which he argued that greater equalisation of income and wealth could be obtained through growing prosperity; and that the expansion and improvement of education had a vital part to play in smashing class distinctions. His aim was 'uninhibited mingling between the classes', one of Dalton's favourite phrases.

Crosland drew repeatedly on Dalton's ideas, sometimes challenging them. He was more concerned than Dalton about the distribution of power, and comparatively less concerned to pursue economic equality as an end in itself. Where Dalton wanted to smash the rich, Crosland worried about the political consequences. Where Dalton had abandoned the capital levy reluctantly on economic grounds, Crosland's objection was political. He argued that such an expropriation, if large enough to destroy the rentier class, would overstep 'those crucial though indefinable boundaries of mutual tolerance' on which democracy was based. On the other hand he supported Dalton's other favourite confiscatory scheme (derived from First World War Italian reading), the Rignano Plan for the scaling of death duties.

Like Dalton, Crosland reacted against the view of socialism – widely attributed to Beatrice Webb and her nephew, Sir Stafford Cripps – as state-directed puritanism. Believing in individuality and variety, he saw a need for more open-air cafés, brighter and gayer streets at night, later closing hours for public houses. He concluded his book by pointing to the lead that Dalton had given during his Chancellorship, in his generosity to universities and in the Land Fund, as a pioneer of 'cultural' socialism.[90]

The Future of Socialism was published in the autumn of 1956. It was greeted with enthusiasm by the Labour Right, which pointed triumphantly to Crosland's attack on indiscriminate nationalisation. It was denounced by many on the Left, who saw it as a polemic against eternal verities. Where did that place its author? 'He held the old Left in contempt', writes Susan. ' ... Yet his credentials as a democratic socialist could not be doubted. His toughmindedness made him impatient with the Right's caution ... He said he was an egalitarian and meant it.'[91] It is a description which fits Dalton, as well as Crosland, precisely.

The Suez affair stirred Dalton far less than international crises in the past. He was unashamedly pro-Israel, and anti-Egypt. When Arthur Henderson ('Little Arthur') criticised Gaitskell's comparison between Nasser and Hitler, Dalton scolded him. 'You should not talk like that. Your father was never afraid to tell the truth.'[92] Dalton was delighted by the early success of the Israeli attack which, he felt, would make Israel more secure than at any time since 1948.[93] He also urged Gaitskell not to appear to be anti-Israeli. 'I consider that the Israelis have a very strong case for their entry into Egypt, in self defence after repeated and intolerable provocation', he wrote to the Party Leader.[94] But he accused the Tories of hypocrisy in suddenly taking up the Israeli case having previously ignored it, and he opposed the Anglo-French attack – especially after the U.N. Security Council condemnation.

On the second day of the Suez debate he roared jovially at an old S.O.E. employee, Bickham Sweet-Escott, over lunch at the Special Forces Club, that an ample amount of wine was needed so that he could go and 'shout against the Tories'.[95] To Beaverbrook he put it slightly differently. He was, he declared, 'quite speechless with anger' about the state of the world. But this did not prevent an extremely affable correspondence with the old magnate, who felt that Eden's mistake had not been to invade, but to call a cease-fire.[96] Ruth wrote to Hilde Auerbach, 'Our rage and humiliation over Eden's criminal idiocy have blotted out most other things from my thoughts.'[97] In fact, Hugh was much more interested in the publication of *The Fateful Years*. 'Bombs away!', he wrote to Gaitskell when the book went off to the printers in July.[98] He looked forward eagerly to more ruffled feathers. Extracts were serialised in the *Evening Standard* in March 1957. One of these dealt with Morrison's abortive last minute bid to oust Attlee and grab the Leadership just after the 1945 election. Dalton waited for a reaction. He was not disappointed. 'The story is very inaccurate and unreliable', Morrison told the press, adding waspishly, 'though I cannot comment on Mr. Dalton's own lively activities on the telephone and otherwise, as stated by him.' ' "None of us can escape history", said Abraham Lincoln', replied Dalton.[99] Encouraged by the publicity, the *Standard* decided on five instalments instead of three. When Morrison rose to speak in the House, there was a bantering cheer.[100] Appearing on television the same night, Dalton told the interviewer: 'I don't want to have a row with Mr. Morrison. I am very fond of him.'[101] There was talk of an official reprimand by the Shadow Cabinet, or even the P.L.P.[102] But nothing came of it.

The Fateful Years received higher praise than any of Dalton's previous books. A. J. P. Taylor accused him of energy without leadership or ideas,[103] Christopher Hollis wrote an acid satire in *Punch*,[104] and Michael Foot declared that the portrait of Labour in the 1930s was so extraordinary as to be unrecognisable.[105] On the other hand, John Raymond called the book far and away the best volume of memoirs since Churchill's *The Gathering Storm* and contrasted Dalton's speeches with those of the current Party Leader: 'They make Mr. Gaitskell's oratory sound like that of a man with a heap of wood-shavings in his mouth.'[106] John Freeman pointed out that Dalton wrote as well as he talked; 'and he is one of the best talkers in the world – shrewd, good tempered, indiscreet, generous (sometimes over-generous) to his friends and not cruel to his enemies.'[107] Francis Williams described the book as egotistical, noisy, rumbustious, con-spiratorial, and impolite – like its author.[108] 'Dr Dalton is one of the relatively few contemporary politicians ... with a well-defined per-sonality', remarked Malcolm Muggeridge. 'He is a card.'[109]

'Please make a note of the numbers of the pages which make you cry', Dalton wrote to Catherine Walston.[110] He immediately em-barked on Volume III, to be called *High Tide and After* covering the period since 1945. He also set about planning his retirement from Parliament. Predictably, this was bound up with an intrigue.

In June, he told Gaitskell that he intended to announce his departure after Conference,[111] 'otherwise some poor B.A. delegate would be surrounded like a honeypot by bees'.[112] He colluded first with Sam Watson, the miners' leader, so as to outwit local Bevanites over the new selection. It was, like Operation Avalanche, to be a 'planned sunset'.

'Most of my contemporaries bore me stiffer and stiffer', Dalton explained to Gaitskell. 'But I still like younger people with attractive qualities, and I still enjoy discovering new ones.'[113] Here was a chance to bequeath to one of the younger people a most treasured possession: his seat. The heir needed to be chosen carefully. It had to be somebody of whom he was fond, whom he could trust, and who could be expected to rise far and fast within the Party. Dalton thought first of Tony Crosland. But Crosland had interests elsewhere, and declined. So he turned to Brian Abel-Smith, 'rather shyly young & a little twisty faced & spotty complexioned',[114] who had helped him with the new edition of *Public Finance*. That summer, Dalton varied his recent pattern of making foreign trips alone and took Abel-Smith with him on an extended holiday in Italy. The Italian government laid on cars, and they travelled together inspecting re-forestation schemes – with good lunches, wines and walking.[115] Dalton found in his companion ('not only young, but charming and handsome, energetic, quick at every uptake, easily amused and amusing')[116] an ideal combination of qualities. When they returned, Big Hugh eagerly contacted Little Hugh. 'I want to fix a lunch with you & Brian Abel-Smith, my favourite, so far, as my successor', he wrote. 'If you like him, we must commend him to Sam Watson, & arrange a meeting.'[117]

On 19th October, as planned, Dalton announced his retirement at a meeting of the Bishop Auckland G.M.C.[118] In his speech he referred to his age (70) and hinted that others should follow his example. Shinwell was asked by the press to comment. 'Dalton's been old for years', he replied.[119] A few days later, Dalton was admitted to hospital for a short course of treatment. Shinwell, Ede and Grenfell, the Father of the House, sent a barbed telegram: 'Best wishes from Old Guard for a speedy recovery and full return to your parliamentary responsibilities.'[120]

Meanwhile Dalton moved behind the scenes to tie up the selection, sending Abel-Smith's curriculum vitae to Gaitskell, and urging the Party Leader to get Transport House to tighten up the constitution of the Bishop Auckland party before the selection began. He also arranged for Abel-Smith to meet Sam Watson and address a meeting of miners in County Durham. Abel-Smith travelled north, spoke, and received Watson's blessing. All seemed to be proceeding smoothly.

There now occurred a hitch. Abel-Smith, who had gone along with Dalton's plans up to now, suddenly changed his mind. He decided that he did not want to be a politician after all. When he broke this unwelcome news to his benefactor in Ashley Gardens, Dalton refused to believe it, then flew into a rage. Finally he tried flattery and bribery: he would extract from Gaitskell a firm promise that once in Parliament, Abel-Smith would not stay on the backbenches for long. None of this worked. Ruth showed the young man out after his ordeal. 'I can guess what that was all about', she said. 'You've turned him down.' 'Yes', said Abel-Smith. 'Thank God', she replied. 'I remember another enthusiastic young socialist years ago in the same situation. He's a very different man today. I'm referring to Hugh Gaitskell.'

Dalton soon forgave his young friend. Next day he sent a copy of *The Fateful Years* (forgetting he had already given one) inscribed 'Storm is over. Hugh'.[121] Later he praised Abel-Smith to Beaverbrook, and took him for a weekend party at Cherkeley.[122] No other promising young man presented himself, so Dalton switched his support to Jim Boyden, a 47-year-old adult education lecturer at Durham University. Boyden was selected in June 1958 on the first ballot, beating local Bevanite opposition. Dalton handed over constituency casework to the new prospective candidate, and disengaged completely.[123]

He had been disengaging in other ways too. He attended the 1957 Conference, and was pleased by the failure of 'shit-faced Mikardo' to push Crossman off the N.E.C., and by the evident deterioration of Morrison and Shinwell.[124] His absences from Parliament were becoming more frequent, and caused comment. In January a sharp attack of sciatica confined him to bed and kept him away from the House for a month on doctor's orders. This provoked an embarrassing row with Ted Short, the Northern Area Whip, who had previously tolerated absences due to authorship but who now brusquely accused him of malingering.

In April, Dalton reappeared at a P.L.P. meeting in order to congratulate Bevan on opposing unilateral nuclear disarmament. Unilateralism, Dalton declared, might appeal to 'small groups of excited people, mostly middle class'; but it would never get accepted by the Durham miners or by any Workmen's Club he had ever been in. His speech was greeted by cheers. 'Isn't it better to do it only occasionally', he said to Gaitskell afterwards, 'but then rather well?' Except when the House was in session, he stayed in Wiltshire with his diary, his memoirs and his trees.

Dalton's circle of friends was getting narrower. Mike Williams-Thompson, a young man he had met during the war who was now in public relations, became one of his most frequent companions. There were weekends at Cherkeley with Beaverbrook and at Newton Hall with the Walstons. Dalton's working-class contacts, on the other hand, dwindled.

George Brown took him to task on this subject. At Hugh's suggestion, the Browns were invited for a weekend at Newton Hall. It was a mistake. Before they went, Sophie Brown protested that 'She didn't want to come, the Walstons were not the sort of people she wanted to be with, not what she meant by socialism, etc.' At Newton, George told Catherine Walston: 'I'm only a lorry driver's son, not rich like you.' The Browns left feeling uncomfortable. Afterwards, Brown complained that all Dalton's really intimate friends were public school and university men, and that the exclusive XYZ Club contained not a single trade unionist among its members. Dalton – who counted several trade union M.P.s, including Brown, Alf Robens and Arthur Bottomley, among his protégés – found it impossible to understand Brown's difficulty or see the importance of what he said.[125]

Unlike the Hampstead socialists, privately educated but generally opposed to public schools, Dalton defended independent, or at any rate boarding, education. In October 1958 he wrote to Gaitskell applauding the conclusions of an N.E.C. working party, with Tawney as a member, which rejected abolition. Boarding schools, he had always believed, gave young people a healthy taste of communal living ('classless mingling') and should be available to all: Eton and King's for the masses. He also believed, or said he believed, that a commitment to abolition would arouse fiercer resistance than any other Labour proposal since 1945 and lose Labour the next election.[126]

Perhaps this last opinion was a symptom of his declining powers. Attacks of illness were becoming more frequent. So were bouts of absent-mindedness, involving trivial mistakes, like leaving his mackintosh in Gaitskell's car, dropping his wallet in the street and not noticing, or forgetting to take his pyjamas and plimsolls home after a Fabian summer school.[127] His letters, still vivid and witty in parts, were becoming as repetitive as gramophone records. Increasingly, he was living his life through the careers of those on whom he had visited his affections, and who no longer always welcomed the intrusion. Busy with political work and self-advancement, younger friends started to find his company less fun and more of a penance. Gaitskell, preoccupied by the approach of an election at which he would lead the Labour Party with every hope of winning, began gently but firmly to turn down Dalton's insistent requests to meet for lunch or dinner. People who were prepared to take him in and offer company were rewarded with gratitude and warmth. But they also felt, as most did, that he was a lonely and unloved man.[128]

Booking seats for younger comrades, as he put it, remained a major diversion. Michael Barnes, later M.P. for Brentford and Chiswick, was a beneficiary of this Daltonian hobby in its final phase. After graduating from Oxford, Barnes decided he wanted to be an M.P., and wrote to the author of *The Future of Socialism*, a book which he had admired, with this in mind. Crosland promised to put him in touch with Dalton, 'the great encourager of the young'. A few months later, Barnes received a call from a man with a booming voice: 'Hugh Dalton here. Can you come and have lunch at the Akropolis?' They met, and Dalton took Barnes's as yet non-existent political career in hand. Young, good-looking, intelligent, public school educated, Barnes had all the appropriate qualifications, as Crosland doubtless realised. Visits to West Leaze and the Durham Miners' Gala, and introductions to union and party organisers, followed. There was little discussion of issues. They talked instead about constituencies and vacancies. 'At times it seemed as if he was more interested in my career than I was', Barnes recalls. Dalton's attempt to find him a hopeless seat for the 1959 election failed, which was hardly surprising considering that Barnes only joined the Labour Party in 1957. But contacts acquired during this bizarre training course helped Barnes indirectly to get selected for a better constituency thereafter.[129]

In February 1959 Tony Crosland, out of Parliament since the previous election, was chosen for the safe seat of Grimsby. After the publication of *The Future of Socialism*, Dalton had written: 'It may yet make trouble for him at a Selection Conference'.[130] He was wrong – the Grimsby selection went without a hitch. No news could have delighted him more. 'So now this most gifted political problem-child, this all-but-statesman already at 40, so outstandingly able, astringent, brave, integral, quick, gay – such fun to have about – is on the high road up', he wrote to Gaitskell. 'Great success, given a flick of luck, is easily within his powers.'[131]

On 23rd March, Dalton suffered a stroke. For three days his speech was blurred and he became clumsy on his left side. Ruth, who for so long had lived a separate life, moved in and took control. 'Speech normal, brain a bit slow. Movement of left leg almost normal ... ' she wrote to Gaitskell on 11th May, adding poignantly, 'Doctor thinks that his brain will be almost as good as before.' Hugh was told that it was just a 'spasm of the blood vessels'. Only Gaitskell, Crosland and Abel-Smith were allowed to know the true diagnosis. 'When he returns to the House & people observe that his mental processes are less lively', Ruth wrote, 'let us hope that they will merely think that "he has aged a good deal lately".'[132] That, alas, was precisely what they did think. On 23rd June he made a painful visit to the House for a meeting of the P.L.P., hobbling on a stick. He dined with Bevan, Strachey, Crossman and the former Solicitor-General, Lynn Ungoed-Thomas. Crossman wrote cruelly, 'Suddenly, over dinner, we discovered that Dalton, mumbling about his memoirs, is now deaf and hardly articulate. Nye thought him drunk but he is only, quite suddenly, gaga.'[133]

Recovery was slow, and never complete. Dalton hated being ill. As he told Gaitskell on the telephone at the beginning of June, 'Rude health from puberty into the seventies, with no serious illness, is a bad training for later life.'[134] In July he accepted the Mastership of the Drapers' Company, proudly following in his father's footsteps.[135] At the end of the month he invited himself to stay with the Walstons.[136] Then he spent most of the summer at West Leaze, working on the final volume of his memoirs. By September he was well enough to offer Little Hugh advice on the coming election. 'I think that Macmillan may easily put a foot, or even two feet, wrong during the fight', he wrote. 'I hope you'll be prepared, if he gives you an unguarded opening, to knock him about and to laugh at him too. He hates that and finds it very disconcerting.'[137] But Dalton knew that he was not the man he had been before the attack. At the end of the year, he still had difficulty walking, and felt muzzy, deaf and slow on the uptake.[138]

The election was held in October. It was the first without Attlee as Labour Party Leader since 1931. It was also the first since 1918 without Dalton as a parliamentary candidate. He missed the Dissolution on purpose. 'I don't like funerals', he told Gaitskell, 'and I recall Rupert Brooke once writing to me, "Cambridge must be full of people one knows; perhaps it is nicer not to be there".'[139] During the campaign he went to Bishop Auckland briefly, 'to push the boat off' for Jim Boyden, making a few speeches.[140] Then he retired to Wiltshire until

it was over. He spoke several times for the Devizes candidate, in his
capacity as honorary President of the Devizes constituency party,
and for Philip Noel-Baker's son Francis, standing at Swindon. He
particularly enjoyed a meeting in Marlborough Town Hall, half full of
boys from the public school. Yet at one meeting he had to speak sitting,
being too exhausted to stand. ' "Non sum qualis eram" ', he wrote, 'I
tire much too easily and my points go over less well.'[141]

Dalton's main interest during the campaign was in Gaitskell. 'My
very dear Hugh', he wrote three days before the poll. 'This is much the
most personal election of my long career. I've never had one of my
younger friends running for P.M. before.'[142] There also flickered a
wistful, passing half-hope that – despite his anti-age campaign and
trumpeted retirement – Gaitskell might make him a Minister without
Portfolio in the Lords. It was not to be. Hugh and Ruth sat up until
2.30 a.m. with pens poised to note Labour gains from Tory, but the
movement was all the other way. The morning after, Big Hugh spoke
to Dora on the telephone. She asked: how did he feel? 'Very angry
with the electors and very proud of Hugh', he replied.[143]

XXXIV

Finale

As soon as the results were known, Gaitskell held a post-mortem at his home in Frognal Gardens, Hampstead. The invitation list was short, restricted to close friends and retainers. Core members of the Hampstead Set were there: Douglas Jay, Patrick Gordon Walker, Roy and Jennifer Jenkins, Tony Crosland. So was Herbert Bowden, the Chief Whip. Though no longer an M.P., Dalton was also asked. Crosland drove him over. It was a time for licking wounds, and for reappraisals. How to prevent Labour staying in Opposition for ever? Jay offered a plan: the Party must drop nationalisation, change its name, and break the link with the unions. Dalton was appalled: 'pouring out the baby with the bath water and throwing the bath after him', he called it. When Jay followed this up by writing an article in the Labour journal *Forward* suggesting that the Party had become too rigidly associated with the working class, Dalton protested vehemently to Gaitskell. The Party Leader replied 'that he couldn't accept that Left (Tribune) could continually attack and Right never reply'.[1]

A few years earlier Dalton might have upbraided Gaitskell for tying himself to a faction, and warned against the danger of a Party split. Now he no longer had the will to make opponents of his friends. He hesitated. Then he moved strongly and loyally behind the Party Leader. At the Blackpool Party Conference at the end of November, Gaitskell attacked proposals for further nationalisation, and criticised Clause IV of the Party Constitution, which laid down that public ownership was one of the Party's fundamental aims. The Party centre, as well as the Left, felt uneasy. Dalton, on the other hand, was full of congratulations. ' ... [Y]ou'll get the Constitution Revised sooner than I thought likely', he wrote, sending an item from Molly Hamilton's biography of Arthur Henderson which showed that Uncle Arthur, co-author of the original Clause IV, had been in favour of revising it nine years after its adoption.[2] Dalton told a Fabian audience at the L.S.E. that he himself preferred the formula contained in the old 'Fabian Basis', which he and Rupert Brooke had signed before the First World War. This had called for the transfer 'of such industrial capital as can conveniently be managed socially'.[3]

After Blackpool, Dalton rushed angrily to the defence of his cubs. He was no longer a politician. But he still had opinions and did not hesitate to express them. An article in the *New Statesman* attacking 'a small and much disliked group of anti-Socialist zealots', which he took as a thinly veiled reference to Jay, Jenkins and Crosland, aroused him to particular fury.[4] 'Without such men as these', he wrote in the *Evening Standard*, ' ... the Labour Party would be much poorer ... Thank God there are a number of other able and promising younger men in the Parliamentary Party – George Brown, James Callaghan and Denis Healey, to mention only three of the best of them. These could hold their own in any Cabinet. And their time will come ... '[5] He wrote bitterly to Crosland about the 'deep faithlessness in John Freeman', now editor of the *New Statesman* and 'Crossman's CROOKED conscience'. 'Labour Politics is fuller now of personal stinks and stinkers than ever before', he declared. 'I don't know why, but I'm sure it is so.'[6]

He was pleased by Gaitskell's Shadow Cabinet, and by some of the junior appointments. 'I'm so glad that you've brought in several young (< 40) Trade Unionists', he told the Party Leader, '& that you haven't over-invested in the Hampstead Set'. He wrote congratulatory notes to Fred Peart, George Chetwynd, Kenneth Robinson, Christopher Mayhew, Roy Mason, Tony Benn and Reg Prentice, all of whom he privately called 'my poodles'. He was gratified by the progress of Denis Healey and Denis Howell, and he considered that Benn was 'maturing in judgment & range of interests'.[7] But he saw less of all of them now that he was out of the Commons.

He told Gaitskell he wanted to go to the Lords, so as to keep in touch with young friends along the corridor. On the Party Leader's recommendation, he was given a life peerage in the 1960 New Year's Honours List, thirty years after he had first been offered an hereditary title by Ramsay MacDonald. He took the title 'Lord Dalton of Forest and Frith in the County Palatine of Durham', choosing the name of the highest parish in Upper Teesdale, which contained the hotel at which he and Ruth had stayed in 1928 when Ruth was asked to be candidate for Bishop Auckland.[8] Ruth wrote to Hilde Auerbach, a trifle disingenuously. 'It will bore me dreadfully to be called Lady Dalton!'[9] Lord Beaverbrook sent a telegram:

WELCOME HUGH STOP YOU WILL BRING REALITY TO A HOUSE OF MAKE BELIEVE MAX. [10]

As soon as he had taken his seat, Dalton began making irreverent jokes about his new abode, calling it 'a placid sort of Life-After-Death' and 'my "Elysian Dormitory"'. [11] 'Bishops in one corner, diplomats in another', he commiserated with Beaverbrook, 'old fuddy duddies in between and the drinking facilities for one used to the other place are derisory.' [12] He delivered his maiden speech in March – castigating the Government for its failure to administer his own Distribution of Industry Act with sufficient vigour. [13] Then he made himself audible in the dining room, presenting Tony Benn's father, Lord Stansgate, to a friend as 'a member of the Lords Labour League of Youth', [14] and loudly announcing to Harry Walston the details of the private lives of the occupants of each other table in turn. [15]

'I shouldn't hang around the place, or listen through key holes, or run about picking up gossip, or trying to influence details', Dalton promised Gaitskell before becoming a peer. 'I was *retired*, & now the younger ones must run the show.' [16] He kept his word. Most of his energies were devoted to literary activities. He struggled on with his memoirs and wrote a few articles for the press. He also sent a series of letters to the Party Leader, full of school-masterly encouragement and advice, not all of it redundant. In April he passed on a story about a young Labour M.P., eager for a personal word with Gaitskell, being told politely that an interview could be arranged in three weeks' time. 'I wish I could be sure that this tale was totally untrue and quite misleading!' Dalton scolded. 'You've allowed yourself to walk much too much by yourself, when many others would have liked to walk with you.' [17]

Against unilateralism, the other issue – apart from Clause IV – that divided the Party after the 1959 election, Dalton felt the stirrings of an old passion. As a member of the Defence Committee in 1948, he had opposed the manufacture of a British atomic bomb – but on financial, not moral, grounds. [18] In the 1930s he had resisted one-sided disarmament. He did so still. In May, he advised Gaitskell to give a public warning that he would resign as Leader if the Party went unilateralist. 'Speak as the Leader of the Party, firm and clear', he urged before the Brighton Conference debate in the autumn. ' ... A strong response will come to that.' [19] At Brighton, the Party voted to give up nuclear weapons, after Gaitskell had promised to 'Fight, fight and fight again'. 'I grieve much for Hugh in his ordeal, and for the Labour Party', Dalton wrote to Catherine Walston. He added a phrase borrowed from his favourite poem by Rupert Brooke: 'There are so many ...

who have toiled so long and seen no daybreak.'[20] To Gaitskell, he sent lines from Swinburne learnt at Eton more than half a century before: 'Wrecked hope and passionate pain shall grow, Like tender things and a spring tide seen.'[21]

Both his letters and his conversation were becoming more long-winded, and increasingly spiced with expletives and obscenities. On one occasion, in a hotel, he issued such loud and unrestrained oaths that Crosland, who was with him, had to shut him up.[22] The final retirement, death, was much in his mind. 'I don't want to go on too long, certainly not past 80', he wrote at the beginning of 1960, '& best stop short of Four Score, & I don't want to become a too senile bore & burden, and I hope not to have much pain.'[23] He told Catherine Walston that he was not sure he wanted to live through the next winter. 'Wouldn't it be nice just to sleep through it, like some animals do? Isn't "being alive" a crude illusion anyhow?'[24]

'Unilateralism is not internationalism', he wrote to the *Daily Telegraph* in October. 'It is nationalist egoism gone mad.'[25] In February 1961 he ended many months of absence from public platforms to take the chair at a rally called by the Campaign for Democratic Socialism, an anti-unilateralist pressure group organised by William Rodgers, Dick Taverne, Tony Crosland and others and aimed at reversing the 1960 Conference decision. Speaking 'in a voice that made the heckling of the unilateralists seem like squeals', Dalton recalled Party Conference in 1933, when a pacifist resolution had been adopted only to be reversed the following year.[26] This public appearance, widely reported, had a symbolic value for C.D.S. For Dalton, too, it was important, because it was his last.

Alone with Ruth at West Leaze for most of the year, he lived for little now except the final volume of his memoirs. Work on this project had become difficult and slow. In December 1960 he wrote to Gaitskell: 'I'm in the last stage of pregnancy, heavy with my Volume III.'[27] He finished at last in March. He felt a deep relief, and his depression briefly lifted. Then, as though an internal clock had noted that his life's tasks were complete, his fragile system fell apart.

On 8th May 1961, Hugh wrote in his diary cryptically: 'Washout & Passout'. Three days later, Ruth fell down stairs and broke her femur badly. She was admitted to University College Hospital where she spent three months before being released on crutches. Meanwhile, on 15th May, Hugh fainted again, and without Ruth to look after him, he was admitted to the nursing home in Fitzroy Square where he had been treated before.[28] On 26th May he wrote to Catherine Walston expressing concern about Ruth, and saying that they were having their worst summer ever.[29] 'I have been kidding myself that I am very fit', he told a reporter. 'But now I have to confess that I am not.'[30]

There was a brief recession in his illness. In mid-June he was back in Ashley Gardens reading proofs of *High Tide and After*,[31] while the *Evening Standard* serialised extracts. With Ruth still in University College Hospital with her leg in a sling, Hugh returned to Wiltshire. He told the press: 'The weather is perfect. I am sitting in the garden in the sun waiting for the men to come and cut the hay.'[32] There were a few, loyal visitors – Mike Williams-Thompson, Fred and Ann Kendall, Ian Little, Brian Abel-Smith, Desmond Donnelly. Proofs were sent back to the publishers at the beginning of August. On one of Dalton's good days, Tony Crosland, who was staying half an hour's drive away, came over and fetched him. On the way back, Dalton talked ceaselessly and repetitively.[33]

There were alternations between periods of lucidity, and periods when his memory failed him. Ruth became worried. The housekeeper wrote that she had found Hugh wandering up and down the garden aimlessly late at night. Ruth feared that Hugh's behaviour might cause the housekeeper to leave, and tried desperately to organise domestic arrangements in Wiltshire from her London sick-bed.[34] At last, on 12th August, she was driven down by the Frasers, with a nurse in attendance. The next few weeks were filled with doctors, nurses and physiotherapists, attending to both of them. Gradually, Ruth moved from heavy to light crutches, and then to sticks. Hugh made less progress. Denied alcohol, and with nothing to do, he sat silently at his desk, staring out at the Downs and his trees.[35] The weather was hot and clear. 'But physically', Hugh wrote in an unsteady hand, 'Ruth & I have had a FART of a SUMMER'.

When he was lucid, his mind was on youth. He noticed the marriage of Douglas Jay's son Peter to James Callaghan's daughter Margaret, reported in a Sunday paper. 'Why aren't all the Labour Party under forty (? 30) as good looking as that?' he wrote to Gaitskell. 'Then we should win, not only all elections, but all Life's Golden Apples.'[36] He still had energy for his favourite pastime, helping the young. He sent Michael Barnes advice on the next step to take in pursuit of a parliamentary seat. 'I still want – very badly – to see a swarm of bright, fresh, interesting, young, effective Labour candidates preparing to go into action and give us a Labour Majority next [time] & you one of that gay gang of winners,' he wrote.[37]

He returned to Ashley Gardens at the end of September and was immediately laid low with sciatica. 'Then R. nursed me beautifully & collected young friends', he recorded gratefully at the end of the year.[38] Of his contemporaries Bill Piercy came, and so did Willie Hall.

But nearly all his visitors were younger by one generation or even two – Gaitskell, Davenport, Wilmot, the Frasers, Jebb, Williams-Thompson, de Freitas, George Brown, Michael Barnes, Denis Howell, George Chetwynd, John and Marina Vaizey, Abel-Smith, Dick Taverne, Dick Marsh.

'Middlesbrough E. I wish we could get this for some one young, lively & loyal', he wrote reflectively to Gaitskell in December; 'of course Bill Rodgers would be tops, if he could get it. He would be most useful & efficient in the House ... Do Try for him. At Lincoln, I hear from Geoffrey de Freitas, we shall probably have choice of two good Labour Lawyers as candidates. NIALL MacDermot [sic] or DICK TAVERNE, one of your young CAMPAIGNERS. Either good, but *I* should prefer TAVERNE.' Taverne got Lincoln, but something else cropped up. One of Dalton's visitors was George Chetwynd, his old P.P.S. Chetwynd told him that he had decided to resign his seat, Stockton-on-Tees, in the north-east. This was Dalton territory, and it provided the chance to render a last political service.

Dalton had long had his eye on William Rodgers, the fervent young Gaitskellite who was General Secretary of the Fabian Society, and now the mastermind of C.D.S. Before the 1959 election Dalton had been pushing Rodgers for the Bosworth constituency – only to find himself in collision with Gaitskell, who had secretly been pushing Woodrow Wyatt.[39] Early in December, Dalton rang Rodgers: 'I've somebody I'd like you to meet. Can you come to tea?' Rodgers went to Ashley Gardens, and found Chetwynd already there. Dalton said: 'My friend George Chetwynd tells me he's resigning. We think you should have his seat.' Contacts were provided, and Rodgers won the selection.[40]

The Daltons were driven down to West Leaze by their friends the Kendalls for Christmas and the New Year. Gloomily, Hugh surveyed the past twelve months. '1961 was a bad year', he noted, 'we were both ill, in Hospital, nursing homes etc. We incurred large personal health expenditure, including private nurses at W.L. etc.'[41] On 4th January they returned to London. Advance copies of Volume III of the memoirs, entitled *High Tide and After*, arrived four days later.

By then, Hugh had started to decline fast, losing control physically and mentally. His last week in the flat, irrational and almost mad, flinging objects around the room, was terrible.[42] Despite a stiff and painful leg, Ruth managed him efficiently and with tenderness. On Sunday, 14th January he was admitted to a private ward at University College Hospital. But he made so much noise that he was moved to St Pancras Hospital,[43] into a public geriatric ward with 28 other men.[44] On 20th January the press reported that Lord Dalton had had two heart attacks and was seriously ill.[45]

Tony Crosland visited him on 24th January.[46] Ruth turned other visitors firmly away. 'Why don't they let him die?' she asked friends. Waiting for the end, and desperate for something to do, she bought some branches of pine, symbolising his love of trees, to decorate the cortège. Then his condition stabilised for a few days, and she was left with pine needles on the carpet.[47] In the hospital there was another touch of black humour, reported by Ruth to a friend. One morning a nurse explained to Hugh that she had to give him an enema so as to give him a motion. Hugh's voice reverberated through the ward: 'You can't have a motion without a debate!'[48]

The radio carried daily bulletins. Hugh's sister, widowed ten years and out of contact with her brother for eighteen, heard them. For a week in the Forbes Watson house there were silent purposeful games of bezique. Georgie's daughter, Heather, who had never met her uncle, offered to drive her mother to the hospital. But Georgie shook her head and refused.[49]

On 1st February, the *Guardian* carried a note on Dalton's last serious piece of writing. This was a review, published in *Political Quarterly*, of a new book called *Parliamentary Socialism* by Ralph Miliband, a Marxist theoretician. The book was critical of the Labour Party, and Dalton was critical of the book. Miliband had found both the Labour Party and the Labour Left guilty of addiction to 'parliamentarism'. Dalton posed the question: what were the alternatives?

> Industrial action for economic ends? ... Violence ·organised and prepared beforehand? Wisely he does not say so. But, if not this mad nightmare, then what? I feel that most of Mr. Miliband's criticisms of the 'Labour Left' relate to tactics, not principles, and are weakened by a lack of inside knowledge and experience of politics.[50]

High Tide and After was published on 5th February. The political scientist Robert McKenzie called it 'the most important contribution to an understanding of the post-war political scene so far made by any of those who played a part in it.'[51] Others used it as an opportunity for obituary, anticipating the end. 'Most people will be embarrassed by the recurring panegyrics of youth in which he drowns the inner sighs of personal unhappiness', wrote Hugh's old friend and critic John Freeman. ' ... Dalton is traditionally accused by his many enemies of insincerity, of cynicism, of malice. Look deeper, and you find a man of feeling, humanity, and unshakeable loyalty to people which matched his talent.'[52]

On 12th February 1962 Hugh Dalton died. In accordance with his wishes, he was cremated, and his ashes scattered at West Leaze. Ruth showed little emotion, brushing aside condolences.[53] She found the funeral service and cremation ludicrous, like a French farce.[54] Both she and Hugh had been atheists, with no belief in an after-life. At the end of March she told her teacher friend Hilde Auerbach that she had recovered from the shock and fatigue. 'I quite understand how rushed you are, so that you missed the splendid tributes to Hugh in the Guardian and the Observer', she wrote. 'By the way I hope you have persuaded the school to take the Guardian. It is particularly interesting for older girls, as its women's page often contains excellent accounts of interesting women who do fine things.'[55] A pile of letters arrived. 'There was no one it was so much fun to be with – laughing & uninhibited fun', wrote Crosland. ' ... Nobody outside my family has ever done so much so willingly for me.'[56]

Hugh left £25,425 (£19,700 after estate duty and expenses). His own money had never greatly interested him and he had lost some of his capital by misguidedly investing in 'Daltons', the government stock he had himself launched. Everything went to Ruth, except the letters from Rupert Brooke which were donated to King's College, Cambridge, and Canon Dalton's letters from members of the Royal Family, which were left to Georgie.[57] Hugh's papers, including his huge unpublished diary, were handed over by his literary executors to the London School of Economics. Ruth no longer had an address for Georgie, and there was some initial difficulty in tracing her.

After his death, Ruth came to revere Hugh's memory and achievements, proudly showing his books to friends and citing his opinions. Yet it was a relief, at first, when he was gone. The strain of the last months had been hard to bear.

She soon returned to her old routine of committees and semi-public functions – taking an active, initiating role on the Arts Council, the Board of the Royal Ballet, and the Executive of the National Trust. It was a life whose quiet, conscientious regularity suited her temperament. Before long, she seemed happier than for years past. She was completely on her own – no children, siblings, close relatives to soften the isolation she had felt all her life. But she was self-contained in her loneliness, and drew satisfaction from public duties. More than ever she turned to younger friends, mainly women. She was eager, as Hugh had been, to offer what she had of advice, encouragement, help with careers. There were many women of her daughter Helen's generation or younger who discovered beneath the chilly, bird-like exterior reserves of generosity and kindness.

Ruth let West Leaze for most of the year, and took an L.S.E. student as a lodger at Ashley Gardens, to help pay the rent. She planned to leave West Leaze to Tony Crosland – Hugh's adopted son – and in July 1964 she made a will to this effect. But the frugality of her own existence was not enough to compensate for the impact of inflation on her dwindling private income, and so she decided instead to sell. When the time came to move out, she stood in the large front room of the empty house, beside the huge glass table that once provided a ringing echo to Hugh's voice and laughter, and looked out silently at the pines and sorbuses marking the sharp slope down to Aldbourne. Fred Kendall, who had driven down to fetch her, watched. 'She was taking in the view, thinking "This is the last time"', he recalls. Then she turned and said briskly, 'Right Fred. We're off.' They drove away with never a look back.[58]

Ruth was pleased by the 1964 election result, watching on television the comings and goings in Downing Street of the young men Hugh had pushed forward ten or twenty years before. Some of these remembered the debt. 'This is my first letter in the Chancellor's chair!', Jim Callaghan wrote to her. 'I know Hugh would have been pleased and if he had been here we would have had lots of fun.'[59] Later, when Tony Crosland was promoted to the post of Secretary of State for Education and Science, she told his new wife Susan that he would enjoy being in the Cabinet in ways he could not yet imagine: 'The authority, the briefings, being looked after, the car ... '[60]

At the beginning of 1965 Ruth went on holiday to Morocco with two friends, Ethel Whitehorn and Enid MacLeod, who shared her love of French culture. While they were there, Ethel and Enid bought her a jewel as a present. She was happy and excited like a little girl. 'This is the only jewel I have ever had, apart from an aqua marina which Hugh gave me', she said. 'And *that* the window-cleaner stole.' She enjoyed the travelling and the companionship. Her friends noticed, however, tell-tale signs of illness: shortness of breath and a reluctance to walk more than a few yards.[61]

An exploratory operation revealed nothing. At first Ruth thought she was getting better. Then stomach cancer was diagnosed. Knowing that death was near, she settled her affairs. First, she made a new will, making bequests to women friends, and leaving the bulk of her estate to the Israeli ambassador to buy English books for libraries in Israel. Then she went to a well-known charity that dealt with international relief. She wanted, she said, to aid a specific project. 'How much do you need?' she asked. '£250', replied an official. She wrote out a cheque on the spot.[62]

She refused further medical attention, preferring to make private arrangements for a nurse to take care of her needs at the very end. Then, without telling friends, she withdrew into her bedroom at the Ashley Gardens flat and on 15th March 1966 she died. According to the nurse, in her final delirium she called out for her lost daughter.[63]

There was no ceremony or music at the funeral in Golders' Green Crematorium. The coffin sat in the middle of the room in silence. Then it disappeared noiselessly and in a minute all was over.[64] The Public Trustee was sole executor. Furniture, clothes, books, political mementoes, together with the relics of Dalton ancestors, were shifted to a government warehouse, where they were placed alongside the worldly possessions of other anonymous or heirless deceased.[65] Friends named in the will were permitted to come and make selected pickings. A few books and items of furniture were distributed in this manner. What remained was sold and the proceeds were added to the value of the estate.

Three weeks after Ruth's death, the Labour Party won another election victory, with the biggest majority since 1945. Harold Wilson, once Hugh's employee at the Board of Trade, formed his second Cabinet. Its members included Arthur Bottomley, George Brown, James Callaghan, Barbara Castle, Anthony Crosland, Richard Crossman, Denis Healey, Douglas Jay, Roy Jenkins, Lord Longford and Fred Peart – each and every one a Dalton poodle.

NOTES

The following abbreviations are used frequently in the Notes:

CBY   *Call Back Yesterday*
FY   *Fateful Years*
HC Debs   House of Commons Debates, Fifth Series (Hansard)
HD   Hugh Dalton
HDD   Hugh Dalton's diary
HTA   *High Tide and After*
L.P.A.C.R. Labour Party Annual Conference Report
RA   Royal Archives

For other abbreviations and full titles of works cited in shortened form, see the Bibliography, pp. 717–31. BT, CAB, FO, HLG, PREM and T references are to papers in the Public Record Office, Kew.

I *The Royal Connection*

1 J. N. Dalton to Eliza Dalton, 1st September 1887 (Joyce Parker Letters).
2 RA GV AA6/369.
3 Prince George to J. N. Dalton, 16th September 1887 (RA GV AA6/369).
4 RA 2101/16.
5 RA GV AA6/370.
6 So Hugh's sister told her children. (Ian Forbes Watson, Heather Forbes Watson: interviews.)
7 27th July 1929, ed. M. Cole, *Beatrice Webb: Diary 1924–1932*, Longman, 1949, pp. 209–10.
8 A. C. Benson, *The House of Quiet: An Autobiography*, John Murray, 1906, p. 6. The following account of Dalton's ancestry is largely based on information from *The Journal of The Dalton Genealogical Society*. I am particularly grateful to the editor, Michael Neale Dalton, and to Morag Simpson and Joyce Parker, Committee members of the Society.
9 E. A. Towle, *John Mason Neale D.D.: a Memoir*, Longman, 1906, p. 1. John Mason Neale, Cornelius's son, wrote one eighth of *Hymns Ancient and Modern*, including 'Jerusalem the Golden'.

10 Apart from Hugh Dalton's own recollections of his uncle (*Call Back Yesterday*, Muller, 1953, p. 23, henceforth CBY), there is an interesting pen-portrait by one of Cornelius's grandsons, Lord Cross, in *The Journal of the Dalton Genealogical Society* (Vol. II, No. 1, 1982). The impression is of a typical Victorian senior civil servant – scholarly, mild-mannered, unostentatious, living comfortably but modestly in Hampstead.

11 'The Intellectual Aristocracy' in (ed.) J. H. Plumb, *Studies in Social History*, Longman, 1955, pp. 243–87.

12 Queen Victoria's Journal (RA). There is a further reference on 30th April: ' ... Church to Whippingham, where Mr. Prothero as usual performed the sermon and preached, being assisted by Mr. Dalton.'

13 In appointing Dalton, what selection procedures were adopted? With the whole of the British Empire at her disposal, it is hardly credible that Queen Victoria should have picked a country curate just because she liked the way he preached. There is even some doubt about who actually did the picking. King George VI's biographer claimed that the Prince of Wales chose Dalton 'with care and anxiety', but gives no source. (J. W. Wheeler-Bennett, *King George VI – His Life and Reign*, Macmillan, 1958, p. 23.) Others have assumed that Dalton was Queen Victoria's choice, possibly after consulting Prothero. (J. Gore, *King George V: A Personal Memoir*, Murray, 1941, p. 18; see also J. E. Vincent, *H.R.H. Duke of Clarence and Avondale – A Memoir*. Murray, 1893.) Or were there others who recommended him? (See p. 79.)

14 Harold Nicolson, unpublished diary, 14th April 1949.

15 Gore, *King George V*, p. 19.

16 1st June 1874. Queen Victoria's Journal (RA).

17 Cited in H. Nicolson, *King George the Fifth – His Life and Reign*, Constable, 1952, p. 6.

18 Prince George to J. N. Dalton, 9th August 1877 (Joyce Parker Letters).

19 Nicolson, *King George*, pp. 12–20; P. Magnus, *King Edward the Seventh*, Murray, 1964, pp. 158–9. On 19th May 1879, the Cabinet recommended, on grounds of safety, that the Princes should be separated and that two warships should be provided. The Prince of Wales, who disagreed, sent for the Prime Minister, who apologised and gave way. Thereupon Dalton, who had demanded two ships, handed in his resignation, but was persuaded to change his mind less than a week before the ship's departure. When the ship did sail, it carried a complement of officers and tutors virtually hand-picked by himself.

20 Nicolson, *King George*, p. 21.

21 Gore, *King George V*, p. 47.

22 Magnus, *King Edward*, p. 169.

23 11th July 1883, cited in Gore, *King George*, p. 58.

24 A. V. Baillie, *My First Eighty Years*, Murray, 1951, pp. 175–6.

25 R. Thorndike, *Children of The Garter*, Rich & Crown, 1937, p. 96.

26 2nd January 1888 (RA GV AA6/371).

27 CBY, p. 14.

28 18th January 1885, Queen Victoria's Journal (RA).

29 Cited in G. Battiscombe, *Queen Alexandra*, Constable, 1969, p. 162.

30 23rd June 1885, Queen Victoria's Journal (RA).

31 A knighthood followed later.

32 Charles Evan-Thomas had worked the Gnoll pit, coal being conveyed through the town of Neath in carts, until differences with the local corporation led to the closure and dismantling of the colliery.

33 D. Rhys Phillips, *The History of the Vale of Neath*, published by the author, Swansea, 1925, p. 380. (I am grateful to Joyce Parker for this reference.) See also J. and J. B. Burke (eds.), *A Genealogical and Heraldic Dictionary of the Landed Gentry of Great Britain and Ireland*, Vol. II, Henry Colburn, 1853.

34 22nd June 1887 (RA GV AA6/367).

35 CBY, p. 17. It is not known whether this was Kitty Dalton's second or third confinement. The baby is believed to have been a boy (*Dictionary of National Biography* 1961–1970, Oxford University Press, 1981, p. 266).

36 Heather Forbes Watson (daughter of Georgie Forbes Watson, née Dalton), interview.

37 CBY, p. 14.

38 Ian Forbes Watson, Heather Forbes Watson, interviews.

39 Hugh Dalton's unpublished diary (henceforth HDD), 22 March 1944.

40 CBY, p. 14.

41 Thorndike, *Children*, p. 89.

42 J. N. Dalton to Prince George, 8th December 1887, 20th May 1888 (RA GV AA6/370, 373).

43 Prince Albert Victor to J. N. Dalton, 9th November 1888 (RA GV AA6/377).

44 11th December 1888, Prince George's Journal (RA).

45 CBY, p. 15.

46 Sir Walford Davies, organist in the Chapel, gave this version: 'Queen Victoria told one of her ladies in waiting that she asked dear Canon and Mrs. Dalton to tea, but they were bringing "that odious little son of theirs with them".' (Recalled by Commander Crichton Maitland, 28th January 1952; Vidler papers.) This should be compared to stories, referred to later (see p. 416), about George V's hostility to Canon Dalton's 'anarchist son'. The theme is always the same: the Canon is acceptable; the son an outcast.

47 In a letter to her niece, cited in F. E. Leaning, 'The Dalton Book' (unpublished typescript), 1951.

48 Joyce Parker, Morag Simpson, interviews. Gertrude, daughter of the Canon's parson brother (and hence a first cousin of Hugh) was one who held this view.

49 Information about Georgie and her attitude to Hugh is mainly derived from interviews with two of her children, Heather and Ian Forbes Watson.

50 Magnus, *King Edward*, p. 169; H. Nicolson, unpublished diary, 16th February 1949.

51 Lady Geraldine Somerset's diary, cited in G. St. Aubyn, *The Royal*

George, Constable, 1963, p. 299.

52 N. Nicolson (ed.), *Harold Nicolson: Diaries and Letters 1945–1962* Collins, 1968, p. 167.

53 Cited in H. Montgomery Hyde, *Their Good Names*, Hamish Hamilton, 1970, p. 97.

54 H. Montgomery Hyde, *The Cleveland Street Scandal*, W. H. Allen, 1976; see also H. Nicolson, unpublished diary, 16th February 1949.

55 The death occurred during an influenza epidemic. However, a prescription found among Eddy's doctor's papers suggests that he suffered from a gonorrheal infection (Hyde, *Their Good Names*, p. 77). Within the Dalton family, it was always believed that the prince died from syphilis, contracted in the West Indies during the *Bacchante* voyage, while under the Canon's care.

56 19th March 1892, Queen Victoria Journal (RA).

57 H. Bolitho, *Older People*, Cobden-Sanderson, 1935, p. 111.

58 The Rev. Canon S. G. B. Exham, 5th February 1953 (Vidler Papers).

59 Bolitho, *Older People*, p. 114.

60 A. C. Deane, *Time Remembered*, Faber, 1945, p. 212.

61 Baillie, *My First Eighty Years*, pp. 172–3, 175.

62 M. C. Boyle, 31st November 1952 (Vidler Papers).

63 Bolitho, *Older People*, pp. 115–16.

64 James Webb Jones (Vidler Papers).

65 Rev. Anthony Tremlett (Vidler Papers).

66 James Webb Jones (Vidler Papers).

67 Bishop of Willesden (Vidler Papers).

68 Thorndike, *Children*, p. 81.

69 Bolitho, *Older People*, p. 115.

70 Lady Walford Davies (Vidler Papers).

71 Thorndike, *Children*, p. 81.

72 Bishop of Willesden (Vidler Papers).

73 Rev. Canon Exham (Vidler Papers).

74 CBY, p. 24.

II *Boyhood*

1 The uniqueness of this status is revealed in the school register for 13th September 1895 (courtesy of Mr. Widgeway).

2 R. Thorndike, *Children of the Garter*, Rich & Crown, 1937. See especially p. 200.

3 J. Barham Johnson, 'Boyhood Reminiscences of St. George's School, Windsor' MS. (Vidler papers).

4 Thorndike, *Children*, p. 89. Thorndike added: 'This was only natural, considering his father put him to Euclid at the age of four.'

5 G. Boas, *A Teacher's Story*, Macmillan, 1963, p. 14.

6 Sir James Montagu Butler in R. Usborne, *A Century of Summer Fields*, Methuen, 1964, p. 54.

7 Usborne, *Summer Fields*, p. 35.
8 E. Waugh, *The Life of the Right Reverend Ronald Knox*, Chapman & Hall, 1959, p. 48. Knox was unstinting in his praise for the school.
9 Usborne, *Summer Fields*, p. 22.
10 Prince George to J. N. Dalton, 25th March, 27th April 1897 (RA GV AA6/475, 496).
11 CBY, p. 16.
12 Boas, *A Teacher's Story*, pp. 14–15.
13 CBY, p. 16.
14 Waugh, *Knox*, p. 48.
15 *Summer Fields School Magazine*, 1900.
16 Only eight immediately (*Eton College Calendar*, 1901).
17 *Summer Fields School Magazine*, 1901.
18 A correspondent to *The Times* in 1884, cited in L. S. R. Byrne and E. L. Churchill, *Changing Eton*, Jonathan Cape, 1937, p. 55.
19 CBY, pp. 26, 27.
20 Lord Lambton recalls the late Lord Allendale telling this story (interview).
21 *Granta*, 6th November 1906.
22 Major W. G. McMinnies, private correspondence with the author.
23 CBY, pp. 27–8. Bourne later became a Tory M.P.
24 N. Mosley, *Julian Grenfell: His Life and The Times of His Death; 1888–1915*, Weidenfeld & Nicolson, 1976, p. 90.
25 L. E. Jones, *A Victorian Boyhood*, Macmillan, 1955, pp. 180–1.
26 CBY, p. 26.
27 1st, 14th June 1903, Prince George's journal (RA).
28 CBY, p. 34.
29 *Granta*, 6th November 1909.
30 CBY, p. 27.
31 Cited in N. Wood, *Communism and British Intellectuals*, Gollancz, 1959, p. 113.
32 C. Connolly, *Enemies of Promise*, Deutsch, (1973 ed.), p. 235.
33 Jones, *A Victorian Boyhood*, p. 194.
34 CBY, pp. 27–34.
35 *St. George's School Magazine*, 1904; *Eton School Register*, Part VII, 1899–1909; Spottiswoode, Ballantyne & Co., 1922.
36 *Granta*, 6th November 1909.
37 *Eton College Chronicle*, October 1905, February 1906. Dalton incorrectly gives the date of his second performance as June 1906 (CBY, p. 31).
38 Prince George to J. N. Dalton, 6th April 1906 (RA GV AA6/519).
39 CBY, pp. 33–5.
40 *Evening Standard*, 24th April 1948.

III *Golden Time*

1 In a paper, delivered in 1903 to a small Cambridge gathering. Cited in

P. N. Furbank, *E. M. Forster: A Life*, Oxford University Press (1979 ed.), p. 105.
2 CBY, pp. 53–5.
3 Ibid., p. 38.
4 Amber Blanco-White, interview.
5 E. Marsh (ed.), *The Collected Poems of Rupert Brooke: With a Memoir*, Sidgwick & Jackson, 1918, p. xxx.
6 CBY, p. 16.
7 *Cambridge Review*, 8th November 1906, *Granta* 10th November 1906. He spoke against a motion 'That this House would welcome the development of a national rather than an imperial ideal'.
8 CBY, p. 44.
9 R. C. K. Ensor, *England 1870–1914*, Oxford University Press, 1936, p. 386.
10 E. R. Pease, *The History of the Fabian Society*, A. C. Fifield, 1916, pp. 37–9.
11 R. Barker, *Political Ideas in Modern Britain*, Methuen, 1978, p. 29.
12 N. MacKenzie (ed), *The Letters of Sidney and Beatrice Webb, Vol. II, Partnership 1892–1912*, Cambridge University Press, 1978, p. 219.
13 Pease, *Fabian Society*, p. 166.
14 N. and J. MacKenzie, *The First Fabians*, Weidenfeld & Nicolson, 1977, p. 34.
15 Pease, *Fabian Society*, pp. 269, 188–9.
16 CBY, p. 44. E.T.[ownshend] (ed.), *Keeling Letters and Recollections*, Allen & Unwin, 1918, p. xi. The words are those of H. G. Wells.
17 *Cambridge Review*, 1st November 1906.
18 *Keeling Letters*, pp. ix, 13–14.
19 *Letters of Sidney and Beatrice Webb*, Vol. II, p. 315.
20 *Keeling Letters*, pp. 13–14, 3.
21 *Granta*, 30th May 1908. Gerald Shove received similar treatment; see C. Hassall, *Rupert Brooke: A Biography*, Faber, 1964, pp. 176–7.
22 Lord Noel-Baker, interview.
23 CBY, p. 36.
24 R. Rhodes James (ed.), *Memoirs of a Conservative: J. C. C. Davidson's Memoirs and Papers 1910–1937*, Weidenfeld & Nicolson, 1969, p. 8.
25 T. Rogers (ed.), *Rupert Brooke: A Reappraisal and Selection*, Routledge & Kegan Paul, 1971, p. 24.
26 *Granta*, 6th November 1909.
27 *Cambridge Review*, 14th February 1907.
28 CBY, p. 46.
29 F. Brockway, *Inside the Left*, New Leader, 1942, p. 17.
30 *Keeling Letters*, p. 11.
31 Rhodes James (ed.), *Memoirs of a Conservative*, p. 8.
32 CBY, p. 46.
33 *Granta*, 2nd March 1907, *Cambridge Review*, 28th February 1907.
34 *Granta*, 2nd March, 4th May 1907.
35 *Cambridge Review*, 28th February 1907.

36 An entry in Prince George's journal for 12th June 1907 reads: 'Dalton and his son who is now at Cambridge dined with us. Bed at 11.30'. (RA). There is no mention of any other guests.
37 *Granta*, 26th October 1907, 15th, 22nd February 1908.

IV *Comrade Hugh*

1 17th April 1908, in G. Keynes (ed.), *The Letters of Rupert Brooke*, Faber, 1968, p. 125.
2 T. Rogers (ed.), *Rupert Brooke: A Reappraisal and Selection*, RKP, 1971, p. 24. Under the poster was the legend: 'Forward the day is breaking'.
3 Brooke to Mrs Brooke, 11th May 1908, in *The Letters of Rupert Brooke*, p. 127.
4 Keeling to Mrs Townshend, 11th June 1909, in E.T[ownshend] (ed.), *Keeling Letters and Recollections*, Allen & Unwin, 1918, pp. 22–3.
5 C. Hassall, *Rupert Brooke: A Biography*, Faber, 1964, p. 166.
6 End of July 1908 [?], in *The Letters of Rupert Brooke*, p. 135.
7 Beatrice Webb's diary, cited in N. and J. MacKenzie, *H. G. Wells: A Biography*, Simon and Schuster, 1973, p. 234.
8 B. Webb to M. Playne, 21st August 1907, September 1908, in N. Mac-Kenzie (ed.), *Letters of Sidney and Beatrice Webb*, Vol. II, *Partnership 1892–1912*, Cambridge University Press, 1978, pp. 272, 316.
9 Beatrice Webb, unpublished diary, 15th September 1908. See also B. Drake and M. Cole (eds.), *Our Partnership by Beatrice Webb*, Longman, 1948, pp. 414–5.
10 B. Webb to M. Playne, September 1908, *Letters of Sidney and Beatrice Webb*, Vol. II, p. 316.
11 Keeling to Mrs Townshend, 21st July, 13th September in *Keeling Letters*, pp. 30, 37.
12 *Keeling Letters*, p. 44.
13 Brooke to HD, 18th August 1908, in *The Letters of Rupert Brooke*, pp. 139–40.
14 R. W. Service, *Songs of a Sourdough* (7th ed.) T. Fisher Unwin, 1908, pp. 20–1.
15 2nd February 1909, 21st July 1908 in *Keeling Letters*, pp. 46, 31.
16 CBY, p. 56.
17 Furbank, *Forster*, p. 60.
18 D. Proctor (ed.), *The Autobiography of G. Lowes Dickinson*, Duckworth, 1973, p. 13.
19 M. A. Hamilton, *Uphill All the Way*, Jonathan Cape, 1953, p. 28.
20 Proctor (ed.) *The Autobiography of G. Lowes Dickinson*, p. 13.
21 Hassall, *Rupert Brooke*, p. 154.
22 M. Holroyd, *Lytton Strachey: A Biography*, Penguin, 1971, p. 280.
23 R. F. Harrod, *The Life of John Maynard Keynes*, Macmillan, 1951, pp. 147–8, 131.
24 CBY, pp. 60–2.

25 Cited in N. and J. MacKenzie, *The First Fabians*, Weidenfeld & Nicolson, 1977, p. 354.
26 See P. Thane, *The Foundations of the Welfare State*, Longman, 1982, pp. 88–90; S. Checkland, *British Public Policy, 1776–1939*, Cambridge University Press, 1983, pp. 246–7.
27 Obituary of Churchill by Dalton, written in 1957 and published in the *New Statesman*, 29th January 1965 (after Dalton's own death). Dalton recalled the meeting as having taken place after Churchill had become President of the Board of Trade. Other evidence suggests that it took place in March, a few weeks before Churchill took office (J. Harris, *William Beveridge*, Oxford University Press, 1977, p. 139; J. Beveridge, *An Epic of Clare Market*, L.S.E., 1960, p. 75). Beveridge took up his new post in July. But see also Drake and Cole (eds.), *Our Partnership*, p. 435, diary entry for 3rd October 1909, which describes a dinner at which the Webbs recommended Ben Keeling to Churchill for the job of manager of a labour exchange.
28 MacKenzie, *The First Fabians*, pp. 360–7.
29 16th April 1909, in *The Letters of Rupert Brooke*, p. 167.
30 Sir Geoffrey Keynes, interview.
31 M. Gilbert (ed.), *Plough My Own Furrow: The story of Lord Allen told through his writings and correspondence*, Longman, 1965, p. 11.
32 L. Manning, *A Life for Education*, Gollancz, 1970, pp. 35–7.
33 *Granta*, 20th February, 29th May 1909.
34 In CBY (p. 51), Dalton admits to only two defeats.
35 J. R. M. Butler papers.
36 Brooke to HD, 16th April 1909, Brooke to Schofield, June 1909, in *The Letters of Rupert Brooke*, pp. 167, 171.
37 CBY, p. 36.
38 Hassall, *Rupert Brooke*, p. 185.
39 5th July, 1909 (Brooke Papers: Dalton Bequest, Da 2).
40 Brooke to Ka Cox, June 1909, in *The Letters of Rupert Brooke*, p. 172.
41 Hassall, *Rupert Brooke*, p. 195.
42 23rd July 1909, cited in M. Holroyd, *Augustus John: A Biography*, Vol. I, Heinemann, 1974, p. 256.
43 August 1909, in *The Letters of Rupert Brooke*, p. 174.
44 *Keeling Letters*, p. 54.
45 Brooke to Marsh, August 1909. Brooke to Ward, 25th August 1909, in *The Letters of Rupert Brooke*, pp. 174, 176.
46 Hassall, *Rupert Brooke*, pp. 196–7.
47 *Granta*, 6th November 1909.
48 Brooke to HD, end of 1909 (Brooke Papers: Dalton Bequest, Da 2).
49 *Granta*, 5th February 1910.
50 CBY, p. 58.
51 A. C. Pigou, *Wealth and Welfare*, Macmillan, 1912, p. 488.
52 CBY, p. 56.
53 J. Saltmarsh and P. Wilkinson, *Arthur Cecil Pigou 1877–1959*, Cambridge University Press, 1960, p. 19.

54 CBY, p. 57.
55 Brooke to Erica Cotterill, 9th January 1910, in *The Letters of Rupert Brooke*, p. 206.
56 CBY, p. 63.
57 Brooke to HD (Brooke Papers: Dalton Bequest, Da 2).
58 Brooke to Frances Cornford, 16th March, to HD, 23rd March 1910, in *The Letters of Rupert Brooke*, pp. 228–30.
59 Hassall, *Rupert Brooke*, p. 220.
60 *Nation*, 1st May 1915, cited in ibid., p. 221.
61 Beatrice Webb: unpublished diary, 27th December 1909.
62 Drake and Cole (eds.), *Our Partnership*, pp. 456–7.
63 CBY, p. 49.
64 Beatrice Webb, unpublished diary, 4th September 1910.
65 Hassall, *Rupert Brooke*, p. 232.
66 So Sir Geoffrey Keynes, who edited Brooke's letters, recalled in an interview with the author on 11th January 1980. Although Sir Geoffrey was unable to shed light on the whereabouts of this letter, which was not one of those used in his edition, his recollection fits other known facts: the presence of James Strachey in a stable, and the fact that Brooke corresponded with Ward on other matters at this time. Sir Geoffrey recalled that, according to the letter, Dalton was naked, presumably dressing in the early morning. He was not certain of the exact phrase, but it was either 'his enormous steaming penis' or 'his huge penis steaming'.
67 CBY, p. 62.
68 R. Rhodes James (ed.), *Memoirs of a Conservative: J. C. C. Davidson's Memoirs and Papers*, Weidenfeld & Nicolson, 1969, p. 8.
69 CBY, p. 62.

V *Ever Young*

1 HD to Geoffrey Keynes, 4th August 1950 (Brooke Papers Da 3).
2 See N. Davenport, *Memoirs of a City Radical*, Weidenfeld & Nicolson, 1974, pp. 73, 174–5. S. Crosland, *Tony Crosland*, Jonathan Cape, 1982, pp. 48, 54. Susan Crosland suggests that Dalton was a 'repressed' homosexual.
3 P. Fussell, *The Great War and Modern Memory*, Oxford University Press, 1975, p. 281.
4 T. d' Arch Smith, *Love in Earnest*, Routledge & Kegan Paul, 1970, p. 3.
5 M. Holroyd, *Lytton Strachey: A Biography*, first published 1966–7, Penguin, 1971, p. 282.
6 S. Hynes, *Edwardian Occasions*, Routledge & Kegan Paul, 1972, p. 146.
7 C. Connolly, *Enemies of Promise*, Routledge, 1938, p. 190.
8 CBY, p. 43.
9 D. Newsome (ed.), *Edwardian Excursions: From the Diaries of A. C. Benson 1898–1904*, Murray, 1981, p. 24; D. Newsome, *On The Edge of Paradise: The Diarist A. C. Benson*, Murray, 1980, p. 230.

10 A. C. Benson, *Memories and Friends*, Murray, 1924, p. 327.
11 September 1912, in G. Keynes (ed.), *The Letters of Rupert Brooke*, Faber, 1968, p. 400.
12 Fussell, *The Great War and Modern Memory*, pp. 229–300. Fussell comments: 'One of the period's most vigorous exponents of naked bathing was Rupert Brooke … ' (p. 301).
13 d' Arch Smith, *Love in Earnest*, pp. 191–2.
14 CBY, p. 22.
15 6th November 1870 (Carpenter Collection).
16 Cited in S. Rowbotham and J. Weeks, *Socialism and the New Life*, Pluto Press, 1977, p. 36.
17 P. N. Furbank, *E. M. Forster: A Life*, Oxford University Press (1979 ed.), Vol. I, pp. 256–7.
18 S. Pierson, *British Socialists: The Journey from Fantasy to Politics*, Harvard University Press, 1979, p. 35.
19 J. N. Dalton to E. Carpenter, 21st August 1920, 27th August 1921 (Carpenter Collection).
20 28th December 1907 in E.T[ownshend] (ed.), *Keeling Letters and Recollections*, Allen & Unwin, 1918, p. 20.
21 Keeling to B. Townshend, 3rd April 1910 in *Keeling Letters*, p. 62.
22 Keeling to Mrs Townshend, 12th August 1916, in *Keeling Letters*, p. 310.
23 D. Proctor (ed.), *The Autobiography of G. Lowes Dickinson*, Duckworth, 1973, p. 157.
24 'Body and Soul. A Dialogue' in ibid., pp. 273–83.
25 G. L. Dickinson, 'Edward Carpenter as a Friend' in G. Beith (ed.), *Edward Carpenter: In Appreciation*, Allen & Unwin, 1931, pp. 35–7.
26 E. Carpenter, *My Days and Dreams*, Allen & Unwin, 1916, p. 77.
27 E. Carpenter, *The Intermediate Sex: A Study of Some Transitional Types of Men and Women*, Swan Sonnenschein & Co., 1908, p. 115.
28 E. Carpenter, *Towards Democracy* (ed. G. Beith), Allen & Unwin, 1949, p. 253.
29 E. Delavenay, *D. H. Lawrence and Edward Carpenter: A Study in Edwardian Transition*, Heinemann, 1971, p. 232.
30 CBY, p. 22.
31 Furbank, *Forster*, p. 256.
32 J. N. Dalton to E. Carpenter, 12th, 22nd June 1923 (Carpenter Collection).
33 HDD, 25th–29th June 1923.
34 C. F. Sixsmith, 'Edward As I Knew Him', in G. Beith (ed.), *Edward Carpenter*, pp. 225–6.
35 Box 8/61–3, Carpenter Collection.
36 Rowbotham and Weeks, *Socialism and the New Life*, p. 31.
37 It should be noted that the most recent biography of Carpenter accepts, and repeats uncritically, the information given in the Beith envelope, taking the dates on the two single portraits (1875) as the date of the job offer. (C. Tsuzuki *Edward Carpenter 1844–1929: Prophet of Human*

Fellowship, Cambridge University Press, 1980, p. 77.)

VI *L.S.E. and A.S.C.*

1 CBY, pp. 69–70.
2 'The London School of Economics, 1895–1945' *Economica*, Vol. XIII, No. 49, 1946.
3 *The Gownsman*, 8th November 1910.
4 Brooke to Dalton, 17th October 1910 (Brooke Papers: Dalton Bequest, Da 2).
5 Brooke to Dalton, 7th August 1912 in G. Keynes (ed.), *The Letters of Rupert Brooke*, Faber, 1968, p. 392.
6 Brooke to Dalton, January 1913 (Brooke Papers: Dalton Bequest, Da 2).
7 Brooke to Dalton, 5th July 1913, in *The Letters of Rupert Brooke*, p. 480.
8 W. Pember Reeves to S. Webb, 1st August 1912. Minute Book of the 'Hutchinson Trustees' (L.S.E. School Archives, Vol. c. item 2.).
9 CBY, p. 114.
10 T. E. Gregory and H. Dalton (ed.), *London Essays in Economics: In Honour of Edwin Cannan*, Routledge, 1927, pp. 9, 21–2.
11 *Clare Market Review*, February 1913, Vol. 8, No. 2, p. 43.
12 N. and J. MacKenzie, *The First Fabians*, Weidenfeld & Nicolson, 1977, pp. 377–81.
13 Keeling to Mrs Townshend, 14th June 1914 in E.T[ownshend] (ed.) *Keeling Letters*, pp. 175–6.
14 CBY, p. 70.
15 *The Hunt 1898–1937*, Pelican Press, 1937, pp. 5, 13. Other Kingsmen made the same trip: Dudley Ward in 1911 and Nigel Crompton (a former Carbinaro) in 1913 (Ibid., pp. 5–6). I am grateful to Martin Bulmer for drawing my attention to this booklet.
16 Dalton to Cannan, 13th December 1913; Cannan Papers, 1022f. 75.
17 CBY, p. 70.
18 J. Beveridge, *An Epic of Clare Market*, G. Bell, 1960, p. 83.
19 Beatrice Webb, unpublished diary, 20th October 1936.
20 C. R. Attlee, *As It Happened*, Odhams, 1956, p. 40. See also CBY, p. 71.
21 Brooke to Dalton, 5th July 1914 in *The Letters of Rupert Brooke*, p. 597.
22 C. Hassall (ed.), *Rupert Brooke: A Biography*, Faber, 1964, p. 454.
23 *The Letters of Rupert Brooke*, pp. 671–2.
24 *Keeling Letters*, p. 183.
25 Major A. F. Becke, *History of the Great War: Order of Battle of Divisions*, Part 3B, H.M.S.O., 1945, pp. 57–8.
26 Brig-Gen. Sir J. E. Edmonds, *History of the Great War: Military Operations in France and Belgium 1916*, Macmillan, 1932, pp. 100–1.
27 HDD, 25th, 26th January; 1st, 22nd February; 16th March; 5th, 15th April; 21st May; 24th June; 1st, 13th, 20th, 23rd July; 26th August 1916.
28 *Keeling Letters*, Keeling to Mrs Green, 8th August 1916, p. 309.
29 HDD, 6th September; 30th August; 27th, 6th September 1916.

30 Dalton to Cannan, 25th October 1916 (Cannan Papers 1023ff. 71/75).
31 CBY, p. 87.

VII *Blasting and Bombardiering*

 1 Sir J. E. Edmonds and H. R. Davies, *History of the Great War: Military Operations in Italy 1915–1919*, H.M.S.O., 1949, pp. 24–35.
 2 HDD, 11th, 14th July 1917.
 3 H. Dalton, *With British Guns in Italy*, Methuen, 1919, p. 16.
 4 HDD, 18th July 1917.
 5 Dalton, *With British Guns*, p. 70.
 6 Mrs E. Davison, private correspondence with the author.
 7 W. H. Spedding, interview.
 8 G. M. Trevelyan, *Scenes from Italy's War*, T. C. & E. C. Jack, 1919, p. 140.
 9 Dalton, *With British Guns*, p. 75.
10 Edmonds and Davies, *History of the Great War*, p. 36.
11 HDD, 27th August 1917.
12 Dalton, *With British Guns*, pp. 81–2.
13 Trevelyan, *Italy's War*, p. 162.
14 Interview.
15 HDD, 19th October 1917; Dalton, *With British Guns*, p. 95; Lord Noel-Baker, interview.
16 HDD, 4th August, 18th October 1917.
17 See Archbishop Randall Davidson to Lord Stamfordham, 29th August 1917 (RA GV I/1171/7).
18 Queen Alexandra to Canon Dalton, 16th November 1917 (RA GV AA 6/547).
19 HDD, 15th, 20th, 21st, 22nd, 25th October; Dalton, *With British Guns*, p. 95.
20 Trevelyan, *Italy's War*, p. 163.
21 HDD, 27th October 1917.
22 Trevelyan, *Italy's War*, pp. 165–6.
23 Dalton, *With British Guns*, p. 108.
24 HDD, 27th, 28th, 30th October 1917; Dalton, *With British Guns*, pp. 122–34.
25 Dalton, *With British Guns*, p. 142; HDD, 14th, 17th, 23rd, 29th November, 10th December 1917, 4th January 1918.
26 Medal Citation (Dalton Papers).
27 Dalton, *With British Guns*, pp. 169–71.
28 Interview.
29 HDD, 2nd February 1918. This is the final entry in the third volume of Dalton's diary. The fourth volume was destroyed by shell-fire (see CBY, p. 87).
30 14th July 1918 (Joyce Parker Letters). This is the only reference to a wartime illness which (rather oddly) is not mentioned in Dalton, *With*

British Guns, or in Dalton's memoirs.

31 Dalton, *With British Guns*, pp. 179, 216, 241–51, 256–8.
32 H. Dalton, *Towards the Peace of Nations: A Study in International Politics*, Routledge, 1928, p. ix.
33 CBY, pp. 100–1.
34 Interview.
35 HDD, 18th July 1917.
36 Dalton, *With British Guns*, pp. 260–1.
37 Wyndham Lewis, *Blasting and Bombardiering*, Eyre and Spottiswoode, 1937, p. 122. See also, B. Bergonzi, *Heroes' Twilight*, Constable, 1965, p. 164.
38 L. Housman (ed.), *War Letters of Fallen Englishmen*, Gollancz, 1930, p. 73.
39 Lewis, *Blasting and Bombardiering*, p. 121.
40 Dalton, *With British Guns*, pp. 82–4.
41 CBY, pp. 87–8, 39.
42 Cited in Bergonzi, *Heroes' Twilight*, p. 41.
43 HDD, 27th October 1917.
44 Dalton, *With British Guns*, pp. 148, 137. Dalton believed that in Brooke's early poetry and writings 'dawn' and 'daybreak' were symbols of social revolution (CBY, p. 42). Thus there seems to be an interesting analogy between military and social victory, a connection we shall return to later. This particular passage in Dalton's war book concludes with a reference to the rich reward, 'when, a year later, the dawn broke in all its glory'. Brooke's poem looks forward to 'the light, Returning ... in the great dawn!'
45 Cited in CBY, p. 63.
46 R. H. Mottram, *The Spanish Farm Trilogy 1914–1918* (first published 1927), Penguin, 1979, p. 210.
47 CBY, p. 102.
48 See the list of Carbonari in ibid., pp. 39–40.
49 Dalton, *With British Guns*, pp. 259–60.
50 Queen Alexandra to Canon Dalton, 11th December 1918 (RA GV AA 6/549).
51 HDD, 11th to 14th, and 29th December 1918.

VIII *In Pursuit of Politics*

1 See C. A. Cline, *Recruits to Labour: The British Labour Party 1914–31*, University of Syracuse Press, 1963, passim.
2 HDD, 31st December 1918, 3rd, 23rd, 26th January, 23rd March 1919; CBY, p. 102.
3 *The Times*, 24th July 1919; HDD, 5th May, 25th April, 26th May, 8th, 13th, 18th June, 5th, 16th July 1919; CBY, p. 125.
4 HD to Cannan, 3rd July 1919 (Cannan Papers 1024 f. 44).
5 HD to Cannan, 19th January 1920 (Cannan Papers 1025 f. 43).

6 HDD, 19th June 1919.
7 Leah Manning, *A Life for Education*, Gollancz, 1970, pp. 58–9; Cambridge County Archives (information about the invitation to Dalton to attend the selection meeting kindly supplied by Mrs Eileen Price); the Hon. Helen Pease, interview.
8 HDD, 2nd, 3rd May 1920.
9 Manning, *A Life for Education*, p. 59.
10 HDD, 4th June 1920. In CBY (p. 110) Dalton incorrectly gives the date of this appointment as 1922.
11 HD to Cannan, 22nd August 1920 (Cannan Papers 1025 f. 45).
12 *Daily Chronicle*, 9th September 1920.
13 'The Measurement of the Inequality of Incomes', *Economic Journal*, September 1920. This was later included as an appendix in the second edition of Dalton's book on inequality, which will be discussed in Chapter 10.
14 HDD, 31st December 1920.
15 Dora Russell, *The Tamarisk Tree*, Elek/Pemberton, 1975, p. 153.
16 Baroness Wootton, interview.
17 HDD, 21st June, 27th July to 26th September 1921.
18 E. F. Penrose, private correspondence with the author.
19 HDD, 30th February to 15th March 1922; CBY, p. 132.
20 Manning, *A Life for Education*, pp. 59–60.
21 *Cambridge Daily News*, 2nd, 14th March 1922.
22 HDD, 16th, 17th March 1922.
23 Penrose, private correspondence with the author.
24 HDD, 21st March, 5th February 1922.
25 C. P. Scott, unpublished diary, 28th February 1922 (Scott Papers, 1911–28).
26 Clifford Smith, private correspondence with the author.

IX *Ruth and Helen*

1 'Oral history' is a euphemism for gossip. (But what are published reminiscences other than gossip?) In this chapter, faced with a conflict between the historian's duty to stick to hard evidence and the biographer's instinct to use an interesting and possibly significant story, I have permitted instinct to prevail. I am, however, aware of the fallibility of memories of events and conversations which in some cases took place more than half a century ago, particularly where the conversations were themselves about memories. Some matters (for example, the basic details of the progress of Helen's illness, the later stages of which Hugh himself carefully recorded) are more securely based than others (such as relationships within the Fox household, for which there is no written evidence, other than a few oblique comments in Hugh's diary). Much of the information in this chapter is based on interviews (and correspondence)

with Marjorie Durbin, Sir Robert and Lady Fraser, Mary Grant, Pat Herbert, Peggy Jay, Marion Miliband, Joyce Parker, Helen Pease, Joan Radice, Josephine Smith, George and Irene Wagner, Heather Forbes Watson, Ian Forbes Watson and others. In some cases the amount of information supplied was slight, in others more substantial, but no individual was the source for more than a small proportion of the whole.
2 HDD, 15th May 1922.
3 *The Times*, 16th May 1922.
4 HD to Cannan, 19th January 1920 (Cannan Papers 1025 f. 43).
5 Beatrice Webb, unpublished diary, 20th June 1927.
6 HDD, 5th September 1921.
7 Georgie Forbes Watson to an aunt, 1918 (Joyce Parker Letters).
8 HDD, 26th, 27th–31st March, 12th, 13th, 16th, 17th, 20th–21st, 29th May, 6th, 14th, 21st June 1922, 26th July 1929, 30th April 1931; CBY, p. 136.
9 Beatrice Webb, unpublished diary, 20th June 1927.
10 HDD, 9th March 1930.

X *Class Traitor*

1 *Morning Post*, 10th November 1922; *Kent Messenger and Maidstone Telegraph*, 11th November 1922.
2 HDD, 30th December 1922.
3 J. Harris, *William Beveridge*, Clarendon Press, 1977, p. 262.
4 Lord Beveridge, *The London School of Economics and its Problems 1919–1937*, Allen & Unwin, 1960, p. 21.
5 W. A. Robson, interview.
6 Eveline Burns, private correspondence with the author.
7 Lord Robbins in *The Times*, 20th February 1962.
8 Clifford Smith, E. Warren, private correspondence with the author.
9 Eveline Burns, private correspondence with the author.
10 Ruth Gilmour, private correspondence with the author.
11 Freda Mautner, private correspondence with the author.
12 N. Lourie, private correspondence with the author.
13 Lord Robbins, *Autobiography of an Economist*, Macmillan, 1971, pp. 75–7.
14 H. Dalton, *Principles of Public Finance*, Routledge, 1922, pp. v–vi; for a list of foreign translations, see January 1939 impression, p. iv; 'to excite ... tediously': the words of Francis Bacon, cited by Dalton in his preface.
15 Routledge, 1920.
16 *The Times*, 20th February 1962.
17 H. Gaitskell, *Recent Developments in British Socialist Thinking*, Co-operative Union, 1956, p. 21.
18 See, for example, A. B. Atkinson (ed.), *Welfare, Incomes and Inequality*,

Penguin, 1973. He cites H. Dalton, *Some Aspects of the Inequality of Incomes in Modern Communities*, Routledge, 1920, as a major contribution in the field and uses Dalton's article on the measurement of inequality as the basis for his own discussion of the subject ('On the Measurement of Inequality', *Journal of Economic Theory*, Vol. 2, 1970, pp. 244–63). Amartya Sen discusses Dalton's writings in conjunction with those of Pigou, in *On Economic Inequality*, Oxford University Press, 1973, pp. 27–47.

19 Dalton, *Inequality of Incomes*, p. vii.
20 W.A.R. (probably W. A. Robson) in *Fabian News*, January 1921.
21 Dalton, *Inequality of Incomes*, pp. 242, 284–5.
22 Ibid., pp. 339–40, 348, 350–1. See also D. Winch, *Economics and Policy: A Historical Study*, Hodder and Stoughton, 1969, p. 45.
23 Alfred A. Knopf, 1923.
24 See C. A. Cline, *Recruits to Labour: The British Labour Party 1914–1931*, Syracuse University Press, 1963, p. 59.
25 A. C. Pigou, *A Capital Levy and a Levy on War Wealth*, Oxford University Press, 1919, p. 263.
26 J. M. Keynes, *The Economic Consequences of the Peace*, Macmillan, 1919, p. 263.
27 R. Blake, *The Unknown Prime Minister*, Eyre & Spottiswoode, 1955, p. 401.
28 See M. Cowling, *The Impact of Labour 1920–1924*, Cambridge University Press, 1971, p. 287.
29 F. W. Pethick Lawrence, *The Capital Levy: How the Labour Party Would Pay the War Debt*, Co-operative Printing Society, 1919.
30 Cline (*Recruits to Labour*, p. 64) even suggests that the Capital Levy issue helped to bring Dalton back into the Labour Party after the War. It may have been one factor, though as we have seen, there were other reasons as well.
31 HDD, 11th February 1922.
32 See Beatrice Webb, unpublished diary, 22nd June 1922; Dalton to J. S. Middleton, 16th December 1922 (Middleton Papers, JSM/ADM/12).
33 G. W. Gough, in *Lloyd George Liberal Magazine*, December 1922.
34 H. Dalton, *Practical Socialism for Britain*, Routledge, 1935, p. 327.
35 H. Dalton, *Principles of Public Finance*, Routledge & Kegan Paul, 1954 ed., pp. 193–4. Nicholas Kaldor was advocating 'an old-fashioned capital levy' as a means 'to start a strong heave towards equality', at about the same time (*New Statesman*, 2nd July 1955).
36 Harris, *William Beveridge*, p. 291.
37 Beveridge wrote later that he liked Dalton 'at first sight and thereafter' (*London School of Economics and its Problems*, p. 21).
38 HDD, 12th February 1923; CBY, p. 120; *The Economist*, 3rd February 1923.
39 Cited in Harris, *William Beveridge*, p. 292.
40 HDD, 12th February, 25th–29th May, 6th–8th October, 18th November 1923.

41 HD to C. P. Trevelyan, 21st December 1923 (C. P. Trevelyan Papers, Letter 105).
42 HDD, 8th, 12th December 1923.
43 'Report of a conversation between Lord Stamfordham and Mr. Hugh Dalton', 26th December 1923 (RA GV 0 1905/2).
44 HDD, 27th December 1923 to 3rd January 1924.
45 M. Cole (ed.), *Beatrice Webb: Diaries 1924–1932*, Longman, 1956, p. 26 (2nd May 1924).
46 HD to C. P. Trevelyan, 21st December 1923 (C. P. Trevelyan Papers, Letter 105).
47 HDD, 29th June, 2nd February 1924.
48 *Spalding Standard*, 19th July 1924. Dalton lost his temper with such violence on one occasion that stories about the incident were still circulating locally five years later. (See *Boston Guardian*, 5th January 1929.)
49 *Daily Herald*, 29th June 1924.
50 Labour Party N.E.C. Minutes (By-Election Reports), 23rd July, 2nd September 1924.
51 HD to Pethick Lawrence, 10th August 1924 (Pethick-Lawrence Papers P-L1/177).
52 *Spalding Standard*, 9th, 28th August 1924.
53 HDD, 2nd August 1924.
54 HD to Pethick Lawrence, 10th August.
55 HDD, 4th June 1925.
56 *South London Press*, 24th, 31st October 1924.
57 A. C. King, private correspondence with the author.
58 *South London Press*, 7th November 1924.

XI *Mosley and Keynes*

1 Entry for 5th April 1927 in M. Cole (ed.) *Beatrice Webb: Diaries 1924–32*, Longman, 1949, p. 138.
2 CBY, p. 199.
3 *Evening News*, 15th April 1926.
4 HDD, end of 1927.
5 Beatrice Webb, unpublished diary, 20th June 1927.
6 F. Brockway, *Towards Tomorrow*, Hart Davies & MacGibbon, 1977, p. 64. Having first joined the I.L.P. as an undergraduate and subsequently allowed his membership to lapse, Dalton rejoined in 1923.
7 HDD, 1st–5th October 1928.
8 Sir Oswald Mosley, *My Life*, Nelson, 1970, p. 218.
9 HDD, 10th January 1930.
10 *Political Quarterly*, Vol. 29, No. 4, October–December 1958.
11 Lord Brockway, interview.
12 Mosley, *My Life*, p. 218.
13 E. Wertheimer, *Portrait of the Labour Party*, Putnam, 1929, p. 128.
14 R. Skidelsky, *Oswald Mosley*, Macmillan, 1975, pp. 133, 138.

15 Dalton served on the I.L.P. committee which produced *The Living Wage*. (See I.L.P. National Administration Committee minutes for 1926).

16 30th May 1924. Cited in R. E. Dowse, *Left in the Centre*, Longman, 1966, p. 106.

17 HD to Pethick Lawrence, 5th March 1924 (Pethick-Lawrence Papers, PL I 176 (1)).

18 *Labour Magazine*, February 1926.

19 *New Leader*, 7th October 1929 (cited in Skidelsky, *Oswald Mosley*, p. 151).

20 13th, 26th April 1927, HC Debs. [205] cols. 498, 716–17.

21 HDD, end of 1927.

22 13th April 1927, 5th February 1926, HC Debs [205] col. 489, [191] col. 513.

23 CBY, p. 60.

24 Keynes Papers. According to Keynes's register of undergraduate attendances, Dalton attended only 9 lectures out of a possible 16.

25 Engagement diaries in Keynes Papers.

26 HD to Keynes, 14th November 1918 (Keynes Papers).

27 Keynes Papers.

28 *New Leader*, 30th May 1924.

29 Colin Clark, private correspondence with the author.

30 See Fabian Lecture Notes, 19th November 1924 (Fabian Collection c62/1/229).

31 D. Winch, *Economics and Policy*, Hodder & Stoughton, 1969, pp. 148–9.

32 T. E. Gregory and H. Dalton (eds.), *London Essays in Economics: In Honour of Edwin Cannan*, Routledge, 1927, p. 7.

33 See pp. 217–23.

34 See HD to Beveridge, 19th June 1926 (Beveridge Papers IIb 25, Box 62).

35 HDD, 10th April 1926. See also Lord Robbins, *Autobiography of an Economist*, Macmillan, 1971, chapter 5; CBY, pp. 114–16.

36 CBY, pp. 115–16.

37 S. Howson and D. Winch, *The Economic Advisory Council 1930–1939*, Cambridge University Press, 1977, pp. 60–3.

38 Robbins, *Autobiography*, p. 151.

39 HDD, 23rd, 29th October 1930.

XII *Grass Roots*

1 A. C. King, conversation with the author.

2 *South London Press*, 28th November 1924, 14th August 1925.

3 W. A. Sibbs, private correspondence with the author.

4 Mrs J. M. Brown, private correspondence with the author (in response to a request for information about Dalton published in the *News of the World*).

5 *South London Observer, Camberwell and Peckham Times*, 15th May 1926.

6 *South London Press*, 14th May 1926.

7 Ibid., 21st December 1926; *List of Organisations Affiliated to the Labour*

Party, The Labour Party, 1928.

8 CBY, pp. 184–5.
9 HD to A. Creech Jones, 10th November 1924 (Creech Jones Papers: ACJ 7/1 f 96).
10 HDD, end of 1925.
11 Ibid.
12 *South London Press*, 5th February 1926.
13 Conversation with the author.
14 J. H. Hopkins, private correspondence with the author.
15 A. C. King, conversation with the author.
16 HDD, 2nd February 1928.
17 *South London Press*, 9th August 1927.
18 HDD, 19th March, 23rd April 1928. Meanwhile some members were resigning from the Peckham party in disgust and others were being expelled (HD to A. C. King, 21st March 1928, E. Baldwyn to A. C. King, 5th April 1928 [letters lent to the author by A. C. King]; Labour Party N.E.C. Organisation Sub-Committee minutes, 1st May 1928).
19 *South London Press*, 24th July 1928. This was published after the dispute had been resolved in Baldwyn's favour.
20 HDD, 26th, 27th April, 5th, 23rd May 1928.
21 N.E.C. Sub-Committee Report (N.E.C. minutes, July 1928).
22 HDD, 23rd May, 11th, 23rd June 1928.
23 A. C. King, private conversation with the author.
24 N.E.C. Sub-Committee Report.
25 HDD, 28th June, 11th–12th July 1928.
26 Labour Party N.E.C., Organisation Committee minutes, 20th January 1932.
27 J. H. Hopkins, private correspondence with the author.
28 CBY, p. 201, HDD, 18th July 1928.
29 *Auckland and County Chronicle*, 18th, 21st June, 25th July 1928; HDD, 18th, 20th–21st, 24th July 1928; CBY, p. 201.
30 *Auckland and County Chronicle*, 13th September 1928.
31 HDD, 7th October 1928; CBY, p. 202.
32 *Auckland and County Chronicle*, 27th December 1928.
33 I.L.P. National Administration Council minutes, 1922, 13th–14th February 1926.
34 *Auckland and County Chronicle*, 21st June 1928.
35 HDD, 27th December 1928; *Auckland and County Chronicle*, 3rd January 1929.
36 *Daily Herald*, 31st December 1928.
37 23rd January 1929.
38 *New Leader*, 18th January 1929.
39 *Manchester Guardian*, 23rd January 1929.
40 *Auckland and County Chronicle*, 7th February, 31st January 1929.
41 *New Leader*, 18th January 1929.
42 *Daily Herald*, 2nd February 1929.
43 Mrs Florence Davis, interview.

44 Ruth obtained 14,797 votes against 7,725 for the Liberal with the Conservative running third. The Labour majority increased from 2,918 in 1924 to 7,072.
45 HDD, 9th February 1929.
46 *The Miner*, 26th January 1929.
47 13th March 1929, HC Debs [226] col. 1166.
48 HDD, 13th March 1929; CBY, p. 209.
49 Mrs Florence Davis, manuscript notes.
50 The result was as follows: H. Dalton 17,838; A. C. Curry (Liberal) 9,635; H. Thompson (Unionist) 4,503.
51 Mrs Margaret Gibb, interview.
52 Hugh Dalton, *The Fateful Years: Memoirs 1931–1945*, Muller, 1957 (henceforth, FY), pp. 85, 86.
53 Interview.
54 Tom Anderson, interview and unpublished memorandum. Dalton discouraged invitations to other M.P.s to speak in the division, on the grounds that 'they all expect me to pay a return visit – which is, very often, a waste of my energies' (HD to W. Davis, 22nd March 1949; Davis Letters).
55 Mrs Margaret Gibb, interview.
56 Tom Anderson, interview; Bishop Auckland Divisional Labour Party: annual reports and minute books.
57 Harry Clements, interview.
58 James Mudd, interview.
59 J. R. S. Middlewood, interview.
60 Arthur Cheesemond, interview.
61 Mrs Florence Davis, interview.
62 Harry Russell, interview.
63 HD to Will Davis, 13th November 1948 (Davis Letters).
64 Bishop Auckland Divisional Labour Party Annual Reports, 1950, 1951. By 1954 there were 30 local polling district and ward parties functioning in the constituency (which by then had different boundaries) compared with 12 in 1938 (Annual Reports).
65 Tom Anderson, interview.
66 Tom Anderson, unpublished memorandum.

XIII *Towards the Peace of Nations*

1 *Foreign Affairs*, October 1928, Vol. 7, No. 1, p. 63.
2 See for example 11th March 1926, HC Debs [192] col. 2729.
3 Allen & Unwin, 1923.
4 A. J. P. Taylor, *The Trouble Makers* (first published Hamish Hamilton, 1957) Panther, 1969, p. 165.
5 11th March 1926, 11th July 1927, 22nd, 12th March 1928, HC Debs [192] col. 2732; [208] col. 1832; [215] col. 642; [214] col. 1554. See also 11th March 1926, HC Debs [192] cols. 2734–5.

6 *Contemporary Review*, November 1926.
7 CBY, p. 167.
8 *Contemporary Review*, November 1926.
9 HDD, 1926 holiday diary, pp. 18–24.
10 The book which influenced Dalton most directly in writing *Towards the Peace of Nations* was H. N. Brailsford, *The War of Steel and Gold: A Study of the Armed Peace*, Bell, 1914. Dalton did not, however, accept all Brailsford's conclusions.
11 Taylor, *The Trouble Makers*, p. 158.
12 H. Dalton, *Towards the Peace of Nations. A Study in International Politics*, Routledge, 1928, especially pp. 24–5, 304–5, 46. Dalton continued to hold the same view when he became a Foreign Office Minister in the second Labour administration. 'If some measure of disarmament is visibly proceeding the atmosphere may gradually become less unpropitious for frontier revision', he minuted during a discussion of proposed frontier concessions to Germany. 'But meanwhile the initiative is, in my view, neither to be taken by us nor encouraged in others.' (FO 800/288 X/P 7362.)
13 Dalton, *Towards the Peace of Nations*, pp. 114, 290.
14 Lord Noel-Baker, interview.
15 HDD, 6th February 1928, 1st June 1929.
16 Walter Citrine, unpublished diary, 5th June 1929 (Citrine Papers, 7/8).
17 HDD, 6th, 5th, 7th June 1929; CBY, pp. 214–15.
18 See D. Carlton, *MacDonald versus Henderson: The Foreign Policy of the Second Labour Government*, Macmillan, 1970, p. 16.
19 HDD, 9th March 1931.
20 *Political Quarterly*, October–December 1931, pp. 492, 495, 304.
21 C. L. Mowat, *Britain Between the Wars 1918–1940*, Methuen, 1955, p. 372.
22 M. A. Hamilton, *Remembering My Good Friends*, Jonathan Cape, 1944, p. 187.
23 M. A. Hamilton, *Arthur Henderson: A Biography*, Heinemann, 1938, p. 288.
24 E. Wilkinson, *Peeps at Politicians*, Philip Allen, 1930, p. 29.
25 14th May 1930, HC Debs [238] col. 1858.
26 *Political Quarterly*, 1931, p. 490.
27 HDD, 2nd May 1930, 4th December 1929, 9th April 1930.
28 *The Memoirs of Lord Gladwyn*, Weidenfeld & Nicolson, 1972, p. 39.
29 HDD, 11th May 1929.
30 11th January 1929 (FO 371/13695).
31 20th June 1929 (Dalton Papers, IIA 1/1 ff 1/24).
32 HDD, 29th June 1929.
33 Wilkinson, *Peeps at Politicians*, pp. 28–9.
34 FO 800/280 X/P 7351; *The Times*, 10th August 1929.
35 HD to Sir R. Lindsay, 15th August; Lindsay to HD, 16th August 1929 (Dalton Papers IIA 6/1).
36 HDD, 20th, 22nd August, 4th, 8th November 1929.

37 Lord Vansittart, *The Mist Procession*, Hutchinson, 1958, p. 398.
38 HDD, 19th, 25th November 1929; CBY, pp. 248–9.
39 *Morning Post*, 11th September 1929.
40 HDD, 19th December 1929.
41 Ibid., 3rd–9th March, 29th December 1930.
42 Ibid., 14th December 1929, 24th–25th April 1930.
43 F. Macmanus, interview.
44 HDD, 31st August, 15th–16th November, 28th May 1930.
45 Sir Geoffrey de Freitas, interview.
46 HDD, 3rd–5th July 1931.
47 West Leaze Visitors' Book (kindly lent to the author by Marion Miliband).
48 HDD, 24th December 1929, 18th April, 28th July 1931.
49 H. Nicolson, *George V*, p. 452.
50 HDD, 27th, 28th July 1931.
51 CBY, p. 266.
52 H. Nicolson, *King George the Fifth*, p. 432.
53 D. Marquand, *Ramsay MacDonald*, Jonathan Cape, 1977, p. 576.
54 HDD, 16th–17th, 22nd July, 5th February, 11th June, 23rd, 24th, 27th August 1931.
55 *The Times*, 2nd September 1931.
56 *North Eastern Gazette*, 2nd September 1931.
57 C. Cross, *Philip Snowden*, Barrie & Rockliff, 1966, p. 302.
58 Beatrice Webb, unpublished diary, 20th September 1931.
59 M. Bondfield, *A Life's Work*, Hutchinson, 1948, p. 317.
60 10th October 1931. M. Cole (ed.), *Beatrice Webb's Diaries, 1924–1932*, Longman, Green & Co., 1949, p. 291.

XIV *Practical Socialism*

1 Arthur Henderson was elected Party Leader in succession to MacDonald. He retained this post, despite losing his seat in the general election, until October 1932, when he resigned to make way for Lansbury.
2 FY, p. 20.
3 *Clem Attlee: The Granada Historical Records Interview*, Panther Record, London 1967, p. 12.
4 E. Estorik, *Stafford Cripps: A Biography*, Heinemann, 1949, p. 82.
5 Leah Manning, *A Life for Education*, Gollancz, 1970, p. 81.
6 FY, pp. 148–9, 41.
7 M. Cole, *The Life of G. D. H. Cole*, Macmillan, 1971, p. 178.
8 HD to G. D. H. Cole, 13th April 1931 (Fabian Collection).
9 Friday Group (N.F.R.B.) minutes, 13th May 1931 (Fabian Collection).
10 Labour Party N.E.C. minutes, 22nd June 1932.
11 HD to Pethick Lawrence, 15th May 1932 (Pethick-Lawrence Papers).
12 HD to G. D. H. Cole, 30th May 1932 (Cole Papers).
13 HDD, 8th October 1932.

14 Beatrice Webb, unpublished diary, 22nd February 1932.
15 HDD, 5th July 1932.
16 FY, pp. 26–7.
17 I am grateful to Mr. Jasper Ridley for showing me these extracts from his father's letters to his mother, written during the Russian visit.
18 Dame Margaret Cole, interview.
19 HD to Ruth, 10th July 1932 (Dalton Papers 5/1 (1)); HDD, 3rd, 13th, 14th July 1932.
20 HD to Ruth, 10th July, August 1932 (Dalton Papers 5/1, (1) and (2)).
21 HD to Lord Ponsonby, 4th September 1932 (Ponsonby Papers, 674/1).
22 Cole, *The Life of G. D. H. Cole*, p. 159.
23 M. Cole (ed.), *Twelve Studies in Soviet Russia*, Gollancz, 1933, pp. 16–34. David Caute (*The Fellow Travellers – A Postscript to the Enlightenment*, Weidenfeld and Nicolson, 1973, p. 70) accuses Dalton of having 'refused to see or, alternatively, insisted on blandly condoning' the destruction of trade union wage-bargaining powers in the Soviet Union. It is true that trade union rights was not a subject which Dalton investigated closely. However, this was not part of his New Fabian brief; and there is no evidence at all that he either turned a blind eye to uncomfortable aspects, or 'blandly condoned' them. On the contrary, his writings show that he was very conscious of the loss of freedom in the Soviet Union and of the need to ensure that any British experiment in planning avoided this aspect.
24 Cited in *North Eastern Gazette*, 15th October 1932.
25 HDD, 16th December 1931.
26 Ian Mackay in *News Chronicle*, 1st April 1935. At first the Chairmanship of the Policy Committee went with the Chairmanship of the N.E.C., changing annually. In 1936, Dalton was appointed Chairman and held this post until 1944, when he became chairman of the International Sub-Committee instead.
27 HD paper on 'Cabinet Reconstruction' (N.F.R.B. Friday Group minutes, 10th November 1932; Fabian Collection, J13).
28 N.E.C. Finance and Trade Sub-Committee minutes, cited in Elizabeth Durbin, *New Jerusalems: The Fabians, Mr. Keynes and the Economics of Democratic Socialism*, Routledge & Kegan Paul (forthcoming).
29 B. Wootton, *Plan or No Plan*, Gollancz, 1934, p. 307.
30 HD to Ponsonby, 5th December 1932 (Ponsonby Papers).
31 FY, pp. 33–5; HDD, 30th December 1932.
32 HD to William Gregory, 7th December 1932 (letter kindly lent by Mr. Gregory to the author).
33 H. Dalton (ed.), *Unbalanced Budgets: A Study of the Financial Crisis in Fifteen Countries*, Routledge, 1934, pp. 453–8.
34 R. Jenkins, *The Pursuit of Progress*, Heinemann, 1953, p. 60.
35 H. Dalton, *Practical Socialism for Britain*, Routledge, 1935, pp. 26–7, 244n, 113–15, 213, 261, 197, 300, passim. See also Elizabeth Durbin, *New Jerusalems*, chapter 8. As Donald Winch (*Economics and Policy: A Historical Study*, Hodder & Stoughton, 1969, p. 345) points out, even in the 1936 edition of *Principles of Public Finance*, Dalton included no

mention of the multiplier.
36 *Spectator*, 19th August 1935.
37 Gollancz, 1934. James Jupp (*The Radical Left in Britain 1931–1941*, Frank Cass, 1982, pp. 157–8) provides an interesting discussion of Mitchison's book. According to Jupp, *The First Workers' Government* had sufficient resemblances to Labour's developing plans 'to suggest the existence of a common approach'. Jupp, however, puts the cart before the horse as far as influences are concerned. 'Anticipating *Labour's Immediate Programme* of two years later', he wrotes, 'Mitchison supported the formation of a National Investment Board to control new investment.' In fact, it was Mitchison who was anticipated. The National Investment Board had already appeared in *For Socialism and Peace*.
38 *The Next Five Years – An Essay in Political Agreement*, Macmillan, 1935, p. 313.
39 *The Economist*, 24th April 1935.
40 *The Next Five Years*, p. 313.
41 A. Marwick, 'Middle Opinion in the Thirties: Planning, Progress and Political "Agreement" ', *English Historical Review*, 1964, p. 293.
42 Hugh Dalton, 'The Popular Front', *Political Quarterly* (October–December 1936, p. 487).
43 *The Next Five Years*, pp. 11, 5, 3. There were, of course, other differences between Labour Movement and 'capitalist' approaches to planning. See, for example, K. Middlemas, *Politics in Industrial Society: The Experience of the British System Since 1911*, Deutsch, 1979, pp. 223–4, and chapter 8, passim. For an excellent discussion of the different, and often contradictory, 'planning' traditions in the 1930s, see D. Winch, *Economics and Policy*, especially chapter 10.
44 *Practical Socialism*, pp. 5, 3, 248, 7 and n., 343.
45 *Daily Herald*, 24th June 1935.
46 *The Next Five Years*, p. 5.
47 Beatrice Webb, unpublished diary, 20th May 1934, 14th January, 1st March 1935.
48 Beatrice Webb, unpublished diary, 16th February 1936.
49 W. T. Rodgers (ed.), *Hugh Gaitskell*, Thames and Hudson, 1964, p. 69.
50 HDD, 11th September 1931.
51 See Durbin, *New Jerusalems*, chapter 8.
52 Nicholas Davenport, interview.
53 N. Davenport, *Memoirs of a City Radical*, Weidenfeld & Nicolson, 1974, p. 95. For a comment on the influence of XYZ, see Francis Williams, *Nothing So Strange*, Cassell, 1970, p. 112.
54 Durbin, *New Jerusalems*, chapter 11.

XV *Anti-Appeaser*

1 M. A. Hamilton, *Remembering My Good Friends*, Jonathan Cape, 1944, p. 290.

2 H. Dalton, *Practical Socialism for Britain*, Routledge, 1935, pp. 368–75.
3 HDD, 29th, 30th April 1933; FY, pp. 37–41.
4 *Daily Herald*, 6th May 1933.
5 Draft speech, August 1933 (Dalton Papers II 6/2).
6 See R. Bassett, *Democracy and Foreign Policy: A Case History. The Sino-Japanese Dispute 1931–33*, Longman, 1952, pp. 554–5; L.P.A.C.R. 1933, p. 185.
7 HDD, 29th September 1933.
8 HD to Frank Hardie, 1st December 1933 (letter kindly lent by Mr. Hardie to the author).
9 HDD, 19th January 1934.
10 Cited in K. Martin, *Editor*, Penguin, 1969, pp. 186–7.
11 *Sunday Times*, 22nd September 1935.
12 Beatrice Webb, unpublished diary, 1st October 1935.
13 HDD, 5th to 6th October 1935.
14 Beatrice Webb, unpublished diary, 28th September 1935.
15 HDD, 27th May, 5th to 6th October 1935. In 1932 Dalton described Morrison privately as 'intellectually able, but aggressive' (HDD, 8th October).
16 *Daily Herald*, 4th November 1935.
17 HDD, 15th November 1935.
18 Francis Williams, *Nothing So Strange*, Cassell, 1970, p. 135.
19 HDD, 5th to 6th October 1935.
20 Beatrice Webb, unpublished diary, 2nd February 1936.
21 J. F. Naylor, *Labour's International Policy: the Labour Party in the 1930s*, Weidenfeld & Nicolson, 1969, p. 135.
22 Quoted in *Daily Herald*, 20th December 1935.
23 *Daily Telegraph*, 7th May 1936.
24 Beatrice Webb, unpublished diary, 29th May 1936.
25 Lord Ponsonby to HD, 10th May 1936 (Ponsonby Papers).
26 26th March 1936, HC Debs [310] col. 1454–5.
27 FY, p. 88.
28 J. Symons, *The Thirties*, The Crescent Press, 1960, p. 118.
29 FY, pp. 96–7. He did, however, express the view privately that 'if Franco won in Spain, Germany would use him to squeeze France'. (Entry for 16th March 1937 in J. Harvey (ed.), *The Diplomatic Diaries of Oliver Harvey 1937–1940*, Collins, 1970, p. 28.)
30 Laski to Felix Frankfurter, 1st May 1938, in K. Martin, *Harold Laski 1893–1950: A Biographical Memoir*, Gollancz, 1953, p. 112.
31 Beatrice Webb, unpublished diary, 16th April 1937.
32 HD to L. Woolf, 24th September 1936 (Berg Collection). Woolf was Secretary of the Labour Party Advisory Committee on International Questions.
33 HDD, 2nd to 4th March 1936.
34 See D. M. Roberts, 'Hugh Dalton and the Labour Party in the 1930s', unpublished Ph.D. thesis (C.N.A.A.), 1978.
35 K. Martin, *Critic's London Diary: From the New Statesman 1931–1956*,

Secker & Warburg, 1960, p. 32.

36 FY, pp. 95–6.
37 HDD, 27th March 1936.
38 *New Statesman & Nation*, 24th October 1936.
39 *Daily Telegraph*, 19th September 1936.
40 J. T. Murphy, *New Horizons*, John Lane, 1941, p. 321.
41 L.P.A.C.R., 1936, p. 228.
42 *Manchester Guardian*, 18th January 1937.
43 See Elizabeth Durbin, *New Jerusalems*, Routledge & Kegan Paul (forth-coming), especially chapter 15, for an excellent examination of *Labour's Immediate Programme* and its origins.
44 Draft paper in Dalton Papers II A 3/1, cited in Durbin, *New Jerusalems*.
45 *Daily Herald*, 17th, 7th November 1936.
46 FY, p. 128.
47 L.P.A.C.R., 1936, p. 257.
48 N.E.C. minutes, 24th March 1937.
49 HDD, 19th January 1934.
50 *Revally*, London May 1937 (copy in Dalton Papers II 5/4).
51 P. Strauss, *Bevin and Co. The Leaders of British Labour*, Putnam, 1941, p. 177.
52 M. Foot, *Aneurin Bevan: A Biography*, MacGibbon & Kee, 1962, Vol. I, p. 245.
53 *Manchester Guardian*, 12th April 1937.
54 *Daily Herald*, 19th April 1937.
55 F. Brockway, *Inside the Left*, Allen & Unwin, 1942, pp. 269–70.
56 *Daily Express*, 22nd July 1937. See also *Manchester Guardian*, 23rd, 26th July 1937. Baldwin's friend Thomas Jones had noted earlier the same month: 'Attlee cannot control his men. He is pushed from behind.' (*A Diary with Letters 1931–50*, Oxford University Press, 1954, p. 358.)
57 Foot, *Aneurin Bevan*, Vol. I, p. 264. Foot's suggestion that Dalton 'lobbied his friends without putting his opponents ... on their guard', may be discounted – unless his opponents had failed to read the morning's newspapers.
58 23rd, 26th July 1937.
59 HD to Martin, 26th July 1937 (Dalton Papers II 5/2).
60 See Naylor, *Labour's International Policy*, chapter 7.
61 L.P.A.C.R., 1936, p. 247. For a fuller discussion of the Constituency Parties' Movement, see my *Labour and the Left in the 1930s*, Cambridge University Press, 1977, pp. 111–40.
62 FY, p. 116; N.E.C. minutes 23rd June 1937.
63 Ben Greene to Charles Garnsworthy, 2nd June 1937 (Garnsworthy Papers).
64 FY, p. 145.
65 Beatrice Webb, unpublished diary, 14th December 1937.
66 FY, p. 118.
67 Lord Morrison of Lambeth, *Herbert Morrison: An Autobiography*, Odhams Press, 1960, p. 306.

68 FY, p. 117.
69 *Herbert Morrison*, p. 305.
70 HD to Mayhew, 26th October 1937 (Lord Mayhew Letters).
71 L.P.A.C.R., 1937, p. 208.
72 FY, p. 145.
73 6th, 5th October 1937.
74 A. J. P. Taylor, *The Trouble Makers*, Panther, 1969 (first published Hamish Hamilton, 1957), pp. 191, 197.
75 Ibid., p. 175, 181.
76 L.P.A.C.R., 1937, p. 138.
77 *New Statesman & Nation*, 30th October 1937.
78 16th March 1937. J. Harvey (ed.), *The Diplomatic Diaries of Oliver Harvey 1937–1940*, Collins, 1970, p. 27.
79 H. Macmillan, *Winds of Change 1914–39*, Macmillan, 1966, p. 550.

XVI *Towards War*

1 The Left Book Club, closely linked to the British Communist Party, distributed large numbers of magenta-covered monthly 'choices', selected by Victor Gollancz, Harold Laski and John Strachey. By the end of 1937, there were 730 Left Book Club discussion groups, including many overseas. In the late summer of 1937 Dalton had been involved in a skirmish with Gollancz and Laski over an offer by the Club to carry out propaganda work for the Labour Party. (See my *Labour and the Left in the 1930s*, Cambridge University Press, 1977, pp. 160–1.)
2 HDD, end of November, 21st, 27th, 30th December 1937, 1st March, 17th February, April 1938; HD to Ruth Dalton, 16th, 17th December 1937 (diary letter, Dalton Papers); FY, pp. 153–5.
3 P. Einzig, *In the Centre of Things*, Hutchinson, 1960, p. 205; HD to Einzig, 28th July 1938 (Einzig Papers).
4 25th May 1938. HC Debs. [336] col. 1233–53.
5 *Spectator*, 27th May 1938.
6 *Daily Telegraph*, 30th May 1938.
7 *Tribune*, 27th May 1938.
8 HDD, April 1938.
9 HD to Noel Buxton, 26th May 1938 (Buxton Papers).
10 CBY, pp. 247–8.
11 Lord Noel-Baker, interview; HDD, September 1938.
12 *Daily Herald*, 10th September 1938. Dalton told Vansittart a few days later that the Godesburg proposals for cession of Czech territory were 'like pulling the shell from the crab's back' (HDD, 24th September 1938).
13 HDD, 17th, 19th, 25th September 1938.
14 See C. L. Mowat, *Britain Between the Wars, 1918–1940*, Methuen, 1955, pp. 609 ff.
15 HD to Mayhew, 15th September 1938 (Lord Mayhew Letters).
16 *The Memoirs of Lord Gladwyn*, Weidenfeld & Nicolson, 1972, p. 81.

17 See H. Dalton, 'The Popular Front', *Political Quarterly*, October–
    December 1936, p. 487.
18 *News Chronicle*, 18th June 1938.
19 HDD, 20th September 1938.
20 FY, pp. 209 f.
21 Quoted in *The Times*, 4th October 1938.
22 Entry for 3rd October 1938 in D. Dilks (ed.), *The Diary of Sir Alexander
    Cadogan 1938–1945*, Cassell, 1971, p. 112.
23 HDD, 3rd October 1938; FY, pp. 198 ff. Macmillan recalled a more
    sympathetic response on the Labour side than Dalton's own account in
    FY seems to suggest. (H. Macmillan, *Winds of Change*, Macmillan, 1966,
    p. 569).
24 HDD, 6th October 1938.
25 *Manchester Guardian*, 9th October 1938.
26 FY, p. 207.
27 John Parker, unpublished memoir (typescript); private correspondence
    with the author.
28 HD Note, 23rd January 1939 (Dalton Papers 3/1 (27), (28)).
29 Lord Cecil to HD, 28th November 1938; HD to Cecil, 1st December
    1938 (Dalton Papers 5/2 (18), (20)).
30 Lord Sandys, interview.
31 FY, p. 199.
32 Earning a rebuke from the National Agent, as a result. See D. M.
    Roberts, 'Hugh Dalton and the Labour Party in the 1930s', unpublished
    Ph.D. thesis (C.N.A.A.), 1978, p. 151.
33 Cripps Memorandum (N.E.C. minutes, January 1939).
34 HD Notes, 19th, 23rd January 1939 (Dalton Papers 3/1 (24), (25), (27),
    (28)).
35 FY, pp. 212–13.
36 *Daily Herald*, 27th February 1939.
37 *New Statesman & Nation*, 3rd June 1939.
38 L.P.A.C.R., 1939, pp. 227–32.
39 HDD, 26th May–2nd June 1939.
40 Ibid., 6th October 1938.
41 *Sunday Chronicle*, 4th December 1938.
42 See, for example, *Evening Standard*, 19th December 1938: 'Hugh Dalton
    … would like to lead the Labour Party'. The *Evening News*, which con-
    sidered the possibility of a Dalton candidature on the same day, concluded
    that he was probably too forceful to succeed. 'Mr. Attlee pleads or
    admonishes mildly', its commentator observed, 'when Mr. Dalton would
    slap, in dealing with Party offenders.'
43 Beatrice Webb, unpublished diary, 9th July 1939.
44 HDD, 26th May to 2nd June 1939.
45 14th June 1949; FY, p. 224.
46 HDD, November 1939 (dictated in December).
47 *Daily Herald*, 16th November 1939.
48 FY, p. 250.

49 28th June 1939, PREM 1/325/3.
50 Jean Seaton and Ben Pimlott, 'The Struggle for Balance: the BBC and the Labour movement in the 1930s and 1940s' (as yet unpublished paper).
51 HDD, 25th to 30th August 1939; HD note, 2nd–3rd September 1939 (Henderson Papers, Labour Party Archives, HEN/16/iv–vi); I. Kirkpatrick, *The Inner Circle*, Macmillan, 1959, p. 143.

XVII *Old Limpet*

1 L. S. Amery, *My Political Life*, Vol. III, *The Unforgiving Years 1929–1940*, Hutchinson, 1955, p. 308.
2 HDD, 25th August, 9th October 1939.
3 See Report of Conference on the Labour Party in Wartime, 16th March 1940 (Fabian Collection, 949/1/1).
4 HDD, 25th, 19th September 1939.
5 E. Spears, *Assignment to Catastrophe*, Vol. I, *Prelude to Dunkirk, July 1939–May 1940*, Heinemann, 1954, p. 39.
6 HDD, 28th–31st October 1939.
7 30th November 1939. HC Debs [355] col. 302.
8 H. Dalton, *Hitler's War: Before and After*, Penguin, 1940, p. 164.
9 HDD, 10th April, 17th March 1940.
10 *Daily Herald*, 30th April 1940.
11 *Reynolds News*, 14th April 1940; *Daily Herald*, 22nd April 1940.
12 HDD, 17th March 1940.
13 Beatrice Webb, unpublished diary, 12th April 1940.
14 HDD, 24th February 1940.
15 *Sunday Express*, 25th February 1940.
16 16th March 1940 (Fabian Collection 9/49/1 [item 1]).
17 See P. Addison, *The Road to 1945*, Quartet, 1977 (first published Jonathan Cape, 1975).
18 HDD, 1st May 1940.
19 W. P. Crozier (ed. A. J. P. Taylor), *Off the Record: Political Interviews 1933–1943*, Hutchinson, 1973, p. 167.
20 Addison, *The Road to 1945*, p. 92.
21 H. Macmillan, *The Blast of War: 1939–1945*, Macmillan, 1967, p. 71.
22 HDD, 8th May 1940.
23 Amery, *My Political Life*, Vol. III, p. 371.
24 HDD, 9th, 10th, 8th May 1940.
25 R. A. Butler to Lord Halifax, cited in Earl of Birkenhead, *The Life of Lord Halifax*, Hamish Hamilton, 1965, p. 453.
26 HDD, 10th May 1940.
27 B. Donoughue and G. W. Jones, *Herbert Morrison: Portrait of a Politician*, Weidenfeld & Nicolson, 1973, p. 275.
28 HDD, 2nd May 1940: Addison, *The Road to 1945*, p. 101.
29 Donoughue and Jones, *Herbert Morrison*, p. 275.
30 F. Williams, *A Prime Minister Remembers*, Heinemann, 1961, p. 31; *Clem*

Attlee: The Granada Historical Records Interview, Panther Record, 1967, p. 22; Amery, *My Political Life*, Vol. III, p. 371; FY, p. 309n. Amery (p. 370) was told that Greenwood and some other Labour front benchers wanted him as Chamberlain's successor.

31 HDD, 1st, 2nd, 8th May 1940.
32 Earl of Birkenhead, *Life of Lord Halifax*, p. 433.
33 HDD, 9th May 1940.
34 Cited in I. MacLeod, *Neville Chamberlain*, Muller, 1961, p. 291.
35 FY, p. 312.
36 HDD, 10th, 11th, 12th, 13th, 14th May 1940.
37 John Parker, interview.
38 V. Brittain, *Pethick-Lawrence: A Portrait*, Allen & Unwin, 1964, p. 117.
39 HDD, 14th May 1940.

XVIII *Blockade*

1 L.P.A.C.R., 1940, p. 188.
2 See W. N. Medlicott, *The Economic Blockade*, Vol. I, H.M.S.O., 1952. I have made extensive use of Medlicott's study in preparing this chapter.
3 *The Times*, 15th April 1940.
4 Douglas Jay in W. T. Rodgers (ed.), *Hugh Gaitskell 1906–63*, Thames & Hudson, 1964, p. 86.
5 *Economic Journal*, September 1953.
6 FO 837/1A X/M 03068, p. 13.
7 Medlicott, *The Economic Blockade*, Vol. II, p. 2.
8 See Dalton Papers 7/2 (46); also CAB 127/204.
9 HDD, 21st October 1941. Dalton also gave as a reason that he had 'a very good band of officials'.
10 Sir Noel Hall, interview.
11 Sir Frederick Leith-Ross, *Money Talks: Fifty Years of International Finance*, Hutchinson, 1968, p. 287.
12 HDD, 16th May 1940.
13 Leith-Ross, *Money Talks*, p. 287.
14 Private information. This story was in wide circulation among M.E.W. staff at the time.
15 FY, p. 334.
16 *Economic Journal*, September 1953.
17 Sir Patrick Hancock, interview.
18 *Economic Journal*, September 1953.
19 Sir Noel Hall, interview.
20 Geoffrey Crowther, *Ways and Means of War*, Oxford University Press, 1940, p. 57. ' ... [A] large amount of routine and administrative detail has disappeared,' Dalton wrote on 27th June, 'and, consequent on this, I have much less to supervise in this field ... ' ('Note on the Present Position and Probable Future of Economic Warfare', CAB 127/204).
21 Sir Noel Hall, interview.

22 Dalton Papers 8/1 (26).
23 D. Dilks (ed.), *The Diary of Sir Alexander Cadogan*, Cassell, 1971, p. 294. Entry for 5th June 1940.
24 'Notes on a Conversation', 22nd July 1941 (FO 837/1221).
25 HDD, 31st August 1940.
26 Dalton Papers 7/2 (13); Note, 17th October 1941, in CAB 127/204.
27 Sir John Lomax, *The Diplomatic Smuggler*, Arthur Barker, 1965, pp. 76, 80.
28 'Notes on a Conversation' 3rd July 1940 (Dalton Papers 7/3 (4); see also FO 837/1218).
29 Medlicott, *The Economic Blockade*, Vol. I, p. 562.
30 FO 837 1A X/M 03068.
31 'Food and the Blockade', Memorandum by the Minister of Economic Warfare, 7th August 1940 (CAB 127/204). See also War Cabinet Minutes, 9th August 1940, WP (G) (40) 208.
32 HC Debs [364] col. 1162.
33 See FO 837/1218: Lord Lothian to HD, 27th October 1940; HD undated minute ('Food Blockade to Europe').
34 Sir Noel Hall, interview.
35 Medlicott, *The Economic Blockade*, Vol. I, pp. 581–2. 'It will be necessary to strengthen the blockade against unoccupied France and to assert effectively our rights of contraband control', the Prime Minister wrote in a personal minute on April 2nd. 'I shall be glad if the Admiralty will make sure they have the necessary ships at Gibraltar to arrest and overhaul all French ships.' (PREM 3/74/7/32).
36 HDD, 12th January 1942. Cabinet had decided that one cargo of 8,000 tons of wheat should be sent to Greece, where deaths from starvation were reported. In February, in response to pressure from the Greek Prime Minister, Dalton suggested further shipments to Greece, while maintaining the principle of a full blockade elsewhere ('Greece: The Blockade', 14th February 1941, CAB 127/204).
37 HD to Attlee, 27th May 1940 (Dalton Papers 8/1 (3)).
38 HDD, 27th May 1940.
39 3rd June 1940 (Dalton Papers 7/2 (2)). At the end of May, Dalton was privately urging Maisky, the Soviet ambassador, to persuade his government to stop supplying Germany with oil (25th May 1940, CAB 127/204).
40 Dilks (ed.), *The Diary of Sir Alexander Cadogan*, p. 295.
41 FY, p. 345.
42 HDD, 8th June 1940.
43 Sir Arthur Harris, *Bomber Offensive*, Collins, 1947, p. 45.
44 Sir Charles Wheeler and N. Frankland, *The Strategic Air Offensive against Germany 1939–1945*, Vol. IV, H.M.S.O., 1961, pp. 214–19.
45 *The Times*, 10th June 1940.
46 Harris, *Bomber Offensive*, pp. 46–7.
47 A. S. Milward, *The German Economy at War*, Athlone Press, 1965, pp. 115–16.
48 In 1941, 32 ships were known to have tried to run the blockade from

South America; of these, 14 were intercepted (FO 837 1A X/M 03068).

49 Medlicott, *The Economic Blockade*, Vol. II, pp. 643–6, 2.

50 HDD, 31st May 1940.

51 HDD, 1st, 5th, 21st June 1940. 'Have a drink with C. Stuart [Sir Campbell Stuart, head of EH (Electra House) which dealt with propaganda] who is all for G.J. taking over some important work in which we are both interested', Dalton noted on 5th June. 'Go on to dine with G.J., who would like to do it, but must speak first to Cadogan … ' On 21st June, Dalton recorded: 'G.J. came to see me. He has been offered a job of some importance under Monckton in connection with press censorship. He and Cadogan are trying to think out a plan for better control of problems of common interest to me and others.' Jebb went on to mention a proposal for joint control with Eden, adding that 'it might be useful to have a relatively junior person from the F.O. as liaison with the new organisation'.

52 Dilks (ed.), *The Diary of Sir Alexander Cadogan*, p. 308.

53 HDD, 21st, 29th June 1940 (see n. 51).

54 Dalton Papers 7/3 (2).

55 HDD, 1st July 1940.

56 Cited in M. R. D. Foot, *SOE in France*, H.M.S.O., 1968, p. 8.

57 HDD, 1st, 9th, 10th July 1940.

58 A. V. Alexander Papers (Ref.: 5/4/39). (Dalton's underlining).

59 Dilks (ed.), *The Diary of Sir Alexander Cadogan*, p. 312. Entry for 11th July 1940.

60 HDD, 12th July 1940.

61 FY, p. 366.

XIX *S.O.E.*

1 R. Usborne, *Clubland Heroes*, Barrie & Jenkins (1974 ed.), p. 1. See also M. Wheeler, 'The SOE Phenomenon', in W. Laqueur (ed.), *The Second World War: Essays in Military and Political History*, Sage, 1982, p. 195, where the passage is cited.

2 M. Wheeler, 'The SOE Phenomenon', p. 196.

3 Cited in Brigadier P. Young (ed.), *The Almanac of World War II*, Hamlyn, 1981, p. 67.

4 Sir Robin Brook, interview.

5 M. R. D. Foot, quoted in B. Davidson, *Special Operations Europe: Scenes from the Anti-Nazi War*, Gollancz, 1980, p. 72.

6 M. Wheeler, 'The SOE Phenomenon', p. 197.

7 ' … [I]s there a single Buchan heroine', asks Usborne, 'who is not at some time praised for her boyish looks, lines, stride, manner, health or hips?' (*Clubland Heroes*, p. 98.)

8 HDD, 11th September, 10th October 1941.

9 H. Dalton, *With British Guns in Italy*, Methuen 1919, pp. 65–6.

10 Cited in D. Stafford, *Britain and European Resistance, 1940–1945: A*

Survey of the Special Operations Executive, with Documents, Macmillan, 1980, p. 26.

11 See M. R. D. Foot, 'Was SOE Any Good?', in Laqueur (ed.), *The Second World War*, p. 24; also Dalton Papers 7/3 (2).

12 M. R. D. Foot, *SOE in France*, H.M.S.O., 1966, p. 2.

13 HD to Sir Robert Vansittart, 24th August 1940 (Dalton Papers 7/3 (19)).

14 B. Sweet-Escott, *Baker Street Irregular*, Methuen, 1965, p. 56.

15 HDD, 9th November 1940; FY, p. 288.

16 J. Astley, *The Inner Circle*, Hutchinson, 1971, p. 34.

17 J. Amery, *Approach March: a Venture in Autobiography*, Hutchinson, 1973, pp. 212–13.

18 Bickham Sweet-Escott, George Taylor, interviews. See also Sweet-Escott, *Baker Street Irregular*, pp. 20–1, 38–9.

19 HD to Sir Robert Vansittart, 24th August 1940 (Dalton Papers, 7/3 (18)).

20 HD to Gladwyn Jebb, 8th November 1940 (Dalton Papers, 7/3 (37)).

21 HDD, 18th, 25th November 1940.

22 Two essays in the same volume give different figures. 'At its peak strength in the autumn of 1944 S.O.E. employed some 10,000 persons', writes Mark Wheeler (Laqueur (ed.), *The Second World War*, p. 196). 'Its total strength has never been established', writes M. R. D. Foot. 'It appears to have contained 10,000 men and 3,000 women.' (Ibid., p. 246.) One senior S.O.E. officer, Sir Robin Brook, however, considers that these estimates are too low. (Interview.)

23 Sweet-Escott, *Baker Street Irregular*, p. 123.

24 C. Gubbins, 'S.O.E. and the Co-ordination of Regular and Irregular War', in M. Elliott-Bateman (ed.), *The Fourth Dimension in Warfare*, Manchester University Press, 1970, pp. 85–7.

25 George Taylor, interview.

26 Bickham Sweet-Escott, George Taylor, interviews.

27 HDD, 10th December 1940.

28 Lord Gladwyn (formerly Gladwyn Jebb), interview.

29 Sir Robin Brook, interview.

30 George Taylor, interview.

31 Sweet-Escott, *Baker Street Irregular*, p. 123.

32 Bickham Sweet-Escott recalled only one visit. (Interview.)

33 Sir Robin Brook, interview. (The knighthood came later.)

34 Sir Colin Gubbins to J. E. S. Peart-Binns, July 1975. (Letter kindly lent to the author by Mr. Peart-Binns.)

35 B. Sweet-Escott, 'S.O.E. in the Balkans', in P. Auty and R. Clogg (eds.), *British Policy towards Wartime Resistance in Yugoslavia and Greece*, Macmillan, 1975, p. 6.

36 George Taylor, interview.

37 D. Stafford, 'S.O.E. and British Involvement in the Belgrade Coup d'État of March 1941', *Slavic Review*, Vol. 36, No. 3, September 1977, pp. 417–19.

38 HDD, 27th March 1941.

39 To some extent, the two approaches were combined: in February 1941

Dalton asked for bombing raids against Rumanian oilfields 'if only on a light scale, as a prelude to subversive activities in Rumania which are timed to begin on 28th February' (FO 371/30000/196).

40 Dalton Papers 18/1.
41 HDD, 16th June 1941.
42 E. Barker, *British Policy in South-East Europe in the Second World War*, Macmillan, 1976, p. 40.
43 Stafford, *Britain and European Resistance*, p. 54.
44 HDD, 1st December 1941.
45 Stafford, *Britain and European Resistance*, pp. 70–1.
46 HDD, 26th September 1941.
47 Stafford, *Britain and European Resistance*, p. 71.
48 *The Memoirs of Lord Chandos*, Bodley Head, 1962, p. 239.
49 Sweet-Escott, *Baker Street Irregular*, p. 65.
50 HDD, 2nd May 1941. It seems likely that the banker in Dalton's diary and the banker in Sweet-Escott's account are the same; it is possible, however, that two separate incidents (and rejections) were involved.
51 Sweet-Escott, *Baker Street Irregular*, pp. 73–6 et seq.
52 K. Young (ed.), *The Diaries of Sir Robert Bruce Lockhart*, Vol. II, *1939–1965*, Macmillan, 1980, p. 112. (Entry for 4th August 1941.)
53 *The Memoirs of Lord Gladwyn*, p. 103.
54 Dalton Papers, 18/3 (44).
55 HDD, 12th November 1941.
56 George Taylor, interview.
57 Gubbins to Peart-Binns, July 1975.
58 Dalton Papers, 18/2 (40), (41). Nelson's remarks were made at a meeting on 30th October.
59 Dalton Papers, 18/2 (42)–(54).
60 Stafford, *Britain and European Resistance*, p. 57. The following discussion is largely based on Professor Stafford's illuminating account (ibid., pp. 57–68).
61 August 1941, cited in E. H. Cookridge, *Inside S.O.E.: The Story of Special Operations in Western Europe 1940–1945*, Arthur Barker, 1966, p. 26.
62 Stafford, *Britain and European Resistance*, pp. 58–60.
63 See 'The Distant Future', extract from the Joint Planning Staff's Review of Future Strategy, 14th June 1941, JP(41)444 in CAB 79/12. (Reprinted in ibid., pp. 234–8.)
64 Stafford, *Britain and European Resistance*, p. 63. Yet as late as October 1941 the Polish Prime Minister-in-exile, General Sikorski, wrote to Dalton thanking him for help in getting Air Ministry agreement for special flights to Poland (20th October 1941; CAB 127/207).
65 HDD, 9th January 1942.
66 See Davidson, *Special Operations Europe*, p. 71.
67 Ibid., pp. 71–2.
68 HDD, 24th, 25th November 1941.
69 Sweet-Escott, *Baker Street Irregular*, p. 116. Dalton's idea was that

S.O.E. should infiltrate its trainees among the workers taken into Axis countries from enemy-occupied Europe for forced labour. But nothing came of it. Dalton also tried to persuade Halifax to make more use of leading left-wing Belgian politicians-in-exile (HD to Halifax, 11th October 1940, CAB 127/205).

70 And, according to some, in saving Europe from Soviet domination. See M. R. D. Foot, 'Was S.O.E. Any Good?', in Laqueur (ed.), *The Second World War*, p. 249. For a list of S.O.E.'s alleged successes, see ibid., pp. 248–50.

XX *Black Propaganda*

1 C. Cruickshank, *The Fourth Arm: Psychological Warfare 1938–1945*, Davis-Poynter, 1977, pp. 17 et seq.
2 S. Delmar, *Black Boomerang*, Secker & Warburg, 1962, p. 6.
3 Perhaps rightly. See K. Young (ed.), *The Diaries of Sir Robert Bruce Lockhart*, Vol. II, *1939–1965*, Macmillan, 1980, p. 56. Entry for 17th May 1940.
4 Ibid., p. 78. Entry for 15th September 1940. See also ibid., p. 68, entry for 19th June 1940, which provides earlier evidence of Leeper's low opinion of Dalton.
5 *Memoirs of Lord Gladwyn*, p. 102.
6 HDD, 25th July 1941.
7 Jebb minute to HD, 21st August 1940 (Dalton Papers 7/3 (10)).
8 HD to Sir Robert Vansittart, 24th August 1940 (Dalton Papers 7/3 (18)).
9 Bruce Lockhart considered Crossman the outstanding figure in the organisation of wartime propaganda. (R. Bruce Lockhart, *Giants Cast Long Shadows*, Putnam, 1960, p. 96.)
10 HDD, 19th–25th May, 5th, 8th July 1941. See also HD to Cadogan, 30th June 1941; HD to Eden, 4th July 1941 (Dalton Papers 18/2).
11 *Memoirs of Lord Gladwyn*, p. 102.
12 Young (ed.), *The Diaries of Sir Robert Bruce Lockhart*, Vol. II, p. 85. Entry for 26th November 1940.
13 Sir Hugh Greene, *The Third Floor Front: A View of Broadcasting in the Sixties*, The Bodley Head, 1969, p. 21.
14 R. H. S. Crossman, 'Psychological Warfare', *Journal of the Royal United Service Institution*, Vol. XCVII, August 1952, p. 321.
15 Cruickshank, *The Fourth Arm*, p. 111.
16 FO 898/69/42. Perhaps some of these were believed; however, Dalton had his doubts, and in March 1941, in an effort to improve quality, he ordered that the production of sibs should be cut by one third (Cruickshank, *The Fourth Arm*, p. 109).
17 16th May 1941, cited in Cruickshank, *The Fourth Arm*, p. 106.
18 'PROPAGANDA POLICY (PWE) Memorandum by the Minister of Economic Warfare' (initialled 'H.D.'), 6th December 1941 (FO 898/11/477-80).
19 Delmar, *Black Boomerang*, p. 62.
20 B. Sweet-Escott, *Baker Street Irregular*, Methuen, 1965, p. 69.

21 George Wagner, interview.
22 Crossman, 'Psychological Warfare', p. 321.
23 Cited in M. Balfour, *Propaganda in War 1939–1945*, Routledge & Kegan Paul, 1979, p. 91.
24 HDD, 2nd, 22nd November 1940.
25 PREM 7/3.
26 See R. Bruce Lockhart, *Comes the Reckoning*, Putnam, 1947, pp. 116–17.
27 D. Cooper, *Old Men Forget: The Autobiography of Duff Cooper*, Rupert Hart-Davis, 1953, p. 288.
28 HDD, 24th June 1941.
29 Ibid., 16th July 1941.
30 C. Lysaght, *Brendan Bracken*, Allen Lane, 1979, pp. 143, 148, 177, 146, 196, 14, 182. The description of Bracken's hair is by General Louis Spears, cited in ibid., pp. 176–7. The quotation from *Brideshead Revisited* is cited in ibid., p. 275.
31 HDD, 20th, 27th February 1941.
32 Young (ed.), *The Diaries of Sir Robert Bruce Lockhart*, Vol. II, pp. 113, 110. 8th August, 23rd July 1941.
33 Andrew Boyle, *Poor Dear Brendan: The Quest for Brendan Bracken*, Hutchinson, 1974, p. 281.
34 Bruce Lockhart report to Eden, week ending 28th July 1941 (FO 898/9/167).
35 HDD, 28th July 1941.
36 FO 898/9 X/M OS 668.
37 6th August 1941 (FO 898/12 X/M OA 679).
38 HDD, 8th August 1941.
39 FO 898/9 X/M OS 668.
40 FO 898/9/167.
41 20th August 1941 (Dalton Papers 18/3).
42 HDD, 21st August 1941.
43 Cruickshank, *The Fourth Arm*, p. 26.
44 HDD, 10th September 1941.
45 HC Debs [374] col. 294.
46 HDD, 10th September 1941.
47 Cited in K. Harris, *Attlee*, Weidenfeld & Nicolson, 1982, p. 190.
48 HDD, 11th September 1941.
49 Memorandum marked 'C.H.Q. 20.9.41' in HDD.
50 HDD, 20th September 1941.
51 Young (ed.), *The Diaries of Sir Robert Bruce Lockhart*, Vol. II, p. 119. Entry for 20th September 1941.
52 HDD, 9th October 1941.
53 Boyle, *Poor Dear Brendan*, pp. 273–4.
54 George Taylor, interview.
55 HDD, 13th October 1941.
56 Young (ed.), *The Diaries of Sir Robert Bruce Lockhart*, Vol. II, p. 125. Entry for 21st October 1941.
57 Dilks (ed.), *The Diary of Sir Alexander Cadogan*, Cassell, 1971, p. 409.

Entry for 21st October 1941. This meeting was described by no fewer than three of those present in their respective diaries. Dalton wrote in his: '[Bracken] brings no papers, has studied nothing, is arrogant, rude, inconsequent, critical, purely destructive' (HDD, 21st October 1941).

58 HDD, 24th October 1941.
59 Josephine Smith, Peggy Jay, interviews.
69 George and Irene Wagner, interviews.
61 HDD, 7th June 1940.
62 Ibid., 25th January 1941.
63 Josephine Smith, interview.
64 *The Times*, 12th May 1941.
65 HDD, 11th May 1941.
66 Josephine Smith, interview.
67 Davenport, *Memoirs of a City Radical*, Weidenfeld & Nicolson, 1974, p. 173. Davenport suggests that the incident occurred when Dalton was President of the Board of Trade. By then, however, the Daltons had already vacated the Carlisle Mansions flat. Nevertheless, the identification of the raid that caused Ruth's decision with the heavy raid of 10th–11th May is based only on circumstantial evidence: Hugh's vivid account of returning to Victoria, and viewing the ruins, does not mention Ruth.
68 See ibid. Ruth told Josephine Smith the same.
69 HDD, 22nd June 1941.
70 Josephine Smith, interview.
71 HDD, 20th August, 23rd, 28th October 1941.
72 See p. 313.
73 HDD, 11th, 14th November 1941.
74 Young (ed.), *The Diaries of Sir Robert Bruce Lockhart*, Vol. II, p. 129. Entry for 3rd November 1941.
75 HDD, 18th, 19th November 1941; 18th October 1940; 23rd, 25th November, 25th December, 15th November 1941; 1st, 6th January, 5th February 1942.
76 Young (ed.), *The Diaries of Sir Robert Bruce Lockhart*, p. 138. Entry for 3rd February 1942.
77 HDD, 3rd, 21st February, 5th December 1942.
78 J. Harvey (ed.), *The War Diaries of Oliver Harvey*, Collins, 1978, p. 100.
79 Young (ed.), *The Diaries of Sir Robert Bruce Lockhart*, Vol. II, p. 143. Entry for 2nd February 1942.
80 See P. Addison, *The Road to 1945*, Jonathan Cape, 1975, p. 198.
81 Young (ed.), *The Diaries of Sir Robert Bruce Lockhart*, Vol. II, p. 147. Entry for 25th February 1942.

XXI *Coalition Poker*

1 HDD, 21st May, 26th June 1940.
2 *The Memoirs of Lord Gladwyn*, Weidenfeld & Nicolson, 1972, p. 106.
3 HDD, 3rd April 1941.

4 K. Young (ed.), *The Diaries of Sir Robert Bruce Lockhart*, Vol. II, *1939–1965*, Macmillan, 1980, p. 121. Entry for 5th October 1941.

5 Sir John Wheeler-Bennett (ed.), *Action This Day: Working with Churchill*, Macmillan, 1968, p. 105.

6 George Taylor, interview. Taylor's source was Desmond Morton. See also Young (ed.), *The Diaries of Sir Robert Bruce Lockhart*, p. 89. (Entry for 28th January 1941), for Morton's comment that 'Dalton bores [Churchill], and no man wants to see bores'.

7 B. Sweet-Escott, *Baker Street Irregular*, Methuen, 1965, p. 122.

8 HDD, 22nd November 1940, 21st February, 2nd, 3rd March, 15th May 1941.

9 Young (ed.), *The Diaries of Sir Robert Bruce Lockhart*, Vol. II, p. 89. Entry for 28th January 1941.

10 J. Colville, *The Churchillians*, Weidenfeld & Nicolson, 1981, p. 59. Churchill's dislike of Dalton does not, however, explain his lack of interest in S.O.E. after February 1942 when Dalton ceased to be responsible for the organisation.

11 HDD, 15th May 1941.

12 D. Cooper, *Old Men Forget*, Hart-Davis, 1953, p. 288.

13 C. Lysaght, *Brendan Bracken*, Allen Lane, 1979, p. 208.

14 Chuter Ede, unpublished diaries, 24th February 1942.

15 Sir Frederick Leith-Ross, *Money Talks*, Hutchinson, 1968, p. 293.

16 Dalton Papers, 7/4 (1) n.d.

17 HDD, 3rd, 11th March 1942.

18 Dalton Papers, 7/4 (1) n.d.

19 HDD, 2nd, 5th March, 7th April 1942.

20 J. Harris, *William Beveridge*, Oxford University Press, 1977, p. 377.

21 Lord Beveridge, *Power and Influence*, Hodder & Stoughton, 1953, pp. 287–8.

22 HDD, 6th May 1942.

23 H. Wilson, *New Deal for Coal*, Contact, 1945, p. 59.

24 Cited in Philip M. Williams, *Hugh Gaitskell: A Political Biography*, Jonathan Cape, 1979, p. 112.

25 Chuter Ede, unpublished diaries, 25th April 1942.

26 W. H. B. Court, *Coal*, H.M.S.O., 1951, p. 161.

27 'I am not at all convinced we should be wise to pull the Army to pieces at the present time', Churchill minuted to the Lord President on 30th March, after Dalton had urged the Lord President's Committee to release all ex-miners from the Army (PREM 4/9/8).

28 HDD, 17th, 21st April 1942.

29 Court, *Coal*, p. 159.

30 Mass Observation, cited in H. Pelling, *Britain and the Second World War*, Fontana, 1970, pp. 157–8.

31 P. Goodhart and V. Branston, *The 1922*, Macmillan, 1978, p. 115.

32 HDD, 30th, 28th April, 6th May 1942.

33 R. Page Arnot, *The Miners in Crisis and War*, Allen & Unwin, 1962, p. 337 n.

34 HDD, 12th, 17th May 1942.
35 Court, *Coal*, p. 162.
36 HDD, 20th April, 20th May 1942. See also A. Horner, *Incorrigible Rebel*, MacGibbon & Kee, 1960, p. 164.
37 HDD, 21st May, 19th March 1942.
38 FY, p. 391.
39 See D. R. Grenfell, *Coal*, Gollancz, 1947, pp. 95–7.
40 HDD, 26th May 1942.
41 See W. P. Crozier (ed. A. J. P. Taylor), *Off the Record*, Hutchinson, 1973, p. 323 n.
42 Cited in M. Foot, *Aneurin Bevan: A Biography*, Vol. I, *1897–1945*, MacGibbon & Kee, 1962, pp. 358–9.
43 HDD, 31st May 1942.
44 Cited in Williams, *Hugh Gaitskell*, p. 114.
45 HDD, 12th June 1942.
46 Ibid., 22nd October 1942.
47 FY, p. 415. On one occasion, the Prime Minister even issued a personal command that he should produce more playing cards, for the amusement of troops (26th July 1943. CAB 127/204).
48 HDD, 21st June 1943; E. L. Hargreaves and M. M. Gowing, *Civil Industry and Trade*, H.M.S.O., 1952. A shortage of rubber, which was the cause of the corset crisis, also hit the contraceptive industry. In 1944, Lord Horder, who was President of the Family Planning Association, approached Dalton on the strength of Ruth's interest in birth control. Dalton acted, production of condoms and dutch caps increased, and the F.P.A. recorded a vote of thanks to Ruth, who had used her influence on their behalf (private information).
49 *Daily Express*, 5th August 1943.
50 W. K. Hancock and M. M. Gowing, *British War Economy*, H.M.S.O., 1949, pp. 493–5.
51 BT, 64/1730 X/P 7759.
52 FY, p. 410.
53 *News Chronicle*, 19th March 1943.
54 *Daily Express*, 16th February 1943.
55 *Manchester Guardian*, 10th March 1943.
56 *The Times*, 10th March 1943.
57 *Daily Express*, 18th March, 6th April 1943.
58 *New Statesman & Nation*, 13th November 1943.
59 *Daily Herald*, 22nd February 1945.
60 HDD, 21st June, 18th February 1943, 16th August 1942, 8th July, 27th June, 22nd March 1943.
61 Chuter Ede, unpublished diaries, 8th May 1943.
62 HDD, 24th, 26th, 16th May 1943, 26th–27th February, 19th July, 26th September, 28th November, 11th December 1944, July 1945. See also P. Addison, *The Road to 1945*, Quartet, 1977 (first published Jonathan Cape, 1975), pp. 234–5.
63 T. Fraser to J. S. Peart-Binns, 16th October 1973. (Letter kindly lent to

the author by Mr Peart-Binns.)

64 See J. M. Lee, *The Churchill Coalition 1940–1945*, Batsford, 1980, p. 125.
65 HDD, 14th July 1943.
66 Cripps to Beatrice Webb, 23rd June 1939, cited in Addison, *Road to 1945*, p. 193.
67 'Note for War Cabinet by the Minister of Economic Warfare: Trade Talks with Russia.' CAB 127/204.
68 HDD, 17th, 18th, 27th May 1940.
69 Cited in Addison, *Road to 1945*, p. 199.
70 HDD, 4th, 9th, 19th February 1942.
71 HD to Beatrice Webb, 14th June 1942 (Passfield Papers II 4m 107).
72 HDD, 19th, 29th May, 24th August 1942.
73 Cited in Addison, *Road to 1945*, p. 210.
74 HDD, 9th, 21st–22nd November, 28th October, 7th December 1942, 22nd March 1943.
75 B. Donoughue and G. W. Jones, *Herbert Morrison*, Weidenfeld & Nicolson, 1973, pp. 327–8.
76 HDD, 14th June 1943.
77 FY, p. 413.
78 HDD, 1st July 1940.
79 Bevin shared Dalton's concern about the Whitehall machine. (See Bevin to Dalton 7th July 1944; Bevin Papers (3/2).
80 HDD, 6th July, 22nd November 1944.
81 FY, p. 460.

XXII *Pig*

1   See Sir Frederick Leith-Ross, *Money Talks*, Hutchinson, 1968, p. 281.
2   Sir Noel Hall, interview.
3   Sir Harry Lintott, interview.
4   Memorandum by Gaitskell (n.d.) in Dalton Papers 7/4 (1).
5   G. J. Macmahon, interview.
6   Dame Alix Meynell, interview.
7   FY, p. 388 n.
8   HDD, 5th March 1945.
9   James Meade, interview.
10 HDD, 15th September 1942.
11 Ibid., 13th March 1944.
12 Sir Edmund Parker, private correspondence with the author.
13 A. E. Welch, private correspondence with the author.
14 G. C. Allen, private correspondence with the author.
15 Sir Harry Lintott, interview.
16 H. A. R. Binney, private correspondence with the author.
17 Dame Alix Meynell, interview.
18 Captain Charles Waterhouse to J. E. S. Peart-Binns, 9th April 1974. (Letter kindly lent by Mr. Peart-Binns.)

19 Mrs Margaret Dean, interview.
20 Dame Alix Meynell, interview.
21 Sir Anthony Percival, private correspondence with the author.
22 George Wansbrough, private correspondence with the author.
23 Sir Edmund Parker, private correspondence with the author.
24 G. C. Allen, private correspondence with the author.
25 James Meade, unpublished diaries, 28th January 1945.
26 HDD, 24th February 1942.
27 James Meade, interview.
28 W. L. B. Fairweather, private correspondence with the author. Fairweather was a principal concerned with Development Area surveys.
29 James Meade, interview.
30 HDD, 22nd February 1942.
31 G. C. Allen, private correspondence with the author.
32 *Daily Herald*, 13th December 1941; *News Chronicle*, 18th April 1942.
33 HDD, 22nd January 1942.
34 Ruth Dalton to Hilde Auerbach, c. 1943 (Auerbach Letters).
35 HDD, 18th April 1944.
36 Ruth Dalton to Hilde Auerbach, 27th December 1942 (Auerbach Letters); HDD, 25th December 1942.
37 HDD, 29th June 1943.
38 Ruth Dalton to Hilde Auerbach, 17th October 1943, 4th March 1944 (Auerbach Letters).
39 HDD, 14th March 1944.
40 Leith-Ross to HD 27th April, HD to Leith-Ross 8th May 1944 (Dalton Papers 8/1 (71), (72)).
41 Ruth to Hilde Auerbach, 18th June 1944 (Auerbach Letters); *Sunday Dispatch*, 24th December 1944.
42 HDD, 8th June 1944.
43 Pearl Jephcock, private correspondence with the author.
44 HDD, 24th July 1944.
45 Ibid., 11th August 1943.
46 John Freeman, interview.
47 B. Reed and G. Williams, *Denis Healey and the Policies of Power*, Sidgwick & Jackson, 1971, pp. 45–8.
48 HDD, 12th November 1943.
49 Sir Robert and Lady Fraser, interviews.
50 Rosalind Gilmore, interview. Interestingly, Dalton recorded this tale when he first told it. (HDD, 12th December 1943.)
51 Sir Robert and Lady Fraser, interviews.
52 HDD, 28th September, 30th October 1944.
53 Draft of letter, HD to Lord Horder, 3rd November 1944 (Dalton Papers 8/1 (66)).
54 HDD, 10th November 1944.

XXIII *Planning for Post-War*

1 Douglas Jay, *Change and Fortune: A Political Record*, Hutchinson, 1980, p. 110.
2 H. Dalton, *Hitler's War*, Penguin, 1940, p. 141.
3 28th August 1942 (Dalton Papers 7/4 (79)).
4 D. E. Moggridge, 'Economic Policy in the Second World War', in (ed.) M. Keynes, *Essays on John Maynard Keynes*, Cambridge University Press, 1975, p. 194.
5 HDD, 18th November 1942.
6 8th January 1943 (CAB 87/3).
7 HDD, 21st June, 27th August 1942.
8 Dalton's suspicions had some basis. Fundamental to Keynes's thinking on reparations was the view that post-war policy should favour German economic reconstruction, so that Germany could resume the role of economic leadership which Keynes regarded as essential for the economic health and political stability of Europe. (See D. E. Moggridge, *Keynes*, Macmillan, 1976, p. 139.) This was precisely the attitude which Dalton rejected.
9 HDD, 10th November 1942.
10 13th March 1944 (Dalton Papers 8/1 (21)). See also HD to Beatrice Webb 14th June 1942 (Passfield Papers II 4 m 107).
11 HDD, 5th January, 23rd April, 26th July 1943.
12 HTA, p. 166 (cited in V. Rothwell, *Britain and the Cold War 1941–1947*, Jonathan Cape, 1982, p. 316).
13 L.P.A.C.R., 1944, pp. 4–9, 140.
14 FY, p. 427. Dalton's Palestine paragraph was unusually specific. Much of Labour's foreign policy document amounted to a *carte blanche* to a Labour Foreign Secretary to do whatever he considered fit, as T. D. Burridge has pointed out (*British Labour and Hitler's War*, Deutsch, 1976, p. 119).
15 See A. Sargent, 'The Labour Party and Palestine', unpublished Ph.D. thesis (London), 1981, p. 256.
16 HDD, 28th April 1944. See also the *New Judaea* (London), June–July 1944.
17 Dalton Papers, n.d. 7/10 (43), and see Sargent, 'The Labour Party and Palestine'.
18 28th October 1944. (Dalton Papers 8/1 (99).)
19 K. Harris, *Attlee*, Weidenfeld & Nicolson, 1982, p. 390.
20 HTA, p. 147.
21 J. M. Lee, *The Churchill Coalition 1940–1945*, Batsford, 1980, p. 129.
22 Labour Party N.E.C. minutes, 21st July 1943; HDD, 20th October 1943.
23 J. Harris, 'Beveridge, William Henry, Baron Beveridge (1879–1963)', in *The Dictionary of National Biography 1961–70*, Oxford University Press, 1981, p. 106.
24 HD to Sir William Jowitt 6th December 1942 (CAB 117/209; cited in Addison, *Road to 1945*, p. 216).

25 Harris, 'Beveridge, William Henry', p. 106.
26 HDD, 24th February 1943.
27 J. Harris, *William Beveridge: A Biography*, Oxford University Press, 1977, p. 430.
28 Dalton, however, regarded Beveridge's definition of 'full employment' – one and a half million out of work – as unduly pessimistic. (HD to Morrison 24th January 1944. Dalton Papers 8/1 (92)).
29 HDD, 11th, 25th January, 4th, 5th March 1944.
30 FY, p. 422.
31 *The Times*, 19th October 1942.
32 HDD, 20th December 1942.
33 p. 243.
34 E. Durbin, *What Have We to Defend?*, Routledge, 1942, pp. 74–7.
35 6th September 1942 (Durbin Papers).
36 F. L. Block, *The Origins of International Economic Disorder: a study of United States international monetary policy from World War II to the present*, University of California Press, 1977, pp. 47–8.
37 R. N. Gardner, *Sterling-Dollar Diplomacy*, McGraw-Hill, 1969, p. 103.
38 26th and 29th August 1942 (BT 11/2000 X/P 7759).
39 James Meade, interview.
40 HDD, 11th November 1942.
41 Sir Frederick Leith-Ross, *Money Talks*, Hutchinson, 1968, p. 293.
42 Gardner, *Sterling-Dollar Diplomacy*, p. 103 and passim.
43 27th May 1943 (CAB 87/13 X/P 07917).
44 See D. Maclennan and J. B. Parr (eds.), *Regional Policy: Past Experience and New Directions*, Martin Robinson, 1979, pp. 5–6.
45 See FY, pp. 434–54; Jay, *Change and Fortune*, pp. 111–26.
46 HDD, 14th, 9th, 13th September 1943.
47 Jay, *Change and Fortune*, p. 112.
48 FY, p. 419.
49 HDD, 2nd, 3rd November 1943.
50 FY, p. 419.
51 Cited in Jay, *Change and Fortune*, p. 113.
52 *Labour's Immediate Programme*, The Labour Party, London 1937, p. 7.
53 Jay, *Change and Fortune*, pp. 114–16.
54 'Location of Industry and its Control' 2nd September 1943 (CAB 87/13 X/P 07917).
55 *Daily Herald*, 9th June 1945.
56 Jay, *Change and Fortune*, p. 118.
57 HDD, 13th May 1943, 5th January 1945.
58 See pp. 559–63.
59 See FY, pp. 446–54. Also to pushing a Restrictive Practices Bill, which he was eventually forced to abandon.
60 HD to Churchill, 21st November 1944 (in HDD).
61 Jay, *Change and Fortune*, p. 121.
62 HDD, 11th December 1944; FY, p. 448.
63 Jay, *Change and Fortune*, p. 121.

64 21st March 1945 H.C. Debs [409] col. 837.
65 See FY, pp. 451–2.
66 Harold Nicolson, unpublished diary, 21st March 1945.
67 *Daily Herald*, 22nd March 1945.
68 Jay, *Change and Fortune*, pp. 120–2, 213.
69 J. D. McCallum, 'The Development of British Regional Policy', in Maclennan and Parr (eds.), *Regional Policy*, p. 8.
70 *Sunday Chronicle*, 7th May 1944.
71 *Sunday Express*, 17th June 1945.
72 It is interesting that the editors of an otherwise excellent history of regional planning should have been under the mistaken impression that Dalton's Act was passed by the *Labour* government, rather than by its predecessor. (Maclennan and Parr (eds.), *Regional Policy*, p. 7.) ' ... [F]ollowing the election in 1945 of a Labour Government strongly committed to an activist economic policy', they write, 'came the Distribution of Industry Act 1945.'
73 L.P.A.C.R., 1944, pp. 4–9.

XXIV *The Switch*

1   HDD, 28th May 1945.
2   Dame Alix Meynell, interview.
3   HDD, Summer 1945.
4   *The Times*, 28th June, 5th July 1945.
5   HDD, Summer 1945.
6   West Leaze Visitors' Book.
7   FY, p. 466.
8   HDD, 16th May 1945.
9   CRA to HD, 13th July 1945 (Dalton Papers). See also A. Bullock, *The Life and Times of Ernest Bevin*, Vol. II, Heinemann, 1967, p. 393. The mid-July correspondence between Dalton and Attlee disposes of a later suggestion by Morgan Phillips (referred to by Dalton in FY, p. 474) that Attlee had for some time intended to make Bevin Foreign Secretary and Dalton Chancellor in the event of a Labour victory and only wobbled temporarily after Bevin had indicated his own preference for the Exchequer on 26th July.
10 HDD, 27th July 1945, FY, pp. 468–9.
11 HDD, 27th July 1945.
12 *Tribune*, 21st November 1952. According to Morgan Phillips, Attlee lunched alone with his wife (FY, p. 474).
13 Douglas Jay, *Change and Fortune*, Hutchinson, 1980, pp. 129–30.
14 Lord Morrison of Lambeth, *Herbert Morrison: An Autobiography*, Odhams Press, 1960, pp. 246–7.
15 HDD (Note), 11th December 1956.
16 Bullock, *Bevin*, Vol. II, p. 39.
17 FY, p. 382.

18 Diary, 26th July 1945, cited in Earl of Avon, *Memoirs of the Rt. Hon. Sir Anthony Eden K.G., P.C., M.C.: The Reckoning*, Cassell, 1965, p. 551.
19 N. Davenport, *Memoirs of a City Radical*, Weidenfeld & Nicolson, 1974, p. 148.
20 Lord Gladwyn, interview.
21 D. Dilks (ed.), *The Diaries of Sir Alexander Cadogan*, Cassell, 1971, p. 776.
22 Cited in J. W. Wheeler-Bennett, *George VI: His Life and Reign*, Macmillan, 1958, p. 638.
23 *Observer*, 23rd August 1959, cited in HTA, p. 12.
24 HTA, p. 10.
25 The Duke of Windsor, *A Family Album*, Cassell, 1960, p. 78.
26 Denis Craig, private correspondence with the author.
27 H. Nicolson, unpublished diary, 14th April 1949.
28 P. M. Williams (ed.), *The Diary of Hugh Gaitskell*, Jonathan Cape, 1983, pp. 249–50, 4th May 1951.
29 HDD, 25th, 26th March 1944. The entries appear to have been dictated on 30th March.
30 *The Times*, 27th March 1944.
31 Ian Forbes Watson, interview.
32 Cited in P. Addison, *The Road to 1945*, Quartet, 1977, p. 214.
33 HDD, 29th, 28th, 30th March 1944.
34 Apart from those already mentioned, and clothing, which was left to Ruth. (Will of Catherine Alicia Dalton, Somerset House.)
35 Ian Forbes Watson, interview.
36 Heather Forbes Watson, interview.
37 George and Irene Wsgner, interviews.
38 HTA, p. 9.

XXV *Behold the Dawn Appear*

1 In 1946 Wilson Smith retired, and Sir Eric Bamford and J. I. C. Crombie were appointed to Third Secretaryships.
2 Lady Trend, interview. (Lady Trend, as Miss Shaw, was Assistant Private Secretary to Dalton as Chancellor.)
3 Lord Trend, interview.
4 Charles Wintour in the *Evening Standard*, 27th November 1946.
5 Lord Trend, interview.
6 Sir Thomas Padmore, interview. Padmore worked for Dalton as Principal Private Secretary in the summer of 1945.
7 Lord Trend, interview.
8 Sir Thomas Padmore, interview.
9 Lord Trend, interview.
10 H. Dalton, *Principles of Public Finance*, Routledge (1954 ed.), p. 229.
11 Sir Noel Hall, interview.
12 R. F. Harrod, *The Life of John Maynard Keynes*, Macmillan, 1951, p. 596.

13 Meade Papers (1/4 p. 125).
14 Sir Richard Clarke (ed. Sir Alec Cairncross), *Anglo-American Economic Collaboration in War and Peace 1942–1949*, Oxford University Press, 1982, p. 71.
15 James Meade, interview.
16 Lord Trend, interview.
17 Harrod, *Keynes*, p. 596.
18 R. N. Gardner, *Sterling-Dollar Diplomacy: Anglo-American collaboration in the reconstruction of multilateral trade*, Clarendon Press, 1956, p. 193.
19 A. Grant, interview.
20 Gardner, *Sterling-Dollar Diplomacy*, pp. 191–4.
21 Lord Keynes to HD, 26th September 1945 (T247/47/2).
22 Lord Keynes to HD, 1st October 1945 (T247/47/4).
23 *Note by Chancellor of the Exchequer to the four Ministers* (n.d.; T236/439).
24 HD to Lord Keynes, 2nd October 1945 (T247/47/5).
25 HD telegram to Lord Halifax, No. 10094 PRISEC, 8th October 1945 (T236/439).
26 HD telegram to Lord Halifax, No. 10024 PRISEC, 12th October 1945 (T236/439).
27 HTA, pp. 73–5.
28 Gardner, *Sterling-Dollar Diplomacy*, p. 194.
29 HTA, p. 77.
30 Lord Robbins, *Autobiography of an Economist*, Macmillan, 1971, p. 207.
31 HDD, 7th December, 6th November 1945.
32 D. Jay, *Change and Fortune*, Hutchinson, 1980, p. 137.
33 HDD, 7th December 1945.
34 Lord Trend, interview.
35 J. C. R. Dow, *The Management of the British Economy, 1945–60*, Cambridge University Press, 1964, p. 18n.
36 Robbins, *Autobiography*, p. 209.
37 13th December 1945. HC Deb. [417] col. 439.
38 Lord Kahn blames Keynes for the severity of the terms. Kahn, at the time a temporary civil servant in the Board of Trade, recalls receiving a telegram on the subject of the convertibility clause from Keynes 'who gave us about half an hour in which to make up our minds'. Kahn considers that Keynes was making an error 'in supposing that our negotiating position was quite so weak as his concessions suggest ... ' (A. P. Thirlwall (ed.), *Keynes and International Monetary Relations*, Macmillan, 1976, p. 58.)
39 HTA, p. 86.
40 Dow, *Management of the British Economy*, p. 18.
41 Jay, *Change and Fortune*, p. 139.
42 13th December 1945. HC Deb. [417] col. 440–2.
43 HTA, pp. 73, 84–5.
44 See T. Brett, S. Gilliatt and A. Pople, 'Planned Trade, Labour Party

Policy and U.S. Intervention: The Successes and Failures of Post-War Reconstruction', *History Workshop Journal*, 1982, p. 135.

45 Harrod, *Keynes*, pp. 600–1.
46 Clarke, *Anglo-American Economic Collaboration*, pp. 52–4, 145, 152.
47 Memorandum by Lord Keynes to Sir Edward Bridges, 8th February 1946 (T247/47/14).
48 Clarke, *Anglo-American Economic Collaboration*, pp. 57–8. Clarke felt, however, that 'this was no backstop for Ministers on a failure to get adequate terms under "Justice", no alternative to "Austerity"'.
49 *New Statesman & Nation*, 8th, 15th December 1945.
50 HDD, 7th December 1945.
51 Jay, *Change and Fortune*, p. 139.
52 Lord Trend, interview.
53 Gardner, *Sterling-Dollar Diplomacy*, p. 206.
54 Clarke, *Anglo-American Economic Collaboration*, p. 56.
55 P. Einzig, *In The Centre Of Things*, Hutchinson, 1960, p. 265.
56 Clarke, *Anglo-American Economic Collaboration*, pp. 55–6.
57 L. S. Amery, *The Washington Loan Agreements*, Macdonald, 1946, p. 151. Beaverbrook argued the same case in a speech (reprinted as a pamphlet) at the end of 1945. 'There is no need to take the money', he declared. 'And if it is accepted, the nation will be plunged into difficulties instead of reaping any benefits or advantages.' (Copy in T247/47).
58 Clarke, *Anglo-American Economic Collaboration*, p. 71.
59 HD to Lord Keynes, 5th December 1945. (Keynes Papers.)
60 Jay, *Change and Fortune*, p. 139.
61 HD to J. T. Sheppard, 29th April 1946. (Sheppard Papers.)
62 Robbins, *Autobiography*, pp. 211–12.
63 HTA, p. 5.
64 Sir Hartley Shawcross's actual words, on the Third Reading of the Trade Disputes and Trade Unions Bill in April 1946, were: 'We are the masters for the moment – and not only for the moment, but for a very long time to come.' (Cited in A. Howard, 'We are the Masters Now', in M. Sissons and P. French (eds.), *Age of Austerity 1945–1951*, Hodder & Stoughton, 1963, p. 29).
65 James Callaghan, interview.
66 *Daily Herald*, 8th February 1946.
67 M. Foot, *Aneurin Bevan: A Biography*, Vol. II, *1945–1960*. Davis-Poynter, 1973, pp. 35–6.
68 Michael Foot, interview.
69 *Observer*, 15th December 1946.
70 Cited in *Tribune*, 7th February 1947.
71 Lord Trend, interview.
72 *Sunday Pictorial*, 30th March 1947.
73 *New York Herald Tribune*, 29th June 1946.
74 *Sunday Express*, 30th June 1946.
75 *New Statesman & Nation*, 29th June 1946.
76 Sir Geoffrey de Freitas, interview.

77 Lord George-Brown, James Callaghan, Lord Robens, interviews.
78 Sir Geoffrey de Freitas, John Freeman, interviews.
79 Kenneth Robinson, Roy Jenkins, interviews.
80 Lord Robens, interview.
81 Sir Oswald Mosley, *My Life*, Nelson, 1968, p. 218.
82 (Lord) Wilson, interview.
83 Lord Robens, interview.
84 John Freeman, interview.
85 Josephine Smith, interview; Ruth Dalton to Hilde Auerbach, 6th May 1945 (Auerbach Letters).
86 Auerbach Letters.
87 Josephine Smith, interview.
88 Auerbach Letters.
89 HD to Evan Durbin, 28th December 1945 (Durbin Papers).
90 Ruth Dalton to Hilde Auerbach, 2nd January 1946 (Auerbach Letters).
91 Enid MacLeod, interview.
92 Irene Wagner, interview.
93 Ruth Dalton to Hilde Auerbach, 14th April 1946 (Auerbach Letters).

XXVI *Socialist Chancellor*

1 HTA, p. 4.
2 A. Shonfield, *British Economic Policy since the War*, Penguin, 1958, p. 160.
3 *The Times*, 23rd November 1945.
4 A. Howard, 'We are the Masters Now', in M. Sissons and P. French (eds.), *Age of Austerity 1945–51*, Hodder & Stoughton, 1963, p. 15.
5 D. Coates, *The Labour Party and the Struggle for Socialism*, Cambridge University Press, 1975, p. 47.
6 Cited in A. A. Rogow and P. Shore, *The Labour Government and British Industry 1945–1951*, Blackwell, 1955, p. 13.
7 S. H. Beer, *Modern British Politics*, Faber, 1965, p. 193.
8 HD to Durbin, 26th September 1945 (Durbin Papers).
9 P. Einzig, *In the Centre of Things*, Hutchinson, 1960, p. 262.
10 H. Dalton, *Principles of Public Finance*, Routledge (1954 ed.), p. 228.
11 See I. Little, 'Fiscal Policy', in G. Worswick and P. Ady (eds.), *The British Economy 1945–50*, Oxford University Press, 1952, p. 165.
12 Lecture to the Fabian Society, 13th November 1946 (Fabian Collection (Nuffield) 64/2 Item 3).
13 9th April 1946. HC Debs [421] col. 1825 (cited in J. C. R. Dow, *The Management of the British Economy*, Cambridge University Press, 1964, p. 19).
14 Dalton had told officials of his intention to revise and develop death duties, providing his own detailed schemes for doing so, at the end of

1945. See a note by the Chancellor entitled 'Inclinations for New Year's Budget' (T171/388).

15 HTA, p. 223.

16 As we shall see, American tobacco imports were a major cause for concern. In January 1947 Dalton indicated his strong agreement with a Board of Trade comment that 'if we go on at our present rate, one fifth of the American Loan will, quite literally, go up in smoke.' (18th January 1947; T171/389/196).

17 Lecture to the Fabian Society.

18 'An Economist', *Tribune*, 11th February 1949. Dalton quotes this passage, while concealing the identity of the author, in HTA (p. 184).

19 HTA, p. 27.

20 See *Tribune*, 23rd May 1947. Dalton's taxation policy, this newspaper declared, had 'speeded up the process of getting greater equality in the distribution of all income.'

21 M. Lindsay, 'Socialism and Pseudo-Socialism', *Political Quarterly*, Vol. xix, No. 2, April–June 1948, p. 154.

22 Lecture to the Fabian Society.

23 Nevertheless, he continued to contemplate taxes that were similar in effect to the capital levy: for example, a Supplementary Estate Duty. See 'Two more possibles for Autumn Budget'. HD note (? October) 1947 (T171/393/437).

24 At the end of 1946 the Chancellor noted his intention to look again at the possibility of an 'inheritance levy' (i.e. a levy on the whole excess of a net inheritance over a given figure) in the New Year (T171/391/158). He was unable to get support for the scheme, however, and so it was decided to take no action (T171/391/163).

25 HTA, p. 116.

26 HD note to Sir E. Bridges (n.d.; T171/388).

27 HD to Earl of Crawford, 11th July 1946 (CAB 127/204).

28 In his capacity as Chairman of the Trustees of the National Gallery in the late 1950s (cited in HTA, p. 119).

29 Cited in HTA, pp. 109–10.

30 *Sunday Graphic*, 14th July 1946.

31 *Daily Telegraph*, 29th October 1946.

32 *The Economist*, 1st March 1947.

33 Sir Thomas Padmore, interview.

34 *Spectator*, 2nd November 1945.

35 S. Pollard, 'The Nationalisation of the Banks', in D. Martin and D. Rubinstein (eds.), *Ideology and the Labour Movement*, Croom Helm, 1979, pp. 167–90.

36 N. Davenport, *Memoirs of a City Radical*, Weidenfeld & Nicolson, 1974, pp. 49–50.

37 H. Dalton, *Practical Socialism for Britain*, Routledge, 1935, p. 207.

38 Cited in C. N. Ward-Perkins, 'Banking Developments', in Worswick and Ady (eds.), *The British Economy 1945–1950*, p. 217.

39 HTA, pp. 41–2.

40 27th November 1945. CAB 128/2/34.
41 Davenport, *Memoirs*, pp. 154–5, 161.
42 S. Strange, *Sterling and British Policy*, Oxford University Press, 1971, pp. 231–2.
43 HTA, p. 43.
44 R. S. Sayers, *Modern Banking*, Oxford University Press, 1967, pp. 72–3.
45 Dalton, *Principles of Public Finance* (1954 ed.), p. 231.
46 'Random Reflections from a Visit to the U.S.A.' Memorandum for the Chancellor of the Exchequer by Lord Keynes, 4th April 1946 (T247/47/18).
47 The following account draws heavily on C. M. Kennedy, 'Monetary Policy', in Worswick and Ady (eds.), *The British Economy 1945–50*, pp. 188–206.
48 Dalton, *Principles of Public Finance* (1954 ed.), p. 254.
49 15th April 1947. HC Debs [436] col. 61.
50 Cited in H. Dalton, *Financing Labour's Plan*, Labour Party, 1946, p. 3.
51 *The Times*, 24th October 1945.
52 Davenport, *Memoirs*, pp. 156–7.
53 HDD, 12th April 1946.
54 16th October 1946. HC Debs [427] col. 904.
55 Cited in *Picture Post*, 2nd November 1946.
56 Davenport, *Memoirs*, p. 157.
57 Dalton, *Principles of Public Finance* (1954 ed.), p. 239.
58 Cited in Davenport, *Memoirs*, p. 159.
59 Kennedy, 'Monetary Policy', pp. 201, 195.
60 *Tribune*, 11th February 1949.
61 Davenport, *Memoirs*, pp. 157–8.
62 Political and Economic Planning, *Government and Industry*, PEP, February 1952, pp. 40–1.
63 Joan Robinson, cited in Kennedy, 'Monetary Policy', p. 206.
64 A. Bevan, *In Place of Fear*, Heinemann, 1952, p. 10 (cited in Coates, *The Labour Party*, p. 44).
65 Rogow and Shore, *The Labour Government*, p. 13.
66 B. Donoughue and G. W. Jones, *Herbert Morrison*, Weidenfeld & Nicolson, 1973, p. 349n.
67 H. Morrison, *Economic Planning*, Institute of Public Administration, 1947, p. 9.
68 H. Morrison, *Socialisation and Transport*, Constable, 1933, pp. 294–5.
69 Dalton, *Practical Socialism*, pp. 312–14.
70 Sir E. Bridges, *Treasury Control*, Athlone Press, 1950, p. 15.
71 Rogow and Shore, *The Labour Government*, p. 190.
72 A. Booth, 'The "Keynesian Revolution" in Economic Policy-Making', *Economic History Review*, Vol. xxxvi, No. 1, February 1983, p. 119.
73 *Evening Standard*, 15th January 1947, cited in Donoughue and Jones, *Herbert Morrison*, p. 625.
74 Lord Trend, interview.
75 Donoughue and Jones, *Herbert Morrison*, p. 348.

76 H. Morrison, *Government and Parliament: A Survey from Inside*, Oxford University Press, 1954, p. 308 (cited in Dow, *Management of the British Economy*, p. 14).
77 Morrison, *Economic Planning*, p. 4.
78 Sir H. Henderson, *The Uses and Abuses of Economic Planning* (Rede Lecture, 9th May 1947), Cambridge University Press, 1947, p. 14.
79 Bridges, *Treasury Control*, pp. 24–5.
80 D. N. Chester, 'Machinery of Government and Planning', in Worswick and Ady (eds.), *The British Economy 1945–1951*, pp. 338–9.
81 Dow, *Management of the British Economy*, p. 8.
82 Bridges, *Treasury Control*, pp. 15–16.
83 James Meade, interview.
84 Robbins, *Autobiography*, p. 188.
85 Morrison, *Economic Planning*, p. 9.
86 James Meade, interview.
87 Donoughue and Jones, *Herbert Morrison*, p. 350; Booth, 'The "Keynesian Revolution"', p. 120.
88 James Meade, interview.
89 James Meade, unpublished diary, 30th June 1946.
90 Lord Trend, interview.
91 James Meade, unpublished diary, 20th October 1945, 13th January 1946; interview.
92 Booth, 'The "Keynesian Revolution"', pp. 103–23 passim.
93 Professor Sir Austin Robinson, interview.
94 Robbins, *Autobiography*, p. 211.
95 G. D. N. Worswick, 'Direct Controls', in Worswick and Ady (eds.), *British Economy 1945–1951*, p. 312.
96 Beer, *Modern British Politics*, p. 194.
97 *Spectator*, 25th March 1949.
98 R. Skidelsky, 'Is Keynes Still Relevant?', *Encounter*, April 1979, Vol. LII, No. 4, p. 35.
99 Beer, *Modern British Politics*, p. 195.
100 R. Harrod, *And So It Goes On*, Rupert Hart-Davis, 1951, p. 69. Harrod's remarks first appeared in January 1949 in a review of a book by Meade (see below).
101 In *Planning and the Price-Mechanism: The Liberal–Socialist Solution* (Allen & Unwin, 1948) Meade argued in favour of a relaxation of controls and return to the market. Unlike many Keynesians, however, he supported measures to reduce large personal fortunes, and advocated a capital levy.
102 See Booth, 'The "Keynesian Revolution"', *passim*.

XXVII *Crisis*

1 HTA, pp. 93, 131, 59, 153–5.
2 27th September 1946. T236/473.

3   HDD, 26th September 1946.
4   HTA, pp. 187, 254.
5   Susan Cooper, 'Snoek Piquante', in M. Sissons and P. French (eds.), *The Age of Austerity: 1945–1951*, Hodder & Stoughton, 1963, p. 47.
6   HD to Attlee, 19th November 1946 (Dalton Papers 9/2 (72)).
7   Attlee to HD, 21st November 1946 (Dalton Papers 9/2 (76)).
8   Philip M. Williams, *Hugh Gaitskell: A Political Biography*, Jonathan Cape, 1979, pp. 134–6.
9   *The Times*, 29th, 30th January, 6th, 8th February 1947.
10 HDD, 6th February 1947.
11 *The Times*, 12th, 13th February 1947.
12 D. Jay, *Change and Fortune*, Hutchinson, 1980, p. 162.
13 *The Times*, 18th February 1947.
14 *Textile Bulletin*, March 1947.
15 HDD, 10th February 1947.
16 F. Williams, *A Prime Minister Remembers*, Heinemann, 1961, p. 221.
17 Sir Richard Clarke, *Anglo-American Economic Collaboration in War and Peace 1942–1949*, Oxford University Press, 1982, p. 85, n. 5.
18 HDD, 1st August 1946.
19 Dr Urwick, private correspondence with the author.
20 HDD, 28th April 1947.
21 HTA, p. 193–4.
22 HD to Attlee, 20th January 1947 (Dalton Papers 9/3 (2)).
23 HTA, p. 197.
24 HDD, 27th January 1947.
25 HTA, p. 254.
26 HDD, 21st March 1947.
27 18th January 1947. T171/389/196.
28 *The Economist*, 19th April 1947.
29 HTA, pp. 206–9. Sir Richard Clarke suggested that, by demonstrating that the British would not go on accepting commitments which did not represent national interests, the Government's decision may, in addition, have helped create the climate of opinion in U.S. political circles which led to the Marshall Plan (*Anglo-American Economic Collaboration*, p. 8, n. 6).
30 CAB 128/10/28.
31 HDD, 13th June 1947.
32 J. C. R. Dow, *The Management of the British Economy 1945–60*, Cambridge University Press, 1964, pp. 23–4.
33 Memorandum, 2nd May 1947 (Dalton Papers 9/3 (15)).
34 Helen Pease, interview.
35 HTA, p. 5.
36 Lord Trend, interview.
37 8th July 1947, HC Debs, [439], 2158 (cited in Dow, *The Management of the British Economy*, p. 23).
38 24th July 1947. Harold Nicolson, unpublished diary.
39 HDD, 25th July 1947.

40 R. N. Gardner, *Sterling-Dollar Diplomacy* (first published Oxford University Press, 1956), McGraw-Hill, 1969, p. 312.
41 CAB 128/10/90.
42 Cabinet Memorandum by the Chancellor of the Exchequer, C.P. (47) 221 (PREM 8/489).
43 HDD, 30th July 1947.
44 HTA, p. 259.
45 HDD, 8th August 1947.
46 HTA, p. 259.
47 HDD, 30th, 31st July 1947.
48 CAB 128/10/100.
49 CAB 128/10/111.
50 7th August 1947, HC Debs [441], col. 1664.
51 HDD, 8th, 12th August 1947.
52 PREM 8/489.
53 Philip M. Williams (ed.), *The Diary of Hugh Gaitskell, 1945–56*, Jonathan Cape, 1983, p. 24, 12th August 1947.
54 HTA, p. 261.
55 Gardner, *Sterling-Dollar Diplomacy*, p. 312.
56 Jay, *Change and Fortune*, p. 165.
57 Cited in Gardner, *Sterling-Dollar Diplomacy*, p. 323.
58 HTA, p. 262.
59 *Daily Mail*, 23rd August 1947.
60 HTA, p. 254.
61 D. Butler and A. Sloman, *British Political Facts 1900–1979*, Macmillan, 1980, p. 341.
62 Clarke, *Anglo-American Economic Collaboration*, pp. 177, 180.
63 HC Debs [441], cols. 1660, 1488.
64 Jay, *Change and Fortune*, p. 139.
65 Dalton was himself an admirer of Gardner's book, which he described as 'very well, simply and clearly written' (HTA, p. 69n.). He did not, however, refer to it in his own account of the convertibility crisis.
66 Gardner, *Sterling-Dollar Diplomacy*, p. 311.
67 18th July 1947. HC Debs [440], cols. 741–2 (cited in ibid., p. 311).
68 S. P. Chambers, 'The Economic Crisis', 1st November 1947 (T172/2023).
69 HD to John Snyder, 15th April 1947 (T171/390/170).
70 Lord Trend, interview.
71 HC Debs [441], col. 1762.
72 HD to John Snyder, 25th November 1946 (Dalton Papers 9/2 (71)).
73 Gardner, *Sterling-Dollar Diplomacy*, pp. 316 et seq.
74 CAB 128/10/121-4.
75 Gardner, *Sterling-Dollar Diplomacy*, p. 319.
76 HC Debs [441], col. 1475.
77 N. Davenport, *Memoirs of a City Radical*, Weidenfeld & Nicolson, 1974, p. 167.
78 HTA, p. 255. See also H. Dalton, *Principles of Public Finance*, Routledge (1954 ed.), p. 244.

79 HDD, 30th July 1947.
80 Dow, *Management of the British Economy*, p. 23.
81 Gardner, *Sterling-Dollar Diplomacy*, pp. 206–7, 325 et seq.
82 Clarke, *Anglo-American Economic Collaboration*, p. 56.
83 HTA, p. 82.
84 Gardner, *Sterling-Dollar Diplomacy*, pp. 327–8.
85 James Meade, cited in HTA, p. 83.
86 Lord Robbins, *Autobiography*, Macmillan, 1971, pp. 211–12.
87 Lord Robbins, interview.
88 Cobbold to Sir Wilfrid Eady, 16th October 1947. Cited in Clarke, *Anglo-American Economic Collaboration*, p. 184.
89 Dow, *The Management of the British Economy*, p. 23.
90 HDD, 8th August 1947.
91 See Jay, *Change and Fortune*, p. 164; also Dow, *The Management of the British Economy*, p. 25.

XXVIII *Insolence of Office*

1 Lord Trend, interview.
2 M. Foot, *Aneurin Bevan: A Biography,* Vol. II, 1945–1960, Davis-Poynter, 1973, pp. 35, 138.
3 HDD, 20th May 1946.
4 Woodrow Wyatt, 'Sir (Richard) Stafford Cripps (1889–1952)', in E. T. Williams and H. M. Palmer (eds.), *The Dictionary of National Biography 1951–1960*, Oxford University Press, 1971, p. 273.
5 Philip M. Williams (ed.), *The Diary of Hugh Gaitskell, 1945–56*, Jonathan Cape, 1983, p. 26, 12th August 1947.
6 H. Dalton, *Practical Socialism for Britain*, Routledge, 1935, pp. 145–6.
7 HTA, p. 136.
8 HDD, 12th April 1946, 28th April 1947.
9 See B. Donoughue and G. W. Jones, *Herbert Morrison: Portrait of a Politician*, Weidenfeld & Nicolson, 1973, pp. 400 et seq., for a fuller account of the iron and steel controversy.
10 Cabinet minutes, 7th August 1947 (CAB 128/10/118).
11 HDD, 17th January 1947.
12 'If Congress Rejects the Loan'. Lord Keynes memorandum to Sir D. Waley, R. W. B. Clarke and Mr. Rowe-Dutton, 22nd February 1946 (T247/47/16).
13 HDD, 17th January 1947.
14 Cabinet minutes, 28th January 1947 (CAB 128/9/55).
15 See HTA, Chapter XXIII, 'Fight Against Military Expenditure', passim.
16 CAB 128/9/55.
17 Foot, *Aneurin Bevan*, Vol. II, p. 90.
18 HDD, 29th November 1946.
19 *New Statesman & Nation*, 9th August 1947.
20 Lord Trend, interview.

21 Sir Richard Clarke, *Anglo-American Economic Collaboration*, Oxford University Press, 1982, pp. 78–9.
22 J. M. Lee, *Reviewing the Machinery of Government 1942–1952: An Essay on the Anderson Committee and its Successors* (mimeo), 1977, p. 40. See also H. Pelling, 'The Labour Government of 1945–51: The Determination of Policy', in M. Bentley and J. Stevenson (eds.), *High and Low Politics in Modern Britain: Ten Studies*, Oxford University Press, 1983, p. 272.
23 *The Economist*, 30th August 1947.
24 J. Jewkes, *Ordeal by Planning*, Macmillan, 1948, p. 100.
25 Donoughue and Jones, *Herbert Morrison*, pp. 391–6.
26 HDD, 1st April 1946, 5th, 24th February 1947.
27 Ruth Dalton to Hilde Auerbach, 25th February 1947 (Auerbach Letters).
28 HDD, 1st August 1946.
29 *Sunday Express*, 30th March 1947.
30 HDD, 5th February, 28th April, 2nd, 1st May 1947.
31 Lord Trend, interview.
32 Donoughue and Jones, *Herbert Morrison*, p. 406.
33 HDD, 1st May 1947.
34 HD to E. Durbin, 9th March 1947 (Durbin Papers).
35 Lord George-Brown, interview.
36 HDD, 25th, 26th, 28th July 1947.
37 From Wells's own account, *Evening Standard*, 7th June 1961.
38 George Brown, *In My Way*, Gollancz, 1971, Penguin, 1972, p. 51.
39 Lord George-Brown, interview.
40 HDD, 30th July, 6th October, 31st July, 1st August 1947.
41 Ruth Dalton to Will Davis, 28th August 1947 (Davis Letters).
42 N. Davenport, *Memoirs of a City Radical*, Weidenfeld & Nicolson, 1974, p. 171.
43 HDD, 25th August 1947.
44 Davenport, *Memoirs of a City Radical*, p. 171.
45 HDD, 5th September 1947.
46 Most of the evidence for this affair comes from Dalton's diary and from HTA (pp. 236–47). Donoughue and Jones add some points of detail from Morrison's papers (*Herbert Morrison* pp. 413 et seq.).
47 CAB 128/10/144.
48 HDD, 5th, 8th, 9th September 1947.
49 Williams (ed.), *Diary of Hugh Gaitskell*, p. 36, 14th October 1947.
50 D. Jay, 'Civil Servant and Minister', in W. T. Rodgers (ed.), *Hugh Gaitskell 1906–1963*, Thames & Hudson, 1964, p. 90.
51 Williams (ed.), *Diary of Hugh Gaitskell*, p. 24, 12th August 1947.
52 Foot, *Aneurin Bevan*, Vol. II, pp. 93–4; Michael Foot, interview.
53 HDD, 17th August 1947.
54 *Time and Tide*, 8th February 1962.
55 *Royal Commission on the Press: Minutes of Evidence*, 28th April 1948 (Cmd. 7475), H.M.S.O., 1949, pp. 9–10.
56 Foot, *Aneurin Bevan*, Vol. II, p. 89.
57 Cabinet minutes, 20th September 1947 (CAB 128/10/149).

58 *The Times*, 1st October 1947.
59 CAB 128/10/160.
60 HDD, 2nd October 1947.
61 P. Noel-Baker to HD, 9th October 1947 (Dalton Papers 9/3 (37)).
62 G. Brown to HD, 3rd October 1947 (Dalton Papers 9/3 (35)).
63 HDD, 12th October 1947; Attlee to Morrison, 3rd October 1947 (Morrison Papers).
64 *New Statesman & Nation*, 11th, 4th October 1947.
65 Williams (ed.), *The Diary of Hugh Gaitskell*, p. 36, 14th October 1947.
66 Lord Trend, interview.
67 N. Nicolson (ed.), *Harold Nicolson: Diaries and Letters 1945–1962*, Collins, 1968, p. 111, 8th October 1947.
68 HDD, 12th October 1947.
69 *Tribune*, 2nd March 1962.
70 HD to F. Williams, 26th September 1947 (Francis Williams Papers, FWS 8/5).
71 CAB 129/10/165.
72 Mr. Gorell-Barnes to C. R. Attlee, October 1947 (PREM 8/494).
73 Economic Planning Board Report, 16th September 1947, contained in the minutes of the first meeting of the Cabinet Economic Policy Committee, 9th October 1947 (PREM 8/494).
74 CAB 128/10/175 (C.P. (47) 283).
75 HDD, 20th October 1947.
76 *New Statesman & Nation*, 1st November 1947.
77 H.C. Debs [443] cols. 398–400.
78 Sir E. Bridges to HD, 25th October 1947 (Dalton Papers 9/3 (33)).
79 HDD, 24th October 1947.
80 *Daily Telegraph*, 3rd November 1947.
81 HD to W. Davis, 6th November 1947 (Davis Letters).
82 Ian Mikardo, 'Was it a Workers' Budget?', in *Tribune*, 21st November 1947.
83 *New Statesman & Nation*, 8th November 1947.
84 *Financial Times*, 12th November 1947. See also *The Economist*, 8th November 1947.
85 Lord Trend, interview.
86 D. Jay, *Change and Fortune: A Political Record*, Hutchinson, 1980, p. 167.
87 H.C. Debs [444] cols. 390–8.
88 *Daily Telegraph*, 13th November 1947.
89 *The Report of the Select Committee on the Budget Disclosures*, H.M.S.O., 1947, p. 23.
90 H.C. Debs [444] col. 405.
91 *Daily Telegraph*, 13th November 1947.
92 *The Economist*, 15th November 1947.
93 *Financial Times*, 13th November 1947.
94 *Manchester Guardian*, 15th November 1947.
95 This argument is developed by Anthony Crosland, writing anonymously as 'An Economist' in *Tribune*, 11th February 1949.

96 J. C. R. Dow, *The Management of the British Economy 1945–60*, Cambridge University Press, 1964, p. 28.
97 H.C. Debs [444] col. 439.
98 HTA, p. 275.

XXIX *A Single Sentence*

1 *The Report of the Select Committee on the Budget Disclosures*, H.M.S.O., 1947, p. 4.
2 P. Einzig, *In the Centre of Things*, Hutchinson, 1960, p. 265.
3 *Report of the Select Committee*, pp. 24, iii.
4 Robert Carvel, interview.
5 *Report of the Select Committee*, p. v.
6 Robert Carvel, interview.
7 *Evening Standard*, 12th November 1947.
8 Robert Carvel, interview.
9 *Report of the Select Committee*, p. 10.
10 Robert Carvel, private correspondence with the author.
11 Robert Carvel, interview. The *Spectator* suggested that 'a journalist in such circumstances would be at the telephone within sixty seconds'. (21st November 1947). In view of the distance, and the need to negotiate a lift, this is unlikely.
12 *Report of the Select Committee*, p. 25.
13 This fits Dalton's own evidence that he spoke to Carvel between 3.0 and 3.15, and that he was on the Front Bench by 3.20; also Carvel's statement that he finished telephoning around 3.15 to 3.20. (*Report*, pp. 1, 8). We may therefore discount Jay's recently published recollection that the Dalton–Carvel exchange did not take place until 3.26 or 3.27 (*Change and Fortune*, Hutchinson, 1980, p. 167).
14 *Report of the Select Committee*, pp. 20, 8, 22, 21.
15 Robert Carvel, interview.
16 *Report of the Select Committee*, p. 11.
17 Einzig, *In the Centre of Things*, pp. 265–6. We may deduce that Einzig and Carvel passed each other during Carvel's second trip because Einzig makes no reference to Robert, Robert has no memory of seeing Einzig, and Einzig gave the time as 'shortly before 3.30 p.m.'.
18 *Report of the Select Committee*, pp. 20, 22.
19 H.C. Debs [444] col. 390.
20 *Report of the Select Committee*, pp. 25–6, 47–51.
21 Sir Trevor Evans, interview.
22 *Report of the Select Committee*, pp. 49–51.
23 Jay, *Change and Fortune*, p. 169.
24 *Report of the Select Committee*, pp. 18–19.
25 The explanation for this story may be that at Bouverie Street (but not at the Wharf), the *correction* to the Carvel story was added when the machine was stopped, routinely, for the racing results. It should be borne in mind that Dalton did not *finish* listing tax changes until almost

4.30, so copies which reached the streets before that time anticipated at least part of the Chancellor's announcement. Moreover, somebody reading the Carvel fudge at, say, 4.0 p.m., would have been twenty minutes or half an hour ahead of anybody listening to the Chancellor in the House. This bears on the 'chance-in-a-million' theory. Quick responses in the *Star* office were needed to get the 'forecast' on to the streets by 3.53. But Carvel, the *Star* office, and the printers would have had to be extraordinarily, indeed negligently, slow not to have made it well in advance of 4.30.

26 Robert Carvel, interview, and private correspondence with the author.
27 Sir Victor Raikes, interview.
28 Robert Carvel, interview.
29 Philip M. Williams (ed.), *The Diary of Hugh Gaitskell, 1945–1956*, Jonathan Cape, 1983, p. 45, 14th November 1947.
30 CAB, 128/10/200.
31 HTA, p. 276.
32 *Report of the Select Committee*, p. 1.
33 Lord Trend, interview.
34 PREM 8/435.
35 HTA, pp. 276–7.
36 Jay, *Change and Fortune*, pp. 167–8.
37 *Daily Mail*, 14th November 1947.
38 H.C. Debs [444] col. 551.
39 Jay, *Change and Fortune*, p. 168.
40 Williams (ed.), *The Diary of Hugh Gaitskell*, p. 45, 14th November 1947.
41 Lord Morrison, *Herbert Morrison: An Autobiography*, Odhams Press, 1960, p. 262.
42 Robert Carvel, interview.
43 *Daily Mail*, 15th November 1947.
44 *Daily Express, Daily Mail*, 14th November 1947.
45 If what Dalton told the inquiry was accurate, it was barely three hours. See also HTA, p. 280, where Dalton quotes the findings of the Report – and the note from Helsby to Attlee (PREM 8/435) – which proposes 2.15 p.m. as the time of the original meeting between Dalton and the Prime Minister.
46 HTA, pp. 278–9.
47 Dr Urwick, private correspondence with the author.
48 HTA, p. 280.
49 Dalton Papers, 9/3 (67).
50 HTA, p. 285. According to *The Times* (14th November 1947), the Prime Minister had an audience with the King at 6 p.m. This presumably followed the acceptance of Dalton's resignation.
51 Morrison, *Herbert Morrison*, p. 262.
52 Sir Victor Raikes, interview.
53 Einzig, *In the Centre of Things*, p. 266.
54 *Report of the Select Committee*, p. 13.
55 HTA, p. 279.

56 *Report of the Select Committee*, p. 31.
57 17th November 1947 (PREM 8/435 and CAB 27/240 Y/P 7659).
58 H. Macmillan, *Tides of Fortune 1945–55*, Macmillan, 1969, p. 59.
59 Harold Nicolson, unpublished diary, 14th November 1947.
60 Macmillan, *Tides of Fortune*, p. 59.
61 Lord Moran, *Winston Churchill: The Struggle for Survival*, Constable, 1966, p. 378. Entry for 7th December 1947.
62 Macmillan, *Tides of Fortune*, p. 59.
63 John Parker, interview.
64 *Sunday Dispatch*, 16th November 1947; Macmillan, *Tides of Fortune*, p. 59.
65 Williams (ed.), *The Diary of Hugh Gaitskell*, p. 45, 14th November 1947.
66 *Financial Times*, 17th November 1947.
67 *Clem Attlee: The Granada Historical Records Interview*, Panther Record, 1967, p. 45.
68 R. Blake, *The Unknown Prime Minister*, Eyre & Spottiswoode, 1955, p. 147.
69 17th November 1947. Attlee's leniency towards Alexander (in contrast to his toughness towards Dalton) is the more remarkable because it occurred less than two months after a stern warning by the Prime Minister on the subject of Cabinet security. On 16th June, Morrison had complained of leakages of his affairs to Sunday newspapers. The Prime Minister responded a week later with a printed Cabinet Paper (C.P. (47) 186) complaining of recent 'serious leakages' and urging greater discretion by ministers (PREM 8/436). Perhaps this warning was in Attlee's mind when he sacked Dalton. If so, it is notable that he took no action against Alexander for a breach which might have caused damage of a far more serious nature.
70 *New Statesman & Nation*, 22nd November 1947.
71 Cited in 'American Press Survey', prepared by the American Information Department of the Foreign Office, 15th November 1947 (Dalton Papers).
72 *Granada Historical Records Interview*, p. 45.
73 HD to Louis Spears, 22nd November 1947. Spears Papers (SPRS 1/102).
74 *Observer*, 16th November 1947.
75 Williams (ed.), *The Diary of Hugh Gaitskell*, p. 46, 14th November 1947.
76 HTA, p. 281.
77 Michael Foot, interview.
78 F. Williams, *Nothing So Strange*, Cassell, 1970, p. 226.
79 Williams (ed.), *The Diary of Hugh Gaitskell*, p. 46, 14th November 1947.
80 Sir Geoffrey de Freitas, interview.
81 HTA, p. 279. Macmillan speculated in his memoirs that 'the Dalton–Cripps manoeuvres to remove [Attlee] from the Leadership' may have had something to do with the Prime Minister's decision (*Tides of Fortune*, p. 60).
82 *Daily Mail*, 15th, 17th November 1947.
83 *Tribune*, 21st November 1947.

84 *New Statesman & Nation*, 22nd November 1947.
85 Michael Foot, interview.
86 *The Economist*, 22nd November 1947.
87 *Manchester Guardian*, 15th November 1947.
88 *Observer*, 16th November 1947.
89 K. Harris, *Attlee*, Weidenfeld & Nicolson, 1982, p. 110.
90 See F. Williams, *A Prime Minister Remembers*, Heinemann, 1961, p. 224.
91 *Financial Times*, 17th November 1947.
92 American Press Survey (Dalton Papers). This passage has been marked, presumably by Dalton himself.
93 N. Davenport, *Memoirs of a City Radical*, Weidenfeld & Nicolson, 1974, p. 171.
94 HDD, 4th April 1948.
95 HTA, p. 6.
96 Lord Trend, interview.
97 F. Williams, *The Triple Challenge*, Heinemann, 1948, p. 50.
98 *New Statesman & Nation*, 22nd November 1947.
99 22nd November 1947. There was one odd incident which may have been somewhere in Dalton's mind. Secrecy over the Chancellor's suspension of convertibility broadcast on August 20th (secrecy which, as we have seen, was dangerously breached by a politician, Alexander) had brought an angry reaction from the B.B.C. and Fleet St. Sir Edward Bridges had responded appeasingly. In future, he promised the Editor of B.B.C. News, information about a key ministerial broadcast would be supplied *an hour and a quarter* in advance of its delivery. (A. P. Ryan to Sir Edward Bridges 21st August 1947; Treasury minute 14th October 1947. B.B.C. Archives R 51/55.) The Budget speech was Dalton's first major ministerial announcement after this row. When Carvel asked about the Budget only minutes before the House was due to be informed (and, by a coincidence, *precisely an hour and a quarter* before the Chancellor finished speaking), was Dalton, in answering him, unconsciously reacting to the complaints of twelve weeks before?
100 HD to Leonard Woolf, 22nd November 1947 (Berg Collection, New York Public Library).
101 F. Williams, *A Prime Minister Remembers*, Heinemann, 1961, p. 222.
102 Williams (ed.), *The Diary of Hugh Gaitskell*, p. 57, 16th February 1948.
103 HTA, pp. 291–2.
104 Davenport, *Memoirs of a City Radical*, p. 172.
105 HTA, p. 6.
106 In asking the Parliamentary Question which brought the Chancellor down, Raikes stated that newspapers containing the disclosure were on sale for fifteen minutes before the start of the Chancellor's announcement. Nobody challenged this. The inquiry revealed that the maximum conceivable length of time was eight minutes.
107 Williams (ed.), *The Diary of Hugh Gaitskell*, p. 57, 16th February 1948.
108 HTA, p. 6.

109 HDD, 14th November 1948.
110 *Manchester Guardian*, 15th November 1947.
111 D. Marquand, 'Sir Stafford Cripps', in Sissons and French (eds.), *The Age of Austerity*, Hodder & Stoughton, 1963, p. 176.
112 HD to Evan Durbin, 9th March 1947 (Durbin Papers).

XXX *Aftermath*

1 Lord Trend, interview.
2 Enid MacLeod, interview.
3 Olga Davenport, interview.
4 *The Times*, 1st November 1947.
5 Sir Thomas Padmore, interview.
6 N. Davenport, *Memoirs of a City Radical*, Weidenfeld & Nicolson, 1974, p. 173; Olga Davenport, interview.
7 *Daily Express*, 17th November 1947.
8 HTA, pp. 282–3.
9 Auerbach Letters.
10 Josephine Smith, interview.
11 E. Durbin to C. R. F. Beards, 12th January 1948 (Attlee Papers, Box 5).
12 Lady Brook, interview.
13 HTA, pp. 282–3.
14 Robert Carvel, interview.
15 John Carvel to HD, 13th November 1947 (Dalton Papers 9/3 (68)).
16 Robert Carvel, interview.
17 John Freeman, Sir Trevor Evans, interviews.
18 Robert Carvel, interview.
19 Such resignations are, indeed, comparatively rare. In *British Political Facts 1900–1979*, Macmillan, 1980, (pp. 81–3) David Butler and Anne Sloman list a number of cases of resignation 'where the individual actions of ministers have been thought impolitic or unworthy'. Of ten ministers whose resignations clearly fall into this category between 1914 and 1979, Dalton was the only one ever to hold ministerial office again.
20 John Freeman, interview.
21 HTA, p. 287.
22 *Manchester Guardian*, 15th November 1947.
23 HTA, p. 280; *News Chronicle*, 18th November 1947; *Observer*, 23rd November 1947. The original of Dalton's diary for late November, part of which is quoted in HTA, has disappeared.
24 Trevor Evans in *Daily Express*, 14th November 1947; *Observer*, 23rd November 1947.
25 Philip M. Williams (ed.), *The Diary of Hugh Gaitskell, 1945–1956*, Jonathan Cape, 1983, pp. 49–50, 4th December 1947.
26 *Observer*, 23rd November 1947.
27 Michael Foot, interview.
28 Wilson Broadbent, *Daily Mail*, 17th November 1947.

29 *Observer*, 23rd November 1947.
30 Cited in HTA, p. 300. Meanwhile behind the scenes, Douglas Jay (who had become Economic Secretary at the Treasury) had been encouraged by Dalton to press for the inclusion in the Budget of a wealth tax of 1 per cent on personal capital fortunes as defined for death duties (Jay, *Change and Fortune*, Hutchinson, 1980, p. 184).
31 *Daily Telegraph*, 9th April 1948.
32 Colin Brogan in *Daily Telegraph*, 13th April 1948.
33 Harold Nicolson, unpublished diary, 8th February 1948.
34 HDD, 4th April 1948. The italics are Dalton's own.
35 Attlee to HD, 30th December 1947 (Dalton Papers 9/4 (2)).
36 One junior minister, Hector MacNeil, privately predicted Dalton's return because of the speech. (Williams (ed.), *The Diary of Hugh Gaitskell*, 23rd April 1948, p. 61.)
37 HDD, 13th, 15th and 16th April 1948.
38 *Out of Doors* (London), July–August 1948.
39 *Socialist Advance*, July 1951.
40 *Out of Doors*, July–August 1948.
41 HDD, 26th May, 1st June 1948.
42 Downing Street statement, cited in *Daily Telegraph*, 1st June 1948.
43 Sir Norman Brook to Attlee, 1st June 1948 (PREM 8/722).
44 *Sunday Pictorial*, 6th June 1948.
45 HDD, 2nd June 1948. See also *Daily Mail*, 2nd June 1948.
46 *Tribune*, 4th June 1948.
47 Dalton did what little was required of him in connection with the Duchy well, and was regarded by officials as a 'good Chancellor'. (Sir Robert Somerville, interview.)
48 Sir Thomas Padmore, interview. For Dalton's committees, see PREM 8/722 (9th June 1948).
49 F. Williams, *The Triple Challenge*, Heinemann, 1948, pp. 44–5.
50 *Evening News*, 1st June 1948.
51 HDD, 11th September 1948.
52 Ibid., 14th November 1948.
53 *Daily Graphic*, 2nd October 1948. The others were Morrison and Shinwell.
54 See John Gross, 'The Lynskey Tribunal', in Sissons and French (eds.), *The Age of Austerity*, Hodder & Stoughton, 1963, pp. 266–86, passim.
55 *Star*, 7th December 1948.
56 *Evening Standard*, *Evening News*, 7th December 1948.
57 HDD, end of 1948; Lord Shawcross, interview. But the Lord Chancellor, Lord Jowitt, advised Dalton that if his conscience was clear he should say 'cross-examine and be damned!' HD to Attlee, 22nd December 1948 (Dalton Papers 9/4 (142)).
58 *Report of the Tribunal appointed to inquire into Allegations reflecting on the Official Conduct of Ministers of the Crown and other Public Servants* (Cmd. 7617), H.M.S.O., 1949, pp. 71–3; *Daily Herald*, 15th December 1948.
59 Lord Shawcross, interview.

60 Harold Nicolson, unpublished diary, 15th December 1948.
61 *Evening Gazette* (Middlesbrough), 17th December 1948.
62 HD to Will Davis, 4th January 1949 (Davis Letters).
63 *Daily Mirror*, 21st December 1948.
64 HD to Attlee, 22nd December 1948 (Dalton Papers 9/4 (139)).
65 24th January 1949. H.C. Debs. [460] col. 563.
66 K. Lewin to HD, 3rd January 1949 (Dalton Papers 9/6 (22)).
67 Dalton had earlier written that he intended not to speak in this debate 'unless provoked' (HD to Will Davis, 28th January 1949 (Davis Letters)).
68 3rd February 1949. H.C. Debs. [460] cols. 1896–1903.
69 *Daily Mirror*, 5th, 11th February 1949.
79 HD to Will Davis, 7th January 1949 (Davis Letters).
71 *The Times*, 12th February 1949.
72 HD to Will Davis, 4th January 1949 (Davis Letters).
73 *News Chronicle*, 12th February 1949.
74 Lord Lambton, interview.
75 F. Williams, *Triple Challenge*, Heinemann, 1948, p. 168.
76 Cited in *Daily Express*, 8th March 1949.
77 *Daily Telegraph*, 1st December 1948; *Report of the Tribunal*, p. 72.
78 This is clear from Dalton's diary and from a letter produced at the Tribunal dated 9th April, in which Dalton wrote 'I can look in next Thursday at 3 o'clock or 3.30'. Dalton saw Attlee at 3. (HDD, 15th April 1948; *Daily Telegraph*, 15th December 1948; *Report of the Tribunal*, p. 72).
79 HDD, 15th, 16th April 1948.
80 Sissons and French (eds.), *Age of Austerity*, p. 284.
81 L. Ruddock to S. R. Raffan, 23rd December 1948 (Dalton Papers 9/6 (25)).
82 HD to Will Davis, 28th March 1947 (Davis Letters).
83 HD to Attlee, 22nd December 1948 (Dalton Papers 9/4 (140)).
84 Tom Anderson, unpublished memorandum.
85 Statement for the Tribunal of Enquiry (Dalton Papers 9/6 (12)).
86 *Sunday Express*, 5th June 1949.
87 HDD, 15th April 1951.
88 Ibid., end of 1948, 20th March 1949.
89 Morrison to Attlee (memo), 29th November 1947 (Morrison Papers f 27).

XXXI *Duchy*

1 H. A. Schmitt, *European Union*, Van Nostrand Reinhold, 1969, p. 37.
2 HTA, pp. 313–14.
3 HDD, 21st November 1948.
4 *Daily Mail*, 15th November 1948.
5 HDD, 19th November 1948.
6 HTA, pp. 316–18.
7 *The Memoirs of Lord Gladwyn*, Weidenfeld & Nicolson, 1972, p. 223.

8 A. H. Robertson, *The Council of Europe*, Stevens, 1956, pp. 3–9.
9 Lord Gladwyn, *The European Idea*, Weidenfeld & Nicolson, 1966, p. 48.
10 Schmitt, *European Union*, p. 39.
11 Nicholas Davenport, interview.
12 HDD, end of 1948.
13 *Observer*, 8th May 1949.
14 HTA, p. 323.
15 H. Macmillan, *Tides of Fortune*, Macmillan, 1969, pp. 180–4.
16 *Daily Telegraph*, 9th September 1949.
17 HTA, p. 334.
18 Nicholas Davenport, interview.
19 HD to Attlee, 10th September 1949 (Dalton Papers 9/7 (45)).
20 HDD, 15th June 1949.
21 'The Dollar Situation' (draft memo) in HDD, 1st July 1949.
22 HDD, 19th July 1949.
23 So Jay later told Dalton (HDD, 12th September 1949).
24 D. Jay, *Change and Fortune*, Hutchinson, 1980, p. 187.
25 Philip M. Williams (ed.), *The Diary of Hugh Gaitskell, 1945–56*, Jonathan Cape, 1983, p. 131, 3rd August, 1949.
26 HDD, end of July 1949.
27 Philip M. Williams, *Hugh Gaitskell*, Jonathan Cape, 1979, p. 199.
28 B. Donoughue and G. W. Jones, *Herbert Morrison*, Weidenfeld & Nicolson, 1973, p. 438; Jay, *Change and Fortune*, p. 186 et seq.; Cabinet minutes 17th September 1949 (CAB 128/16/51).
29 D. Marquand, 'Sir Stafford Cripps', in Sissons and French (eds.), *The Age of Austerity*, Hodder & Stoughton, 1963, pp. 194–5.
30 Williams, *Hugh Gaitskell*, pp. 200, 204.
31 HDD, 11th, 12th, 13th October, 7th December 1949, 27th January 1950.
32 Jay, *Change and Fortune*, p. 176.
33 HDD, 24th, 27th January 1950.
34 Williams (ed.), *The Diary of Hugh Gaitskell*, p. 164, 1st February 1950.
35 The southern part of the former Barnard Castle constituency (including the market and residential town of Barnard Castle, 150 sq. miles of agricultural land, and 'some of the wildest and most beautiful fell country in England') came into the Bishop Auckland division. The new territory contained no industry and little mining, and the change, which added some 5,000 electors to Dalton's constituency, was believed to be to his disadvantage (HTA, p. 305).
36 Tom Anderson, interview.
37 Douglas Jay, interview.
38 *Tribune*, 21st October 1949.
39 Not all of this was popular locally. In the run-up to the 1950 election, Dalton was keen to keep secret Silkin's plan for a major expansion of Aycliffe (HD to Will Davis, 5th November 1949 (Davis Letters)).
40 *Daily Telegraph*, 31st January 1950.
41 *Evening Gazette* (Middlesbrough), 16th February 1950.
42 Tom Anderson, interview.

43 HDD, end of September to early October 1949; 27th February 1950, 10th December 1949, 27th January 1950.
44 HD to Attlee, 28th February 1950 (Dalton Papers 9/9 (18)).
45 HDD, 28th February 1950.
46 See *Manchester Guardian*, 1st March 1950.
47 HDD, 28th February 1950.
48 HD to Gaitskell, 5th March 1950 (Gaitskell Papers).

XXXII *Call of the Wild*

1 Baroness Sharp, interview.
2 HDD, 25th March 1951.
3 (Sir) George Chetwynd, interview.
4 Baroness Sharp, interview.
5 Later in the year, he delayed publication of the North East Development Plan, causing some of the planners to accuse him of dirty work behind the scenes. (June–September 1950; 27th October 1950. Pepler Papers, Drawer 7/3/10.)
6 *Observer*, 12th March 1950.
7 Baroness Sharp, interview.
8 *Country Life*, 23rd April 1950.
9 *Daily Telegraph*, 5th June 1950.
10 *Socialist Advance*, July 1951.
11 *Observer*, 21st April 1950.
12 *Daily Telegraph*, 17th June 1950.
13 Geoffrey Wakeford in *Daily Mail*, 17th June 1950.
14 A. H. Robertson, *The Council of Europe*, Stevens, 1956, p. 92.
15 *Manchester Guardian*, 13th June 1950.
16 *News Chronicle*, 20th June 1950.
17 N. Nicolson (ed.), *Harold Nicolson: Diaries and Letters 1945–1962*, Collins, 1968, 15th June 1950, p. 190.
18 *Manchester Guardian*, 19th June 1950.
19 *Daily Telegraph*, 17th June 1950.
20 HDD, 19th, 25th June 1950.
21 'Note by the Minister of Town and Country Planning'; speech, 22nd July 1950. (Dalton Papers 9/11 (15), 9/23 (15)).
22 H. Macmillan, *Tides of Fortune*, Macmillan, 1969, p. 216.
23 *Daily Herald*, 10th April 1950.
24 HD to Bevin, 21st August 1950 (Dalton Papers 9/9 (60)).
25 *Observer*, 20th August 1950.
26 HD to Gaitskell, 2nd September 1950 (Gaitskell Papers).
27 HTA, p. 331.
28 HD to Crosland, 25th November 1950 (Crosland Papers).
29 HTA, p. 331.
30 James Callaghan, interview.
31 HDD, 8th September 1950.

32 HD to Geoffrey Keynes, 4th August 1950 (Brooke Papers, Dalton Bequest: Da 3).
33 HDD, 11th, 12th September 1950.
34 HD to Crosland, 25th November 1950 (Crosland Papers).
35 HDD, 18th September 1950.
36 (Sir) George Chetwynd, interview.
37 HDD, 27th September 1950.
38 *Manchester Guardian*, 7th October 1950.
39 HDD, 18th August, 19th October 1950.
40 HD to Gaitskell, 19th October 1950 (Gaitskell Papers).
41 Gaitskell to HD, 30th October 1950 (Dalton Papers 9/9 (100)).
42 HDD, 19th October 1950.
43 Roy Jenkins, interview.
44 Macmillan, *Tides of Fortune*, p. 324. (Diary note, 10th April 1951.)
45 Philip M. Williams, *Hugh Gaitskell*, Jonathan Cape, 1979, p. 236.
46 Ibid., p. 240. The civil servant was William Armstrong.
47 Susan Crosland, *Tony Crosland*, Jonathan Cape, 1982, p. 49.
48 HD to Crosland, 29th September 1948 (Crosland Papers).
49 Roy Jenkins, interview.
50 Crosland to HD, 4th April 1949 (Crosland Papers). See also S. Crosland, *Tony Crosland*, p. 50.
51 HD to Crosland, 25th November 1950 (Crosland Papers). Dalton claimed to have made the remark before Crosland's election.
52 *Tribune*, 11th February 1949.
53 HD to Crosland, 17th November 1949 (Dalton Papers 9/7 (62)).
54 HDD, 1st July 1951.
55 HD to Gaitskell, 28th June 1951 (Gaitskell Papers).
56 Crosland to Ruth Dalton, February 1962 (Dalton Papers 16/1).
57 N. Davenport, *Memoirs of a City Radical*, Weidenfeld & Nicolson, 1974, p. 171; N. Davenport, interview.
58 Lord Vaizey, interview.
59 Michael Young, in 'Anthony Crosland & Socialism', *Encounter*, August 1977, Vol. XLIX, No. 2, p. 85.
60 Susan Crosland, interview.
61 Roy Jenkins, interview.
62 HD to Crosland, 25th January 1951 (Crosland Papers).
63 Susan Crosland, interview.
64 HDD, 30th October 1951.
65 Crosland, *Tony Crosland*, p. 34; Crosland Papers.
66 Crosland, *Tony Crosland*, p. 55.
67 Crosland Papers. Extracts from this letter are also quoted by Susan Crosland in *Tony Crosland*, pp. 55–6.
68 HD to Attlee, 30th November 1950 (Dalton Papers 9/9 (108). Dalton's italics).
69 See M. Foot, *Aneurin Bevan*, Vol. II, Davis-Poynter, 1973, p. 309 and n.
70 HD to Crosland, 2nd, 25th January 1951 (Crosland Papers).
71 Olga Davenport, interview.

72 Lord Walston, interview.
73 HDD, 8th February, 26th June 1951.
74 CBY, p. 88.
75 Michael Young, *Encounter*, August 1977, p. 83.
76 J. Vaizey, *In Breach of Promise*, Weidenfeld & Nicolson, 1983, p. 86.
77 HD to Crosland, 5th December 1951 (Crosland Papers).
78 HD to Attlee, 21st October 1950 (Dalton Papers 9/9 (102)).
79 HDD, 31st December 1950.
80 Philip M. Williams (ed.), *The Diary of Hugh Gaitskell*, Jonathan Cape, 1983, p. 228, 24th January 1951.
81 HDD, 31st December 1950; Williams (ed.), *The Diary of Hugh Gaitskell*, p. 228, 24th January 1951; Attlee to HD, 21st December 1950 (Dalton Papers 9/9 (117)).
82 See *News Chronicle*, 18th January 1951.
83 *Yorkshire Observer*, 19th January 1951.
84 Macmillan, *Tides of Fortune*, p. 419.
85 HDD, 25th March 1951.
86 HD to Attlee, 23rd December 1950 (Dalton Papers 9/9 (118)).
87 HDD, 25th March 1951.
88 Baroness Sharp, interview.
89 HDD, 25th March, 28th January, 9th, 19th, 20th February, 10th March 1951.
90 K. Harris, *Attlee*, Weidenfeld & Nicolson, 1982, p. 472.
91 HD to Sir Gladwyn Jebb, 11th March 1951 (Dalton Papers 9/18 (92)).
92 H.C. Debs [485] col. 1721 (14th March 1951).
93 HDD, 14th March 1951.
94 H.C. Debs [485] col. 1971. Hansard simply records: *'Interruption'*.
95 HDD, 15–16th, 22nd March 1951; HTA, p. 359.
96 Michael Stewart to J. S. Peart-Binns, 3rd September 1975. Dalton also made a case for the elderly. Supporting Gaitskell in Cabinet on 22nd March, he argued that pensions were a higher priority than free pre-scriptions (CAB 128/19/110).
97 On this Michael Foot's account which presents Dalton as *plus royaliste que le roi*, is misleading. (*Aneurin Bevan*, Vol. II, p. 319 et seq.)
98 HDD, 4th, 5th, 6th April 1951.
99 HD to Bevan, 7th April 1951. Letter kindly lent to the author by Michael Foot. (A draft copy is also to be found in Dalton Papers 9/18 (36)).
100 CAB 128/19/129.
101 HDD, 9th April 1951.
102 *Daily Express*, 12th April 1951.
103 *Observer*, 15th April 1951.
104 HDD, 10th, 11th, 14th April 1951.
105 HD to Attlee, 15th April 1951; Attlee to HD, 16th April 1951 (Dalton Papers 9/18 (20), (22)); HDD, 19th April 1951.
106 HD to Meade, 19th April 1951 (Dalton Papers 9/18 (123)).
107 CAB 128/19/143.
108 HDD, 20th April 1951.

109 Williams, *Hugh Gaitskell*, p. 258.
110 HDD, 22nd April 1951.
111 John Freeman, interview.
112 Freeman to HD, 23rd April 1951 (Dalton Papers 9/19 (78)).
113 HDD, 23rd, 25th April 1951.
114 Cited in Williams, *Hugh Gaitskell*, p. 266.
115 HDD, 6th April 1951. See also Cabinet minutes for 22nd March (CAB 128/19/110) and 9th April (CAB 128/19/128).
116 K. Harris, *Attlee*, p. 473.
117 Williams, *Hugh Gaitskell*, p. 264.
118 HTA, p. 159.
119 *People*, 19th August 1951.
120 *New Statesman & Nation*, 9th June 1951; see also *Evening News*, 17th September 1951.
121 *Daily Telegraph*, 22nd June 1951.
122 HDD, 1st June 1951.
123 *Observer*, 1st July 1951.
124 HDD, 21st June, 2nd August, 24th July 1951. Michael Foot, having himself inspected Dalton's diary while writing about Aneurin Bevan, later wrote of Donnelly as the 'compulsive informer in our midst who reported our proceedings to Hugh Dalton and thereby to the Whips'. (*Bevan*, Vol. II, p. 358 and n.) Foot, who concluded that leakages did not begin until after the election, evidently missed Dalton's diary entry for 24th July, which shows that they had begun by the summer.
125 HDD, 13th October 1951.
126 HD to Mrs M. Felton, 12th June 1951 (Dalton Papers 9/24 (10)); L. Manning, *A Life for Education*, Gollancz, 1970, pp. 196–7.
127 *Daily Telegraph*, 2nd August 1951.
128 HDD, 28th July 1951.
129 *Daily Mail*, 15th September 1951.
130 *The Economist*, 22nd September 1951.
131 *Daily Worker*, 3rd October 1951.
132 HDD, 4th, 13th October, October–November 1951.
133 Williams, *Hugh Gaitskell*, p. 283; Macmillan, *Tides of Fortune*, p. 355.
134 *Daily Telegraph*, 2nd October 1951.
135 Tom Anderson, interview.
136 *Daily Herald*, 25th October 1951.
137 HDD, end of October, 29th, 27th October 1951.

XXXIII *Sunset*

1 HDD, 10th November 1951.
2 *The Times*, 17th March 1966.
3 Ruth Dalton to Hilde Auerbach (n.d.; Auerbach Letters).
4 *Daily Mirror*, 11th January 1952.
5 HDD, 10th November 1951.

6 J. Morgan (ed.), *The Backbench Diaries of Richard Crossman*, Hamish Hamilton and Jonathan Cape, 1981, p. 34, 12th November 1951.
7 HDD, 10th November 1951, 1st May 1952.
8 See B. Jones, *The Russia Complex: The British Labour Party and the Soviet Union*, Manchester University Press, 1978, passim.
9 HDD, mid-February 1951.
10 Philip M. Williams, *Hugh Gaitskell*, Jonathan Cape, 1979, p. 246.
11 Morgan (ed.), *The Backbench Diaries of Richard Crossman*, p. 57, 19th December 1951.
12 HDD, 3rd January, 7th February, 13th May 1952.
13 M. Foot, *Aneurin Bevan*, Vol. II, Davis-Poynter, 1973, p. 374.
14 See P. Foot, *The Politics of Harold Wilson*, Penguin, 1968, pp. 23–49.
15 HDD, 3rd December 1951.
16 Roy Jenkins to HD, 31st October 1950 (Dalton Papers 9/10 (39)).
17 *Sunday Pictorial*, 4th May 1952.
18 HDD, 25th June 1952.
19 Len Williams, interview.
20 HDD, 25th June 1952.
21 HDD, 26th June 1952; *Sunday Express*, 4th May 1952.
22 HDD, 11th, 26th, 28th, 30th June, 1st, 7th, 17th, 24th July 1952.
23 *New Statesman & Nation*, 2nd June 1952.
24 HDD, 4th August 1952.
25 *Manchester Guardian*, 25th August 1952.
26 *Observer*, 31st August 1952.
27 HDD, September 1952.
28 James Callaghan, interview.
29 HDD, 25th September 1952.
30 HD to Sir Gladwyn Jebb, 26th October 1952 (Dalton Papers 9/25 (42)).
31 Tom Anderson, interview.
32 HDD, 30th September 1952.
33 Foot, *Aneurin Bevan*, Vol. II, p. 379.
34 D. Jay, *Change and Fortune*, Hutchinson, 1980, p. 223.
35 G. Wakeford, *The Great Labour Mirage*, Robert Hall, 1969, p. 218.
36 HDD, 1st October 1951.
37 Wakeford, *The Great Labour Mirage*, pp. 225–6.
38 HDD, 11th November 1952.
39 HD to Brian Abel-Smith, 31st October 1952 (Dalton Papers 9/25 (50)).
40 HD to Crosland, 23rd September 1952 (Crosland Papers).
41 S. Crosland, *Tony Crosland*, Jonathan Cape, 1982, pp. 60–1.
42 Ruth Dalton to Hilda Auerbach, 21st December 1952 (Auerbach Letters).
43 *Jewish Vanguard* (London), 13th February 1953.
44 HDD, 9th January, 28th February, 25th March 1953.
45 HD to Crosland, 7th June 1953 (Crosland Papers).
46 HDD, 30th April 1953.
47 *Observer*, 3rd May 1953.
48 HDD, 30th April 1953.

49 *The Current*, 6th May 1953.

50 *New Statesman & Nation*, 9th May 1953.

51 Morgan (ed.), *The Backbench Diaries of Richard Crossman*, p. 143, 26th September 1952.

52 HD to Colonel Grover, 15th May 1953 (Brooke Papers Da 5).

53 HD to Catherine Walston, 27th July 1953 (Walston Letters); and Rupert Brooke's poem, 'Day That I Have Loved', in G. Keynes (ed.), *Poems of Rupert Brooke*, Nelson, 1952, p. 26. Perhaps Dalton had seen this recent edition, in which Geoffrey Keynes wrote that Brooke's 'affairs of the heart' still remained for the most part 'in the privacy of his unpublished letters and in the memories of those of the sharers of his love and friendship that are yet alive' (p. xvi).

54 HDD, 6th–7th November 1953.

55 Foot, *Aneurin Bevan*, Vol. II, p. 425.

56 *Manchester Guardian*, 16th January 1954.

57 *Daily Worker*, 18th January 1954.

58 Morgan (ed.), *The Backbench Diaries of Richard Crossman*, p. 102, 29th April 1952.

59 HDD, 24th March, 11th April 1954.

60 *Sunday Express*, 9th May 1954.

61 *Tribune*, 2nd June 1954.

62 *Sunday Citizen*, 9th May 1954.

63 HDD, 4th June, 16th, 24th April, mid-October 1954.

64 Ruth Dalton to Hilde Auerbach, 28th December 1954 (Auerbach Letters).

65 HDD, 14th, 20th November, 25th December, Christmas 1954.

66 Morgan (ed.), *The Backbench Diaries of Richard Crossman*, p. 43, 3rd December 1951.

67 HDD, 3rd November 1952, 29th October 1953, mid-October 1954, 28th February, 31st March 1955.

68 Philip M. Williams (ed.), *The Diary of Hugh Gaitskell*, Jonathan Cape, 1983, p. 387, 25th March 1955.

69 HDD, 31st March, 28th April 1955.

70 HD to Crosland, 3rd May 1955 (Crosland Papers).

71 HDD, 7th May 1955.

72 Ibid., 1955 General Election.

73 HD to Hugh Gaitskell, 30th May 1955 (Gaitskell Papers).

74 HDD, 1st June 1955.

75 Morgan (ed.), *The Backbench Diaries of Richard Crossman*, p. 422, 6th June 1955.

76 HTA, pp. 414–15.

77 *Manchester Guardian*, 4th June 1955.

78 *Daily Mail*, 10th June 1955.

79 HTA, p. 420.

80 *Daily Mirror*, 27th June 1955.

81 HDD, 9th June 1955.

82 *Daily Herald*, 12th October 1955.

83 HDD, end of October 1955.
84 John Parker, interview.
85 HDD, end of February, 2nd February, 2nd March 1956.
86 *Manchester Guardian*, 21st September 1955.
87 HD to Lord Beaverbrook, 29th September 1955 (Beaverbrook Papers BBK c/109).
88 HD to Catherine Walston, 28th August 1956 (Walston Letters).
89 See comments by Daniel Bell in 'Anthony Crosland & Socialism', *Encounter*, Vol. XLIX, No. 2, August 1977, p. 91.
90 C. A. R. Crosland, *The Future of Socialism*, Jonathan Cape, 1956, pp. 13, 19, 113, 308–18, 527.
91 S. Crosland, *Tony Crosland*, p. 71.
92 Williams (ed.), *The Diary of Hugh Gaitskell*, p. 569, 1st August 1956.
93 HDD, 3rd November 1956.
94 HD to Gaitskell, 5th November 1956 (Gaitskell Papers).
95 Bickham Sweet-Escott, interview.
96 HD to Beaverbrook, 29th November 1956; Beaverbrook to HD, 3rd December 1956 (Beaverbrook Papers BBK c/109).
97 Ruth Dalton to Hilde Auerbach, 21st November 1956 (Auerbach Letters).
98 HD to Gaitskell, 23rd July 1956 (Gaitskell Papers).
99 *Daily Express*, 12th March 1957.
100 *Manchester Guardian*, 13th March 1957.
101 *Daily Mirror*, 13th March 1957.
102 *Daily Sketch*, 13th March 1957.
103 *Observer*, 7th May 1957.
104 *Punch*, 17th April 1957.
105 *Tribune*, 12th April 1957.
106 *Sunday Times*, 7th April 1957.
107 *New Statesman & Nation*, 6th April 1957.
108 *Forward*, 19th May 1957.
109 *News Chronicle*, 8th April 1957.
110 HD to Catherine Walston, June 1957 (Walston Letters).
111 HD to Gaitskell, 21st June 1957 (Gaitskell Papers).
112 HDD, 21st July 1957.
113 HD to Gaitskell, 21st June 1957 (Gaitskell Papers).
114 HDD, 1st November 1952.
115 Brian Abel-Smith, interview.
116 HTA, p. 436.
117 HD to Gaitskell, 4th October 1957 (Gaitskell Papers).
118 HTA, pp. 437–8.
119 *Daily Mail*, 21st October 1957.
120 *Daily Herald*, 31st October 1957.
121 Brian Abel-Smith, interview.
122 HD to Lord Beaverbrook, 30th June 1958 (Beaverbrook Papers BBK c/109).
123 Jim Boyden, interview.

124 HD to Gaitskell, 4th October 1957 (Gaitskell Papers).
125 HDD, 1957, 2nd April 1958.
126 HD to Gaitskell, 7th October 1958 (Gaitskell Papers).
127 HDD, 18th June 1958; HD to Hugh Gaitskell, 21st September 1957 (Gaitskell Papers); HD to J. Feeling, 20th December 1957 (letter kindly lent by Mr. Feeling); Dick Leonard to HD, 26th August 1958 (Fabian Collection 928/3 f 87).
128 Lord Walston, interview.
129 Michael Barnes, interview.
130 HDD, 27th October 1956.
131 HD to Gaitskell, 14th February 1959 (Gaitskell Papers).
132 Ruth Dalton to Gaitskell, 11th, 30th May 1959 (Gaitskell Papers).
133 Morgan (ed.), *The Backbench Diaries of Richard Crossman*, p. 761, 23rd June 1959.
134 HD to Gaitskell, 2nd June 1959 (Gaitskell Papers).
135 HD to Lord Beaverbrook, 7th July 1959 (Beaverbrook Papers BBK c/109).
136 HD to Catherine Walston, 21st July 1949 (Walston Letters).
137 HD to Gaitskell, 13th, 9th September 1959 (Gaitskell Papers).
138 HDD, 1st January 1960.
139 HD to Gaitskell, 13th September 1959 (Gaitskell Papers).
140 *Evening Standard*, 18th September 1959.
141 HDD, 8th October 1959.
142 HD to Gaitskell, 5th October 1959 (Gaitskell Papers).
143 HDD, 16th, 8th October 1959.

XXXIV *Finale*

1 HDD, 1st, 16th October 1959; see also D. Jay, *Change and Fortune*, Hutchinson, 1980, p. 272.
2 HD to Gaitskell, 29th November 1959 (Gaitskell Papers).
3 Fabian Lecture at the L.S.E., 31st October 1960 (Dalton Papers 13/11).
4 HD to Gaitskell, 31st January 1960 (Gaitskell Papers).
5 *Evening Standard*, 28th June 1960.
6 HD to Crosland, 20th March 1960 (Crosland Papers).
7 HD to Hugh Gaitskell, 14th, 29th November 1959 (Gaitskell Papers).
8 HTA, p. 305.
9 Ruth Dalton to Hilde Auerbach, 6th January 1960 (Auerbach Letters).
10 Lord Beaverbrook to HD, 1st January 1960 (Beaverbrook Papers BBK c/109).
11 HD to Gaitskell, 31st January, 19th December 1960 (Gaitskell Papers).
12 HD to Beaverbrook, 10th June 1960 (Beaverbrook Papers BBK c/109).
13 *Daily Telegraph*, 16th March 1960.
14 Pat Haynes, private correspondence with the author.
15 Lord Walston, interview.
16 HDD, 16th October 1959.

17 HD to Gaitskell, 4th April 1960 (Gaitskell Papers).
18 A. Bullock, *Ernest Bevin: Foreign Secretary 1945 to 1951*, Heinemann, 1983, p. 352.
19 HD to Gaitskell, 5th May, 22nd September 1960 (Gaitskell Papers).
20 HD to Catherine Walston, 10th October 1960 (Walston Letters).
21 HD to Gaitskell, 22nd September 1960 (Gaitskell Papers).
22 Susan Crosland, interview.
23 HDD, 1st January 1960.
24 HD to Catherine Walston, 23rd January 1960 (Walston Letters).
25 *Daily Telegraph*, 25th October 1960.
26 *Manchester Guardian*, 3rd February 1961.
27 HD to Gaitskell, 19th December 1960 (Gaitskell Papers).
28 Dalton Papers 13/3, 15/5.
29 HD to Catherine Walston, 26th May 1961 (Walston Letters).
30 *Daily Express*, 10th June 1961.
31 (Sir) George Chetwynd, interview; Dalton Papers 13/3.
32 *Evening Standard*, 17th June 1961.
33 Susan Crosland, interview.
34 Marion Miliband, interview.
35 Michael Barnes, interview.
36 HD to Gaitskell, 17th September 1961 (Gaitskell Papers).
37 HD to Michael Barnes, 25th September 1961 (Barnes Letters).
38 Dalton Papers 15/3.
39 HD to Gaitskell, 1st December 1961, 13th April, 2nd June 1959 (Gaitskell Papers).
40 William Rodgers in conversation with the author. See also Rodgers to Ruth Dalton, 23rd February 1962 (Dalton Papers 16/1).
41 Dalton Papers 15/3.
42 Brian Abel-Smith, interview.
43 Lord Taylor, private correspondence with the author.
44 Lord Vaizey, interview; *Daily Express*, 20th January 1962.
45 *Daily Express*, 20th January 1962.
46 Crosland engagement diary, 1962 (Crosland Papers).
47 Enid MacLeod, interview.
48 Private information.
49 Heather Forbes Watson, interview.
50 *Political Quarterly*, January–March 1962.
51 *Observer*, 4th February 1962.
52 *New Statesman*, 9th February 1962.
53 Marion Miliband, interview.
54 Pat Herbert, interview.
55 Ruth Dalton to Hilde Auerbach, 26th March 1962 (Auerbach Letters).
56 Crosland to Ruth Dalton, February 1962 (Dalton Papers 16/1).
57 Will, dated 13th October 1950 (Dalton Papers 15/3, and Somerset House).
58 Fred Kendall, interview.
59 J. Callaghan to Ruth Dalton, 19th October 1964 (Dalton Papers 15/3).
60 S. Crosland, *Tony Crosland*, Jonathan Cape, 1982, p. 140.

61 Enid MacLeod, interview.
62 Ann Kendall, interview.
63 Private information.
64 Jack Rathbone, interview.
65 Lord and Lady Vaizey, interviews. Her estate was valued for probate at £30,228 (Somerset House).

SELECT BIBLIOGRAPHY

Below are sources cited in the Notes and a few others that have been especially valuable as background. Smaller private collections of letters, and the names of people interviewed, are not included. These are listed in the Acknowledgments at the beginning of the book.

PRIVATE PAPERS

1 Dalton Papers

Dalton's papers were deposited by his literary executors at the British Library of Political and Economic Science (B.L.P.E.S.) after his death. Apart from his diary, which begins in 1916 and continues until the late 1950s, there is virtually nothing earlier than 1929. Thereafter coverage is patchy, most material (letters, notes, memoranda) relating to the 1940–51 period. Smaller collections are to be found in the papers of Rupert Brooke (Brooke's letters to Dalton), Anthony Crosland, Hugh Gaitskell and Lord Pethick-Lawrence, in particular. For these and other useful collections, see below.

2 Other Private Papers

A. V. Alexander papers (Churchill College, Cambridge).
C. R. Attlee papers (Churchill College, Cambridge and Bodleian Library, Oxford).
Lord Beaverbrook papers (House of Lords).
Berg Collection, for Hugh Dalton–Leonard Woolf correspondence (New York City Library).
Lord Beveridge papers (B.L.P.E.S.).
Ernest Bevin papers (Churchill College, Cambridge).
Rupert Brooke papers (King's College, Cambridge).
J. R. M. Butler papers (Trinity College, Cambridge).
Noel Buxton papers (McGill University).

Edwin Cannan papers (B.L.P.E.S.).
Edward Carpenter collection (Sheffield Central Library).
Walter Citrine diary, in Lord Citrine papers (B.L.P.E.S.).
G. D. H. Cole papers (Nuffield College, Oxford).
Arthur Creech Jones papers (Rhodes House Library, Oxford).
Sir Stafford Cripps papers (Nuffield College, Oxford).
Anthony Crosland papers (courtesy of Susan Crosland).
Hugh Dalton diary and papers (B.L.P.E.S.).
Evan Durbin papers (courtesy of Marjorie Durbin).
J. Chuter Ede diary and papers (British Library).
Paul Einzig papers (Churchill College, Cambridge).
Hugh Gaitskell diary and papers (courtesy of Philip M. Williams).
Charles Garnsworthy papers (B.L.P.E.S.).
Arthur Henderson papers (Labour Party Library).
Lord Keynes papers (King's College, Cambridge, Marshall Library, Cam-
     bridge, and T247, Public Record Office).
James Meade diary, in Meade papers (B.L.P.E.S.).
James Middleton papers (Labour Party Library).
Herbert Morrison papers (Nuffield College, Oxford).
Harold Nicolson unpublished diary (Balliol College, Oxford).
Passfield papers, including Beatrice Webb unpublished diary (B.L.P.E.S.).
George Pepler papers (University of Strathclyde).
Lord Pethick-Lawrence papers (Trinity College, Cambridge).
Arthur Ponsonby papers (Bodleian Library, Oxford).
J. T. Sheppard papers (King's College, Cambridge).
Sir Charles Trevelyan papers (University of Newcastle upon Tyne).
Vidler papers (St George's Chapel, Windsor).
Francis Williams papers (Churchill College, Cambridge).

PUBLIC AND INSTITUTIONAL RECORDS

1 *State Papers*

State papers are now available at the Public Record Office, Kew, for all of
Dalton's periods of ministerial office.

Papers consulted include minutes and papers of the Cabinet and its com-
mittees (CAB); the Prime Minister's office (PREM); the Foreign Office,
M.E.W., S.O.E. and P.W.E. (FO); the Board of Trade (BT); the Treasury
(T); Housing and Local Government (HLG).

CAB 127/206, 208 and 210 (relating to S.O.E.) and 212 (relating to the
publication of Dalton's memoirs) are closed, 'for security reasons'. I am
grateful to the Departmental Record Officer of the Cabinet Office for giving
me special permission and facilities to see CAB 127/204, 205 and 207. Most
of this material relates to less sensitive aspects of S.O.E.

2 *Other Records*

B.B.C. Written Archives (Caversham Park).
Bishop Auckland Divisional Labour Party annual reports and minute books (Bishop Auckland Constituency Labour Party).
Cambridge County Archives.
Fabian Collection (Nuffield College, Oxford).
Independent Labour Party National Administration Committee minutes (on microfilm at B.L.P.E.S.).
Labour Party National Executive Committee and sub-committee minutes and papers (Labour Party Library).
L.S.E. School Archives (B.L.P.E.S.).
Royal Archives (Windsor Castle).
St George's Choir School register (courtesy of Mr. Widgeway).

3 *Published Official and Party Documents*

Hansard: House of Commons Debates (HC Debs), Fifth Series.
Labour Party Annual Conference Reports, Labour Party, London.
Report of the Select Committee on the Budget Disclosures, H.M.S.O., 1947.
Report of the Tribunal appointed to inquire into Allegations reflecting on the Official Conduct of Ministers of the Crown and other Public Servants (Cmd. 7617). H.M.S.O., 1949.
Royal Commission on the Press: Minutes of Evidence 1948 (Cmd. 7475). H.M.S.O., 1949.

THE PRESS AND PERIODICAL LITERATURE

Foreign and National (Daily and Sunday)

Daily Chronicle, Daily Express, Daily Graphic, Daily Herald, Daily Mail, Daily Mirror, Daily Sketch, Daily Telegraph, Daily Worker, Evening Standard, Financial Times, Manchester Guardian, Morning Post, New York Herald Tribune, News Chronicle, Observer, People, Reynolds' News, Star, Sunday Chronicle, Sunday Citizen, Sunday Dispatch, Sunday Express, Sunday Pictorial, Sunday Times, The Times.

Local and Regional

Auckland and County Chronicle, Boston Guardian, Camberwell and Peckham Times, Cambridge Daily News, Evening Gazette (Middlesbrough)*, Kent Messenger and Maidstone Telegraph, North Eastern Gazette, Northern Echo, South London Observer, South London Press, Spalding Standard, Yorkshire Observer.*

Journals and Periodicals

Banco Nazionale del Lavoro: Quarterly Review, Cambridge Review, Clare

*Market Review, Contemporary Review, Country Life, Current, Dalton
Genealogical Society Journal, Economic Journal, Economica, Economist,
Eton College Calendar, Eton College Chronicle, Fabian News, Foreign
Affairs, Fortnightly Review, Forward, Gownsman, Granta, Jewish Vanguard,
Labour Magazine, Lloyd George Liberal Magazine, Miner, New Judaea,
New Leader, New Statesman & Nation, Out of Doors, Picture Post, Political
Quarterly, Punch, Revally* (Labour Candidates' Magazine), *St George's
School Magazine, Socialist Advance, Socialist Review, Spectator, Summer
Fields School Magazine, Textile Bulletin, Time and Tide, Tribune.*

PUBLISHED WORKS BY HUGH DALTON

1 *Books and Pamphlets*

With British Guns in Italy: A tribute to Italian achievement, Methuen, London,
1919.
Some Aspects of the Inequality of Incomes in Modern Communities, Rout-
ledge, London, 1920. (The 1925 edition includes Dalton's *Economic
Journal* article, 'The Measurement of the Inequality of Incomes'.)
Principles of Public Finance, Routledge, London, 1922 (revised eds. 1922,
1929, 1936 and 1954).
The Capital Levy Explained, Labour Publishing Co., London, 1923.
Public Finance. A syllabus for classes and students, Labour Research Depart-
ment, London, 1924.
London Essays in Economics. In Honour of Edwin Cannan (ed. T. E. Gregory
and Dr H. Dalton), Routledge, London, 1927.
Towards the Peace of Nations. A Study in International Politics, Routledge,
London, 1928.
(ed.) *Unbalanced Budgets. A Study of the Financial Crisis in Fifteen Countries*,
Routledge, London, 1934.
Practical Socialism for Britain, Routledge, London, 1935.
Hitler's War: Before and After, Penguin, Harmondsworth, 1940.
Financing Labour's Plan, Labour Party, London, 1946.
Call Back Yesterday: Memoirs 1887–1931, Muller, London, 1953.
The Fateful Years: Memoirs 1931–1945, Muller, London, 1957.
High Tide and After: Memoirs 1945–60, Muller, London, 1962.

2 *Longer Articles and Essays*

'The Measurement of the Inequality of Incomes', *Economic Journal*, Vol. 30,
September 1920.
'The Financial Situation', *Contemporary Review*, CXXIII, May 1923.
'A Labour Majority Next Time?', *Socialist Review*, March 1926.
'The Theory of Population', *Economica*, March 1928.
'British Foreign Policy 1929–1931', *Political Quarterly*, October–December
1931.
'Financial Institutions in Transition', in *Where Stands Socialism Today?*

(Preface by G. B. Shaw), Rich & Crown, London, 1933.

'A general view of the Soviet Economy, with special reference to planning', in M. Cole (ed.), *Twelve Studies in Soviet Russia*, Gollancz, 1933.

'The Present International Situation', *Political Quarterly*, July–September 1935.

'The Popular Front', *Political Quarterly*, October–December 1936.

'Our Financial Plan' in Fabian Society, *Forward to Victory! Labour's plan: six essays*, Gollancz, London, 1946.

SECONDARY SOURCES

1 *Biography, Diaries, Letters and Memoirs*

J. Amery, *Approach March: A Venture in Autobiography*, Hutchinson, London, 1973.

L. S. Amery, *My Political Life*, Vol. III: *The Unforgiving Years 1929–1940*, Hutchinson, London, 1955.

J. Astley, *The Inner Circle*, Hutchinson, London, 1971.

C. R. Attlee, *As It Happened*, Odhams, London, 1956.

Clem Attlee: The Granada Historical Records Interview, Panther Record, London 1967.

Earl of Avon, *Memoirs of the Rt. Hon. Sir Anthony Eden K.G., P.C., M.C.: The Reckoning*, Cassell, London, 1965.

A. V. Baillie, *My First Eighty Years*, John Murray, London, 1951.

G. Battiscombe, *Queen Alexandra*, Constable, London, 1969.

G. Beith (ed.), *Edward Carpenter: In Appreciation*, Allen & Unwin, London, 1931.

A. C. Benson, *The House of Quiet: An Autobiography*, John Murray, London (second ed.), 1906.

——, *Memories and Friends*, John Murray, London, 1924.

J. Beveridge, *An Epic of Clare Market*, L.S.E., London, 1960.

Lord Beveridge, *Power and Influence*, Hodder & Stoughton, London, 1953.

——, *The London School of Economics and its Problems 1919–1937*, Allen & Unwin, London, 1960.

Earl of Birkenhead, *The Life of Lord Halifax*, Hamish Hamilton, London, 1965.

R. Blake, *The Unknown Prime Minister. The Life and Times of Andrew Bonar Law 1858–1923*, Eyre & Spottiswoode, London, 1955.

G. Boas, *A Teacher's Story*, Macmillan, London, 1963.

H. Bolitho, *Older People*, Cobden-Sanderson, London, 1935.

M. Bondfield, *A Life's Work*, Hutchinson, London, 1948.

A. Boyle, *Poor Dear Brendan. The Quest for Brendan Bracken*, Hutchinson, London, 1974.

V. Brittain, *Pethick-Lawrence: A Portrait*, Allen & Unwin, London, 1964.

F. Brockway, *Inside the Left*, New Leader, London, 1942.

——, *Towards Tomorrow*, Hart-Davis & MacGibbon, London, 1977.

G. Brown, *In My Way*, Penguin, Harmondsworth, 1972 (first published Gollancz, 1971).

R. H. Bruce Lockhart, *Comes the Reckoning*, Putnam, London, 1947.

——, *Giants Cast Long Shadows*, Putnam, London, 1960.

A. Bullock, *The Life and Times of Ernest Bevin*, Vol. II, *Minister of Labour*, Heinemann, London, 1967.

——, *Ernest Bevin: Foreign Secretary 1945–1951*, Heinemann, London, 1983.

E. Carpenter, *My Days and Dreams*, Allen & Unwin, London, 1916.

The Memoirs of Lord Chandos, Bodley Head, London, 1962.

Sir Richard Clarke (ed. Sir Alec Cairncross), *Anglo-American Economic Collaboration in War and Peace 1942–1949*, Oxford University Press, London, 1982.

M. Cole (ed.), *Beatrice Webb Diaries 1924–32*, Longman, Green & Co., London, 1949.

M. Cole, *The Life of G. D. H. Cole*, Macmillan, London, 1971.

J. Colville, *The Churchillians*, Weidenfeld & Nicolson, London, 1981.

C. Connolly, *Enemies of Promise*, Routledge, London, 1938.

C. Cooke, *The Life of Richard Stafford Cripps*, Hodder & Stoughton, London, 1957.

D. Cooper, *Old Men Forget: The Autobiography of Duff Cooper*, Rupert Hart-Davis, London, 1953.

S. Crosland, *Tony Crosland*, Jonathan Cape, London, 1982.

C. Cross, *Philip Snowden*, Barrie & Rockcliff, London, 1966.

W. P. Crozier (ed. A. J. P. Taylor), *Off the Record: Political Interviews 1933–1943*, Hutchinson, London, 1973.

N. Davenport, *Memoirs of a City Radical*, Weidenfeld & Nicolson, London, 1974.

B. Davidson, *Special Operations Europe: Scenes from the Anti-Nazi War*, Gollancz, London, 1980.

A. C. Deane, *Time Remembered*, Faber, London, 1945.

S. Delmar, *Black Boomerang*, Secker & Warburg, London, 1962.

D. Dilks (ed.), *The Diary of Sir Alexander Cadogan 1938–1943*, Cassell, London, 1971.

B. Donoughue and G. W. Jones, *Herbert Morrison: Portrait of a Politician*, Weidenfeld & Nicolson, London, 1973.

B. Drake and M. Cole (eds.), *Our Partnership by Beatrice Webb*, Longman, Green & Co., London, 1948.

P. Einzig, *In the Centre of Things*, Hutchinson, London, 1960.

E. Estorick, *Stafford Cripps: A Biography*, Heinemann, London, 1949.

M. Foot, *Aneurin Bevan: A Biography*, Vol. I, *1897–1945*, MacGibbon & Kee, London, 1962.

——, *Aneurin Bevan: A Biography*, Vol. II, *1945–1960*, Davis-Poynter, London, 1973.

P. Foot, *The Politics of Harold Wilson*, Penguin, Harmondsworth, 1968.

M. Gilbert (ed.), *Plough My Own Furrow: The Story of Lord Allen told through his writings and correspondence*, Longman, London, 1970.

The Memoirs of Lord Gladwyn, Weidenfeld & Nicolson, London, 1972.

J. Gore, *King George V: A Personal Memoir*, John Murray, London, 1941.

M. A. Hamilton, *Arthur Henderson: A Biography*, Heinemann, London, 1938.

——, *Remembering My Good Friends*, Jonathan Cape, London, 1944.

——, *Uphill All the Way*, Jonathan Cape, London, 1953.

Sir Arthur Harris, *Bomber Offensive*, Collins, London, 1947.

J. Harris, *William Beveridge: A Biography*, Clarendon Press, Oxford, 1977.

K. Harris, *Attlee*, Weidenfeld & Nicolson, London, 1982.

R. F. Harrod, *The Life of John Maynard Keynes*, Macmillan, London, 1951.

J. Harvey (ed.), *The Diplomatic Diaries of Oliver Harvey 1937–1940*, Collins, London, 1970.

—— (ed.), *The War Diaries of Oliver Harvey*, Collins, London, 1978.

C. Hassall, *Rupert Brooke: A Biography*, Faber, London, 1964.

M. Holroyd, *Lytton Strachey: A Biography*, Penguin, Harmondsworth, 1971 (first published Heinemann, 1967–8).

——, *Augustus John: A Biography*, Vol. I, Heinemann, London, 1974.

A. Horner, *Incorrigible Rebel*, MacGibbon & Kee, London, 1960.

L. Housman (ed.), *War Letters of Fallen Englishmen*, Gollancz, London, 1930.

D. Jay, *Change and Fortune: A Political Record*, Hutchinson, London, 1980.

L. E. Jones, *A Victorian Boyhood*, Macmillan, London, 1955.

T. Jones, *A Diary with Letters 1931–50*, Oxford University Press, London, 1954.

G. Keynes (ed.), *The Letters of Rupert Brooke*, Faber, London, 1968.

I. Kirkpatrick, *The Inner Circle*, Macmillan, London, 1959.

Sir Frederick Leith-Ross, *Money Talks: fifty years of international finance*, Hutchinson, London, 1968.

W. Lewis, *Blasting and Bombardiering*, Eyre & Spottiswoode, London, 1937.

Sir John Lomax, *The Diplomatic Smuggler*, Arthur Barker, London, 1965.

C. Lysaght, *Brendan Bracken*, Allen Lane, London, 1979.

N. MacKenzie (ed.), *The Letters of Sidney and Beatrice Webb*, Vol. II, *Partnership 1892–1912*, Cambridge University Press, Cambridge, 1978.

N. and J. MacKenzie, *H. G. Wells: A Biography*, Simon & Schuster, New York, 1973.

I. MacLeod, *Neville Chamberlain*, Muller, London, 1961.

H. Macmillan, *Winds of Change 1914–39*, Macmillan, London, 1966.

——, *The Blast of War 1939–45*, Macmillan, London, 1967.

——, *Tides of Fortune 1945–55*, Macmillan, London, 1969.

P. Magnus, *King Edward the Seventh*, John Murray, London, 1964.

L. Manning, *A Life for Education: an Autobiography*, Gollancz, London, 1970.

D. Marquand, *Ramsay MacDonald*, Jonathan Cape, London, 1977.

E. Marsh (ed.), *The Collected Poems of Rupert Brooke: With a Memoir*, Sidgwick & Jackson, London, 1918.

K. Martin, *Harold Laski 1893–1950. A Biographical Memoir*, Gollancz, London, 1953.

——, *Critic's London Diary: From the New Statesman 1931–1956*, Secker & Warburg, London, 1960.

——, *Editor*, Penguin, Harmondsworth, 1969.

D. E. Moggridge, *Keynes*, Macmillan, London, 1976.

Lord Moran, *Winston Churchill. The Struggle for Survival 1940–1965*, Constable, London, 1966.

Janet Morgan (ed.), *The Backbench Diaries of Richard Crossman*, Hamish Hamilton and Jonathan Cape, London, 1981.

Lord Morrison of Lambeth, *Herbert Morrison: An Autobiography*, Odhams Press, London, 1960.

N. Mosley, *Julian Grenfell: His Life and the Times of his Death 1888–1915*, Weidenfeld & Nicolson, London, 1976.

Sir Oswald Mosley, *My Life*, Nelson, London, 1970.

R. H. Mottram, *The Spanish Farm Trilogy 1914–1918* (first published Chatto & Windus, London, 1927) Penguin, Harmondsworth, 1979.

J. T. Murphy, *New Horizons*, John Lane, London, 1941.

D. Newsome, *On the Edge of Paradise: The Diarist A. C. Benson*, John Murray, London, 1980.

—— (ed.), *Edwardian Excursions: From the Diaries of A. C. Benson 1898–1904*, John Murray, London, 1980.

H. Nicolson, *King George the Fifth: His Life and Reign*, Constable, London, 1952.

N. Nicolson (ed.), *Harold Nicolson: Diaries and Letters 1945–1962*, Collins, London, 1968.

D. Proctor (ed.), *The Autobiography of G. Lowes Dickinson*, Duckworth, London, 1973.

B. Reed and G. Williams, *Denis Healey and the Policies of Power*, Sidgwick & Jackson, London, 1971.

R. Rhodes James (ed.), *Memoirs of a Conservative: J. C. C. Davidson's Memoirs and Papers 1910–1937*, Weidenfeld & Nicolson, London, 1969.

Lord Robbins, *Autobiography of an Economist*, Macmillan, London, 1971.

W. T. Rodgers (ed.), *Hugh Gaitskell*, Thames & Hudson, London, 1964.

S. Rowbotham and J. Weeks, *Socialism and the New Life*, Pluto, London, 1977.

D. Russell, *The Tamarisk Tree*, Elek/Pemberton, London, 1975.

G. St. Aubyn, *The Royal George*, Constable, London, 1963.

J. Saltmarsh and P. Wilkinson, *Arthur Cecil Pigou 1877–1959*, Cambridge University Press, Cambridge, 1960.

R. Skidelsky, *Oswald Mosley*, Macmillan, London, 1975.

——, *John Maynard Keynes*, Vol. I, *Hopes Betrayed 1883–1920*, Macmillan, London, 1983.

E. Spears, *Assignment to Catastrophe*, Vol. I, *Prelude to Dunkirk July 1939–May 1940*, Heinemann, London, 1954.

P. Strauss, *Bevin and Co. The Leaders of British Labour*, Putnams, New York, 1941.

B. Sweet-Escott, *Baker Street Irregular*, Methuen, London, 1965.

H. Thomas, *John Strachey*, Eyre & Methuen, London, 1973.

R. Thorndike, *Children of the Garter*, Rich & Crown, London, 1937.

E. A. Towle, *John Mason Neale D.D.: a Memoir*, Longman, Green & Co., London, 1906.

E.T[ownshend] (ed.), *Keeling Letters and Recollections*, Allen & Unwin, London, 1918.

G. M. Trevelyan, *Scenes from Italy's War*, T. C. & E. C. Jack Ltd., London, 1919.

C. Tsuzuki, *Edward Carpenter 1844–1929: Prophet of Human Fellowship*, Cambridge University Press, Cambridge, 1980.

R. Usborne (ed.), *A Century of Summer Fields*, Methuen, London, 1964.

J. Vaizey, *In Breach of Promise*, Weidenfeld & Nicolson, London, 1983.

Lord Vansittart, *The Mist Procession*, Hutchinson, London, 1958.

J. E. Vincent, *H.R.H. Duke of Clarence and Avondale: A Memoir*, John Murray, London, 1893.

E. Waugh, *The Life of the Right Reverend Ronald Knox*, Chapman & Hall, London, 1959.

Sir John Wheeler-Bennett (ed.), *Action This Day: Working with Churchill*, Macmillan, London, 1968.

J. W. Wheeler-Bennett, *King George VI: His Life and Reign*, Macmillan, London, 1958.

E. J. Williams and C. S. Nicholls (eds.), *Dictionary of National Biography 1961–1970*, Oxford University Press, London, 1981.

F. Williams, *A Prime Minister Remembers*, Heinemann, London, 1961.

——, *Nothing So Strange*, Cassell, London, 1970.

Philip M. Williams, *Hugh Gaitskell: A Political Biography*, Jonathan Cape, London, 1979.

—— (ed.), *The Diary of Hugh Gaitskell 1945–1956*, Jonathan Cape, London, 1983.

The Duke of Windsor, *A Family Album*, Cassell, London, 1960.

K. Young (ed.), *The Diaries of Sir Robert Bruce Lockhart*, Vol. II, *1939–1965*, Macmillan, London, 1980.

2 Other Books

P. Addison, *The Road to 1945*, Quartet, London, 1977 (first published Jonathan Cape, 1975).

L. S. Amery, *The Washington Loan Agreement*, Macdonald & Co., London, 1946.

A. B. Atkinson (ed.), *Welfare, Incomes and Inequality*, Penguin, Harmondsworth, 1973.

P. Auty and R. Clogg (eds.), *British Policy towards War-time Resistance in Yugoslavia and Greece*, Macmillan, London, 1975.

M. Balfour, *Propaganda in War 1939–1945*, Routledge & Kegan Paul, London, 1981.

E. Barker, *British Policy in South-East Europe in the Second World War*, Macmillan, London, 1976.

R. Barker, *Political Ideas in Modern Britain*, Methuen, London, 1978.

R. Bassett, *Democracy and Foreign Policy: A Case History. The Sino-Japanese Dispute 1931–33*, Longman, Green & Co., London, 1952.

Major A. F. Becke, *History of the Great War: Order of Battle of Divisions*, Part 3B, H.M.S.O., London, 1945.

S. H. Beer, *Modern British Politics: A Study of Parties and Pressure Groups*, Faber, London, 1965.

M. Bentley and J. Stevenson (eds.), *High and Low Politics in Modern Britain: Ten Studies*, Oxford University Press, London, 1983.

B. Bergonzi, *Heroes' Twilight*, Constable, London, 1965.

A. Bevan, *In Place of Fear*, Heinemann, London, 1952.

F. L. Block, *The Origins of International Economic Disorder: a study of United States international monetary policy from World War II to the present*, University of California Press, Berkeley, 1977.

H. N. Brailsford, *The War of Steel and Gold: A Study of the Armed Peace*, Bell, London, 1914.

Sir E. Bridges, *Treasury Control*, Athlone Press, London, 1950.

S. Brittan, *Steering the Economy: The Role of the Treasury*, Penguin, Harmondsworth, 1971 (first published as *The Treasury under the Tories, 1951 to 1964*, Penguin, 1964).

J. and J. B. Burke (eds.), *A Genealogical and Heraldic Dictionary of the Landed Gentry of Great Britain and Ireland*, Vol. II, Henry Colburn, London, 1853.

T. D. Burridge, *British Labour and Hitler's War*, André Deutsch, London, 1976.

D. Butler and A. Sloman, *British Political Facts 1900–1979*, Macmillan, London, 1980.

L. S. R. Byrne and E. L. Churchill, *Changing Eton*, Jonathan Cape, London, 1937.

D. Carlton, *MacDonald versus Henderson: The Foreign Policy of the Second Labour Government*, Macmillan, London, 1970.

E. Carpenter, *The Intermediate Sex: A Study of Some Transitional Types of Men and Women*, Swan Sonnenschein & Co., London, 1908.

——, *Towards Democracy* (ed. G. Beith), Allen & Unwin, London, 1949.

D. Caute, *The Fellow Travellers: A Postscript to the Enlightenment*, Weidenfeld & Nicolson, London, 1973.

S. Checkland, *British Public Policy 1776–1939*, Cambridge University Press, Cambridge, 1983.

Sir Norman Chester, *The Nationalisation of British Industry 1945–51*, H.M.S.O., London, 1975.

P. Clarke, *Liberals and Social Democrats*, Cambridge University Press, Cambridge, 1978.

C. A. Cline, *Recruits to Labour: The British Labour Party 1914–31*, University of Syracuse Press, N.Y., 1963.

D. Coates, *The Labour Party and the Struggle for Socialism*, Cambridge University Press, Cambridge, 1975.

G. D. H. Cole, *A History of the Labour Party since 1914*, Routledge & Kegan Paul, London, 1948.

M. Cole (ed.), *Twelve Studies in Soviet Russia*, Gollancz, London, 1933.

W. H. B. Court, *Coal*, H.M.S.O., London, 1951.

M. Cowling, *The Impact of Labour 1920–1924*, Cambridge University Press, Cambridge, 1971.

C. A. R. Crosland, *The Future of Socialism*, Jonathan Cape, London, 1956.

G. Crowther, *Ways and Means of War*, Clarendon Press, Oxford, 1940.

C. Cruickshank, *The Fourth Arm: Psychological Warfare 1938–1945*, Davis-Poynter, London, 1977.

J. Curran and J. Seaton, *Power without Responsibility: the Press and Broadcasting in Britain*, Fontana, London, 1981.

T. d'Arch Smith, *Love in Earnest*, Routledge & Kegan Paul, London, 1970.

E. Delavenay, *D. H. Lawrence and Edward Carpenter: A Study in Edwardian Transition*, Heinemann, London, 1971.

J. C. R. Dow, *The Management of the British Economy 1945–60*, Cambridge University Press, Cambridge, 1964.

R. E. Dowse, *Left in the Centre*, Longman, London, 1966.

Elizabeth Durbin, *New Jerusalems*, Routledge & Kegan Paul, London (forthcoming).

Evan Durbin, *What Have We to Defend?*, Routledge, London, 1942.

Brig-Gen. Sir J. E. Edmonds, *History of the Great War: Military Operations in France and Belgium 1916*, Macmillan, London, 1932.

Sir J. E. Edmonds and H. R. Davies, *History of the Great War: Military Operations in Italy 1915–1919*, H.M.S.O., London, 1949.

M. Elliott-Bateman (ed.), *The Fourth Dimension in Warfare*, Manchester University Press, Manchester, 1970.

R. C. K. Ensor, *England 1870–1914*, Oxford University Press, London, 1936.

Eton School Register, Part VII 1899–1909, Spottiswoode, Ballantyne & Co., Eton, 1922.

M. R. D. Foot, *S.O.E. in France*, H.M.S.O., London, 1968.

P. Fussell, *The Great War and Modern Memory*, Oxford University Press, London, 1975.

H. Gaitskell, *Recent Developments in British Socialist Thinking*, Co-operative Union, London, 1956.

R. N. Gardner, *Sterling-Dollar Diplomacy. Anglo-American collaboration in the reconstruction of multilateral trade*, McGraw-Hill, New York, 1969 (first published Oxford University Press, London, 1956).

Lord Gladwyn, *The European Idea*, Weidenfeld & Nicolson, London, 1966.

P. Goodhart and V. Branston, *The 1922*, Macmillan, London, 1978.

Sir Hugh Greene, *Third Floor Front: A View of Broadcasting in the Sixties*, The Bodley Head, London, 1969.

D. R. Grenfell, *Coal*, Gollancz, London, 1947.

W. K. Hancock and M. M. Gowing, *The British War Economy*, H.M.S.O., London, 1949.

E. L. Hargreaves and M. M. Gowing, *Civil Industry and Trade*, H.M.S.O., London, 1952.

R. F. Harrod, *And So It Goes On*, Rupert Hart-Davis, London, 1952.

Sir Hubert Henderson, *The Uses and Abuses of Economic Planning*, Cambridge University Press, Cambridge, 1947.

F. H. Hinsley et al., *British Intelligence in the Second World War*, Vols. I, II, H.M.S.O., London, 1979, 1981.

S. Howson and D. Winch, *The Economic Advisory Council 1930–1939*, Cambridge University Press, Cambridge, 1977.

The Hunt 1898–1937, Pelican Press, London, 1937.

H. M. Hyde, *Their Good Names*, Hamish Hamilton, London, 1970.

——, *The Cleveland Street Scandal*, W. H. Allen, London, 1976.

S. Hynes, *Edwardian Occasions*, Routledge & Kegan Paul, London, 1972.

D. Jay, *The Socialist Case*, Faber, London, 1937.

R. Jenkins, *The Pursuit of Progress*, Heinemann, London, 1953.

J. Jewkes, *Ordeal by Planning*, Macmillan, London, 1948.

B. Jones, *The Russia Complex: The British Labour Party and the Soviet Union*, Manchester University Press, Manchester, 1978.

J. Jupp, *The Radical Left in Britain 1931–1941*, Frank Cass, London, 1982.

G. Keynes (ed.), *Poems of Rupert Brooke*, Nelson & Sons, London, 1952.

J. M. Keynes, *The Economic Consequences of the Peace*, Macmillan, London, 1919.

——, *The General Theory of Employment, Interest and Money*, Macmillan, London, 1936.

M. Keynes (ed.), *Essays on John Maynard Keynes*, Cambridge University Press, Cambridge, 1975.

W. Laqueur (ed.), *The Second World War: Essays in military and political history*, Sage, London, 1982.

J. M. Lee, *Reviewing the Machinery of Government 1942–1952: An Essay on the Anderson Committee and its successors* (mimeo, available from the author), 1977.

——, *The Churchill Coalition 1940–1945*, Batsford, London, 1980.

N. and J. MacKenzie, *The First Fabians*, Weidenfeld & Nicolson, London, 1977.

D. Maclennan and J. B. Parr (eds.), *Regional Policy: Past Experience and New Directions*, Martin Robertson, Oxford, 1971.

D. Martin and D. Rubinstein (eds.), *Ideology and the Labour Movement*, Croom Helm, London, 1979.

A. Marwick, *Britain in the Century of Total War*, Bodley Head, London, 1968.

J. E. Meade, *Planning and the Price Mechanism: The Liberal-Socialist Solution*, Allen & Unwin, London, 1948.

W. N. Medlicott, *The Economic Blockade*, Vols. I and II, H.M.S.O., London, 1952, 1959.

K. Middlemas, *Politics in Industrial Society: The Experience of the British System since 1911*, Deutsch, London, 1979.

A. S. Milward, *The German Economy at War*, Athlone Press, London, 1965.

H. Morrison, *Socialisation and Transport*, Constable, London, 1933.

——, *Economic Planning*, Institute of Public Administration, London, 1947.

——, *Government and Parliament: A Survey from Inside*, Oxford University Press, London, 1954.

C. L. Mowat, *Britain Between the Wars 1918–1940*, Methuen, London, 1955.

J. F. Naylor, *Labour's International Policy: The Labour Party in the 1930s*, Weidenfeld & Nicolson, London, 1969.

R. Page Arnot, *The Miners in Crisis and War*, Allen & Unwin, London, 1962.

E. R. Pease, *The History of the Fabian Society*, A. C. Fifield, London, 1916.

H. Pelling, *Britain and the Second World War*, Fontana, London, 1970.

——, *The Labour Governments 1945–51*, Macmillan, London, 1984.

F. W. Pethick Lawrence, *The Capital Levy: How the Labour Party Would Pay the War Debt*, Co-operative Printing Society, London, 1919.

S. Pierson, *British Socialists: The Journey from Fantasy to Politics*, Harvard University Press, Cambridge, Mass., 1979.

A. C. Pigou, *Wealth and Welfare*, Macmillan, London, 1912.

——, *A Capital Levy and a Levy on War Wealth*, Oxford University Press, London, 1919.

B. Pimlott, *Labour and the Left in the 1930s*, Cambridge University Press, Cambridge, 1977.

—— (ed.), *Fabian Essays in Socialist Thought*, Heinemann, London, 1984.

B. Pimlott and C. Cook (eds.), *Trade Unions in British Politics*, Longman, London, 1982.

Political and Economic Planning, *Government and Industry*, P.E.P., London, 1952.

D. Rhys Phillips, *The History of the Vale of Neath*, published by the author, Swansea, 1925.

A. H. Robertson, *The Council of Europe*, Stevens, London, 1956.

T. Rogers (ed.), *Rupert Brooke: A Reappraisal and Selection*, Routledge & Kegan Paul, London, 1971.

A. A. Rogow and P. Shore, *The Labour Government and British Industry 1945–51*, Blackwell, Oxford, 1955.

V. Rothwell, *Britain and the Cold War 1941–1947*, Jonathan Cape, London, 1982.

R. S. Sayers, *Modern Banking*, Oxford University Press, London, 1967.

H. A. Schmitt, *European Union*, Van Nostrand Reinhold, New York, 1969.

A. Sen, *On Economic Inequality*, Oxford University Press, London, 1973.

R. W. Service, *Songs of a Sourdough* (7th ed.), T. Fisher Unwin, London, 1908.

A. Shonfield, *British Economic Policy since the War*, Penguin, Harmondsworth, 1958.

M. Sissons and P. French (eds.), *The Age of Austerity*, Hodder & Stoughton, London, 1963.

R. Skidelsky, *Politicians and the Slump: the Labour Government 1929–31*, Macmillan, London, 1967.

D. Stafford, *Britain and European Resistance 1940–1945. A Survey of the Special Operations Executive, with Documents*, Macmillan, London, 1980.

S. Strange, *Sterling and British Policy*, Oxford University Press, London, 1971.

J. Symons, *The Thirties*, The Crescent Press, London, 1960.

A. J. P. Taylor, *English History 1914–45*, Clarendon Press, Oxford, 1965.

——, *The Trouble Makers*, Panther, London 1969 (first published Hamish Hamilton, 1957).

P. Thane, *The Foundations of the Welfare State*, Longman, London, 1982.

A. P. Thirlwall (ed.), *Keynes and International Monetary Relations*, Macmillan, London, 1976.

R. Usborne, *Clubland Heroes*, Barrie & Jenkins, London, 1974 ed. (first edition published 1953).

G. Wakeford, *The Great Labour Mirage*, Robert Hall & Co., London, 1969.

D. C. Watt, *Personalities and Policies: studies in the formulation of British foreign policy in the twentieth century*, Longman, London, 1965.

E. Wertheimer, *Portrait of the Labour Party*, Putnam, London, 1929.

Sir Charles Wheeler and N. Frankland, *The Strategic Air Offensive against Germany 1939–1945*, Vol. IV, H.M.S.O., London, 1961.

E. Wilkinson, *Peeps at Politicians*, Philip Allen & Co., London, 1930.

F. Williams, *The Triple Challenge*, Heinemann, London, 1948.

H. Wilson, *New Deal for Coal*, Contact, London, 1945.

——, *The Governance of Britain*, Weidenfeld & Nicolson, London, 1976.

D. Winch, *Economics and Policy: A Historical Study*, Hodder & Stoughton, London, 1969.

N. Wood, *Communism and British Intellectuals*, Gollancz, London, 1959.

B. Wootton, *Plan or No Plan*, Gollancz, London, 1934.

G. Worswick and P. Ady (eds.), *The British Economy 1945–1950*, Oxford University Press, London, 1952.

M. Young, *Labour's Plan for Plenty*, Gollancz, London, 1947.

Brigadier P. Young (ed.), *The Almanac of World War II*, Hamlyn, London, 1981.

3 *Articles and Essays*

N. Annan, 'The Intellectual Aristocracy', in J. H. Plumb (ed.), *Studies in Social History*, Longman, Green & Co., London, 1955.

A. B. Atkinson, 'On the Measurement of Inequality', *Journal of Economic Theory*, Vol. 2, 1970.

T. Balogh, 'Britain's Foreign Trade Problem: A Comment', *Economic Journal*, Vol. LVIII, 1948.

D. Bell, J. Vaizey and M. Young, 'Anthony Crosland & Socialism', *Encounter*, Vol. XLIX, August 1977.

A. Booth, 'The "Keynesian Revolution" in Economic Policy-Making', *Economic History Review*, Vol. XXXVI, 1983.

T. Brett, S. Gilliatt and A. Pople, 'Planned Trade, Labour Party Policy and US Intervention: the successes and failures of post-war reconstruction', *History Workshop Journal*, 1982.

D. Bruce, 'A review of Socialist Financial Policy, 1945–1949', *Political Quarterly*, October–December 1949.

R. H. S. Crossman, 'Psychological Warfare', *Journal of the Royal United Service Institution*, Vol. XCVII, August 1952.

J. T. Grantham, 'Hugh Dalton and the International Post-War Settlement', *Journal of Contemporary History*, XIV, 1979.

M. Lindsay, 'Socialism and Pseudo-Socialism', *Political Quarterly*, XIX, April–June 1948.

A. Marwick, 'Middle Opinion in the Thirties; Planning, Progress and Political "Agreement"', *English Historical Review*, April, 1964.

B. Pimlott, 'The Socialist League: Intellectuals and the Labour Left in the 1930s', *Journal of Contemporary History*, VI, 1971.

——, 'The Labour Left', in C. Cook and I. Taylor, *The Labour Party: An Introduction to its History, Structure and Politics*, Longman, 1980.

——, 'Hugh Dalton's diaries', *Listener*, 17th July 1980.

L. Robbins, 'Inquest on the Crisis', *Lloyd's Bank Review*, Vol. 6, 1947.

J. Seaton and B. Pimlott, 'The Struggle for Balance: the B.B.C. and the Labour movement in the 1930s and 1940s', in J. Seaton and B. Pimlott (eds.), *The Media in British Politics* (forthcoming).

R. Skidelsky, 'Is Keynes Still Relevant?', *Encounter*, Vol. LII, April, 1979.

D. Stafford, 'S.O.E. and British Involvement in the Belgrade Coup d'État of March 1941', *Slavic Review*, Vol. 36, September 1977.

D. C. Watt, 'American Aid to Britain and the problem of Socialism', *American Review*, Vol. 11, March 1963.

4 *Unpublished Theses, etc.*

T. Anderson, 'Hugh Dalton' (memorandum lent by the author).

F. E. Leaning, 'The Dalton Book' (typescript, the British Library).

D. M. Roberts, 'Hugh Dalton and the Labour Party in the 1930s' Ph.D. (C.N.A.A.), 1978.

A. Sargent, 'The Labour Party and Palestine', Ph.D. (London University), 1981.

Index

Index